Encyclopedia of
Rural America
The Land and People

Encyclopedia of Rural America

The Land and People

Volume 1

A-L

Gary A. Goreham

Editor

ABC-CLIO

Santa Barbara, California
Denver, Colorado
Oxford, England

Library of Congress Cataloging-in-Publication Data

Encyclopedia of rural America : the land and people / Gary A. Goreham,
    general editor.
        p. cm.
    Includes bibliographical references (p.   ) and index.
    ISBN 0-87436-842-1 (alk. paper)
    1. Country life—United States—Encyclopedias. 2. United States—
Rural conditions—Encyclopedias. 3. United States—Geography—
Encyclopedias. I. Goreham, Gary.
    E169.12.E5   1997
    973'.09173'4—dc21   97-23320
                                                             CIP

04 03 02 01 00 99 98 97 10 9 8 7 6 5 4 3 2 1

ABC-CLIO, Inc.
130 Cremona Drive, P.O. Box 1911
Santa Barbara, California 93116-1911

This book is printed on acid-free paper ⊚ .
Manufactured in the United States of America

CONTENTS

List of Entries   *ix*
Introduction   *xiii*
Acknowledgments   *xv*

Encyclopedia of
Rural America
The Land and People

Volume 1: A-L   1
Volume 2: M-Z   439

Selected Bibliography   *789*
Illustration Credits   *809*
About the Contributors   *811*
Index   *825*

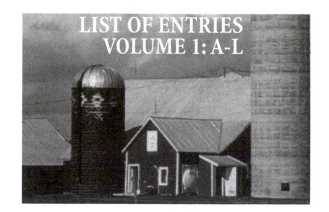

Addiction
Adolescents
African Americans
Agrichemical Industry
Agrichemical Use
Agricultural and Resource Economics
Agricultural Engineering
Agricultural Law
Agricultural Prices
Agricultural Programs
Agriculture
Agriculture, Alternative
Agriculture, Hydroponic
Agriculture, Structure of
Agro/Food System
Agronomy
American Indians
Animal Rights/Welfare
Apiculture
Aquaculture
Architecture
Arts
Asian Pacific Americans

Bank Lending Practices
Barns
Biodiversity
Biotechnology

Camps
Careers in Agriculture
Cemeteries
Churches
Climatic Adaptability of Plants
Clothing and Textiles
Community
Community, Sense of
Community Celebrations
Computers
Conservation, Energy
Conservation, Soil
Conservation, Water

Consumer-Goods Advertising
Consumerism
Cooperative State Research, Education,
    and Extension Service
Cooperatives
Corn Industry
Cowboys
Crime
Crop Surplus
Cropping Systems
Cultural Diversity
Culture

Dairy Farming
Dairy Products
Decentralization
Dental Health Care
Dependence
Desert Landscapes
Development, Community and
    Economic
Division of Household Labor
Domestic Violence
Drought
Dryland Farming

Education, Adult
Education, Special
Education, Youth
Educational Curriculum
Educational Facilities
Elders
Electrification
Employment
Entrepreneurship
Environmental Protection
Environmental Regulations
Ethics
Ethnicity

Family
Farm Finance

Farm Management
Farms
Feedlots
Films, Rural
Financial Intermediaries
Folklore
Food Safety
Foreclosure and Bankruptcy
Forest Products
Foresters
Forestry Industry
Forests
Fringe Benefits
Future of Rural America
Futures Markets

Gambling
Games
Government
Grain Elevators
Grain Farming
Greenhouses
Groundwater

Health and Disease Epidemiology
Health care
History, Agricultural
History, Rural
Home Economics
Home-based Work
Homelessness
Horse Industry
Horticulture
Housing
Hydrology

Impact Assessment
Income
Inequality
Infrastructure
Injuries
Insurance

Intergenerational Land Transfer
Irrigation

Labor Force
Labor Unions
Land Reform

Land Stewardship
Land Values
Land-Grant Institutions, 1862
Land-Grant Institutions, 1890
Landownership
Latinos

Leadership
Literacy
Literature
Livestock Industry
Livestock Production

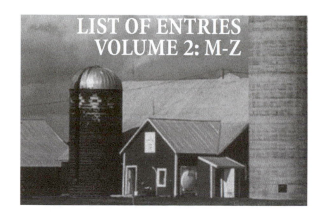

Manufacturing Industry
Marijuana
Marketing
Markets
Marriage
Mechanization
Media
Mental Health
Mental Health of Older Adults
Migrant Farm Workers
Migration
Military Personnel and Industry
Miners
Mining Industry
Mountains
Municipal Solid Waste Management
Music

Natural Resource Economics
Nursing and Allied Health Professions
Nursing Homes
Nutrition

Organic Farming

Parks
Pasture
Pest Management
Petroleum Industry
Plantations
Policing
Policy, Agricultural
Policy, Economic
Policy, Environmental
Policy, Food
Policy, Health Care
Policy, Rural Development

Policy, Socioeconomic
Policy, Telecommunications
Politics
Poultry Industry
Poverty
Public Libraries
Public Services

Quality of Life

Ranching
Recreational Activities
Refugee Resettlement
Regional Diversity
Regional Planning
Religion
Restaurants
Retail Industry
Rice Industry
River Engineering
Rural, Definition of
Rural Demography
Rural Free Delivery
Rural Sociology
Rural Women

Sawmilling
Senior Centers
Service Industries
Settlement Patterns
Signs
Social Class
Social Movements
Soil
Sport
Stock Car Racing
Sugar Industry

Taxes
Technology
Technology Transfer
Telecommunications
Temperate Fruit Industry
Textile Industry
Theatrical Entertainment
Theology of the Land
Tillage
Tobacco Industry
Town-Country Relations
Trade Areas
Trade, International
Trade, Interregional
Transportation Industry
Trees

Underemployment
Urbanization

Value-Added Agriculture
Values of Residents
Vegetable Industry
Voluntarism

Water Use
Weather
Wetlands
Wheat Industry
Wilderness
Wildlife
Wine Industry
Wool and Sheep Industry
Work
Workers' Compensation

INTRODUCTION

The *Encyclopedia of Rural America* is dedicated to the land and its people. Rural America is characterized by its vast expansiveness and its diversity. Of the nation's 1.9 billion acres, 1.8 billion acres are in rural areas or federal lands. It is a land of crop and pasture land, forests and wetlands, mountains and deserts, sea coasts and inland plains. And of America's 249 million people, 62 million people live in rural areas. They represent scores of races, ethnic backgrounds, religious groups, and cultures. The *Encyclopedia of Rural America* is a resource of information on the land and its people. It includes topics ranging from production agriculture and a variety of other rural industries to rural youth, elderly, women, and minority groups to the culture, music, and the arts of rural America.

A variety of definitions are used for "rural." Some definitions emphasize the population in an area. For instance, the U.S. Census Bureau defines any community with a population of less than 2,500 as rural. Other definitions emphasize the economic nature of an area. Places that rely primarily on agriculture, fishing, forestry, mining, or energy—the land-based or extractive industries—typically are rural. Some definitions highlight the ecological, social, or organizational characteristics of places with low population densities, that is, places where substantial distances must be traveled to obtain medical care, to shop, or to go to school or church. Still other definitions are based on the culture or the mind set of the people themselves. The variety of understandings of "rural" often leads to differences in how the rest of the nation relates to the land and its people. The policies and programs made by state and national legislators, educators, medical and religious officials, and business and industry leaders for rural areas are heavily influenced by their understanding of what is "rural." (*See entry* Rural, definitions of.)

Rural sometimes is viewed as synonymous with agriculture. Agriculture is extremely important to rural America; it has been the mainstay of many rural communities, and continues throughout much of rural America as the predominant economic sector. But other economic sectors also are vital. Many regions depend primarily on forestry, fishing, energy, mining, manufacturing, tourism, or other industries. Thus, the *Encyclopedia of Rural America* includes articles describing these diverse industries and the roles they play in the lives of rural people.

The encyclopedia was prepared using a multi-phase process. Phase 1 involved a selection of terms and subterms about which topical articles would be written. The terms were selected by general editor and the Advisory Board with recommendations and advice from people in several areas of rural study. Terms were collected from lists obtained from sources such as Agricultural On—line Access (AGRICOLA), various volumes of the U.S. Department of Agriculture *Yearbook of Agriculture*, and Current Research Information System. We planned to cover as broad of a range of topics as possible, including agriculture, the arts, business and economics, the environment, health and medicine, humanities, policy issues, and social sciences. We recognized at the outset that the volume could not be exhaustive, yet it was to be as inclusive as possible. Phase 2 involved selecting authors who had extensive expertise in each of the topical areas. This involved conducting literature reviews of research journals, periodicals, and computer on—line services. The final phase was to contact potential authors and work with them as they wrote the articles.

The encyclopedia is intended for several audiences. The academic world consisting of faculty, researchers, and undergraduate and graduate students need handy reference to information that may be outside of their immediate area of expertise. Another audience is people who work with rural residences or in rural areas, including county commissioners, newspaper editors, clergy, legal staff, government officials, librarians, teachers, county Extension staff, counselors, change agents, and industry leaders.

Until the second decade of this century, the majority of Americans lived on farms or in rural communities. Today, although only one-quarter of Americans are rural, urban residents still maintain many close connections with rural America. Many urbanites idealize rural America as "America as it should be." Some vacation in sparsely populated parks or visit friends and family who reside in rural communities. Others conduct business with or provide services to people in rural places. And rural people maintain their urban connections with personal and business visits to the city. Numerous interconnections exist between rural and urban America. For this reason, the *Encyclopedia of Rural America* is a needed resource for both urban and rural audiences.

The encyclopedia is arranged alphabetically. Each article begins with a concise definition of the term, and is followed with an article abstract or overview. Some arti-

cles have extensive citations referring to data, research findings, and quotations; others have fewer citations, but may include data from the public domain, such that from the Census Bureau. All articles end with a list of references that were cited in the narrative as well as "must read" items. The reference sections serve as a guide and place to start. Readers may use the reference sections as a resource of materials to read for more information. A general index is provided to cross—reference terms or topics. Several articles include graphs, tables, and photographs for illustration.

It is our hope that the *Encyclopedia of Rural America* will be used to gain a greater understanding and appreciation of the beauty, vastness, and diversity of our nation's land and its people.

—*Gary A. Goreham*
Department of Sociology/Anthropology
North Dakota State University, Fargo

ACKNOWLEDGMENTS

The Encyclopedia of Rural America's Advisory Board was instrumental in helping me select article topics and approach authors who had expertise in each of the topical areas. The Board consisted of Don E. Albrecht (Texas A&M University), Michael D. Boehlje (Purdue University), Emmett P. Fiske (Washington State University), Cornelia Butler Flora (Iowa State University), Lorraine E. Garkovich (University of Kentucky), William D. Heffernan (University of Missouri, Columbia), Patrick C. Jobes (Montana State University), Martin Kenney (University of California, Davis), Phyllis Gray-Ray (North Carolina Central University), and Sonya Salamon (University of Illinois).

I had library assistance from Donna Graber, Lorrettax Mindt, and Deb Sayler, North Dakota State University Library. Department of Sociology/Anthropology graduate assistants Laura Demke, Viki Johnson, Jason Kramer, and Maureen Lucas helped to track references. Department of Sociology/Anthropology department heads, George Youngs, Jr. and Jeffrey Clark, and College of Humanities and Social Science deans, Thomas Isern and Thomas Riley, provided much helpful guidance and support. Kate Ulmer (Department of Sociology/Anthropology) provided technical computer assistance.

I am grateful to the nearly 230 authors who contributed articles to the Encyclopedia of Rural America. Without their expertise and the time they spent writing their articles, this project could not have been accomplished.

Finally, I wish to thank my wife, Jonna Goreham, and daughters, Jessica and Julie Anne Goreham, from whom I received overwhelming encouragement and moral support throughout this project. They cheerfully and consistently endured me as I read and edited manuscripts on evenings, weekends, and holidays.

—*Gary A. Goreham*

Encyclopedia of
Rural America
The Land and People

Addiction

An excess, compulsion, and inability to control a specific harmful behavior; an uncontrollable, incurable, and inherited disease. After introducing the concept of addiction, this entry provides an overview of rural addiction in the following areas: addiction patterns, programs and services, attitudes and resources related to addiction, and future trends. Drug and alcohol use serve as examples since more information is available about those addictions.

Difficulties in Definition

Discussions on addiction often focus on behaviors that are viewed as negative or harmful. But there is another side to addiction that can be positive. There are individuals who take time every day or every other day to exercise. This behavior usually is encouraged as a way to maintain health. But what happens when exercising is increased to twice a day or three times a day? Is this an addiction? Is it an addiction or a good habit that went bad? What is labeled an addiction may not always be easy to distinguish from normal behavior. The choice can depend on perspective, setting, culture, circumstances, and degree of harm.

Addictions have been classified as genetically transmitted disorders, learned behaviors, maladaptive coping strategies, or a combination of all three. There are those who would limit the use of the addiction label only to compulsive involvement with mind- and mood-altering drugs. Others extend compulsivity to a variety of behaviors, including sex, eating, gambling, sensation seeking, and work, that could have the potential to alter brain chemistry.

There is a widespread belief that rural areas offer protection from problems. The idea that rural areas are protective and that rural people know each other well perpetuates the belief that there are fewer addictions in rural than in urban areas. However, a closer examination of addictive behaviors in rural areas, especially alcohol abuse, about which more is known than other addictions, reveals discrepancies in the perception that addictive behaviors are less common. There are few differences in the way urban and rural people look at addictions and cope with both the good and bad habits.

America's interest in addictions fluctuates and is fueled largely by political interest, celebrity involvement, and crime associated with addictions, especially to drugs. Thus, addictions to drugs, alcohol, tobacco, gambling, sex, and eating move in and out of the media spotlight. There are few, if any, distinctions made between rural and urban addictions, and a majority of the information has been developed with urban populations. Information about addiction in rural areas, which is clustered in the area of alcohol and drug abuse, is limited. In addition, many studies are of a purely descriptive nature and geographically limited. For gambling, sexual, and eating addictions, this also is the case for urban areas.

Rural Patterns

Incidence and prevalence data for addictions other than alcohol, tobacco, and other drugs are sparse, especially for behavioral addictions. The belief that addiction levels are lower in rural areas is not supported for alcohol and tobacco use. However, although alcohol use is high, there is a comparatively lower level of marijuana and cocaine use in very rural areas of under 2,500 people (Leukefeld, Clayton, and Meyers 1992). Alcohol and drug addiction in rural America differs from that found in urban areas, even as city problems continue to seep into rural areas. This finding is supported by Blazer et al. (1985), who reported that alcohol and marijuana were more prevalent in rural areas, whereas drug abuse/dependence and depression were more prevalent in urban areas.

In a comparison of adolescents from smaller and larger rural towns with those in urban communities,

Peters, Oetting, and Edwards (1992) reported that there were some significant differences at eighth grade for drug use by city size, but the differences vanished by twelfth grade. After reviewing 65 research reports on the use of alcohol, marijuana, and hard drugs by rural adolescents, Donnermeyer (1992) concluded that alcohol use is the same for rural and urban youths, rural youths are closing the gap on marijuana use, and the use of hard drugs (for example, heroin, cocaine, crack) is lower among rural youths. Sarvela et al. (1990) reported that over 40 percent of rural junior and senior high school students admitted to driving under the influence. The role of peer group influence on drinking behavior has been confirmed among both rural and urban youths (Tolone and Dermott 1975; Pruitt et al. 1991).

Rural Programs and Services

Rural addiction treatment services usually consist of outpatient counseling, with fewer staff than urban programs. Inpatient treatment for detoxification, residential treatment, and therapeutic community treatment generally are provided in the nearest large city. Productivity of rural substance abuse programs appears to be lower than urban programs because of the geographic distances that treatment staff frequently must travel to area offices in order to provide accessible treatment.

In addition to alcohol use, rural Americans receiving addictions treatment reported marijuana as the primary drug of abuse, while urban clients were more likely to have used opiates (Brown, Voskuhl, and Lehman 1977). A Government Accounting Office Report (1990) found that 80 percent of treatment admissions in the surveyed rural states were for alcohol treatment. Key informant data collected in rural eastern Kentucky support the finding that alcohol is the primary drug of choice and add that it often is mixed with marijuana and opiates by men and with benzodiazapines (for example, Xanax and Valium), obtained primarily on prescription, by women. Anecdotal evidence from treatment providers who see both rural and urban populations indicates that compulsive involvement with sexual and gambling behaviors is seen more often in urban individuals, while addictive eating, sensation seeking, and addictions to work are seen equally in both groups. Cadoret et al. (1985) reported that adoptees raised in rural environments had a much higher rate of alcoholism when exposed to it in their adoptive family than did those raised in urban settings.

A major force influencing urban addictions treatment is the relationship of drug abuse to crime, a rela-
tionship that appears to be more obvious in urban areas. A study of arrest data found that drug use in rural areas was much higher than generally perceived and quite similar to drug use of urban arrestees (Belyea and Zingraff 1985). Therefore, it seems ill advised to suggest that there are differences between rural and urban areas in the link between drug use and crime (Leukefeld et al. 1992). However, treatment programs targeted to substance abusers involved in the criminal justice system are much more likely to be an urban phenomenon.

Rural Attitudes and Resources

Rural life has advantages and disadvantages for treatment and other interventions focused on addictions. In general, rural people and rural communities have a more suspicious view of mental health services, including those for addiction (Sullivan, Hasler, and Otis 1993). This point of view can dampen help-seeking behavior in rural areas. An additional factor is that treatment, intervention resources, and self-help support groups, such as Alcoholics Anonymous and Overeaters Anonymous, are fewer and are spread thin over a wider geographic area. Thus, addicted persons must travel further to obtain the help and assistance they need to establish and maintain recovery. Given the ambivalence many individuals experience in early recovery, this distance may have a significant impact on recovery for addicted individuals in rural areas.

Rural treatment and other rural institutions tend to be more personal and informal than urban institutions. The rural, small-town culture can enhance the personal involvement of such institutions as courts, physicians, and churches in the addiction recovery process. There also are added benefits of community organizations working more closely together than in urban settings. However, roles and issues can overlap. For example, a physician may serve on the School Board, Savings and Loan Board, and the Community Mental Health Center Board and also be prominent in a political party. This complexity requires sensitivity to community concerns and particular attention to confidentiality. Thus, community relationship skills may be more important in rural areas than in urban areas in order to provide the most effective interventions for addicted people.

Future Trends

A major issue for the future is the limited resources available to rural Americans coupled with a need to know more about rural addictions. Resources in rural America are scarce, and professional help and self-help groups may not be available locally. People will probably continue to travel long distances to obtain treatment. They will have limited local aftercare or treatment follow-up services to enhance recovery and decrease the chance of relapse. It is important to recognize that one treatment or intervention may not be appropriate for all rural Americans who need addictions treatment. For example, Appalachian east Kentuckians culturally are very different from Alaska Natives. Addiction services that do not take into account cultural differences will not be effective.

Future rural addictions issues will be shaped by multiple forces, including the following (Leukefeld et al. 1992): (1) Contrary to popular belief, there is much drug use in rural areas, particularly alcohol and tobacco abuse. (2) As the proportion of older rural residents continues to increase, expertise will be needed to provide services for older people. (3) Based on National Household Survey data, rural residents often do not seek treatment for their addiction to drugs. Thus, rural areas have a hidden group of abusers. Effective outreach for this group could help to meet community-based drug and alcohol problems. However, given the scarcity of resources in rural areas, such outreach may not be a reality. Identification through traditional methods such as Driving Under the Influence programs could be most useful for beginning interventions. (4) Rural residents reported a high level of heated arguments related to substance abuse. (5) Additional attention and treatment interventions should be targeted toward rural drug and alcohol users. Ritson and Thompson (1970) identified an additional important issue that will continue to influence the course of addictions in rural America for the future—the difficulty of a person receiving anonymous care. (6) Finally, those who examine future trends and develop rural addiction interventions must remember that rural people consider themselves to be self-reliant, that rural populations are diverse, and that rural people pride themselves on being independent.

—Carl G. Leukefeld and Theodore Godlaski

See also
Adolescents; Crime; Mental Health; Policy, Health Care; Public Services.
References
Belyea, Michael J., and Matthew T. Zingraff. "Monitoring Rural-Urban Drug Trends: An Analysis of Drug Arrest Statistics, 1976–1980." *International Journal of the Addictions* 20, no. 3 (1985): 369–380.
Blazer, Dan, Linda K. George, Richard Landerman, Margaret Pennybacker, Mary L. Melville, Max Woodbury, Kenneth G. Manton, K. Jordan, and B. Locke. "Psychiatric Disorders: A Rural/Urban Comparison." *Archives of General Psychiatry* 42, no. 7 (1985): 651–656.
Brown, Barry S., Thomas C. Voskuhl, and Paul E. Lehman. "Comparison of Drug Abuse Clients in Urban and Rural Settings." *American Journal of Drug Abuse* 4, no. 4 (1977): 445–454.
Cadoret, Remi J., Thomas W. O'Gorman, Edward Troughton, and Ellen Heywood. "Alcoholism and Antisocial Personality: Interrelationships, Genetic and Environmental Factors." *Archives of General Psychiatry* 42 (February 1985): 161–167.
Donnermeyer, Joseph F. "The Use of Alcohol, Marijuana, and Hard Drugs by Rural Adolescents: A Review of Recent Research." *Drugs and Society* 7 (1992): 31–75.
Government Accounting Office. *Rural Drug Abuse: Prevalence, Relation to Crime, and Programs.* Washington, DC: U.S. Government Printing Office, 1990.
Leukefeld, Carl, Richard R. Clayton, and Jo Ann A. Meyers. "Rural Drug and Alcohol Treatment." *Drugs and Society* 7 (1992): 95–116.
Office of Technology Assessment. *Health Care in Rural America.* Washington, DC: U.S. Government Printing Office, 1990.
Peters, Victor J., Eugene R. Oetting, and Ruth W. Edwards. "Drug Use in Rural Communities: An Epidemiology." *Drugs and Society* 7 (1992): 9–29.
Pruitt, Buzz E., Paul M. Kingery, Elaheh Mirzaee, Greg Heuberger, and Robert S. Hurley. "Peer Influence and Drug Use among Adolescents in Rural Areas." *Journal of Drug Education* 21 (1991): 1–11.
Ritson, E. Bruce, and C. P. Thompson. "Planning a Rural Alcoholism Program." *British Journal of Addictions* 65 (1970): 199–202.
Sarvela, Paul D., Deborah Pape, Justin Odulana, and Srijana Bajracharya. "Drinking, Drug Use, and Driving among Rural Midwestern Youth." *Journal of School Health* 60, no. 5 (1990): 215–219.
Sullivan, William P., M. Diane Hasler, and Alisha G. Otis. "Rural Mental Health Practice: Voices from the Field, Families in Society." *Journal of Contemporary Human Services* 74, no. 8 (1993): 493–502.
Tolone, William L., and Diane Dermott. "Some Correlates of Drug Use among High School Youth in a Midwestern Rural Community." *International Journal of Addictions* 10, no. 5 (1975): 761–777.

Adolescents

Those in the developmental stage of adolescence, starting at puberty and continuing to maturity or the legal age of majority; typically children aged 10 through 17. This entry addresses strong families as the best environment in which to raise children. Contemporary changes in family structure have dramatic effects on children, and factors such as poverty, discrimination, and distressed communities put adolescents at risk. A national agenda that supports adolescents and families can reverse this trend.

Strong Families

The National Commission on Children (1991a) noted that many fathers and mothers lack the ability and commitment to be responsible parents. In a final report, the commission recommended that individuals and society reaffirm their commitment to forming and supporting strong families as the best environment for raising children.

When families are strong and stable, young people have a basis to succeed in life. When families are vulnerable, children are less likely to achieve their potential. In 1990, 1.7 million families nationwide started with the birth of a new baby. Almost half (45 percent) of these families started at a disadvantage; the mother had not finished high school at the time of the child's birth, the parents were not married, or the mother was under the age of 20. Twenty-four percent of the families had at least two of these disadvantages, and 11 percent had all three (Center for the Study of Social Policy 1993). Some of these families will succeed, but many are at risk of instability and breakup, dependence on public assistance, and financial insecurity.

The family is a powerful institution for helping children develop the skills they need to succeed in life. The early years are critical. Consistency and predictability are essential in helping children develop a sense of mastery and control over their world. Experiences from the early years form the building blocks for sound physical health, intellectual achievement, and social and emotional well-being during adolescence. If such experiences teach lessons in character building and getting along with others in the home, children learn the fundamentals for functioning in the wider world.

Child development begins before birth and continues into adulthood. If all goes well and children achieve successful milestones at each stage, they enter adolescence motivated to learn and equipped with skills to relate well with others. Problems that are unresolved in early stages may reappear and become greater problems in later life.

The Nation Commission on Children (1991b) believes that children and adolescents need clear, consistent messages about personal conduct and responsibility associated with living in community. Developing moral values and personal standards enables them to live in harmony with their families and others, a significant step in achieving a sense of positive development. Families do not live in isolation. The development of children and adolescents is shaped by inherited characteristics and influences inside and outside the home, including the church, school, and neighborhood. These factors interact to determine individual development. Changes in today's family affect the lives of children and adolescents. A father's absence correlates with emotional and financial deficits for children that are hard to overcome.

The Effects of Changes in Family Structure

The American family has experienced many changes in recent years. More families are raising children today without the support and presence of a father in the home. As a result, many children enter adolescence with a deficit of the emotional and financial support they need to succeed in life. One in four adolescents grows up in a single-parent family, which is more likely to be poor than families in which both parents are present. The vast majority of children in single-parent families are in female-headed families. In 1988, nearly one-half of the children living in families headed by a female were living in families with yearly income levels below $7,500, or about $625 per month.

Women generally earn less money than men, and absent fathers pay little child support. Two-thirds of female-headed families received no child support in 1990. That same year, 3.5 million 12- to 17-year-old youths lived in poverty (Sherman 1992). Although many parents of poor adolescents work, most have limited financial resources and less time to devote to the supervision, education, and nurturing of their children. Thus, the healthy development of many youths is in jeopardy. This is especially true of children in rural areas, where nearly 15 million (22.9 percent of the nation's children) lived in 1991.

In 1990, 23 percent of rural children younger than 18 lived in poverty, even though 65 percent of them had one or more family members who worked. Sherman (1992) found that children in rural areas received less help from the government than children in metropolitan areas. Most poor rural children did not receive Aid to Families with Dependent Children. Rural children were more likely to live in a home with an adult head who had not finished high school. The majority of rural children lived with both parents; however, 19 percent lived in a female-headed home in 1990, up from 10.3 percent in 1970. About 22 percent of children in metropolitan areas lived in female-headed families.

Since 1990, rural areas had the fastest growth in the proportion of children in female-headed families. This might be a reflection of the decline in wages and employment opportunities during the 1980s. Earnings in rural areas are less than metropolitan levels. In 1990, 500,000 rural parents were looking for employment and the median income for rural families was $28,272, or 75 percent of metropolitan figures (Sherman 1992).

At-Risk Factors

Many youths are at risk of not developing their potential to lead productive lives. Loyer-Carlson and Willits (1993) found such factors as poverty, discrimination, parental unemployment, and disintegrating communities significant in impairing the physical and emotional health of adolescents. These factors create a lack of self-motivation needed to succeed in school and in the workforce. One in four adolescents in this country, nearly 7 million between the ages of 10 and 17, engage in social behavior that can lead to serious, long-term problems: dropping out of school, premature sexual activity, juvenile delinquency, crime and violence, and drug abuse (Dryfoos 1990).

Nationwide, 3 million teenagers contract a sexually transmitted disease each year, which makes them more vulnerable to HIV, the virus that causes AIDS. In 1992, nearly 10,000 young adults under the age of 25 had been diagnosed with AIDS. Most of them contracted HIV during their teen years.

Over a half million babies are born to teenage girls each year in this country, with great costs to society. A greater proportion of births in rural areas (15 percent of all births) than in metropolitan areas (12 percent) are to teen mothers. Research shows that high teen birth rates correlate to increased poverty and low educational attainment. National studies indicate that children of teen mothers are at risk of developmental delays, behavior problems, early parenthood, academic failure, or delinquency. Over three-fourths of unmarried teen mothers receive welfare at some point in their lives. One out of three female-headed families started with a teen birth, and almost half of all teen mothers are poor (Center for the Study of Social Policy 1993).

Increasingly, the workforce demands better-educated employees. In 1990, more than 14 percent of 18- and 19-year-olds had not graduated from high school and were not in school. Although rural areas experienced a decline prior to 1990 in the number of students who drop out of school, the numbers are still more than their metropolitan counterparts because rural youths are more likely not to complete their education by either returning to school or getting a general equivalency diploma. In this country, male high school dropouts between the ages of 20 and 24 can expect to earn about $8,349 per year. However, female dropouts earn only $3,109 per year (Children's Defense Fund 1992). In 1993, the Center for the Study of Social Policy found a large number (628,000) of 16- to 19-year-olds across the country not engaged in productive roles, whether in school, working, in the military, or as homemakers. Not participating in mainstream society has implications for most social ills. Examples these researchers cited included crime and delinquency,

substance abuse and drug trafficking, alienation and hopelessness, and mental illness.

In 1991, 130,000 youths, 10 to 17 years of age, were in custody for violent crimes: rape, robbery, homicide, or aggravated assault. This was an increase of 48 percent since 1986, or 42,000 more arrests. Many of these were drug-related arrests (Center for the Study of Social Policy 1993). In 1988, rural eighth graders were just as likely as eighth graders in metropolitan areas to indicate that they felt unsafe at school, that they had been threatened, or that someone had offered to sell them drugs. Rural communities, although experiencing a higher rate than in the past, have fewer reported problems with handgun crimes than do metropolitan areas (Sherman 1992).

Dryfoos (1990) found few research studies on the behavior of rural adolescents. However, one study (Crockett 1987) suggested that rural adolescents with high grades and heavy involvement in academics are less likely to be sexually active than are those with poor academic performance and low expectations for the future. This suggests the importance of a rigorous course of study for all students and the need to create more positive youth-development opportunities.

A New Agenda
The Center for the Study of Social Policy (1993) called for a national agenda that supports families so that fewer children will grow up in poverty. This will mean that community institutions, the family, and employers forge new partnerships to strengthen families. This agenda is neither new nor radical, according to these researchers. It is about renewing our commitment to help families succeed. Free public schools, disabled veteran pensions, settlement houses, child labor laws, an eight-hour work day, minimum wage, aid to dependent children, mortgage deductions, and even the traditional school-year calendar (which gave summers off for farmwork) examples of public-policy initiatives designed to help families meet the needs of their children. Social policies must reflect the realities of American families. Helping adolescents to succeed is in the best interest of the nation. The future of the country depends on all of our young people, not just those who are better educated and more advantaged.

—*Irene K. Lee*

See also
Addiction; Camps; Domestic Violence; Education, Special; Education, Youth; Family; Homelessness; Policy, Socioeconomic; Poverty; Recreational Activities; Rural Demography.

References

Center for the Study of Social Policy. *Kids Count Data Book: State Profiles of Child Well-Being.* Washington, DC: Center for the Study of Social Policy, 1992.

———. *Kids Count Data Book: State Profiles of Child Well-Being.* Washington, DC: Center for the Study of Social Policy, 1993.

Children's Defense Fund. *The State of America's Children.* Washington, DC: Children's Defense Fund, 1992.

Commission on Behavioral and Social Sciences and Education National Research Council. *Losing Generations: Adolescents in High-Risk Settings.* Washington, DC: Commission on Behavioral and Social Sciences and Education National Research Council, 1993.

Crockett, L. "Educational Plan, Current Behaviors, and Future Expectations among Rural Adolescent Girls." Unpublished paper, 1987.

Dryfoos, Joy G. *Adolescents at Risk: Prevalence and Prevention.* New York: Oxford University Press, 1990, pp. 240–250.

Lee, Irene K. "Adolescent Dependencies." *What's New in Home Economics* 24, no. 4 (March/April 1991): 24-25.

———. "Education for Parenting." *Forecast for Home Economics* (October 1995): 33–35.

———. "You Can't Go Forward with the Brakes on: Adolescent Pregnancy Prevention." *Sensitive to the Educational Needs of Growing Americans (SENGA)* 1, no. 2 (Spring 1991): 22–27.

———. "Teens and Steps to Pregnancy Prevention." *What's New in Home Economics* 20, no. 3 (December 1985): 6–9.

Loyer-Carlson, Vicki. L., and Fern. K. Willits. "Introduction and Overview." Pp. 5–12 in *Youth-at-Risk: The Research and Practice Interface.* Edited by V. L. Loyer-Carlson and F. K. Willits. University Park, PA: Northeast Regional Center for Rural Development, 1993.

National Commission on Children. *Beyond Rhetoric: A New American Agenda for Children and Families.* Washington, DC: U.S. Government Printing Office, 1991a.

———. *Speaking of Kids: A National Survey of Children and Parents.* Washington, DC: U.S. Government Printing Office, 1991b.

Sherman, Arloc. *Falling by the Wayside: Children in Rural America.* Washington, DC: Children's Defense Fund, 1992.

African Americans

A racial group with ancestral heritage to Africa; also known as Black people. This entry covers the various events and struggles that have been encountered by African Americans, as well as the effects of race relations, political struggles, African American subcultures, health care, and the educational system on rural African Americans. The major focus of this entry, therefore, is on various institutions as they relate to African Americans in rural America.

Race Relations

The southern region of the United States currently is home to 93 percent of rural African Americans (Ghelfi 1986). According to the U.S. Bureau of the Census (1990), 18.5 percent of the population in southern states is African American (compared with 11.0 percent in the Northeast, 9.6 in the Midwest, and 5.3 percent in the West). Of the entire Black population in the United States, 52.8 percent resides in the South. African Americans are one of the most disadvantaged ethnic minorities due to a lack of institutional and personal resources. Negative race relations keep them from overcoming impoverishment. The development of the "New South" eluded many rural African Americans, who, like their ancestors, continue to be severely hampered by social and economic deprivation, negative social prejudices, and various patterns of discrimination. The economic and social hardships faced by the rural African American population, "which some regard as a continuing legacy of the southern slave and plantation economy" (Lichter 1989, 445), remains as prominent today as ever.

Life chances for rural African Americans historically have been restricted. They experienced systemic barriers and deprivation. Rural African Americans were violently attacked and intimidated for many years. They also had no protection or support from the legal system. This was evidenced by the passage of "Jim Crow laws," which established the legal basis for the segregation of the races. Jim Crow laws affected all parts of rural African Americans' lives from birth until death. African Americans were completely segregated in all public accommodations and common carriers in the South. African Americans were born in "Negro hospitals" and buried in "Colored" cemeteries.

Political Struggles

African Americans in the rural South experienced restrictions of political rights and participation. During Reconstruction, however, the Fourteenth and Fifteenth Amendments were added to the Constitution to protect the voting rights of all male citizens, including African Americans. After these two amendments were ratified, African Americans actively participated in political affairs. Blacks were appointed or elected to such public offices as lieutenant governor, state treasurer, supreme court justice, superintendent of public instruction, and secretary of state. However, these gains soon disappeared as a result of the Compromise of 1877, which required the Union to remove troops from the South that had been sent to protect African American citizens.

To circumvent the Fourteenth and Fifteenth Amendments, Whites implemented such practices as the

Legally enforced segregation, as shown in this 1945 photograph, was just one of the barriers to economic progress faced by African Americans in the rural South.

"Grandfather clause," poll taxes, and reading comprehension tests. The Grandfather clause, introduced in the 1880s, stated that persons could vote only if their grandparents had voted. Most African Americans had no such eligible ancestors. Acting as prerequisites, exorbitant poll taxes and reading comprehension tests often prohibited the majority of this racial group from voting. The Supreme Court finally declared these practices unconstitutional in 1915. Although the guise of discrimination has changed over the years, the rural African American is living proof of the perpetuation of a rather unsightly past.

Economic Conditions

Rural African Americans are confronted by severe economic conditions, which are magnified within the rural Black farm population. The rural South contains approximately 40 percent of all farms in the United States, where nearly 95 percent of the entire nation's Black-owned operations are located (Beaulieu 1988). The majority of Black-operated farms historically have been, and still are, dedicated to tobacco, livestock, and cash grain. These are agricultural industries with which African Americans traditionally are most familiar and are considered relatively secure, even though they may not be very monetarily rewarding (Beauford and Nelson 1988).

Farmers in the South have the highest dependence on off-farm employment. Secondary income is far more critical to southern farmers than to those operations in other segments of the country. For example, approximately 41 percent of southern farm operators worked 200 days or more in 1987 in nonfarming occupations. This is due mainly to the fact that 82 percent of southern farms are small scale and have an annual sales of less than $40,000 (Beaulieu 1988). Overall, the composite picture of the southern Black farmer is "one of low income, limited education, advancing age, and inferior social status" (Rogers et al. 1988, 331). Therefore, the rural South continues to be the most impoverished area in the country.

One of the major barriers to economic development in rural areas is the lack of new technology industries. New industries are reluctant to invest the time, energy, and money in an area that is economically underdeveloped and has race relations problems. The rural South traditionally has had many race relations problems and is therefore far behind the rest of the country in level of economic development. Several factors associated with past and present race relations in rural areas may explain this deficiency. A high concentration of impoverished African Americans and racial conflicts have contributed to the lack of rural economic development. Prospective industries often are reluctant to relocate or remain in areas of rampant racial conflicts. These factors make an area unattractive to industries that require skilled laborers. Racist power structures have directly or indirectly ignored poor African Americans and have failed to include them in rural economic development (Gray 1991).

Migration

Southern rural African Americans historically have been affected by the problem of out-migration. Because of economic conditions, those promising individuals who possessed leadership skills, and therefore were able to have an impact within the community, moved north. Out-migration of the southern rural black farm population has taken place on a large scale since the 1920s. More than 750,000 Blacks left the South in the 1920s and headed to other areas of the country. Much of this population moved to northern cities, creating northern Black ghettos (Rogers et al. 1988). However, out-migration of these potential leaders from this aggregate of society has ceased. The current trends show that there is an influx of Blacks to the South, providing potential leadership to overcome economic, political, and educational disparities.

During the period between 1980 and 1985, the rural southern Black population increased by approximately 87,000 people (Robinson 1986). The most recent analysis of rural population trends in the late 1980s suggests that the worst of the out-migration is now over. The introduction of industry to rural southern areas has caused an influx of Blacks. This in-migration partially has been attributed to the economic reawakening of the South and the poor living conditions of the interclass in the north-

ern cities (Kasarda, Irwin, and Hughes 1986). However, the rural population growth continues to lag well behind that of urban areas, and the inequality between the rural rich and poor continues to widen (Galston 1992).

Southern rural African Americans continue to have a grievance with higher rates of poverty and lower levels of income than the general population. Poverty levels were higher and median family incomes were lower in the South compared with other regions of the country in 1970 as well as in 1980. In 1989, the median Black family income was $18,083, or 59 percent of the White family income of $30,406. Thirty-five percent of the Black population lived in poverty. The median family income was lowest for the South in comparison with other regions, and the South's poverty level remained the highest (U.S. Bureau of the Census 1990). Even with the economic growth of the 1970s, the per capita income of southern rural African Americans just reached 30 percent of the U.S. standards in 1980 (Beaulieu 1988). The percentage of African Americans living below the poverty level ranges from a high of 64 percent in Tunica County, Mississippi, to a low of 13 percent in Chatham County, North Carolina (Beauford and Nelson 1988).

Health Care

A minimal total volume demand for health care services exists due to the small scattered population of rural regions. Although multiple factors contribute to the persistent health disadvantages of Blacks, poverty may be the most profound and pervasive determinant. African Americans in some rural communities are denied health care services based on the low level of economic development in their area (Cosby et al. 1992).

The African American population has benefited from advances in medical care. However, Blacks at each stage of the life cycle still die at higher rates and suffer disproportionately from a wide range of adverse health conditions. African Americans often do not have a regular source of medical care; emergency room care may be the only care available. The barriers to health care for Blacks are prevalent for those living in the South, especially the rural South. Those African Americans who are uninsured have an even greater difficulty getting health care (Jaynes and Williams 1989). The recent trend of stabilization or decline in the number of Black health professional students signals the continuation of further access problems, especially in poor rural areas. African Americans thus are placed at a relative disadvantage in obtaining quality health care in America.

Education

Like medical facilities, the public educational system in the United States is dependent on a secure tax base. Most rural areas lack such a tax base. Therefore, the educational systems are in desperate need of a significant overhaul. Since a poor education is provided by most rural school systems, a good education is attainable only through private institutions. A dependence on private institutions further segregates rural African Americans because of the economic discrepancies between Blacks and Whites. This situation is saturated with irony in that if all parents could afford to send their children to private schools, then the tax base would be strong enough to support an excellent public school system. The low level of attainable education for the average rural Black child usually will place him/her in the same situation as the parents. If rural areas could offer excellent public schools for children, producing a well-educated workforce, there would be hope (Cosby et al. 1992).

Voluntary Organizations and Churches

African Americans formed a subculture within the larger society where their institutions flourished. Since participation in White associations was denied, African Americans formed associations geared toward their interests and the progress of the race. The first of these organizations were professional groups of the early Black elite such as the Prince Hall Masons and the National Medical Association. There are still many active African American volunteer and professional groups, including the Prince Hall Masons, the National Medical Association, the Knights of Peter Claver, the National Bar Association, the Elks, and various church- and academic-related groups. African Americans also have had several institutions with political agendas, such as the National Association for the Advancement of Colored People, the Black Panthers, the National Urban League, and the Congress of Racial Equality. Although these groups have important influence in the Black community, it is overshadowed by the significance of the church in rural Black America.

The church has been the single most-important institution in rural Black society. The rural Black church provided the foundation for the Civil Rights Movement, and the Black pastor/minister became an icon within the rural setting. Thus, rural preachers received unwavering respect. The church historically lent itself to moral guidance and social control over the congregation. The role of the church since the Civil Rights Movement has diversified somewhat. The Congress of National Black Churches, the Southern Christian Leadership Conference, and the National Committee of Black Churchmen all have had profound effects on the African American religious experience. The church provides a significant supply of support services and spiritual guidance, particularly for the poor (Jaynes and Williams 1989).

Family

The family is another important institution in rural Black America. Today, over one-half of all African American children are living in female-headed households. This can be attributed to the rapid growth in the proportion of parents who are separated, divorced, or never married. The African American female, as head of the family, has had to fill the role that carries out the instrumental as well as the expressive function of the family (that is, the activities carried out by the institution of the family to care for its own members as well as those directed at concerns beyond its own members, such as neighborhoods, churches, and voluntary organizations). This can be a monumental task for the rural African American female. It creates an environment where rural African American children are four times more likely to live in poverty than those in the general population (Gooley 1989).

The absence of the father from the rural Black family does not necessarily mean that his family does not exist. The father may not be present in the home because of structural reasons (e.g., governmental regulations) rather than cultural ones. Although the single-parent, female-headed household is now the most common family structure of rural Black families, the two-parent rural family has not vanished (Gray 1991).

At the same time, the extended family is an important element in the rural Black family (as well as throughout the Black community). This aspect of family life can be traced to cultural experiences during slavery. The extended family is important throughout Black society, especially in the rural Black family. The fact that roughly 86 percent of all children will spend at least part of their lives in a single-parent household gives an indication of how much extended families are needed among rural African Americans (Jaynes and Williams 1989). The church plays an important role in fostering extended families as the core of rural Black communities. There also are private and state organizations that provide help with parenting. The most successful programs have been community-based private groups that foster hope, provide role models, and boost morale. But unfortunately the local programs that have the best chance of succeeding often are forced out of business for lack of funds, while the larger bureaucracies continue to dispense handouts and destroy hope.

—Phyllis Gray-Ray, Melvin C. Ray,
Ronnie B. Tucker, and Terri L. Earnest

See also
Cultural Diversity; History, Rural; Land-Grant Institutions, 1890; Music; Plantations; Poverty; Social Class.

References
Beauford, E. Yvonne., and Mack. C. Nelson. "Social and Economic Conditions of Black Farm Households: Status and Prospects." Pp. 99–110 in *The Rural South in Crisis: Challenges for the Future.* Edited by L. J. Beaulieu. Boulder, CO: Westview Press, 1988.

Beaulieu, Lionel. J. "The Rural South in Crisis: An Introduction." Pp. 1–12 in *The Rural South in Crisis: Challenges for the Future.* Edited by L. J. Beaulieu. Boulder, CO: Westview Press, 1988.

Cosby, Arthur. G., Mitchell W. Brackin, T. David Mason, and Eunice R. McCulloch. *A Social and Economic Portrait of the Mississippi Delta.* Mississippi State: Mississippi State University, 1992.

Galston, William A. "Rural America in the 1990s: Trends and Choices." *Policy Studies Journal* 20 (1992): 202–211.

Ghelfi, Linda M. *Poverty among Black Families in the Nonmetro South.* Washington D.C.: U.S. Department of Agriculture, Economic Research Service, 1986.

Gooley, Ruby. "The Unique Status of Black Women in American Society." Paper presented at the Mid-South Sociological Association, Baton Rouge, LA, 1989.

Gray, Phyllis. "Economic Development and African Americans in the Mississippi Delta." *Rural Sociology* 56 (1991): 238–246.

Jaynes, Gerald David, and Robin M. Williams. *A Common Destiny: Blacks and American Society.* Washington, DC: National Academy Press, 1989.

Kasarda, John D., Michael D. Irwin, and Holly L. Hughes. "The South Is Still Rising." *American Demographics* 8 (1986): 32–39.

Lichter, Daniel T. "Race, Employment Hardship, and Inequality in the American Nonmetropolitan South." *American Sociological Review* 54, No. 3 (1989): 436–446.

Molnar, Joseph J., and William D. Lawson. "Perceptions of Barriers to Black Political and Economic Progress in Rural Areas." *Rural Sociology* 49 (1984): 261–283.

Robinson, I. "Blacks Move Back to the South." *American Demographics* 8 (1986): 40–43.

Rogers, Everett M., Rabel J. Burdge, Peter F. Korsching, and Joseph F. Donnermeyer. *Social Change in Rural Societies: An Introduction to Rural Sociology.* 3d ed. Englewood Cliffs, NJ: Prentice-Hall, 1988.

Summers, Gene F. "Minorities in Rural Society." *Rural Sociology* 56 (1991): 177–188.

U.S. Bureau of the Census. *Current Population Reports.* Washington, DC: U.S. Government Printing Office, 1990.

Agrichemical Industry

A sector of the economy that manufactures and sells chemical products for agricultural uses. The two main categories of agricultural chemicals are pesticides and fertilizers. The historical patterns of pesticide and fertilizer use are described in this entry, followed by a discussion of agrichemical manufacture, health and safety concerns, international issues, and regulation.

Historical Patterns of Pesticide Use

The increase in agricultural chemical use since World War II is part of a technological revolution in agricultural production that is continuing today. New technology tends to use more capital, machinery, and chemicals and less labor. In addition to technology, government programs have stimulated pesticide and fertilizer use. The greater use is caused by farmers increasing input use in response to higher prices or farming remaining acres more intensively as land is removed from production (Lin et al. forthcoming).

According to the United States Department of Agriculture (USDA), pesticide use on major crops increased from 233 million pounds in 1964 to 612 million pounds in 1982. Overall use has since leveled off, declining to 574 million pounds in 1992. Herbicides constitute the greatest use of pesticides in U.S. agriculture, followed by insecticides, then fungicides and rodenticides.

By the 1950s, insecticide was widely used and at a fairly stable level for high-value, insect-susceptible crops, such as cotton, tobacco, and vegetables. During the late 1950s and early 1960s, insecticide use for corn increased, raising the overall level of insecticide use greatly. Today, over 80 percent of the total quantity of insecticide used is on the major field crops: cotton, corn, and soybeans. Zilberman et al. (1991) found that the incremental benefits of pesticides are estimated to far exceed cost. They noted that $1.00 in pesticide expenditures is estimated to raise the value of gross output between $3.00 and $6.50.

Historical Patterns of Fertilizer Use

Fertilizer use in agriculture began moving sharply upward in the 1960s, when total annual use stood at about 7.5 million tons (Taylor 1994). By the time fertilizer use peaked in 1981, total use was about 23.7 million tons of total nutrient. The Payment in Kind program was designed to reduce government stocks and pay farmers to keep land out of production. The resulting drop in production caused a drop in overall input use in agriculture. As a result, fertilizer use fell by 25 percent. Since then, fertilizer use has rebounded and stayed fairly constant at between 19 and 22 million tons annually.

Since 1960, the use of nitrogen fertilizer has

increased over 335 percent and now accounts for more than one-half of total fertilizer use. Taylor (1994) attributes this growth to a more favorable response by crops to nitrogen. Potash and phosphate, or macronutrients, have also increased, although not as dramatically. Potash accounts for about 25 percent of total annual use and phosphate about 21. Secondary and micronutrient use has never risen much above 2.7 million tons and stood at 2.5 million tons in 1993.

Farmers use more fertilizer on corn than on any other crop. The most current statistics show corn accounting for about 40 percent of total nutrient use, more than twice as much as is used on the next heaviest user, wheat. Fertilizer use also varies by geographical area, with the heaviest use in the midwestern corn belt.

The country's international trade in fertilizer varies widely by nutrient (Vroomen and Taylor 1993). The United States became a net importer of nitrogen in 1983, although it still exports significant quantities of anhydrous ammonia, urea, and ammonium sulfate. The United States is the world's largest exporter of phosphate, with 5.57 million tons (on a plant nutrient basis) in 1991, and the world's largest importer of potash, with 4.61 million tons the same year.

Agrichemical Manufacturing

During the 1960s, most agrichemical companies concentrated on the large and growing U.S. market with little thought for the rest of the world. New openness in international trade has made more countries global food exporters, thus increasing competitive pressures to use the most efficient farming technology. As a result, the U.S. agrichemical business has become a global industry. The National Agricultural Chemical Association reached its highest membership in 1976, with 120 member companies. The 1980s were a time of downsizing and consolidation of the industry. Part of the reason for these trends was the increasing cost of bringing new chemicals to market. The industry itself estimates that it costs $40 million to bring a new product to market and that sales of $500 million to $1 billion are needed to manage ongoing development. Some estimates are even higher. New research looks for chemicals that are species-specific and therefore are more environmentally benign. Industry sources expect the trend toward consolidation to continue, with eventually fewer than 12 companies existing worldwide (Miller 1987).

According to Ward's Business Directory (1995), there were 43 U.S. companies with over 20,000 employees producing nitrogen fertilizers in 1995. The top three companies, Terra Industries, C. F. Industries, and Arcadian Corporation, controlled 41 percent of the sales attributable to U.S. companies. The U.S. does import significant quantities (about 20 percent of the total) of ammonia and urea, two sources of nitrogen fertilizer. Standard and Poor's reports that, although some capacity has been added to existing facilities, no new plants have been constructed in the United States since 1979.

Similar measures for phosphorus producers indicate that 81 percent of the business is controlled by Freeport McMoRan Resource Partners, LESCO, and Mobile, the top three of the ten U.S.-based companies. Total employees in that segment of the industry total about 2,200. Standard and Poor's reports that profitability in this sector has improved since 1993 as a result of higher phosphorus prices.

Exports account for about one-third of domestic U.S. potash production. In spite of the growing export market in Asia, potash capacity in the United States has declined since 1993. North America's largest potash producer, Canpotex, is in Saskatchewan, Canada. The fertilizer mixing sector, with a U.S. total of 65 companies, is marked by a large number of cooperatives. The top three companies are Cenex/Land O'Lakes Ag Services, Tennessee Farmer's Cooperative, and Royster-Clark, which together control 65 percent of the U.S.-based business.

Worldwide sales of pesticides was estimated at $25.3 billion in 1993 (Standard and Poor's). The same year, U.S.-based companies had $8.89 billion in sales, with more than three-quarters sold domestically. Of the $6.81 billion of pesticides sold in the United States in 1993, $5.45 billion were manufactured in the United States. Exports of $2.08 billion exceeded imports, valued at $1.36 billion. A surprising 17 percent of total sales went for nonagricultural uses, such as home and garden or industrial. In 1995 in the United States, there were 68 companies that reported producing agricultural chemicals, the category that includes herbicides, insecticides, and fungicides. The top three U.S. companies, Rhone-Poulenc, Monsanto Co. Agricultural Group, and Dow Elanco, accounted for 81 percent of the U.S. business in 1995.

Health and Safety Concerns

Although pesticides have contributed to increased productivity in agriculture, they are being scrutinized because of potential chronic health problems and toxicity to farmworkers, concern for food safety, ground and surface water pollution, and possible effects on wildlife.

Partly because of these concerns, the USDA plans to have 75 percent of U.S. crop acreage under Integrated Pest Management (IPM) by the year 2000 (Delvo and Lin 1995). IPM is a strategy to reduce farm use of pesticides. It includes monitoring of pests to determine when the population has reached an economically damaging threshold (scouting), crop rotations, and field sanitation (Vandeman et al. 1994).

Public concern over agriculture's impact on groundwater began with the 1979 discovery of aldicarb in the groundwater of Suffolk County, New York. Since then, the Environmental Protection Agency (EPA) and other groundwater surveys have discovered some local problems, mostly with nitrogen fertilizer, but nothing that could be called catastrophic. In 1985, 18 percent of the U.S. population depended on private wells. Kellogg, Maizel, and Goss (1992) developed an estimate of pesticide-leaching potential for broad areas of the United States based on chemical-leaching properties of pesticides, leaching characteristics of soils, rainfall, and the chemicals normally applied to the crops grown in the areas. Kellogg and colleagues found that the potential for pesticide contamination of groundwater is greatest in the Midwest, the coastal plains of the South and East, and the irrigated areas of the West. Regarding the detection of contaminants, Batie (1988, 5) contended that "our current ability to detect pesticides and nitrates in groundwater far exceeds our understanding of their significance."

Several states have passed laws designed to protect groundwater. By 1988, Arizona and California, two states heavily dependent on groundwater for drinking, had discovered contamination and passed laws for groundwater protection. Connecticut passed a law in 1982 holding farmers responsible for contamination of groundwater, no matter how much caution was exercised in the use of chemicals. The law has been modified, but some farmers still may be liable for damages under limited circumstances.

Runoff of surface water also is causing concern. The EPA (1990) reported that siltation and nutrients are the pollutants causing the greatest share of water quality impairment to the nation's water. The pollutants are primarily of nonpoint source origin (that is, there is no single specific point from which the pollutants originated), with agriculture contributing 55 percent of the water quality impairment to the nation's rivers. The offsite cost of agricultural nutrient and sediment pollution in U.S. rivers and lakes is estimated to cost some $4 to $16 billion per year (Ribaudo 1986).

The most common method for measuring agrichemical use is the total quantity of active ingredient applied. This measure does not give a good estimate of safety or environmental damage without being coupled with measures of the toxicity of the ingredients and the exposure of individuals or ecosystems to these ingredients. The measure may not tell decisively if pesticide use actually has changed at all. Since modern pesticides generally are applied at a much lower rate, acreage treated could be going up, while pounds of active ingredient applied is falling. Another method for measuring use is acre-treatments, or the number of acres treated times the number of applications. Although this measure provides another gauge of farm chemical use, data have been gathered on acre-treatments only since the 1970s.

International Issues

Several industrialized countries have introduced national-level chemical-use fees. Austria, Denmark, Finland, Norway, and Sweden all have a system of taxes on fertilizer and/or pesticide use (Organization for Economic Cooperation and Development [OECD] 1993). In spite of the existence of these laws, some in the United States fear that domestic agriculture will be at a disadvantage in international trade because of more lax foreign environmental laws. A related food safety aspect of this phenomenon is sometimes referred to as the "circle of poison." Under the circle of poison scenario, chemical companies, unable to market their pesticide in the United States because of stricter food safety laws, sell the same chemical to foreign producers, which then export food containing residuals of the banned chemical back to the United States. In the meantime, domestic producers have lost business and domestic consumers are no safer. Empirical evidence of such a phenomenon has been scarce.

At the same time, increasing worldwide trade has spawned growing interest in harmonizing and coordinating regulations for chemical registration and use among trading nations. In investigating this issue, the General Accounting Office found a high degree of uniformity among OECD countries in the types of tests required to have pesticides approved for use. However, much of the similarity was superficial since there was divergence on what testing approaches were acceptable, what constituted an acceptable level of risk, and how transparent each country's procedures were.

Many European countries use a threshold model to assess cancer risk, which assumes that there is some safe level of exposure. The United States still uses a quantitative model, which makes a linear extrapolation from animal studies to the smaller quantities to which humans normally are exposed. Furthermore, most European countries, in addition to toxicology, review a chemical's efficacy on the assumption that effectiveness will limit a pesticide's use. The EPA, the agency in the United States charged with evaluating pesticides, assumes cost-minimizing farmers will limit use to the lowest effective dosage and therefore tests only for toxicity.

Regulation

Pesticides available to farmers have been limited since regulations began in earnest in the 1970s. Gianessi (1993) pointed out that many of the government's research dollars in recent years have been spent on finding substitutes for chemical pest control. Nonpesticide options to control insects include eradication, a policy currently enjoying some success in the South against the cotton boll weevil; cultural practices, including crop rotation; and organic techniques, including the use of parasitic insects to control target pests. In spite of the effort, nonchemical alternatives available to farmers still are quite limited. Because of the high cost of regulatory approval, crop protection alternatives are being lost at a faster rate than they are being replaced. Biological alternatives are also not without difficulties. Some biological controls, originally thought to have been benign, have been implicated in the eradication of several species worldwide. In addition, natural compounds that are used as pesticides have raised human health and environmental concerns. Some restrictions also have been placed on fertilizer use, but they have not been as limiting as have the pesticide restrictions.

On the national level, pesticide use is regulated by the EPA, which can remove a chemical from use if it is found to be dangerous. The EPA's methodology, which by law cannot take into account the benefits of a chemical deemed dangerous, has been criticized but as of this writing has not been changed. Thus, it is argued, farmworkers may be no safer if the chemical that is banned or not approved is replaced by one that is more harmful (this may happen if the replacement chemical has prior approval) or if the banned chemical is replaced by several that are needed to accomplish the job that one did before. For the same reasons, consumers' food may be no safer, and they may be denied the quantity of fruits or vegetables, for example, that they had before. The net change in human health may indeed be negative.

One regulatory concern is that "minor-use" pesticides may be lost. Because the sales volume of some chemicals is so low, chemical companies do not find it economically justifiable to go through the approval process. This leaves some farmers, for whom the crop in question is "major," without a suitable means of pest control.

Estimates of economic losses due to regulations vary as a result of different assumptions as to which chemicals are restricted and by how much. For instance, in a scenario that assumed a 100 percent pesticide ban, Knutson at al. (1990) estimated that yields would be 35 to 50 percent lower and that food price inflation would exceed 10 percent.

There are presently no national policies that restrict the level of fertilizer use, either through taxes or direct restriction. Forty-six states, however, have in place at least nominal taxes on fertilizer sales to help pay for programs of environmental protection and environmental research (EPA 1992). States also have been active in regulating pesticides. California voters approved Proposition 65 in 1986. That law required the governor to publish a list of carcinogens and reproductive toxicants, which businesses were forbidden to discharge into public drinking water sources, either groundwater or surface water. The law contained a "bounty hunter" provision that allowed any private party bringing a successful suit to collect up to 25 percent of any assessed fine.

—*C. Matthew Rendleman*

See also

Agrichemical Use; Agriculture, Alternative; Agro/Food System; Biotechnology; Environmental Regulations; Food Safety; Organic Farming; Pest Management; Policy, Environmental.

References

Batie, Sandra S. "Agriculture as the Problem." *Choices* 3, no. 3 (1988): 4–7.

Delvo, Herman, and Biing–Hwan Lin. "Module 3.2: Pesticides." In *Agricultural Resources and Environmental Indicators*. Washington, DC: U.S. Department of Agriculture, Economic Research Service, 1995.

Environmental Protection Agency. *National Water Quality Inventory: 1988 Report to Congress*. EPA 440–4–90–003. Washington, D.C.: Environmental Protection Agency, April 1990.

———. *The United States' Experience with Economic Incentives to Control Environmental Pollution*. Report 230–R–92–001. Washington, DC: Environmental Protection Agency, Office of Planning, Policy, and Evaluation, July 1992.

General Accounting Office. *Pesticides: A Comparative Study of Industrialized Nations' Regulatory Systems*. Washington, DC: General Accounting Office, Program Evaluation and Methodology Division, July 1993.

Gianessi, Leonard. "The Quixotic Quest for Chemical-Free Farming." *Issues in Science and Technology* (Fall 1993): 29–36.

Kellogg, Robert L., Margaret Stewart Maizel, and Don W. Goss. *Agricultural Chemical Use and Groundwater Quality: Where Are the Potential Problem Areas?* Washington, DC: U.S. Department of Agriculture, Soil Conservation Service, December 1992.

Knutson, Ronald D., C. Robert Taylor, John B. Penson, and Edward G. Smith. *Economic Impacts of Reduced Chemical Use.* College Station, TX: Knutson and Associates, 1990.

Lin, Biing-Hwan, Harold Taylor, Herman Delvo, and Len Bull. "Factors Influencing Herbicide Use in Corn Production in the North Central Region." *Review of Agricultural Economics* (forthcoming).

Miller, Dale. "A Changed Agrichemical Industry." *Choices* 2, no. 2 (1987): 16–18.

Organization for Economic Cooperation and Development. *Environmental Taxes in OECD Countries: A Survey.* Environment Monographs No. 71. Paris: OECD, 1993.

Osteen, Craig D., and Philip I. Szmedra. *Agricultural Pesticide Use Trends and Policy Issues.* Agricultural Economic Report No. 622. Washington, DC: U.S. Department of Agriculture, Economic Research Service, September 1989.

Ribaudo, Marc O. "Consideration of Offsite Impacts in Targeting Soil Conservation Programs." *Land Economics* 62 (November 1986): 402–411.

Standard and Poor's. *Industry Surveys.* New York: Standard and Poor's, 1995.

Taylor, Harold H. *Fertilizer Use and Price Statistics, 1960–93.* Statistical Bulletin No. 893. Washington, DC: U.S. Department of Agriculture, Economic Research Service, September 1994.

Vandeman, Ann, Jorge Fernandez-Cornejo, Sharon Jans, and Biing-Hwan Lin. *Adoption of Integrated Pest Management in U.S. Agriculture.* Agriculture Information Bulletin No. 707. Washington, DC: U.S. Department of Agriculture, Economic Research Service, September 1994.

Vroomen, Harry, and Harold Taylor. *Fertilizer Trade Statistics, 1970–91.* Statistical Bulletin No. 851. Washington, DC: U.S. Department of Agriculture, Economic Research Service, January 1993.

Ward's Business Directory of U.S. Private and Public Companies. Vol. 5. New York: Gale Research, 1995.

Zilberman, David, Andrew Schmitz, Gary Casterline, Erik Lichtenberg, and Jerome B. Siebert. "The Economics of Pesticide Use and Regulation." *Science* 253 (1991): 518–522.

Agrichemical Use

Use of chemicals (pesticides and fertilizers) to maintain the desired environment for crops and animals, combat disadvantageous elements (insects, weeds, and diseases) in nature, and thus increase productivity and decrease risks on farms. This entry addresses the historical aspects of agrichemical use. In addition, the costs and benefits of agrichemical use are identified to develop a better understanding of agrichemical use on farms.

Pesticides

Prior to 1870, cultural and physical control methods were used to combat pest damage in crop production. These methods included crop rotation, destruction of crop refuse, timing of planting dates, use of trap crops, pruning and defoliation, and isolation from other crops (Osteen and Szmedra 1989). Although these cultural methods provided marginal suppression of pests, additional controls were sought further to increase productivity and decrease risks. In 1870, chemical pest control was used to control the potato beetle through development of paris green (copper acetoarsenite) (Osteen and Szmedra 1989). Although this technology showed promise, the losses due to pests were still high. According to the House Committee on Agriculture (U.S. Congress, House 1945), in 1944 the average annual loss in farm income from pests was approximately $360 million. The modern age of chemical pesticides began when organochlorine and organophosphorus insecticides were discovered and synthetic hormone-based herbicides were developed in the early 1940s.

Synthetic organic materials applied to agricultural systems increased rapidly from the late 1940s to the early 1980s and then stabilized. More specifically, the use of insecticides has increased, herbicide usage has grown dramatically, and the use of fungicides and other pesticides on major crops has remained relatively stable. In 1964, it was estimated that 116.7 million pounds of insecticide active ingredients were applied to major crops (Osteen and Szmedra 1989). This figure increased to 130.3 million pounds in 1976 (Osteen and Szmedra 1989). More recent estimates indicate an increase in insecticide use, with 185 million pounds of active ingredients of insecticides applied in 1988 (Environmental Protection Agency [EPA] 1991).

Changes in insecticide use can be attributed to differences in the composition of the compounds used. Technology has reduced the amount of chemical used but has not reduced the overall toxicity of the compounds. The toxicity of some insecticides has increased at least tenfold (Pimentel et al. 1991). For example, "In 1945 DDT was applied at a rate of 2 kg/ha [kilograms/hectare], but today similar effective control is achieved with pyrethroids and aldicarb applied at 0.1 kg/ha and 0.05 kg/ha, respectively" (Pimentel et al. 1991, 681–682).

Herbicide usage also has increased dramatically. According to Osteen and Szmedra (1989), 70.5 million pounds of active ingredients were applied to major crops in 1964. By 1976, this figure had risen to 373.9 million pounds. Currently it is estimated that approximately 510 million pounds of active ingredients of herbicides are used in agriculture (EPA 1991).

Fertilizers

In addition to the suppression of pests, farmers also have sought to increase productivity through the use of fertil-

Cropdusters like this one disperse insecticides and herbicides to prevent crop loss.

izers. As early as 1913, Dupont Nitrate Company began operations and quickly became a major producer of nitrates in the United States. After World War II, the development of synthetic ammonia and increased production of nitrate resulted in an increase of fertilizer production. With this huge capacity for production, revolutionary changes occurred with the usage of fertilizers in the 1950s. These changes resulted in the formation of mixed fertilizers with nitrogen, phosphorous, and potassium formulations. "U.S. consumption of nitrogen, phosphate, and potash for all purposes rose from 7.5 million nutrient tons in 1960 to a record high of 23.7 million nutrient tons by 1981, an increase of over 217 percent" (Taylor 1994, 1–2). In 1983, a decrease in fertilizer use can be attributed to a decrease in crop acreage because of the government program Payment in Kind. Between 1984 and 1993, the tons of nutrients applied remained relatively stable, with 20.9 million nutrient tons applied in 1993 (Taylor 1994).

Usage

Currently agrichemicals are used on crops and domestic animals throughout the United States. Insecticides are used on field crops, including cotton, corn, soybeans, sorghum, rice, tobacco, peanuts, wheat, other small grains, alfalfa, and other hay and pasture. Cotton, corn, and soybeans account for 82 percent of the total insecticide used on major crops (Osteen and Szmedra 1989). In addition, insecticides are important in fruit and vegetable crop production. Methods of application for all these crops include seed treatments, preplant incorporation, planting time treatments, chemigation, ground applications, and aerial spraying treatments.

Herbicides are used primarily on soybeans and corn, constituting 81 percent of herbicide applications in 1982 (Osteen and Szmedra 1989). The application methods include preplant incorporation, planting time treatments, cultivation time treatments, ground applications, and aerial applications. Livestock receiving insecticide applications include cattle, hogs, sheep, and poultry. The methods of applications include dipping, dusting, pour-on treatment, direct spraying, and treated ear tags. Fertilizers are used primarily on four crops: soybeans, corn, wheat, and cotton. Corn receives more fertilizer than any other crop (34 percent of the nutrient consumption) (Taylor 1994). The methods of application include ground broadcast, banding, injection, and chemigation.

Costs

Associated with these agrichemical usage trends are increasing costs. The first and most obvious cost is the price of chemical usage. According to Pimentel et al. (1991), approximately 700 million pounds are used in the United States each year, at a cost of $4.1 billion (including application costs). In Iowa, the costs of pesticide use (including application costs) average about $33.31 per acre for medium- to large-sized farms (Duffy and Vontalge 1995).

These costs may be justified because they help increase productivity and decrease private risk. However, indirect costs associated with agrichemical usage are not easily determined. These indirect costs come in the form of environmental and social costs, which include "impacts on human health, livestock product losses, increased control expenses resulting from pesticide-related destruction of natural enemies and from the development of pesticide resistance, crop pollination problems and honeybee losses, crop product losses, fish, wildlife, and microorganism" (Pimentel et al. 1993, 48). In addition, water quality is a concern. The EPA estimates that about 10.4 percent of the 94,600 community wells contain one or more pesticides, 52.1 percent contain nitrates, and 7.1 percent contain both (U.S. Congress, Senate 1991).

Indirect environmental and social costs also are associated with fertilizer use. It has been estimated that 50 to 70 percent of the nutrients found in water supplies are a result of agriculture (U.S. Congress, House 1990). In addition, the direct costs of fertilizer application can be high. According to Chase et al. (1991), the average costs of phosphorous and potassium treatments per acre can be as high as $45. Furthermore, regular maintenance applications of fertilizer treatments are not always needed, and these unwarranted applications result in additional costs for the farmer.

Benefits

The obvious benefit is that chemical control is a labor-saving technology. Because the costs of pesticide applica-

tion are lower than nonchemical methods (labor), pesticides are commonly substituted for labor. In addition, the use of pesticides often results in higher, less variable yields, and "in general, each dollar invested in pesticide control returns about $3 to 5 in crops saved" (Pimentel et al. 1991, 679).

Fertilizers also provide benefits to the farmer through increased yields. For example, a study in corn grown in central Indiana showed that increasing fertilizer from 100 to 125 kilograms of nitrogen per hectare raises corn yields by 832 kilograms per hectare (Crispeels and Sadava 1994). Thus, with this cost-effective technology, profitability has increased as a result of reduction in the cost per unit of output. Agrichemical use continues to provide farmers with solutions to their challenges with the natural elements.

Conclusion

Agrichemical use continually changes and evolves. The government programs that require conservation compliance have had an impact on agrichemical use. In Iowa, for example, farmers are shifting from row-planted to solid-seeded soybeans to increase residue cover. As a result more herbicides are applied and less row cultivations are used (Duffy 1995). The use of no-till or reduced tillage practices to fulfill conservation plans also has changed herbicide practices. Environmental concerns have focused attention on agrichemical use and led to changes in use patterns. These concerns have led to regulations and, in some cases, to the banning of certain materials.

It is important to understand the use of agrichemicals in farming. Domesticated crops require pest management and nutrients. Today, farmers have four methods available to meet these needs: chemical, cultural, mechanical, and biological. Agrichemicals have assisted in increasing productivity and decreasing risks. They have allowed crop rotations that would not be possible without them. Agrichemicals have also decreased much of the hard labor in farming and helped reduce some types of risk. If agrichemicals are used in an integrated crop management approach, that is, as a part of an overall plan based on needs and efficacy, their use can be cost effective, and if safely used, indirect costs can be minimized.

—Michael Duffy and Carol Simmons

See also
Agrichemical Industry; Agriculture, Alternative; Environmental Regulations; Organic Farming; Pest Management.

References

Chase, C., M. Duffy, J. Webb, and R. Voss. "An Economic Assessment of Maintaining High Phosphorous and Potassium Soil Test Levels." *American Journal of Alternative Agriculture* 6 (1991): 83–86.

Crispeels, Maarten J., and David E. Sadava. *Plants, Genes, and Agriculture*. Boston: Jones and Bartlett, 1994.

Duffy, M. "Economic and Social Challenges in Weed Management." Paper presented at the Next Generation of Weed Management, National Soil Tilth Lab Conference, Ames, IA, June 1995.

Duffy, M., and A. Vontalge. "Estimated Costs of Crop Production in Iowa 1995." Ames: Iowa State University, University Extension, Fm–1712, January 1995.

Environmental Protection Agency. "EPA's Pesticide Programs." 21T-1005. Washington, DC: Environmental Protection Agency, 1991.

Osteen, Craig D., and Philip I. Szmedra. "Agricultural Pesticide Use Trends and Policy Issues." Agricultural Economic Report No. 622. Washington, DC: U.S. Department of Agriculture, Economic Research Service, 1989.

Pimentel, David, H. Acquay, M. Biltonen, P. Rice, M. Silva, J. Nelson, V. Lipner, S. Giordano, A. Horowitz, and M. D'Amore. "Assessment of Environmental and Economic Impacts of Pesticide Use." Pp. 47–84 in *The Pesticide Question*. Edited by D. Pimentel and H. Lehman. New York: Champman and Hall, 1993.

Pimentel, David, L. McLaughlin, A. Zepp, B. Lakitan, T. Kraus, P. Kleinman, F. Vancini, W. J. Roach, E. Graap, W. S. Keeton, and G. Selig. "Environmental and Economic Impacts of Reducing U.S. Agricultural Pesticide Use." Pp. 679–718 in *The Handbook on Pest Management in Agriculture*. Edited by D. Pimentel. Boca Raton, FL: CRC Press, 1991.

Taylor, Harold. H. "Fertilizer Use and Price Statistics, 1960–93." Agricultural Economic Report No. 893. Washington, DC: U.S. Department of Agriculture, Economic Research Service, 1994.

U.S. Congress. House. Committee on Agriculture. *Formulation of the 1990 Farm Bill*. 101st Cong., 2d sess., March 15, 1990.

———. Committee on Appropriations, Subcommittee on Agriculture. *Agriculture Department Appropriation Bill for FY 1946*. 79th Cong., 1st sess., February 17, 1945.

U.S. Congress. Senate. Committee on Agriculture, Nutrition, and Forestry. *Circle of Poison: Impact on American Consumers*. 102d Cong., 1st sess., September 20, 1991.

Agricultural and Resource Economics

The use of economic principles to help identify and solve rural problems. As a profession, agricultural economics is closely associated with the land-grant university system and had its formal beginnings in the early part of the twentieth century. Initially emphasizing farm management, the field today includes commodity processing and marketing, agricultural policy analysis, rural and community development, and natural resource and environmental economics. Agricultural economists serve rural areas through teaching, research, public outreach, foreign service, and farming and agribusiness. This entry addresses the history of the discipline, agricultural and resource economics training, rural services, and the national professional association.

History

Early economists such as Adam Smith and David Ricardo were greatly concerned with agricultural problems. As a profession, however, agricultural economics did not emerge until the early years of the twentieth century. Its origin owed much to the Morrill Act of 1862 and Hatch Act of 1887, which established land-grant colleges of agriculture and provided federal funds for their agricultural experiment stations. By the turn of the century, agricultural production specialists with an interest in economics and economists with an interest in farming were collaborating to introduce agricultural economic curricula at the land-grant colleges.

These pioneer agricultural economists sought mainly to improve the welfare of the family farm. The majority wanted to concentrate on farm management skills and in 1910 organized the American Farm Management Association. A smaller group, the American Association of Agricultural Economists, favored concentrating on broader economic concepts. In a compromise move, the two groups merged to form the American Farm Economic Association in 1919. Its *Journal of Farm Economics,* also launched in 1919, was one of the first professional economics journals in the United States. Inauguration of the Bureau of Agricultural Economics in the U.S. Department of Agriculture (USDA) in 1921 further stimulated farm economic research and helped to secure agricultural economics as a profession distinct from general economics.

Throughout the 1940s, agricultural economists' work continued to emphasize farm management. However, there was growing attention to agricultural marketing, national agricultural policy, land value, and rural development issues as well. Department names in the land-grant colleges illustrated this variety: farm management, rural economy, marketing, or agricultural economics. The 1950s brought greater attention to microeconomic theory both in the classroom and in the formation of research hypotheses. Linear programming came into use as a way of applying the theory to practical problems. Econometric methods, whose scope and rigor had been advanced by the Cowles Commission, the U.S. Department of Agriculture, and other researchers, became widely employed (Hildreth n.d.). Reflecting this increased stress on economic theory, farm management and marketing departments merged into departments of agricultural economics. In 1968, the American Farm Economic Association became the American Agricultural Economics Association (AAEA); its journal became the *American Journal of Agricultural Economics.*

Since the 1970s, agricultural economics has broadened beyond commercial agriculture, land economics, and rural development to include resource and environmental economics. Professional associations specializing in geographic regions and in subject matter subfields have appeared to cater to the increased diversification. Regional agricultural economics associations are now active in the West, South, and Northeast, each publishing its own academic journal; another is published in the north-central region. Professional societies and journals have been established in such subfields as resource economics, futures markets, international trade, economic development, marine economics, and agribusiness. Academic departments once again go under a plethora of names, including agricultural and resource economics. At the same time, the demand for applied economists outside the university has risen relative to the academic demand. The agricultural economics profession is struggling to accommodate the increased variety of its members' interests.

Training

Some rural students receive their first limited exposure to agricultural economics through a high school 4-H or Future Farmers of America (FFA) program. However, because U.S. high schools provide little economics training of any sort, a person's first formal introduction to agricultural economics usually occurs at a land-grant or other state university. Interested students often may major either in agricultural economics itself or in the allied field of agricultural business management (ABM). An agricultural economics major involves more courses in economic principles and theory, whereas ABM gives greater attention to business courses and to production specializations such as animal science and horticulture. Many departments now offer a field in resource or environmental economics, which appeals especially to the growing number of agricultural economics students from urban areas.

Over 70 U.S. universities grant an M.S. degree in agricultural economics or agribusiness. Most are land-grant universities, although some are state or private institutions oriented principally to teaching. A limited number of M.S. programs involve coursework only; most require completion of a thesis as well. M.S. degrees provide students with postbaccalaureate exposure to eco-

nomic theory, quantitative methods, and research and serve as an entree to jobs both in the commercial and academic sectors.

Approximately 35 land-grant universities offer a Ph.D. degree in agricultural or resource economics. Ph.D. students often take economic theory courses and some quantitative methods training (especially in econometrics and mathematical programming) in the university's economics or statistics department. Specialty courses and dissertation research are provided in the agricultural economics department. An average of 170 Ph.D. degrees are conferred each year, more than one-half of them to foreign students. Most foreign Ph.D.'s return to work in their home countries.

Rural Services

Teaching and Research. Agricultural economics departments are housed in the university's college of agriculture, along with production specialty departments such as plant and animal science. Professors teach undergraduate and graduate courses, engage in organized research projects, and conduct cooperative extension (outreach) programs. The three functions complement one another to some degree. Usually, a professor will have an appointment in both teaching and research, teaching and outreach, or outreach alone.

An agricultural economist normally specializes either in commercial agriculture, in natural resource and environmental economics, or in economic and rural development, although these areas overlap significantly. A research project in commercial agriculture might examine the effects of the North American Free Trade Agreement on the U.S. beef industry, the implications of federal tax policies for the profitability and competitive position of U.S. farming, or the impacts of technical change on U.S. grain and oilseed marketing systems. Natural resource–environmental projects include evaluation of the groundwater quality effects of alternative irrigation strategies, benefits and costs of public policies to promote plant and animal diversity, or demand for selected public recreation facilities. Rural development economists investigate such topics as the impacts of farm technical change on rural community welfare, the implications of the national food stamp program for child nutrition, and the local economic effects of relocating key firms or industries.

Outreach. Agricultural economic outreach specialists in land-grant universities conduct teaching programs for farmers, agribusiness personnel, and community and government decision makers. They also provide support for extension economists working at the county level. State and county outreach projects directed to farmers and small agribusinesses include such topics as financial and tax management, use of management information systems, and state and federal health and safety regulations. Some outreach specialists develop and disseminate software to support commodity marketing decisions, or conduct workshops in futures market hedging.

Outreach programs in natural resource economics have grown rapidly. They include extramural courses in federal lands management, river and marine fisheries conservation, and citizen participation in solving local natural resource problems. Some rural development outreach economists conduct seminars for community leaders on managing economic or regulatory change. Others educate policymakers and voters about consequences of state and local tax policies or about zoning regulations.

Public economic outreach is less involved than in earlier years with direct services to individual farmers and agribusinesses. Specific financial, tax, and farm management advice is increasingly available from private consultants and from fertilizer, seed, and pesticide distributors. Rather, extension specialists emphasize services, especially general economic education, that might not be provided by the private sector. The potential for competition with the private sector is forcing a rethinking of cooperative extension activities.

Government. The Economic Research Service (ERS) of the USDA has employed numerous agricultural economists to advise the federal government on the welfare of farm and agribusiness sectors and rural communities and to provide analytical support in the development of federal farm policy. The ERS is now declining substantially in size, and employment opportunities in the department have fallen accordingly. Yet there is growing government demand for resource economists specializing either in the environmental cost of agribusiness activity or in the economic cost of laws seeking to regulate such activity.

International Employment Opportunities. American agricultural economists work extensively in the emerging economies of Eastern Europe, Africa, and Asia. Principal employers are private consulting firms, universities, international agricultural research centers, the U.S. government, U.N. agencies, and nonprofit organizations. A development economist might advise a national department of agriculture about the effects of price deregulation, assess impacts of exchange-rate policies on farm income,

or examine the economic implications of irrigation and pest control programs. Others provide economic and management training for agricultural extension personnel, conduct seminars for entrepreneurs initiating small businesses, or help develop marketing systems for newly profitable farm commodities. International assistance programs lately have shifted somewhat from Africa and Asia to Eastern and Central Europe.

Commercial Employment Opportunities. Agribusiness firms hire agricultural economists to perform a number of key jobs. Important functions include economic analysis for a bank, commodity broker, trade association, or farm supply or marketing firm. Firm-level agricultural economists help assess the technical efficiency of the company's operations, examine whether inputs are deployed in a cost-minimizing or profit-maximizing way, and advise management on the significance of national and international economic events. Consulting firms employing agricultural economists offer advice to agribusiness concerns that do not have adequate in-house staff for the purpose. Many consultants use large-scale econometric models to provide price forecasting services. Trade association economists, such as in the wine, dairy, or beef cattle industries, help anticipate effects of economic changes or of proposed government policies on the welfare of an entire agricultural sector.

National Professional Association

The American Agricultural Economics Association has close to 4,000 members, of whom 66 percent are in academia, 23 percent in government or international service, and 11 percent in the private sector. Twenty percent of AAEA members are non-U.S. economists working in their home countries, a reflection of the central role that the United States occupies in the worldwide agricultural economics profession. Besides the *American Journal of Agricultural Economics*—intended for an academic audience—the AAEA publishes the quarterly magazine *Choices,* which reviews for an informed lay audience a wide range of farm and natural resource issues. The AAEA also publishes a bimonthly *Newsletter* and conducts an annual professional meeting attracting from 1,500 to 2,000 participants.

Through a committee structure, the AAEA assists member activities in agribusiness industries, economic education, statistics development, and other areas. The AAEA Foundation fosters professional growth through travel grants, support for undergraduate programs such as the Academic Bowl, and contributions to economic networking infrastructure in developing economies. The AAEA's recently formed Council on Food, Agriculture, and Resource Economics coordinates government, foundation, and academic efforts to increase the public profile of the agricultural and resource economics profession. Further information about AAEA activities may be obtained from AAEA Business Office, 1110 Buckeye Ave., Ames, IA 50010-8063. Phone 515-233-3202. Fax 515-233-3101.

—*Steven T. Buccola*

See also

Agricultural Prices; Agricultural Programs; Careers in Agriculture; Development, Community and Economic; Farm Management; Financial Intermediaries; Land Values; Natural Resource Economics; Policy, Agricultural.

References

AAEA Newsletter. Ames, IA: American Agricultural Economics Association, bimonthly.

American Journal of Agricultural Economics 75 (October 1993): 1-91.

Carstensen, Vernon. "An Historian Looks at the Past Fifty Years of the Agricultural Economics Profession." *American Journal of Agricultural Economics* 42 (December 1960): 994-1006.

Choices: The Magazine of Food, Farm, and Resource Issues. Ames, IA: American Agricultural Economics Association, quarterly.

Hildreth, Clifford. "The Cowles Commission in Chicago, 1939-1955." Lecture notes in Economics and Mathematical Systems, No. 271. New York: Springer-Verlag, n.d.

Agricultural Engineering

A unique branch of engineering that deals with the application of engineering practices and principles to biological systems. This entry examines the occupational activities for agricultural engineers, their career prospects, and their professional training. Three classes of undergraduate and graduate programs are discussed, which include agricultural engineering, biological systems engineering, and food and biological materials engineering. Besides professional engineering and teaching, agricultural engineers are involved in research and extension work.

Occupational Activities

Agricultural engineers are unique in that their discipline requires them to be able to understand not only engineering principles but also how these principles can be applied to a variety of operations within a biological system. The profession of agricultural engineering is closely allied with various land-based industries. It has its origins in the development of mechanized systems to support production agriculture, and although this is still a focus, the profession has greatly expanded its scientific base to include the mechanization of various biological systems, in addition to production agriculture.

Agricultural engineering is a very diverse discipline offering the engineer opportunities to apply engineering at a variety of levels to some biological system. For example, some agricultural (biological) engineers are involved with the development of processes to modify or measure cellular changes within a biological system. Others apply engineering principles to processes designed to operate with whole structures or species within a biological system. Animal and plant species usually are associated with such operations. Such processes might involve the establishment of mechanically assisted growing, regulating, harvesting, storage, and/or processing systems for the species or commodities involved.

Some examples of the work conducted by agricultural engineers illustrates the broad theme of engineering for biological systems. Agricultural engineers are involved in the use of biological materials for industrial applications. Some develop new extruded materials using combinations of long chain molecular materials as feed inputs. Others design extrusion machines for specific industrial applications. Agricultural engineers also work closely with polymer chemists to design biological materials with unique properties, such as gels and gums. Others work with transducers to measure physical parameters associated with biological systems, such as cellular-level changes that occur during crop growth and soil stresses under tractor tires. Others develop skills that enable them to write computer software for modeling and analysis of some aspect of a biological system. Some use their computer software skills to digitize and analyze images from machine vision cameras.

Agricultural engineers are also design engineers. They design structures and ventilation systems for livestock confinement housing, crop irrigation systems, and equipment to support the growth, harvesting, storage, and processing of various crops and other biological commodities. Agricultural engineers are involved with soil scientists and agronomists in using computers and electronics to enable farmers to produce their crops more efficiently and with less damage to the environment. This is achieved by monitoring resource inputs and crop yields over small subunits within a field and is referred to as site-specific farming. Satellites are used to position field equipment, and sensors provide records of resource inputs and yields. A series of overlaying field maps are generated to provide important information on productivity variations within a field. Other agricultural engineers are concerned with mechanical handling and packaging systems for biological materials or with various processes for chemically, biologically, or mechanically altering biological materials, such as fermentation, separation, drying, or sterilization.

Career Prospects

Agricultural engineering is an exciting, dynamic discipline that transcends many boundaries both in the engineering and biological sciences. Career prospects for agricultural engineers continue to expand and grow as the discipline of agricultural engineering further evolves and interacts with a broad range of engineering and biologically based industries. Industries that employ agricultural engineers include the food processing industry, environmental engineering firms and consultants, materials-handling industries, irrigation equipment manufacturers, water supply agencies, equipment manufacturers, instrumentation companies, computer companies and consultants, building designers, and waste handling companies. High school students interested in agricultural engineering as a career will need high school courses in math and science, including biology. In addition, the agricultural engineering departments at land-grant universities can provide course and career information and tours of their facilities.

Professional Training

The agricultural engineering profession is supported by ASAE, formerly the American Society of Agricultural Engineers and now the Society for Engineering in Agricultural, Food, and Biological Systems. ASAE provides various services for its members, including annual and regional meetings, the publication of industry standards, a job service for employers of agricultural engineers, accreditation throughout the United States of agricultural engineering programs through the Accreditation Board for Engineering and Technology, and liaison with related national and international groups, agencies, and individuals. ASAE also supports the various student branches of ASAE located throughout the United States and Canada.

There are, at present, a total of 68 academic departments of agricultural engineering (or similarly named departments) at universities throughout the United States and Canada. Of these, 59 are located in the United States and 9 are in Canada. The only states that do not offer agricultural engineering programs are Alaska, Connecticut, Delaware, Massachusetts, Nevada, New Hamp-

shire, Rhode Island, Vermont, West Virginia, and Wyoming.

The development of the discipline of agricultural engineering and the increased emphasis on the concept of engineering for biological systems have resulted in changes in both teaching and research for many agricultural engineering departments. For a number of departments, agricultural engineers more appropriately are identified as biological systems engineers. Their view of the agricultural engineering discipline is reflected in the biological emphasis of their research and in the integration of biology for engineers into the curriculum. Other departments follow a more traditional model, with agricultural engineering defined by its interaction with the agricultural industry. The view of agricultural engineering adopted by a department often is reflected in the structure of the programs offered.

Undergraduate Programs. These programs in agricultural engineering can be categorized in one of three ways: programs in agricultural engineering, programs in biological systems engineering, and programs in food engineering. A department of agricultural engineering simply may offer one or more of these programs as discrete entities. Other departments have options or streams within a primary program structure, essentially allowing the student to specialize in any one of the three types of programs. There are similarities among the three types in that each has a core of mathematics, basic science, engineering science, humanities, and social science courses. They also have in common a computer programming course, a sequence of capstone design courses, and an upper-level instrumentation course. They differ in terms of the required and elective discipline-related courses. The essential characteristics of programs in each of the three classes is as follows:

Agricultural Engineering. This is the traditional, broad-based agricultural engineering program. In addition to the foundation courses in math and engineering topics, it includes courses at the junior and senior levels that deal with irrigation engineering; soil and water engineering; engineering for agricultural structures, including ventilation and thermal considerations; engineering related to food processing and storage; and engineering related to the design of agricultural power units and machines. There are also a number of technical electives that allow a student to achieve greater technical depth in soil and water engineering, structures and environment, processing, or power and machinery.

Biological Systems Engineering. Programs in biological systems engineering differ from the traditional agricultural engineering program in the focus given to engineering with biological systems. Foundation courses in biological science and organic chemistry are used to complement courses dealing with engineering properties of biological materials, biology for engineers, transport processes, and instrumentation for biological systems. Areas of emphasis within a biological systems engineering program typically deal with biological processing, plant and animal environments, environmental engineering, and waste treatment. An increasingly important area of involvement for agricultural engineers with a specialization in biological systems engineering is natural resource engineering. These engineers work with conservation management specialists to investigate the environmental impacts of agriculture, industry, and commerce on the quality of our natural resources. They design systems to mitigate the effects of environmental contamination, and they design monitoring systems to measure the changes in the levels of pollutants in soils, groundwater, and ecosystems.

Food and Biological Materials Engineering. Programs in food and biological materials engineering differ in that there is more preparation in the biological sciences in addition to courses in engineering science. Courses in biology, microbiology, organic chemistry, thermodynamics, and food chemistry serve as prerequisites for junior- and senior-level courses that deal with unit operations, properties of biological materials, food processing, extrusion, and food quality. Areas of emphasis within food and biological materials engineering typically focus on processing of dairy products, meat processing, storage and refrigeration, and waste engineering.

Research and Extension. In addition to providing undergraduate programs, the majority of agricultural engineering departments also have research and extension programs that work in areas designed to support food, agriculture, and various related industries. Faculty in agricultural engineering departments have responsibility for one or more research projects. These projects are funded by government agencies, foundations, or private industry. Other faculty are extension specialists. They are employed by the Cooperative Extension Service to provide technical support for the agricultural industry. There are intrinsic advantages to undergraduate students of having departmental faculty involved in research and extension projects. These projects often provide opportunities for undergraduate student participation in research, with credit given for the work undertaken. Fac-

ulty involvement in research also adds to the overall academic credibility of agricultural engineering departments. Their research is important for maintaining the effectiveness and viability of agriculture and its related industries; protecting and utilizing natural resources; and adopting innovative practices and techniques.

Research and extension projects in agricultural engineering departments may deal with a wide range of issues and problems. They can be broadly categorized as dealing with environmental and natural resource problems, including soil, air, and groundwater contamination; machine design, which includes various instrumentation-related investigations; the design of storage systems and structures for agricultural commodities and rural industries; information technology for monitoring the performance of various biological systems; and biological materials engineering, which includes the various unit operations associated with food engineering.

Department Names. The changes in program and curricula emphases that have occurred in recent years have resulted in a number of departments adopting different names. These name changes have been implemented to better reflect the content of the associated teaching, research, and extension programs. The two most common department names currently are agricultural engineering and biological and agricultural engineering. The other names in use are bioresource engineering and biological systems engineering. A somewhat confusing element is that many departments have made substantial program and curricula changes without changing the name of the department. Program names also vary. The degree names commonly in use tend, however, to reflect the department names.

Graduate Programs. These are offered by nearly all agricultural engineering departments. Graduate programs enable students with a bachelor of science degree in agricultural engineering, or a related discipline, to obtain further qualifications at the M.S. level. This is usually a two-year program involving a combination of coursework and a research thesis. A number of departments also offer the Ph.D. This normally takes three years beyond the master's degree and also involves a combination of coursework and a research thesis. Both M.S. and Ph.D. programs allow a student to undertake a detailed examination of a particular area of interest. Students also take research tool courses in areas such as statistics, numerical methods, and computer programming. Graduate degrees enable students to develop very specific technical skills in their area of concentration. Study to the

Ph.D. level also enables an individual to obtain a position as a researcher, either in industry or in academia.

Agricultural engineers are in demand, in part because they have a specialization in biological systems and in part because the engineering curriculum requires students to have hands-on experiences in laboratory environments. The practice of agricultural engineering embraces an ever-widening range of specializations, enabling graduates to find employment with companies and agencies specializing in a variety of disciplines. The unique feature of agricultural engineering degrees is that they prepare graduates as engineers with the capability of working with biological systems.

—*Ralph Alcock*

See also
Agriculture, Structure of; Careers in Agriculture; History, Agricultural; Mechanization; Technology; Tillage.
References
Cuello, Joel. "Faces of Change." *Resource* (January 1995): 12–14, and (February 1995): 10–12.

Agricultural Law

The study and practice of a distinct variety of law that is unique because of the influence agriculture and law have had on each other. This entry examines how law and agriculture have coexisted and evolved over time. It describes some of the factors that have made the practice of agricultural law the independent discipline it is today.

Definitions

Scholars have labored over defining the fundamental basis of agricultural law. In one sense, it is the study of the law's effects on the ability of the agricultural sector of the economy to produce and market food and fiber. Other scholars take a more functional perspective, saying that the academic recognition of the existence of agricultural law as a distinct area of study confirms the opinion of many rural lawyers that their farming clients require special treatment (Looney et al. 1990). Yet another way to define agricultural law is to describe it in terms of its outcomes or results. This school of thought appears to follow the maxim "By their fruits ye shall know them" but neglects to consider how law has shaped the practice of agriculture, particularly in this century.

Agricultural law also recognizes and implements government policy in addressing the significant role that agriculture plays in the economic affairs of the nation. It undertakes the task of protecting the safety, abundance, and security of the national food supply and strikes a balance between competing societal goals and needs.

Agricultural law may best be viewed as a unique symbiotic relationship in which the law responds to the factors that distinguish agriculture as a productive and social enterprise from other areas of American life; agriculture, in turn, responds to the law. These unique mechanisms and systems have become institutionalized and are the basis for the study of what we call agricultural law.

Agricultural law as a distinct branch of legal study and practice may also be understood as having evolved with the law itself. From its earliest days, the law had to intervene in the problems and order the relationships of people connected with the land, the land itself, the things on it, and sometimes the things underneath it and above it. Early cases from the English and colonial courts illustrate the principle. In 1615, Richard Godfrey, a landlord, took two cows belonging to Robert Bullen because Bullen owed money for what were essentially grazing fees. A fine was assessed against all of Bullen's fellow members in the leet, or manor court, because of Bullen's nonpayment of the debt. The controversy in the case centered over whether a fine could be assessed jointly or severally. In a 1680 order of the governor of Martha's Vineyard, Simon Athearn of Tisbury, "[b]eing legally convicted of committing a riot, by unlawfully and by force, entering into an enclosure, or Corn Field, belonging to certain Indians, with force of arms, threatening and affrighting the possessors, is adjudged to pay a fine of five pounds, or a public acknowledgment and fifty shillings" (Dukes County, Massachusetts Registry of Deeds, Liber 1, 4).

In what may be one of the first agricultural nuisance cases reported, an Englishman named William Aldred sued Thomas Benton in the year 1610 for trespass because Benton had erected a hog pen next to Aldred's house. Benton contended that the law ought not to favor the dainty nose or discourage worthwhile and productive enterprises. The judge found, among other things, that the right to wholesome air is unquestioned. William Aldred's case illustrates that the competing interests of agriculture and other land uses are not unique to this age.

Sometimes the needs of agriculture and the legal structure that evolved with it have proved destructive and futile; enforced peonage is a commentary in some respects on the co-evolution of agriculture and law. As uncomfortable as this subject may be, it is a part of our past and ought not to be overlooked in our understanding of the relationship between agriculture and law.

A group of Iowa farmers gathered at the state capitol in 1983 to lobby for minimum prices on corn and soybeans and for a moratorium on farm foreclosures.

John Davidson, University of South Dakota, identified six factors that contribute to the unique nature of agricultural law as a study of social, economic, and political impacts (Hamilton, 1990a). They are (1) ownership and control of land, (2) dominance of the biological cycle in the production of agricultural commodities, (3) the overwhelming importance of government regulation in determining the operating environment, (4) high levels of competitiveness in agriculture, (5) cultural and social factors relating to the family farm, and (6) the significance of structural changes associated with the commercialization of agriculture. There are other uniquely agricultural factors to consider in an evaluation of the relationship between law and agriculture. Some of these include (1) agriculture's dependence on marginally controllable natural phenomena that affect the productive process; (2) extensive and extractive use of natural resources in the production process; (3) the influence of biological-temporal factors such as the crop cycle, gestation periods, and the photoperiodicity (or relative lengths of alternating periods of light and darkness that affect growth), of plants; (4) reliance on free public inputs such as sunlight, air, and, to some extent, water; (5) dependence on a finite land base; (6) the relatively short time that elapses between first inputs and harvest; (7) globalization of world agricultural markets; (8) massive dependence for price setting on speculative trading floors; (9) a unique mix of short- and long-term financial needs related to the purchasing of land, production inputs, and equipment; (10) perishability of the end product; (11) the importance generally of food and other natural products to national well-being and security; and (12) relatively high levels of technical innovation.

As much as law has changed to harmonize with

agriculture, it has changed the face of agriculture itself. Areas of law that have molded agriculture are (1) credit and financial rules such as the Uniform Commercial Code, which standardized agricultural finance; (2) laws providing for the orderly transfer of interests in land; (3) landlord-tenant law, which makes possible a predictable system of leased land farming; (4) securities and commodity trading laws; (5) legal rules that allow the transfer of farm businesses as going concerns; (6) contract law that regularizes the purchase and sale of necessary inputs; (7) corporation law that facilitates the formation of businesses; (8) the operation of federal and state farm programs; (9) federal and state antitrust laws such as the Packers and Stockyards Act; (10) federal environmental statutes such as the Clean Water Act and the Federal Insecticide, Fungicide, and Rodenticide Act; and (11) international agreements such as the General Agreement on Tariffs and Trades, Codex, and the North American Free Trade Agreement, which are changing the practice of agriculture as we move into a world market and American farmers attempt to meet world market demands.

Practice

One of the most significant things that distinguishes the practice of agricultural law from its town counterpart is agriculture's dependence on land utilization as a primary input in the production cycle. Adaptation of legal doctrines that address the issues of ownership, succession, taxation, use, nuisance, and preservation and reclamation of the physical and social environment all have their influence on the law and the policy that ultimately must decide legal issues for or against those involved in agriculture. Agricultural law adapts itself to the changing economic needs of persons concerned with the land in the application of probate, contract, business, and tax law to the desire of many farmers to keep landholdings in the immediate family and to promote an orderly transfer of interest to younger persons with the desire to farm. Proper application of these fields of law allows older farmers to retire with much less financial uncertainty than previously. It facilitates newer farmers' land use by means of land leases and contract sales or by the formation of closely held farm corporations. In this respect, the law molds itself to agricultural practice as a facilitating mechanism by which the financial goals of farmers and their families are reached.

Recent developments in the emergent field of alternate dispute resolution (ADR) suggest that agricultural lawyers must rethink the utility of their previous adver-

sarial role and instead focus on their ability to be problem solvers. In the aftermath of the farm crisis of the 1980s, many states enacted statutory ADR processes designed to mediate disputes between farmers and creditors. This served farmers' needs by providing opportunities to resolve financial issues with creditors and avoid needless foreclosures. ADR approaches serve the agriculturally related business community by reducing expensive, time-consuming litigation and by establishing a forum to resolve other disputes among rural people. As part of the Department of Agriculture Reorganization Act of 1994, the U.S. Department of Agriculture offered mediation as a first step to resolve program determination disputes without the expensive appeals process.

Land Ownership Rights

The difficulties created by the divergence between the source of law and the point of application cannot be understated. In this half of the twentieth century, law, for the most part, is made by urban people and institutions and reflects largely the concerns of those constituencies. Urban residents have become more concerned over environmental degradation and destruction of species and habitat than many in agriculture and other extractive industries, such as logging and mining, historically have been. This urban concern has been expressed in law and legislation that some in agriculture view as inimical to its interests. Nevertheless, the question of whether the farmer has any duty of stewardship or responsibility toward the land has been addressed in some state courts. Iowa courts particularly expressed strong opinions on the issue. In Woodbury County Soil Conservation District v. Ortner (1981), the Iowa Supreme Court found that the state had a right to insist on soil protection as the fundamental base of its agriculture. In that case the court upheld the constitutionality of a state statute that lays a duty of soil conservation on all Iowa landowners. Iowa courts held that farm tenants are obliged to practice good farm management to prevent deterioration of the soil and can be held to pay money damages for a loss in property value where topsoil has been lost due to erosion. In *Benschoter v. Hakes* (1943), the court stated that those who control the production of food and fiber have a special responsibility to protect the health of the lands under their control.

The considerable body of law that exists on the subject suggests that, contrary to popular opinion, landownership is not a blanket dispensation to landowners to do as they wish within their own borders.

Landowners have never been permitted to do in private what they cannot do in public. Reasonable environmental restrictions on land use, with or without compensation, will continue to be a feature of the agricultural landscape and a feature of federal and state agricultural programs and statutes, although farmers are concerned that the government has been inconsistent in its application of such policy instruments.

A further source of concern for farmers is that governmental environmental policy toward agriculture has been inconsistent in its application, creating mistrust and suspicion. The resistance some farmers have toward land use law perceived as having it origin somewhere in a city has been harnessed by some groups with a more obscure agenda. This view finds its expression in a willingness to assert uninformed (from a legal point of view) takings arguments in any forum available and a fundamental misunderstanding and consequent misapplication of obsolete common law doctrines. Under the Fifth Amendment to the Constitution, private property may not be taken for public use without compensation. Such takings find their expression in the doctrine of eminent domain, which permits government to command the use or destruction of private property. Regulatory takings occur when regulations deprive the property owner of the value of property, either by a direct effect on the property in question or by some government action having that subsidiary effect. The constitutional requirement that the government pay just compensation is conditioned by the police power to regulate the public health, safety, welfare, and morals. For example, this power may be expressed by orders to abate a nuisance or law that regulates the use of public resources such as irrigation water. In such cases, compensation may or may not be paid for the consequent diminution in value to the landowner. Similarly, if a legal restriction inheres to a land title, takings claims by subsequent landowners may be disallowed because landowners are charged with knowledge of the applicable law at the time of purchase. For these reasons, takings arguments that conflict with the reasonable exercise of police power are likely to be unsuccessful.

Livestock, Nuisance, and the Right to Farm

Since the days of Robert Bullen and William Aldred, the law has intervened in the issues of livestock and grazing. Today, grazing rights on federal lands are an issue of great interest to western cattle growers. Many of them feel threatened by the prospect of restriction of what some regard almost as a birthright. In addition, the ever-present antipathy of farm and ranch operators to perceived environmental and nuisance problems caused by concentrated feeding operations has given pause to many in agriculture and to those in the agricultural law community.

In response to the pressure thus put on agriculture, all 50 states have enacted some form of right-to-farm protection. Of course there is no "right to farm" any more than there is a "right to operate an auto muffler shop" or a "right to dry clean." What the statutes afford is a measure of protection from nuisance actions to agricultural operators if they can satisfy the requirements to be afforded nuisance lawsuit protection. Right-to-farm statutes come in several distinct varieties, and they fall into six general categories. First, traditional right-to-farm laws require only that the farm or operation be in existence some time prior to the change in the locale that gave rise to the nuisance action. These statutes codify the common law defense of coming to the nuisance. They afford little protection to the operation that was a nuisance at its outset or is negligently or otherwise improperly operated. Second, some statutes afford protection from nuisance suits to the operator who complies with generally accepted agricultural management practices. The main objection to these statutes is that often these practices are either not defined at any level or are placed in the hands of agencies such as the Extension Service, which may be ill-suited to assume a rule-making role. Farming methods are subject to much interpretation; one farmer's good practice may be criticized as wasteful and backward by neighbors. Third, some right-to-farm statutes enumerate and specifically protect certain discrete types of operations and agricultural practices. Fourth, some livestock operation and feedlot statutes protect the operator from nuisance suits arising from storage and disposal of manure and the odors produced by large numbers of confined animals or poultry. These operations are the source of a great majority of agricultural nuisance suits. Fifth, some states have enacted districting statutes that allow the formation of agricultural districts, enterprise zones, or reserves that offer nuisance protection to the operator. These statutes have considerable potential for controversy. In many cases, they may remove the power to zone away a nuisance from local and county authorities. Sixth, local ordinance delegation, such as California's, allows each county to decide the extent of nuisance protection it wishes to afford to agricultural operations.

Livestock nuisance cases may also arise and the operator may not qualify for the nuisance suit protection afforded by right-to-farm statutes because either the type of livestock (e.g., canines, waterfowl, or exotic species) does not qualify the operation for nuisance protection or the operation has in some way (either in scope, conduct, size, date of establishment, or scale) been statutorily defined out of the safe harbor afforded by right-to-farm laws. Additionally, persons within city limits who own livestock or poultry may be prosecuted for violations of municipal animal nuisance laws. Challenges to these statutes usually fail since such regulation is within the police power to regulate the public health, safety, and welfare.

Recent well-publicized problems with manure spills in Iowa, North Carolina, and elsewhere bolstered the view many have, justified or not, that agribusiness and government are aligned against local interests and small-time family farm operators. In this politically charged climate, the consequences for elected officials who ignore these perceptions are likely to be significant and may weigh against too liberal an interpretation of nuisance protection statutes.

The New Agriculture and New Law

As agriculture underwent fundamental changes in the last 30 years, particularly those relating to contract production of crops and livestock, genetic engineering, vertical integration, global markets, and the reduction of the federal role in farm programs, the law and the rural lawyer had to adapt themselves to a changing agricultural, technical, and legal environment. American agriculture has seen a rapid increase in production contracting. Until recently, production contracting was used for seed reproduction; now it dominates the poultry industry and seems likely to make significant inroads in the hog and specialty crop market and in the production of "identity-preserved" crops. Identity-preserved crops are those that are intimately associated with a brand name or a particular seller, thus implying a particular feature or quality not found elsewhere. As purchasers look to contracting to reduce their risks, assure supplies, and protect proprietary genetic resources, farmers have looked to production contracting to assure income and thus tenancy of the land or to help young farmers start farming. However, with the possibility of increased income has come a significantly higher level of risk than previously existed for the farmer.

When farmers make the decision to become contract growers, they are at the mercy of those who, in most cases, have superior legal knowledge of the law of contracts. Farmers often must make a significant long-term investment in facilities that have no other practical use than the purpose for which they are designed; in the process farmers lose most of the management autonomy they previously enjoyed. Farmers usually do not have title to the crops they raise and thus may be in the position of an unsecured creditor in the event that the purchaser experiences financial trouble. Farmers also may lose the ability to use the land for purposes other than those of the contract. Many genetic advancements that are part of the contract production equation are proprietary to the owner of the technology and confer no benefit to the contract producer beyond payment for services rendered. Misappropriation of the contractor's proprietary genetic resources may constitute a cause of action under the production contract.

Contract production farmers often do business with vertically integrated producers who control most aspects of production and distribution of the particular commodity at issue. This introduces a significant power disparity into the contractual relationship. The disparity in bargaining power introduces inequities that properly may become the concern of the agricultural lawyer serving rural citizens. In some cases, for example, the sellers of genetically engineered seed and livestock may contractually obligate the independent purchaser of such products to produce the offspring only for market, give the seller unlimited right of entry in following crop years, and bar independent producers from using such resources to improve or reseed their own operation. In other cases, grain elevators may refuse to take delivery of or store transgenic crops that have had foreign genetic material introduced to their line.

These factors have introduced a new element of wariness into rural legal practice and have placed on farmers the responsibility to be far more conversant with legal matters than in the days when a handshake between neighbors was as good as money in hand. Rural practitioners have had to become significantly more sophisticated in the emergent discipline of interpreting crop production contracts to adequately protect the interests of their clients. Agricultural attorneys have had to educate their clients about the new environment of risk imposed on them by the new age of globalization, decreasing federal program guarantees, and vertical integration. In short, the future environment will demand heightened knowledge of and ability to deal with the heightened levels of risk on the part of the farmer. This environment will demand from the agricultural law practitioner a greater level of ability to operate in a multidisciplinary legal environment than has been the case to date.

—Neil Hamilton and Robert Luedeman

See also
Cooperatives; Environmental Regulations; Feedlots; Foreclosure and Bankruptcies; Intergenerational Land Transfer; Landownership; Land Reform; Policy (various); Taxes.
References
Hamilton, Neil. *A Farmer's Legal Guide to Production Contracts.* Philadelphia: Farm Journal, 1994.
———. "Feeding Our Future: Six Philosophical Issues Shaping Agricultural Law." *Nebraska Law Review* 72 (spring 1993): 210–257.
———. *A Livestock Producer's Guide to Nuisance, Land Use Control, and Environmental Law.* Des Moines, IA: Drake University, Agricultural Law Center, 1992.
———. "The Role of Law in Shaping the Future of American Agriculture." *Drake Law Review* 38 (1988/1989): 573–587.
———. "The Study of Agricultural Law in the United States: Education, Organization, and Practice." *Arkansas Law Review* 43 (1990a): 503–522.
———. "The Value of Land: Seeking Property Rights Solutions to Public Environmental Concerns." *Journal of Soil and Water Conservation* 48 (July/August 1993): 280–284.
———. *What Farmers Need to Know about Environmental Law.* Des Moines, IA: Drake University, Agricultural Law Center, 1990b.
Looney, J. W., et al. *Agricultural Law: A Lawyer's Guide to Representing Farm Clients.* Chicago: American Bar Association, Section of General Practice, 1990.
Reisner, Marc. *Cadillac Desert: The American West and Its Disappearing Water.* New York: Penguin Books, 1993.
Urban, Thomas. "Agricultural Industrialization—It's Inevitable." *Choices* 6 (4th Quarter 1991): 4–6.
Court Cases
Benschoter v. *Hakes,* 8 N.W. 2d 481 (Iowa 1943).
Clark v. *Wambold,* 160 N.W. 1039 (Wis. 1917).
Moser v. *Thorp Sales Corp.,* 312 N.W.2d 881 (Iowa 1981).
Richard Godfrey's Case, 11 Co. Rep. 42 (1615).
Rylands v. *Fletcher,* L.R. 1 Ex. 265 (1866).
Spur Industries v. *Del E. Webb Development Co.,* 494 P. 2d 700 (Ariz. 1972).
William Aldred's Case, 77 Eng. Rep. 816 (1610).
Woodbury County Soil Conservation District v. *Ortner,* 279 N.W.2d 276 (Iowa 1981).

Agricultural Policy
See Policy, Agricultural

Agricultural Prices
The prices farmers receive for their products. This entry addresses, first, why these prices vary and, second, how they are determined in the market. Agricultural prices

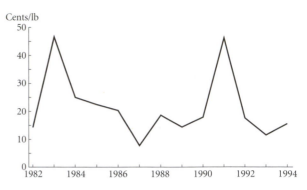

Marketing Year Average Price, Tart Cherries, United States, 1982–1994
Source: National Agricultural Statistics Service, U.S. Department of Agriculture, Agricultural Prices, 1994 Summary, Pr 1-3(95), July 1995, p. A40.

fluctuate more widely and more frequently than do the prices of most other goods and services. A commodity price may change 5 percent from one day to the next and 50 or more percent from one year to the next. For example, the average price of tart cherries in the United States increased from $0.18 to $0.46 per pound (155 percent) from 1990 to 1991, but dropped back to $0.18 in 1992. In contrast, prices of products such as autos and toothpaste change perhaps 5 percent once in a year's time. Manufactured goods and services have fixed prices, and farm commodities have flex prices. Farmers usually cannot post a price for their products and expect buyers to pay it. Farm commodity prices are determined largely by competitive market forces.

A discussion of farm prices is of more than academic interest. Changes in the level of prices received by farmers relative to the prices paid by farmers can be politically sensitive. Declines in prices received relative to those paid were influential in the development of the Granger movement, the Populist party, and New Deal farm policy. In the 1970s, when food prices rose sharply relative to other prices, consumers organized boycotts of meat purchases. Changes in farm prices influence the level of farm incomes, the welfare of consumers, and export earnings (import costs) and consequently influence production and consumption decisions.

Why Prices Vary
Farm commodities have complex arrays of individual prices, and it is helpful to visualize both an average (representative) price and a distribution of prices about the average. When a representative price is observed frequently (say, daily), it appears to be related to the price yesterday, perhaps also to prices two or more days ago, and it has considerable random (that is, seemingly unpre-

dictable) variability. For annual average prices, it is common to see periods of quiet, sometimes related to a government price support program, with prices bouncing along a floor, like the edge of a cross-cut saw. For both daily and annual prices, quiet periods are interrupted by large changes.

Variability about the average price ebbs and swells with the passage of time. For daily prices, these ebbs and swells are related partly to the flow and assimilation of new information. Also, farm prices vary geographically (spatially); the price of number two yellow corn in Ames, Iowa, is not the same as the price of number two yellow corn in Batavia, New York. Spatial prices differ because of differences in regional supplies and demands and transportation costs. Moreover, prices in a particular area on any day are likely to have a range reflecting different transactions. Differences in quality across lots of the product are one reason for such price differences.

The emphasis here, however, is on price behavior for a representative quality and location. Such a price series contains systematic and random components, and the systematic portion is often categorized as trend, seasonal, and cyclical. Since many farmers are selling the same commodity, individual farmers have little influence on the prices they receive. Price behavior is explainable in terms of changes in current and expected supply and demand.

An obvious feature of the supply of farm commodities is the biological production process. Significant time lags exist between a decision to produce and the realization of output. Farmers' production decisions are based partly on their expectations about future yields and prices of the alternative commodities that they might produce. Since these expectations are not always realized, price and yield risks exist in farming. The way expectations are formed and acted upon by farmers may affect a cyclical component to supply and prices.

The nature of resources, like land and equipment, used in farming is such that producers cannot easily make major changes in production plans in response to price changes. Given a change in the price that farmers expect to prevail, the change in quantity supplied, at least in the short run, is relatively small (where both changes are measured in percentage terms); supply is said to be price inelastic.

Farm commodities are the raw materials used to manufacture a large variety of end products; they are also exported and stored for future use. Farm-level demand is derived from this broad array of uses, and the magnitude of these uses depends on such factors as population size and income levels. Like supply, the demand for most commodities is price inelastic. Changes in prices have relatively small effects on the quantity consumers are willing to buy, and small percentage changes in supply result in relatively large percentage changes in price. When crop prospects deteriorate, large and rapid increases in prices occur. If one small crop is followed by a second, so that stocks are depleted, extraordinary peaks in prices occur.

Trends in prices arise when supply grows (or declines) systematically relative to demand, or vice versa. For example, technological improvements in the broiler industry over a period of years reduced the costs of producing chicken, and consequently supply grew relative to demand. Thus, the price of chicken, especially when adjusted for the overall rate of inflation, trended downward. Trends need not persist indefinitely because the underlying causes of trends change.

Commodity prices often have a seasonal component. Most crops and some livestock products have seasonality in output. For annual crops, prices are lowest at harvest, tend to rise during the storage season, and then drop as the next harvest approaches. However, unpredictable changes in demand or in expectations about the next year's harvest can occur during the storage season; consequently, prices do not always rise in a smooth seasonal pattern. Moreover, when commodities are perishable or semiperishable—that is, have limited storage life—seasonal prices are highly dependent on current production.

Random behavior in farm prices arises from many sources. Supply is affected by unanticipated changes in growing conditions (for example, weather or pests). Demand also is affected by unexpected events. Given the internationalization of commodity markets, these events can occur anywhere in the world. An exceptionally good soybean crop in Brazil reduces the export demand for soybeans produced in other countries and hence reduces the prices of oilseeds in the United States. The threat of war in some distant land affects expected demand, thus causing grain prices to rise. Since changes in macroeconomic policies of governments influence the incomes of consumers and exchange rates among currencies, they, too, can affect commodity prices. Finally, there is a random element in individual human behavior. Buyers and sellers have different degrees of access to information, and they interpret existing information differently. Thus, even if economic conditions did not change, individual transaction prices would not be identical.

Price Discovery

The institutional arrangements for assessing information and establishing prices are called price discovery methods. Many price discovery methods exist, but most can be classified under three headings: auctions, negotiation, and administration. Auctions discover prices through explicit rules that use bids (and perhaps offers) from market participants. Many kinds of auctions exist (for example, sealed bidding is a type of auction). Negotiated prices include private bargaining between a buyer and a seller, with no formal rules, and organized bargaining between a group of sellers and one or more buyers. The negotiation may result in a formula or contract for setting price. Administered prices include price lists and posted prices established by managers of firms and prices set or regulated by governments.

Organized futures markets are an important price discovery method for major farm commodities in the United States. They establish prices for contracts for future delivery of a commodity. The contracts on a specific market have identical delivery terms, except the date of delivery. The Chicago Board of Trade corn contract, for example, specifies that 5,000 bushels of number two yellow corn be delivered in an approved warehouse in Chicago, St. Louis, or Toledo; contracts are traded for delivery in March, May, July, September, and December. A seller of December corn has made a legal contract to deliver corn before a specific date in December.

Because of the specificity of futures contracts, well-known and precisely defined prices result. Hence, futures prices are a good base for setting prices for other qualities, locations, and times of delivery. Buyers of corn use the price for the nearby delivery month to set their posted bid price; this local cash price reflects differences in location and time of delivery relative to those in the futures contract. Although the bid is a posted price, it is closely linked to an auction market price. Futures markets are called double auction markets because traders can make both bids and offers.

Farmers have had concerns about the fairness of prices. One concern has been that large buyers may manipulate futures prices to keep them lower than they otherwise would be. Although little evidence exists to support such allegations, they have resulted in government regulations and programs. The Commodity Futures Trading Commission, for example, has the explicit task of regulating futures and options markets. The federal government also plays a major role in providing information for market participants.

Governments attempt to influence at least some farm prices in most countries. Government intervention in the United States usually has had the purpose of enhancing farm incomes. Sometimes, the government intervenes to hold down or freeze prices in response to pressures from consumers. Over- or underpricing commodities relative to their market values is a political decision.

One definition of fair prices for farmers is parity prices. A parity price is the price that gives a commodity the same purchasing power today as it had in a base period when prices received and paid by farmers were judged to be equitable. It is extremely difficult, however, to make and maintain fair purchasing-power comparisons; the quality and type of items bought and sold by farmers change through time. Thus, even though parity prices are still computed by the U.S. Department of Agriculture, they have been largely abandoned as a basis for setting price supports. Support levels are now established by legislative mandates or by the secretary of agriculture within limits set by Congress.

For some commodities, farmers are eligible to receive a government loan equal to their production, say of wheat, multiplied by a loan rate (support price). The crop is the collateral for the loan. If market prices are below the loan rate, farmers then have an incentive to take the loan, not repay it, and let the government keep the collateral. Thus, the loan rate tends to set a floor under market prices.

Market prices are often above support levels, but based on concerns that market prices do not always provide a fair return to farmers, target prices became another component of farm programs. Target prices are set higher than the loan rate, and if market prices fall below the target, then program participants receive a direct payment from the government; it is based on the difference between the target price and an average market price. Government programs evolve and can be complex, and potential changes in government policy can create risks that influence prices and the decisions of farmers. Target prices and loan rates may become historical concepts as farm policy changes. To summarize, a complex array of forces determines agricultural prices. These forces include political and random events as well as conventional determinants of supply and demand. Consequently, we should not be surprised that changes in farm prices are difficult to forecast.

—*William G. Tomek*

See also

Agricultural and Resource Economics; Agricultural Programs; Agro/Food System; Farm Finance; Futures Markets; Income; Policy, Agricultural; Value-Added Agriculture.

References

Allen, P. Geoffrey. "Economic Forecasting in Agriculture." *International Journal of Forecasting* 10 (1994): 81–135.

Cramer, Gail L., and E. J. Wailes, eds. *Grain Marketing.* 2d ed. Boulder, CO: Westview Press, 1993.

Goodwin, John W. *Agricultural Price Analysis and Forecasting.* New York: John Wiley and Sons, 1994.

Lesser, William H. *Marketing Livestock and Meat.* Binghamton, NY: Food Products Press, 1993.

Tomek, William G., and Kenneth L. Robinson. *Agricultural Product Prices.* 3d ed. Ithaca, NY: Cornell University Press, 1990.

Tomek, William G., and Robert J. Myers. "Empirical Analysis of Agricultural Commodity Prices: A Viewpoint." *Review of Agricultural Economics* 15 (1993): 181–202.

Agricultural Programs

Mechanisms to transfer benefits from government to agricultural producers through price supports or direct payments that began with the 1933 Agricultural Adjustment Act and will continue at least until 2002. The main reason for agricultural programs during the Roosevelt administration was to make farm income comparable to urban income. That goal was largely accomplished in the 1970s and 1980s, yet the mechanisms and programs remained in place until early 1996. Farm programs continue as financial transfers to agricultural producers, but the goals are less clear and less clearly met today. This entry discusses the history of these programs and some of their key components.

Initial Objectives

The original agricultural programs, enacted during Franklin Roosevelt's administration, had the objectives of raising rural incomes, providing a countercyclical influence on returns from the agricultural sector, and ensuring an adequate and reasonably priced food supply for the nation. The last goal of an adequate food supply has been met for the United States and for part of the rest of the world through American exports and food aid. This success is due to long-term public investment in agricultural technology and to a vast resource base of high-quality farmland in the United States. These two factors provided a continuing ability to overproduce that fed the United States and part of the rest of the world but made the increasing and stabilizing of rural incomes all the more difficult.

The objective of raising rural incomes was met ini-tially through programs that supported agricultural commodity prices. Later, direct payments were made to farmers. Other devices, such as marketing orders that allowed producers to restrict the quantity of their commodity on the market, have also helped raise income. Marketing orders have been used for specialty crops such as navel oranges that could be differentiated or have a market niche. Sometimes combinations of these have been used, as in the case of dairy. Marketing orders segregate the market and discriminate between fluid milk sold to consumers directly at a higher price and the milk that goes to manufactured products such as cheese. Price supports are then used to raise the price of one or more of the component uses, which then, like a tide, lifts all boats.

Nonrecourse Loans

The key price support mechanism in place until 1996 was the nonrecourse loan. This device was also countercyclical. After harvest, a farmer had the opportunity to take out a loan with the crop pledged as security against that loan. The government set a loan price for the crop, initially proposed at the long-run moving average of prices for that crop. Having taken the loan, the farmer had the option to pay back the loan sometime within the year or to default on the loan, at which point the government took possession of the farmer's crop. The program was tied to specific crops, and the amount of price support or income assistance that the farmer received was directly related to the level of crop production. Large-scale farms received larger payments than small-scale farms. In this sense the program was not designed to help low-income farmers with limited production. Benefits were bid into the value of farmland. As the government program brought higher income from production, the value of that land increased to the benefit of the original landowner. Programs tied to land benefit the initial recipients and landholders but are not necessarily effective in raising returns over time. Succeeding farmers just pay more in costs for the asset (land) with the government program income attached and do not necessarily realize higher returns on their investment and labor.

This simple mechanism, put in place when Henry A. Wallace was secretary of agriculture (1933-1940), accomplished many ends. The original loan placed cash into the farmer's hands at a critical time of the year when market prices may have been driven to low levels after a big harvest, thus being countercyclical and potentially income enhancing. Depending on the level that the government set for the loan rate, the amount transferred to the farmer might enhance income over a number of years, in comparison to world prices, or only smooth the cyclical variation between years and the seasonal variation. In times of overproduction of commodities the program also built government stocks. This occurred when the government took delivery on the grain pledged as security by farmers who took the option of defaulting on their loans when the loan rate set by the government was higher than the market price. When prices were high, the government sold the stocks to recover the money it loaned. Sometimes, U.S. stocks were so large that they met world and national needs. When they were sold in times of high prices, they helped ease national and world shortages. The nonrecourse loan mechanism thus was also an automatic countercyclical stocks policy.

The Loan Rate

The choice of the loan rate, that value the government set on a commodity pledged against a nonrecourse loan, has been critically important. Much of the criticism of farm programs has stemmed from this choice. When Congress wanted to transfer money to farmers, it raised loan rates or put pressure on the secretary of agriculture to do so. When the loan rate was above the long-term average world price, the government payments to farmers increased their incomes above what the world prices would have brought, and the government accumulated stockpiles. To dispose of these, the government used surplus commodities for the early food stamp programs or Food for Peace and other aid programs. In the 1980s, the loan-based price support mechanism put government-supported commodity prices above world price levels, and American price supports and stock accumulation in turn helped raise world prices and kept U.S. grain in storage rather than being exported. Other countries produced more than they would have without American support of world prices and sold their grain at a few cents less than the American loan rate to undercut it.

Acreage Diversion

The original agricultural program, the Agricultural Adjustment Act, included direct reduction of supply as part of the effort to raise prices. The experience of the Federal Farm Board after the disastrous drop in farm prices in the 1920s showed that trying to support farm prices without concern about increased supply was a budget buster. However, the Supreme Court struck down these early direct-supply control efforts as too intrusive upon individual freedoms. Farm programs were made

voluntary, and land reduction, rather than product quotas, was tied to the benefits of joining the program and obtaining price support. To take advantage of the nonrecourse loan, the farmer had to be willing to set aside some cropland. Through this device, the secretary of agriculture could reduce supply during periods of high production and low prices. In addition to this land diversion or set-aside (later called the Acreage Reduction Program), supply control was accomplished as farmers set aside additional land that was subject to erosion or had other characteristics critical for conservation or water quality. Payments were made to farmers for these and other voluntary conservation-enhancing efforts, which also increased farm income. The most recent of these is the Conservation Reserve Program, which continues with a goal of holding 36 million acres in conserving uses.

Target Prices

In the 1970s, a target price concept was introduced under which the U.S. Department of Agriculture made direct payments to farmers who signed up for farm programs. The farmer received the difference between the loan rate, or the world price if it was higher than the loan rate, and a target price set by the secretary of agriculture and/or Congress. The loan rate could then be set low, usually below the expected average world price, so that government stocks would not accumulate often. Farm income could still be supported partially through the loan rate mechanism if world prices were extremely low; then countercyclical stocks would be accumulated. As a result of the target price mechanism, income support became the act of writing a check to farmers for the difference between the world price and the target price, a price Congress set based on commodity interest arguments about what was fair to farmers.

The cost of target payments is usually lower than the cost of comparable income support through nonrecourse loans. One reason is the cost to accumulate and manage stocks for loan programs. Although target prices are more cost effective, they are more transparent as a government transfer payment to farmers. Such a program device would not have been possible to implement in the 1930s; it would have been called socialism or even communism. Henry Wallace's political genius was in calling for fair prices for farmers, not income payments.

Who Was Included?

When farm programs first were put in place under the Agricultural Adjustment Act, they included basic commodities such as corn and wheat. Special attention was paid to cotton, rice, peanuts, and tobacco because of the political power of the rural South. Recent farm legislation deals straightforwardly and briefly with corn, wheat, and soybeans. Many more pages of legislation are necessary for the detailed special provisions and enhancements for cotton, rice, tobacco, and others that have had especially strong regional support. There is little willingness on the part of these interests to allow much discretion or generic treatment of their interests. Other special programs included such things as honey price supports and the beekeepers' indemnity. These programs were recently ended by Congress, along with the wool program that existed to keep the U.S. sheep industry viable.

Sugar represents a special case. It was not originally included in farm programs, but sugar growers and processors lobbied to have it included. Taxpayers do not pay for price supports for sugar. Instead, tariffs are set to prevent foreign sugar from coming into the United States. This tariff policy keeps domestic sugar prices above world markets and benefit both producers and processors. Sugar consumers pay for the program. So whereas budget concerns may change other commodity programs, only consumer pressure can change the sugar program. The sugar program also provides a price umbrella for corn sweeteners, now used extensively in processed foods. Corn producers and processors strongly support the sugar program. Without it their more costly sweeteners would have difficulty competing with world market–priced sugar.

The New Structural Changes in Farm Programs

Major structural change occurred in agricultural programs in 1996, representing a departure from the programs that had existed since 1933. This change was driven by new circumstances in agriculture, concerns with the budget deficit, and the election of a Congress wanting to reduce the role of government.

The 1996 Federal Agricultural Improvement and Reform Act (FAIR) changed previous programs in very fundamental ways. The basic concept of the new legislation is that the dollars available for agricultural commodity programs under the budget reduction plan (1995–2002) will be paid to farmers in gradually declining lump sums over this seven-year period on the following basis. First, payments will be made in most cases irrespective of what the farmers grow and without requirements of land set-asides. The government role of supply control through land retirement will thus be abandoned and payments

will be decoupled from most commodities. Thus, farmers who received target payments for a certain number of acres of corn in the past will receive similar payments through the year 2002 without having specifically to grow corn.

Second, farmers still must comply with conservation and environmental standards. However, the requirements to preserve wetlands and noncropland conversion to cropland have been eased. Third, payments will be based on the land and its former involvement in government programs. This will benefit landowners in terms both of rent levels and the value of the payments that will be capitalized into the value of the land. Fourth, payments will not depend on the level of prices. Over this seven-year period payments will be made to those taking the responsibility and risk for land formerly in government programs without regard to world prices. Thus, the countercyclical role of government will be abandoned. In 1996 and 1997, farmers received an estimated $7.8 billion and $7.6 billion, respectively (U.S. Department of Agriculture, 1997) payments in spite of prices that would have resulted in little or no payments under the old farm programs. As a result, the seven-year bill, while meeting the initial budget reduction targets, will likely result in more income transfer to farmers than would have been the case under the old program. And fifth, whereas the new program retains the nonrecourse commodity loans, limits placed on loan rates for most commodities and specific provisions preventing stock accumulation will prevent countercyclical stock accumulation and sale.

The FAIR legislation was represented as being an end to farm programs, a buyout according to which farmers are alone on the free market after 2002. It was represented this way to the public by most of the press and politicians. However, in the final days of debate, in March 1995, the basic historical legislation that had provided the umbrella for all farm bills since 1949 was placed in the new legislation. Thus, if nothing is done explicitly to end farm programs in 2002, the United States reverts to the old farm programs.

There are important questions to be asked as the new programs begin to operate. Will world prices remain high and provide adequate incomes for farmers? Will only the largest farmers survive? If so, will help be available for those pushed out of farming as they adjust to other jobs similar to that available for some industrial workers? Will the end of supply controls and countercyclical price supports result in more market variability and dangerous risk for producers, input suppliers, and processors? Will agriculture operate in the nation's best interest under a hands-off free-market environment? Congress may adjust the new programs as the new bill operates and questions like these are answered.

—Otto C. Doering III

See also
Agricultural and Resource Economics; Agricultural Prices; Crop Surplus; Farm Management; Marketing; Policy, Agricultural; Trade, International.
References
Cochrane, Willard W. *The Development of American Agriculture.* 2d ed. Minneapolis: University of Minnesota Press, 1993.
General Accounting Office. *U.S. Agriculture: Status of the Farm Sector.* GAO/RCED–95–104FS. Washington, DC: General Accounting Office, March 1995.
Hallberg, Milton C. *The U.S. Agricultural and Food System: A Postwar Historical Perspective.* Publication No. 35. University Park: Pennsylvania State University, Northeast Center for Rural Development, 1988.
Schlesinger, Arthur M. *The Coming of the New Deal.* Boston: Houghton Mifflin, 1958.
U.S. Department of Agriculture. *Agricultural–Food Policy Review: Commodity Program Perspective.* Agricultural Economic Report No. 530. Washington, DC: U.S. Department of Agriculture, Economic Research Service, July 1985.
———. *Background for 1995 Farm Legislation* (by Commodity Names). Agricultural Economic Reports Nos. 707–716. Herndon, VA: U.S. Department of Agriculture, Economic Research Service, National Agricultural Statistics Service, April 1995.
———. *The Basic Mechanisms of U.S. Farm Policy.* Miscellaneous Publication No. 1479. Rockville, MD: U.S. Department of Agriculture, Economic Research Service, National Agricultural Statistics Service, January 1990.

Agriculture

The domestication of plants and animals for use by humans. This entry describes the historical development of American agriculture and the factors that have resulted in its tremendous productivity at the current time. In addition, the entry examines the present structure of U.S. agriculture and discusses some of the major issues likely to affect agriculture in the future.

Historical Development

The historical emergence of agriculture was among the most prominent events shaping the development of human societies. Agriculture transformed human societies in at least two major ways. First, when compared to hunting and gathering techniques as a mean for obtaining sustenance, agriculture greatly increased the amount of food that could be produced and made food production more consistent and dependable. With a more dependable food source, the population that the earth could support increased significantly. Compared to agriculture, a subsistence based on hunting and gathering could support only a tiny fraction of the world's current population (Vasey 1992). Second, agriculture made permanent settlement feasible since it was no longer necessary for humans to follow herds of animals or go out in search of edible plants.

In addition to these major historical implications, changes in the process by which agricultural production occurs have been among the most vital forces shaping the United States (Cochrane 1979). It could be argued that the history of rural America is largely parallel to the history of agricultural change.

When Europeans first arrived in North America, they brought a primitive form of agriculture from their homeland. Despite learning some new farming techniques and adopting new crops from Native Americans, the first Europeans engaged in subsistence farming in which most families were able to produce only enough for their own consumption, with little left for the marketplace. Consequently, most families were involved in agricultural production. When the first U.S. census was taken in 1790, 96 percent of Americans lived in rural areas and most of them were involved in agriculture. Since then, a variety of factors have resulted in tremendous increases in the productivity of American agriculture. The westward expansion of the new nation brought new and extremely fertile land into production. New plant and animal varieties enabled the amount of production per acre to increase dramatically. Perhaps most important, the development of new machines allowed human labor to be replaced in the production process. With fewer workers needed in agriculture, many Americans could pursue other endeavors.

While the productivity of American agriculture was steadily increasing, a growing industrial sector in urban areas was attracting displaced farmworkers. In 1880, the nonfarm population surpassed the farm population for the first time, and by 1920 the urban population exceeded the rural population. It has been since 1940, however, that agricultural change has been most pronounced in this country. In 1940, there were over 6 million farms in the United States and the farm population exceeded 30 million. Since then, the mechanization process has greatly reduced the labor needs of American agriculture. With machines doing much of the work, farmers were able to operate much larger acreages than in previous years. As a consequence, the average farm size increased substantially, while there was a rapid decline in the number of

One of the myriad techniques used in agriculture, the skip-row planting method by mid-South cotton growers produces greater yields.

farms. By 1992, the number of farms in this country had declined to 1.9 million, while the farm population had been reduced to 3.9 million. Farmers now make up only about 2 percent of the population.

An equally dramatic consequence of the industrialization of U.S. agriculture was that it resulted in farmers and their families becoming a small minority of the population even in rural areas. Despite the loss of jobs in agriculture, and the subsequent migration of rural people to urban areas, the population of rural America remained remarkably consistent through the decades of declining farm numbers. This was possible because the net out-migration was offset by a natural population increase of births exceeding deaths, and as agricultural employment declined, there was a corresponding increase in the number of jobs in manufacturing and the service industries. By 1990, less than 10 percent of the rural labor force was employed in agriculture and the number of rural workers employed in both the manufacturing and service industries far exceeded the number employed in agriculture.

Productivity

American agriculture is the most productive the world has ever known (Paarlberg 1980). This tremendous productivity allowed America to make the transition from a farm to an urban society. American agriculture is now so productive that it is possible for a relatively few farmers to feed our own population and have a surplus remaining for extensive exports abroad. Several factors have combined to result in American agriculture becoming so productive. Perhaps most important are the vast stretches of land in the United States that are ideally suited for agricultural production. Huge tracts of land combine the three characteristics necessary for dependable crop production: good moisture conditions, deep and moisture-retentive soils, and flat or gentle slopes. Some parts of the midwestern states of Iowa and Illinois contain some of the most productive farmland anywhere in the world.

U.S. agricultural policies have played a prominent role in the productivity of American agriculture. One policy that played a paramount role in the development of American agriculture was getting the prime agricultural land into the hands of individuals, primarily family farmers. The opportunity to own one's own land was the magnet that drew thousands of immigrants from Europe to the United States, and there is little question that a system of private ownership provided the motivation for these farmers to be as productive as possible. This policy is perhaps best exemplified by the Homestead Act of 1862, which made it possible for a settler, after paying a registration fee of $10 to $25 and residing on and working 160 acres of land for five years, to gain clear title to the land.

U.S. policy also emphasized agricultural development, especially through research and education. In 1862, the Department of Agriculture was created and the Morrill Act was passed, which established the land-grant university system. The goals of these policies were to increase farm production and stabilize the welfare of farm families. Later policies built upon the foundation set in 1862. The Hatch Act of 1887 provided federal funds for research at agricultural experiment stations associated with the land-grant universities. In 1890, the land grant concept was extended to the Black colleges in the South. The organizational base for the threefold mission of today's land-grant system was completed in 1914 with passage of the Smith-Lever Act, which provided federal funds for agricultural extension. These initiatives had impressive results. Experiment stations developed new agricultural sciences, and the Cooperative Extension Service disseminated this science to farmers. The result was that the efficiency of agricultural production greatly increased the total supply of food and fiber products.

U.S. farm policy initially provided agriculture with numerous advantages not provided to other industries that added to its productivity. These included social security exemptions, exemptions from many labor laws, and exemptions from many environmental laws. In addition, agriculture greatly benefited from the commodity programs that emerged during the 1930s. These programs established a bottom level below which farm prices cannot fall and attempted to keep farm prices high by limiting production. The effect of the commodity programs has been to remove much of the risk from farming and greatly increase the income of farm families. With declining numbers of farms and farm families and a corresponding loss of political clout, there have been important changes in the direction of U.S. farm policy in recent years. Growing environmental interests and increased concern about the health risks from exposure to agrichemicals have resulted in the passage of farm bills that have made the receipt of most federal farm program benefits contingent upon the producers' utilization of selected environmental and conservation management practices.

Technological development and extensive mechanization greatly contribute to the productivity of American agriculture. The major impact of mechanization has been to reduce the amount of human labor required to produce a given level of output. It is estimated that there were about 30 billion hours of human labor used in agricultural production in 1930. By 1984, this number had been reduced to 3.7 billion. In 1940, the average farmer produced enough food and fiber to supply 10.7 persons; in 1984 the average farmer could supply 77 persons. With modern technology, a farmer can now accomplish in 1 hour what took 14 hours in 1920 (Bertrand 1978; Poincelot 1986).

Structure

Throughout most of American history, the typical farm could be described as medium sized, full time, and diversified relative to the commodities produced. On the typical farm, the family provided most of the needed labor, and the farm provided most or all of the family's economic sustenance. Of course, there were exceptions to this general farm structure rule, and the exceptions were more common in some parts of the country than others. For example, large plantations and a slave labor force existed in the South prior to the Civil War. After the Civil War, slave labor was replaced by a system of sharecropping. California has always been dominated by large farms and a hired labor force (Pfeffer 1983).

Since about 1940, the U.S. farm sector has gone through a period of dramatic restructuring as attempts have been made to adjust to vastly different technological, population, economic, and world markets circumstances (Lasley et al. 1995). Between 1940 and 1970, the major change was the loss of vast numbers of small farms and a rapid trend toward fewer and larger farms (Albrecht and Murdock 1990). During this time, the total number of farms declined from 6.1 million to 2.7 million and the size of the average farm increased from 175 acres to 390 acres. Small farms were especially vulnerable, and the number of farms with 49 or fewer acres declined from 2.3 million in 1940 to 635,000 in 1969, a decline of 72 percent. In comparison, the number of medium-sized farms (50–499 acres) declined by 52 percent, and the number of farms with 500 acres or more increased by 38 percent.

The direction of farm structural change altered after 1970 as American agriculture became increasingly dominated by trends toward dualism and concentration. The trend toward dualism consisted of a growing proportion of very small farms, a growing number of very large farms, and a continuing decline in the number of medium-sized farms that once had been the heart of American agriculture. Regarding the small farm trend, an increasingly large proportion of American farms could be considered as hobby, leisure, or retirement farms where the major objective of the operator is something other than agricultural production. Many of these farms are operated by families where either the farm operator, the operator's spouse, or both have employment off of the farm. Between 1969 and 1982, the number of American farms declined from 2.7 million to 2.2 million, yet the number of farms with 49 or fewer acres actually increased. During the 1980s, however, there was once again a reversal in the fortunes of small farms, and the dualism trend may be over. Between 1982 and 1992, the number of farms with 49 or fewer acres declined from 637,000 to 554,000, a decline of 13 percent.

The other major trend in U.S. agriculture consisted of a relatively small but growing number of very large, highly capitalized farms that are producing an increasingly large share of this country's agricultural commodities. A growing number of these large farms are corporately owned, and most are dependent on hired labor rather than family labor. In 1992, only 2.4 percent of American farms had gross farm sales of $500,000 or more. These farms, however, had about 46 percent of this nation's farm sales. The emergence of such farms can be traced to technological developments that allow production to occur in an assembly-like fashion and allow a more efficient use of farm labor. Since some commodities are more amenable to such capitalized forms of production than others, the extent to which production is concentrated varies greatly from commodity to commodity. In this regard, agricultural enterprises requiring large tracts of land, such as the production of most crops, are less likely to become concentrated than those commodities more dependent on capital (Mann and Dickinson 1978).

The dairy industry provides a graphic example of the trend toward concentration in agriculture. At one time in this country, most family farms had a few dairy cows that were used to provide milk, butter, and cheese for the farm family. The 1950 census of agriculture reported that there were over 3.6 million American farms with dairy cows and the average farm had 5.8 cows. In the years since, technological developments, policy decisions, breakthroughs in veterinary medicine, the record-keeping capacity of computers, and other factors have combined to greatly change the dairy industry (Gilbert and Akor 1988). By 1992, there were just 155,879 farms with dairy cows (a 96 percent decline from 1950) and these farms had an average of 61 cows each. Even though many American dairy farms remain as family farms, a number of large-scale, highly capitalized dairy farms have emerged in recent years. These farms specialize totally in dairy production, purchase most or all of their feed, and rely heavily on hired farm labor. In 1992, only 1.1 percent of dairy farms had 500 or more cows, but 18 percent of the dairy cows were on such farms. One-half of the dairy cows in this country are now on farms with 100 or more cows.

The dairy industry is not alone in the trend toward increased concentration. In 1992, over 69 percent of the hogs sold in the United States were produced on specialized hog plants that sold 1,000 or more hogs. Other researchers have described the concentration occurring in the poultry industry (Heffernan 1984) and in the production of several types of fresh fruits and vegetables (Friedland, Barton, and Thomas 1981).

Future Trends

The history of American agriculture has been a story of continued change in response to technological developments, changes in the availability of resources, economic changes, and policy changes. No doubt, American agriculture in the future will look substantially different from agriculture today. Speculating on the direction of agricultural change is risky business. In fact, speculation on which factors may be important may be futile. Nevertheless, from an examination of the horizon, three factors will likely play a major role in the future of American agriculture. First, technological developments have always played a prominent role in agricultural change and will probably continue to do so. Specifically, developments in biotechnology are likely to have a major impact on the future of agriculture. Second, the emergence of a truly world economy is likely to have massive implications for farm prices and the production of commodities in many local communities. Third, the depletion of the world's resources and the transfer of resources from agriculture to industries that can bid a higher price will drastically affect agriculture in the years to come.

—*Don E. Albrecht*

See also
Agriculture, Alternative; Agriculture, Hydroponic; Agriculture, Structure of; Cropping Systems; Dairy Farming; Dryland Farming; Farms; Grain Farming; Mechanization; Organic Farming; Value-Added Agriculture.

References
Albrecht, Don E., and Steve H. Murdock. *The Sociology of U.S. Agriculture: An Ecological Perspective.* Ames: Iowa State University Press, 1990.

Bertrand, Alvin L. "Rural Social Organizational Implications of Technology and Industry." Chapter 5, pp. 75-88 in *Rural U.S.A.: Persistence and Change.* Edited by Thomas R. Ford. Ames: Iowa State University Press, 1978.

Cochrane, Willard W. *The Development of American Agriculture: A Historical Analysis.* Minneapolis: University of Minnesota Press, 1979.

Friedland, William H., Amy E. Barton, and Robert J. Thomas. *Manufacturing Green Gold: Capital, Labor, and Technology in the Lettuce Industry.* New York: Cambridge University Press, 1981.

Gilbert, Jess, and Raymond Akor. "Increasing Structural Divergence in U.S. Dairying: California and Wisconsin since 1950." *Rural Sociology* 53, no. 1 (1988): 56–72.

Heffernan, William D. 1984. "Constraints in the U.S. Poultry Industry." Pp. 237–260 in *Research in Rural Sociology and Development.* Vol. 1: *Focus on Agriculture.* Edited by Harry K. Schwarzweller. Greenwich, CT: JAI Press.

Lasley, Paul F., Larry Leistritz, Linda M. Lobao, and K. Meyer. *Beyond the Amber Waves of Grain.* Boulder, CO: Westview Press, 1995.

Mann, Susan A., and James M. Dickinson. "Obstacles to the Development of a Capitalist Agriculture." *Journal of Peasant Studies* 5, no. 4 (1978): 466–481.

Paarlberg, Don. *Farm and Food Policy: Issues of the 1980s.* Lincoln: University of Nebraska Press, 1980.

Pfeffer, Max J. "Social Origins of Three Systems of Farm Production in the United States." *Rural Sociology* 48, no. 4 (1983): 540–562.

Poincelot, Raymond P. *Toward a More Sustainable Agriculture.* Westport, CT: AVI, 1986.

Vasey, Daniel E. *An Ecological History of Agriculture, 10000 B.C.–A.D. 10000.* Ames: Iowa State University Press, 1992.

Agriculture, Alternative

An agriculture that will provide current and future generations with ample, wholesome food in ways that are economically viable, environmentally sound, and socially responsible. Interest in alternative agriculture has grown, largely in response to the limitations and unforeseen adverse side effects of modern conventional agriculture. This entry discusses the nature of alternative agriculture and why it has gained national attention; the connections between alternative agriculture and rural communities; and future prospects for alternative agriculture.

The Nature of Alternative Practices

Farmers' adoption of alternative agricultural practices continues to be restrained by lack of research-based information on such practices; by customs, institutions, and government policies that historically have supported conventional agriculture; and by lack of consensus concerning the goals of alternative agriculture, especially those of a social nature. Growing awareness of the meaning and mission of alternative agriculture not only could help to lower those restraints but also begin a process of revaluing rural communities and reshaping American culture.

Alternative farms are generally more diversified and smaller than conventional farms (Bird, Bultena, and Gardner 1995). Alternative farmers favor use of integrated production methods that will conserve soil and water, protect the environment, and, to the extent possible, substitute renewable resources and human skills for purchased, nonrenewable resources. Alternative farmers seek to minimize or exclude the use of synthetic chemical pesticides and fertilizer. Production, to them, is not a factorylike process of converting inputs into outputs. Stewardship of the land is as important as profitable farming.

Other schools of thought and farming approaches included under the alternative umbrella include organic, regenerative, ecological, biodynamic, low input, perennial polyculture, and biological agriculture. In recent years, sustainable agriculture has become an especially popular term.

Gains in Attention

Fueled by science, technology, and favorable government policies, extraordinary gains in food production at home and abroad have repeatedly quelled doubts about the ability of farmers and our natural resources to meet the food needs of the world's expanding population. Why then is there interest in alternative agriculture? One reason is uncertainty as to whether conventional agriculture will always be able to produce as abundantly as it has in the past. More widely publicized concerns are raised about these effects of conventional agriculture: (1) farmers' heavy reliance on nonrenewable energy sources for fuel, fertilizer, and other inputs to farm production; (2) excessive loss of topsoil from erosion; (3) declining soil quality as a result of salinization, compaction, and pollution by toxic chemicals; (4) surface and groundwater pollution from environmentally harmful chemical pesticides and fertilizers; (5) depletion of underground aquifers as a result of continued expansion of irrigated farming; (6) health and safety risks to farmers, hired farmworkers, and consumers as a result of use of chemicals in both the production and processing of food; (7) loss of fish and wildlife habitats caused by monocultural and chemical-intensive farming practices; (8) farmers' dependence on federal price and income support programs for many commodities, programs that have rewarded high yields through intensive farming practices and discouraged diversified agriculture; (9) the demise of owner-operated family farms as a result of chronically low incomes caused by escalating costs of land, production inputs, and the financing of both and persistent downward pressure on the prices farmers receive for their products; and (10) the increasing size of remaining farms and the rising average age of surviving farmers.

Until recently, such concerns were repeatedly overshadowed by the importance the nation attached to increasing food production and by faith that science and technology would always be able to mend whatever adverse effects a productive agriculture might have. Alternative agriculture was regarded as a fringe idea. For example, in 1980 the U.S. Department of Agriculture (USDA) published a detailed report on organic farming, including recommendations for research on the subject. A year later, a new secretary of agriculture who spoke for conventional agriculture referred to organic agriculture research as a dead end.

But interest in alternatives was not to fade. Congress passed the Food Security Act of 1985 urging USDA researchers to give the subject more attention. A few years later, the National Academy of Sciences released a major study entitled *Alternative Agriculture* (National Research Council 1989). And Congress appropriated funds to support the research on alternative farming systems that it had authorized in 1985. Doing so, it launched a new and visible program, now called the USDA Sustainable Agriculture Research and Education Program.

At first, many farmers, agricultural organizations, the farm press, and colleges of agriculture interpreted alternative agriculture as unfair criticism of the nation's modern and highly productive agriculture. They said that they, too, supported soil and water conservation, environmental protection, and food safety, adding that unproved alternative farming methods would only cut farmers' profits, lower production, increase the cost of food, and invite hunger and starvation. Yet concerns about conventional agriculture continued to surface as a result of recurring fears, if not disturbing evidence, of pesticide residues in food, groundwater pollution, excessive soil erosion, and other adverse economic, environmental, or social effects of conventional farming. Proponents of

alternative agriculture became more organized and vocal. In 1990, major farm legislation passed by Congress reaffirmed federal support for sustainable agriculture research and education and offered farmers additional incentives to conserve soil and water, protect wetlands and other wildlife habitats, and experiment with environmentally beneficial farming practices.

Connections with Rural Communities

While public attention has centered largely on environmental concerns and the desire for safe and wholesome food, growing support for alternative agriculture also reflects concern about the steady weakening of traditional economic and social ties between farmers and rural communities. The trend began decades ago. To be profitable, farmers adopted more specialized and efficient methods, bought more of their production inputs, and sold more of their products outside their immediate communities. To stay competitive and prosper, they increased the size of their farms by purchasing neighboring farms. As a result, the total number of farms in the United States is now roughly 2 million, down from a peak of nearly 7 million in the mid-1930s. The drop came gradually, but its ultimate impacts on both rural and urban America were enormous. During the 30-year period from 1945 to 1975, "the largest migration in the history of mankind occurred in the U.S., when 20 million persons left the farms and ranches of this country and went elsewhere looking for a job" (Bergland 1992, 65).

Changes in the number and size of farms are among the more visible signs of what is now often referred to as the industrialization of American agriculture. There are other signs, such as a steady shift in the control of farming from farmers to other people and organizations. Huge companies, such as ConAgra and Philip Morris, now own, operate, or otherwise control not only the production of crops and livestock but also the shipping, processing, and retailing of final food products. More and more farmers who produce broilers, eggs, turkeys, beef, hogs, fruits, and other commodities do so under contract with large corporations. The firms supply inputs, tell farmers what production practices to use, and market the resulting products.

Farmers contract their production of crops and livestock for several reasons. Some are no longer willing or able to cope with the managerial, financial, or technical risks of modern agriculture. Contracting, they hope, will ease those burdens and provide them with a decent and predictable income. Others have done so because the merging of competing local marketing firms in their areas has closed off past markets, leaving them with no choice but to contract with a surviving firm, learn to produce and market other products, or go out of business.

Gains in efficiency and profit are major rewards of industrialized agriculture. Unfortunately, they often invite offsetting problems. For example, large-scale confinement feeding of livestock tends to increase disease risks and create major waste and other environmental problems as a result of the unnatural concentration of animals. The economic and social impacts of agricultural industrialization are among the least well understood. Smith (1992) sees today's industrialized agriculture as an advanced stage of a process through which most of the farming activities once performed by farmers are now carried out by firms that make and sell production inputs and market farm products.

The process began long ago when farmers replaced animal power with tractors and, more recently, substituted synthetic chemical pesticides and fertilizers for crop rotations and other nonchemical methods of controlling insects, weeds, and diseases. As a result of those trends, Smith estimates that only 9 percent of the total dollar returns paid to participants in the food system now go to those directly involved in farming activities (farmers, farmworkers, and farm service providers). Participants in the input manufacturing and distribution sector get 24 percent and those in the marketing sector, 67 percent.

On the surface, those shifts tell only a story of progress. Thanks to the efficiencies they have made possible, we are among the best-fed people in the world. But the true cost of that progress has not been fully recognized. For example, as control of farming continues to shift from the farming sector to input and marketing sectors, the farmer becomes more of a hired laborer. Proponents of alternative agriculture fear that as a result the watchful eyes of the farmer are being replaced by those of corporate analysts and managers who work in distant office buildings and are more interested in maximizing company profits than in ensuring the survival of environmentally beneficial farming. Of course, even on farms that are still owned and operated by farm families, physical absence is no longer uncommon. More and more family farmers must now work part time off the farm to help pay the bills.

These developments have been steadily redefining traditional ties between agriculture and rural communities in ways that may benefit neither. Studies of the impacts of agricultural industrialization on rural areas

"generally suggest that it is not so much the scale of operation but the social organization of the farm that influences rural communities. Large farms with industrial-type relationships tend to have negative influences, while owner operator farms generally have positive influences" (Browne et al. 1992, 31).

A related change over recent decades has been the steady influx of manufacturing and service industries into rural areas. Today, only one out of six counties in the United States is economically dependent on farming (that is, receives at least 20 percent of its earned income from farm wage or salary jobs and self-employment). Increasingly, farmers who supplement their incomes with off-farm employment have jobs in nonagricultural fields, which is another reason that the "culture" in "agriculture" is undergoing changes never imagined.

Future Prospects

Support for alternative agriculture is growing. More and more farmers appear to be aware of, and are experimenting with, environmentally beneficial production practices. Soil erosion rates are down. Agricultural research and extension programs are generating and disseminating credible information on alternative farming systems. Sales of organically grown food, though still a tiny fraction of consumers' food expenditures, increased 20 percent a year during the early 1990s. At the same time, evidence of significant change in the way farmers farm is spotty. Existing data show no appreciable drop in farm use of synthetic chemical pesticides and fertilizers, and the trend toward industrialization is, if anything, accelerating.

Important barriers to adoption of alternative agriculture include a lack of science-based information on alternative farming systems and practices, inadequate market outlets for alternative crop and livestock products, and the persistence of farm and other public policies that give artificial advantage to conventional agriculture. The importance of these barriers varies from one part of the country to the next. They are least restraining in areas characterized by diversified family farming with close ties to neighboring rural communities. They are formidable in parts of the country dominated by large-scale, industrialized, monoculture serving distant markets. The nation's heartland, a vast area of corn and soybean production, is a case in point. Corn and soybeans dominate Midwest agriculture not only because of favorable soils and climate, but also because of economic efficiencies that provide farmers with good access to inputs of seed, fertilizer, pesticides, equipment, know-how, and credit, as well as markets for their crops. Federal commodity and related support programs, as well as the research and educational assistance of the land-grant colleges of agriculture, also have favored corn-soybean agriculture.

Contributing importantly to each of the barriers to adoption of alternative agriculture in the United States is a basic lack of consensus concerning the ends or goals of such an agriculture and therefore agreement on specific changes needed in conventional agriculture. Ambiguities continue to frustrate meaningful discourse on the subject, thwarting development of public policies needed to support adoption of alternatives. Misuse of the popular term *sustainable agriculture* exacerbates the problem. The term was embraced in the 1980s by proponents of alternative agriculture who believed that the yardstick of sustainability provided a pathway for research to support the scientific legitimacy of alternative farming systems. But the term's meaning has been weakened by lack of consensus as to what should be sustained and for whom. Moreover, the term is now used routinely to describe not only farming practices expected to contribute to sustainability but also unproved practices that people hope will do so. In many cases, little thought is given to how so-called sustainable practices will affect other parts of the total farm system.

For example, enthusiasts of no-till farming, an effective way to reduce soil erosion, often equate the practice with sustainable agriculture. But if no-till farmers use more synthetic chemical herbicides to control weeds previously killed by cultivation, as many are inclined to do, the net effect may not be a truly sustainable agriculture. Precision farming is another example. By using high-technology methods and sophisticated equipment, precision farming increases the efficiency of production. Manufactured fertilizer inputs can be reduced with the help of equipment that adjusts fertilizer applications to within-field differences in nutrient requirements. But while impressive, those efficiencies may be offset partially by increased reliance on costly equipment or off-farm expertise. Precision farming also tends to postpone consideration of more fundamental changes that might eliminate the need for manufactured fertilizer inputs, such as crop-livestock diversification and extensive use of rotations.

The future of alternative agriculture is clouded especially by lack of agreement on what is meant by the common assertion that alternative, and sustainable, agriculture must be socially responsible. To some, it means simply an agriculture that favors family farming and enhances the quality of rural life. Others (for example, Allen and Sachs 1993) believe alternative agriculture lacks true meaning unless it deliberately seeks to ensure social justice and equity and satisfies requirements such as humane treatment of animals.

Perhaps the most important unanswered question is whether adoption of an environmentally sound, productive, and economically viable agriculture automatically will lead the way to an agriculture that is socially responsible. The belief that it might is expressed by Kirschenmann, a farmer and spokesperson for alternative agriculture. He (1992, 33) writes that "if behavior, at least in part, changes values, then alternative agriculture practices, poised on the principle of restraint, may give birth to revitalized rural communities; revitalized in the sense of having a new sense of purpose and a new set of values that could reshape American culture and revalue rural communities. It is reasonable to predict that if sustainable agriculture is successful, it could create an alternative future in which rural America could lead the way to a cultural renaissance of the human spirit in which self-sufficiency, happiness, and security are redefined."

—*Neill Schaller*

See also

Biodiversity; Conservation, Soil; Cropping Systems; Environmental Protection; Food Safety; Groundwater; Land Stewardship; Organic Farming; Pest Management; Policy, Agricultural.

References

Allen, Patrick, and Carolyn Sachs. "Sustainable Agriculture in the United States: Engagements, Silences, and Possibilities for Transformation." Pp. 139–167 in *Food for the Future: Conditions and Contradictions*. Edited by Patrick Allen. New York: John Wiley and Sons, 1993.

Bergland, Bob. "The USDA Structure of Agriculture Study and Other Lessons from the Past." Pp. 64–72 in *Alternative Farming Systems and Rural Communities: Exploring the Connections*. Greenbelt, MD: Institute for Alternative Agriculture, 1992.

Bird, Elizabeth A. R., Gordon L. Bultena, and John C. Gardner, eds. *Planting the Future: Developing an Agriculture That Sustains Land and Community*. Ames: Iowa State University Press, 1995.

Browne, William P., Jerry R. Skees, Louis E. Swanson, Paul B. Thompson, and Laurian J. Unnevehr. *Sacred Cows and Hot Potatoes*. Boulder, CO: Westview Press, 1992.

Kirschenmann, Frederick. "What Can Alternative Farming Systems and Rural Communities Do for Each Other?" Pp. 25–38 in *Alternative Farming Systems and Rural Communities: Exploring the Connections*. Greenbelt, MD: Institute for Alternative Agriculture, 1992.

National Research Council. Board on Agriculture. *Alternative Agriculture*. Washington, DC.: National Academy Press, 1989.

Smith, Stewart. "Farming Activities and Family Farms: Getting the Concepts Right." United States Congress. Hearing before the Joint Economic Committee, Congress of the United States, One Hundred Second Congress, Second Session, October 21, 1992. *Joint Economic Committee Symposium on Agricultural*

Industrialization and Family Farms: The Role of Federal Policy.
Washington, DC: Government Printing Office, October 1992
(Y4.EC 7: AG 8/19).

U.S. Department of Agriculture. *Report and Recommendations on
Organic Farming.* Washington, DC: U.S. Department of Agriculture, July 1980.

Agriculture, Hydroponic

The growing of crops without soil; also termed soilless agriculture when a nonsoil medium is used. This entry examines the nutrient solutions required for hydroponic agriculture and the various hydroponic systems that are used in vegetable production. Issues related to the types of training needed by hydroponic growers is addressed. The entry concludes with a discussion of the economic impact of hydroponic agriculture on rural communities.

Basis

Pure hydroponics uses a water-nutrient solution only. The most widely used methods are peatlite (mixes of sand, peat, vermiculite/perlite), sawdust, sand, rockwool, and nutrient film technique (NFT) cultures. Peatlite culture is used principally to grow potted houseplants and bedding plants. Vegetables, such as tomatoes, cucumbers, peppers, lettuce, spinach, and herbs, are grown in the other cultures. The majority of hydroponic crops are grown in greenhouses to extend the growing season to year-round.

Nutrient Solutions

Nutrient solutions contain 13 of the 16 essential elements for plant growth (those elements plants require to complete their life cycle). Essential elements fall into two groups: macroelements (those required in relatively large amounts) and microelements (those needed in relatively small amounts). Macroelements include carbon, hydrogen, and oxygen, which come from water, carbon dioxide, and the oxygen in the atmosphere. The remaining macroelements must be present in the nutrient solution and available for plant root uptake. These include nitrogen, phosphorus, potassium, calcium, magnesium, and sulfur. Microelements include iron, manganese, copper, zinc, boron, molybdenum, and chlorine. The specific level of each of the 13 essential elements in the nutrient solution is the nutrient formulation. The levels vary from in excess of 400 parts per million (ppm) for potassium in a tomato formulation to as low as 0.02 ppm of molybdenum (Resh 1989).

Raw water is analyzed for the presence of any of these elements, and the formulation is adjusted accordingly to prevent toxicities, especially in the case of the microelements. The nutrient solution is made up from highly soluble fertilizer compounds. The acidity or basic level of the solution (pH) determines the availability of the elements to the plants. Solutions to grow most vegetable crops should have a pH between 6.0 and 6.5.

The pH and total dissolved solutes of the nutrient solution is monitored with a pH meter and electrical conductivity meter. The pH is adjusted by addition of an acid or base. Nutrient solutions become imbalanced as a result of the differential uptake of the elements by the plants. A complete nutrient analysis may be carried out on the solution by a commercial laboratory. The grower can then adjust the nutrient solution to make up for the elements in nonoptimum levels. The precise management of the nutrient solution is the key to successful hydroponic growing.

Systems

The following description focuses on systems used in vegetable production. The most common systems include sand, sawdust, rockwool, and NFT.

Sand Culture. This system has been the most suitable method for desert areas where sand is abundant. However, even in areas where sand is of sedimentary origin (calcareous), rather than igneous (volcanic) origin, the calcareous sand creates a high pH in the nutrient solution, reducing nutrient uptake. This leads to nutrient deficiencies in the plants. Any nutrient imbalance in the plant greatly reduces productivity. With proper testing and adjustment of the pH, the nutrient solution may be stabilized. Sand culture has been very successful in Arizona, where several greenhouse operations of 10 or more acres are operated. Similar facilities have been established in Abu Dhabi, Iran, Kuwait, and Saudi Arabia.

Although sand culture may be set up as beds, the more common method is to line the entire floor with black polyethylene, place drainage pipes 5 or 6 feet apart, and backfill the area with 12 inches of sand. Drip irrigation lines are located beside the plant rows. The drip system consists of nutrient tanks, a fertilizer injector, filters, pumps, solenoid valves, and a controller that regulates the irrigation cycles to each section of plants. Nutrient solutions are prepared as concentrated stock solutions (usually 200 times normal strength) in several large tanks in addition to holding facilities of an acid component to adjust the pH. The injector measures and places the correct volume of stock solutions into the flowing raw water as it passes through the injection loop to achieve a 1:200

dilution of stock solution to water. This results in the normal-strength nutrient solution going to the plants. Downstream, the pH and EC may be monitored by a computer that makes changes in the injection rates to adjust the solution.

Sawdust Culture. This system is used commonly in areas having a forest industry of softwood lumber. Douglas fir and hemlock sawdusts are used because other species, such as pine, contain chemicals that inhibit plant growth. This culture has been used extensively in British Columbia because of the presence of the large forest industry that has made sawdust readily available. Sawdust culture is not being replaced by rockwool culture.

Sawdust culture is set up similarly to sand culture but uses polyethylene plastic bags rather than polyethylene floor covering. The greenhouse floor is covered with a 6-milliliter thick, white-on-black polyethylene liner. Polyethylene bags, measuring about 30 inches long and 8 to 10 inches wide, are heat-sealed on one end. They are filled with sawdust (a hopper and chute are used to do so); then the other end is heat-sealed. Small drainage holes are punched in the bottom sides of the bags. They are placed on top of the liner in the greenhouse in rows at the appropriate crop spacing. Seedlings are started in growing blocks such as rockwool and transplanted to the top of the bags through a hole cut in the bag; the transplant with its block is placed on top. Plants are individually fed with a spaghetti drip line at the base of the plant. The nutrient system is similar to that of sand culture using stock tanks or a large central nutrient solution tank.

Rockwool Culture. This system rapidly is becoming the most widely used system of hydroponics. The Netherlands, which has the largest greenhouse industry in the world, uses 5,000 acres of rockwool. It is an inert, sterile material made from volcanic rock, limestone, and coke melted at high temperatures and extruded as fine threads that are pressed into loosely woven sheets. Four products are made for horticultural uses: granusis, cubes, blocks, and slabs. The granular form is used for potted plants, whereas the cubes and blocks are used for seedlings. The slabs were designed specifically to grow vine crops. The slabs are similar in size to sawdust culture bags and are wrapped with a white polyethylene. Slabs are placed on top of a polyethylene liner on the floor, as was done for the sawdust bags. The slabs are presoaked with nutrient solution prior to transplanting. Seedlings are started in rockwool blocks and transplanted to the slabs similar to the procedure used with sawdust culture.

Irrigation is by a drip spaghetti system. The nutrient solution drains from the slabs through slits made at their base and then through other slits made in the floor liner to an underlying drainage system. Alternatively, slabs are placed in a gutter that recycles the solution back to the tank. With a recirculation or closed system, a normal-strength nutrient solution is stored in a large tank. The nutrient solution is adjusted with stock solutions from an injector. This can be monitored and controlled by a computer. To eliminate disease organisms, the recycled solution is sterilized by ozonation, ultraviolet light exposure, or heat pasteurization as it returns to the storage tank.

Nutrient Film Technique. NFT is a water culture system that uses no medium. Plants are grown in a channel or gutter in a closed recirculating system. Seedlings are started in rockwool or other synthetic blocks and transplanted to the gutters once they develop three or four true leaves. As with a recirculating rockwool system, the solution is stored in a large tank and monitored and adjusted by use of a computer. Sterilization of the nutrient solution each time it passes through the tank is important to prevent diseases. The nutrient film technique has universal application since it is not dependent on a medium. It may be operated on a small, relatively simple scale in Third World countries or in a highly technical, large commercial production facility.

Grower Training

Whatever hydroponic system is used, growers must have a thorough understanding of basic chemistry. They must be able to calculate changes in the nutrient formulation. Variations in plant health expressed as color change, leaf curling or wilting, or poor flower and fruit formation indicate a problem. Quick recognition of problems and implementation of remedial measures will prevent production losses. Growers must correctly identify pests, understand their life cycle, and know which pesticides and/or biological control agents may be applied in their control. Courses in entomology and pest management practices are an asset.

Previous growing experience with a particular crop increases the potential success through familiarity with some of the problems associated with the crop, particularly the common pests and diseases of the crop. Growers must have knowledge of the cultural practices for the plants. Tomatoes, cucumbers, and peppers, for instance, require vertical training and suckering (or pruning). Seeding and transplant timing is important in the regulation of crop cycles. Growers must understand the operations of a greenhouse and be handy in repairing its components. They should have previous work experience in the greenhouse industry.

Potential Economic Impact on Rural Communities

The greenhouse industry, together with soilless culture, is present in almost every country of the world. It is used in desert areas such as the Middle East as well as tropical areas of Mexico, Central and South America, Australia, and islands in the Atlantic, Caribbean, and Pacific. Work is being done in Alaska and Antarctica. Europe and North America have the largest greenhouse industries.

Even though many large commercial greenhouse hydroponic operations exist throughout North America, there is a rapid growth in the hobby and small commercial "mom and pop" operations. Hobbyists wish to grow clean, high-quality vegetables for their own use. The number of people now involved in hydroponics has supported the development of small businesses that provide information and supplies to the backyard grower. Small commercial growers (under 1 acre of greenhouses) have found market niches in supplying local stores with produce. These growers can supply a high-quality product since the vegetables can be harvested as vine ripened and delivered to the grocers in short time, unlike the larger commercial growers, which must ship products not only out of their local community but also to large wholesalers and supermarkets across the country or even abroad.

The general public is aware of healthful foods. Greenhouse-produced vegetables are almost pesticide free as a result of integrated pest management using natural predators. Many people grow their own vegetables hydroponically in small backyard greenhouses. Co-generation projects continue to develop where greenhouses use waste heat from power generation stations and other industries. Natural geothermal sites can be harnessed to heat greenhouses.

The environmental impact of agriculture on groundwaters is forcing restraints on the industry. Recycling hydroponic nutrient solutions in greenhouses is increasingly important to prevent groundwater pollution. These hydroponic methods will be in high demand to conserve water and fertilizers. Hydroponic research has been proceeding with the space program by providing food for astronauts. Closed systems use wastes from the astronauts to provide nutrition to the plants. The goal of controlled ecological life support systems is to recycle mass and provide self-sufficiency.

Hydroponics is a universal method of agriculture that is particularly suitable for the growing of high-value crops and ornamentals. Nonetheless, it may be applied to growing most crops if it is economically feasible. It is particularly suited to the greenhouse industry and other controlled environment agriculture and probably will become an integral part of human exploration of space in the future.

—*Howard M. Resh*

See also
Greenhouses; Horticulture; Temperate Fruit Industry; Vegetable Industry.
References
Bridwell, Raymond. *Hydroponic Gardening*. Santa Barbara, CA: Woodbridge Press, 1990.
Cooper, A. *The ABC of NFT*. London: Grower Books, 1979.
Mason, John. *Commercial Hydroponics*. Kenthurst, NSW, Australia: Kangaroo Press, 1990.
Muckle, M. Edward. *Basic Hydroponics*. Princeton, BC: Growers Press, 1982.
Resh, Howard M. *Hydroponic Food Production*. 4th ed. Santa Barbara, CA: Woodbridge Press, 1989.
———. *Hydroponic Home Food Gardens*. Santa Barbara, CA: Woodbridge Press, 1990.
———. *Hydroponic Tomatoes for the Home Gardener*. Santa Barbara, CA: Woodbridge Press, 1993.
Smith, Denis L. *Rockwool in Horticulture*. London: Grower Books, 1987.

Agriculture, Structure of

The control and organization of resources needed for farm production. The first section of this entry describes the changes that took place in the number and size of farms, with particular emphasis on the last half of the twentieth century. The second section pertains to government policies, generally supported by the American people, that influenced many of the changes in farm structure.

Historical Changes

Changes in the size of farms and in ownership are major themes for an understanding of the structure of agriculture. Government policies have had, and continue to have, an ineradicable influence on agriculture. Major changes in farm structure took place at about the time of the American Revolution, the Civil War, and World War II. At the time of the American Revolution, farmers made up 95 percent of the workforce. When the British government attempted to control farm structure by forbidding settlement west of the Allegheny Mountains, thus limiting the land available to farmers, taxing the export of farm products, and imposing small permanent "quit rents" or taxes on land occupied by farmers, this policy harmed the economic interests of the colonial settlers.

After the revolution, these disabilities were brought to an end. Their end did not mean sharp increases in productivity, but it did mean substantial changes in farm structure. The emphasis on each farmer owning his own land was a goal that was never achieved. At the same time, the number of farms increased rapidly as the growing population, including many immigrants, moved west and bought land from the government and speculators or simply settled without title. There were 335,000 farms in 1800, with a farm population of 4.3 million. Those numbers jumped to 1.1 million farms in 1840, with a farm population of 12.3 million.

Farms typically were not large, except in the South, where plantations were worked by slaves. Land generally was readily available, and in much of the eastern United States the size of the farm was limited by the difficulty of clearing land of timber. During this early period, Thomas Jefferson extolled the virtues of the self-sufficient, independent farmer, although he operated a large plantation with slave labor.

By 1850, the nation counted 1.4 million farms, averaging 203 acres in size; the farm population was at 15.8 million; and farmers made up 64 percent of the labor force. The Civil War demanded food and agricultural products for export. At the same time, farmworkers were entering the military and the urban labor force. These countervailing forces brought about major changes in structure. Many farmers increased production by increasing the size of farms and by replacing hand labor with horse-drawn machinery. The result was that after the war these farmers were caught up in commercial agricultural production to pay for their land and machinery. By 1870, there were 2.7 million farms, averaging 199 acres in size. However, although the farm population increased to 20.1 million, farmers as a percentage of the total labor force dropped to 58 percent.

Congress contributed to the change in structure by passing three laws in 1862 all aimed at encouraging family farms. The first established the U.S. Department of Agriculture (USDA) to develop useful information and carry it to the farmers. Second, the Homestead Act offered 160 acres of unclaimed western land without charge to anyone willing to improve the land and live on it for five years. And third, each state was offered land to establish a college to teach agriculture, mechanical engineering, and military science. Over the years, these institutions made

substantial contributions to farm structure, helping to make U.S. agriculture competitive in world markets. The changes that took place in agricultural structure around the Civil War, primarily the change from hand power to horse power, make up what has been called the first American agricultural revolution.

In 1900, the 38 percent of the labor force on the nation's 5.7 million farms was entering what has been called the "Golden Age of American Agriculture," the period from 1900 to 1914. Over 31 million American lived on farms (41.9 percent of the total population). The structure of agriculture was in balance, producing the food and fiber for which there was a reasonable market. The Great Depression had an acute impact on agriculture and led the federal government to pass a series of laws aimed at agriculture and rural life; passage began with the Agricultural Act of 1933. Most of these laws have been modified but are still in effect. They provided for support of prices for major crops, soil conservation, rural electrification, and loans to purchase farms. These laws had major impacts on farm structure, primarily by providing a price base, incentives for better land use, and opportunities for poor families to buy farms. The farm population in 1935 stood at 32.2 million (25.3 percent of the total population) and lived on 6.8 million farms, the largest number of farms in America before or since.

Revolutionary structural changes took place around World War II, including the change from horse power to mechanical power, the use of new productive seeds and strains of livestock, the proper application of fertilizer, irrigation when and where necessary, and the productive use of livestock feed. Making the most of such a combination of factors required management skills and led to problems of structure quite different from those previous decades. Three facts define the changes in structure during the past half century. First, between 1950 and 1995 the average size of farms in the United States increased by one-half, jumping from an average of 216 acres to an average of 469 acres. Second, the number of farms declined by over one-half, from 5.4 million farms in 1950 to 2 million farms in 1995. The rural farm population fell from 23 million (15.3 percent of the total population) in 1950 to 3.9 million (1.6 percent of the total population) in 1990. And third, both total production and productivity increased during this period. The American people are interested in securing a safe, sure supply of food at a reasonable cost to consumers and the government. The family farm as an agricultural structure ranks high in public esteem as a source of food, even as the family farm may be disappearing.

Current Problems

Six million farms produced the nation's food and a substantial amount of food and other products for export during World War II. Fifty years later, a commercial agricultural sector of less than 1 million farms accounted for more than 95 percent of all farm production. Another 1 million part-time farming operations added to the total, although the operators of these farms earned more from employment off the farm than on it. Together, the income from commercial farming and from off-farm work brought farm household incomes near to the national average of all U.S. households, a goal long sought.

During the 1950s and 1960s, several proposals were made to strengthen the family farm and end rural poverty. Little of substance resulted, although some rural development programs started by the USDA and some state land-grant universities remain in limited existence. Industries were encouraged to move to rural areas and provide employment to members of farm families who would continue to live on their farms. These programs frequently were opposed by city interests, which had their own poor groups to accommodate. The programs soon became ways to improve the social and educational structure of rural areas. Some farm programs of this era had little relevance to the very large producers and processors of farm products. The programs were directed instead to national and world markets.

The total amount of land in farms, slightly under 1 billion acres in 1995, decreased somewhat between 1960 and 1995. The major decrease took place in midsized farms, with the large farms remaining about the same and the small farms increasing in size and number. Small farms in 1995 (those with sales between $1,000 and $9,999) averaged 101 acres in size and made up nearly one-half of the nation's total farms. Midsized farms (those with sales of $10,000 to $99,999) averaged 497 acres in size and made up 35 percent of the total number of farms. Large farms (those with sales of $100,000 and over) averaged 1,522 acres in size and made up 16 percent of all farms in the United States. Although it is difficult to determine the number of farms that are business corporations (many farm families incorporate for tax or inheritance purposes), certainly fewer than 5 percent are business corporations. However, these corporations produce a substantial percentage of the total farm output.

The USDA and other government agencies generally encouraged people to stay on their farms through price supports, loan programs, subsidization of electricity, payments to carry out soil conservation programs, and irrigation facilities. These programs were aimed primarily at, but not limited to, the midsized farms, giving their operations control over the resources needed for farm production. However, these programs did not stop the continued exodus of people from the farms. Changes in farm structure over the past half century have permitted farmers to meet the needs of the nation for agricultural products, while achieving something of an economic equilibrium.

—*Wayne D. Rasmussen*

See also
Agricultural Programs; Agriculture; Agro/Food System; Farms; History, Agricultural; History, Rural; Landownership; Mechanization; Policy, Agricultural; Rural Demography.
References
Cochrane, Willard W. *The Development of American Agriculture, A Historical Analysis.* 2d ed. Minneapolis: University of Minnesota Press, 1979.
Danbom, David B. *The Resisted Revolution: Urban America and the Industrialization of Agriculture, 1900–1930.* Ames: Iowa State University Press, 1979.
Dyson, Lowell K. *Farmers' Organizations.* Westport, CT: Greenwood Press, 1986.
Hallam, Arne. *Size, Structure, and the Changing Face of American Agriculture.* Boulder, CO: Westview Press, 1993.
Hurt, R. Douglas. *American Agriculture: A Brief History.* Ames: Iowa State University Press, 1994.
Rasmussen, Wayne D., ed. *American Agriculture: A Documentary History.* 4 vols. New York: Random House, 1975.
———. "Public Experimentation and Innovation: An Effective Past but Uncertain Future." *American Journal of Agricultural Economics* 69 (1987): 890–899.
———. *Taking the University to the People: Seventy-Five Years of Cooperative Extension.* Ames: Iowa State University Press, 1989.
U.S. Congress. Office of Technology Assessment. *Agriculture, Trade, and Environment: Achieving Complementary Policies.* Washington, DC: U.S. Government Printing Office, 1995.
———. *A Time to Choose: Summary Report on the Structure of Agriculture.* Washington, DC: U.S. Department of Agriculture, 1981.
———. Senate. Committee on Agriculture, Nutrition, and Forestry. *Farm Structure: A Historical Perspective on Changes in the Number and Size of Farms.* Washington, DC: U.S. Government Printing Office, 1980.

Agro/Food System

The organizational arrangement through which food moves from the production stages, to the processing stages, and then to the distributions stages that make food available to consumers. Throughout most of history, the agro/food system was very simple since families produced, processed, and consumed their own food in their home setting. With the Industrial Revolution, a movement toward increased specialization introduced new stages through which food products proceeded on their way to distant consumers. Early in this new system, a number of firms competed at each stage and many new stages were developed. However, in the past two or three decades control of these stages narrowed. Increasingly, a limited number of food firms control the entire process from "seed to shelf." Throughout this evolution, many opposed this system because of its negative social, economic, and political consequences. As a result, a new social movement is growing that attempts to develop an alternative food system.

History

When Europeans began to farm in North America, farm families purchased very few items for their farms and sold very few products from their farms. For the most part, farm families produced what the family consumed and consumed what the farm produced. This subsistence food system provided few surpluses of food or fiber products for those who were not farming. The coming of the Industrial Revolution to the United States brought with it the demand for surplus food to be produced on farms, freeing others to move to the industrializing cities. Thus, social, political, and economic forces emerged to begin the development of a commercial agriculture system that could produce sufficient supplies to be sold in the growing cities.

Commercial farmers in the United States began by using hand tools and simple equipment that animals pulled. Much of the equipment could be made at the local blacksmith shop. However, the production of more sophisticated equipment, such as the steel plow used to break up the prairie sod of the Plains, was soon produced in specialized factories following the industrialized model. For example, John Deere, originally a local blacksmith in Illinois, was one of the first to develop a steel plow, which he soon began to produce for a mass market. The company he founded is today one of the four farm equipment firms that dominate sales in the United States. The need for increasingly sophisticated, mass-produced equipment encouraged farmers' dependence on purchased inputs for their farms.

Increasing Complexity

The need for other inputs followed the need for more sophisticated equipment. Farmers learned that their animals were more productive when their feed rations included all of the necessary dietary ingredients, such as a balance of protein, vitamins, and minerals. Commercial feeds and feed premixes to fortify farmers' homegrown feeds were developed. Soon special seeds, especially hybrid seeds and now genetically engineered seeds, became available. Fertilizers followed by agricultural chemicals became major purchased inputs after World War II. These purchased inputs required increasing amounts of capital, and thus borrowed capital became another major input.

Today, farmers purchase a host of other inputs ranging from fuel and animal health products to computers and satellite guidance systems. What was once a rather simple food system in which most of the food was produced, processed, and consumed by the family in the home became increasingly complex as the industrialized model, with its emphasis on specialization, began developing in the food system. As the input portion of the agricultural sector increased and farm families were able to produce more products, movement of products to cities became more important. Farmers could not sell directly to consumers or retail stores in distant cities as they could in their local community. They were increasingly dependent on a wide array of brokers, transportation firms, and processing firms. These agribusiness firms, rather than consumers in distant places, became the farmers' markets. Often these agribusiness firms were called "middlemen" because they operated between producers and food consumers. Farmers became so dependent on the agribusiness firms for purchased inputs and for markets for their outputs that farms today are sometimes compared to assembly plants like those found in the automobile system.

Specialization in food production, processing, and distribution by different persons and firms led to an identification of different stages in the food system that extended from the extraction of iron ore and petroleum to produce and provide energy for farm equipment to retail food stores. Firms that were directly producing goods and services for the production stage, such as farm equipment, and those that did the original processing of the farm commodity became known as agribusiness firms. At the national level early in the development of the industrialized food system, a host of firms evolved in most of the stages. A sufficient number of firms existed so that no one firm sold or purchased enough of a commodity at any stage to influence the price of the commodity. Firms easily entered or exited the system, a characteristic of a competitive economic system. For this reason, the agricultural sector is often used as an example of a competitive economic system.

However, in many local areas the input and output stages were dominated by a few firms from the beginning of commercial agriculture. In many local areas and for many commodities, the lack of an economically viable transportation system or market meant farmers had only one or very few alternatives. For example, if there was only one railroad passing through an area with no other transportation source capable of moving the food product to distant cities, the farmer and the agribusiness firm did not enter into price negotiation from an equal power position. Furthermore, the special relationship between railroads and the government was such that the government would not provide economic assistance to a competing railroad in an area, so another railroad was not free to enter even if the first firm was making very large profits. Farmers were in a much less powerful position than railroads because in any particular time period the railroads did not need the farm products from a single area. They could get the product from another area. The farmers, however, had no choice. Most of them had to sell their product the year it was produced for whatever price the railroad offered for the product or charged for transporting it to market, even when the resulting price was well below the cost of production.

Increased Tensions

As the agribusiness portion of the food system evolved, tensions often developed between farmers and agribusinesses. The tensions resulted from the unequal power distribution between the farmers and the agricultural business firms upon which they depended for their livelihood and much of their quality of life. Even in areas where there were many firms within reasonable access to farmers during the early stages of the evolution of agribusiness firms, the trend was toward a reduced number of firms. As a consequence, the power relationship in the exchange of goods and services increasingly favored the agribusiness firms. This can be seen in the differences in the return on investments received by food firms and farmers. The major food firms in United States, many of which are listed in the table, expect to provide stockholders with a 20 percent or greater return on their investments. Food firms receive about a 50 percent greater return on their investments than is typical of other manufacturing firms. In marked contrast, farm management records indicate that on average, well-managed farms can expect to receive a 3 to 5 percent return.

Most of the nation's farm movements, which led to the formation of many national general farm organizations, such as the existing Grange and the National Farmers Union and the now-defunct Farmers Alliance and the Nonpartisan League, trace their origins to the tensions between farmers and agribusiness firms. Railroads, bankers, and farm equipment manufactures were frequently targets of farm movements in the past. Farm organization leaders believed that if farmers across a region or at the national level were to cooperate together, they could equalize the power relationship because the firms could no longer treat farmers in one area differently from those in another.

Farmers established national general farm organizations, cooperatives, and commodity organizations to help equalize the power relationship in the economic exchange of goods and services between farmers and agribusiness firms. However, the continued concentration of ownership and control of agribusiness firms at the national, and now at the international, level counters most of the benefits farm organization leaders hope to achieve. Today the tensions and conflicts seen in the past are still associated with the loss of competition in the food system. This is especially obvious in the broiler, dairy, swine, and beef sectors.

Growing Concentration

Horizontal integration and vertical integration are two processes by which changes are brought into the organization of the food system. Horizontal integration refers to the expansion of a firm in the size of its operation in one stage of the food system, such as the production of agricultural chemicals or the slaughter of beef cattle. As one firm gets larger, the others either get smaller or, more likely, go out of business. Data in the table indicate that the largest four firms in each commodity slaughter 87 percent of the beef cattle, 73 percent of the sheep, 46 percent of the hogs, and 45 percent of the broilers in the United States. Economists suggest that when four firms control 40 percent of a market, the economic system loses the characteristics of a competitive system. This means a change in the power relationship between farmers and agribusinesses.

Control of grain and oil crops processing is just as concentrated as the livestock sectors. Seventy-one percent of the flour in the United States is milled by four firms. The largest four firms own 57 percent of the corn dry milling facilities, and in the wet milling of corn the largest four firms process 74 percent. About 75 percent of soybeans are processed by the largest four firms, and about the same proportion of ethanol is produced by four firms.

Market Share Controlled by Largest Food Firms

Food Sector	Four Largest Food Firms	Market Share (%)
Broilers	Tyson Gold Kist Perdue Farms ConAgra	45
Beef	IBP ConAgra (Monfort) Cargill (Excel) Farmland Industries (National Farms)	87
Pork Slaughter	IBP Smithfield ConAgra Cargill (Excel)	46
Sheep Slaughter	ConAgra Superior Packing High Country Denver Lamb	73
Turkey	ConAgra Rocco Turkeys Hormel (Jennie-O) Carolina Turkeys	35
Flour Milling	ConAgra ADM Cargill General Mills	71
Soybean Crushing	ADM Cargill Bunge Ag Processors	76
Dry Corn Milling	Bunge Illinois Cereal ADM ConAgra (Lincoln Grain)	57
Wet Corn Milling	ADM Cargill Tate and Lyle CPC	74

Source: Heffernan, Constance, Gronski, and Hendrickson, 1996.

The data indicate that not only are firms getting larger in size and smaller in number in each food sector, but also some of the firms are major players in more than one of the commodities. For example, ConAgra ranks in the top four processing firms in beef, pork, broilers, sheep, and seafood. Firms such as Cargill, Archer Daniels Midland, and Iowa Beef Processors also appear in more than one commodity.

The foregoing list focused on the initial processing of the farm commodity. However, a characteristic of the modern food system is the further processing of foods so as to limit preparation time in the home. Although some of the preceding firms are engaged in this further processing of foods, another set of firms is also involved. The largest food firm in the United States is Philip Morris, which claims it gets $0.10 of every $1.00 that U.S. consumers spend on food. Some of Philip Morris's brand names are General Foods, which include Post Cereals; Miller Brewing Company; Kraft USA, which includes Velveeta and Cracker Barrel; Kraft General Foods International, which includes Maxwell House, Tang, Miracle Whip, and Philadelphia Cream Cheese; Oscar Mayer Foods; Kraft General Foods of Canada; and Kraft General Frozen Foods, which includes Jell-O, Tombstone Pizza, and Breyers.

A recent example from the dairy sector underscores the concerns farmers have with the increased concentration of markets. Dairy farmers again face very low prices for their product and the accompanying economic hardship. They have taken their case to the government and have also dumped one day's milk supply to draw public attention to their plight. They blame the low price of milk on the dominance of the National Cheese Exchange by Kraft Foods (i.e., Philip Morris), which is allegedly able to manipulate prices to its advantage during trading activities.

Vertical integration occurs when two or more stages of the food system are controlled by a single firm. The movement to commercial agriculture led to a proliferation of stages and participants in the food system at the outset, but the trend today is toward a joining of the various stages. This process of vertical integration received the most attention when it began in the broiler sector in the 1950s. Feed companies often began the process by agreeing with a farm family to provide the birds, feed, and medical inputs necessary to raise broilers if the family would construct the buildings, equip them to the firm's specifications, and provide the labor. This was a means by which the feed firm could gain access to a steady market for its feed and the farmers did not need to generate all of the capital necessary to produce broilers. In this arrangement, the integrating firm makes all of the major decisions and agrees to pay the farm family. The birds are never sold because the grower never owns the birds. Thus, the grower family is an employee of the food firm and is being paid on a piece-rate basis.

Often horizontal integration and vertical integration proceed simultaneously. Today the largest 4 broiler firms produce and process about 50 percent of the broilers in the United States. About 40 firms produce and process 97 percent of all the broilers in the country. These 40 firms have their own breeding flocks and hatcheries to produce chicks and operate their own feed mills. Since the mid-1980s broiler growers in the southeastern United

States have complained that they have not received any increase in their compensation in the last 15 years. They sought a court action to correct this and other grievances, including errors in the weighing of feed and of broilers.

In the Midwest, opposition and controversy surround the vertical and horizontal integration occurring in pork production. Contracts and other forms of formal integration between farmers and processing firms and the increased size of a few megahog production facilities created increasing controversy. Because of the impact these new structures have on local communities and their environments, most of the opposition in communities and across the region involves many rural nonfarm persons and even some persons from urban areas.

Farther west, farmers and ranchers in the Plains states are angered and tensions are rising. Many feel that low beef prices are the result of three firms controlling 81 percent of beef slaughter and also much of the feedlot production. Cattle in feedlots, which are controlled by slaughtering firms, are called "captured supply" because they are not bought or sold on an open market and the price received is not reported publicly. Some observers of the beef industry suggest that cow/calf producers will begin to form alliances with participants in other stages of the production by the end of the century because this is the only stage that is not yet vertically integrated. Tensions arise because ranchers argue that today's low cattle prices are the result of the large net imports of beef into the country, of vertical integration of the production and processing stages of the beef sector, and of the lack of public disclosure of the price paid for a large proportion of cattle going to market. Food firms, however, argue that low cattle prices are the result of the "cattle cycle" being at a high point in the number of cattle and the lack of a well-integrated system, like that of the broiler industry.

ConAgra, the second largest food firm in the United States, provides an example of the vertical and horizontal integration processes existing simultaneously in the food system. ConAgra is the largest distributor of agricultural chemicals in North America, one of the largest fertilizer producers, and in 1990 it entered the seed business. ConAgra owns more than 100 elevators; some are terminal elevators from which the company ships grain to other countries, and some are local elevators through which the company sells its inputs and buys grain from farmers. ConAgra owns 2,000 railroad cars and 1,100 barges to transport its grain. ConAgra is the largest of the three firms that mill over three-fourths of the wheat in North America. ConAgra is the largest turkey producer and processor and the fourth largest broiler producer. It produces its own feed and owns and operates hatcheries that supply baby chicks. ConAgra hires growers to raise its birds and then processes the birds in its own facilities. This poultry meat is then sold as fryers under the brand name Country Skillet or as further processed food such as frozen dinners and pot pies under the labels of Banquet and Beatrice Foods. Other brand names that are a part of ConAgra include Healthy Choice, Wesson, Swiss Miss, Kid Cuisine, Swift, Butterball, Hunt's, Peter Pan, and Orville Redenbacher.

The increased vertical integration of agribusiness firms providing inputs, producing the commodity, and processing and distributing the final product raises questions as to whether firms such as ConAgra, Cargill, Archer Daniels Midland, and others should be called agribusiness firms or food firms. The term *agribusiness* implies intricate involvement with commercial family farms. Yet these firms are involved in the entire food system from "seed to shelf." Although most of the retail stage is not yet formally integrated with the rest of the system, the representatives of the food firms sometimes have the right to arrange the supermarket displays that feature their products. Furthermore, with the dominant structure in animal production sectors moving from a family farm structure to an industrial model, the term *food firms* seems the more precise name for these companies. Although most of the crop sectors are not yet as vertically integrated as the animal sectors, farmers purchasing their inputs from the same firms to which they sell their products are participating in an obviously unequal power relationship.

The Emerging Global System

The most recent change in food firms involves their global reach. For example, Cargill operates in over 60 countries around the world, and ConAgra has operations in 23 countries. These firms travel the world to locate areas where they can "source" their products as cheaply as possible. The products are then sold in countries that can afford the food. The global beef sector provides a good example of the emerging global food system.

Not only do Iowa Beef Processors, Cargill, and ConAgra process 81 percent of the beef in the United States, but they also now have feedlots and slaughtering plants in Canada and about the same market dominance there. With the passage of the North America Free Trade Agreement, beef can easily travel back and forth across the border. One of the very difficult questions to answer is, In which country was the beef produced? It is possible for a 500-pound calf to move from Canada to the United States to be raised as a stocker animal to 800 pounds, sent back across the border to be fattened in a feedlot, returned across the border to be slaughtered, and sent back across the border once more as meat to be consumed. Although food firms do not engage in raising a feeder calf, they may purchase it as a 500-pound animal, thereby gaining possession of it, or engage in a formal contract with another firm that gives them virtual control over the animal. Obviously, the boundaries between the United States and Canada are blurred. Moreover, in the past decade ConAgra also bought Elders in Australia to become the dominant slaughterer of beef in that country. Cargill bought a smaller firm, and Mitsubishi, the largest banker in the world, recently built feedlots and slaughtering facilities in Australia. Today these three firms dominate the Australian beef sector, the largest exporter of beef in the world. Japan is Australia's largest beef importer, followed by the United States. These firms also have beef operations in Mexico, Brazil, Honduras, and other countries.

The trend toward a few global food firms dominating the food system takes many forms. For example, Cargill, Continental, and Archer Daniels Midland handle over three-fourths of the grain exchanged on the global market. At the other end of the food system, the five largest food/beverage firms in the world are Nestle, Philip Morris, Pepsi Co., ConAgra, and Unilever. The independent farmer is rapidly being lost as the system both expands globally and integrates vertically from the production of genetic material to delivery of the food in retail stores. Farms and agribusiness firms are rapidly being formally integrated into a food system where they lose their identity. As in the case of broilers, there is no market for independent producers. However, these very same conditions have seemed to increase the tensions between food firms and farmers and a host of other organizations and groups.

Thus, we might say that a social movement that is challenging the global food system on a variety of grounds is evolving. It includes groups and organizations focusing on concerns such as the environment, social justice, food safety, food quality, the sustainability of the food system, humane animal treatment, and quality of life in rural communities. The movement is attempting to develop alternative food systems that focus on more locally produced food. Two food systems or a dual food system appears to be emerging. One system includes the global mass-production system; the second system places more attention on a locally produced, less centralized system, with more flexibility for the product, a system that some argue is more compatible with the information age. Clearly, the food system continues to change.

—*William D. Heffernan*

See also
Agrichemical Industry; Agricultural and Resource Economics; Agriculture, Structure of; Careers in Agriculture; Cooperatives; Feedlots; Grain Elevators; Livestock Industry; Marketing; Poultry Industry; Value-added Agriculture.

References
Bonanno, Alessandro, Lawrence Busch, William Friedland, Lourdes Gouveia, and Enzo Mingione. *From Columbus to ConAgra: The Globalization of Agriculture and Food.* Lawrence: University Press of Kansas, 1994.

ConAgra. *1996 Annual Report.* Minneapolis: ConAgra, 1996.

Heffernan, William, Douglas Constance, Robert Gronski, and Mary Hendrickson. "Concentration of Agricultural Markets." Columbia: University of Missouri, Department of Rural Sociology, 1996.

McMichael, Philip. *Food and Agrarian Orders in the World Economy.* Westport, CT: Greenwood Press, 1995.

Mooney, Patrick H., and Theo J. Majka. *Farmers' and Farm Workers' Movements: Social Protest in American Agriculture.* New York: Twayne, 1995.

Sanderson, Steven. "The Emergence of a 'World Steer': Internationalization and Foreign Domination in Latin American Cattle Production." Pp. 123–148 in *Food, the State, and International Political Economy.* Edited by F. L. Tullis and W. L. Hollist. Lincoln: University of Nebraska Press, 1985.

Stull, Donald D., Michael J. Broadway, and David Craig Griffith. *Any Way You Cut It: Meat Processing and Small-Town America.* Lawrence: University Press of Kansas, 1995.

Agronomy

The development and management of plant and soil resources to produce abundant, high-quality food, feed, and fiber crops in a protected environment. The key to an understanding of agronomy is the green plant concept, or the cultivation of green plants where a portion of the plant is used by humans. Humans were hunters and gatherers before this concept was adopted. There were no permanent towns, and a significant portion of each day was spent in food acquisition. This changed when humans became agronomists. Permanent towns and cities evolved, and the agricultural production of a small proportion of the population supported the entire population. This was the beginning of today's society; the underpinning of modern society remains the abundant supply of high-quality food. The science of agronomy is therefore one of the most basic of all industries. This entry discusses the history and development of American agriculture as influenced by agronomy. It addresses agronomy as an academic discipline, training in the science of agronomy, and the national agronomic professional associations.

History

The first White settlers in Jamestown, Virginia, in 1607 knew very little about farming and had no intention of engaging in farming. However, it soon became apparent that they would have to revise their original purpose in coming to the new country. They came expecting to make a quick fortune, while the London Company furnished them with food and other necessities from England. When these supplies failed to arrive and famine threatened, the settlers quarreled over their relative rank in the new society, heedless of the danger that lay about them. Captain John Smith obtained food from the Indians and at that time believed it feasible to compel the Indians to supply all the foodstuff needed. Little did he realize that the Indians' desire for beads, tin bells, and other knickknacks would soon be satiated. The early settlers learned the rudiments of agronomy and started to farm. This began American agriculture's development and the eventual exploitation of the continent. Agriculture progressed from subsistence to self-sustenance to commercial agriculture over the next 250 years. Farmers settled the West and brought their culture and technology to the frontiers. Along the way, American agriculture became the envy of the world and American farmers became some of the most efficient and productive farmers in the world.

Survival was the principal concern of most White settlers from 1607 to 1640. Indians taught the colonists how to plant and cultivate the New World crops. (Plants domesticated by the Indians and embraced by colonists provide 57 percent of the value of total farm production today.) By 1640, there were about 25,000 people in the English colonies. Nine of every ten working persons were on the farm. Tobacco became an important crop in Virginia and provided a more marketable product. Between 1640 and 1780, a few fortunes were made through sale of this surplus. Productive capital of agriculture, including Black slaves, increased rapidly in the older, settled areas near the coast.

In the late eighteenth century, each colonial farm was a self-sustaining unit, growing food for home needs with a little surplus to be traded for sugar and salt. Crop rotations were grain to grass to fallow. Cotton moved into the South, first to South Carolina and Georgia, then westward. The southern climate provided excellent growing conditions for green-seed, short-staple cotton. The problem was separating the seed from the fiber. Eli Whitney's cotton gin solved this problem. This invention separated the seed from the fiber and made short-staple cotton the largest commercial crop in the South. Cotton exports jumped from 1.6 million pounds in 1794 to 6 million pounds in 1795. Rice and sugar production advanced rapidly during the postrevolutionary period. There was a mix of subsistence and commercial agriculture between 1815 and 1860. More of the farms located closer to good transportation were commercial farms.

Agriculture was the basis of the western movement; nearly all pioneers were farmers. A steady stream of settlers were moving west by 1790. From Georgia to New England, settlers moved to new, rich, black ground in the early 1800s. Trees were removed and corn, oats, and barley were grown. Top yields per acre reached 60 bushels of corn, 50 bushels of wheat, and 40 bushels of barley. The thick, matted prairie soils were a formidable challenge to the wooden and cast-iron plows. The fresh prairie soil was fertile and could produce up to 100 bushels of corn per acre.

Eastern agriculture underwent two major changes in the 1840s. In response to a home market, farmers shifted from self-sufficiency to commercial agriculture. John Deere, an Illinois blacksmith, patented his self-scouring moldboard plow in 1837. In 1834, Cyrus McCormick, a Virginian, patented his reaper. The reaper was further improved in 1845, and with it, a farmer could cut about 12 acres of grain per day. After over 200 years of continuous agriculture, eastern Virginia agriculture was in a decline. Edmond Ruffin headed a reform movement in southern agriculture. He suggested the use of marl, manure, and other fertilizers to correct chemical imbalances in the soil. His work laid the foundation of the fertilizer industry.

The Civil War further changed the course of agricultural development. Northern farmers faced reduced demands for their products after the war, whereas southern farmers were demoralized and heavily in debt. The passage of the Homestead Act in 1862 sent many farmers west after the war. Homesteaders established 57 percent of the farms on the frontier. The principal crop was wheat because it could be grown quickly and easily. Unfortunately, these farmers failed to recognize the negative effect of producing the same crop for many years in succession on the same piece of land. Yields decreased and the homesteaders moved to other lands. The positive result of these declining yields was the push for the scientific revolution. Agricultural fairs became important instructional media. The newly formed land-grant colleges educated young people and encouraged the application of practical ideas through farmer institutes.

The twentieth century found free land gone and rapid extensive growth no longer possible. Farmers were no longer just self-sufficient producers. They produced crops and livestock, sold them on the markets, and bought the manufactured goods they required. Farmers became more specialized, devoting money and labor to one of a few commodities. The first 20 years of the century saw the emergence of the tractor and the number of man-hours to produce 1 acre of wheat and corn reduced by more than one-half. More commercial fertilizers, fungicides, weed controls, and insecticides were used. Better understanding of genetics led to plant hybridization and improved varieties. Numbers of farms decreased, whereas farm size increased and production of crops and livestock increased rapidly.

Roosevelt's New Deal moved agriculture away from the grave economic problems brought about by the Dust Bowl and Depression. World War II brought easing of crop controls, and U.S. agriculture moved into the role of world food and fiber provider, making America the "breadbasket of the world." Much of the increased production can be attributed to greater use of lime and fertilizer. Fifteen million horses and mules disappeared from the farm, releasing land to grow feed for an equivalent number of productive livestock.

The adoption of hybrid seed meant more bushels per acre. About 78 percent of the corn produced in 1942 was from hybrid corn. Between 1950 and 1975, corn yields almost doubled, from 50 to over 90 bushels per acre. Other crops also saw yield increases. Cotton yields more than doubled from 219 pounds to 520 pounds per acre. Wheat yields rose from 16 bushels per acre to 32 bushels and soybeans, from 22 to 28 bushels per acre. Tillage, planting, and cultivation equipment paved the way for more efficient crop production. The application of pesticides became more scientific and produced better results. Scientists developed increasingly more sophisticated compounds with improved selectivity and effectiveness.

Since 1975, a new concern for a quality environment has been influencing American agriculture. This concern stems from philosophical beliefs and practical self-interests. Sustained yields of wholesome agriculture products depend on a healthy environment. Environmentalists'

concern about upsetting the balance of nature prompted close investigation of many pesticides and banning of some. Guidelines for runoff and erosion control were implemented by the Environmental Protection Agency. Erosion, sediment, pesticide, and nutrient management plans became commonplace in American agriculture.

The potential to increase crop production in the next century is endless. The potential of a new generation of more benign chemicals and the untapped potential of biotechnology lead the way. Other possibilities include wider application of high-level management skills using the computer and global positioning and hybrid varieties of wheat, barley, and soybeans. A new generation of more benign chemicals will provide farmers with environmentally sensitive disease and pest control. The untapped potential of biotechnology may lead to nitrogen-fixing cereals and a higher protein content in grains. This technology will lead to greater insect and disease resistance in plant varieties.

As agronomists move into the fourth century of crop production in America, many exciting changes are on the horizon. The power of the computer to model and predict is moving to the farm. The use of satellites in global positioning to finely tune fertility and weed control and enhance pest management practices is already being tested in the Midwest and South. American agriculture, led by agronomic science, will continue to change with time and continue to be a highly efficient agricultural system.

Academic Discipline

Agronomists are professionals who deal with the resources of soils and crops. Agronomists are concerned with the theory and practice of crop production and soil and water management. They apply the science of their profession to increase crop production for many uses while conserving our natural resources. Agronomists provide consumers with low-cost food and fiber and help producers increase profitability and efficiency. This unique dual contribution of agronomists creates a mounting demand for their services at home and abroad.

Many agronomists secure employment with fertilizer, lime, chemical, seed, or crop-processing companies. Some farm, whereas others work with banks, crop insurance companies, farm management organizations, and golf courses. Opportunities exist in government services such as cooperative extension, soil conservation, land-use planning, and crop reporting. There are also many opportunities for international employment.

Some students receive limited training and experience in agronomy in high school programs and on-farm experience, but these are the exceptions, not the rule. Most students receive their first formal introduction to agronomy at a land-grant or other state college or university. The departments at these universities and colleges may be listed as agronomy, plant science, soil science, plant and soil science, crop and soil environmental science, or some other combination. Agronomy students need a strong background in the natural sciences, biological sciences, and mathematics. Many departments offer options in crop production (agro-ecology), soils, turf, environmental sciences, or international agriculture. Many institutions offer master's and doctoral degrees in agronomy or related areas such as plant breeding, soil science, and plant biotechnology. Most master's degree programs require classwork and a thesis on research conducted by the student. However, some institutions also offer nonthesis master's degree programs. The doctoral degree requires a dissertation and evidence of research accomplishments.

National Professional Associations

Agronomists are professionally represented by the American Society of Agronomy (ASA), the Crop Science Society of America (CSSA), and the Soil Science Society of America (SSSA). All three societies share a close working relationship and the same headquarters and staff because of their common interests. However, each of the three societies is autonomous, has its own bylaws, and is governed by its own board of directors. The ASA, founded in 1907, has more than 12,200 members worldwide and consists of 8 divisions of interest, plus a student activities subdivision. The CSSA, founded in 1955, has 4,700 members and has 8 divisions of interest. The SSSA has over 6,000 professionals throughout the world and has 11 interest divisions. The ASA publishes the *Agronomy Journal, Soil Science Journal, Journal of Environmental Quality, Journal of Production Agriculture, Journal of Natural Resources and Life Sciences Education,* and many other publications. These titles illustrate the ASA's diversity.

—*James R. McKenna*

See also

Biodiversity; Careers in Agriculture; Conservation, Soil; Cropping Systems; Environmental Protection; Land Stewardship; Pest Management; Soil.

References

Carrier, Lyman. *The Beginnings of Agriculture in America.* New York: McGraw-Hill, 1923.

Carstensen, Frederick V., Morton Rothstein, and Joseph A. Swanson. *Outstanding in His Field: The Henry A. Wallace Series.* Ames: Iowa State University Press, 1993.

Cochrane, Willard W. *The Development of American Agriculture: A Historical Analysis.* Minneapolis: University of Minnesota Press, 1979.

Conrat, Maisie, and Richard Conrat. *The American Farm: A Photographic History.* San Francisco: California Historical Society, 1977.

Edwin, Ed. *Feast or Famine: Food, Farming, and Farm Politics in America.* New York: Charterhouse, 1974.

Ferleger, Lou. *Agricultural and National Development: Views on the Nineteenth Century.* Henry A. Wallace Series. Ames: Iowa State University Press, 1990.

Grigg, David B. *The Dynamics of Agricultural Change: The Historical Experience.* New York: St. Martin's Press, 1982.

Heiser, Charles B. Jr. *Seed to Civilization. The Story of Food.* San Francisco: Freeman and Company Press, 1981.

Hurt, R. Douglas. *American Agriculture: A Brief History.* Ames: Iowa State University Press, 1994.

Rasmussen, W. Douglas. *Readings in the History of American Agriculture.* Urbana: University of Illinois Press, 1960.

Rupnow, John, and Carol W. Knox. *The Growing of America: Two Hundred Years of U.S. Agriculture.* Ft. Atkinson, WI: Johnson Hill Press, 1975.

American Indians

One of the aboriginal, or native, peoples of the Americas. As the first occupants of this country, American Indians have had an influence on much of rural America, even though they were decimated by warfare and disease during the nineteenth century through contact with the whites. Today, only a tiny fraction of their original lands remain in officially designated reservations. Although these reservations sometimes have abundant natural resources, American Indians are one of the poorest groups in American society. In response to these problems, many reservations are actively trying to develop their economies. Some of these efforts have been highly controversial, especially projects involving gambling or hazardous waste disposal.

A Rural Population

For about 15,000 years and perhaps as long as 40,000 years, American Indians occupied what is now considered rural America. American Indians continue to be concentrated in rural areas more than any other racial or ethnic minority. The total Native American population (including American Indians and Alaska Natives) numbered slightly over 2 million in 1990. Of this number, about 49 percent (980,015) were living outside of metropolitan areas. This reflects a slight change from a decade earlier; in 1980 about 51 percent of the American Indian population was in nonmetropolitan locations. Nonetheless, this concentration in nonmetropolitan areas is substantial compared with other groups. For example, in 1990 only 16 percent of African Americans, 24 percent of Whites, and 10 percent of Latinos lived in nonmetropolitan areas.

Besides their long-standing presence, rural American Indians are significant because a substantial number reside on federal reservations and tribal trust lands. Again, in 1990 the number of American Indians occupying these lands was 437,771. This reflects an increase since 1980, when about 386,000 American Indians lived on reservations and other trust lands, but in percentage terms it was about the same in 1990 as it had been in 1980. There are also large numbers of American Indians, perhaps another 15 percent, who lived in places adjacent to or nearby reservations as of 1990.

Historical Background

At the founding of the United States, it was obvious even then that some sort of accommodation with American Indians would have to be reached if the nation was to continue its growth. Relations between the colonists and American Indians in the East were strained and sometimes violent. This situation worsened after the Revolutionary War as the nation grew in population. The acquisition of the Louisiana territory in 1803 offered a solution to what was becoming known as the "Indian problem." It was a place where tribes in the East could be removed to and resettled away from the rapid expansion in states such as Georgia and Tennessee. This resulted in the creation of Indian Territory in what is now the state of Oklahoma.

Beginning in the 1830s, large numbers of American Indians were removed from the Southeast to Indian Territory. Within a few decades, the region east of the Mississippi River was emptied of its Indian population. The creation of Indian Territory proved to be no more than a temporary solution, however. Continued westward expansion by Anglo Americans and other immigrant groups forced new confrontations with American Indians throughout the West. As these conflicts escalated, the federal government intervened by negotiating land cessions and by dispatching military force. Throughout most of the nineteenth century, the West, especially the Plains, was dotted with military outposts assigned the duty of subduing tribal resistance. After the Civil War, President Ulysses S. Grant formulated what became known as his Peace Policy, genuinely intended to ease hostile relations with American Indians. Ironically, Grant's Peace Policy inaugurated two decades of bloody conflict across the Plains and the Southwest.

By the mid-1880s, nearly the entire American Indian population had been resettled in Indian Territory or on reservations in remote regions of the West. Reservations were located in places distant from American cities and in places considered unfit for habitation by White Americans. In particular, the government created reservations using land that at the time seemed worthless and devoid of resources. In many instances, this valuation proved accurate, but in a few notable cases it turned out to be greatly in error.

By the end of the nineteenth century, the conventional wisdom among influential observers was that American Indians were destined for distinction. Ultimately, the race would disappear, and in the interim the only humane recourse was to "civilize" American Indians so that they would be fit for citizenship and would become contributing members of society. A prevailing motto of the time was "Kill the Indian and save the man." One part of this plan was the creation of the boarding school system, which was designed to detribalize and indoctrinate American Indian children in Anglo American culture.

Another part of the plan was the infamous allotment legislation. The General Allotment Act of 1887, also known as the Dawes Act (the bill was sponsored by Senator Henry Dawes), mandated that communally owned tribal lands be allotted as private property to individual Indian families. The rationale behind this measure was to detribalize American Indians by making them owners of private property. According to this thinking, as landowners American Indians would assume more of the values identified with the White middle class. Reservation Indians were expected to become economically self-sufficient farmers once given a tract of land, thereby eliminating their dependence on government aid.

The allotment of tribal lands was halted by the Roosevelt administration in 1934. Near the end of the policy's enactment, it proved a disappointment for its proponents and a disaster for American Indians. For its supporters, allotment did little to detribalize American Indians. For American Indians not inclined to farm before allotment, few became farmers after receiving their land titles; tribal traditions and lifestyles remained relatively unchanged. Allotment did not make American Indians economically self-sufficient; rather, it increased their collective impoverishment.

The General Allotment Act and subsequent related legislation caused massive land losses. Allottees sometimes sold all or part of their land simply to have money for food and clothing. Others were unaware of property taxes and so did not have money to pay these taxes; this resulted in frequent property seizures and tax auctions. In other instances, some American Indians lost their allotments through criminal fraud. By 1934, American Indians had lost about two-thirds of the land they possessed in 1887, about 90 million acres.

Reservation Resources

Modern reservations still bear the legacy of allotment through a complicated set of land tenure arrangements. Many reservations have a "checkerboard" pattern of landownership. Some land is owned as private property by individual landholders. This land can be bought and sold regardless of its location within reservation boundaries. Tribal trust lands and family trust lands belong to American Indian tribes and families, respectively. However, because the federal government exercises a trust responsibility over these lands, they cannot be bought or sold or used as collateral to secure loans.

Although American Indians have much less land than at the turn of the century, it nonetheless represents their most precious asset. Reservation lands have a variety of resources, which vary tremendously with respect to their development potential. Some reservations have few, if any, resources worth developing, while others are abundantly endowed. The resources that most commonly are found on reservations include agricultural land, water, timber, and minerals.

Agriculture is a major source of employment for American Indians. About 34,000 American Indians worked in commercial agriculture, and another 45,000 were dependent on small-scale subsistence agriculture, to augment their income in 1989. Agricultural production on American Indian land was valued at $621 million in 1988. Most of this income, $431 million, or 69 percent, passed into non-Indian hands. There is a simple reason that non-Indians receive the majority of income from agricultural production on American Indian land. About two-thirds of the land that can be used for profitable dryland farming is leased and farmed by non-Indians. In contrast, livestock grazing is considerably less lucrative than dryland farming, but this is the type of production in which American Indians are concentrated; about 85 percent of reservation grazing land is operated by American Indians.

Because most reservations are located in arid regions of the West, access to water for irrigation can be one of the largest obstacles to increased agricultural production. In 1908, the Supreme Court ruled in *Winters v. United States* that American Indian water rights claims have a priority over the claims of later settlers. Subsequent Supreme Court decisions affirmed *Winters* but limited these rights to water for which there was a "reasonable use" on the reservation. Determining the water needs of reservations appears to be a nearly endless source of litigation.

In one case, the Wind River reservation spent $9 million in legal fees to establish its water rights in Wyoming. The enforcement of water rights has been in many instances important for tribal developments. For example, the Ak Chin reservation in Arizona made a successful claim that led to water rights and a $40 million settlement. With sufficient capital and water for irrigation, this reservation launched a highly successful farming project. However, some tribes have not been as successful in claiming their water rights. One of the best known examples is the Navajo Indian Irrigation Project. This project was promised to the Navajo in exchange for other water rights authorized by Congress in 1962, but it still has not been completed.

Timber is a third important resource for many reservations. About 200 tribes are involved in timber production. The income from this production is not inconsequential; it reached $91.3 million in 1991. However, most of this production and subsequent income is concentrated among a few tribes. Ten tribes located in the Pacific Northwest and the upper Midwest account for 86 percent of timber production. Despite the fact that a few of these tribes have very high volumes of timber production, none is currently involved in the most profitable sector of the lumber industry—the production of finished goods such as plywood. A few reservations, such as the Menominee in Wisconsin, have mills to produce rough lumber, but most Indian timber is shipped off the reservation for processing as wood products or pulp for paper goods.

The equipment required for the production of finished wood products entails a substantial capital investment. The lack of capital is one of the main reasons that most tribes do not further process the wood produced on their reservation. This lack of capital is also one of the main reasons that tribes do not develop and process the mineral resources found on their reservations. There are several reservations with substantial deposits of coal, uranium, zinc, and copper, but these resources are leased and developed exclusively by outside corporate interests.

Some of these mineral deposits have immense value. Some estimates indicate that 40 percent of all uranium and 30 percent of strippable coal west of the Mississippi River is sited on reservation land. Yet under the auspices of the Bureau of Indian Affairs (BIA), these resources have been badly managed and have yielded few benefits to the tribes. For example, in the 1970s coal leases were yielding only pennies per ton, a tiny fraction of their true value. In the wake of congressional investigations and tribal complaints about BIA mismanagement, many of these leases were renegotiated, and tribal representatives now have a greater role in lease negotiation than in the past. Nonetheless, it still remains true that reservations are not realizing the full value of their resources in the same way they would if they developed these mines themselves.

Social and Economic Development

Despite the fact that some reservations have substantial amounts of potentially valuable natural resources, American Indians are still among the poorest groups in American society. And among American Indians, those living on reservations are the most likely to be living in poverty. The per capita income for American Indians living on reservations and trust lands was $4,478 in 1989. At the same time, about 51 percent of these American Indians were deemed to have incomes below the official poverty threshold. In contrast, Whites in nonmetropolitan areas had per capita incomes of $11,687 and a poverty rate of 13.5 percent. To add context, American Indians living on reservations and trust lands had lower per capita incomes and higher poverty rates than African Americans living in central cities ($8,713 and 28 percent, respectively).

The economic hardship facing reservation Indians can be more easily understood from the standpoint of educational qualifications and job opportunities. School dropout rates are high on many reservations. About 18 percent of reservation youths between the ages of 16 and 19 are out of school without a diploma. This is approximately twice the rate for White youths of the same ages. It is hardly surprising that a large segment of the adult American Indian population has less than 12 years of schooling. In 1990, 46 percent of American Indians age 25 and over and living on reservations or trust lands had not completed high school. Less than 19 percent of White Americans have not completed high school.

Many tribal governments established active campaigns to stem the dropout problem and keep their students in school. However, it can be difficult to make a compelling argument about the economic benefits of staying in school when there are few jobs to be found. Job opportunities are so scarce on many reservations that they do not represent a realistic incentive to stay in school. The unemployment rate for reservations in 1990 was 25.6 percent, and many reservations had unemployment rates exceeding 50 percent—this at a time when unemployment was around 6 percent for the rest of the nation. The few job opportunities that exist on reservations are often provided by federal agencies such as the Indian Health Service, the Bureau of Indian Affairs, or the local tribal government. On most reservations, public-sector employment is usually the only source of well-paid white-collar jobs. Likewise, these agencies are frequently the primary source of reservation employment, and sometimes they are the only source; 46 percent of reservation workers are hired by federal, state, and tribal governments.

The heavy dependence of reservation workers on public-sector employment means they are highly vulnerable to the changing political fortunes that affect the funding of government programs. Tribal leaders aggressively pursued economic development projects that might lesson this dependence and create new jobs on their reservations. Besides developing natural resources, some reservations initiated projects that proved extraordinarily controversial. For example, the Campo Rancheria in California allowed the development of a landfill over the objections of nearby non-Indian communities. The Mescalero Apaches initiated studies to determine the feasibility of siting a nuclear waste disposal facility on their reservation, against the strenuous objections of the state of New Mexico.

Apart from these isolated instances, the development of reservation gaming, especially casino gambling, caused perhaps the most widespread controversy. Reservation gaming was launched by two court cases in the mid-1980s. In 1986, the Florida Supreme Court upheld the Seminoles' claim that the doctrine of tribal sovereignty extended their jurisdiction over reservation gambling and hence allowed them to operate a high stakes bingo hall. A short time later, the Cabazon band in California won a similar case against the state that allowed it to offer casino games. In the wake of these court cases, state and local governments vigorously lobbied Congress to restrict reservation gaming. Congress refused to outlaw tribal gaming operations, but it did pass the Indian Gaming Regulatory Act of 1988, which set certain conditions and limits on reservation gaming.

Since 1988, casinos and high stakes bingo halls have proliferated quickly. In 1994, the National Indian Gaming Association listed 136 reservations as members. The Foxwoods Complex in western Connecticut and the Mystic Lake Casino outside Minneapolis are possibly the largest operations and gross millions of dollars annually. Although Foxwoods, Mystic Lake, and a few others have been spectacularly successful, gaming operations are considerably less lucrative on other reservations, and about one-half of all reservations have no gambling whatsoever. Nonetheless, proponents of reservation gaming argue that it is an important economic resource. Gaming provides jobs to tribal members and non-Indians alike and generates revenues for tribal government services. Gaming, along with many other recent developments on reservations, underscores the fact that American Indians will remain an enduring presence in rural areas for the foreseeable future.

—*C. Matthew Snipp*

See also

Culture; Development, Community and Economic; Employment; Gambling; History, Rural; Landownership; Poverty; Settlement Patterns.

References

Ambler, Marjane. *Breaking the Iron Bonds: Indian Control of Energy Development.* Lawrence: University Press of Kansas, 1990.

Hoxie, Frederick E. *A Final Promise: The Campaign to Assimilate the Indian, 1880–1920.* Lincoln: University of Nebraska Press, 1984.

O'Brien, Sharon. *American Indian Tribal Governments.* Norman: University of Oklahoma Press, 1989.

Prucha, Francis P. *The Great Father: The United States Government and American Indians.* Lincoln: University of Nebraska Press, 1984.

Snipp, C. Matthew. *American Indians: The First of This Land.* New York: Russell Sage Foundation, 1989.

Thornton, Russell. *American Indian Holocaust and Survival: A Population History Since 1492.* Norman: University of Oklahoma Press, 1987.

Utley, Robert M. *The Indian Frontier of the American West, 1846–1890.* Albuquerque: University of New Mexico Press, 1984.

White, Robert H. *Tribal Assets: The Rebirth of Native America.* New York: Henry Holt, 1990.

Animal Rights/Welfare

A movement and a belief system that propose a different standard for moral treatment of animals than that widely held in European-based cultural traditions. This entry focuses on the philosophy of animal rights activists and organizations. Animal activists, particularly those who believe in animal rights, have an organized philosophy that differs distinctly from other widely held worldviews, are concerned with a variety of issues affecting animals, and can tap a large body of resources (money, volunteers, organizations). Activists generally focus on changing the way humans use animals for food, research, hunting, and entertainment; activists have had different degrees of success with each issue.

Organized Philosophy

The moderate wing of the animal movement primarily concerns itself with protecting animals from suffering and cruelty, an aim little different than the original goals of the American Humane Association (AHA), founded in 1877, and the American Society for the Prevention of Cruelty to Animals (ASPCA), founded in 1866. Then and now, moderates largely accept that humans should manage and use animals. Animal welfare groups tend to be relatively pragmatic, accept compromise, and avoid the more extreme tactics of the animal rights groups, tactics that include confrontation, civil disobedience, and, at the most extreme end, break-ins and vandalism. Animal pragmatists can point to more legal and economic victories, but pressure from animal rights groups has fundamentally changed the debate on how humans should treat animals.

Animal rights philosophies are closer to a medieval view of animals in that both treat animals and humans as similar in morally relevant ways. In medieval Europe, animals were executed for murder, bestiality, and theft under the same legal system that applied to humans. Today's animal rights activists argue that animals have the same right to be treated with respect that humans do; the more comprehensively committed animal rights activist will not eat meat, wear leather, drink milk, hunt, fish, go to zoos, have pets, or support any research that involves animals, from developing and testing drugs to basic research.

Singer (1990) and Regan (1983), two philosophers, set the stage for much of the modern discussion of the moral status of animals. Singer, a utilitarian philosopher, argued that animals that can feel pain have interests in increasing pleasure and decreasing pain. Moral actors—humans—should include animals' interests in decisions that would affect animals' overall pleasures. Complex animals (for example, pigs, cows, and dogs) are close enough to humans for us to assume that these animals have a simple form of self-awareness as beings with futures and pasts. Humans should consider animals' preferences before taking actions that affect them. Killing any mammal, including cows, pigs, dogs, and so on, is wrong when the killing would, on balance, deny the animal more future pleasure than pain. Singer shaded his argument for chickens; their nervous system may not be developed enough to be self-aware. Regan, a rights philosopher, argued that individuals who are self conscious—mentally complex enough to start actions in the present with the intention of satisfying their desires in the future—have a basic right to respectful treatment, which includes a prima facie right not to be harmed. He assumed all mammals are conscious of a self. Chickens and turkeys may not be complex enough to have inalienable rights.

Organizations

The animal rights movement includes 7,000 different groups that collectively have 10 million members and an estimated budget of $50 million. The most widely known groups generally work on a variety of animal issues; these include both moderates (AHA, ASPCA) and fundamentalist groups (People for the Equal Treatment of Animals [PETA] and the Animal Liberation Front). There are, however, groups for every major issue, such as companion animals, sports, entertainment, farm animals, marine life, wildlife, and laboratory animals; groups for specific professions, such as veterinarians and lawyers; and groups for specific purposes, such as lobbying, legislation, and animal sanctuary. The oldest organizations (AHA and ASPCA) are still actively protecting animals today. However, several moderate groups formed after World War II became increasingly active and radical in the 1970s. In the 1980s, groups that were explicitly animal rights organizations, including PETA and Trans-Species Unlimited, began to dominate the debate and publicity on animal issues.

Laws

In 1955, the two federal laws that protected animals both regulated shipping. From 1958 to 1993, Congress passed an additional 13 laws. The most important of these are the Animal Welfare Act, which regulates a wide range of activities from housing laboratory animals to using the mail to promote dogfights; the Humane Slaughter Act, which requires packers to anesthetize or stun animals before slaughter; and several acts that protect endangered or wild animals, including the Endangered Species Act.

Confinement Farming

Both welfare and rights activists object to animal confinement systems. Animal advocates argue that confinement farming, which keeps animals in limited floor or cage space, interferes with animals' social needs. The

stress and boredom of being confined increase aggression, which in turn leads animals to peck, gore, and bite each other. Thus, animals' natural reaction to crowding leads to additional cruelties, such as debeaking chickens and docking pigs' tails. Stress also lowers immune system responses. As bacteria build up, crowding allows diseases to spread rapidly, forcing farmers to use more antibiotics. Concentrated by-products, such as ammonia in poultry operations, pose additional health hazards. Furthermore, activists argue, confinement-raised animals eat food that humans could eat. Since animals are inefficient energy converters and since Western agriculture depends on nonrenewable fossil fuel, the raising of animals for food wastes energy. Finally, confined animals produce a large amount of manure in one localized spot and can easily pollute water.

Agriculture's most common response to animal activists is emotional rather than logical, and none of the arguments from agriculture today truly address animal fundamentalists' concerns. Agricultural representatives largely defend confinement systems on two grounds: animal comfort and a global need for food. The confinement system argument generally starts with the (easily countered) assumption that farm animals will not produce efficiently unless their needs are met, so humane handling can be measured in terms of productivity and economic gain. Even though a few farmers may be grossly cruel to animals, they will be stopped either by existing laws or by market forces. Agriculturalists argue that confinement farming enhances animals' welfare by reducing disease; providing better protection against predators and extremes of weather; freeing animals from scratching for grubs or insects; and providing better sanitation and nutrition. Current large-scale production systems are necessary for efficient food production, which in turn is necessary to feed a growing and increasingly urban population. Such systems also enhance the life of the producer by reducing labor, while providing a higher quality product at a cheaper price. With the exception of veal production, animal activists have had little impact to date on agricultural production or consumer eating habits. In the long run, animal activists' educational work might reduce meat consumption, but medical warnings on high cholesterol have had a greater impact on the average consumer.

Entertainment

Animal activists generally oppose using animals for entertainment, particularly if the activity can cause suffering or death (for example, bullfights, cockfights, dog

An overview of the Jeckel farm. Russell J. Jeckel, one of the originators of confinement hog production, is credited with many innovations in the management and housing of hogs. Animal rights activists oppose such production systems for a variety of reasons.

fights, and bird shoots). Animal activists carefully watch dog and horse races, rodeos, circuses, carriage services, and zoos for individual cases of abuse. Many animal rights activists are against using animals in any way, arguing that even if the animals are not directly suffering, using animals for purposes such as silly dog tricks deprives animals of dignity. Zoos, another form of entertainment, are a more tricky case. Zoos educate, increase sympathy for and knowledge about animals, and, as institutions, help preserve different species. Animal activists who oppose zoos argue that keeping animals in captivity is intrinsically immoral. The animal rights movement probably has heightened attention to animal comfort; certainly rodeo and fair organizers are aware that they are being watched. Disclaimers on movies indicating that the animals were not harmed during filming are now quite common. And zoos, in particular, have made dramatic efforts in recent year to simulate animals' natural habitat.

Pets

Many in the animal rights movement, certainly those in the protectionist/welfare segment, approve of pets (non-human companion animals) for many of the same reasons they approve of zoos. Pets help people understand human/animal relationships, help humans learn to value animals, and provide companionship. Some activists, however, object to the servant/master relationship implied by pet ownership.

Hunting

Animal rights activists generally oppose all hunting for recreation, arguing that the enjoyment that hunters receive is trivial compared to an animal's life. Both the utilitarian and the rights' philosophies would potentially allow hunting to save human life. Animal rights groups, however, have criticized the Nature Conservancy for hunting feral pigs in Hawaii to control population, fish and game officers who hunted mountain lions threatening children in California, and controlled black bear sport hunting in Oregon and other Western states. The powerful National Rifle Association leads the legal fight against animal activists, and activists have won only a handful of battles. Animal activists also have occasionally harassed hunters in the wild, trying to reduce hunters' enjoyment of the sport.

Trapping and Furs

Animal activists also object to trapping, which they claim kills animals for trivial reasons such as fur and meat. Animal welfarists, as well as animals rightists, strongly oppose steel-jaw traps, which are extremely painful for the trapped animal. A handful of states have banned these traps. The same general argument, that animals are harmed for trivial reasons, also is made against fur farming, which produces roughly 80 percent of all furs. The antifur campaign has had some success: fur sales have steadily declined in the United States and Europe; the decline in Europe has been particularly dramatic. Activists' success with furs is probably due to several factors. There are relatively few moral arguments in favor of fur use. Fur consumers live in the same type of urban areas as the majority of animal rights sympathists and hence are more likely to be exposed to animal rights arguments. Finally, the increased number of demonstrations, coupled with fear that activists might mark and ruin furs, makes wearing furs a financial and social risk rather than the sign of wealth and privilege it once was.

Research

Animal activists continue to object to both routine testing and basic research. In response, many companies have stopped tested cosmetics and household products on rabbits (to check for eye irritation). Cosmetics companies have been particularly responsive—their patrons can easily stop using cosmetics or switch, and "cruelty-free" product advertising gives some companies a market edge. However, animal activists have been far less able to stop efficacy and safety testing for individual batches of drugs. The activists' main argument, that animals are not a good model for checking drug safety for humans, has gathered relatively little support. Animal activists also question the morality of doing basic research with animals. After all, they say, laboratory animals suffer, while humans benefit. Fundamentalists want all research using animals stopped; moderates have successfully lobbied for stricter laboratory care standards. The animal research controversy has probably increased scientists' concern with animal comfort; universities are paying more attention to explaining research and to examining the value of research projects. However, extreme groups, such as PETA, have increased the emotionalism and antagonism between scientists and their critics.

—*Ann Reisner*

See also
Agricultural Law; Agro/Food System; Dairy Farming; Feedlots; Horse Industry; Livestock Industry; Livestock Production; Poultry Industry; Wildlife; Wool and Sheep Industry.

References

Jasper, James M., and Dorothy Nelkin. *The Animal Rights Crusade: The Growth of a Moral Protest.* New York: Free Press, 1992.

Regan, Tom. *The Case for Animal Rights.* Berkeley and Los Angeles: University of California Press, 1983.

Singer, Peter. *Animal Liberation.* New York: Avon Books, 1990.

Apiculture

Bee-keeping, bee culture, and the care and management of honeybee colonies. The name comes from the scientific name for honeybee (*Apis mellifera*), Latin for "honey maker." This entry addresses the modern apiculture industry, bee colony management, and honey and bee products. It discusses two potential problems: stings and the Africanized bee.

The Modern Industry

Prior to becoming beekeepers, people hunted bees and robbed their nests. A Spanish cave painting, dating about 7000 B.C., is the earliest record of humans robbing a beehive. Beekeeping advanced when people learned to move wild nests and keep bees in primitive, destruct-harvest fashion. Honeybees were carried to new settlements during western colonization. Records of bee colonies in Virginia date to 1622.

L. L. Langstroth discovered the principle of bee space in 1851 and produced the first practical beehive with removable combs. Bees leave space open for movement by constructing their nests with a space between parallel, vertically hanging combs of beeswax. Hives with removable beeswax comb led to the development of a honey extractor, which uses centrifugal motion to spin honey-filled combs in a metal basket. Honey can be removed and the intact combs returned to hives for the bees to refill in nondestruct harvest.

Today there are an estimated 250,000 U.S. beekeepers. Once largely rural, beekeepers can now be found in suburban areas as well. In the 1990 census, 1.3 percent of U.S. farms had bee colonies, down from 1.85 percent five years earlier. Of the estimated 3 million U.S. bee colonies, 70 percent are maintained by commercial beekeepers, who manage several hundred to 50,000 or more colonies. Commercial beekeepers migrate with their colonies from one floral source location to another and rent their bees to farmers who rely on bee pollination. Bee-keeping operations have become larger and more specialized; the two largest U.S. beekeepers each manage 65,000 colonies, keeping bees in a dozen or more states during the year.

Bee-keeping remains a sideline for other individuals. They may have 10 to 25 or as many as 300 colonies, often managed at permanent sites, although some move colonies short distances to pollinate local crops. The largest group of beekeepers is the hobbyists whose objective is less to make money than to harvest a product for their own tables.

An industry of national and regional companies has developed to sell bees, beekeeping equipment, and supplies. Individuals may purchase everything needed to begin a bee hobby for between $150 and $200. Additional colonies can be started for under $100, bees included.

Honeybees have become greatly valued in American agriculture, particularly with the multitude of changes in agriculture since World War II. They pollinate many important fruit, vegetable, and nut crops. Planned pollination using honeybees produces nearly $10 billion in commodities annually. Growers interplant compatible varieties by mixing pollen-producing (male) flowers in sufficient quantity to ensure pollination of pistillate (female) flowers to produce a commercial crop. Bee colonies are moved to the growers' sites at or just before the blooming period and are then removed after bloom to allow the producers to apply pesticides. Bees contribute to the overall environmental balance by pollinating plants that produce many wild seeds, berries, and fruits used by wildlife.

Bee Colony Management

Bee-keeping requires bees, beehives, a location (or apiary), personal protective equipment, and knowledge about bee biology. A person can start bee-keeping by buying an established colony (or nucleus) or a new package of bees and equipment or by capturing a feral colony. Unlike other animals in human care, the honeybee has not been domesticated.

A beehive is a series of boxes (or supers). The boxes may be of varying depths, with equal length and width. Wooden or plastic frames suspend the beeswax combs inside the boxes. These combs are drawn by the bees from a beeswax or plastic template (or foundation). When completely drawn, each beeswax comb is a bee space away from the adjacent one. The frames are suspended in the box to ensure bee space around all surfaces of the completed comb.

Beekeepers use smokers to reduce colony defense at the time of hive opening and a hive tool to pry and manipulate the frames. Beekeepers also use protective clothing, such as gloves, coveralls, and a bee veil that covers the face and head, to reduce stings.

Managed beehives must be maintained in movable comb hives, as mandated by state laws, that allow inspection for infectious diseases. There are few regulations on location of apiaries. Some large cities and towns have restrictive ordinances or zoning interpretations that exclude bee colonies or prevent problem situations such as too many colonies in a small suburban lot.

Fall management ensures that colonies have honey stores; are free of pests, diseases, and mites; and have a compact, ventilated brood pattern. Beekeepers reduce the size of the colony entrance to exclude mice and medicate their colonies to control for parasitic tracheal and Varroa mites. Beekeepers historically wrapped colonies in preparation for winter, but few do so today. Migratory beekeepers move their colonies to the South, where winters are less severe and fewer winter honey stores are required.

Honeybees cluster on their beeswax combs to conserve warmth during winter. The huddled bees eat honey to produce enough warmth to keep alive. As the days lengthen, the bees begin to rear more immature brood in the beeswax cells. Over one-half of the colonies are rearing brood by February. Once pollen sources can be gathered in the spring, brood rearing increases rapidly. At this time, 10 to 15 percent of the colonies may die from starvation or lack of an adequate adult population to keep the bees and their brood warm and supplied with honey. Disease and mite infestation may increase the likelihood of heavier winter loss.

Spring management involves boosting bee colonies that are slow to rear brood and keeping colonies from swarming. Swarming can be prevented through use of young queens and provision of adequate space for colony expansion and ventilation. Preflow colony management of late spring and summer involves swarm control management and expansion of the number of adult worker bees. Beekeepers add more boxes to strong colonies for storage of the now-plentiful nectar resources foraged by the adult population. They attempt to increase the bee population to coincide with the major nectar flow. Postflow management is less intensive. The season is completed when the beekeeper evaluates honey reserves and harvests the surplus. Many beekeepers employ part-time help for the labor-intensive activities of removing honey-filled supers (or filled frames), uncapping the filled frames, and extracting and processing the honey and beeswax for sale.

Honey and Bee Products

Honey is a low moisture (18.6 percent or less water), viscous sugar solution. It contains a small (less than 3 per-cent) amount of acids, minerals, along with aroma and taste components directly from the nectar source collected by the bees. The flowers from which bees gather nectar largely determine the color, flavor, and aroma of honey. Well-known floral sources are orange blossom, blackberry, buckwheat, sage, and clover. Some honey is a blend of floral types that beekeepers designate as wildflower honey. Clovers and alfalfa honey constitute over one-half of the honey produced in the United States.

Honey is marketed in four forms: liquid, comb, chunk, and creamed. Extracted honey is liquid honey separated from storage combs. Comb honey is sections of beeswax comb that contain honey stored by the bees. Combs may be stored in wooden boxes, circular plastic rings, or containers of various sizes. Chunk honey is a piece of comb surrounded by liquid in a wide-mouthed container and is popular for selling orange blossom honey in Florida and sourwood honey in the Appalachians. Creamed honey, common in the northern states and Canada, is crystallized honey with the consistency of butter.

Beeswax is obtained when the wax covering (or cappings) is removed from honey cells prior to extraction. For every 100 pounds of honey, 1 or 2 pounds of lemon-yellow colored beeswax are obtained. The price varies widely but usually is four to six times the value of honey. Beeswax is used for products such as candles, cosmetics, wax, polish, and comb foundation. Other bee products include pollen and propolis, which worker bees forage outside the beehive, and royal jelly, which is a protein-rich glandular substance worker bees produce to feed to queen larvae. All three products are consumed by humans or fed to pets as a medicine. Pollen can be a source of protein in the diet. Bee venom is collected and injected for treatment of human arthritis or applied directly in bee venom therapy.

Bee Stings

Colonies of honey bees sting intruders to defend their nests. A normal reaction consists of pain, formation of a wheal with redness, development of swelling, and itching. Symptoms may include minor pain to prolonged swelling and itching persisting several days. An allergic reaction to a bee sting is an exaggerated response that is immediate and pronounced. The allergic reaction may range from swelling to anaphylactic shock (shock that results from hypersensitivity to foreign proteins or drugs), which may be life threatening. An allergic reaction can occur with a single sting. A toxic reaction may also occur if a person receives too many stings in too short a period of time. Many beekeepers develop immunity to bee stings and reduced discomfort after repeated stings.

Africanized Bees

Africanized bees, named "killer bees" by the media, developed from bees brought from Africa to Brazil by a genetist who attempted to breed bees better suited to the American tropics. They are well known for their defensive behavior, and colonies are easily disturbed. Worker bees quickly respond to release of the alarm pheromone by immediately searching in the vicinity of the hive and stinging potential threats. Although innocent humans and animals have suddenly been stung by these bees, some suffering toxic reactions, they are not a public health hazard.

With their defensive behavior, Africanized bees are more difficult to manage than other honeybees. Apiary sites need to be isolated and management activities carefully planned to avoid accidental stinging attacks. The bees are ecologically dominant in a tropical/semitropical environment. They spread from the initial escape and now occupy South America, except extreme southern Argentina and Chile; Central America; several islands of the Caribbean; and some parts of the southern United States. The eventual extent of their spread in North America and the impact they will have is a topic of debate.

—*Dewey M. Caron*

See also
Biodiversity; Horticulture; Sugar Industry; Temperate Fruit Industry; Vegetable Industry.
References
American Bee Journal.
Bee Culture.
Bee Science.
Free, John B. *Insect Pollination of Crops.* London: Academic Press, 1992.
Graham, Joe M., John T. Ambrose, Lorenzo L. Langstroth eds. *The Hive and the Honey Bee.* Hamilton, IL: Dadant and Sons, 1992.
Morse, Roger A., and K. Flottum, eds. *The ABC and XYZ of Bee Culture.* 40th ed. Medina, OH: Root, 1990.
Morse, Roger A., and T. Hooper, eds. *The Illustrated Encyclopedia of Beekeeping.* New York: Dutton, 1985.
Seeley, Thomas D. *Honeybee Ecology.* Princeton, NJ: Princeton University Press, 1985.
Snodgrass, Robert E. *Anatomy of the Honey Bee.* Ithaca, NY: Cornell University Press, 1956.
Speedy Bee.
Winston, Mark L. *The Biology of the Honey Bee.* Cambridge, MA: Harvard University Press, 1987.
———. *Killer Bees: The Africanized Honey Bee in the Americas.* Cambridge, MA: Harvard University Press, 1992.

Aquaculture

The raising or fattening of fish in enclosures, usually ponds, cages, tanks, or raceways. The first part of this entry describes industry trends for several major and emerging species of fish. The major species have been catfish, trout, salmon, and shrimp, and emerging species are mollusks, tilapia, ornamental fish, and crawfish. The second part of the entry examines factors affecting the growth of American aquaculture. These include externalities, infrastructural issues, supply response and boom-bust cycles, and food safety.

Industry Trends

The growth of aquaculture has been dramatic during the 1990s. Growth in U.S. aquaculture has centered on the catfish industry in the south-central states, with only fragmented, mixed results involving other species and areas. The public image of aquaculture has been hurt by some negative consumer reaction to the safety and quality of fish and seafood supplies in general, as well as to growing evidence that aquaculture has the potential to cause some perceived or actual negative externalities (that is, costs to the well-being and beauty of the environment that are not usually calculated as part of the cost of production). Nonetheless, growing population, changing nutritional habits, increasing income, relatively constant catch from capture sources, and water pollution all suggest that the share of fish and seafood coming from culture sources will increase.

Major Species. Aquaculture is a major source of commercial fish and seafood production from fresh and brackish water. Even recreational catch is based on frequent restocking from aquaculture operations.

Catfish. Mississippi produces three-fourths of the nation's catfish. The other leading catfish-producing states are (in order) Alabama, Arkansas, Louisiana, California, and Missouri. Dramatic growth has occurred since the 1980s reaching 460 million pounds in 1993. The average size of farms and average sales per operation have continued to edge higher; in 1993 there were 1,404 operations, averaging 108 acres per operation, resulting in total acreage of about 150,000.

Trout. The growth of trout culture has remained steady since 1990, with an average of 56 million pounds. The primary states involved with trout production are Idaho, Utah, North Carolina, California, and Virginia. Idaho is responsible for 72 percent of U.S. production. Trout farming requires cold-water temperatures and flowing water with a high oxygen content.

Salmon. Estimates of farm-raised Atlantic salmon production in the United States were 26 million pounds in 1993. Virtually all U.S. production is in Maine and Washington. In Maine, the contribution of farm-raised Atlantic salmon to the value of the state's seafood industry is second only to wild-caught lobsters. Although the domestic farm-raised salmon industry is expected to expand, its rate of growth in coming years will likely be much slower because of a lack of high-quality sites and the cost of obtaining new farming permits. Almost all of the increase in production since 1990 has been at existing leases, not through additional lease sites. Another major factor in the slowdown is increasing foreign competition from Canada, Chile, and Norway.

Shrimp. In 1993, U.S. culture of shrimp was approximately 6.6 million pounds, about 2 percent of the U.S. wild-caught shrimp quantity. Expansion of U.S. shrimp aquaculture is limited because of the low cost of production in foreign countries and the large U.S. wild catch. It has been suggested that the country's comparative advantage may lie in the technical aspects of producing disease-free postlarvae for foreign shrimp industries or in providing hatchery technology for production of postlarvae.

Emerging Species. *Mollusks.* Culture of oysters, mussels, and clams is small compared to the wild catch, but aquaculture is growing because of reduction in available oyster and clam stocks and aquaculture's ability to supply a steady high-quality product that can command a premium price. In 1993, total oyster sales in the United States were approximately 32 million pounds, valued at $98 million. The two greatest constraints to expansion of mollusk culture are the limited number of suitable sites and food safety related to consumption of raw mollusks, particularly oysters and clams.

Tilapia. The outlook for tilapia production in the United States is good for several reasons. Tilapia can be polycultured (cultured in the same pond with other fish species), it can be grown profitably on diets of less expensive vegetable protein, it can be bred easily and quickly, and its flesh is mild and can be substituted for a number of other traditional seafood species. However, there are limitations to U.S. culture of tilapia, foremost being the species' intolerance to water temperatures below 45 degrees Fahrenheit. This temperature constraint gives tropical producers a major advantage; domestic producers might be expected to target fresh fillet markets.

Ornamental Fish (Tropical Fish). The ornamental fish industry is centered in Florida, particularly in the Tampa and Miami areas. These products are considered luxury items that may decline during recessions, as in 1992, when imports were down 12 percent. Producers are concerned about the Food and Drug Administration applying the same rules for therapeutic chemical use in food fish production to the ornamental fish industry. The forecast for U.S. exports of ornamental fish indicates continued expansion, but net trade will continue to be negative.

Crawfish. Of all the freshwater species, culture of crawfish is probably the most heavily affected by wild production of the same species. Wild production occurs during the same season as aquaculture production. Because wild harvests are dependent on water temperature and the volume of water moving through the swamp areas of Louisiana, production has experienced wide annual swings, from 18 million pounds in 1991 to 69 million pounds in 1993. This supply fluctuation is a serious limitation to crawfish market development because the food industry wants a product that is in constant supply, has good quality, and has a relatively stable price. Crawfish are not available year-round, which makes it difficult to build a steady market. Seasonal harvesting patterns, along with a considerable wild catch, means there are huge swings in prices throughout the season. The advantages of crawfish culture are the relatively low fixed costs of production, natural reproduction, and ability to double-crop crawfish with rice.

Factors Affecting Growth

Aquaculture is closely linked to capture fisheries (Anderson and Wilen 1986). The development of aquaculture is greatly enhanced through selection of a species with a strong history of consumption. The shrimp and salmon aquaculture industries have grown in response to deficits in the supply of these species. The consistent quality and quantity that can be made available to the market through culture are a further advantage. Catfish production has been hindered by a lack of a history of consumption in many areas of the United States. Catfish promotion and advertising programs have been needed to improve the catfish's image. Aquaculture is able to break the seasonal and geographical limits historically imposed by capture sources.

Externalities

Aquaculture generates, and is affected by, a number of externalities—that is, environmental impacts not usually calculated as part of the cost of production— that could have profound impacts on the sustainability of the industry. Environmental pollution associated with pond efflu-

Fish hatcheries like this salmon farm in Alaska have provided an excellent solution to the problems of declining fish populations and pollution inherent in fishing at sea.

ent, discharge from processing plants, and sedimentation in coastal areas are pressing issues that have to be resolved. Competition for water with other uses could become an important constraint. Aesthetic objections represent another class of problems for U.S. aquaculture, especially related to the raft culture of shellfish in the Pacific Northwest. Coastal residents find rafts, pens, and other facilities unsightly. Zoning, licensing, and other restrictions have been placed on the industries.

Common property resources, such as wild-caught postlarval shrimp, represent another class of externalities. Postlarval shrimp obtained from the oceans are used by shrimp farmers in many parts of the world to seed their ponds. Increased harvests of the postlarvae reduce the wild catch of adult shrimp. There is growing concern that shrimp aquaculture is causing a rapid depletion of natural shrimp populations. The importance of postlarval shrimp in the food chain of many marine fish species raises additional concerns. Reduced shrimp populations may adversely affect fish populations of important com-

mercial, ecological, recreational, or aesthetic value. Increased development of shrimp hatcheries can reduce dependence on an uncertain seed supply and eliminate the threat to the regeneration of wild stocks.

Aquaculture may be adversely affected by externalities generated by other enterprises. Fish health, growth rate, and human safety may all be compromised by pesticides, fertilizers, and industrial pollutants in streams and groundwater. Catfish farms often are in close proximity to chemical-intensive row crop operations such as cotton, soybeans, and peanuts. Agricultural runoff, crop dusting, chemicals leaching into the groundwater, and chemical residues from former crops are all potential vectors of contamination. Major problems for mollusks are generated by their dependence on water quality because they are filter feeders that concentrate toxins.

Infrastructure
A minimum flow of product creates benefits for all producers in the production area in the form of infrastruc-

ture (transport, diagnostic labs, processors), availability of specialized services and inputs (credit, equipment, feed, medicines), and generation of and access to new information. Infrastructure facilitates the flow of aquacultural products between buyers and sellers. Specialized research facilities, industry trade associations, extension services, physical facilities such as feed mills, fish disease diagnostic laboratories, supply firms specializing in aquacultural inputs, live-haul and other transportation services, and processing plants are all important elements of the infrastructure supporting aquaculture. Because aquaculture is relatively new, many of the components of infrastructure that are taken for granted in other industries either do not exist or are still in developmental stages. Fragmentation has been a problem for some segments of the aquaculture industry because there has not been a sufficiently concentrated production area to create the foregoing benefits.

Vertical integration, production and marketing contracts, and cooperatives can be implemented as a means of lowering costs or enhancing price. The broiler industry may serve as a model for the catfish industry, suggesting its eventual evolution into a fully integrated production system. Contracts or integration offer a mechanism for assuring a continual supply of the size and type of fish desired by the processor. Farmers gain through year-round markets at known prices. Cooperatives and bargaining associations permit fish farmers to exert greater control over the pricing and marketing of their products.

Supply Response and Boom-Bust Cycles

Aquaculture has been described as simply another form of livestock production and as such should receive the same treatment as the more traditional forms of agriculture. Livestock development evolved from hunting to domestication of animals, and the fishing industry is following a similar path. Modern fishing fleets have developed the capacity to harvest fish faster than they can reproduce, resulting in depletion of ocean fish populations. Farming trials to evaluate wild fish species' suitability for culture have been conducted for centuries in China and since the 1980s in many Western countries. Even though a number of fish species are now farmed, in many cases the genetic stock is still basically that of the wild population. Using the same type of genetic selection that has increased the efficiency of livestock and poultry production, aquaculture operations should also be able to increase their efficiency.

Another comparison often made between aquaculture and livestock production involves cyclical, or boom-bust, production cycles. Cyclical production has been experienced in the catfish industry, but it has been overshadowed by the overall growth of the industry. For example, from 1991 through 1993 production increased very rapidly, resulting in dramatically falling farm prices. In response, producers reduced stocking rates and some growers left the industry. After a period of time, stocks of available fish were reduced and farm prices rose. As prices improved, the growers remaining in the industry gradually increased production. If prices remain above the average cost of production for an extended period of time, new growers will enter the industry. With new growers entering the industry and established growers expanding production, prices will begin to fall, and the cycle will start all over again.

Now that the aquaculture industry has got past the initial phase of working out basic production techniques, it seems to be following the type of development seen in the livestock and poultry industries: larger production units, higher concentration of production, more vertical integration, rising production efficiencies, and declining real costs (after inflation is considered). Over the long term, real prices for livestock and poultry products have declined. This trend also has occurred in the catfish industry, where the real farm price fell from $0.80 per pound in 1980 to $0.40 per pound in 1992. This long-term decline in real prices means that growers will be pressured to adopt new efficiency-increasing technologies, that the price of farmed products will become more competitive with the wild harvest, and that aquaculture production will become a major factor in those markets.

However, aquaculture may develop differently from the livestock and poultry industries because of its wider range of species. In this sense, aquaculture could be more closely compared with the fruits and vegetables industry. Some aquaculture species appear to be developing into major industries, such as catfish and trout, and they will likely follow the path taken by the livestock and poultry industries. For many other aquaculture species, production will remain much lower, and they will be marketed more as specialty products.

Aquaculture is a major challenge for economic management (Hatch and Kinnucan 1993). Ecology, monitoring, and feed utilization require additional sophistication that is not essential for other animal production systems. Because of the sensitivity of aquatic species to temperature and other environmental conditions (for example, dissolved oxygen, ammonia, salinity, and pH), the complex interaction of ecological factors can have a significant impact on the growth (Boyd 1990; Cacho 1990; Cuenco, Stickney, and Grant 1985) and profitability of aquaculture (Cacho, Hatch, and Kinnucan 1990). The difficulty of monitoring the grow-out of a population that cannot be seen or handled is probably the most crucial management problem. The producer cannot determine the number of animals and their health at any given time. The density of fish that is necessary to make closed systems profitable has tended to lead to a myriad of problems related to waste removal. Salmon culture has been quite successful in cages placed in bays (Bjorndal 1990); however, even this success has been mitigated by problems with disease and waste disposal.

Feed utilization is another source of uncertainty for the manager of an aquacultural production facility because the amount of feed actually consumed by the fish can be observed only in a qualitative way as they come to the surface to feed but cannot be known with much precision (Lovell 1989). Loss of nutrients occurs quickly after feed is in the water. Feed not consumed within a few hours decomposes, decreasing available dissolved oxygen and other water quality factors. Low dissolved oxygen levels decrease fish appetite and growth and increase risk of fish mortality.

Food Safety

Food safety is one of the key consumer issues of the 1990s. Media attention given to food contamination incidents has sensitized consumers to food quality and safety. The perishability of fish, coupled with their tendency to absorb and concentrate some pollutants, makes the issue of food safety especially germane to aquaculture. Brooks (1993) found that 38 percent of consumers had seen or heard news stories on some negative aspect of seafood. Actual risks have been measured to be substantially less than consumers' perceptions, however. The greater control over the culture process as compared to the total lack of control over the capture process should be emphasized to allay consumer safety concerns.

Quality control and consumer apprehension about the supply of fish and seafood may become an important comparative advantage for U.S. aquaculture. For example, perceptions that shrimp produced under the intensive Taiwanese system may cause health problems are resulting in greater care on the part of processors and exporters in their purchasing decisions. Consumers may be willing to pay extra for fish and seafood that are certified to be of high quality and pathogen-free. Proximity to the final consumer may make this certification process easier to implement. This quality issue may result in a more distinct separation in the bulk market and high-quality market niches.

—Upton Hatch

See also
Agricultural and Resource Economics; Food Safety.
References
Anderson James L., and James E. Wilen. "Implications of Private Salmon Aquaculture on Prices, Production, and Management of Salmon Resources." *American Journal of Agricultural Economics* 68 (1986): 866–879.
Bjorndal, Trond. *The Economics of Salmon Aquaculture.* Cambridge, MA: Blackwell Scientific Publications, 1990.
Boyd, Claude E. "Water Quality in Warm Water Fish Ponds." Auburn: Auburn University, Alabama Agricultural Experiment Station, 1990.
Brooks, P. M. "The Northeast U.S. Market for Blue Mussels: Consumer Perceptions of Seafood Safety and Implications for Aquaculture." Pp. 247–269 in *Aquaculture: Models and Economics.* Edited by Upton Hatch and Henry W. Kinnucan. Boulder, CO: Westview Press, 1993.
Cacho, Oscar. "Protein and Fat Dynamics in Fish: A Bioenergetic Model Applied to Aquaculture." *Ecological Modeling* 50 (1990): 33–56.
Cacho, Oscar, Upton Hatch, and Henry Kinnucan. "Bioeconomic Analysis of Fish Growth: Effects of Dietary Protein and Ration Size." *Aquaculture* 88 (1990): 223–238.
Coomber, James, and Sheldon Green. *Magnificent Churches on the Prairie.* Fargo: North Dakota State University, Institute for Regional Studies, 1996.
Cuenco, Michael L., Robert R. Stickney, and William E. Grant. "Fish Bioenergetics and Growth in Aquaculture Ponds: I. Individual Fish Model Development." *Ecological Modeling* 27 (1985): 169–190.
Hatch, Upton, and Henry Kinnucan. *Aquaculture: Models and Economics.* Boulder, CO: Westview Press, 1993.
Lovell, Tom. *Nutrition and Feeding of Fish.* New York: Van Nostrand Reinhold, 1989.
U.S. Department of Agriculture. "Aquaculture: Situation and Outlook Report." Washington, DC: U.S. Department of Agriculture, Economic Research Service, 1993.

Architecture

The process of thoughtfully creating spaces, specifically buildings, to serve human purposes. It is necessary in rural settings to differentiate between high-style architecture, whose appearance and ornamentation derive from academic styles, and vernacular architecture, which reflects problem-solving ingenuity on the part of builders who learned their craft from practice and observation. Although one may think first of agricultural buildings on the rural landscape, rural architecture includes a wide variety of building types in towns, as well as architectural traditions adapted from foreign precedents. The first part of this entry address academic styles and vernacular types of rural architecture and their regional and ethnic variations. In the second part, the impact of rural residents' creative processes and functional performance on rural architecture is discussed. Finally, commercial and industrial architecture in small towns is noted.

Academic Styles and Vernacular Types

Several factors have influenced the historical development and patterns of rural architecture in North America. Among them are design styles, ethnic traditions, construction technology, regional environmental variations, and a continuing need for straightforward solutions to day-to-day problems. In small towns and the rural countryside, rural architecture includes a wide range of building types, such as farmhouses, barns, buildings for main street businesses, train depots, country churches, schools, and buildings for processing agricultural products. The vast majority of rural architecture may be referred to as vernacular; that is, it was designed and built by people who were not trained in architectural schools. Instead, most builders of rural architecture were carpenters, farmers, or small-town business people who learned about constructing buildings from experience and observation. Only a small percentage of rural buildings—mostly constructed since the late 1800s—were designed by people formally educated as architects. This should in no way diminish our appreciation of the rich, imaginative rural architectural solutions that were built by the more commonplace tradition.

Regional Variations

One way of examining rural architecture is to consider regional differences and variations among buildings. Historically, rural areas of North America tended to be settled by settlers moving westward from established communities along the eastern coast. As they moved westward, people brought with them familiar ways of designing and constructing buildings that often reflected the place from which they had moved. Thus, scholars of rural architecture have noted similarities in architecture from New England transplanted first to the Ohio Valley region and eventually to Iowa, Wisconsin, and Minnesota, where the architectural landscape is occasionally referred to as New England extended. Middle Atlantic architectural traditions may be found extending into Kentucky, Tennessee, and Missouri, whereas the architectural practices of Virginia and the lower Chesapeake were spread throughout the southern states by the time of the American Civil War. Some aspects of these historical architectural traditions continue today, and these variations provide a fascinating example of regional distinctiveness. Architecture is one strong, visible manifestation of the concept of cultural diffusion, or passing characteristics and components of one culture to another.

Regional variations in rural architecture are reinforced by the practical uses of buildings and by the demands of the physical environment. Barns built to dry tobacco are noticeably different from those in which dairy cattle are kept. Half-buried potato warehouses are distinct from cotton sale-barns. Houses in the humid South often evolved with long porches to take advantage of shading and prevailing breezes, whereas buildings with a similar function in the North often had compact floor plans and very small windows on the north or west. Local, indigenous materials frequently were used for rural architecture; often brick, adobe, or stone structures rather than wooden occur where those respective materials were available. Availability of materials and technological development of new construction technologies can be detected among patterns of buildings regionally. Scholars of rural architecture often find such patterns more revealing than one-of-a-kind buildings.

Academic Styles

Although preferences for particular architectural styles also may be detected regionally, style is largely a product of acquired tastes that change over time. Because the first purpose of rural architecture usually is to fulfill a practical need, the desire for familiar styles and ornamental embellishment is sometimes less obvious than other factors that affect the design of rural buildings. Nevertheless, a strong desire for popular styles, like the wide spread of neoclassical motifs that revived interest in the architecture of Greece and Rome following the 1893 Columbian Exposition in Chicago, is often visible in more ornamented rural buildings such as houses, churches, and schools. Not surprisingly, the desire for socially appreciated architectural styles tends to be more noticeable in rural towns than on farms in the countryside, although there are many exceptions to this general principle. One architectural style that consciously endeavored to respond to unique conditions of dispersed, rural architecture was the Prairie School style (with its low, horizontal character and broad overhanging roof lines), which originated in the Midwest and was spread by such proponents as Frank Lloyd Wright and the regional firm of Purcell and Elmslie.

Ethnicity and Imported Traditions

An additional factor with a profound effect on design of vernacular, rural architecture is the effect of national building traditions among ethnic groups that emigrated to North America. Immigrants often were brought directly from East Coast ports by railroads to homesteads or small towns in North America, with little exposure to New World ideas along the way. Frequently the possessions they carried with them included memories of familiar ways of designing and planning buildings and specialized skills in the kinds of hand craft needed to construct them. Until very late in the nineteenth century, farm families emigrating from northern Europe tended to build large barns of carefully joined heavy timbers, often with stone foundation walls. These barns frequently exhibited a gambrel roof that the farmers knew to be an efficient shape within which to store hay. Where local conditions allowed it, the barns were sometimes built into a hillside to allow wagon access to the upper loft. Immigrants from other regions, such Ukrainians and Black Sea German-Russians who settled on the Great Plains, brought along house designs in their minds with low earthen walls and heavy earthen roofs that they knew to be well suited to harsh environmental conditions similar to their homelands. In recent years, a great deal of systematic study of rural buildings has helped us to better understand the variations in rural architecture among distinct immigrant groups.

Creative Processes

Many different methods or processes have been used to design and construct rural architecture. Some authors draw distinctions between folk methods that borrow from traditional, conservative ways of doing things; popular designs that borrow freely from tastes, styles, and preferences shared by many people; and academic design processes that are learned from books or in a formal school of architecture. Farmers, and many other people who live in rural settings, have gained reputations as tinkerers who are fond of experimenting and refining solutions to practical problems. This same method has been applied frequently to architectural problem solving. Farmers recognized the need to create large hay storage mows in dairy barns and as a result developed a wide variety of constructional systems. Many such barn-building technologies were even patented and marketed by their inventors, including barns framed with complex wood trusses; glue-laminated, arched wood timbers; and, in recent times, pole barns and steel-framed loafing sheds with precast concrete feed bunks for livestock.

Other rural buildings have been significantly influenced by pattern books and premanufactured systems of construction. In the nineteenth century, pattern books for residential design were widely distributed by architect-builders such as A. J. Downing and George and Charles Palliser. Country churches and schools likewise benefited from plan services that published books illustrating a variety of way to construct and ornament rural architecture. Frequently these design prototypes were modified and adapted to unique local requirements by carpenter-builders, school boards, or church congregations. Perhaps a surprising influence on the process of designing and building rural architecture, houses in particular, was the marketing of precut buildings by mail-order suppliers such as Sears, Roebuck and Company. As building technology, functional requirements, and architectural licensing laws have become more complex, the role of professionally trained architects has become much more widespread, especially for public buildings. Extension services at many land-grant universities, and even local lumber yards, continue to develop and distribute packaged designs for many agricultural building types.

Functional Performance

Style and cultural preferences aside, most rural architecture is expected to be functionally well suited to a particular activity. On farms and in small towns, various types of working buildings have evolved where they may support either the agricultural infrastructure or other aspects of rural community. Farmhouses, combination barns that function as both stables and granaries, grain storage structures, and quonsets or other machine storage buildings are the principal functional types on farms, although in the broader sense rural architecture might also include groupings of farmstead buildings and even alterations to the physical landscape, such as shelterbelt windbreaks, livestock confinement structures, and drainage ways.

Farmhouses, in particular, afford an example of evolution in utilitarian suitability of a building type. The earliest farmhouses generally consisted of simple single-pen and double-pen structures (with one or two rooms, respectively) or dogtrot buildings, differentiated by an open breezeway between two dwelling cells. Two-story I-houses and more elaborate hall-and-parlor arrangements expanded the house plan upward. Throughout the 1800s, T- or L-shaped farmhouse plans were commonplace throughout the Midwest, with strong orientation of interior spaces toward the farmyard and advancements in food-processing facilities in the kitchen. As a result of numerous cultural and technological factors, the American Foursquare style of house was built increasingly after 1900. Sometimes described as the Cornbelt Cube, this ubiquitous house type comprised four upstairs bedrooms above four ground-floor rooms. Today, ramblers and one-story ranch-style houses are found throughout the North American landscape.

The distinctive architectural type most associated with agricultural infrastructure in rural communities where grain handling predominates is the grain elevator, a vertically structured grouping of bins for storing various grains, served by an elevator lift mechanism for sorting called a grain leg. Within those broad functional requirements, myriad variations in color, material, shape, arrangement, and construction technology may be noted. From about 1870 until well into the twentieth century, most elevators were built of wood side walls consisting of dimensionally milled lumber, laid crib-fashion; that is, placed flat and nailed together to contain the outward pressure of grain. In more recent times, many newer grain storage structures have been constructed of combustion-resistive, slip-formed concrete or corrugated steel. Numerous photo essays and publications in the popular press have surveyed this distinctive architectural type and characterized it as "the skyscraper of the prairie."

Small-Town Constructions

Rural architecture does not, however, consist exclusively of agricultural structures. Even the layout and configuration of many small towns west of the Mississippi were results of conscious, formulaic architectural planning by railroad entrepreneurs. Rural towns include many interesting architectural constructions that serve and support these communities. The closely spaced, two-story buildings of many small-town main streets have become virtual icons of small-town America, sometimes reproduced in theme parks around the world as symbols of a vanishing landscape. Much of the architectural character of these structures derives from premanufactured material systems, such as wood millwork, pressed metal ornament, cast iron, and glass display windows that have been distributed throughout the United States from the 1870s to the present day. In many respects, the widespread distribution network for standardized products is both a unifier and destroyer of regional variations in architecture. The boomtown fronts (two-story rectangular facades applied to the front of one-story, gable-roofed buildings) on many wood-framed, western rural businesses reflect a desire for an architectural expression of importance and permanence consistent with more established communities.

Rural architecture may be examined and better understood from many perspectives. Over time, rural architecture has evolved in response to diverse influences that reflect cultural values, functional requirements, and stylistic preferences. In the late twentieth century, architecture is frequently thought of as both a professional discipline and a service industry. Contemporary construction techniques, economics, and material technologies have grown to be major influences on architectural design judgments. These observations aside, an enduring and richly varied architectural legacy remains visible throughout the rural American landscape.

—*Steve C. Martens*

See also
Barns; Churches; Culture; Housing; Plantations.
References
Arthur, Eric, and Dudley Witney. *The Barn: A Vanishing Landmark in North America*. New York: Arrowood Press, 1988.
Brand, Stewart. *How Buildings Learn*. New York: Penguin Books, 1995.
Hart, John. F. *The Look of the Land*. Englewood Cliffs, NJ: Prentice-Hall, 1975.
Kniffen, Fred B. "Folk Housing: Key to Diffusion." Pp. 3–26 in *Common Places: Readings in American Rural Architecture*. Edited by D. Upton and J. M. Vlach. Athens: University of Georgia Press, 1982. (See also Introduction and other articles in the same volume.)
Longstreth, Richard. *The Buildings of Main Street: A Guide to American Commercial Architecture*. Washington, DC: Preservation Press, 1987.
McMurry, Sally. *Families and Farmhouses in Nineteenth-Century America*. New York: Oxford University Press, 1988.
Meinig, D. W., et al., ed. *The Interpretation of Ordinary Landscapes*. New York: Oxford University Press, 1979.
Noble, Allen. *Barns of the Midwest*. Athens: Ohio University Press, 1995.
Peterson, Fred W. *Homes in the Heartland*. Lawrence: University Press of Kansas, 1992.
Rapoport, Amos. *House Form and Culture*. Englewood Cliffs, NJ: Prentice-Hall, 1969.
Upton, Dell, ed. *America's Architectural Roots: Ethnic Groups That Built America*. Washington, DC: Preservation Press, 1986.

Arts

One of the ways in which the cultural values of a community are identified, conserved, celebrated, and transmitted. There have been numerous influences on the development of the arts in rural communities, the most important of which is known as the community arts movement. The historical roots of this movement go back at least to the early nineteenth century, beginning with the Lyceum movement; moving to the Chautauqua, particularly the Tent Chautauqua Circuit; then to the development of community art schools and arts centers; right after that to the community theater movement; and finally, to the more recent development of community arts agencies. This entry reviews these influences on the development of the arts in rural communities.

General Background

From the time of the earliest colonies, the arts have been a vital part of the culture of rural communities. The arts have a long, rich heritage of innovative individuals, philosophical traditions, and creative community efforts whose existence continues to change the face of America's rural landscape today. Each region has its own unique history and cultural touchstones. Folk arts, including song, stories, and dance and traditional arts, including crafts, furniture making, quilts, carving, and woodworking, were brought by the immigrants when they arrived on the continent. As the westward expansion continued, individuals carried their cultural traditions with them to their new communities, providing a bridge between the Old and New Worlds. Many rural communities began as communal colonies of immigrants from one particular country or region, and the arts and the cultural traditions of these communities strongly reflected this influence. These cultural traditions continue today and can be found flourishing in rural communities all across America.

In addition to the arts transplanted from Europe, these new communities, in their struggle to carve a life out of the wilderness, created unique arts traditions. Individuals in these communities began to create their own cultural traditions, providing them with the opportunity to communicate their singular experiences in their own voice. In addition, the arts and culture of African Americans and Native American indigenous traditions added their influence to the emerging rural communities. All of this contributed to the unique role the arts played in identifying, conserving, celebrating, and transmitting the cultural values of these communities.

The Lyceum and the Chautauqua

The Lyceum began in 1828 when Josiah Holbrook, a farmer, organized his neighbors in Millbury, Massachusetts, into an association of adults for the purpose of self-education. Inviting professors and educators from surrounding schools and colleges, Holbrook and his neighbors met in Holbrook's parlor to explore, discuss, and learn about various cultural issues and traditions. They wanted to learn about culture and be educated; they had to be creative and persistent for this to occur. What began as one individual's desire for self-improvement quickly grew and expanded to other rural areas. By 1831, the movement had become formalized, and the American Lyceum Association came into existence. By 1850, there were over 3,000 Lyceums across the country in communities of every size. The purpose of these associations was the self-improvement and cultural enrichment of its members through discussion and education.

Many of the Lyceum sponsoring organizations broke down or ceased to exist with the start of the Civil War. Because many were never reactivated, lecturers started to make their own speaking arrangements. This led to the Lyceum Speaker's Bureau, which was a systematic attempt to introduce culture into rural communities. This was the first of many times when programs initiated to meet rural needs for self-improvement and self-education were transformed into commodity-based, profit-making experiences.

Recognizing the potential of the Lyceum, the need for speakers, and some means to deliver services, James Redpath revolutionized the movement. In 1867, he created the Chicago Redpath Lyceum Speaker's Bureau, which became the chief booking office for people such as Mark Twain, Josh Billings, and Wendell Phillips. The Redpath Bureau streamlined the booking process by making the most efficient use of the time and talent of the speakers on tour. Communities with rail lines were fortunate enough to be placed on the bureau's circuit, leaving most of the rural communities without the resources to continue their efforts. The Lyceum Speaker's Bureau continued into the early twentieth century.

Concurrent with this movement, another very important cultural influence on the arts and culture of rural communities emerged—the Chautauqua. Beginning in 1874 as a Methodist Sunday school camp at Lake Chautauqua in rural western New York, the Chautauqua soon became synonymous with culture. Started by Dr. John Heyl Vincent, a Methodist minister, the Chautauqua became one of the most vigorous, private movements in popular education developed in the United States. One influence of the Chautauqua that rapidly reached rural communities was the Chautauqua Literary and Scientific Circles. Dr. Vincent believed that there needed to be

Quilting is a traditional art form in many rural areas. Here, Cajun women quilt at a farm near Arnaudsville, Louisiana.

resources to assist individual study of the cultural traditions that had become so much a part of the Chautauqua experience. Small parlor gatherings in rural communities used published Chautauqua material as a resource for self-education. By 1878, 84,000 people, mostly from the Midwest, who joined these self-improvement circles and continued the tradition of art and culture in rural communities for self-education and self-improvement.

Keith Vawter became the manager of the Redpath Chicago Lyceum Bureau in 1902. He recognized that the Independent Chautauqua could be addressed by better planning and use of more speakers, and he had Lyceum speakers who were available to him in the summer. Vawter combined the Lyceum Speaker's Bureau with the Chautauqua traveling shows. In addition, he knew that most rural communities did not have the facilities to accommodate even the touring Chautauqua experience. To remedy this and increase his potential market, Vawter purchased a used circus tent to provide a meeting place for the pro-

gram. The tent symbolized the combined adventure of the circus and the tradition of the religious revival and helped break through what had been a difficult audience to reach. For a long time, the fine arts, especially theater, were not strongly supported in rural communities. Vawter used the indirect certification of the original Chautauqua because it started as a Methodist church training experience, even though the Tent Chautauqua had no connection whatsoever to this original movement. Chautauqua provided one of the first opportunities for people in rural communities to experience the arts and culture on a personal basis by being members of an audience.

The Visual Arts

It is more difficult to talk about movements when it comes to visual art; so much of visual art is related to the success of individual artists. One influence that continues to affect visual art in rural communities is the development of individual art centers. These centers focus on visual art but frequently serve as the focal point for all of the arts disciplines in these communities. Many of the Carnegie libraries built in rural communities are experiencing a new life during the second half of the twentieth century as they are being transformed into community and visual art centers. In addition, the National Guild of Community Schools of the Arts, formerly part of the Settlement Music School movement, supports the work of the visual art centers and schools for visual art in rural communities.

The real influence of visual art comes from the artists themselves. One of the most noted Midwest regional artists is George Caleb Bingham, whose art depicted the social and political life of the rural frontier. His engravings based on his paintings, especially *The County Election* and *Stump Speaking,* give some of the earliest glimpses of what life was like in rural America in the nineteenth century. Bingham's depiction of trappers and boatmen who populated Missouri's great rivers and his background landscapes portray the Midwest and the people who inhabited it.

Other nineteenth-century regional artists, known as the western artists, include Fredric Remington, Charles Marion Russell, and N. C. Wyeth. Remington was best known for his action-oriented paintings, with their portrayals of military, Indian, and cowboy existence. Russell gained his reputation for paintings and illustrations documenting the daily life of Indian and White people on the frontier of the 1870s and 1880s. N. C. Wyeth served as a bridge between the nineteenth and twentieth centuries, with his early work dominated by western images. He eventually turned away from the western art tradition and began the work he is most well known for: his New England landscapes. These three artists were known as much for their illustrations of the West published by popular magazines (*Harper's Weekly* and the *Saturday Evening Post*), as for their paintings.

The twentieth century has produced several noted visual artists whose work represents the continuing tradition of regional art. These artists include John Steuart Curry, a Kansas artist, and his contemporary, Grant Wood, who portray the transition of American life from the rural-based community to the urban-industrialized society. Their art preserves many of the idealized images that have been identified with the values of small-town existence. Perhaps one of the most influential and well-known artists of the twentieth century is Thomas Hart Benton, a painter and muralist whose work portrayed rural life during the first part of this century. These indi-

vidual regional artists and many others like them played a vital role in depicting and preserving what life was like in rural America.

The Community Theater Movement

Several factors influenced the development of the community theater. The most important factor is the introduction of theater college courses in 1905 by George Pierce Baker at Harvard University. With compulsory education enabling rural students to attend college, more of them were exposed to theater. This provided an incentive to participate in theatrical productions when they returned to their rural communities. The little theater movement (later called the community theater movement) assisted in making theater more available in rural communities. This, combined with the steady influence of the Tent Chautauqua, which increasingly added theatrical productions to its programming, helped make theater more socially acceptable and helped overcome long-entrenched negative attitudes by people in rural communities about theater and the people who participated in it.

Two individuals contributed greatly to the influence of community theater on the community arts movement. The first is Alfred Arvold. Working with the North Dakota Agricultural College in Fargo in 1923, Arvold designed programs to unleash the creative potential of individuals in rural communities throughout the state. Another major figure in this movement is Robert Gard, founder of the Wisconsin Idea Theater, who created an extension outreach program in the College of Agriculture, University of Wisconsin. His commitment to train rural playwrights who could develop the regional voice expanded later to promote all of the arts in rural Wisconsin communities.

The community theater movement combined the self-improvement and self-education goals of the Lyceum and Chautauqua experiences with the opportunities to participate in the arts and experience them on a personal basis. It created a balance between art-as-product and art-as-process. For many people, this was their first experience with the arts.

The Contemporary Community Arts Movement

The most recent influence on the development of the arts in rural communities is the emergence of community arts agencies, schools, and centers. Beginning with the Works Progress Administration and the many visual arts projects it conducted in rural communities, increasing emphasis has been placed on nurturing and celebrating the arts in rural communities. In the mid-1960s, this effort expanded with the creation of the National Endowments for the Arts and the Humanities. Subsequent to these national endowments, state agencies for the arts and humanities were created, providing new public funding sources to support the arts and humanities all across America. Many rural communities benefited from public funding support provided by these agencies.

Because of these new funding resources and the recognition of what the arts contribute to the community setting, a new rural profession emerged under the name *community arts administrator*. With the steady increase of new rural community arts agencies led by these community arts administrators, the arts continue to thrive in rural communities. As a result, new opportunities are created for an active and vital process that brings into existence new means for revitalizing our rural communities. Each region has its own unique history to be identified and reclaimed. Each community has its own cultural roots to be remembered, restored, and celebrated.

In the history of these movements in the arts, four patterns can be distinguished. The first is a pattern of creativeness and innovation at the community level that translates into new ways for meeting community needs. It is an approach to art and culture as a process of self-improvement, self-expression, and self-education. This pattern represents the value of art as a process to be participated in and experienced on a personal basis.

A second pattern is that of individuals outside rural communities who took early efforts at self-improvement and self-expression and turned them into moneymaking ventures that changed the value of art from process and participation to that of commodity or product. Several times, what started out as celebration of community and self-expression quickly became an entrepreneurial venture that contradicted the original purpose of the arts. The "art merchants" who promote art as a product to be bought and sold have always found rural communities an excellent marketplace.

A third pattern, which emerged through the efforts of people such as Alfred Arvold and Robert Gard, is the valuing of art and culture as both process and product; this pattern kept the arts centered in the community and central to the life of the people who lived there. This tradition continues today with those working in the arts who try to balance bringing art into the community with bringing art out of the community, that is, sharing a community's art with others outside of that community. It is this pattern upon which the value system and philosophical foundation of the community arts movement are based.

A fourth pattern is the continuing uneasy and tenuous relationship between the arts and the church. The nation's early Puritan-influenced value system viewed the arts as potential expressions of evil and wickedness, which threatened the piety of the individual. This value system conflicted with the value system that promoted the arts as a means of self-education and self-expression. This conflict continues to manifest itself today in public controversy about the arts, making them a means by which rural communities identify and address cultural conflict.

There is ample evidence to support the conclusion that the arts in rural communities have enriched the cultural development of the arts in all communities, large and small. The community arts movement has always understood that along with the cultural treasures brought into the community, there are cultural treasures created by the community, and these need to be nurtured and valued as well. This dual focus of process and product continues to be the guiding force behind the development of arts in rural communities all across America.

—Patrick Overton

See also
Films, Rural; History, Rural; Literature; Music; Theatrical Entertainment.

References

Arvold, Alfred. *The Little Country Theater*. New York: Macmillan, 1923.

Brownell, Baker. *Art Is Action*. New York: Harper and Brothers, 1939.

———. *The Human Community*. New York: Harper and Brothers, 1950.

Gard, Robert, and Kolhoff, Ralph. *The Arts in the Small Community: A National Plan*. Reprint, Washington, DC: National Assembly of Local Arts Agencies, 1984.

Gould, Joseph E. *The Chautauqua Movement*. Albany: State University of New York Press, 1961.

Harrison, Harry P. *Culture under Canvas*. New York: Hastings House, 1958.

Mackaye, Percy. *The Civic Theater*. New York: Mitchell Kennerley, 1912.

Overton, Patrick. *Grassroots and Mountain Wings: The Arts in Rural and Small Communities*. Columbia, MO: Columbia College, 1992.

———. *Rebuilding the Front Porch of America: Essays on the Art of Community Making*. Columbia, MO: Columbia College, 1996.

Asian Pacific Americans

Ethnic groups that trace their origins to Asia and the Pacific Islands. This entry briefly describes the dispersion of Asian Pacific Americans and the impact of immigration and laws affecting Asian Pacific American immigration and highlights the rural experiences of five important Asian Pacific American ethnic groups. It concludes with an examination of future trends affecting Asian Pacific Americans.

Number and Dispersion

There were 7,273,662 Asian Pacific Americans, represented by 30 Asian and 21 Pacific Islander ethnic groups, in 1990. Between 1960 and 1990, the Asian Pacific American population increased from 1 million to well over 7 million and constituted 2.9 percent of the nation's population.

Chinese Americans constituted the largest Asian Pacific American population, with 1,645,472 individuals (22.6 percent of all Asian Pacific Americans) in 1990. Closely following them were Filipino Americans, with a population of 1,406,700 (19.3 percent of all Asian Pacific Americans). In descending order by proportion of the Asian Pacific American population were Japanese Americans (847,562), Asian Indian Americans (815,447), Korean Americans (798,849), Vietnamese Americans (615,547), Hawaiian Americans (211,014), Laotian Americans (149,014), Cambodian Americans (147,411), Thai Americans (91,275), Hmong Americans (90,082), Samoan Americans (62,964), Guamanian Americans (49,345), and Tongan Americans (17,606). The remainder of other Asian Pacific Americans was 326,304.

Although 94 percent of Asian Pacific Americans reside in metropolitan areas today, their initial association was with rural America. These immigrants played a pivotal role in the economic and agricultural development of the United States, developed new agricultural crops and varieties, played major roles in agricultural unionization movements, and created vibrant ethnic communities. The story of Asian immigrant groups in America in the first half of this century involved their challenging many discriminatory barriers. In the process, each of these groups used or developed strategies for group survival that have relevance to questions related to rural and community development today.

Asian Pacific Americans are, by and large, heavily concentrated on the western and eastern seaboards of the United States. More than one-half the nation's Asian Pacific Americans live in the West, where their share of the population, 7.7 percent, is now higher than the percentage of African Americans. In contrast to earlier periods when occupations such as railroad construction, levee building, salmon processing, tenant farming, and farm labor associated the Asian presence with rural America in the West, Asian Pacific Americans are now concentrated in metropolitan areas where, compared to non-Hispanic Whites, a disproportionate number live in central cities.

Impact of Immigration and Immigration Laws

Asian Pacific Americans are affected by immigration more than any current racially identified group. In comparison to the record high percentages of immigration during the 1980s and 1990s, Asian Pacific Americans never reached more than 0.25 percent of the total U.S. population before 1940, despite several waves of immigration from Asian and Pacific countries. Racist legislation that minimized Asian immigration was repeatedly passed and amended to bar Asians and Pacific Islanders of various nationalities and classes from entering the United States and supposedly competing with native-born White workers.

There are many examples of such discriminatory anti-Asian immigration laws. The Chinese Exclusion Act of 1882 barred most Chinese immigration and was not repealed until 1943. The Gentleman's Agreement of 1908 limited Japanese immigration and was in effect until 1952. The Johnson-Reed Act of 1924 excluded Asian immigration because Asians were ineligible for citizenship. The Tydings-McDuffy Act of 1934 closed the door to Filipino nationals trying to enter the United States. Substantial Asian and Pacific Island immigration to the United States did not begin again until the passage of the Immigration and Nationality Act Amendments of 1965. Despite these discriminatory measures, many Asian Pacific Americans found labor opportunities in rural America; many became leaseholders and farm owners. These rural ethnic enterprises were important to the development of Asian Pacific American communities and to the economic upward mobility of subsequent generations.

Chinese Americans

Chinese Americans were crucial to California's agricultural development. They are credited with saving the state from economic disaster in the 1870s and 1890s and with providing 75 percent of California's agricultural labor force. Chinese immigrant labor reclaimed 88,000 acres of rich swampland in the San Joaquin–Sacramento Delta, where they stayed as farmworkers or tenant farmers. They introduced strawberries, sugar beets, celery, and asparagus—all part of the pantheon of today's California agricultural exports. Horticulturalist Ah Bing bred a new cherry variety known across the country as the Bing

Cherry. By 1877, Chinese American farmers were producing two-thirds of all vegetables in California.

Japanese Americans

Discriminatory laws at the turn of the century drove Japanese into rural occupations. They settled on marginal lands, choosing crops requiring little capital or land. Overcoming obstacles and attaining moderate degrees of success led to resentment that fueled legislation such as the 1913 Alien Land Law, which forbade persons ineligible for citizenship from leasing or owning land. Foreign-born Asian Americans were ineligible for citizenship as a result of the Naturalization Act of 1790, which restricted naturalization and therefore citizenship and voting rights to immigrant White males. California's 1913 Alien Land Law was specifically anti-Japanese. It was modified more stringently in subsequent enactments elsewhere in the West.

Nevertheless, immigrant farmers from Japan played an important role in agriculture, particularly on the West Coast. Japanese immigrant farmers responded with a prodigious output to the nation's need for food when the United States entered World War I in 1917. They accounted for 90 percent of California's production of celery, asparagus, onions, tomatoes, berries, and cantaloupes; 70 percent of the floriculture; 50 percent of the seeds; 45 percent of the sugar beets; 40 percent of leafy vegetables; and 35 percent of grape production. One-half of all Japanese males were involved in some phase of farming on the eve of World War II.

They produced one-half of California truck crops in 1941. They produced all of the green beans, celery, peppers, and strawberries; 50 to 90 percent of artichokes, cauliflower, cucumbers, spinach, and tomatoes; and 25 to 50 percent of asparagus, cantaloupes, carrots, lettuce, onions, and watermelons. All of this was produced on a very small proportion of California's farmland. Because of restrictions in the amount of land that they could lease and because of discrimination (having to pay much higher rental rates on prime agricultural lands), Japanese American farmers used practices that maximized what resources they had by developing lands that were considered unusable or marginal. Half a century ago, Los Angeles was California's leading agricultural county, the result in large part of the productivity of Japanese American farmers, who sold from over 1,000 fruit and vegetable stands placed at their farm gates. Japanese American farmers chose crops that brought the most income on the least space, used irrigation and fertilizers much more extensively than other farmers, used family labor, and sold directly to consumers. Similar concepts are part of current efforts to promote a more sustainable system of food production.

People of Japanese ancestry were evacuated to concentration camps with the advent of World War II. Although some Japanese Americans returned to their rural or agricultural bases after the war, they never recovered the dominance exhibited in places such as Los Angeles County. Many lost too much capital and resources to restart farming operations. The most manageable start-up related to their past expertise was in garden care. Seventy-five percent of Japanese Americans in Los Angeles operated or worked in gardening and nurseries in the 1960s. Their influence on residential landscaping has been widespread.

Filipino Americans

Filipino Americans did not become a U.S. census category until 1950, although their settlements date back to the eighteenth century when "Manilamen" left the harsh treatment on the Spanish galleons to settle around New Orleans. Chinese were recognized in the census in 1870; Japanese, in 1890; Hawaiians, in 1960; Koreans, in 1970; and Vietnamese, Asian Indians, Guamanians, and Samoans, in 1980. The "Other" category added in 1990 includes Cambodians, Hmong, Lao, and Thai. The first sizable numbers of Filipinos to arrive in America went to the sugar plantations in Hawaii. The working conditions under which Filipino immigrants have labored (e.g., in Hawaii, Northwest salmon canneries, and West Coast farmlands) have been such that Filipinos have been involved in unionization movements in all these places. By the 1920s, Filipino Americans were the primary farm labor force in Hawaii and on the West Coast. Several circumstances prevented Filipino Americans from moving up the agricultural ladder, from worker to leaseholder to owner. They were cut off from forming families by the blockage of female immigrants and antimiscegenation laws. This restricted Filipino Americans to oppressive work stations; they resisted by organizing the Filipino Federation of Labor on the Hawaii sugar plantations, the Filipino Salmon Cannery Workers, and the Filipino Labor Union among lettuce pickers in Salinas, California. Farm labor organizing continued through the 1960s when Filipino Americans joined Mexican American workers to form the United Farm Workers, led by César Chávez and Larry Itliong.

In addition to the difficulties created by restrictive

laws, discrimination, and oppressive working situations, Filipino Americans (as well as other Asian Americans) lacked access to credit. Money was needed to move out of the labor cycle and into small business and entrepreneurship. But mainstream lending agencies remained hostile to Asian immigrant requests. The rotating credit association, a social and cultural formation common to Asian Pacific immigrants, became an important source of start-up capital. Close friends or associates from similar hometowns or regions pooled an agreed-upon amount each month to be loaned on a lottery or bidding system. As the money was repaid and the pool increased, others received loans. This system of money pooling went by different names—*tanomoshi* in Japanese, *hui* in Chinese, *bui* in Vietnamese, *hulugan* in Tagalog, and *gae* in Korean. The main collateral, in addition to the shares contributed, was peer pressure and honor. This system of credit access was a key factor in the start-up of small businesses in Asian Pacific American communities. A variation of this concept is now used by many developing and low-income communities.

Sikh Americans, Hmong Americans, and Laotian Americans

Although the majority of Asian Pacific Americans are in metropolitan areas, particularly in central cities and suburbs, today there are unique pockets in rural areas. Two of these are the Sikh Americans in Yuba City and the Hmong Americans around Fresno, both in California's Great Central Valley. The Sikhs are only 2 percent of India's population but have been one of its major immigrant groups to America. Although no longer the dominant immigrant Asian Indian group, they still make up 30 percent of the South Asian immigrant population. The Sikhs from the Punjab were originally employed for their irrigation and farm labor skills. Many towns in California's Central Valley are sites of a *guardwara,* a Sikh temple of worship. Yuba City in Sutter County, a rice- and peach-growing center, is home to some 10,000 Sikhs. Estimates place more than one-half of the peaches in Sutter County as being grown by Sikh Americans.

As a result of the aftermath of the Vietnam War, many Hmong and Lao refugees resettled in America and have centered their communities in agricultural regions that reflect their past agricultural experience. Between 1980 and 1990, the Hmong American population in the United States grew by 1631 percent and Laotian Americans grew 213 percent. Nearly one-half of the 90,082 Hmong immigrants live in California's agricultural Cen-

tral Valley. The largest concentration is a group of 18,000 around Fresno. In a 1992 survey, agricultural extension agents identified nearly 800 refugee farmers in Fresno County, the leading county nationally in value of agricultural production. Of these farmers, 62 percent were Hmong American and 30 percent were Laotian Americans (Ilic 1992). Most had started farming within the three years prior to the study. The size of their operations ranges from 3 to 5 acres of rented land, with six family members helping on the farm. Most finance their operations themselves with loans from relatives. They market their produce with Southeast Asian wholesalers or, when the price is high, sell directly to buyers who come to their farm. These Hmong Americans and Laotian Americans have reestablished their traditional identity through a rural and agricultural way of life, as did other Asian groups before them.

Future Trends

Population Growth. The Asian Pacific American population was estimated at 8.8 million in the 1994 Current Population Survey. In 1994, as in 1990, they were roughly 3 percent of the nation's population. Since 1990, the Asian Pacific American population has grown by an average of 4.5 percent per year. Eighty-six percent of the growth is attributable to immigration, with the remainder resulting from natural increase. Asian Pacific Americans continue to become ever-more urban. By 1994, 96 percent of all Asian Pacific Americans lived in metropolitan areas.

By the year 2000, Asian Pacific Americans are projected to reach 12.1 million and represent 4.3 percent of the nation's population. By 2050, the Asian Pacific American population will be five times its 1995 size. By then, it will make up 10 percent of the total U.S. population and approach 60 million individuals.

Regionally, the western states, particularly California, will continue to be the favorite locations of Asian Pacific Americans. Between 1993 and 2020, the western Asian Pacific American population will increase by 8 million people. By the year 2000, 40.5 percent of all Asian Pacific Americans will live in California, compared to 40.0 percent in 1995 and 39.1 percent in 1990. By the year 2000, California is projected to have almost 10 million Asian Pacific Americans. By 2020, Texas and New York will each have more than 1 million Asian Pacific Americans.

The rural to urban shift will not be solely because Asian Pacific Americans moved from rural areas to metropolitan cities and suburbs. Instead, former rural areas where rural Asian Pacific Americans reside will increasingly be incorporated into the growing boundaries of urbanized areas. Historically, this happened for Japanese Americans, Filipino Americans, and Chinese Americans in Los Angeles and Santa Clara Counties in California and probably will happen for Hmong Americans and Laotian Americans in Fresno, Merced, and Stockton Counties.

Intermarriage. Intermarriage adds another dimension of diversity to the Asian Pacific American population. Among Asian Pacific Americans, 31.2 percent of all Asian Pacific American husbands and 40.4 percent of all Asian Pacific American wives were intermarried in 1990. Among Asian Pacific American husbands, 18.9 percent were interethnically married and 12.3 percent were interracially married. Among the interracially married, 9.9 percent of these husbands married non-Hispanic Whites. Among Asian Pacific American wives, 16.2 percent were interethnically married and 24.2 percent were interracially married. Among the interracially married, 20.8 percent of Asian Pacific American wives married non-Hispanic Whites. Japanese American wives and Filipina American wives had the highest proportion of interracial marriages (51.9 percent and 40.2 percent, respectively). The high proportion of interracial marriages among Japanese Americans is due in part to the large presence of wives of U.S. servicemen.

Acknowledgment of this aspect of Asian Pacific diversity shows in the emergence on various college campuses of student associations that go by such names as "Hapa" (meaning half Asian Pacific–half other) clubs. These groups are testimony to the important role biracial and multicultural identity plays in the lives of a new generation of Asian Pacific Americans. There is also a rise in panethnicity among Asian Americans that is beginning to play out in major universities in Asian American studies and ethnic studies and in the development of Asia-Towns that go beyond the more ethnically specific Little Tokyos, Chinatowns, Manilatowns, Little Saigons, and Koreatowns. This pattern of panethnicity is evidenced in the growing rates of interethnic marriages among Asian Pacific Americans.

Poverty. Despite higher educational attainments and a similar median family income, the poverty rate for Asian Pacific American families (14 percent) was higher than that of non-Hispanic White families (8 percent) in 1993. Between 1990 and 1994, poverty among Asian Pacific American families rose from 11.9 to 13.5 percent. Among individuals, it rose from 14.1 percent to 15.3 percent. Among rural Southeast Asian Americans, the poverty rates were at least double that of the general

Asian Pacific American rate. Factors that need to be watched in relation to differences in poverty rates include language, class divisions, and forces affecting work and entrepreneurial opportunity.

Language. The diversity and challenge of Asian Pacific American groups are captured in the persistence of languages used. In 1990 in California, for example, there were 665,605 households that spoke an Asian Pacific American language. Among these, 32.8 percent were classified as linguistically isolated (that is, no persons in the household over the age of 13 spoke English "well" or "very well"). Of those who spoke an Asian Pacific American language, 18.2 percent aged 5 to 17 years, 24.0 percent aged 18 to 64 years, and 51.3 percent aged 65 years and older responded that they spoke English "well" or "very well." Forty-one percent of persons age 65 and older are in a household where there is no one who speaks English "well" or "very well." Languages spoken at home for persons 5 years and older included Chinese (both Mandarin and Cantonese, 575,447), Vietnamese (233,074), Tagalog (465,644), Korean (215,845), Japanese (147,451), Indic (119,318), and Mon-Khmer (59,622). Rural Asian Pacific American were slightly more linguistically isolated than the general Asian Pacific American population (34.1 percent).

Economic and Political Forces. There are growing class divisions within Asian Pacific American ethnic groups and among Asian American sociocultural groups. For example, East Asian (Chinese, Japanese, Korean) and South Asian (Asian Indian/East Asian) Americans have higher incomes, lower high school dropout rates, and higher educational attainment than Southeast Asian (Cambodian, Laotian, Hmong) American and Pacific Islander groups. Filipino Americans and Vietnamese Americans appear between these two categories.

Asian Pacific Americans may see a major decline in fortunes during the 1990s among unskilled or limited-English-speaking immigrants. Many entrepreneurial opportunities once open to Asian Americans are being taken over by corporate concerns and are being affected by discriminatory licensing laws reminiscent of past anti-Asian laws. Examples of businesses where Asian American entrepreneurs have been adversely affected include video stores, liquor stores, small family-owned and -operated grocery stores, dry cleaning establishments, and donut shops.

At the other end of the scale among the better-educated, successful Asian Americans, both Asian Pacific American females and males have yet to reach economic parity in pay or social parity with non-Hispanic White males. In effect, a glass ceiling appears to limit their opportunities for upward advancement. Many Asian Pacific Americans have sidestepped the discrimination by starting their own ethnic corporate high-technology firms. Many of these firms have become successful and have contributed much to the regional and national economy.

Also, Asian Pacific American communities are increasingly panethnic and transnational in character; choice of residence is increasingly on the West Coast or in New York City. As current immigration laws and preferences are threatened or modified, pressures for naturalization will increase substantially. Naturalization rates among Asian Pacific Americans are already higher than for any other immigrants. Partly because of these changes, the political participation of Asian Pacific Americans will increase markedly. With their metropolitan and Pacific Rim concentrations, their economic capacities and potential, and their growing rates of naturalization and voter participation, Asian Pacific Americans will become a powerful political force in the United States in the 1990s and 2000s.

—*Isao Fujimoto and Larry Hajime Shinagawa*

See also

Cultural Diversity; Culture; Employment; Ethnicity; Family; Inequality; Marriage; Migration; Rural Demography.

References

Chan, Sucheng. *Asian Americans: An Interpretive History*. Boston: Twayne, 1991.

———. *This Bittersweet Soil: The Chinese in California Agriculture, 1860–1910*. Berkeley and Los Angeles: University of California Press, 1986.

Chuman, Frank F. *The Bamboo People: The Law and Japanese Americans*. Del Mar, CA: Publishers Incorporated, 1976.

Gall, Suan, and Irene Natividad. *Reference Library of Asian America*. Detroit: Gale Research, 1995.

Hing, Bill Ong. *Making and Remaking Asian America through Immigration Policy, 1850–1990*. Stanford, CA: Stanford University Press, 1993.

Hune, Shirley, et al., eds. *Asian America: Comparative Global Perspectives*. Pullman: Washington State University Press, 1991.

Ilic, Pedro. "Southeast Asian Farmers in Fresno County: Status Report 1992." Fresno: Fresno County Office of University of California Cooperative Extension, 1992.

Iwata, Masakuzu. *Planted in Good Soil: A History of the Issei in United States Agriculture*. New York: Lang, 1992.

Kitano, Harry H. L. *Asian Americans: Emerging Minorities*. Englewood Cliffs, NJ: Prentice-Hall, 1988.

Ng, Franklin, ed. *The Asian American Encyclopedia*. New York: Michael Cavendish, 1995.

Shinagawa, Larry Hajime, and Michael M. Jang. *Atlas of American Diversity*. Newbury Park, CA: Sage Publications/Altamira Press, 1996.

Shinagawa, Larry Hajime, and Gin Yong Pang. "Asian American Pan-Ethnicity and Intermarriage." *Amerasia Journal* 22, no. 2 (1996): 127–153.

U.S. Bureau of the Census. *The Asian and Pacific Islander Population in the United States: March 1991 and 1990*. Current Population Reports, Population Characteristics, P20–459. Washington, DC: U.S. Government Printing Office, 1992.

———. *Population Profile of the United States, 1995*. Washington, DC: U.S. Government Printing Office, 1995.

———. *Population Projections for States, by Age, Sex, Race, and Hispanic Origin: 1993 to 2020*. Washington, DC: U.S. Government Printing Office, 1994.

———. *Survey of Minority-Owned Business Enterprises: Asian Americans, American Indians, and Other Minorities*. Washington, DC: Government Printing Office, 1991.

Bank Lending Practices

The lending practices of commercial banks. Banking practices are undergoing significant changes. Some of these changes, which are addressed in this entry, include the banking industry structure, loan markets, and loan marketing strategies. The entry also examines environmental rules and regulations, risk, and issues of cost control and containment.

Industry Function and Structure

Rural banking institutions channel funds from savers to borrowers to finance a variety of projects and activities, such as production expenses, capital expenditures, housing, and community development. The major industry for most rural areas is agriculture. Commercial banks historically have been the largest institutional source of non–real estate loans to agriculture and an important source of farm real estate loan funds. On December 31, 1994, commercial banks provided 40 percent of the $148.1 billion total farm debt, excluding operator households.

In terms of numbers, most commercial banks in the United States historically have been "unit" operations. In a unit banking system, an individual bank maintains only one office or place of business. In the past, the laws of many states either prohibited or limited branch banking, or multiple offices of a single firm. However, since the mid-1980s restrictions on branching have eased considerably in many states. Interstate bank branching legislation was passed by Congress in 1994. Such legislation allows banks to purchase and operate banks in all states.

Since then, the number of commercial banks in the United States declined from more than 14,000 in the mid-1980s to 10,675 on 30 June 1994. The number of agricultural banks, as defined by the Federal Reserve Board, declined during that period from more than 4,800 to 3,689. The Board of Governors of the Federal Reserve System classifies banks as agricultural if their ratios of farm loans to total loans exceed the unweighted average of the ratio of all banks on a given date (i.e., 17.4 percent on June 30, 1994). Some forecasters have indicated that the number of U.S. commercial banks will decline to approximately 8,000 by the year 2000. Most of this restructuring will occur from mergers and acquisitions, not from the failure of commercial banks.

Some industry analysts believe that two objectives will guide the management of commercial banks in the future: reduce per dollar volume cost and increase deposit and loan volumes. The management of commercial banks will seek ways to acquire deposits and to provide loans by the least-cost means possible. The result will likely be a banking industry with a small number of large regional banks, but with several smaller banks that serve a niche in the rural market. In addition, the management of commercial banks in rural areas will also be influenced by several driving forces that will help to shape the financing of rural America.

Loan Market

The agricultural loan market, in aggregate, is a mature, slow-growth market at best. Agricultural producers, as well as lenders, have been and probably will continue to be cautious in adding to their debt load, with the objective of maintaining a balance between debt servicing requirements and income generation. Financing demands of the agricultural sector will be modest, fueled more by operating needs and the intergenerational transfer of asset ownership and less by rising asset values and substantial additions to plant capacity.

The agricultural loan market has a diverse customer base in terms of type of business, size of operation, risk characteristics, and collateral available. It is becoming increasingly difficult for commercial banks to serve all segments of this market equally well in a cost-effective manner. Consequently, commercial banks are moving to a focused loan marketing strategy that targets specific segments of the market with specific products and services. This segmented approach is more difficult to implement successfully in a community-based rural bank that is dependent on all segments and sectors of the community for business. But fewer and fewer commercial banks will be focused exclusively on one community as commercial banks merge and consolidate over time. Thus, the market environment will be favorable for a segmented approach to marketing agricultural loans.

Environmental Rules and Regulations

Environmental rules and regulations will continue to have a significant impact on agricultural lending; that impact can be best described as mixed and costly. Such regulations may increase the demand for loan funds to build facilities designed to store and dispose of animal wastes or to comply with regulations on drainage and conservation practices that will reduce or mitigate environmental degradation. Conversely, concerns about environmental liability may make credit for certain uses (e.g., livestock facilities, chemical or fertilizer storage, or application facilities and equipment) more difficult to obtain. Consequently, bank loan officers increasingly will rely on environmental audits or other procedures to reduce the risk of liability. Finally, the cost for those credits that require such procedures probably will increase.

Risk

Managers of commercial banks increasingly are concerned about risk and implementation of procedures to reduce it. For a banker, risk is a function of both credit quality and interest rate fluctuations. The commercial banks that serve rural America continue to implement management strategies and lending policies to reduce their risk exposure. As to credit risk, they continue to increase documentation standards, thus requiring more detailed information on past and projected financial performance of their borrowers. For those not deemed to be creditworthy, rural banks more frequently require private or public guarantees or deny the credit request. Likewise, they continue to expand their use of risk rating or assessment procedures and charge risk premiums or higher interest rates to those borrowers who expose the institution to higher risks.

The risk rating of loans at the customer level has become a common practice in lending to agricultural producers by commercial banks. The ultimate result from risk rating of loans is to use the rating for differential loan pricing. There are a variety of factors associated with differential loan pricing, including deposit balances, loan maturities, loan purpose, loan size, and market competition. However, the most common use of differential loan pricing found in agricultural lending is for differences in customers' credit risks.

As to interest rate risk, commercial banks continue to expand their use of variable rate lending procedures whereby interest rate risk is transferred from the bank to the borrower. They more carefully match the maturity structure of assets (loans and investments) to liabilities (deposits, bonds, or purchased money) so the opportunity exists to reprice assets when liabilities have to be repriced. Generally this strategy results in shorter maturities on loans and/or more volatility in interest rates for borrowers.

Cost Control and Containment

Commercial banks are also facing increased competition and tighter profit margins. To survive and prosper in this kind of environment, they increasingly will focus on cost control and cost containment. The costs a bank incurs in making loans generally can be classified as the costs of money; the costs of origination, delivery, and collection of credits; and the costs of nonperforming loans. Commercial banks have only limited control over their cost of money; rates generally are set in competitive markets, although the bank may manage money costs to a limited degree by monitoring yield curves and choosing maturities on bonds or deposits that generate the lowest cost.

After the cost of money, the most significant cost for the bank is that of credit extension and collection. Thus, the opportunities for cost reductions are typically most promising in this area. Credit delivery is a very labor-intensive process, so one common strategy is increased labor (particularly loan officer) efficiency through the use of well-trained support personnel, increased use of computers, more specialization in loan officers' duties, and better time management and allocation.

The implications are that borrowers may work with more specialized and knowledgeable personnel who have less time available for general discussion and counseling. Borrowers may need to travel farther to talk to the banker and may have to do business with personnel other than their traditional loan officer. Borrowers also will be expected to provide more detailed and complete information on the financial condition of their businesses with less direct input, such as completion of the forms by the banker.

In addition to credit extension and collection costs, commercial bank personnel will monitor carefully the costs of providing services for which they receive little or no income. They may initiate or increase fees for such services as financial counseling, market advisory services, check cashing, and credit cards. Commercial banks also will be cautious in credit extension to reduce the costs of loan losses on nonperforming loans or, alternatively, increase the interest rate for higher-risk borrowers to compensate for the increased risk. Borrowers also may find interest rate discounts or premiums when they apply for a loan. This price differential will be the result of the substantial size economies in lending and the fact that smaller loans generally are more expensive per dollar volume for the bank to deliver and service. Thus, interest rates will be less uniform among bank customers, with smaller and/or high-risk borrowers paying higher rates than their larger and/or lower-risk counterparts.

—*Freddie L. Barnard*

See also

Agricultural and Resource Economics; Farm Finance; Financial Intermediaries; Foreclosure and Bankruptcy; Policy, Economic.

References

Agricultural Income and Finance: Situation and Outlook Report. AIS-52. Washington, D.C.: U.S. Department of Agriculture, Economic Research Service, February 1995.

Barnard, Freddie L. *Banker's Agricultural Lending Manual.* Austin, TX: Sheshunoff Information Services, 1993.

Barnard, Freddie L., Michael Boehlje, Julian H. Atkinson, and Kenneth A. Foster. "Financing Agriculture." In *Indiana Agriculture 2000: A Strategic Perspective.* West Lafayette, IN: Purdue University, Department of Agricultural Economics, June 1992.

Barry, Peter J., John A. Hopkin, and Chester B. Baker. *Financial Management in Agriculture.* 2d ed. Danville, IL: Interstate Printers and Publishers, 1979.

DeVuyst, Cheryl, David Lins, and Bruce Sherrick. "Financing Illinois Agriculture." Pp. 112–120 in *Illinois Agriculture, Agribusiness, and the Rural Economy: Strategic Issues for the Next Century.* Special Publication 85. Urbana-Champaign: University of Illinois, Department of Agricultural Economics, February 1994.

Kohl, David M. *Weighing the Variables: A Guide to Ag Credit Management.* Washington, DC: American Bankers Association, 1992.

Penson, John B., Jr., and David A. Lins. *Agricultural Finance: An Introduction to Micro and Macro Concepts.* Englewood Cliffs, NJ: Prentice-Hall, 1980.

U. S. Department of Agriculture. *Farm Balance Sheet, Including Operator Households, 1960–89: United States and by State.* USDA-ERS Statistical Bulletin No. 826. Washington, DC: U.S. Department of Agriculture, Economic Research Service, August 1991.

Barns

Farm buildings to shelter harvested crops, livestock, or machinery. This entry discusses the history of barn architecture, how American barn design reflects changes in agricultural and building technology over the last two centuries, the decline of traditional barn architecture, and the use of historic barns on farms today.

History

Barns are one of the most visible and most powerful symbols of rural life in America. The history of barn design and construction reflects the development of American agriculture, from early subsistence farming, through mechanization and the "Golden Age of Agriculture," to the megafarms of the 1990s. The sheer size of barns and their simple, functional design have made them treasured architectural landmarks as well as utilitarian structures. Although many barns have been lost to development or neglect, a significant number of farmers across the country have maintained their older barns and adapted them for modern farming uses.

The earliest American barns were simple, gable-roofed structures designed primarily to store grain. They were built of log or stone—whatever materials were available locally. As American agriculture developed, barns incorporated more farming activities. The traditional English, or three-bay, barn of the early nineteenth century included a few stalls for animals and a large floor space for hand threshing of grain. A central driveway allowed the farmer to drive wagons into the barn for loading and unloading. Most early- to mid-nineteenth-century barns were constructed of large timbers, joined by mortise and tenon joints secured with wooden pins. Barn walls, or bents, were assembled on the ground and raised into place. Barn raisings were often community events that including feasting and a dance when the construction was complete.

The development of mechanized farm equipment and scientific farming during the nineteenth century allowed American farms to grow and diversify. Reaping and threshing machines allowed farmers to harvest larger quantities of hay and grain, resulting in a need for more storage space in the barn. An emphasis on raising livestock as well as crops meant that barns had to incorporate new functions. Multipurpose, multistory barns began to replace the smaller barns. Some farmers simply added on to their barns, or raised them up and built a basement underneath, for livestock.

In the late nineteenth century, changes in building

Barns have developed very distinctive structures and styles over time, determined by the type of agriculture as well as the architectural styles of the cultures in which they occur.

technology such as balloon-frame construction and the availability of dimension lumber and wire nails resulted in innovations in barn design. The development of the double-sloped gambrel roof, which is most frequently associated with barns today, allowed as much as 50 percent more hay storage in the mow and eliminated crossbeams, allowing for efficient use of a hay track to load hay. Later developments included arched roofs built with rounded trusses.

Most barns were built by farmers themselves, sometimes with the help of professional barn builders. Some builders developed distinctive styles, which still can be recognized in certain localities. Although most barns had little ornamentation, elements of architectural styles such as Italianate scrollwork, Gothic pointed gables, and even western false fronts sometimes were incorporated into barn design. Some barns also displayed evidence of regional craftsmanship in brick, stone, and woodwork. Cupolas, used for ventilation, provided the farmer or barn builder with an opportunity to add a special flourish to the barn, to distinguish it from surrounding barns.

Land-grant universities had a widespread influence on late-nineteenth- and early-twentieth-century barns. Agricultural engineers developed innovative designs, including round and polygonal barns, for all types of farming purposes. They designed special barns for housing dairy cows, hogs, and horses; storing hay, grain, and machinery; and drying tobacco and distributed the plans to farmers nationwide through the Cooperative Extension Service. With the availability of ready-made plans, and even mail-order barns, barn design became more standardized throughout the country, although regional variations and ethnic building traditions continued well into the twentieth century.

Decline of Traditional Architecture

By the 1950s, construction of the multistory barn had virtually ceased, replaced by the single-story pole barn. Unlike the traditional American barns, which housed several activities under one roof, modern pole barns are specifically designed for a single purpose. They feature huge, open interior spaces, allowing easy access for large machinery. In spite of the predominance of metal-clad pole buildings on farms across America, the traditional gambrel-roofed barn persists as the symbol of American agriculture, appearing in everything from advertising of farm products to logos of agricultural organizations and corporations.

With the decline in the number of individual farms and the total acreage of farmland in the United States since the 1940s, thousands of farmsteads have been abandoned or demolished. Many farms have been lost to development, as cities sprawl outward. A few barns have been saved and adapted for homes, stores, or community centers, but only a small fraction survive when farmland is lost.

The increase in the size of individual farms also has led to destruction of many historic farm buildings. A single modern farm may incorporate a dozen or more traditional 80-acre farms, each with its own set of farm buildings. Because these buildings have no use and are sitting on valuable cropland, they usually are moved or destroyed when farms are consolidated. Even when the farmstead is left intact, traditional barns face an uncertain future. Barns designed specifically for hand threshing of grain, storage of loose hay, or hand milking of cows outgrew their original usefulness a century ago. When the tractor replaced the draft horse for plowing and other farm chores, stalls for horses were no longer needed. Farmers found haymows inefficient and sometimes structurally inadequate for storing baled hay. As agriculture became more specialized, many farmers sold their livestock altogether, and barns that once had been the center of the farm operation stood empty.

Preservation

In spite of the widespread loss, there still are many traditional barns in use on farms and ranches across America. Some have remained in constant use and have been adapted to fit the changes in agricultural practice and technology. For example, in Vermont, 150-year-old dairy barns still serve the descendants of the original barn builders. Wooden stalls gave way to stanchions and later free stalls, mechanical milking and waste removal systems were added and improved over the years, but the barns still retain their original function.

Farmers who own historic barns generally value them for their symbolic, personal, and architectural importance, as well as their practical use on the farm. The massive, traditional barn is often referred to as the "centerpiece of the farming operation" or the "heart and soul of the farm"—labels not used to describe modern pole barns. Although few farmers can afford to preserve barns for sentimental, educational, or aesthetic reasons, many farmers have found traditional barns to be versatile buildings that can be adapted for a variety of uses, often at a fraction of the cost of building a new structure. A 1988 study by the BARN AGAIN! program of *Successful Farming* magazine and the National Trust for Historic Preservation found that farmers saved an average of $2 for every $1 spent rehabilitating an older barn, as compared with building a new structure.

In the Midwest, where many farmers have sold all their livestock and produce only crops, traditional barns have been converted to store large quantities of hay or grain or to shelter and enable repair of farm equipment. These changes usually involve enlarging doorways and sometimes raising or removing the haymow floor to open up the interior space. Traditional barns also have been converted for cleaning, sorting, and packaging seed; raising hogs; and engaging in nontraditional farm activities such as on-farm retail sales, wineries, and food processing. Barns in rural America today are a mix of the old and the new. Preservation of traditional barns alongside modern barns provides a dramatic illustration of the changes in American agriculture over the last two hundred years.

—Mary Humstone

See also
Architecture; Dairy Farming; History, Agricultural.

References
Arthur, Eric, and Dudley Whitney. *The Barn: A Vanishing Landmark in North America*. Toronto: Feheley Arts, 1972.
Ensminger, R. F. *The Pennsylvania Barn: Its Origin, Evolution, and Distribution in North America*. Baltimore, MD: Johns Hopkins University Press, 1992.
Fink, Daniel. *Barns of the Genesee Country, 1790–1915*. Geneseo, NY: James Brunner, 1987.
Hanou, John. *A Round Indiana: Round Barns in the Hoosier State*. West Lafayette, IN: Purdue University Press, 1993.
Halsted, Byron D. *Barn Plans and Outbuildings*. New York: Orange Judd, 1918.
Hubka, Thomas C. *Big House, Little House, Back House, Barn: The Connected Farm Buildings of New England*. Hanover, NH: University Press of New England, 1984.
Humstone, Mary. *BARN AGAIN!: A Guide to Rehabilitation of Older Farm Buildings*. Denver: Meredith Corporation/National Trust for Historic Preservation, 1988.
Noble, Allen G. *Wood, Brick, and Stone: The North American Settlement Landscape*. Amherst: University of Massachusetts Press, 1984.
Sanders, J. H. *Practical Hints About Barn Building*. Chicago: J. H. Sanders, 1875. Microfilm.
Schultz, Leroy G. *Barns, Stables, and Outbuildings: A World Bibliography in English, 1700–1983*. Jefferson, NC: McFarland, 1986.

Biodiversity

Species diversity ranging from the level of genetic material to the level of ecosystems. Attempts to explain why some places have more or different kinds of species than other places have been ongoing in the field of ecology. The explanations usually require consideration of two greatly different time scales—the evolutionary scale and the ecological scale—and sometimes different spatial scales as well (Meffe and Carroll 1994). This entry addresses diversity using these scales and concludes with implications for conservation.

The Evolutionary Scale

The geological record is punctuated by periods of greater or lesser extinction events. These events usually are followed by subsequent expansion or radiation of new groups that produce new patterns of species diversity. Also occurring over long geological periods, landmasses have undergone complex patterns of discontinuity from the breakup of vast, nearly global continents to more local disjunctures, such as the submergence of land bridges or the formation of mountain barriers. The combination of biological processes of extinction and radiation and the ancient geophysical processes of land fragmentation, physical barriers, or migrational corridors results in contemporary biogeographical patterns of biodiversity at higher taxonomic (or the scientific classification of plants and animals) levels (see Table 1).

As two examples will illustrate, these biogeographical patterns are evident in North America. The first example shows the importance of extinction events. As recently as 50,000 years ago, the mammalian fauna of North America resembled that of modern savanna Africa in its rich array of large predators and herbivores. The end of the last northern glaciation cycle was a period of extinction for mammal species in North America. Approximately 43 genera of mammals disappeared, most of them of large size, leaving behind a much impoverished mammalian fauna. The loss of many large vertebrates (often called the Pleistocene Megafauna) from North and South America had an important impact on contemporary processes and patterns of biodiversity. These large browsers, such as the giant ground sloth and mastodon, may have played a role in maintaining a forest-savanna mosaic in North America analogous to the role currently played by elephants and other browsers in Africa.

Barriers and their converse migration corridors also influenced biogeographical patterns. During the Ice Age maxima when the southward expansion of the great glaciers was generating the deep fertile loess soils of the future corn and wheat belt states, western and eastern North America were largely isolated from each other. At the same time, the emergence of the Bering Strait land bridge permitted human colonization, with migrants first penetrating southward through western North America. In addition to people, the large percentage of species in the Pacific states with Asian affiliations (e.g., giant sequoia) is further evidence of the importance of the Bering land bridge to the flora and fauna of Pacific North America.

Biogeographical patterns create a template of species diversity, but they provide only limited information to account for contemporary patterns of local species richness. To answer questions about species richness at a more local scale, the processes that operate in the shorter, ecological time scale must be examined.

The Ecological Scale

Several ecologically based hypotheses have been proposed to explain patterns of species richness. Some, but not all of them, are mutually exclusive, and there is no reason to believe that any one hypothesis can explain all patterns of species richness. Most of the geographical patterns of species richness (see Table 2) are correlated with patterns in the physical environment that set the stage upon which all biological interactions take place.

Five dominant hypotheses—productivity, structural complexity, competition-predation, intermediate disturbance regimes, and stability-time—can be used to explain local patterns of species richness. First, higher productivity results in a larger biomass distributed among more individuals and hence an opportunity to divide resources among a larger number of species. Second, more species are able to coexist in a diversity of environments. Third, if predation keeps population densities low, thereby reducing the strength of competitive interactions, more species will be able to coexist. Fourth, habitats that are frequently disturbed contain species with good colonizing abilities; habitats that are infrequently disturbed contain species with good competitive abilities. Therefore, habitats with intermediate disturbance frequencies should contain a rich mixture of both colonizing and competitive species. And fifth, in contrast to the two previous hypotheses, this one argues that over long stable time periods species evolve greater specialization in the use of resources, and hence more species can coexist in stable habitats. With the exception of the intermediate disturbance hypothesis, these attempts to explain local

Table 1
Species Richness of Major Taxonomic Groups,
United States (Coterminous States) and the World

	United States	World
Vascular plants	17,000	263,000
Insects	163,468	750,000
Freshwater fish	800	8,400
Amphibians	230	4,000
Reptiles	277	6,550
Mammals	346	4,327
Birds	650	9,672

Note: Total area is land area rounded to the nearest 1,000 square miles. Regional species density is the average number of species per 1,000 square miles.
Sources: Nature Conservancy 1993: List of mammal and bird species; Gentry 1986: List of endemic plant species.

Table 2
Regional Species Richness

Selected States	Area	Mammals	Birds	Endemic Plants
Midwestern				
Kansas	82	86	421	0
Nebraska	77	86	419	1
Iowa	56	70	304	0
Illinois	56	60	417	3
Ohio	41	66	308	0
Regional species density: mammals 1.18; birds 5.99				
Eastern				
Pennsylvania	45	74	367	3
New York	47	93	407	1
North Carolina	49	106	412	8
Tennessee	41	80	304	15
Virginia	40	84	400	14
Regional species density: mammals 1.97; birds 8.51				
Western				
Colorado	104	133	384	54
Idaho	83	106	352	37
Oregon	96	147	429	109
Utah	82	130	350	169
Wyoming	97	114	403	19
Regional species density: mammals 1.36; birds 4.15				
Extremes				
Texas	262	158	511	379
California	156	164	445	1,517
Alaska	570	100	383	80

Note: Total area is land area rounded to the nearest 1,000 square miles. Regional species density is the average number of species per 1,000 square miles.
Sources: Nature Conservancy 1993: List of mammal and bird species; Gentry 1986: List of endemic plant species.

patterns of biodiversity ignore the role of colonization (the movement of a species' members to relocate in a new area), extinction, and large-scale landscape effects.

Ecosystem Function
At the level of the ecosystem, the question to be asked is, Are all species equal? Imagine a cosmic game is which

species are randomly removed from an ecosystem and the effects of each removal on every remaining species is measured. Several striking outcomes of this game would be noticed. First, for many species the effects of their removal could be quite small. That is, they are only weakly connected, directly or indirectly, to other species in the ecosystem. Or in some cases, the effects of their removal may be compensated by other species. For example, the removal of one species of decomposer organism may result in increased decomposer activities by other species. Second, the removal of some species may have a very large impact on the remaining species. These are called keystone species to call attention to the key ecological roles they play in ecosystems. Third, the accumulated effects of species removal, even when each separate removal effect is small, eventually may cause a massive change among the remaining species. That is, small cumulative effects can lead to sudden large changes.

Clearly, not all species are equal with respect to their effects on the ecosystem. But the identification of keystone species, or sets of species, is not always obvious. It may seem obvious that the removal of large predators, such as wolves, will have a major effect on their principal prey, vertebrate herbivores. But it is probably less obvious that the elimination of nitrogen-fixing bacteria through the impact of acid precipitation eventually will cause a massive change to forested ecosystems.

Patterns in the United States
The largest number of plant species is in the western and southern states, the fewest in the northern prairie states of Nebraska, North Dakota, and South Dakota. California and Texas each have more than 4,000 species. Oregon, Arizona, New Mexico, Georgia, and Florida each have more than 3,000 native vascular plant species (Morse, Kartesz, and Kutner 1995). Bird and mammal diversity roughly follow similar patterns.

Nearly half (45 percent) of the U.S. land area is in agriculture, with cropland comprising 191 million hectares and pasture/rangeland 238 million hectares (Knutson, Penn, and Boehm 1990). Most of the conversion of natural habitat to agricultural habitat took place in the midwestern states, from the southern plains to the Canadian border. A comparison of potential natural vegetation types to current patterns of land cover shows a north-south swath of landscape that lost between 70 and 100 percent of its natural cover of tall- and short-grass prairie (Loveland and Hutcheson 1995). One major consequence of this conversion has been the decline of some species of birds in the eastern part of the Great Plains. Between 1966 and 1991, data from the annual Breeding Bird Survey indicated average annual population declines for 23 species and increases for 14 species.

Since the 1920s, five historical trends in agricultural lands have influenced the natural biodiversity of the rural landscape. First, the number of farms has declined. Second, the majority of the land has been used to produce fewer kinds of crops. Third, the average farm size has become larger. Fourth, the vegetational diversity on farms has decreased. And fifth, agrichemical applications have increased. The agricultural landscape has become both more uniform and more intensively exploited (Allen 1995). Unproductive farmland in many parts of the eastern and southern states has been abandoned and secondary forests have reestablished. However, in highly productive agricultural regions, farming practices have intensified. So-called clean farming in these regions eliminated brushy field borders and native grass meadows and increased average field size. The loss of edge habitat in the Midwest contributed to the decline of bobwhite quail and cottontail rabbits (78 and 96 percent declines, respectively). Pheasants and native songbirds also declined (Bolen and Robinson 1995).

One of the principal tools of agricultural intensification has been the increased use of agrichemicals, particularly pesticides. Not surprisingly, increased application of toxic chemicals to the land, and therefore indirectly to rivers, streams, lakes, and wetlands, has adversely affected wildlife. The presence in the environment of DDT, DDE, and related organochlorine pesticides and their toxic degradation products has greatly declined since their ban in the 1970s. Newer organophosphorus and carbamate pesticides are now most commonly used to control invertebrate pests in U.S. agriculture. Although these families of chemicals are far less persistent than the organochlorine pesticides, many are quite toxic to humans and other animals. Between 1980 and 1993, 207 organophosphorus or carbamate chemical spills or releases (mortality events) caused the death of thousands of birds and some mammals (Glaser 1995).

On the positive side, the Conservation Reserve Program (CRP), enacted in 1985 to protect agricultural lands vulnerable to erosional soil losses, created new wildlife habitat. In the early 1990s, land use conversion under the CRP included 798,608 hectares for wildlife habitat and 3,424,835 hectares in native grass (U.S. Department of Agriculture 1993). If all types of noncrop cover are included, the CRP provided approximately 14 million

hectares of long-term plant cover (Allen 1995). The CRP supports terrestrial biodiversity by removing land from agricultural production, thereby creating more wildlife habitat for species that can use relatively small patches of grasslands and treelots. Because one major objective of the CRP is to reduce soil erosion, aquatic biodiversity benefits from reduced sediment loads in streams, rivers, and lakes.

In addition to the conversion of upland natural habitat to agriculture, approximately 87 percent of wetland losses are due to agricultural conversion. The Swamp Lands Acts of the mid-nineteenth century encouraged the drainage of "useless wetlands." Conservatively, the precolonial area of forested wetlands was at least 27.2 million hectares. By 1970, about 7.1 million hectares had been converted, largely to agricultural or forest plantations.

The total tree cover in North America north of Mexico has not changed much since the first European contact. However, forest composition and age structure have changed dramatically. About two-thirds of the nation's 298 million hectares of forested land is open to timber extraction. Over 70 percent of that land is privately held and managed primarily for timber. The remaining public timberlands are managed for a variety of purposes, such as recreation, biodiversity protection, and timber extraction. On average, the total timber inventory has remained fairly constant since the 1940s, with some indication of growing inventories in recent years (Darr 1995). Maintaining stable timber inventories is an important economic objective. Although stable timber inventories are better than declining inventories for the protection of forest biodiversity, a mix of relatively young, managed stands that are represented by one or very few tree species shelters far less biodiversity than would be found in a mix of young- and old-growth stands. Timber cover in North America may not be much different than it was in precolonial times; however, the dramatic loss of old-growth forest, the conversion of southern forested wetlands, and the simplification of managed timber stands greatly reduced the ability of timberlands to shelter biodiversity.

Implications for Conservation

The conversion of the rural North American natural landscape to agriculture and managed timberlands affected the processes that maintain natural biodiversity. Because this conversion was nearly completed before the birth of ecology as a science, one can only surmise the extent of the effects of land conversion on biodiversity. Fragmentation and isolation of habitats result in fewer species and slower recolonization rates. Degradation of small habitat patches further reduces biodiversity, although weedy and generalist species may add to the species list. The loss of the most productive land to agriculture may have eliminated many highly productive natural habitats that would have produced migrants to colonize less productive habitats. Hunting reduced keystone predators, and pollution reduced the effectiveness of microorganisms responsible for important ecosystem processes, such as nutrient cycling and decomposition.

What can be done with the natural landscape that remains? The single most important thing is to protect the key remaining pieces. Given limited resources, that fortunately does not mean treating all natural areas equally. A large fraction of the individuals of a species occur in only a few species-rich locations, usually referred to as hotspots. For example, more than 50 percent of all individuals of common passerine (song birds) species were concentrated in a small proportion of the sites where the species occurred (Brown, Mehlman, and Stevens 1995). Some of the hotspots of different species may be positively associated, which raises the question of why some sites are better than others. In most cases, the ecological factors responsible for abundant spatial variation are unknown. But the identification and protection of biodiversity hotspots are a major priority.

—*C. Ronald Carroll*

See also
Climatic Adaptability of Plants; Environmental Protection; Environmental Regulations; Natural Resource Economics; Policy, Environmental; Wetlands.
References
Allen, Arthur W. "Agricultural Ecosystems." Pp. 423–426 in *Our Living Resources: A Report to the Nation on the Distribution, Abundance, and Health of U.S. Plants, Animals, and Ecosystems*. Edited by Edward T. LaRoe, Gaye S. Farris, Catherine E. Puckett, Peter D. Doran, and Michael J. Macs. Washington, DC: U.S. Department of the Interior, National Biological Service, 1995.
Bolen, Eric G., and William L. Robinson. *Wildlife Ecology and Management*. 3d ed. Englewood Cliffs, NJ: Prentice-Hall, 1995.
Brown, James H., David L. Mehlman, and George C. Stevens. "Spatial Variation in Abundance." *Ecology* 76, no. 7 (1995): 2028–2043.
Darr, David R. "U.S. Forested Lands." Pp. 214–215 in *Our Living Resources: A Report to the Nation on the Distribution, Abundance, and Health of U.S. Plants, Animals, and Ecosystems*. Edited by Edward T. LaRoe, Gaye S. Farris, Catherine E. Puckett, Peter D. Doran, and Michael J. Macs. Washington, DC: U.S. Department of the Interior, National Biological Service, 1995.
Gentry, Alwyn H. "Endemism in Tropical versus Temperate Plant Communities." Pp. 153–181 in *Conservation Biology*. Edited by Michael E. Soulé. Sunderland, MA: Sinauer Associates, 1986.
Glaser, Linda C. "Wildlife Mortality Attributed to Organophosphorus and Carbamate Pesticides." Pp. 416–441 in *Our Living Resources: A Report to the Nation on the Distribution, Abundance, and Health of U.S. Plants, Animals, and Ecosystems*. Edited by Edward T. LaRoe, Gaye S. Farris, Catherine E. Puckett, Peter D. Doran, and Michael J. Macs. Washington, DC: U.S. Department of the Interior, National Biological Service, 1995.
Heywood, V. H., ed. *Global Biodiversity Assessment*. New York: Cambridge University Press, 1995.
Knutson, Ronald D., J. B. Penn, and William T. Boehm. *Agricultural and Food Policy*. Englewood Cliffs, NJ: Prentice-Hall, 1990.
Edward T. LaRoe, Gaye S. Farris, Catherine E. Puckett, Peter D. Doran, and Michael J. Macs, eds. *Our Living Resources: A Report to the Nation on the Distribution, Abundance, and Health of U.S. Plants, Animals, and Ecosystems*. Washington, DC: U.S. Department of the Interior, National Biological Service, 1995.
Loveland, Thomas R., and H. L. Hutcheson. "Monitoring Changes in Landscapes from Satellite Imagery." Pp. 468–473 in *Our Living Resources: A Report to the Nation on the Distribution, Abundance, and Health of U.S. Plants, Animals, and Ecosystems*. Edited by Edward T. LaRoe, Gaye S. Farris, Catherine E. Puckett, Peter D. Doran, and Michael J. Macs. Washington, DC: U.S. Department of the Interior, National Biological Service, 1995.
Meffe, Gary K., and C. R. Carroll. *Principles of Conservation Biology*. Sunderland, MA: Sinauer Associates, 1994.
Morse, Larry E., John T. Kartesz, and Lynn S. Kutner. "Native Vascular Plants." Pp. 205–209 in *Our Living Resources: A Report to the Nation on the Distribution, Abundance, and Health of U.S. Plants, Animals, and Ecosystems*. Edited by E. T. LaRoe, G. S. Farris, C. E. Puckett, P. D. Doran, and M. J. Macs. Washington, DC: U.S. Department of the Interior, National Biological Service, 1995.
Nature Conservancy. *Natural Heritage Data Center Network*. Arlington, VA: Nature Conservancy, 1993.
U.S. Department of Agriculture. *Conservation Reserve Program, 12th Sign-up Statistics*. Washington, DC: U.S. Department of Agriculture, Agricultural Stabilization and Conservation Service, 1993.

Biotechnology

A variety of methods for using plants, animals, and microbes to produce substances useful to humans or improve existing species. Biotechnology represents the latest in a long line of technological innovations influencing rural America. The use of biotechnology in agriculture has significant potential that is being realized with a number of newly approved products. This entry defines biotechnology, summarizes the history of its development, and describes those main applications that will affect rural America. Finally, potential environmental, food safety, and socioeconomic impacts and implications of biotechnology are discussed. The entry ends with an overview of prospects for the future.

Definition

Modern agriculture relies extensively on developments in science and technology to feed a rapidly growing world population. Agriculture has entered a new technological era with recent advances in biotechnology. The tools of biotechnology offer a number of opportunities for food and fiber production in the United States and across the globe.

Modern biotechnology has ancient roots. People have been selecting and raising plants and animals to produce food for thousands of years. They have relied on technology to bake bread, brew beer, and make cheese. Although they did not understand the science, our ancestors have been using biotechnology for centuries to modify plants, animals, and food products. Much of the early progress developed because people noticed that certain desirable traits were passed from one generation of plant or animal to the next. The foundations of modern agricultural biotechnology can be traced to 1865 when Gregor Mendel first presented his laws of heredity. He crossed pea plants with different traits to produce unique offspring. Mendel's work was not really recognized until the early 1900s when the term *genetics* first was used.

Another milestone occurred in the 1950s when the structure and function of deoxyribonucleic acid (DNA) was discovered by James Watson and Francis Crick. They proposed the double-helix (spiral) shape of the DNA molecule. Once DNA had been discovered, scientists began to understand the processes for transferring genetic information from one generation to the next. They also learned how to locate specific genes on a chromosome that correspond to specific traits. During the 1970s, enzymes were discovered that cut DNA into smaller pieces, which allowed scientists to isolate specific genes and make duplicate copies (clones). It became possible to combine genes into new arrangements (hence the term *recombinant DNA*). This approach allows for faster and more precise development of microbes, plants, and animals with desirable traits.

Modern biotechnology includes a wide range of techniques, such as genetic engineering, gene transfer, tissue culture, fermentation, embryo transfer, monoclonal antibodies, and bioprocess engineering. Biotechnology draws upon knowledge from a number of scientific disciplines, including molecular biology, biochemistry, genetics, chemical engineering, and computer science. Biotechnology also is based on applied sciences, such as agronomy, plant pathology, entomology, animal science, and food science. In addition, the social sciences (particularly rural sociology and agricultural economics) have made important contributions by assessing the implications and impacts of biotechnology for rural America.

Applications and Uses

The potential benefits of biotechnology in agriculture and food production have been promised since the mid-1980s. Progress did not occur as quickly as was once thought possible because of technical, economic, and regulatory constraints. The year 1994 will be remembered as a watershed in the development of agricultural biotechnology. That was the year that biotechnology's potential became reality, as evidenced by several products developed through biotechnology. First, supplemental bovine somatotropin was approved for use by American dairy farmers. This naturally occurring hormone increases milk production by 10 to 20 percent when administered to well-managed cows. Second, the Flavr-Savr™ tomato was approved for commercial sale in the United States. These tomatoes look and taste better than some other varieties of produce (especially in the winter) because they are allowed to stay on the vine until they are ripe. And third, seven additional biotechnology-produced plants (including tomato, cotton, soybeans, and squash) were approved by the Food and Drug Administration as safe for human consumption. These include varieties that are not damaged by insects, disease, and herbicides.

Many of the goals of biotechnology are the same as those for traditional crop and livestock breeding, namely, increased efficiency and improved quality. Given the long history of breeding and selection, it is important to note that almost all the produce, grains, and meats available to consumers have been modified through traditional methods from the original forms found in nature. So far biotechnology generally focuses on what agricultural scientists have tried to do in the past. Only now scientists can move copies of genes and the associated traits from one species to another. Progress can be more rapid and changes more precise.

Crop Production. Biotechnology is providing farmers with a number to tools for controlling the pests and other stresses that reduce the quantity and/or quality of foods produced. Some of the first commercial plant products of biotechnology are aimed at protecting crop plants from disease and insect damage. Progress is being made on developing crops that have enhanced flavor and nutrition, as well as processing characteristics.

The first viable approach to controlling insects through the use of biotechnology involves a protein from a common soil bacteria known as *Bacillus thuringiensis*. For several decades, home gardeners and others have used a killed version of the bacteria to control insects. Recent advances have allowed scientists to add the gene that kills the insects directly into plants. Tomato, cotton, potatoes, and other crops now can be made self-protecting. As a result, the use of chemical insecticides can be reduced. Scientists have used biotechnology to help protect plants from viruses and other disease-causing organisms. The genes that are modified or added have been shown to have no significant effect on humans, livestock, or wildlife.

Biotechnology provides new approaches to controlling weeds that compete with crops. Farmers have not been able to use most herbicides on crop plants once they emerge because the crops would be destroyed along with the weeds. Scientists have used biotechnology to develop crop varieties that are not damaged by the application of certain herbicides. Farmers gain additional tools and more flexibility in their attempts to control weeds. The herbicides that are used with these plants tend to have more positive environmental features.

New produce varieties, such as the tomato, developed with biotechnology can help meet increasing consumer demands for fresher and better-tasting fruits and vegetables. Scientists also are working to enhance the nutritional value of crops by increasing the protein value or reducing the fat. For example, scientists are developing a higher-starch potato variety that absorbs less oil and will result in lower-fat french fries and potato chips. Soybean oil that contains less saturated fat also has been developed.

Livestock Production. As with crop production, biotechnology generally has tried to address the same types of needs that livestock farmers have had for a long time. One of the first products of biotechnology has been commercial production of naturally occurring protein hormones (or somatotropins) that regulate growth and lactation. Bovine somatotropin, which was found to be safe for cows and human consumption, already is being used in dairy production. A similar compound for swine (porcine somatotropin) will reduce feed consumption and lead to leaner pork when administered to swine.

Efforts are focusing on the development of more disease-resistant and productive livestock. Some vaccines used in livestock production were developed through the use of biotechnology. Tools to diagnose and control animal diseases are being enhanced through the use of biotechnology. Selective breeding, artificial insemination, and other tools to improve reproduction already are being used in livestock production. Food safety will be enhanced as biotechnology leads to more effective tests for the presence in meat and poultry of salmonella and other harmful organisms.

Other Uses. Biotechnology is used in a variety of ways to enhance the taste and nutrition of food through development of flavorings, nutraceuticals, and processing enhancements. The first biotechnology-derived food product was virtually invisible to consumers. Biotechnology was used to produce a synthetic version of rennet, which is an enzyme used in cheese production. The recombinant product has become widely used and replaces the product traditionally obtained from calves' stomachs. Consumers have been very accepting of this product, as well as the others that have been approved for use.

The forest products, turf, and ornamental industries will reap many of the same benefits from biotechnology as crop production has, such as pest protection and enhanced growth. These should provide new opportunities to add value to products from rural America. Work is under way to improve the use of crops and waste materials for fuel, such as ethanol.

The environment can be protected and restored through biotechnology. Many biotechnological efforts are aimed at producing crops that allow reduced chemical pesticide use. Scientists are using biotechnology to modify microbes to prevent pollution or to clean polluted areas more rapidly and safely. For example, new strains of bacteria have been developed that more effectively can break down oil spills, human sewage, animal manure, toxic waste, and other undesirable substances. Biotechnology also aims to improve the ability of plants to withstand drought or make better use of scarce water resources. Such improvements would enable better management of rural water supplies.

Issues and Implications

Any technology, especially a set of tools as powerful and far-reaching as biotechnology, can have a wide range of direct and indirect impacts on the natural and human environments. The application of biotechnology in agriculture could affect many different aspects of rural America. As with earlier advances, many of the impacts will be positive, but concerns have been raised about potential negative impacts. The issues raised about biotechnology tend to focus on environmental and food safety risks, as well as socioeconomic impacts.

Environmental and Food Safety Risks. Biotechnology is emerging at a time of heightened public concern about environmental and food safety risks associated with modern agricultural production. Many of the concerns expressed about the potential risks reflect past experience with other environmental and food safety issues. As a result of public concerns and the attention paid by environmental groups and the media, the early products of biotechnology have undergone extensive scrutiny before they have been approved for use.

The potential for unforeseen environmental and human health risks include specific ecological impacts, such as on native vegetation and wildlife. The potential for allergic reactions to new foods that contain DNA from another species has prompted concerns. Questions have been raised about the relationship between biotechnology and the need for a more sustainable agricultural production system. These and other issues are the subject of much study and debate.

Several government agencies are responsible for evaluating the potential environmental and food safety risks from the products of biotechnology. The U.S. Food and Drug Administration is the primary agency regulating food safety. Its approach is based on the assumption that foods produced through biotechnology will be subject to the same regulations as other foods. Furthermore, the foods will be judged on their individual qualities rather than the process used to produce them. The U.S. Department of Agriculture takes a similar approach in reviewing research projects and commercial use of plant varieties and animal breeds developed through biotechnology. The Environmental Protection Agency, which regulates substances released into the environment, also plays a role in regulating the development and use of certain biotechnology products.

Socioeconomic Impacts. Rural America will be affected by biotechnology as a result of how farmers are affected. History shows that certain groups of farmers usually have benefited from early adoption of new farm practices. Once these practices have been introduced, other farmers then need to adopt the innovations to remain competitive. Farmers who are slow to adopt are at a disadvantage given narrow profit margins. Similar impacts of technological change can be noted in every sector of the economy, including manufacturing and retailing.

Biotechnology could have important implications for ongoing changes in the structure of agriculture. The past decades have seen a trend toward fewer and larger farm operations. Technological change is an important factor in this transition, along with economic and political forces.

The same forces are leading to more specialized, capital-intensive, and vertically integrated operations. However, not all products of biotechnology will have the same impacts. Some products will require more sophisticated management skills as well as additional information and financial resources. These may favor larger and better-managed farms. However, it appears that other types of biotechnology, such as improved seed varieties, may be useful for all farmers regardless of size and skill.

Agribusinesses (agricultural supply industries and processing facilities) will be affected by advances in biotechnology. Firms that are able rapidly to develop and market new biotechnology products will achieve a comparative advantage in the marketplace. The agribusiness sector is becoming more concentrated, with fewer firms controlling a greater share of the market. In the past, the regulatory climate surrounding the introduction of biotechnology raised uncertainty over the prospects for commercialization. However, as the first products have made their way through the government approval process, the potential for future success has been significantly enhanced.

Social scientists have tried to anticipate possible secondary impacts on rural communities, many of which already are affected by changes in the agricultural sector. Earlier agricultural, communication, and transportation innovations reshaped every aspect of rural life. Most rural communities will not benefit directly from biotechnology in terms of economic development. Research and development firms will continue to locate in urban areas. Opportunities do exist for value-added processing facilities in rural areas. Biotechnology may result in regional shifts in production, which will benefit some rural areas at the expense of others. Overall, biotechnology cannot be said to be either good or bad for rural communities. As with other changes, some rural areas reap the benefits of progress, while others bear the costs.

Future Prospects

New products from biotechnology will reach farmers and consumers in increasing numbers. Decision makers must understand and evaluate the potential impacts and opportunities of biotechnology. Each product will have its own unique set of benefits and impacts for urban and rural America. As biotechnology develops, society has the opportunity and responsibility to ensure that the benefits outweigh the costs. The promises of biotechnology depend on ensuring that farmers and consumers receive benefits. There are no simple answers to the complex questions about the impacts of new technology, but the trade-offs need to be evaluated.

Technological change always has had a major influence on rural America in general and agriculture in particular. Disagreements exist over how great the relative impacts of biotechnology will be. Some claim that biotechnology represents a revolution in agriculture that will have more profound impacts than any previous technological development. Others argue that biotechnology will not affect the structure of agriculture as much as the tractor or other innovations. They further claim that the impact of biotechnology on rural communities will be less than that of modern transportation and communication. The consensus seems to be that productivity increases made possible by biotechnology during the 1990s will not be as revolutionary as the gains achieved during the post–World War II period.

Biotechnology became controversial even before the products were actually introduced. Vocal critics arose to challenge the use of technology in agriculture. The average American consumer, however, is not very knowledgeable or concerned about the use of technology in food production. Consumers will continue to demand food that is tasty, nutritious, convenient, safe, readily available, and inexpensive. The fact that technology will play a major role in providing such food is quite acceptable to the majority of consumers. Concerned citizens want the opportunity to make informed decisions about the food they consume. This, in turn, requires a greater commitment to education.

Our society needs more well-informed, open discussion about future directions in biotechnology and other developments, such as information technology. Public officials, universities, industry, and others need to work together to design and implement effective and equitable research, education, and technology transfer programs. The opportunities of biotechnology appear so great that it is in everyone's interest to make sure that effective, safe, and ethically sound products have a chance to reach the marketplace.

—*Thomas J. Hoban*

See also

Dairy Farming; Technology; Technology Transfer.

References

Baumgardt, Bill R., and Marshall A. Martin, eds. *Agricultural Biotechnology: Issues and Choices.* West Lafayette, IN: Purdue University, Agricultural Experiment Station, 1991.

Gendel, Steven M., A. David Kline, D. Michael Warren, and Faye Yates, eds. *Agricultural Bioethics: Implications of Agricultural Biotechnology.* Ames: Iowa State University Press, 1990.

Hoban, Thomas J., and Patricia A. Kendall. *Consumer Attitudes about Food Biotechnology.* Raleigh: North Carolina Cooperative Extension Service, 1993.

Kunkel, Mary Elizabeth. "Position of the American Dietetic Association: Biotechnology and the Future of Food." *Journal of the American Dietetic Association* 93 (1993): 189–194.

MacDonald, June Fessenden. *Agricultural Biotechnology: A Public Conversation about Risk.* Ithaca, NY: National Agricultural Biotechnology Council, 1993.

———. *Agricultural Biotechnology and the Public Good.* Ithaca, NY: National Agricultural Biotechnology Council, 1994.

Molnar, Joseph J., and Henry Kinnucan, eds. *Biotechnology and the New Agricultural Revolution.* Boulder, CO: Westview Press, 1989.

Office of Technology Assessment. *A New Technological Era for American Agriculture.* Washington, DC: U.S. Government Printing Office, 1992.

———. *Technology, Public Policy, and the Changing Structure of American Agriculture.* Washington, DC: U.S. Government Printing Office, 1986.

Camps

Organized, recreational, and educational opportunities for children and adults that provide a sustained, group living experience in an outdoor setting. Camps use trained leadership and the resources of the natural surroundings to contribute to each camper's mental, physical, social, and spiritual growth. After addressing the history of summer camps, this entry discusses youth development outcomes that result from camping experiences. Camp staff and facilities are described, and urban and rural comparisons are made. The American Camping Association's role is examined.

History

Americans displayed their characteristic fascination with the outdoors early on. Clustered in cities along the eastern seaboard, they longed for opportunity and the great open spaces that stretched beyond. Americans began to turn in great numbers to the outdoors for inspiration and recreation in the mid-1800s. At the same time, American education took a new turn. Headmaster Frederick W. Gunn of the Gunnery School, a private boarding school in Connecticut, conceived the idea of taking pupils on a summer outing. Gunn and his wife, Abigail, led a two-week expedition to the beach at Long Island Sound in 1861 that included hiking, boating, sailing, and fishing. The experience proved so effective that they repeated it in 1863 and 1865. A more permanent Gunnery camp was established on an inland lake, where the camp was conducted two weeks each August for 12 years.

The camp idea begun by the Gunnery experience inspired others in the early 1900s to establish private camps, church camps, and fresh-air camps sponsored by youth groups, including the Boy Scouts, the Girl Scouts, the Young Men's Christian Association, and the Camp Fire Girls. Harvard University's president Charles W. Eliot said in 1922, "The organized summer camp is the most important step in education that America has given the world" (Eels 1986, 90).

Today, more than 8,500 day and resident camps of varying types, lengths, and sponsorships flourish in all parts of the country. Summer camps for children, adults, families, and seniors are operated by trained professionals and have volunteer or paid staff to work with their special client groups. Camps may be operated by nonprofit organizations, youth agencies, community or religious organizations, or private concerns. Camps may be found in rural, suburban, or urban communities. They may operate on several thousand backcountry acres or in a city park.

Camps are designed in a variety of styles and formats and provide activities that vary to meet many interests. Most camps offer a general program of outdoor activities of hiking, swimming, sports and games, arts and crafts, and nature awareness. Some camps emphasize programs such as horseback riding, water sports, music, or adventure challenge activities. Camps provide facilities and services for a broad range of children, youths, and adults. Others provide services to special groups, such as seniors, children with cancer, gifted and talented children, youths at risk, diabetics, asthmatics, families, or persons with disabilities.

Resident camps are designed for campers to stay at the camp from several days to eight weeks. They sleep overnight in cabins, tents, tepees, or other forms of shelter and participate in a variety of supervised activities. Day camps offer sessions and age-appropriate programs similar to resident camps. Campers are often transported to camp by a bus or van and return home each day in the late afternoon. Trip camps provide programs where the participants transport themselves to different sites by backpacking, riding, or canoeing. Travel camps often

Camp Watitoh campers experience getting up with the chickens in Becket, Massachusetts.

transport campers by car or bus to geographic and topographic places of interest.

Minimum-impact camping is relatively new in the history of camping skills and has become synonymous with good outdoor living practices. Most camp programs help campers to feel at home in the natural environment and teach environmental awareness and ethics that will carry over to lifelong practices. Many areas have become bare from overuse by people who enjoy camping. Less land is available for outdoor recreation, and more is known about what happens to land and water when they are used carelessly. Improper or overuse of sites, whether established camps or wilderness campsites, can remain ruined for many years and in some environments, for centuries. Minimum-impact camping means using outdoor living skills that affect the soil, water, plants, and animals as little as possible to make the site pleasant for the next campers and to assure campsites for future generations.

Youth Development Outcomes

Parents want the best opportunities for their children and want them to be happy and successful, have good health, and possess the ability to get along with others, thinking and problem-solving skills, and a healthy self-concept. Camp is a community designed specifically to provide children with the essential elements necessary for successful development and daily fun. Psychologist Peter Scales, a Search Institute in Minneapolis senior fellow, says that camp is one of the few institutions where young people can experience and satisfy the need for physical activity, creative expression, and true participation in a community environment, which most schools cannot satisfy (Scales 1976).

Depending on the purpose of the camp, children come from diverse backgrounds—different economic levels, races, religions, level of ability or disability, type of community. Some campers experience being away from home or the city for the first time. Just as rural children may be frightened on their first adventure in a city, urban children may find the nights darker and the sounds of nature a new, perhaps frightening experience. The safe, neutral environment of an organized camp can help children become more comfortable with each other and their new outdoor setting.

Staff and Facilities

Summer camps employ more than 500,000 adults to work as counselors, program/activity leaders, unit and program directors/supervisors, and support staff, such as maintenance, administration, food service, and health care workers. Staff applicants typically are interviewed and screened beginning in January. Resident camp staff live on the site; counselors and other staff are housed with the children they supervise. Day camp staff return home each day. Summer staff who serve as activity leaders in areas of waterfront, archery, horseback riding, climbing, and rappeling usually are required to have certification or documented evidence of their ability to lead the activity. Most camps provide a week-long, precamp staff training for those working in resident camps and 18 or more hours for staff working in day camps. The staff-to-camper ratio varies with the age of the campers and with the camp but is usually one to five for younger children and one to ten for adolescent and teenage campers.

Whereas many activities at day camps and resident camps are similar, the facilities at resident camps must have provisions for meals and sleeping quarters. Depending on the area of the country, weather, and terrain, sleeping facilities may vary from tents, tepees, and screened cabins to year-round cabins or dormitories.

The facilities of many camps can be rented to other groups that wish to provide camping services to their constituents. Some facilities are designed for year-round use. Many facilities are both camps and conferences or retreat centers, with meeting rooms and sleeping and eating accommodations. Camps may provide environmental education or other programs during the school year. Camps may rent their facilities or provide staff to work with teachers and live with the students.

Urban versus Rural Facilities

The camp type, ownership, facilities, and programs will determine much of a camp's goals and philosophy. However, some differences exist in the operation of urban and rural camps. Urban camp directors must be concerned with encroachment and the positive and negative effects of location on the operation. Infrastructure development may bring public roads and recreational facilities, access to medical services and public water, sewage and utilities, and accessibility of supplies and transportation for staff and campers, especially day campers. It may also bring intruders, require more regulation and more costly modern facilities, offer less access to the natural environment, and limit some program possibilities. Urban camps operating in a city, a community park, or a site owned by a school, corporation, or agency may have limited resources for nature and campcraft activities. Campers may need to share program facilities with the general public.

Rural camps must operate more as self-sufficient communities by providing more extensive health services and establishing their own water supply and sewage treatment systems. They may need more food and supplies storage, and delivery may be an issue. Rural camps often have a positive economic impact on the local community. They may have long-term leases to build and operate on U.S. Forest Service or other government-owned property. Rural camps usually have more land and natural features and have more control over the types of programming. In addition to swimming, aquatic activities may include boating, water skiing, canoeing, and fishing. Some rural camps have their own horses and maintain trails for riding, hiking, and overnight camping trips. Children may have an opportunity to take care of farm animals or plant and maintain gardens. Cliffs and ledges provide opportunities to climb and rappel under the direction of a trained staff member. The overall rural environment may be a new adventure to many campers.

American Camping Association

The American Camping Association (ACA) is a private, nonprofit, educational organization with members in all 50 states and several foreign countries. Its members represent a diverse constituency of camp and conference center owners and directors, executives, educators, clergy, business representatives, consultants, staff members, volunteers, students, retirees, and others associated with the operation of camps, conference centers, and retreat centers for children and adults. ACA's professional development opportunities and resources address issues related to all types of camping operations, whether day or resident, nonprofit or for profit, church related or secular, large or small.

The ACA provides accreditation to camps that meet certain criteria. When parents choose an ACA-accredited camp, they have the assurance that the camp complies with up to 300 industry-accepted, government-recognized health and safety and program-quality standards. At least once every three years, a team of trained camping professionals visits the camp to observe its operation while in session to compare its practices with the standards. The ACA's *Guide to Accredited Camps* is available (1-800-428-CAMP) for parents and those who seek summer employment in a day or resident camp.

The ACA offers Outdoor Living Skills training programs to teach children how to visit nature softly and rewards them with colorful patches in five levels of achievement. Whether a simple hike in the park or a multiday trek through the wilderness, all the skills are covered: planning an outing, safety, first aid and sanitation, cooking, equipment, knot tying, map and compass reading, and nature appreciation. This program is a response to the industry's interest in conservation and appropriate land use issues.

—*Connie Coutellier*

See also
Adolescents; Games; Recreational Activities; Sports.
References
American Camping Association. *Standards for Conference Retreat Centers: An Accreditation Program of the American Camping Association*. Martinsville, IN: American Camping Association, 1993.
Chenery, Mary Faeth. *I Am Somebody: The Messages and Methods of Organized Camping for Youth Development*. Durham, NC: Mary Faeth Chenery, 1990.
Ditter, Bob. *Making a Difference Working with Campers and Counselors*. Newton Centre, MA: Little Fox Productions, 1995.
Eells, Eleanor. *Eleanor Eells' History of Organized Camping: The First 100 Years*. Martinsville, IN: American Camping Association, 1986.

Gass, Michael A. *Adventure Therapy: Therapeutic Applications of Adventure Programming.* Boulder, CO: Association of Experiential Education, 1992.

Hammerman, Donald R., William M. Hammerman, and Elizabeth L. Hammerman. *Teaching in the Outdoors.* Danville, IL: Interstate Printing, 1985.

Hammerman, William M., ed. *Fifty Years of Resident Outdoor Education.* Martinsville, IN: American Camping Association, 1981.

Mitchell, Viola, and F. Meier. *Camp Counseling: Leadership and Programming for the Organized Camp.* Madison, WI: Brown and Benchmark, 1983.

Peterson, James A., and Bruce B. Hronck. *Risk Management for Park, Recreation, and Leisure Studies.* Champaign, IL: Sagamore, 1992.

Scales, Peter. "Equipping Children for Success." Keynote speech given at the National Convention of the American Camping Association, San Diego, CA, 28 February 1976.

Storer YMCA Camps. *Nature's Classroom: A Program Guide for Camps and Schools.* Martinsville, IN: American Camping Association, 1988.

Careers in Agriculture

Occupations, jobs, or professions in agriculture or related fields. Changes in the structure of agriculture have led to the emergence and development of a diverse array of careers involving and related to agriculture. As American agriculture continues to grow and change in the future, agricultural careers also will diversify and develop to fit the world's changing needs. Agriculture always will be an important part of the American and world economies as people always will need food and clothing. Agriculture directly and indirectly plays a much larger role in the U.S. economy than often is believed. To provide insight into the importance of agriculture to the nation's economy, this entry discusses careers related to agriculture, the numbers of people employed by agriculture and related industries, and where the areas of growth and jobs are located.

Structural Changes

American agriculture has seen many changes during the twentieth century. The changes can be linked to several factors, such as the increase in technology for agriculture and changes in the structure of the U.S. economy. The economy has gone from one based heavily on subsistence and production from many small family farms to an industrial and service-based economy with agricultural production taking place on fewer and smaller farms. Advancements of technology in areas such as farm machinery and agricultural chemicals have made it possible for farmers to produce agricultural commodities more efficiently. As a result of technological advance-

ments, fewer farms are required to produce food and fiber for the nation. The number of farms in the United States decreased from 6.4 million in 1910 to 2.1 million in 1987 (U.S. Department of Agriculture 1993). Along with the decrease in the number of farms, the average farm size increased from 138 acres in 1910 to 462 acres in 1987 (Hallum 1992).

On the demand side, the impact of demographic and lifestyle changes have led to changing consumer tastes and preferences, which has affected the structure of agriculture. An increase in the number of single-parent households, two-job households, and single households has led to changes in the type of food items consumers are demanding. As a result of the changing lifestyles of Americans today, convenience-food items such as canned and frozen fruits and vegetables, soup starters, packaged mixes, prepared salads, and frozen entrees are in high demand as time has become a precious commodity to the average consumer. In addition to demanding more convenience in food items, consumers are spending more money on food consumed outside of the home.

Employment

Despite the decrease in the number of farms in the United States in recent years, farm and farm-related industries provided 23.2 million jobs in 1989; an increase of 0.3 million jobs over 1988. In 1989, farm and farm-related employment made up 17.3 percent of total U.S. employment. Although recent trends in agriculture show fewer individuals are involved directly in farming, other sectors of the U.S. food and fiber system are growing rapidly. In 1989, farm production employed 3.2 million; agricultural services, 0.8 million; agricultural inputs, 0.3 million; agricultural processing and marketing, 3.2 million; wholesale and retail trade, 13.0 million; and indirect agribusiness, 2.6 million (U.S. Department of Agriculture 1993).

Traditionally, agriculture was thought of only in terms of farm production; however, today's agricultural sector is an enormous, multifaceted industry. Agricultural production depends on inputs such as agricultural credit, farm machinery, agricultural chemicals, feed, and other farm supplies. With today's changing world, the nation's food and fiber sector also relies on output industries to process and market agricultural commodities to meet the consumers' demands. These industries include food processing and marketing, wholesale and retail outlets, and international trade.

As the structure of agriculture has changed over the years, so have the careers in agriculture. Today a wide variety of careers are available to those interested in agriculture. Areas of growth in agriculture are food processing and agricultural inputs such as chemicals, animal health supplies, feed, and farm credit. A growing number of jobs are available each year in these areas.

The agricultural inputs industry is one that continually is growing and provides many opportunities for individuals interested in a career in agriculture. Just a few of the many careers that are available include sales representatives for feed and agricultural chemical companies, crop and livestock management consultants, farm machinery sales representatives, and marketing analysts.

Agricultural credit is another input area that has numerous opportunities for an individual interested in agricultural finance. Because the federal farm credit system has undergone significant consolidation in recent years, many banks now employ an individual to oversee agriculturally related loans and financial analysis. A variety of technical positions related to agricultural inputs also are available, such as engineers needed to design and construct farm machinery, researchers needed to develop and produce agricultural chemicals and animal health products, and veterinarians needed to help livestock producers to maintain animal health. The manufacturing of farm inputs, such as farm machinery and agricultural chemicals, likewise employs a large number of individuals. In 1995, the manufacturing of farm machinery employed approximately 93,600 people (Standard Industrial Classification [SIC] Code 352) and the manufacturing of agricultural chemicals employed approximately 39,100 people (SIC 287) (U.S. Department of Commerce 1997).

Although agricultural inputs contribute significantly to the economy and present numerous career opportunities, the output sector of the agricultural industry plays a much more import role in employment and dollars added to the economy. The output sector is vital to the nation's food and fiber system because it takes the raw agricultural commodities produced by the nation's farmers and ranchers and provides the consumers with the food products they demand. Food processing is a very important part of the output sector of the agricultural industry. Food processing is growing rapidly to meet the continually changing consumer demand for convenience-food items. The importance of the food-processing sector of the economy is evident in the marketing bill. For example, out of every $1 spent on food consumed in the home in 1994, the farmer received only 26 percent, while the processing industry received 33 percent, the retail indus-

try accounted for 25 percent, the wholesale industry received 10 percent, and the transportation industry received 6 percent (Food Institute 1994). In 1995, the food- and kindred-product-processing industry (SIC 20) in the United States employed over15 million people (U.S. Department of Commerce 1997). The three leading areas of food processing in terms of employment were the meat products (SIC 201), preserved fruit and vegetable (SIC 203), and bakery products (SIC 205) industries. The three processing areas employed a total of 859,300 people in 1995, an increase of 56,300 jobs from 1990.

In addition to the food-processing industry, many other facets of agriculture's output sector have a wide array of careers available. Commodity brokerages, the feedlot industry, grain elevators, and agricultural exporters are just a few of the many areas in which opportunities that are directly related to agriculture are available in the industry output sector. Another agriculturally related area of importance to the economy is the wholesale and retail food industry. Wholesale and retail businesses employed the largest number of people in fields related to agriculture in 1989, and 35 percent of the consumer's food dollar goes to this sector of related agriculture. Wholesale and retail businesses associated with agriculture include food distributors, grocery stores, and restaurants. The wholesale and retail industry has become increasingly important in recent years because more consumers are eating out or purchasing take-out dinners.

Additional Employment Opportunities

Individuals interested in a career in agriculture have many choices in addition to those already mentioned. Opportunities are available in many other areas related to agriculture, such as agricultural research, education, and communications. Research is important in agriculture. Researchers are developing new strains of pest-resistant crops, finding more efficient methods for producing livestock that meets the consumer high standard, examining the economic feasibility of new and existing farm policies, or analyzing trends in agricultural production to provide market forecasts. The information that is provided by research helps the U.S. food and fiber industry to be one of the best and most efficient in the world. Research is conducted by the government and by private industries. Agricultural research conducted by the government usually is handled through the U.S. Department of Agriculture (USDA). Research is undertaken by many of the agencies managed by the USDA and at universities with research funding provided by the government. In addition, agricultural research is done by private industry to develop and test new agricultural products and to research new and existing markets for agricultural products.

As a result of the continually changing nature of agriculture, education at the high school and college level is needed in order to prepare the next generation for careers in agriculture. At the high school level, general agricultural education is taught to provide today's youth with the current options available in agriculture today. An integral part of most agricultural education teachers at the high school level is to advise student participation in organizations such as 4-H and Future Farmers of America (FFA). These organizations allow students to become involved with many aspects of agriculture and give them insight into the diversity of agriculture in today's society. A bachelor's degree is required of individuals interested in teaching at the high school level, although many educators today also have a master's degree. At the college or university level, educators are needed to help shape an individual's interest in a particular area of agriculture. Educators are needed in fields such as agronomy, animal science, agricultural economics, education, communications, and horticulture. Most educators at the college or university level will need to have earned an doctoral degree in their chosen field. In addition to education at the college level, many professors are involved in either research or extension work. Agricultural communications are important to spread the word about the importance of agriculture in our society. Journalists and other communicators with an agricultural background are needed by farm publications, farm radio networks, and other broadcast media.

Regional Variations in Employment

A wide array of opportunities exist with agriculture; however, the types of agricultural and related career opportunities will differ in various regions of the United States. For example, the Northeast and north-central portions of the country are involved heavily in dairy production, whereas the Plains states (Kansas, Oklahoma, Texas, Iowa, and Nebraska) are involved primarily in crop and livestock production. Florida, California, and portions of southern Texas produce fruits and vegetables. Poultry production is located mainly in Arkansas and other areas of the Southeast. The majority of the nation's food-processing activities tend to be concentrated in two regions: the Sunbelt and the industrial states around the Great Lakes and in the Northeast (Barkema, Drabenstott, and

Stanley 1990). Individuals interested in a career in agriculture must evaluate the area of agriculture that they wish to be involved in and determine which regions will have the most opportunities in that area.

—*Shida Rastegari Henneberry*
and Michelle Beshear

See also
Agricultural and Resource Economics; Agricultural Engineering; Agricultural Law; Agronomy; Rural Sociology.
References
Barkema, Alan D., Mark Drabenstott, and Julie Stanley. "Processing Food in Farm States: An Economic Strategy for the 1990's." *Economic Review* (Federal Reserve Bank of Kansas City) 75, no. 4 (July/August 1990): 1–23.
Food Institute. *Food Institute Food Retailing Review.* Fairlawn, NJ: Food Institute Information and Research Center, 1994.
Hallum, Arne, ed. *Size, Structure, and the Changing Face of American Agriculture.* Boulder, CO: Westview Press, 1993.
U.S. Department of Agriculture. "U.S. Farm and Farm-Related Employment in 1989: Where Are Jobs in Farming and Its Related Industries Most Important?" Washington, DC: U.S. Department of Agriculture, Economic Research Service, 1993.
U.S. Department of Commerce. *1995 Annual Survey of Manufactures: Geographic Area Statistics.* Document M95(AS)-3. Washington, DC: Bureau of the Census, 1997, Table 2, pp. 14–16.

Cemeteries

A burial ground containing gravemarkers of stone or ornate wrought iron that describe characteristics of a deceased person's life and dates of birth and death. This entry describes cemeteries as a constant, but increasingly fragile, feature of the American rural landscape that present a concentrated resource for the study of history, ethnicity, art, and a variety of evolving cultural values.

The Rural Landscape

Cemeteries, along with churches, schoolhouses, and a select few other constructed features of the cultural landscape, are among the most frequently encountered human elements in America's rural environment and, like them, one of the first to appear when an area has come under settlement. Unlike cemeteries created specifically within, or adjacent to, urban centers, rural burial grounds have seldom tended to be trend setters, choosing rather—in such elements as predominant affiliations, siting choices, internal configurations, and monument types—to reflect and perpetuate patterns that trace back to the earliest graveyards of colonial New England. One of the most conservative elements in the built American landscape, providing valuable insights into community

Cemeteries often are adjacent to country churches, as is the case at Salem Covenant Church in rural Pennock, Minnesota.

and regional history, cemeteries are also, for a variety of reasons, one of the most threatened at the present time.

A semantic problem exists in reference to rural cemeteries in America, for the term *rural cemetery* is often applied to a type of cemetery that, ironically enough, is anything but rural. These large and often corporately maintained establishments, distinguished by their idealized pastoral landscape designs and spectacular monuments, were created in the middle decades of the nineteenth century as "rural" alternatives to the crowded burial grounds that had been established at an earlier point within urban centers and were situated on outlying tracts of land readily accessible by public transportation. Today, these huge, parklike "cities of the dead"—the majority of which are found in the eastern portions of the country—have invariably been surrounded by their expanding metropolitan areas, so that the term *rural,* whatever currency it once might have enjoyed, is now completely anachronistic.

The tens of thousands of cemeteries that dot the landscape of rural America range in size from quite tiny (that is, ten graves or less) to rather large, and in many instances the earliest burials are coincident with initial settlement patterns. A significant proportion began as— and in a number of cases remain—family burial plots on private land claims, a phenomenon clearly reflected in the large number of rural American cemeteries that utilize family surnames as the key identifying element in their titles. Some of these cemeteries eventually would become larger cemeteries under public, or in some cases private, control and serving larger and more diverse segments of the surrounding rural population. Many other rural cemeteries initially were established by town govern-

ments, fraternal groups (in particular, the Masonic orders and the Independent Order of Odd Fellows), churches, or, in some instances, ethnic groups.

Gravemarkers

Although any burial ground has its obvious functional purposes, American rural cemeteries often may be characterized as surprisingly peaceful or even beautiful sites. Regional and topographical variants notwithstanding, they frequently are situated on higher ground—a feature defined by a combination of practical, aesthetic, and spiritual considerations—and are graced by a variety of trees and other ornamental plantings. The style of individual gravemarkers within these cemeteries in some instances may be heavily influenced by any number of local or regional considerations—the lack, or in some cases abundance, of certain materials, ethnic preferences, even prevailing economic patterns—but as a general rule gravemarkers always have conformed as much as possible to the prevailing styles of the time period in which they were erected. Thus, throughout much of rural America one is most likely to encounter stone monuments fashioned of white marble, the material of preference from the late eighteenth to late nineteenth centuries, with a dramatic shift to granite in the twentieth century.

The monuments themselves come in a relatively fixed range of shapes and sizes and correspondingly display a fairly standardized array of carved visual symbols (weeping willows, fingers pointing upward, clasped hands, heavenly gates, roses, and lambs being the most frequently encountered) and conventional epitaph forms. Two important exceptions to this general pattern of uniformity may be observed. The first of these involves instances where strong ethnic influences result in a concentration of unique monument types, such as the iron cruciform markers erected by German/Russian immigrants in certain areas of the northern Great Plains or the seemingly infinite variety of often colorfully embellished concrete markers found throughout the Spanish-speaking areas of the Southwest. A second exception occurs in instances where certain important historical events have imparted a distinctive verbal and visual emphasis to many markers, as, for instance, in the pioneer cemeteries of Oregon, where the proud record of overland emigration is recorded in great detail.

Local Culture

Cemeteries, of whatever type and wherever found, are a vitally important but often overlooked mirror of the cultures that created them, and certainly this is no less true of America's rural cemeteries. It is no accident that writers such as Edgar Lee Masters (*Spoon River Anthology*) and Thornton Wilder (*Our Town*) should have chosen local cemeteries as the focal setting to present powerful glimpses into the essence of American rural life. For cemeteries, the final resting place of the dead, speak, ironically, of life. Within them is recorded not only the factual history of a community but also often a chronicle of the aspirations and sometimes tragedies that have helped to define its values and worldview. To truly understand rural America, therefore, one should not overlook the testimony of its cemeteries.

A Fragile Resource

Given such considerations, it is indeed unfortunate that a disturbingly large number of rural cemeteries are currently at risk. No single cause underlies this situation. In a number of instances, and this is particularly true of smaller family cemeteries, they simply have been abandoned, even forgotten. As the last descendants die out or move to other locales, these once carefully tended sites slowly sink into neglect and decay, often disappearing beneath choking covers of undergrowth. As fraternal organizations and certain church groups, once important creators and maintainers of rural cemeteries, shrink to mere vestiges of their former power and influence, they seek to cede these cemeteries to local governmental authorities, which, their resources already strapped, do not want them. Indeed, these governmental authorities themselves sometimes become the problem, rather than the solution, as they assist in converting these sites into more economically productive uses. Cemetery vandalism is epidemic in many areas of rural America, and too few law enforcement agencies seem either able or willing to do much about it. Where local historical groups and others have formed special associations designed to protect and maintain old cemeteries, these problems often have been overcome or at least diminished, but such efforts have been sporadic at best. Nevertheless, they must serve as a model, for they present what might be the only realistic hope of preserving large numbers of these unique outdoor museums that chronicle so eloquently the history of rural life in America.

—*Richard E. Meyer*

See also
Churches; Culture; Ethnicity; Religion.

References
Bell, Edward L. *Vestiges of Mortality and Remembrance: A Bibliography on the Historical Archaeology of Cemeteries.* Metuchen, NJ: Scarecrow, 1994.
Brown, John Gary. *Soul in the Stone: Cemetery Art from America's Heartland.* Lawrence: University Press of Kansas, 1994.
Jackson, Kenneth, and Camillo José Vergara. *Silent Cities: The Evolution of the American Cemetery.* New York: Princeton Architectural Press, 1989.
Jordan, Terry G. *Texas Cemeteries: A Cultural Legacy.* Austin: University of Texas Press, 1982.
Markers: Journal of the Association for Gravestone Studies. 1980–present.
Meyer, Richard E., ed. *Cemeteries and Gravemarkers: Voices of American Culture.* Logan: Utah State University Press, 1992.
———, ed. *Ethnicity and the American Cemetery.* Bowling Green, OH: Bowling Green State University Press, 1993.
Sloan, David Charles. *The Last Great Necessity: Cemeteries in American History.* Baltimore, MD: Johns Hopkins University Press, 1991.

Churches

Religious organizations whose functions typically include worship, religious socialization of the young and new members, evangelization of nonchurched people, and improvement of society members' quality of life. After comparing the stereotypic images and the realities of rural churces, the history of the church in rural America is examined. The impacts on the rural church by the Rural Life Movement of the early 1900s and the rise of mass society following World War II are discussed, and the rural church's current trends are described.

Image and Reality

The white clapboard meetinghouses with spires puncturing the sky of New England, the modest red brick T-shaped structures with wraparound cemeteries across the South, the gray rock and stained glass transplanted European village churches across the upper Midwest, the earth-tone adobe chapels in the Southwest—such are the images of the rural church across America. Reality is far more diverse. The rural church is probably the most common social institution found in rural America. In 1990, the Glenmary report counted 116,872 congregations in nonmetropolitan counties. Unfortunately, many African American, independent, and fundamentalist congregations did not cooperate in the study. And there may well be half that many more that see themselves as "rural," although they are located in metropolitan counties. (Of course, many of the congregations in the larger towns or rural cities of the nonmetropolitan counties do not readily identify themselves as rural.) It is probable, then, that

A Lutheran church in Viking, Minnesota.

St. Thomas More Catholic Church in DeSmet, South Dakota.

there are well over 200,000 "rural" churches. The churches in the nonmetropolitan counties claim 31.5 million adherents. This is nearly 60 percent of the nonmetro population.

Most counties are dominated by a specific "faith family" or denomination. In New England and the Great Lakes region, it is the Roman Catholics. This is also true along the West Coast and along the southern border all the way back to New Orleans. The upper Midwest is dominated by the Lutherans. The intermountain region is the empire of the Latter-day Saints. The domain of the Methodists runs from Maryland to Colorado, in a strip through the midlands. Portions of this region are shared with the Disciples/Christian churches. And in the South and much of the Southwest lies the heartland of the Baptists. Elsewhere, about 200 hundred scattered counties are dominated by various mainline (United Church of Christ, Presbyterian, and Reformed) and immigrant denominations. However, most nonmetropolitan counties offer greater diversity in denominations now than in 1970.

History

During the colonial period, most colonies established and supported a particular church. Revivalism, immigration, the home mission movement, and territorial expansion modified this considerably since the formation of the United States. Revivalism on the western frontier in the early 1800s sparked a rapid growth of Methodists and Baptists. It gave birth to the Disciples movement. Indirectly, this revivalism birthed the Latter Day Saints. Immigration in the mid- to late nineteenth century brought floods of Roman Catholic and Lutheran farmers to the Midwest and miners to the midlands and Great Plains. In their wake came thousands of pietistic and peace-oriented sectarianists. In that great century of westward settlement, home mission societies strove to plant congregations in the new farm service towns, mining towns, and mill towns that were springing up. Paramount was the American Mission Society, supported primarily by the Congregationalists and the Presbyterians. Second to it was the Northern Methodist Mission Society. This was not an easy task. At first many towns were served by more saloons and brothels than by churches, but in time this usually changed.

Six primary patterns developed. First, the community constructed a building in which a union Sunday school was held, and several different denominations held worship on successive Sundays. If the community grew, then one or all of the denominations formed a separate congregation. Second, a mission society or religious order in Europe or in the East financed the construction of a church house and funded a mission pastor or priest. Often this was an element of the immigration process and a colony would be transported from the Old World to the new. Third, an itinerant preacher came to a community, held a revival meeting, gathered converts, and formed a church. Fourth, an existing congregation encouraged some of its members to form a new congregation in a nearby community and provided financial support. Fifth, earnest laypersons formed a congregation and then asked a denomination to provide a pastor to them or called one from among their own flock. Sixth, a mining or mill company provided churches as a part of the amenities afforded in the company village.

Among African Americans, examples of all six of these patterns can be found following the Civil War. However, they relied largely on indigenous efforts. By 1900, most of the former slaves and their children had become church members. Elsewhere in rural America, some scattered synagogues appeared to serve the many Jewish merchants who settled in the growing towns. Most of the denominations carried on mission activities among the Native Americans on tribal lands seeking to win them to the Christian faith.

In the decades on either side of the beginning of the twentieth century, several new Christian denominations emerged in rural areas. One set sprang from a reaction of modernity, calling for a return to the "fundamental" doctrines of Christianity. A second variety stressed personal holiness and moral perfection. A third stressed the importance of the "gifts of the spirit," particularly the gift of speaking in "unknown tongues." And a fourth, the millennial sects, actively anticipated the coming end of time and the return of Jesus to the earth. (The Churches of Christ, the Church of the Nazarene, the Assemblies of God, and the Seventh-day Adventists, respectively, are prime examples of each of these groups.) These groups soon splintered off of the mainline Protestant denominations. These groups drew heavily upon rural persons, even when they formed city congregations. Almost all of their adherents were poor in the beginning. Over time, many prospered; today, many worship is beautiful church buildings. Each of these four movements have continued to splinter and to grow down to the present. For example, the Assembly of God denomination ranks third behind United Methodists and Roman Catholics in the number of counties where it has a congregation.

The Rural Life Movement

The social gospel movement was launched to respond to the poverty, filth, and crime of the center cities in the latter decades of the nineteenth century. It focused on improving social conditions, addressing social policy, and ministering to personal needs. It sought to apply the Golden Rule to the social order. Soon rural leaders were contending that similar attention should be addressed to rural areas. In 1907, President Teddy Roosevelt called for the Country Life Conference. This became a landmark event for the Cooperative Extension Movement and for the discipline of rural sociology, as well as for the churches. The issues of tenancy, public education, inadequate farm practices, dirt roads, poor hygiene, and the weakness of social institutions, including the churches, were among those addressed.

Most of the major denominations quickly opened a department of rural church work. They addressed social reform and community improvement. They worked with Cooperative Extension in many states to form summer schools to train rural clergy in the social sciences. Many denominational seminaries added staff to teach about how to pastor rural churches and how to work for community development. The denominations opened high schools and colleges in remote places. Where there was more than one congregation for every 1,000 residents, efforts were made to form a federated church to serve several denominations concurrently. Comity agreements were made assigning particular territories to specific denominations, particularly in the West. They cooperated with the area soil and water conservation districts to promote environmental stewardship. The Jeffersonian agrarianism paradigm was wed with a dream that access to the best conveniences of urban America could be made available to rural people. Only much later did the leaders come to realize that the changes they supported were resulting in the depopulation or "unsettling" of much of rural America, in a very real sense destroying what they were working to preserve. It was this movement that caused Charles Galpin to discover rural sociology. Much of the work of rural sociology in the 1920s was sponsored by the denominations and directed by Brunner and others.

The Era of Mass Society

The pull of city jobs and the push of agricultural mechanization drove millions of persons off the land following World War II. Coupled with this movement were improvements in mass communication and distribution of goods and services that seemed to remove differences between urban and rural life. The birthing of the civil rights movement refocused American society on the problems of the cities. Soon seminarians were reading Bensman and Vedich's *Small Town in Mass Society* and concluding that the bloom was off of rural ministry. Differences between rural and urban people soon would be erased. Rural pastoring would become a "maintenance" activity. Consequently, the rural departments of the denominations were cut back, and rural programs in the seminaries were dropped as the professors reached retirement.

However, the fact remained that most of the congregations and many of the members of most denominations were still town and country folk. They needed assistance, too. It came in the mid-1970s with the first of what is now a small library of books on small churches. Recently, several additional books on churches for poor people have appeared. The churches seem to be learning that, although there is now more sameness at one level, there is also more diversity. There are many different kinds of rural communities, rural churches, and rural peoples. No one program will serve them all. Staff persons in national and regional church offices with responsibilities for small churches, or poor churches, or poverty have come to realize that they must know about rural issues and culture as well.

Trends

Although there are still many churches in nonmetropolitan America, many of them are no longer rural in a traditional sense. Many are well staffed and well housed. Yet many are small, and many are poor, and probably most are not well led. In some instances, this is the result of whom they serve. In others, it is because of where they serve. Demographic shifts threaten the continued existence of some congregations in rural settings. Some agricultural and extraction-based communities have lost so much population that once very effective churches find their survival threatened. Others see a surge of new and different people around them even while their traditional membership pool is shrinking. In many rural places, there is a need for urban-style congregations to be formed.

This may mean the refocusing of existing congregations or the planting of new ones. Denominational officers with assignments in rural, small, and poor church work have formed the Rural Church Network. It shares resources, presents joint conferences, and advocates for rural concerns. Several seminaries have added rural church programs. A consortium works with the Appalachian Ministries Educational Research Center in Berea, Kentucky, to provide training for pastoral care of rural and poor congregations. Austin Seminary now offers a D.Min. degree to prepare pastors for the larger town and small city congregations. Others will likely follow. Texas A&M Cooperative Extension launched a Rural Social Science by Education program in 1989 for pastors already in town and country settings, and this is used in many other states. It employs the reflective, small peer group model for education. Courses on community, church, family, and development of community are available.

Difficulty in finding pastoral leadership for many small, poor congregations has been experienced. In 1990, studies indicated that it cost between $60,000 and $100,000 to operate a church with a full-time pastor. Many rural churches are finding themselves "priced out of the market." Several strategies are being used by denominations to address this concern. First, they train leaders from within congregations to function as pastor. Second, they seek retired or bivocational pastoral leadership. Third, yoked churches in a larger field or parish may include from two to ten or more congregations. Often these are of the same denominational family; other times they cross these lines. In some of these arrangements, a staff of ministers with complementary skills is employed. In others, a single person will have a multipoint charge. Fourth, federations of churches of different denominations are being created to serve a community that can no longer support two or three congregations.

Since Vatican II, relationships between Roman Catholic and Protestant congregations have been much improved. This is particularly true in poor, small, declining rural settings. Many rural ministers seem anxious to be involved in community development activities. They can be a valued advocate in such efforts. Often the minister brings a different, more diverse set of experiences to the process, some extralocal resources, and some credibility to the effort.

In much of the South and the Midwest, there seems to be an emerging pattern of micropolitan cities (20,000 to 50,000) having a large (minimega) congregation, the ecclesiological equivalent of a Wal-Mart. Initially, this development had an adverse effect on some of the smaller churches in the city and in the village and open country settings within its trade area. Now some of these congregations that used to service only a township are developing their own "signature" ministry, one that becomes the hallmark of that congregation that draws people from across the trade area. But in spite of the emergence of signature ministries, many village and open country congregations continue to be family chapels. They focus on supporting relationships among the people rather than on being intentional, directional, and goal seeking. They are more interested in being than in becoming. They cannot be closed, and it is difficult to get them to expand their circle to include new members. Another very visible feature of the contemporary rural church is the spread of very conservative, nondenominational congregations. Since these pastors' formal training is often very limited, the quality of their leadership varies considerably.

Rural people historically have been more likely to be connected to a church, and attend with some regularity, than have city people. This continues to be the case. There is evidence that numbers of congregations and membership are increasing and that the ratio of members to the general population is improving.

—Gary E. Farley and David C. Ruesink

See also
Camps; Community, Sense of; Culture; Ethics; History, Rural; Land Stewardship; Religion; Theology of the Land; Values of Residents; Volunteerism.

References
Berry, Wendell. *The Unsettling of America: Culture and Agriculture*. New York: Avon Books, 1977.

Brunner, Edward. *Church Life in the Rural South*. New York: George Dolan, 1923.

Butterfield, Kenyon L. *The Country Church and the Rural Problem*. Chicago: University of Chicago Press, 1909.

Goreham, Gary. *The Rural Church in America: A Century of Writings*. New York: Garland, 1990.

Hassinger, Edward W., John S. Holik, and J. Kenneth Benson. *The Rural Church: Learnings from Three Decades of Change*. Nashville: Abingdon Press, 1988.

Hunter, Kent R. *The Lord's Harvest and the Rural Church*. Kansas City, MO: Beacon Hill Press, 1993.

Jent, J. W. *The Challenge of the Country Church*. Nashville: Sunday School Board, 1924.

Lincoln, C. Eric, and Lawrence H. Mamiya. *The Black Church in African-American Experience*. Durham, NC: Duke University Press, 1990.

Norris, Kathleen. *Dakota: A Spiritual Geography*. Boston: Houghton Mifflin, 1993.

Ray, David R. *The Big Small Church Book*. Cleveland: Pilgrim Press, 1992.

Rich, Mark. *The Rural Church Movement*. Columbia, MO: Juniper Press, 1957.

Schroeder, W. W., and Victor Obenhaus. *Religion in American Culture*. London: Free Press of Glencoe, 1964.

Smith, Rockwell. *The Church in Our Town*. New York: Abingdon Press, 1955.

Street, James. *The Gauntlet*. Garden City, NY: Life Press, 1945.

Surrey, Peter. *The Small Town Church*. Nashville: Abingdon Press, 1981.

Vidich, Arthur J., and Joseph Bensman. *Small Town in Mass Society*. Princeton, NJ: Princeton University Press, 1958.

Class
See Social Class

Climatic Adaptability of Plants

The adaptability of plants to the length of the growing season and to the intervening winters that limit the growing seasons. This entry addresses the notion of growing seasons and then discusses hardiness zones and plant hardiness ratings. Climatic maps make it possible to select adapted plants for any locality.

Growing Seasons

The growing season is the period of time during the year when outdoor conditions favor plant growth. Annual plants and tender perennials are killed by temperatures just a few degrees below freezing, so they can survive and grow only between the last killing frost in spring and the earliest one in autumn. The idea of growing seasons comes from experience, but science adapted growing season information to the planning of crops and gardens. Since frosts do not happen on the same dates every year, climatologists calculate the average (mean) dates of frost (32°F) for all years when records have been kept and define the average growing season as the length of time between the mean last date of occurrence of 32°F in the spring and the mean first occurrence of 32°F in autumn. For example, tomato plants planted in spring on the mean last date of killing frost have a 50 percent chance of being injured or killed by a later frost. Better odds can be attained by the grower waiting patiently until they improve. In most localities, the chance of frost drops to 10 percent about two or three weeks later.

Growing season maps for the United States can be found in extension bulletins, in garden books, and sometimes even on the backs of seed packets. Some maps, usually found in extension bulletins, show growing seasons based on 28°F, or even 24°F, as well as 32°F. These can be helpful because different plants are killed by different temperatures. For example, a 28°F frost, which would kill tomatoes and geraniums, would have little effect on petunias and cabbages. Some root vegetables can be safely left in the ground for much of the winter because there they are protected by the heat of the earth.

Other climatic factors regulate the quality of the growing season. Temperature, as it relates to optimum temperatures for different plants; the amount of rainfall and how much of it is absorbed by the soil rather than running off in a "gully-washer"; and wind all have an effect on the amount and quality of plant growth. Growing season maps are not precise enough to take into account local conditions different from those elsewhere in the same general area. Advice regarding a specific locality's growing conditions may be obtained from others who have greater experience in the locality. The discussion to this point relates primarily to the northern states. In many parts of the South, there are two growing seasons: spring and fall, separated by a summer too long and hot for many plants. In the Deep South, the growing season may extend through winter. It is always a good idea to consult the local sources of information.

Hardiness Zones

Trees, shrubs, and other perennial plants expected to live for years may fail to do so if they are not cold-hardy enough to withstand the lowest winter temperatures in

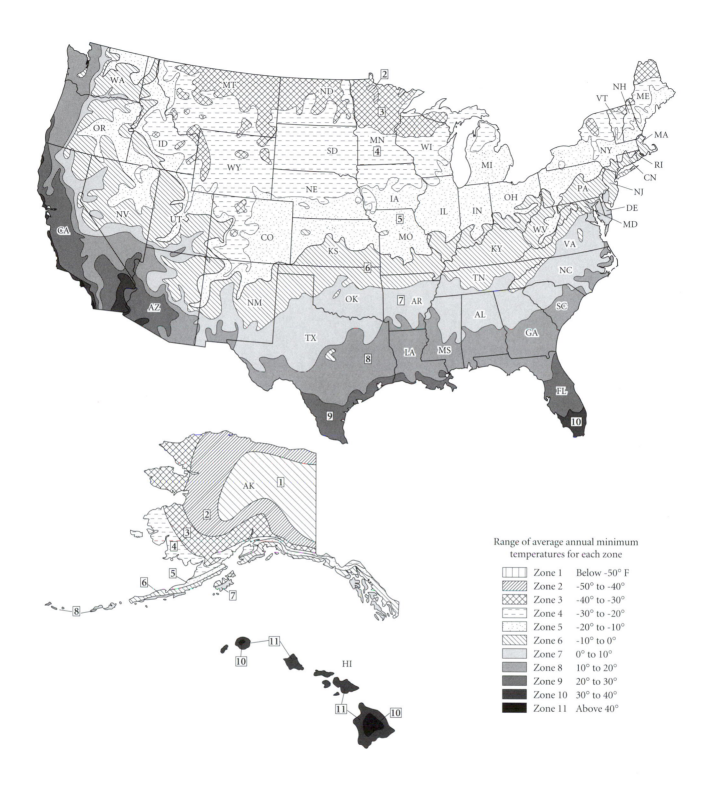

Range of average annual minimum
temperatures for each zone

	Zone 1	Below -50° F
	Zone 2	-50° to -40°
	Zone 3	-40° to -30°
	Zone 4	-30° to -20°
	Zone 5	-20° to -10°
	Zone 6	-10° to 0°
	Zone 7	0° to 10°
	Zone 8	10° to 20°
	Zone 9	20° to 30°
	Zone 10	30° to 40°
	Zone 11	Above 40°

U.S. Department of Agriculture Plant Hardiness Zone Map

Source: Agricultural Research Service, U.S. Department of Agriculture.

the locality where they are growing. To select plants that will live, it is necessary to know about growing seasons and the severity of the winters between them. A plant hardiness zone map is a tool that can help determine what to expect from a local winter climate. Plant hardiness zone maps are based on the average annual minimum temperature (AAMT) for each map point. This is the lowest temperature recorded at a site each year, averaged for all the years for which records exist, for different locations (weather stations) in the map area. Areas with the same AAMT are connected by isotherm lines that serve as boundaries between hardiness zones. In the U.S. Department of Agriculture (USDA) Plant Hardiness Zone Map, for example, southern Iowa and northern Missouri are in Zone 5, where the AAMT ranges between −10° and −20°F, whereas southern Oklahoma and northcentral Texas are in Zone 7, with an AAMT range of +10° to 0°F.

Plant Hardiness Ratings

In many reference books and nursery catalogs, plants are assigned hardiness zone ratings, which show the coldest zones in which they can be expected to be cold-hardy. Sometimes they also are given the numbers of the southernmost zones where they will perform well. Matching one's hardiness zone of a locality, as shown on the map, with the hardiness zone rating of a particular plant, allows a person to predict whether the plant will succeed in that locality. Nothing about plants and climate is perfectly predictable. The hardiness zone does not tell the whole story, for several reasons.

First, in all hardiness zones there are microclimates. Plants in an area exposed to the full force of a northwest wind may not survive even if their hardiness zone rating suggests that they should be safe there. Conversely, some plants that would not be expected to survive may do so in a site sheltered from winter wind and sun or covered by an insulating blanket of deep snow.

Second, many plants are more likely to be damaged or killed by cold in spring or autumn than in winter. For example, in a warm, moist late summer and early fall some shrubs, such as evergreen azaleas, may be stimulated to continue growing well into autumn. Since growth must stop before plants can begin the process of cold-hardening, plants actively growing this late do not harden soon enough to withstand the first hard freeze, even when that freeze would not have been severe enough to injure them had they hardened earlier. Other plants, such as raspberries, peaches, and the flower buds of many early-flowering shrubs, can be activated prematurely by unsea-

sonably warm weather in late winter, predisposing them to injury from severe freezes yet to come during spring.

Third, some evergreen shrubs and trees, such as certain arborvitaes, rhododendrons, and yews, are prone to injury from "fast freezing." During sunny but cold winter days, their leaves often are warmed by heat rays from the sun to temperatures 30° to 40°F higher than that of the surrounding air. Then as the sun's rays are interrupted by the shadow of a cloud or building, the leaves are chilled rapidly back to the air temperature—so fast that their cells cannot make the adjustments that would protect them from slower freezing, and so these plants are killed even though they might easily withstand the same low temperature, applied slowly. In short, just as winter injury does not always happen in winter, it also may have little to do with minimum temperature.

Fourth, many plants are killed or injured by winter conditions not directly related to temperature. Such is the lethal drying experienced by some evergreens exposed to winter sun and wind, especially when their roots are frozen in the ground and unable to absorb water to replace the water that is lost from the leaves by transpiration (evaporation from the leaf surfaces). In spite of all this, hardiness zones are still the best single predictors of plant hardiness in a given locality, and they offer a good way to begin in the selection of plants. A grower can improve a prediction, however, by checking with others who have more experience in the locality.

A note of caution: not all plant hardiness zone maps are the same. The first hardiness zone map in this country was published in 1938 in Wyman's book *Hedges, Screens, and Windbreaks*. This map, called the Arnold Arboretum Hardiness Zone Map, has been republished since in several other books by Wyman and others. In 1960, the U.S. National Arboretum staff published a new plant hardiness zone map, now called the USDA Plant Hardiness Zone Map. This map is an improvement over the Arnold Arboretum map in that it has zones of equal size (10°F, with 5° subzones) rather than zones of variable size. Otherwise, the two maps are so similar that readers may assume they are identical, but different enough to cause serious problems, as shown in the table. For example, the AAMT span of −10° to −20°F, called Zone 4 on the Arnold Arboretum map, corresponds to Zone 5 on the USDA map. If a person living in USDA Zone 4 were to select flowering dogwood (*Cornus florida*) from a source that lists it as hardy to Arnold Arboretum Zone 4 (USDA Zone 5), the decision probably would be fatal for the dogwood. It does not matter which map is used as long as the

Comparisons of Arnold Arboretum and USDA Hardiness Zones

Annual Minimum Temperature (°F)	Arnold Arboretum Hardiness Zone	USDA Hardiness Zone
Below –50	1	1
–50 to –45		2
		2a
–45 to –40		2b
–40 to –35		3a
–35 to –30	3	3b
–30 to –25		4a
–25 to –20		4b
–20 to –15	4	5a
–15 to –10		5b
–10 to –5	5	6a
–5 to 0	6	6b
0 to 5		7a
5 to 10	7	7b
10 to 15	8	8a
15 to 20		8b
20 to 25	9	9a
25 to 30		9b
30 to 35	10	10a
35 to 40		10b

Source: U. S. Department of Agriculture, 1990.

plant ratings published for that specific map also are used; mixing maps and ratings can court disaster.

In 1968, a new and different plant hardiness map was published by the Canadian government in the book *Ornamental Shrubs for Canada,* by Sherk and Buckley of the Canadian Plant Research Institute. This map is based only partly on AAMT in a climatic model that takes into consideration other climatic elements as well. This map works very well if one uses the plant hardiness zone ratings intended for use with the Canadian map.

A revised version of the USDA map was published by the National Arboretum in 1990, with the rationale that, since the 15 years or so prior to publication had included a number of severe winters, at least for most of the eastern United States, a new map was needed. Instead of using data for all years in which records had been kept, the arboretum selected a sample of 13 years (1974–1986), and the resulting map was strikingly different from the 1960 map. This was apparently done in the belief that the climate was cooling in the long run, even though at the same time scientists were beginning to find evidence of global warming. A return to milder-than-normal winters in most of the eastern United States in the decade following (1986–1995) demonstrated that the 1990 USDA map probably is too conservative a predictor of future winters for at least the central and southeastern parts of the country.

Extreme Minimum Temperatures

The USDA map shows residents of southern Michigan, away from the lakes, that they are in Zone 5, where the AAMT ranges from –10° to –20°F. This may surprise older residents of this area who can remember clearly a cold snap to –25° or –30°F! One must remember, however, that the extreme minimum temperature (EMT) for any given locality, that is, the lowest temperature ever recorded, is usually 10° to 20°F lower than the AAMT, averaging about 14° F lower for many different locations. Plant hardiness zone ratings automatically take into account the difference between AAMT and EMT. They are based on actual plant performance in the different zones. Because of this, it does not matter that EMTs much lower than AAMTs can be expected.

—Harrison L. Flint

See also

Agronomy; Horticulture; Temperate Fruit Industry; Vegetable Industry; Weather.

References

Flint, Harrison L. *Landscape Plants for Eastern North America.* New York: Wiley-Interscience, 1983.

Sherk, Lawrence C., and Arthur R. Buckley. *Ornamental Shrubs for Canada.* Ottawa: Canada Department of Agriculture, 1968.

U.S. Department of Agriculture. *Yearbook of Agriculture: Climate and Man.* Washington, DC: U.S. Government Printing Office, 1941.

———. Agricultural Research Service. *USDA Plant Hardiness Zone Map.* A. R. S. Misc. Pub. 1475. Washington, DC: U.S. Government Printing Office, 1990.

U.S. Department of Commerce. Environmental Data Service. *Weather Atlas of the United States.* Detroit: Gale Research, 1975.

Wyman, Donald. *Trees for American Gardens.* 3d ed. New York: Macmillan, 1990.

Wyman, Donald, and Harrison L. Flint. "Plant Hardiness Zone Maps." *Arnoldia* 45 (1985): 32–34.

Clothing and Textiles

Universally used body coverings made from natural agricultural products (such as cotton, linen, ramie, silk, and wool fibers) or manufactured fibers (such as wood pulp or petroleum derivatives). Fibers are formed into fabric for clothing in countless ways. Clothing is essential for

Types of clothing worn by residents on a rural farm.

physical and social survival; people use clothes to express their identity and feelings, communicate their roles and lifestyle, and protect themselves from the environment. For most people, clothing goes beyond strict necessity (Fine and Leopold 1993). New fashions are always welcome because clothes often become psychologically tiresome long before they are worn out. A person may find "nothing to wear" in a whole closet full of clothes! This entry addresses apparel production and consumption in the United States and the roles of apparel in personal identification, communication, and protection.

Apparel Production

During the 1700s, men's tailoring was a skilled craft requiring a long apprenticeship. Women's clothing production was a part of "housewifery." The sewing machine's invention in 1846 hastened the development of the apparel manufacturing industry. Some home sewing persists, but since the money-saving advantages have disappeared, people sew primarily for custom design, a better fit, or creative expression.

Many textile, apparel, or sewn product firms are located in rural communities. The wide distribution of apparel manufacturers across rural America is not well known. For example, Alabama has over 700 and Iowa over 400 textile and apparel-related producers. Innovative firms use teams of workers in modular production or flexible manufacturing systems. Computer-assisted design and a high degree of automation allow production of quality apparel at a price competitive with imports that may require longer production times.

Rural people, women especially, provide an able workforce with a strong work ethic, a need for employ-

ment, and a willingness to work whether in a team environment or for piece-rate wages related to production speed. Fabric manipulation skills developed through home sewing are an asset to manufacturers who provide on-the-job training with specialized equipment. Efficient use of personnel and equipment allows made-to-order manufacturing so that totally new items can be produced and shipped within ten working days. In 1993, 1.9 million people were employed growing cotton and wool or producing fibers, textiles, and apparel in the United States (American Textile Manufacturers Institute 1994).

Apparel Consumption

Many consumers believe clothing prices are high. But the Consumer Price Index (CPI) shows that in recent years clothing prices rose less that other consumer items. In 1993, the CPI for clothing was 130.5, compared with 149.7 for all consumer items, with 1982–1984 as base years (U.S. Department of Labor 1994). Consumer spending does add up, however, so total U.S. consumer expenditures for apparel, not including shoes, was $204.4 billion in 1993 (American Textile Manufacturers Institute 1994). Clothing expenditures as a proportion of total family expenditures have not changed dramatically in recent years. Apparel expenditures of the baby-boom generation households in 1990 were between 5 and 6 percent of all their expenditures regardless of income, the higher number associated with larger family size (Dinkins 1993).

Rural households spend less on apparel and related services than urban households. But the common perception that all rural residents are poor is not accurate. The rural wealthy take extraordinary measures to obtain high-quality merchandise. Some scholars and retail buyers, based on experience in selling apparel, believe that rural residents of the Midwest are more reluctant to risk buying new fashions than urban coastal dwellers. Midwestern store buyers tend to invest less in the trendiest styles. Studies of fashion adoption show young age and high media use as indicators of early adoption, but rural residence was not studied (Behling 1992).

Although rural residence once was synonymous with isolation and lack of access to fashion apparel, modern communication and delivery systems have rendered that notion almost obsolete. Changes in retailing, direct-mail catalog service, and in-home video shopping now bring the world's merchandise to one's community if not one's own living room. With a satellite dish, rural people can get fashion news from Milan, Paris, and New York as it is introduced. However, family income, transportation and mobility, lack of knowledge about sources, or just satisfaction with the status quo may limit consumer choice.

Wal-Mart brought a broader assortment of merchandise to small towns, and its success in promoting low prices is evidence that consumer incomes are important in limiting choice. Other chains expecting lower operating costs, high return on investment, and less-demanding, loyal customers also have opened in rural communities. Discount and outlet malls beside interstate highways and recreation areas provide access for rural consumers as well as transient trade.

Catalog companies geared for quick response to telephone, fax, or mail orders deliver via UPS, Federal Express, or the U.S. Postal Service to remote locations. Database records target customers, and use of samples, fast delivery, and easy return policies facilitate distance shopping. Consumers with access to TV shopping networks, such as QVC and Home Shopping Network, already spend over $2 billion annually for merchandise that includes jewelry and clothes ("Shopping by Television." *Consumer Reports*, January 1995, pp. 8–12); however, the proportion spent by rural compared to urban consumers is unclear.

Identification and Communication

The relationships among clothing and appearance, self-expression, and communication have been studied by many researchers (Roach-Higgins and Eicher 1992). Clothing delivers first impressions to observers. People are more likely to help well-dressed strangers who are stranded along roadsides than poorly dressed ones and are more likely to do so in a rural setting than in urban locations (Mallozzi, McDermott, and Kayson 1990). T-shirts can spell out political beliefs. Diversity of aesthetic expression shown through appearance and dress may be related to differences in cultural or national origin of either the clothing itself or the wearer.

Clothing is a powerful means of expression and nonverbal communication that helps to establish and maintain the self, negotiate identities, define situations, and set the stage for verbal communication. Gender identity through clothing starts in childhood, with baby boys in blue and girls in pink, a differentiation that did not become popular until the 1920s. Whether functional, such as a clean room suit, or special occasion, such as a bridal gown, clothes express a set of expectations that govern social interactions between wearers and viewers. The variety of clothing available in the 1990s allows people to express individuality and communicate in interesting ways.

People with freedom to control what they wear and to choose among satisfying alternatives may or may not conform with group norms. The tension between individual expression or freedom in dress and commonly held notions of appropriate dress can lead to conflict between groups, organizations, or generations. Questions about whose rights are more important arise when a teen whose religious beliefs require a turban is denied admission to a dance club with a dress code that bans hats to foster appropriate behavior. Diversity in cultural values and patterns of dress can easily be misunderstood when parochial views are not extended through education.

Youths often adopt clothing different from that of their parents to express their independence. Despite the lack of research-based evidence that dress codes can reduce violence among teens, school boards impose dress codes, limiting symbols, to discourage gang activity (Holloman 1995). By the time adults understand the meaning of the symbols used by youths, the symbols often have changed. Innocent or accidental use of clothing-related gang symbols can put nongang youths at risk of misidentification and perhaps real danger, so adult concern is not without foundation. There is growing evidence of gang activity in rural communities. Red and blue bandannas, long associated with cowboys and farmers, more recently were used as gang markers among urban youths.

Many organizations require work uniforms, and over 23 million Americans wear them (Soloman 1987). Uniforms help establish identity, show authority, create order, and help equalize social class and income differences among people. Uniforms can improve working relationships and foster the image of standardized service. But they may make individual achievement harder to identify. Military uniform insignia show rank to the troops but may not have meaning for outsiders. Uniform requirements begin in childhood with Little League, band, and scouts.

When uniforms are not required, the tendency to conform with peers often leads to a quasi uniform that may be traditional or transitory as fashions change. Rural football fans wear the traditional school colors even when their team is losing. Midwestern farmers wear promotional baseball-style caps from farm service dealers; cowboy hats are the mark of western ranchers and line dancers. Professional dress (suit, shirt or blouse, and tie) is expected for most job interviews and many offices, whether urban or rural, but some firms are relaxing this standard and encouraging casual dress on designated days. A dress code may define casual, lest the freedom be abused.

Protection

Temperature, fire, water, chemicals, and biological organisms create environmental conditions that may be mediated by clothing and textiles (Raheel 1994). Clothing and protective gear also can mediate the impacts of brute force, small particles, or radiation. Protective clothing is easily accepted when the hazard is obvious and widely understood. Winter coats, hard hats, football helmets, firefighters' protective suits, and medical workers' rubber gloves are examples.

When the hazard is less easily understood and the exposure random or cumulative, protective gear is less readily accepted. Denial of need for protective clothing is widespread. Accidents are chance events and may not happen. Some states have no laws requiring motorcycle helmets, though these could prevent many head injuries. Cumulative effects are not immediately threatening. Long-term sun exposure can lead to skin cancer on the ears and nose that might be prevented by the wearing of wide-brimmed hats, yet they are seldom worn.

Farm pesticide applicators often work alone and are uncertain of the benefit of protective gear, so its use is not guaranteed. The Worker Protection Standard for Agricultural Pesticides regulates pesticide use and requires personal protective equipment in accordance with pesticide labels (Environmental Protection Agency 1993). Surveys show that most agricultural pesticide applicators indicate compliance with pesticide label requirements for chemical resistant glove use, but many express frustrations with glove fit and comfort.

Fabrics with barrier properties designed to resist penetration and permeation of hazardous substances and functional garments requiring specially engineered polymer films, fiber webs, foams, and impact-resistant plastics (perhaps fiber reinforced) are of increasing importance as environmental conditions dictate protection. Choosing protective gear is a challenge because no chemically resistant glove material, for example, resists all chemicals. Protective clothing requires special care to maintain its functional properties. Clothes worn for pesticide application can retain pesticides in more than trace amounts after repeated laundering (Stone, Higby, and Stahr 1992). Careful attention to laundering can reduce residue to minimum levels. Disposable or limited-use protective coveralls, aprons, and gloves eliminate laundering but create contaminated waste for which disposal options are limited.

Rural people choose clothing and textiles not only for aesthetics and design appeal but also for self-identification, communication, and protection. Rural people may wear polyester fleece made from recycled soft-drink bottles, naturally grown colored cotton from Arizona, hand-dyed batiks from Indonesia, and strip cloth from Africa. Garments may be sewn in Wisconsin, Singapore, or Mexico. Clothing and textiles contribute to economic, physical, social, and emotional well-being and rank with food and shelter as necessities of life.

—*Janis Stone*

See also
Consumer-goods Advertising; Culture; Home Economics; Pest Management; Retail Industry; Textile Industry; Wool and Sheep Industry.

References
American Textile Manufacturers Institute. Office of the Chief Economist. *Textile Highlights* (December 1994): 22–23, 33.

Behling, Dorothy U. "Three and a Half Decades of Fashion Adoption Research: What Have We Learned?" *Clothing and Textiles Research Journal* 10 (1992): 34–41.

Dinkins, Julia M. "Expenditures of Younger and Older Baby Boomers." *Family Economics Review* 6 (1993) 2: 2–7.

Environmental Protection Agency. *The Worker Protection Standard for Agricultural Pesticides: How to Comply*. EPA 7354-B-93–001. Washington, DC: Environmental Protection Agency, 1993.

Fine, Ben, and Ellen Leopold. *The World of Consumption*. London: Routledge, 1993.

Holloman, Lillian O. "Violence and Other Antisocial Behaviors in Public Schools: Can Dress Codes Help Solve the Problem?" *Journal of Family and Consumer Sciences* (Winter 1995): 33–38.

Mallozzi, John, Vincent McDermott, and Wesley A. Kayson. "Effects of Sex, Type of Dress, and Location on Altruistic Behavior." *Psychological Reports* 67 (1990): 1103–1106.

Raheel, M. *Protective Clothing Systems and Materials*. New York: Marcel Decker, 1994.

Roach-Higgins, Mary Ellen, and Joanne B. Eicher. "Dress and Identity." *Clothing and Textiles Research Journal* 10 (1992): 1–8.

Soloman, M. R. "Standard Issue." *Psychology Today* (December 1987): 30–31.

Stone, J., P. Higby, and H. M. Stahr. "Pesticide Residues in Clothing: Case Study of Clothing Worn under Protective Cotton Coveralls." *Journal of Environmental Health* 55 (1992): 10–13.

U.S. Department of Labor. Bureau of Labor Statistics. *Consumer Price Index*. Chicago: U.S. Department of Labor, Bureau of Labor Statistics. November 1994.

Community

The interaction among individuals for mutual support. Rural communities are localized systems integrated by means of family and cooperation (Hillery 1968). Different types of community are presented in this entry. Community resources, discussed here as financial, manufactured, human, environmental, and social capital, can enhance or detract from each other. Community power structure and

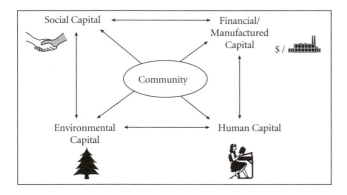

Forms of Capital within Communities

strategies of community change are based on these resources.

Definitions

Almost all definitions of community emphasize the informality and solidarity engendered by relationships and social organization. Communities of interest are composed of interactions among people linked to each other purposively by shared interest and actions. Communities of place are composed of the interactions of individuals who live in a particular locality. As of 1990, there were a total of 23,435 places within the United States. Seventy-seven percent of them (17,953) were outside of urban areas, and 60 percent (14,014) of the places had populations of less than 2,500. Thirty-seven percent of the U.S. population (nearly 90.5 million people) in 1990 lived outside of urban areas, and nearly 25 percent of the U.S. population in 1990 lived in places of less than 2,500, 2 million more than in 1980. Rural communities of place continue to be important for a substantial number of people in the United States. Communities have resources available to them collectively. Resources are either consumed, held in reserve, or invested. When resources are invested, they are used to create new resources and can be referred to as capital.

Financial and Manufactured Capital

Financial capital consists of money or instruments of credit for investment and speculation. Financial capital can be individual or collective (firms or governments). Financial capital is the most mobile of all forms of capital. National boundaries decreasingly influence the flow of financial capital, which can be transferred from Syracuse to Singapore electronically in less than a second. Financial capital is also the least likely to provide a sus-

tainable base for rural communities. International financial markets are governed by the principles of fear and greed; neither one is conducive to community sustainability (*Financial Times,* 30 September 1994).

Manufactured capital is composed of the physical infrastructure, such as machinery, homes, office buildings, schools, roads, sewers, factories, and water systems (Flora et al. 1992). Either the private or the public sector can turn financial capital into manufactured capital. When newly generated manufactured capital can be easily or exclusively captured, or when there is rival consumption for that good or service (that is, if one person consumes it, then no one else can), the manufactured capital tends to be in the private sector. However, when there is open or inclusive access and the possibility of joint consumption, as in the case of most roads, the financial investments often come from the public sector. Manufactured capital can have an enormous impact on other forms of capital, particularly when it is pursued only with the end of increasing financial capital. Although manufactured capital seems relatively immobile, this is only partially true. The sewers and roads constructed by the citizens of a landscape intended to attract a new factory are relatively immobile. However, the factory and machinery within it can be easily dismantled, as many rural communities discovered during the 1980s. Light manufacturing was relocated offshore where wages are lower, environmental restrictions are fewer, and government regulations are less intrusive, but the financial instruments to fund the manufactured capital, in the form of higher taxes, are still in place.

Human Capital

Human capital includes individual capacity, knowledge, training, health, values, and leadership. Embodied in individual human beings, it is also mobile, but not nearly as mobile as financial capital. Economists often use the term *labor,* consisting of the skills, abilities, education, and training that workers possess and bring to their jobs, to signify human capital. Human capital makes financial and manufactured capital more efficient. One of the goals of industrialization is to substitute manufactured capital for human capital. Whereas technology can require higher levels of human capital and make it more efficient, it also can make tasks ever more simple and routine in order to require less skill and less commitment from workers. The implications for a rural community of deskilling labor and making it more mobile are enormous. Public financial capital suffers from high mobility of human capital, particularly that associated with low-wage industrialization. Research by Grey (1995) in Storm Lake, Iowa, related deskilling of labor (with accompanying low wages) to unpaid hospital and clinic bills, increased costs of police and fire protection, and costs of schools. Emphasis on financial and manufactured capital without concern for human capital has long-term implications for rural communities. For instance, pesticides that increase short-term financial capital have long-term negative impacts on human health when used improperly.

Environmental Capital

Environmental capital consists of air quality, water quality and quantity, soil quantity and quality, plant and animal biodiversity, and landscape. Ecological economists refer to this as natural capital (Jansson et al. 1994). The components of environmental capital are highly interrelated and tend to enhance one another. For example, biodiversity helps to maintain soil cover and decrease soil erosion, which in turn contributes to water quality. Deterioration of environmental capital can impact both human and financial capital. Whereas financial capital is saved if air pollution is not remedied or prevented, individuals living in areas of high air quality can expect to lose fewer days from work and to live longer than those living in areas of low air quality. Strip mining can generate immediate financial capital but limit long term capital return. A resort located next to a strip-mined area loses much of its environmental capital and its ability to generate new resources.

Communities can invest in human capital to enhance environmental capital. Much environmental education has been supported to change individual actions toward the environment and to enhance environmental sustainability. However, human capital also can lead to the deterioration of environmental capital. People can be educated to make decisions to enhance financial capital on the assumption that the deterioration of environmental capital can be compensated through the use of manufactured capital. Values that stress the primacy of financial capital, particularly short term, can rapidly decrease environmental capital.

Community Social Capital

Putnam (1993, 35–36) described social capital—collective norms of reciprocity and mutual trust—as "features of social organization, such as networks, norms, and trust, that facilitate coordination and cooperation for mutual benefit. Social capital enhances the benefits of investment in physical and human capital." Social capital often is ignored in economic development; manufactured capital is seen as the important component of community improvement. The way that manufactured capital is enhanced can either help or hurt social capital development. For example, when housing improvements are delivered in a top-down fashion, with the decisions and resources coming totally from outside the community, social capital decreases and dependency increases. Much of urban renewal in the 1960s destroyed social capital in urban communities to deliver short-term manufactured capital. Social capital has a variety of configurations. Each configuration has different implications for community sustainability. Social capital can be horizontal, hierarchical, or nonexistent.

Horizontal Social Capital

Horizontal social capital implies egalitarian forms of reciprocity. Not only is each member of the community expected to give (and gain status and pleasure from giving), but also each is expected to receive. Each person in the community is seen as capable of providing something of value to other members of the community. Contributions to collective projects, from parades to the volunteer fire department and Girl Scouts, is a gift to all. Norms of reciprocity are reinforced, but direct payback to the donor is not required or expected (Allen and Dillman 1994).

Hierarchical Social Capital

Hierarchical or vertical social capital is built on norms of reciprocity and mutual trust or mutual obligation. Traditional patron-client relationships, typical of urban gangs (Portes and Sensenbrenner 1993), Mafia "families," or "boss"-run political machines, are created. Those at the bottom of the hierarchy who are beholden to the few at the top are the majority of the population in such communities. Classic rural community studies, such as Pope's *Millhands and Preachers* (1942) and Goldschmidt's *As You Sow* (1947), demonstrated the detrimental impact of economic power concentration on social capital, environmental capital, human capital, and manufactured capital in rural communities. In communities where power is highly concentrated, the receivers of favors owe incredible loyalty to their patron when time comes to vote for public office, to collect from a loser in the numbers racket, or to settle a score with a rival gang. Those with power actively discourage horizontal networks outside the sphere of influence of the patron. Dependency is created, and mistrust of outsiders is generated. This type of social capital is prevalent in persistent poverty communities (Duncan 1992).

Nonexistent Social Capital

Absence of social capital is characterized by extreme isolation. In these communities, there is little trust and, as a result, little interaction. Bedroom communities, rural communities that become a low-rent haven for jobless urbanites, and many central city neighborhoods, including those undergoing gentrification, fit this pattern. Such communities tend to have high population turnover and high levels of conflict. When middle- and upper-class communities lack social capital, they are able to substitute physical capital for social capital (for example, private guards, fenced neighborhoods, and elaborate security systems). In poorer communities, there are often high levels of crime and delinquency. Fitchen (1981) linked persistent poverty to the decline of an active social community in parts of upstate New York. Putnam (1993) showed that provinces in Italy with low levels of social capital had lower levels of government efficiency, lower levels of satisfaction with government, and slower rates of economic development than did provinces with high levels of social capital. The citizens of these areas with low levels of social capital did not trust others to follow the established rules and were thus less likely to do so themselves. As a result of this heightened level of distrust, there was a high demand for more law enforcement and more demand to incarcerate criminals for longer periods of time, a societal-level manifestation of substituting manufactured capital for social capital.

Interactions of Different Forms of Capital

Each form of capital can enhance the productivity of the other forms of capital. Increasing social capital greatly cuts transaction costs, making other resource use more efficient. Researchers have found that social capital has an independent effect on the functioning of economic systems. Overemphasizing the value of a single form of capital can reduce the levels of other forms of capital. For example, increasing industrial outputs without regard to the pollutants they generate can negatively impact human health in a community; they can decrease water quality or bypass local networks and replace them with impersonal bureaucratic structures with top-down mandates.

Because of the importance for community sustainability, measurement of social capital on a community level should be done. Coleman (1988) identified the kind of social structure that facilitates social capital on the individual level: closure of social networks, meaning that people see each other in more than one setting, such as parents who see their children's friends at home, at church, and at school functions. In the case of community, Flora and Flora (1993) identified entrepreneurial social infrastructure, a basic social structure within a community, as contributing to horizontal community-level social capital development.

Entrepreneurial Social Infrastructure

Entrepreneurial social infrastructure (ESI) is the capacity of a community to initiate and adapt. Key components of ESI are legitimization of alternatives, diversity of community networks, and widespread resource mobilization.

Legitimization of Alternatives. This component means that citizens value different points of view because they increase the alternatives available for the community. Differences are recognized but are not hierarchical. Acceptance of controversy is essential for alternatives to be considered. When differences of opinion within a community are accepted as valid, issues are raised early and alternative solutions are discussed. Such acceptance can be generated when problems ("We need better medical care") are separated from solutions ("We need a doctor"). People who raise issues are not accused of causing problems. Often rules of engagement are in place to discourage personal criticism. Because controversy is accepted and issues are raised early, communities with high levels of ESI depersonalize politics. Burnout of volunteer public officials, which often is related to the amount of abuse they face from their constituents, is reduced. Attention to process helps build ESI. Setting a vision and monitoring progress toward it on a regular basis help increase ESI. Communities that organize communitywide festivals and activities tend to have high ESI.

Diversity of Community Networks. Diverse, inclusive, flexible networks are a crucial part of social capital. Although internally homogeneous groups are often the basis for diversity within the community, there also must be networks within the community that include individuals of diverse characteristics: young and old, men and women, different racial and ethnic groups, different social classes, and newcomers and old-timers. Community networks must be inclusive. Not only are different perspectives present; also other citizens listen to those perspectives.

Gender is particularly important in rural communities. Studies have shown the importance of both male and female networks and the fact that they do not always agree on the direction the community should take. Race is also extremely important, as the dominant group tends to define community interest in terms of its own vested interest.

Horizontal linkages to similar communities and vertical linkages to more inclusive bodies, such as a region, state, or national entity, have been recognized by Warren (1963) and other community scholars as critical to an understanding of communities. Such linkages can contribute to increasing ESI. Communities that develop horizontal networks often take a diverse group of people to a community that has done something they want to emulate. They visit together, ask many questions, and return determined to adapt the idea or do it even better.

Vertical linkages to regional, state, or national entities link many people and groups to resources and markets beyond community limits. Wide access to those vertical networks is crucial. Where there is a single gatekeeper between the community and the outside, no matter how well connected that person is, the concentration of power contributes to hierarchical, not horizontal, social capital. Finally, networks are flexible and finite. People come together when there is something to do.

Widespread Resource Mobilization. The ability of a community to mobilize resources is based on the recognition that many community citizens can contribute to community well-being because they all have resources to give. Equality of access to community resources means that a wide variety of resources, from swimming pools to golf courses and schools, are financed publicly and open to all rather than owned by private individuals or elite social groups. During the 1950s and 1960s, equality of access for African Americans was a major struggle in many rural and urban communities across the United States. Although public facilities officially are open to all, the privatization of schools and recreational facilities maintains separation and inequality in many rural communities. Social class is also a major barrier to access when such facilities are privatized. Access to credit and financial information is limited in a number of communities, as African Americans or individuals from "certain families" are assumed to be poor credit risks. When such discrimination occurs spatially, it is called redlining. In order to enhance equality of access, resource mobilization must include collective investment. Where ESI is high, the community invests in itself through school bonds, public recreation programs, volunteer fire departments, and emergency squads.

Individual investment of private resources is associated with high ESI communities. Banks in such communities have high loan-deposit ratios, choosing to invest locally rather than in safe, but distant government securities. Local entrepreneurs find both equity capital and debt capital through a variety of financial institutions, including community development corporations. Community foundations are increasingly used to mobilize capital for community investment in the public good.

Community Change through the Creation of Social Capital

Increasing social capital takes time. Maintaining groups that are diverse, inclusive, and flexible, with broad and permeable boundaries, requires consistent monitoring and adjustment by local citizens of their own groups. Flexible groups form and reform according to the concerns to be addressed. Activities that foster different groups learning from each other, rather than bringing groups together to listen to experts talk, can be particularly effective in building social capital. Community groups learn best from seeing and discussing on-site rather than in a large lecture hall. Vertical networks are most effective when communities are connected to partner organizations at the state and federal levels through many community members. Community groups must be able to monitor output, such as actual change in environmental quality or increased household well-being, rather than only means. Community social capital is enhanced when there is vision of the ends and flexibility in terms of means. Increasing social capital can challenge existing power relationships. Resistance to giving up power is often strong, if not violent, in some rural communities. In those situations, linkages to the outside increase the negotiating ability for those without power. Despite the importance of community-based resources, linkages to the outside remain critical to increasing the well-being of all rural citizens.

Rural communities are at a crossroads. Some will diminish in size and disappear. Others will become larger and loose their rural identity. For those that are changing and those that are maintaining, investing in local resources can make a difference. Declining communities can link to nearby communities that are growing to increase their boundaries. Growing communities can maintain ways to interact together. Communities that are maintaining population size can increase their individual and collective well-being by working together, a key dimension of community.

—*Cornelia Butler Flora*

See also

Churches; Community Celebrations; Community, Sense of; Development, Community and Economic; Infrastructure; Leadership; Policy, Rural Development; Quality of Life; Regional Planning; Settlement Patterns; Town-Country Relations; Trade Areas; Urbanization; Voluntarism.

References

Allen, John C., and Don A. Dillman. *Against All Odds: Rural Community in the Information Age.* Boulder, CO: Westview Press, 1994.

Coleman, James C. "Social Capital in the Creation of Human Capital." *American Journal of Sociology* 94 Supplement S95–S120 (1988): 95–119.

Duncan, C. M. "Persistent Poverty in Appalachia: Scarce Work and Rigid Stratification." Pp. 111–133 in *Rural Poverty in America.* Edited by C. M. Duncan. New York: Auburn House, 1992.

Fitchen, Janet M. *Poverty in Rural America: A Case Study.* Prospect Heights, IL: Waveland Press, 1981.

Flora, Cornelia B., and Jan L. Flora. "Entrepreneurial Social Infrastructure: A Necessary Ingredient." *Annals of the American Academy of Political and Social Science* 529 (September 1993): 48–58.

Flora, Cornelia Butler, Jan L. Flora, J. D. Spears, and L. E. Swanson, with M. B. Lapping and M. L. Weinberg. *Rural Communities: Legacy and Change.* Boulder, CO: Westview Press, 1992.

Goldschmidt, Walter. *As You Sow: Studies in the Social Consequences of Agribusiness.* Montclair, NJ: Allanheld, Osmun, 1947.

Grey, Mark A. "Pork, Poultry, and Newcomers to Storm Lake, Iowa." Pp. 109–128 in *Any Way You Cut It: Meat Processing and Small Town America.* Edited by D. Still, M. J. Broadway, and D. Griffith. Lawrence: University Press of Kansas, 1995.

Hillery, George A., Jr. *Communal Organizations: A Study of Local Societies.* Chicago: University of Chicago Press, 1968.

Jansson, AnnMari, Monicao Hammer, Carl Folke, and Robert Costanza, eds. *Investing in Natural Capital: The Ecological Economics Approach to Sustainability.* Covelo, CA: Island Press, 1994.

Pope, Liston. *Millhands and Preachers: A Study of Gastonia.* New Haven, CT: Yale University Press, 1942.

Portes, Alejandro, and J. Sensenbrenner. "Embeddedness and Immigration: Notes on the Social Determinants of Economic Action." *American Journal of Sociology* 98, no. 6 (1993): 1320–1350.

Putnam, Robert D. *Making Democracy Work: Civic Traditions in Modern Italy.* Princeton, NJ: Princeton University Press, 1993.

———. "The Prosperous Community: Social Capital and Public Life." *American Prospect* 13 (1993): 35–42.

Warren, Roland. *The Community in America.* Chicago: Rand McNally, 1963.

Wilkinson, Kenneth P. *The Community in Rural America.* New York: Greenwood Press, 1991.

Community, Sense of

To personally experience community, a uniquely human condition that connotes belonging to something larger than oneself to which each individual constitutes an important part, a part that would be missed in the complexity of the whole if for some reason absent. This entry addresses the relationship of one's individualism to the community and how people experience a sense of community. The entry examines the sense of community as it pertains to rural towns and concludes with issues pertaining to social change and its impact on the sense of community.

Individualism in Context

A sense of community cannot be defined simply by the physical location or the size of the town. It is something that must be experienced. A sense of community is understood only by personally experiencing the shared human relationships often associated with certain types of towns that have generically become known as places where community happens.

In the ideological mind's eye of most Americans, rural America represents a place in time in which positive human relationships uniquely occur. Hofstadter (1955) referred to this ideology as the "agrarian myth," the idea that rural places represent both a simpler time and location in Americans' self-image, a time and place where the most virtuous of the American ethos are found. It was in rural America where the honest, hard-working, individualistic frontiersmen who had tempered the steel of America's character and self-image could be found.

There was, however, another side to this rural folk hero. It was the same composite rural citizen who also knew the limits of the individualistic drive and laid it aside to foster the democratic spirit of community. Tocqueville (1960) marveled at rural Americans' ability to weave their individualistic desires with the larger needs of others to form a strong sense of community. That sense demanded vigilant volunteerism and commitment on the part of individuals. It was a major part of their lives, a part that went beyond self. America was great because people in rural villages had the best of both sides of what it truly meant to be an American—rugged individualists, yet devoted community servants. Even today, it is commonly held that the experience of community is nurtured and passed on to each generation primarily in rural America.

Community as an Experience

A sense of community is a shared ideology. It is a human experience or a social condition that can occur in certain places and at certain times. "Community," therefore, is different than "a community," the latter being the place itself, the former being an experience that may be identified with a place. The fundamental nature of the need to experience community has been recognized from the earliest theoretical musings of social philosophers to the present. A common thread ran through the early social philosophers' views and concerns about society. They asked how community could be sustained in the emerging market societies where rights and opportunities were bestowed on individuals as opposed to collectives of individuals. Today, essentially the same question is asked: where are the sense of community and the commitment to the larger good?

Tönnies (1957), one of the most celebrated of the early community social theorists, was interested in how human relationships changed as a result of industrialization, urbanization, and capitalism. He believed certain human relationships represented a "natural will"—the way humans are supposed to relate to each other. Natural relationships were characterized by face-to-face interaction in small groups of people, such as the family, kinship groups, and small villages. Commitment to other members of the group was through honor and was symbolized by one's word. Tönnies called these natural will relationships *Gemeinschaft*, which means "community" relationships. Community relationships were an end in and of themselves and were never used as a means to an end. For Tönnies they embodied the natural strivings of humans as expressed through genuine relationships with each other.

As society diversified through capitalism, urbanism, and industrialization, Tönnies saw natural will being replaced by a rational, artificial, means-end–oriented will. These artificial relationships he called *Gesellschaft*, or "society," that is, an artificial construction of an aggregate of human beings. *Gesellschaft* relationships were characterized by rational means-end orientations. Agreement and commitment were by contract rather than informal honor. An interaction took place through elaborate exchange relations. As *Gesellschaft* relationships began increasingly to dominate community relationships, and thus, social interaction, Tönnies saw people becoming increasingly calloused toward human aspects of interaction, such as face-to-face interactions and informal noncontractual agreements. As they increasingly interacted through rational exchange, community, as an experience, declined.

Rural Town Experience

By the 1940s, Tönnies's argument had become the doctrine of the American ethos—places with small numbers of people who were like each other and who could interact face to face, as opposed to more formal ways, were seen as locales where a sense of community could be experienced. The majority of Americans concluded that rural America epitomized the community experience in contemporary society. The tight ideological relationship among rural places, the Jeffersonian ideal, and community experience became the fabric of the American ethos. Thus, in contemporary American belief the sense of community was strongest in rural American towns.

But do rural residents really have a greater sense of community than do others? There is a second strand to this American ethos that has been developing since the turn of the century. To many urbanites, rural residents are parochial, backward, simplistic, and culturally naive. To urbanites, rural life represents the worst possible scenario in which to experience a sense of community. Such views illustrate at least two things about American's contemporary view of community. First, rural communities are seen as an embodiment of what Americans think they once were—communal, simple, (in a word) nonmodern. Second, Americans' drive toward modernity has increasingly defined their self-image. Their definition of what constitutes a sense of community has become highly variable and is no longer tied to a particular place in time. Thus, ideologies on how a sense of community is experienced are subject to change. Herein is the irony of the community experience: it is a constant human need in all times and in all places, but how that need is fulfilled varies by different time and the types of places that different times create.

Social Change

Today, rural communities experience perhaps more diversity among themselves than with their metropolitan counterparts (Flora et al. 1992). Nevertheless, despite experiencing a number of dramatic social and economic changes, rural residents as a whole continue to show a creative resilience in sustaining their sense of community. One way they have retained their sense of community is through Tocquevillian community involvement. Probably in no other context are local voluntary organizations as visible and active as in rural America. At the entrance in any contemporary rural American town is a sign that lists the unique piece of Americana that town has played or plays (such as "The world's first all-steel bridge" or "Home of the first pony express") to identify it as an important place on the ideological map of America. The sign also may list the fraternal and voluntary organizations active in the town (such as Eastern Star, Lions, and Rotary International). Participation in these voluntary organizations within the community helps to give a strong sense of community to its residents. Because of the smaller physical and population size of rural communities, participation in key organizations often gives the feeling of being involved at the community versus the organizational level. Residents who fail to get involved with some of the organizations often experience less of a sense of community than those who do. Yet the opportunity for a large percentage of citizens to participate at a meaningful level in their community through voluntary organizations remains high in rural towns.

Rural areas, like their urban counterparts, have been incorporated into a mass consumer society (Brown 1993). Most daily consumption needs are purchased through individual interactions in the market. The old communal agricultural villages envisioned by the early social thinkers as harbingers of the community experience are past tense, with a few outstanding exceptions such as the Old Order Amish. But the sense of community has not been lost among rural residents as the number of rural residents directly involved in agriculture has declined. Nor has the local sense of community been lost as main streets steadily lose their business to larger regional centers. But what shapes that experience has changed. Where once rural community events may have included people going to a local movie on a Saturday night, today going to Wal-Mart in a larger town 20 miles away on any night may accomplish the same thing.

Rural residents who participate actively in the consumer-oriented economy are very satisfied with their communities regardless of their economic and demographic characteristics. Yet there is a difference between being satisfied with one's community and experiencing a sense of community there. In reality, rural Americans have no more claim on the ability to experience a positive sense of community than anyone else. However, they do have an American ethos that says they should have a positive sense of community, which may function to bring rural residents to a mutual starting point in interpreting their community experience. As rural people learn ideologically to redefine their experience of community and as their ethos becomes increasingly modern, they may find that they have the same starting point as those who reside in metropolitan contexts.

Hummon (1990) argued that people have different languages of community to interpret what is a positive or negative community experience. The attributes that rural residents believe to be positive expressions of community and that give them a sense of belonging are the same ones

that many urbanites see as stifling a sense of community. For example, a rural resident may interpret a neighbor's comment "We haven't seen you outside for a few days. Is everything okay?" as a caring gesture. But a metropolitan resident may interpret the same comment as overly intrusive. To the metropolitan resident, a sense of community may be experienced by sharing with others of the same ideological persuasion the freedom to be left alone.

Much of the ideology about rural residents experiencing a stronger sense of community than do others is simply not justified, nor is it supported by any empirical evidence. A sense of community is an experience, a sense of social being. It is an uniquely human condition. Such human conditions always have been hard to objectify. The sense of community among rural residents is only as strong as people feel it to be. Does living in a rural area give residents the advantage of experiencing a sense of community more strongly? Yes—if they believes it does!

—*Ralph B. Brown*

See also
Community; Community Celebrations; Culture; Development, Community and Economic; Quality of life; Town-Country Relations; Values of Residents.
References
Brown, Ralph B. "Rural Community Satisfaction and Attachment in Mass Consumer Society." *Rural Sociology* 58 (1993): 387–403.

Flora, Cornelia Butler, Jan L. Flora, Jacqueline D. Spears, Louis E. Swanson, with Mark B. Lapping, and Mark L. Weinberg. *Rural Communities: Legacy and Change.* Boulder, CO: Westview Press, 1992.

Hofstadter, Richard. *The Age of Reform.* New York: Vintage Books, 1955.

Hummon, David M. *Commonplaces: Community Ideology and Identity in American Culture.* Albany: State University of New York Press, 1990.

Tocqueville, Alexis de. *Democracy in America.* New York: Vintage Books, 1960.

Tönnies, Ferdinand. *Community and Society.* Translated by C. F. Loomis. New York: Harper Torchbook, 1957.

Community Celebrations

Stylized public performances that involve participants in dramatic and sometimes entertaining representations of significant social experiences. This entry reviews some of the major theoretical perspectives in sociology and anthropology on collective celebrations. It addresses the extent to which there are distinctively rural characteristics that provide a basis for festive events in contemporary American society. Finally, several issues that reflect the diversity of contemporary American rural community celebrations are discussed, including differences between ritual and play, contrasts between social integration and social conflict in celebratory expression, celebrations as supports of tradition or innovation in local life, and celebration's potential to generate resources that support local community development initiatives.

In the context of contemporary rural community settings, celebrations vary as social forms and are more intriguing for their contradictions than their consistencies. They are impressive in their rich variation—serious and solemn in one setting, riotous and playful in another. This elasticity makes them ideal vehicles for individuals and groups in the communities to confront the contradictory forces of tradition and change in their daily lives.

Theoretical Perspectives

Sociologists and anthropologists long have been drawn to the study of societal celebrations. Early writers drew on the framework of celebration and related issues of the sacred, religious belief, ritual practice, and solidarity in both supernatural and secular contexts. Their concerns centered on the sources of social integration and the critical experiences through which people find meaning in the social world to sustain their relationships and allegiances. Seeing society itself as sacred, sociologists such as Durkheim (1915) discovered an abundance of meaningful attachments in preliterate societies. He worried that shared beliefs and relationships were being crushed in the shift to industrial production.

Whereas the passage of time made it clear that societies would survive the transition to capitalism, researchers continue to search for linkages between the forms and functions of celebrations in nonwestern societies and the experiences of groups and communities in their own milieus. Turner (1969) developed insights on the social importance of a liminal period (or thresholds or new beginning periods of one's life) in life stage transition rituals, such as young peoples' initiation into adulthood (high school graduation and party). Participants were drawn away from the ordinary time and place of their communities to dwell in the symbolic world of the celebration. They were renewed by the fulfilling relationships of their societies and returned to their communities to restore the ongoing social world. Turner discovered these sources of social renewal in the rituals of American society as well. His concept of liminality explains the times of community festivity that participants set apart from ordinary life as important for sus-

A Texas dancer performs in 1981 in the first annual Borderfest, a celebration of local culture featuring music, food, and crafts.

taining individual commitment and reviving the social life of the community.

Geertz (1973) viewed celebrations as experiences that reflect societies' deepest meanings, woven together by and for members into direct expressions of cultural identity. American society gave up mourning for identities lost through social change gradually over the last two-thirds of the twentieth century; instead it discovers in rural and urban settings a wealth of festivals that express emerging identities of ethnic and regional groups in cultural performances rich in customary food, music, and dance.

The Current Rural Context

Before bringing these understandings of celebration into the context of contemporary rural places, one must ask in what sense there is a rural world to celebrate. The decline of farming as a dominant economic activity in many rural areas and the ongoing transition from relatively small family farms to larger, differently structured agricultural enterprises have altered the traditional expectations of rural life. No single rural economic pattern exists. Manufacturing predominates in some areas. Other local economies depend on natural resource exploitation, employment in locally based government institutions, or a mix of tourism and retiree resettlement. Other areas continue to be marked by persistent rural poverty. The majority combines these elements in a way of life that offers only a shadowy link to images of a more traditional rural past. With many rural counties located adjacent to metropolitan areas, patterns of commuting to work, shop, or attend city cultural events bring rural and urban residents into regular interaction.

In the midst of this complex picture of changing rural life, rural locales continue to exist and maintain distinctive identities that their residents experience and dramatize. Americans who live in urban and suburban settings recognize the unique distinctives in many rural communities that they sometimes want to share. Celebrations, as symbolic events, acquire an increased importance since they reflect persisting contrasts between images of rural and urban life that remain an important part of the American national myth. Thus, for rural residents and visitors alike, celebrations offer a variety of important expressive opportunities to define and defend the mix of tradition and change that reflects the current American rural context.

Multiple Characteristics

From the wide variety of celebrations in rural settings, several facets emerge about how celebrations are put together and what kinds of contributions are made to individual and community development. Some facets include (1) differences between ritual and play, (2) the emergence in the festive milieu of social integration and harmony in contrast to social conflict, (3) celebration's definition as a support of tradition or social innovation, and (4) the potential for celebrations to generate economically valuable community outcomes in contrast to less practical experiences of local social identity. Sharp differences may be difficult to observe within the complex experience of these festive events, but by considering opposites a better sense will be developed of the richness and plasticity of celebratory forms.

Ritual and Play. There are differences between ritual and play in societal celebrations. Rituals are practices designed to reflect belief in the basic principles of a social system. Whether in specialized religious experiences of communion or convocation or in the context of political celebrations (for example, speeches, anthems, or patriotic parades), participants engage in formal acts that express affiliation with the authority of the body politic. These rule-bound occasions contrast with the informal, excessive, or even chaotic dimension of more playful celebrations that set aside time from serious or routine pursuits. Playful occasions allow participants to challenge or deny the rules for a while, until they drift back to the greater social conformity of their everyday experience.

In rural settings, the Fourth of July and Memorial Day join participating residents in practices that affirm the values of citizenship and respect for local leaders who share in the authority of local government. Residents of all ages marching behind the nation's flag or gathering at ceremonies in small-town cemeteries to honor soldiers who died in war reflect a more serious ritual side of celebration.

More informal and unique celebrations of rural community identity, such as "old home weeks," fun days, or local fairs where queens are crowned in lavish ceremony, provide playful enactments of the underlying contradictions in local life. These festivities allow make-believe to triumph for a while as residents challenge their places in the community's social hierarchy or make claims about the vigor and independence of their local economies that are often too good to be true.

Social Integration and Social Conflict. A celebration's most valuable contribution may be to foster social integration. By joining in either playful or formal expressions of the local society's deepest social values, residents may be seen as united in support of the local social order. A contrasting perspective by Lukes (1975) argues that many celebrations are based on the steep inequalities of our society's stratification system, which reflects the interests of the privileged and are not likely to represent the true feelings of poor and marginal people. The lines of these divisions can be seen even in intentionally inclusive celebrations, such as a countywide picnic in rural Michigan (Aronoff 1993) where factors such as the cost of tickets for the event, access to transportation, and more deep-seated lifestyle differences screen out participation by the county's poorer residents. As rural county populations become more diverse in relation to race, ethnicity, class, and religion, it is likely that assumptions of celebrations' broadly integrative character will be harder to support.

Support of Tradition or Social Innovation. With the often idealized images of rural communities, the centrality of tradition in celebrations tends to be overstated. There is some evidence that rural residents distinguish themselves from urbanites as more committed to family values and community spirit. The mix of new economic and social adaptations to the pressures of a global economy and the increased presence of newcomers in local communities ensures that the traditional appearance of rural community celebrations is inevitably laced with strong doses of change. Celebration's powerful capacity to reflect what is most significant for residents, rather than what seems to be only literally true, suggests that questions of authenticity may be taken less seriously. Communities will depend on the wisdom of participants to synthesize tradition and change.

In addition to these expressive dimensions, however, celebrations also can play an important innovative role in their local contexts. In the Michigan county picnic just mentioned, for example, a locally invented celebration created a warm, stimulating framework for relationships to promote innovation. It allowed people to relax and overcome past community rivalries in the service of present-day needs. The celebration, initiated at a time of serious local economic crisis, created a context for experimentation with more cooperative, countywide economic development strategies to concentrate county resources and produce additional employment and economic opportunity for area residents.

Celebrations' contributions to community innovation also point to a range of utilitarian economic benefits for local economies, in addition to less practical expressions of local identity. In one midwestern community, for example, civic and business leaders recognized the potential benefit of their local fair and fought to save it from bankruptcy during a period of crisis (Flora and Flora 1991). The fair survived and became a model for other community-based entrepreneurial enterprises that use community resources to generate local benefits.

Community Development. In many other rural communities, fairs and festivals that celebrate rural life or the folkways of area ethnic groups are promoted locally to attract tourists and an inflow of currency into the local economy. At many of these events, both insiders and visitors find ways to enjoy the experience together, even if from somewhat different perspectives. Increasingly, however, the promotion of these events by outside interests, including representatives of government agencies seeking to promote tourism-based economies, may undermine local people's abilities to express the core of local relationships that define the community's special meaning for them.

—*Marilyn Aronoff*

See also
Community; Cultural Diversity; Culture; Development, Community and Economic; Games; Recreational Activities; Sport.
References
Aronoff, Marilyn. "Collective Celebration as a Vehicle for Local Economic Development: A Michigan Case." *Human Organization* 52, no. 4 (1993): 368–379.

Bender, Lloyd D., Bernal L. Green, Thomas F. Hady, John A. Kuehn, Marlys K. Nelson, Leon B. Perkinson, and Peggy J. Ross. "The Diverse Social and Economic Structure of Nonmetropolitan America." Rural Development Research Report No. 49. Washington, DC: U.S. Department of Agriculture, Economic Research Service, 1985.

Durkheim, Émile. *The Elementary Forms of the Religious Life*. Translated by J. W. Swain. London: Allen and Unwin, 1915.

Flora, Jan, and Cornelia Flora. "Local Economic Development Projects: Key Factors." *Rural Community Economic Development*. Edited by N. Walzer. New York: Praeger, 1991: pp. 141–156.

Frese, P. F., ed. *Celebrations of Identity: Multiple Voices in American Ritual Performance*. Westport, CT: Bergin and Garvey, 1993.

Geertz, Clifford. *The Interpretation of Cultures*. New York: Basic Books, 1973.

Humphrey, Theodore C., and Lin T. Humphrey, eds. *We Gather Together: Food and Festival in American Life*. Ann Arbor: University of Michigan Research Press, 1988.

Lukes, Steven. "Political Ritual and Social Integration." *Sociology* 9 (1975): 289–308.

Manning, F. E. "Cosmos and Chaos: Celebration in the Modern World." Pp. 3–30 in *Celebrating Society*. Edited by F. E. Manning. Bowling Green, OH: Bowling Green University Popular Press, 1983.

Turner, Victor W. *The Ritual Process: Structure and Anti-Structure*. London: Routledge and Kegan Paul, 1969.

Community Development

See Development, Community and Economic

Computers

Automatic electronic machines for performing word processing, designing, and complex calculations. Although most farmers still rely on traditional methods for receiving information, computers have gained tremendously in popularity with farmers and ranchers since the machine's introduction in the mid-1970s. Current applications include analysis of cash flow and production costs, enterprise analysis, tracking of the use of pesticides, information gathering, and communication via e-mail. This entry examines the history of computer use among agriculturalists and the rate at which computers have been adopted. AGNET, an agricultural computer network, is described. It notes the growing popularity of computers among agriculturalists, even though most farmers and ranchers rely on other, traditional information sources.

Exploring a Frontier

More than 150 years ago, farmers and ranchers helped explore a geographic frontier as they settled the Great West. Today's farmers, like their urban cousins, are experiencing an Information Age described by one observer as today's frontier—the only place, besides space exploration, where we are not faced by limits (Donnelly 1986). Computers and other electronic technologies have been driving this communication revolution.

In the beginning, personal computers were seen merely as playthings for hobbyists. But the home market began to take off in the mid-1970s thanks especially to Apple Computer. The co-founders of Apple, Steve Jobs and Steve Wozniak, realized that millions of people would purchase personal computers if appropriate software programs were available. Home computers were first used for (1) playing with computing (in the hobbyist sense), (2) playing video games, and (3) doing word processing. Microcomputers were soon adopted in schools and in offices.

Futurists and others predicted early on that every farm would have a computer to assist in record keeping, decision making, and communicating with others in rural and urban areas. Specific benefits cited by researchers and agricultural specialists include enhanced decision-making performance based on the computer's ability to analyze large amounts of information, improved farm management through computer accounting and bookkeeping applications, increased and more efficient operations through computer analysis and evaluation of various production options, and more thorough and efficient market analysis (Davis and King 1994). In addition, the computer has been an evolving innovation, becoming cheaper and more powerful since it became widely available to farmers and ranchers in the early 1980s. It is now more user friendly, has much more flexible and powerful software, and is capable of many more complex operations than were its earlier counterparts.

In light of these benefits, many predicted that farmers would readily adopt and use computer technology. However, recent studies indicate that computer/software adoption has been relatively modest. For example, Abbott and Yarbrough (1992) pointed out that the rate of adoption by farmers and ranchers has been linear and very slow, rising at between 1 and 2 percent per year to a total

of 15 percent by 1989. This slow rate of adoption occurred despite extensive media attention to microcomputers on the farm that peaked in 1984. If current rates of adoption continue, only about 35 percent of farmers will have a microcomputer by the year 2000. By 2005, more than one-half of current Iowa farmers will have reached retirement age, most without ever having adopted a computer.

Rate of Adoption

By 1992, the number of adopters of computers had risen to approximately 22 percent of farmers. A continuation of the adoption rate would put the number of adopters at approximately 28 percent by mid-1995. However, only 7 percent of farmers have a computer with a modem, an essential tool to send and receive electronic mail (Abbott 1995). As a group, farmers who have adopted computers are very different from other farmers. The following factors are consistently associated with greater adoption of computers: higher income, higher education, ages 35 to 44, use of sophisticated management practices, and greater leverage (more acres rented). Thus, computer adopters became an elite group, and the gap in ownership of a microcomputer between the "haves" and the "have-nots" has widened for both the general population and farmers. According to Abbott (1995), the gap will continue to grow as people from land-grant universities and others interested in communicating with farmers find themselves spending more and more time communicating with those who share their technologies (for example, e-mail and fax) and less with their intended audiences.

Abbott and Yarbrough (1993) maintained that the increasing gap in access to and use of computers is due to two major factors: scale of farming operation and skills farmers possess that enable them to envision what these technologies might do that could be useful to them. Although many farmers can improve decision making and management practices by use of a computer, the communication researchers predicted that larger farmers will benefit more from each hour they invest in learning how to use a computer for these purposes. The researchers' data suggested that farmers may need to approach the $200,000 annual farm sales level before they find computers to be truly advantageous to them.

Although adoption of computers by farmers and ranchers continues at a slow but steady pace, a large number of computer users are unfamiliar with any type of agricultural software or have never heard of such software applications. Davis and King (1994) pointed out that many farmers used general application software, such as

Lotus 1-2-3 or DBASE, instead of specifically tailored agricultural products. Initially, most farmers were satisfied with the single-purpose agricultural computer software that was available to them. However, farmers and ranchers became dissatisfied with the agricultural software programs as they saw and experienced the newly developed integrated and multitasking software.

AGNET: An Early Application

One of the earliest computer systems to communicate information to farmers and ranchers was AGNET, an agricultural computer network that began at the University of Nebraska in 1975. Initially, the system responded to growing requests from former students to use interactive computer models developed at the university to teach agricultural economics and agricultural engineering. The first nonuniversity user signed on in 1976. More followed, and by the mid-1980s AGNET had evolved into a totally self-supporting network where public and private sectors worked together to provide management models and time-sensitive information to decision makers. Over 3,000 clients in 27 states, Canada, and other foreign countries paid the entire costs of the network operation, including actual computer and communications resources used, staff salaries, program and system development and maintenance, publication of materials, and rent for office space. At the network's peak, AGNET offered more than 225 programs in three categories (problem solving, marketing information delivery, and conferencing through e-mail) and had six major land-grant universities participating as partners (Montana, North Dakota, South Dakota, Washington, and Wyoming, in addition to Nebraska). Partner status allowed states to modify existing programs and place new programs on the system. Farmers, ranchers, agribusinesses, and other users could access the programs through their County Extension office or on their own computer terminals. As commercial software applications became readily available, AGNET began to lose users and ceased operation in the late 1980s.

Today, farmers use computers for a wide variety of applications, including analyzing cash flow and production costs, comparing profitability of crop and livestock production enterprises, and tracking the efficiency of pesticides, fertilizers, and irrigation. As a communication device, computers are used for e-mailing messages to and from rural and urban residents around the world and tapping vast libraries of information on text-based "Gophers" and on the World Wide Web produced by the U.S. Department of Agriculture, land-grant universities, agribusiness companies, commodity exchanges, and even farm magazines such as *Successful Farming*.

The Popularity of Traditional Methods

Despite the adoption of computers by an increasing number of farmers and ranchers in rural America, most of the information they receive today still comes to them through the traditional methods they have used for many years. Most studies show that farm magazines and radio continue to rank as primary sources of information for most farmers and ranchers on a daily basis, ranking well ahead of computers and other new electronic delivery systems. Traditional farm magazines and other print media will most likely continue to be a major source of information for farmers and ranchers for many years to come. But some publications already are making their issues available to readers via computer, and the day may come when the print version of some publications, including perhaps this encyclopedia, will be only a memory. Instead, readers in both rural and urban America will turn on their computers and access the current issue, back issues, useful articles that never made it into print, and feedback on all of the above.

—Gary L. Vacin

See also
Policy, Telecommunications; Technology; Technology Transfer; Telecommunications.

References
Abbott, Eric A. "The New Technology Dilemma." *ACE* (Agricultural Communications in Education) (March 1995): 3.

Abbott, Eric A., and J. P. Yarbrough. "Inequalities in the Information Age: Farmers' Differential Adoption and Use of Four Information Technologies." *Agriculture and Human Values*, 9 (1992): 67–79.

———. "The Unequal Impacts of Microcomputer Adoption and Use on Farms." Paper presented at International Conference on Information Technology and People, ITAP '93, Moscow, Russia, May 24–28, 1993.

AGNET. *AGNET—The First Decade.* Lincoln: University of Nebraska, 1984.

Davis, Sid, and James King. "An Assessment of Microcomputer Software in the Farm Sector: Is It Meeting Users' Expectations?" *Journal of Agricultural and Food Information* 2, no. 2 (1994): 81–106.

Dillman, Don A. "The Social Impacts of Information Technologies in Rural North America." *Rural Sociology* 50, no. 1 (1985): 1–27.

Donnelly, William J. *The Confetti Generation.* New York: Holt, 1986.

Dutton, William H., Everett M. Rogers, and Suk-Ho Jun. "Diffusion and Social Impacts of Personal Computers." *Communication Research* 14, no. 2 (1987): 219–250.

Kramer, R. C. "The Future of Computers in American Agriculture." *AG Comp Bulletin* 2, no. 2 (1981): 42–52.

Vincent, Gary. "All Ahead Slow! Ag Computerization Steams On." *Successful Farming* 44 (March 1987): 18AR–18AS.

Conservation, Energy

The use of efficient energy practices in producing goods and services. Energy is a vital input to U.S. agriculture. This entry describes the fundamentals of energy use in U.S. agriculture, the costs and other factors that affect energy conservation in U.S. agriculture, and the characteristics of energy use in U.S. agriculture. The entry also describes the current situation and future expectations as well as policy aspects of energy conservation.

Fundamentals of Energy Use

American agriculture relies on nonrenewable sources of energy that are consumed both on the farm and off the farm to provide production inputs. Conservation of energy is a major concern and has been moderately successful. Agriculture can produce renewable energy that can be used on the farm, and energy eventually may become another significant category of agricultural products. Energy is a vital input for agricultural production systems in America, as it is in all industrialized countries. With current practices, farms import and use large amounts of nonrenewable energy in farming operations. The provision of agricultural transportation, the support of farm families, and on-farm processing of agricultural commodities consume additional large quantities of energy.

The nonrenewable forms of energy include the energy commodities derived from crude oil, natural gas, coal, and nuclear sources. Those energy commodities include gasoline, diesel fuel, liquefied petroleum gas, natural gas, electricity, fuel oil, and lubricants. A small portion of agricultural energy consumption currently consists of renewable energy commodities. Energy commodities derived from renewable energy sources include hydroelectric, photovoltaic, and wind-generated electricity; wood and other biomass; alcohol from biomass or wastes; and vegetable oils.

Agricultural production consumes energy both as direct energy in the form of energy commodities used on the farm and as indirect energy. Indirect energy is the energy expended off the farm that enables the provision of inputs used on the farm for agricultural production. This includes energy required for consumable inputs, such as fertilizers, pesticides, packaging materials, small tools, labor, and veterinary supplies. Indirect energy also includes energy used for capitalized inputs, such as machinery, buildings, irrigation systems, and land improvements. Indirect energy consumption for agricultural production in the United States is the hidden energy input that tends to be inadequately accounted for or overlooked. Indirect energy consumed for American agricultural production is about twice the direct energy consumed.

Besides the energy used for agricultural production, rural America also consumes energy for forestry, fisheries, and farm homes. Energy consumed in the home largely supports final consumption rather than agricultural production. But some of the energy consumed in the farm home supports agricultural production by enabling the farmer and farm family to work in agricultural production. That is labor energy input for agriculture.

Costs

Energy conservation varies in response to many factors. The costs of energy are an important, although not the largest, component of total costs of agricultural products. Energy costs increased sharply in 1973 and 1974 and again in 1979 and 1980 as a result of actions by the Organization of Petroleum Exporting Countries, a cartel of oil producers. These increased costs prompted many and diverse efforts to conserve energy in agricultural production. Public funds supported research to conserve energy and to develop renewable energy sources, educational programs disseminated information on conservation practices to farmers, and some conservation practices were adopted by farmers. Also, as American industry became more energy efficient, the energy required to provide some of the inputs to production agriculture was reduced. American agriculture became more energy efficient. Since the early 1980s, however, energy prices have generally moderated, so that inflation-adjusted prices of much agricultural energy today is about what it was before the energy crisis. As nonrenewable energy sources are consumed, energy costs will probably rise again, leading to a renewed emphasis on rural energy conservation. Finally, other costs of energy are the environmental effects of energy consumption, including increased global warming and carbon emissions.

Energy, both that used directly on farms and that used indirectly to supply agricultural inputs, is critical for our industrialized agricultural system to function. Historically, until the energy crisis energy had been cheap and was used liberally. Our agricultural system evolved based on the historic relative costs of numerous inputs, including energy. The infrastructure supporting agriculture developed similarly. It would be very costly and difficult to replace or extensively modify that infrastructure and the capital investments in farm equipment, buildings, and irrigation systems.

The different characteristics of each energy commodity greatly influence the use of energy. Energy density, the quantity of energy per unit volume or weight, is a characteristic favoring gasoline, for example, over wood. Some forms of energy are easier to store than others. For example, it is easier to store diesel fuel in tanks than electricity in batteries. Costs of energy commodities vary; electricity is more costly per unit of energy than diesel fuel. The cost of energy is an important determinant of the costs of agricultural commodities, as energy costs must be included in the total cost of the commodity in order for its production to be profitable and continued. As costs of energy increase, those agricultural commodities requiring more energy will become more expensive, less competitive in the marketplace, and ultimately less available to consumers.

Modes of Usage

The modes of energy use in agricultural production are many. Direct uses include powering engines in mobile field equipment (tractors, combines, and other self-propelled farm equipment) and in farm vehicles, stationary engines using diesel or natural gas to power irrigation pumps, and farmstead equipment. Other direct uses are for electric motors to power farmstead equipment and irrigation pumps and combustion of fuels or electrical resistance heating for crop drying and heating of farm structures. Mobile field equipment uses mostly liquid, high energy density fuels. Indirect energy uses include energy to provide fertilizers, pesticides, and other expendable supplies, capital expenditures, and human labor. The total amount of primary energy, which includes all direct and indirect energy, that is used to support production agriculture is only about 2 or 3 percent of all energy consumed in the United States, or about two quads (quadrillion British thermal units [Btus]). Several patterns characterize agricultural energy use in the United States. Different regions produce different commodities and therefore use different amounts of energy; for example, fruits and vegetables are more energy intensive than field crops. During the year, more energy is consumed at planting and harvesting times than otherwise. Energy must be available in adequate quantities at the times needed for such critical seasonal operations. Available technology influences energy requirements; as technology changes, energy consumption may decrease as improvements are adopted by farmers.

A unique aspect of energy and agriculture is that agriculture is essentially the only industry (other than the energy industry) that can produce energy. Agriculture can produce renewable energy by converting sunlight to carbohydrates through photosynthesis. Several issues exist regarding agriculturally processed energy. One is the relationship between the quantity of energy produced and the quantity of energy required to produce it. The ratio of energy produced to energy consumed must be greater than unity for an energy production system to be viable. A second issue is whether the energy is used on the farm or sold. A third is any wastes and pollution resulting from agricultural energy production. A fourth is that the cost to produce renewable energy must be competitive with the cost of nonrenewable energy. A fifth is the effects of production of renewable energy on the prices of other agricultural commodities. And a sixth is the possible effects of renewable energy production on the sustainability of agricultural systems.

Sources of energy produced within agriculture include wood (consumed in direct combustion or gasification), other biomass, peat, bagasse, and crop residues. Additional sources include wind for electric power or mechanical energy and water pumping, solar thermal (used for grain drying, livestock housing, greenhouses, and water heating), underground tubes for thermal heat exchange, photovoltaic (generation of electricity when light shines on a substance), vegetable oils, ethanol from carbohydrates and celluloses, methane from animal and food-processing wastes, and heat pumps. A few of these are now competitive with the petroleum industry, and more may be in the future.

Current Situation and Future Expectations

The energy situation is dynamic. The focus on energy since the energy crisis of 1973–1974 has shifted from availability of energy supplies, to the cost of energy, to the efficiency of energy use. In the years since the energy crisis, industry has become more efficient in producing many goods and services, including agricultural inputs. Many agricultural inputs now require less energy to manufacture, thereby conserving energy. New technology is continually being developed, some of which conserves energy. Finally, as nonrenewable energy sources are depleted in the future and energy prices increase, there will be a shift from non-renewable to renewable energy.

Energy conservation in rural America has many aspects. The main factor governing what energy conservation practices are adopted by farmers is the practices' economic viability. To be accepted, an energy conservation practice also must save money. A second important factor is how efficiently energy is used in agriculture. The efficiency with which energy is utilized is best measured by energy productivity. Energy productivity is the quotient of the quantity of a specific agricultural product produced and the energy required to produce it. A third factor is that energy and other inputs are partially substitutable for others such as land, labor, and capital. Generally, as the quantity of any one input is increased, the law of diminishing returns results in the productivity of that input decreasing. As the quantity of energy is increased, its productivity decreases and the productivity of other inputs increases.

Effective energy conservation on the farm involves evaluation of many possible energy conservation practices in the context of a specific farm, selection of the best viable practices, and their implementation. Among proved practices to conserve energy is limited tillage, also known as conservation or minimum tillage. Fewer trips are made over the field, reducing liquid fuel consumption. Although herbicide use often is increased, a net reduction of energy inputs usually occurs. Another proved energy conservation practice is reduced inputs of fertilizers by better use of soil testing, following of agricultural consultants and manufacturers' recommendations, and avoidance of overfertilization. Integrated Pest Management generally reduces use of pesticides and may save energy. A continuing shift to more efficient diesel engines in tractors and other equipment has reduced their fuel consumption. Better management of tractors by proper selection of gears and throttle settings and optimum ballast and wheel slip also have conserved energy. Recycling of plant nutrients from livestock operations to replace chemical fertilizers often results in a net saving of energy. Modifications that replace transportation and less than optimum management with information technology can reduce energy consumption. Agricultural utilization of waste low-grade heat from electric power plants and other sources can replace thermal energy fuel to heat greenhouses. Perhaps the most positive prospect for future energy savings is precision farming, based on the use of global positioning systems and geographic information systems. Precision farming is the application of crop inputs in optimum quantities that vary spatially in the field depending on specific parameters determined for different locations. For example, soil type, fertility, and moisture content can be used in conjunction with past yields to determine the optimum levels of application of fertilizers, pesticides, and irrigation.

The idea of energy self-sufficiency, in which a farm would produce all its energy requirements through renewable energy sources and not rely on off-farm sources of energy, has been advocated. But energy self-sufficiency appears to have no more validity than self-sufficiency in any other input, say capital or information. Modern economies have instead developed based on the fact that different entrepreneurs have different advantages and resources and therefore also have advantages in producing selected goods and services. Therefore, various firms and countries are interdependent rather than independent.

Policy

Policy can influence agricultural energy conservation practices by farmers. Energy conservation policy can range from educational programs, to incentives, to subsidies, to allocations, to controls. The Energy Extension Service disseminates information to farmers and agribusinesses to promote effective energy conservation. Funding of agricultural energy research was substantial during the 1970s and early 1980s but has currently moderated. Tax laws can serve as incentive to promote purchase of new equipment that uses less energy by offering investment credits or discourage management practices that promote fuel conservation by decreasing fuel taxes to farmers. All controls, incentives, and subsidies that affect the production levels of agricultural commodities also affect energy consumption since energy consumption varies with commodity. Fuel allocations and price controls would probably be used to cope with more severe energy situations. Current energy policy seems to comprise a moderate educational effort, assurance of energy supplies, and freedom for prices to seek their own levels.

—Richard C. Fluck

See also

Electrification; Environmental Protection; Petroleum Industry; Policy, Environmental.

References

Bhat, Mahadev G., Burton C. English, Anthony F. Turhollow, and Herzon O. Nyangito. *Energy in Synthetic Fertilizers and Pesticides: Revisited.* Oak Ridge, TN: Oak Ridge National Laboratory, 1994.

Federal Energy Administration. *Energy and U.S. Agriculture: 1974 Data Base.* Washington, DC: Superintendent of Documents, 1976.

Fluck, Richard C., ed. *Energy in Farm Production.* Vol. 6 of *Energy in World Agriculture.* Amsterdam: Elsevier, 1992.

Helsel, Zane R., ed. *Energy in Plant Nutrition and Pest Control.* Vol. 2 of *Energy in World Agriculture.* Amsterdam: Elsevier, 1987.

McFate, Kenneth L., ed. *Electrical Energy in Agriculture.* Vol. 3 of *Energy in World Agriculture.* Amsterdam: Elsevier, 1989.

Parker, Blaine F., ed. *Solar Energy in Agriculture*. Vol. 4 of *Energy in World Agriculture*. Amsterdam: Elsevier, 1991.

Peart, Robert M., and R. C. Brook, eds. *Analysis of Agricultural Energy Systems*. Vol. 5 of *Energy in World Agriculture*. Amsterdam: Elsevier, 1992.

Pimentel, David. *Handbook of Energy Utilization in Agriculture*. Boca Raton, FL: CRC Press, 1980.

Rawitscher, Mary, and Jean Mayer. "Nutritional Outputs and Energy Inputs in Seafoods." *Science* 198 (1977): 261–264.

Smil, Vaclav, Paul Nachman, and Thomas V. Long II. *Energy Analysis and Agriculture*. Boulder, CO: Westview Press, 1983.

U.S. Department of Agriculture. *Cutting Energy Costs: The 1980 Yearbook of Agriculture*. Washington, DC: Superintendent of Documents, 1980.

Conservation, Soil

Protection, enhancement, management, and wise use of soil resources to prevent their loss through erosion or degradation. This entry addresses soil erosion as a socioenvironmental issue. It highlights contemporary soil conservation programs and policies and their implications. Alternative soil conservation strategies are discussed, as is the Conservation Title of the 1985 Food Securities Act. Soil conservation initiatives are suggested for future implementation.

Erosion as a Socioenvironmental Issue

Although soil erosion was a serious problem in most agricultural regions of the United States prior to the twentieth century, the environmental costs associated with soil loss were ignored. Three of the most important reasons that soil erosion was permitted to exist at such high rates during this time period were free land in the sparsely settled western frontier, lack of awareness of environmental problems and possible solutions among landowner-operators, and prevailing land tenure laws and attitudes of the general population toward private ownership of land resources.

One of the most significant factors affecting rates of soil loss prior to the closing of the frontier was availability of free land. Many land operators were not concerned about soil erosion because degraded cropland could be abandoned and new farmsteads developed from forests and plains. There were few incentives for land operators to conserve soil resources because fertile land was available at very low prices. The labor required to implement soil conservation programs on highly erodible farmland was considered to be too costly compared with the alternative of abandoning degraded cropland and establishing a new farm on easily accessible frontier land.

A second factor that contributed to soil erosion was lack of awareness of erosion problems and ignorance of technical solutions. Most farmers were not aware of the environmental consequences associated with soil erosion and did not possess the technical expertise required to implement effective erosion control programs. The situation was compounded by the fact that most citizens of the United States were not concerned about environmental quality or about protecting land resources for future generations.

A third factor affecting soil loss on agricultural land was the commitment to protect individual property rights. Society ceded to landowners almost absolute rights to land resources. Although some local jurisdictions prohibited specific types of land uses, national laws gave property owners broad legal rights to use land resources in almost any manner they wished. The only universal constraint on the use of land was nuisance laws that prevented landowners from engaging in actions that would damage other landowners.

Soil and water resources degradation continued unabated for decades under these conditions. However, concern for soil erosion and environmental degradation began to develop during the Great Depression of the late 1920s and early 1930s. Widespread economic deprivation resulted in the emergence of increased government intervention in the economic institutions of society. One of the first government programs to influence future soil conservation programs was the Civilian Conservation Corps (CCC). The CCC was a work relief program, primarily for the unemployed, authorized by the National Industrial Recovery Act of 1933. Program participants implemented conservation control projects within national forests and national parks. Although improvement in environmental quality was a secondary objective to reduction of unemployment, CCC projects generated many environmental benefits and focused public attention on the need to preserve soil and water resources.

Public concern for soil erosion reached its highest level in the United States when the dust storms of the early 1930s billowed across Midwest farmsteads and darkened the skies of urban communities. The environmental consequences of the Dust Bowl changed citizens' attitudes about soil erosion and environmental protection. Residents recognized that abuse of land resources could result in significant reduction in the fertility of farmland and that future food and fiber production could be substantially reduced by inappropriate use of land resources.

The South Dakota Badlands.

Americans were forced to acknowledge that the socioeconomic well-being of the country was dependent on the productive capacities of agricultural land and that it was in the nation's security interests to protect soil resources. The concern for preserving land resources was translated into political action, and Congress authorized the formation of the Soil Conservation Service (SCS) in 1935 via the Soil Conservation Act. The SCS assumed the role of providing technical assistance and financial support to landowners on a voluntary participation basis to encourage adoption of soil conservation production systems at the farm level. SCS program activities traditionally were governed by soil conservation districts, composed primarily of local land operators. This type of social organization gave landowner operators a significant role in the development and implementation of SCS programs at the local community level.

Conservation programs implemented by the SCS were accepted quickly by landowner-operators because most farmers recognized that soil erosion was destroying the future productive capacities of cropland. Landowner-

operators recognized the value of SCS assistance because most farmers did not have the economic resources to adopt conservation practices and technologies, and they did not possess adequate technical skills to implement effective conservation programs.

The initial successes of voluntary methods for implementing soil conservation programs resulted in their widespread use by government conservation agencies for decades. Voluntary SCS programs were supported by farmers because they received many benefits and internalized few costs. After several years of participation in these conservation programs, landowner-operators began to believe that the government was primarily responsibility for abating soil erosion and agricultural pollution.

Few people questioned how soil erosion control programs were implemented. By the mid-1930s, dust storms no longer threatened the topsoil of Midwest farms, water quality in lakes and rivers improved as a result of reduced soil displacement from agricultural land, and future production of food and fiber appeared to be relatively secure from the threat of soil erosion. The subsidy-information dissemination approach used by conservation agencies appeared successful and worthy of financial support. Yet soil erosion continued at rates that society defined as environmentally unacceptable.

Environmentalists questioned why soil erosion remained high even though millions of dollars and thousands of work years were being allocated to address the issue annually. Taxpayers expressed concern about agricultural assistance programs that had been partially justified on the basis of soil conservation benefits. Of particular concern were land diversion programs that authorized cropland to be retired from production. Critics of soil conservation initiatives suggested that programs such as the Agricultural Conservation Program and the Soil Bank Program were not useful for protecting land from soil erosion in the long term. The primary concern expressed by critics of land diversion programs prior to the mid-1980s was the inability of the government to ensure that conservation benefits were maintained once contracts with landowners were completed.

Prior to the Conservation Title of the Food Security Act of 1985, landowners were permitted to reintroduce highly erosive production systems on cropland enrolled in conservation diversion programs without constraint when rental agreements were completed. Critics argued that farmers should be required to operate highly erodible land using conservation production systems once diversion contracts were terminated. The counterargument offered by proponents of voluntary diversion programs was that cropland was rented by the government to control supplies of agricultural commodities rather than protect soil resources. Since land was diverted for supply control purposes, it was argued that government rent payments were not appropriated for the purpose of conservation. Thus, landowner decisions to return cropland to production using erosive practices were not a violation of the intent of land diversion programs.

Concern also was expressed about public investment in on-farm conservation projects designed to reduce soil erosion. Landowner-operators often secured financial subsidies and technical assistance from government agencies to implement soil conservation control programs. However, landowners retained the right to remove conservation structures. Many erosion control structures developed on privately owned land using public subsidies were removed by landowners when these structures were unable to accommodate larger farm technologies introduced at later dates.

Contemporary Programs and Policies

The environmental movement of the 1970s ushered in a new era of environmental awareness and precipitated critical examination of existing soil conservation programs and policies. Conservationists organized themselves into action groups and began to influence public opinion. Environmentalists suggested that government programs implemented in the 1930s no longer were appropriate to address soil erosion problems on agricultural land. Conservation groups suggested that public funds should be allocated for soil conservation research and studies were initiated to assess the nature of soil erosion and the utility of existing conservation programs. Findings derived from these studies significantly redirected soil conservation policies.

Research conducted during the 1970s and 1980s demonstrated that approximately 6 billion tons of topsoil were being eroded from land each year and that a majority of the soil loss was from cultivated cropland (Lovejoy and Napier 1986). Examination of the economics of soil erosion revealed that most of the costs of soil erosion were in the form of off-site damages. Some of the most frequently cited off-site damages were sedimentation of streams, rivers, and lakes; loss of wildlife habitat; loss of recreation use of water resources; costs of purifying contaminated drinking water; disruption of river transportation and shipping; and reduced aesthetic value of water resources. Research revealed that on-site damages were relatively inconsequential. It was also observed that about 90 percent of water-induced soil erosion was confined to about 10 percent of cropland and that highly erodible cropland was widely distributed throughout the United States.

Research revealed that future production of food and fiber was not threatened by erosion in the United States. Projections of grain production losses in the Cornbelt due to soil erosion using 1977 soil displacement rates demonstrated that corn and soybean production probably would decline between 2 and 8 percent over 50 years. It was suggested that production declines of such magnitude would be of relatively little consequence over multiple decades. It should be noted that the magnitude of production losses may be much lower than those projected because erosion rates have declined significantly in recent years. Another reason the projections may be inflated is that they were made without knowledge of the impact on production of improved agricultural technologies.

Other research findings demonstrated that technology transfer programs using the information dissemination approach were basically ineffective. Lack of soil erosion awareness and knowledge of potential solutions were not barriers to adoption of soil conservation practices at the farm level. Farmers were shown to be knowledgeable of soil erosion on their land and aware of the techniques and technologies available to resolve erosion problems (Lovejoy and Napier 1986; Napier 1990a, b; Napier, Camboni, and El-Swaify 1994).

Profitability of soil conservation became an important research topic, and assessments of returns to investments in soil conservation practices were conducted in many geographical regions. Study findings revealed that many soil conservation practices were not profitable in the short term and often not profitable in the long term (Mueller, Klemme, and Daniel 1985; Putnam and Alt 1988). Research findings demonstrated that land operators perceived farming to be a business and that farmers were motivated by profits (Halcrow, Heady, and Cotner 1982; Napier et al. 1994).

Profitability studies strongly suggested that farmers were not adopting soil conservation practices needed to reduce soil erosion to levels desired by society because such practices would not improve the economic viability of the farm enterprise and would not increase net farm income. Adoption decisions relative to conservation practices were shown to be made using the same criteria employed in all farm-level adoption decisions. If a proposed change in production practices was perceived not to be profitable, it would not be incorporated into existing farm production systems. Such findings strongly suggested that landowner-operators did not respond favorably to appeals to change farming practices unless they were adequately compensated for disruptions of farm operations.

Many people assumed that lack of adoption of soil conservation practices at the farm level was a function of attitudes held by farmers about land resources and agricultural pollution. It was argued that farmers would have to possess positive attitudes and perceptions about environmental problems and about stewardship of land resources before they would adopt conservation practices. Research demonstrated that attitudes toward soil conservation were not barriers to adoption of conservation practices at the farm level. Survey findings indicated that farmers held very positive orientations toward protection of land resources and perceived themselves to be stewards of the land, even though they often used production practices that contributed to degradation of soil and water resources (Lovejoy and Napier 1986; Napier 1990a, b; Napier et al. 1994).

Policy and Program Implications

Research conducted during the 1970s and 1980s validated general observations that soil loss from agricultural sources remained quite high after five decades of soil conservation efforts. These findings were used to justify continued public support of soil conservation programs. However, several of the findings from research conducted during this time period suggested that a number of implementation strategies employed by conservation agencies prior to the mid-1980s were inappropriate. The validity of using on-site damages as the primary argument to persuade landowner-operators to adopt soil conservation production systems was challenged. Voluntary conservation programs traditionally had been marketed using protection of future productive capacities of cropland as the primary motivation for farmers to adopt. Study findings indicated that future productivity of cropland was not threatened by erosion. Landowner-operators did not respond to this type of appeal because they were aware that agricultural productivity of their cropland was not being adversely affected by soil erosion.

Soil conservationists often argued that adoption of soil conservation practices would increase profits at the farm level. Landowner-operators were encouraged to adopt conservation practices because such practices were profitable at least in the long term. This intervention strategy was dealt a death blow when it was discovered that many soil conservation practices were not profitable.

Since the 1930s, practically all technology transfer programs designed to facilitate adoption of soil conservation systems have relied heavily on information dissemination to make landowner-operators aware of environmental issues and to create positive attitudes toward the environment. Such strategies were based on the following assumptions: (1) landowner-operators do not adopt conservation production systems because they are ignorant of soil erosion problems and possible solutions, (2) landowner-operators do not possess favorable attitudes toward soil conservation, (3) landowner-operators do not perceive themselves as being stewards of land resources, and (4) structural barriers do not impede adoption of soil conservation systems.

Although information dissemination programs may facilitate adoption of soil conservation programs when these four assumptions are satisfied, research conducted in the 1970s and 1980s revealed that none of the assumptions appeared to be generalizable. Farmers are generally well educated and aware of causes and effects of soil erosion. Agriculturalists are aware of many technological solutions to soil erosion problems and are aware that soil erosion damages cropland. Most landowner-operators support environmental protection programs and perceive themselves as stewards of the land. Programs designed to increase positive attitudes toward soil conservation will have little effect in terms of changing production practices at the farm level because most farmers already have developed favorable attitudes toward environmental protection. The assumption that institutional barriers do not prevent farmers from adopting soil conservation practices is not valid since many farmers do not have access to capital needed to invest in conservation programs. Also, some conservation practices are not appropriate for certain types of farm operations.

Since the assumptions providing the underpinnings of soil conservation programs implemented during the 1930s have been shown to be no longer valid, it should not be surprising that intervention programs using these approaches have not motivated land operators to adopt conservation practices. Conservation programs implemented using a number of these assumptions may have been relevant in the 1930s, but evidence produced in the 1970s and early 1980s challenged past conservation initiatives and provided direction for future soil conservation programs and policies.

Evolution of Alternative Strategies

Dissatisfaction with traditional soil conservation programs and implementation procedures increased, and agitation for change emerged in many sectors of society. Political action by conservation interests resulted in a significant modification of conservation policy included in the Food Security Act of 1985 (FSA 1985). The Conservation Title of the FSA 1985 significantly redirected soil conservation programs. In fact, it may have been the most innovative soil conservation legislation since the authorization of the SCS in 1935.

The most significant change in soil conservation policy contained in the Conservation Title of 1985 was modification of land tenure rights. For the first time, rights of landowner-operators were constrained significantly by the federal government. Landowners no longer possessed the right to cultivate highly erodible land without an approved conservation farm plan. Landowners lost the right to drain wetlands and to cultivate land that had not been previously farmed without approval by federal agencies. The Conservation Title of 1985 introduced the Conservation Reserve Program (CRP), which authorized the federal government to rent highly erodible cropland for a ten-year period. Landowners could enroll highly erodible cropland in the program for yearly payments that were determined on the basis of a bidding system. The federal government established upper bounds of rent prices, and landowners were permitted to submit bids to enroll eligible cropland. The CRP targeted highly erodible land for diversion from crop production and established constraints on the amount of rent a landowner could receive.

The targeting of limited public resources for use on highly erodible cropland was a significant improvement over previous conservation initiatives. Conservation programs developed prior to 1985 made funding for conservation purposes available on a competitive basis to all landowners. Property owners could submit requests for financial support for conservation purposes regardless of the severity of erosion problems. As a result, a large proportion of conservation funding was allocated to conservation efforts on land with relatively insignificant erosion problems.

Another innovation of the CRP was the emphasis placed on conservation relative to other policy objectives. Although the CRP was designed to achieve multiple policy goals (such as commodity supply control, stabilization of commodity prices, and conservation of soil resources), it placed much greater emphasis on conservation. This became one of the most important considerations relative to the reauthorization of the Conservation Title in the 1990 farm bill.

Although a significant portion of highly erodible cropland in the United States is very productive, commodity supply control and price support elements of the CRP would have been substantially enhanced had the criteria used to determine eligibility for inclusion in the program been defined differently. If commodity supply control and price support objectives had been emphasized in the development of the CRP, cropland in the humid Cornbelt would have been targeted for withdrawal from production with significantly fewer acres in the arid west.

Cross-compliance was another innovation included in the CRP. Landowner-operators who violated CRP agreements were subject to penalties. Landowners also were constrained by other components of the Conservation Title from returning highly erodible cropland enrolled in CRP to crop production without use of an approved farm plan. These elements of the Conservation Title were consistent with research findings that demonstrated landowners often wasted public investments in conservation by returning land enrolled in diversion programs to production using highly erosive farming systems.

Environmental Outcomes of the Conservation Title of 1985

The social, economic, and environmental outcomes of the Conservation Title of the FSA 1985 were mixed. Along with many benefits associated with the CRP were several adverse socioeconomic and environmental outcomes. Considerable soil savings were achieved via the CRP but at a very high economic cost. The CRP costs U.S. taxpayers about $2 billion per year in direct payments to landowners, and the administration costs of the program are unknown but are undoubtedly quite high. The socioeconomic costs of retiring large tracts of cropland in rural farming communities were very high. Many rural farming areas in the High Plains suffered significant decline in economic activity as a result of land enrolled in the CRP. Land operators purchased fewer agricultural inputs, and the withdrawal of cropland from production in high enrollment areas negatively affected local land operators who depended on rented land because the price of available rental land was often bid upward (Napier 1990b).

Procedures used to implement the CRP reduced the environmental benefits that could have been achieved with the same level of funding. The CRP was implemented to minimize economic costs rather than maximize environmental benefits. It was designed to maximize soil savings rather than maximize improvement in water quality. Had the goal of the CRP been to maximize improvement in water quality, much of the land in the High Plains would have not been enrolled in the program. CRP benefits would have been distributed more evenly had protection of water quality been emphasized.

Experiences with the Conservation Titles of 1985 and 1990 resulted in the redirection of conservation initiatives designed to address soil and water conservation problems. In the late 1980s, soil erosion began to receive much less attention as an environmental issue in the context of land degradation. However, it received much greater attention in the context of water quality. Future soil conservation programs probably will be focused much more intently on water quality concerns, and the nature of future conservation programs will be significantly affected by this change in emphasis.

Future Initiatives

Realization that it is very difficult to motivate landowner-operators to invest in soil conservation efforts designed to benefit downstream publics has resulted in recent reassessment of conservation policies, programs, and implementation strategies. Increasing attention now is being focused on alternative methods to motivate farmers to adopt soil conservation practices. At least two options have been identified: use of regulations and penalties to force landowner-operators to adopt and privatization of soil and water conservation efforts to make it profitable for landowner-operators to adopt. One or both of these options probably will complement the voluntary approaches presently emphasized.

Regulatory approaches to the reduction of soil erosion are relatively easy to implement, even though they are not popular with landowners. Environmental standards could be established for agriculture, and farmers could be forced to comply. Penalties could be implemented to make it too costly for landowners to violate environmental expectations. Investments in soil conservation production systems would become less costly than penalties assessed for contributing to environmental degradation. Even though monitoring compliance would be expensive, it would be much less costly than the $2 billion per year required to rent highly erodible land enrolled in the CRP. Fines for violation of environmental regulations could be used partially to defer the costs of monitoring compliance.

Regulations to control access to agricultural nutrients also could affect environmental quality. Establishment of nutrient quotas would reduce pounds of fertilizer available for application to cropland. Reduced levels of fertilizers released into the environment would result in lower levels of nutrients that could reach waterways. This assumes that land operators would continue to apply nutrients proportionately to cultivated cropland and would not concentrate available fertilizers on land adjacent to waterways.

There are other regulations that could be established to influence the type of farm production systems adopted at the farm level. Quotas could be established that permit farmers to market a specified amount of food and fiber per year. Such marketing systems could reduce pressure to maximize output and make it possible for land operators to employ production systems that are less erosive. Such a system probably would reduce output but could stabilize commodity prices that would affect farm income in the long term.

It is likely that a number of regulatory approaches will be examined by policy makers in the near term. If federal courts determine that government conservation programs can legally modify property rights to protect environmental quality, it is almost certain that future conservation programs will include regulatory elements.

A second group of policy options that could affect soil erosion programs in the future involves the creation of private conservation markets (Napier 1994). Such approaches would be more acceptable to landowner-operators because they would receive money for selling specific rights to land resources. A market system could be developed for landowners to sell row cropping rights to farmland that contributes to environmental degradation in specific watersheds. Since a very small percentage of cropland contributes the greatest percentage of waterborne erosion, very little land would have to be permanently retired from production to achieve many national environmental goals. Landowners could retain all other rights to land resources under this type of conservation approach.

Wetlands have been shown to be very useful for trapping sediments and nutrients eroded from cultivated farmland. However, most wetlands have been eliminated during the past 200 years. Swamp buster provisions of the Conservation Title prohibit further reduction of wetlands by taking the right to modify wetlands from landowners. This regulatory approach has proved problematic for many landowners who have legitimate reasons to drain existing wetlands. The creation of a private wetland market system could result in positive outcomes for all affected publics. Markets for constructed wetlands could be established that would permit developers and landowners who wish to drain wetlands the opportunity to do so, assuming that they construct comparable wetlands at another site. This type of market system could result in landowners making a large amount of money on a per acre basis by selling the right to build a wetland to developers. Developers could save millions of dollars via such a trading system with the removal of legal barriers to construction. Society would benefit because environmental quality would be maintained (Napier, McCarter, and McCarter 1995).

Soil conservation programs and policies are in the process of radical change in the United States. It is not a question of whether change will occur but rather what the nature of the change will be. Given recent history, regulatory approaches most probably will be more extensively employed in the future unless landowner-operators assume greater responsibility for reducing the incidence of environmental degradation associated with soil erosion. Another option is the creation of private market mechanisms for addressing soil erosion problems and subsequent degradation of water quality. The latter option is much more desirable from the perspective of social acceptability; however, it will demand much greater creativity on the part of interested publics. Regardless of the implementation strategy chosen by society, landowner-operators will be expected to assume a much greater proportion of the costs of controlling environmental degradation produced by soil erosion in the future.

—*Ted L. Napier*

See also
Agricultural Programs; Agriculture, Alternative; Agronomy; Cropping Systems; Environmental Protection; Land Stewardship; Policy, Environmental; Soil; Theology of the Land; Tillage.
References
Halcrow, Harold G., Earl O. Heady, and Melvin L. Cotner, eds. *Soil Conservation Policies, Institutions, and Incentives.* Ankeny, IA: Soil Conservation Society Press, 1982.
Lovejoy, Stephen B., and Ted L. Napier, eds. *Conserving Soil: Insights from Socioeconomic Research.* Ankeny, IA: Soil Conservation Society Press, 1986.
Mueller, D. H., R. M. Klemme, and T. C. Daniel. "Short- and Long-Term Cost Comparisons of Conventional and Conservation Tillage Systems in Corn Production." *Journal of Soil and Water Conservation* 40 (1985): 466–470.
Napier, Ted L. "The Evolution of U.S. Soil Conservation Policy: From Voluntary Adoption to Coercion." Pp. 627–644 in *Soil Erosion on Agricultural Lands.* Edited by J. Boardman, D. L. Foster, and J. A. Dearing. London: John Wiley and Sons, 1990a.
———. "Potential for Public-Private Partnership in Ecosystem Management." Pp. 243–249 in *Ecosystem Management: Status and Potential.* Washington, DC: U.S. Government Printing Office, 1994.
———, ed. *Implementing the Conservation Title of the Food Security Act of 1985.* Ankeny, IA: Soil Conservation Society Press, 1990b.
Napier, Ted L., Sam E. McCarter, and Julia R. McCarter. "Attitudes of Land Owner-Operators toward Participation in a Wetlands Trading Market." *Journal of Soil and Water Conservation* 50 (1995): 502–510.
Napier, Ted L., Silvana M. Camboni, and Samir A. El-Swaify. *Adopting Conservation on the Farm: An International Perspective on the Socioeconomics of Soil and Water Conservation.* Ankeny, IA: Soil and Water Conservation Society Press, 1994.
Putnam, John, and Klaus Alt. "Erosion Control: How Does It Change Farm Income?" *Journal of Soil and Water Conservation* 42 (1988): 265–267.

Conservation, Water

The elimination of wasteful and unnecessary use of water and the effective control of existing water supplies. This entry covers the availability and distribution of water resources in the United States, the role of water in agriculture, methods for improving irrigation water efficiency, practices for managing water in the soil, and institutions for promoting water conservation.

Demand for Resources

Water is essential for all biological systems. Adequate supplies of water for agriculture, industry, and personal consumption are necessary to support the high living standards enjoyed in the United States. The successful management of water resources in U.S. agriculture, the largest consumer of water, has been instrumental in the development of the most productive agricultural production system in the world. However, expanding water demands for urban and environmental needs, higher water costs for available supplies, and limited opportunities for supply enhancement are increasing the pressures on water currently being used in agriculture. How to manage water resources is an important decision for farmers, especially in the arid western states. Farmers who grow crops in potentially water-scarce areas can employ a number of water conservation methods that allow agriculture to be successful over the long term. Governments actively support water conservation through laws and through financial support.

Availability and Distribution

The continental United States receives an average of 30 inches of precipitation per year, or about 4.2 trillion gallons per day. More than one-half rapidly evaporates back into the atmosphere and is unavailable for use. Most of the remaining precipitation becomes part of the surface water system. Rivers and streams carry about 1.3 trillion gallons of water per day. About 100 billion gallons per day infiltrate to underground aquifers. No estimate exists of the total amount of water contained in underground aquifers. However, it is estimated that the portion suitable for irrigating crops that can be tapped with conventional wells and methods totals 9,860 million acre-feet of water. By comparison, large rivers, lakes, and reservoirs (excluding the Great Lakes) contain about 38 million acre-feet under normal conditions.

Despite seemingly abundant supplies, the nation's water resources and supply needs are not distributed evenly. Water shortages of various intensity and duration occur in many parts of the nation, particularly in the arid West. According to the U.S. Geological Survey (1984), the availability of surface water or groundwater in adequate quantity and quality is a concern in most states. Estimates suggest great differences in the ratio of water consumed to available water between the eastern and western United States. In the East, the amounts of water consumed are a small fraction of available water. The total depletion in the West is much greater. It is estimated that

by 2030 water supplies will not be sufficient to meet nonagricultural needs and permit continued irrigation of the existing irrigated acreage if current trends in water demand continue in the Texas-Gulf, Rio Grande, Lower Colorado, and Great Basin river systems (U.S. Department of Agriculture [USDA] 1989).

Groundwater often is seen as an alternative to limited surface water supplies. However, groundwater availability is becoming a concern in 47 states. Intensive pumping has caused water-level declines in 35 states. Although a drawn-down aquifer still may contain adequate supplies of water, the cost of water pumping increases. Major areas of groundwater decline are concentrated in the irrigation-dependent Southwest and southern Plains, including California, Arizona, New Mexico, Texas, and Oklahoma. Groundwater declines also have occurred in Arkansas, Georgia, and Florida.

Water and Agriculture

Precipitation is sufficiently abundant in most areas east of the Mississippi not to be a factor in decisions about which field and forage crops are grown. Farther west, lack of precipitation limits the types of crops that might be grown under dryland (nonirrigated) conditions. In areas where rainfall is inadequate for dryland methods, irrigation is required to grow crops. Major river systems used as a surface water supply of irrigated agriculture include the Columbia, Sacramento, San Joaquin, Colorado, Missouri, Arkansas, Red, and Rio Grande Rivers. Groundwater is a major source of irrigation water in the Plains states and in California. Irrigation also is used in the East to supplement natural rainfall in order to increase the number of plantings per year and crop yields and as a hedge against local droughts during the growing season. The goal of water conservation is to reduce water availability problems through careful planning, management, and application of water conservation practices. Improved management of irrigation water and improved management of soil moisture can bring supply and demand into better balance throughout the growing season, increasing yields and lowering costs.

Irrigation Water Management

Irrigation (water that is withdrawn from the system and not returned to the immediate water environment) accounts for about 81 percent of the total consumptive use of water in the United States (USDA 1994b). Conservation in irrigation becomes an important source of water for downstream users, particularly in the West. An

The sloop Clearwater, *built to champion clean water, sails down the Hudson River past a scrap metal junkyard on its way to Washington, D.C., for the 1970 Earth Day celebrations.*

important means of conserving water is to increase irrigation efficiency. Irrigation efficiency is the percentage of water pumped from groundwater or diverted from surface water that actually is used by the crop. Losses include evaporation, spills, and phreatophytic (wells or deep-rooted plants that obtain water directly from the water table or soil layers immediately above it) consumption. Conservation practices can increase efficiency in delivering water from the diversion point to the farm, in conveying water from the farm headgate or farm irrigation well to the field, and in applying water to the field.

Farmers can increase the off-farm conveyance portion of irrigation efficiency by lining canals to prevent infiltration, converting from open ditches to piping, and clearing noneconomic phreatophytic vegetation. Coordinating the amount and timing of water deliveries with on-farm irrigation needs can increase overall irrigation efficiency. On-farm distribution efficiency can be enhanced by the use of water measurement devices and by the construction of ditches of appropriate length and the proper maintenance of them. Application efficiency is enhanced by selection of the appropriate application technology for given soils, slope, and crops. A more efficient irrigation technology reduces noneconomic water losses to infiltration and evaporation by applying water to the crop when it is needed and in controlled amounts. Sprinkler and drip technologies are more efficient than gravity flow systems in most cases and climates and are the greatest facilitators of irrigation water management because of the ability to control application and timing. The efficiency of gravity systems can be enhanced through various measures. Laser leveling fields can increase greatly the efficiency of flood irrigation. Gated pipe with surge flow is an important innovation in many areas to reduce excess percolation. Shorter furrows can reduce water losses. The use of tailwater pits to capture irrigation runoff at the end of the field allows water to be reused, increasing the application efficiency of all irrigation systems.

Metering and scheduling of improvements can increase overall irrigation efficiency. Soil moisture monitors allow water to be applied only when the plant needs it, as opposed to applying water on a fixed schedule. Flexible water deliveries to the farmgate by water suppliers enhances the producer's ability to implement irrigation water management measures. Overall irrigation efficiency has been increasing in the United States. A national average of 47 percent irrigation efficiency was achieved in 1985, up from 41 percent in 1981 (USDA 1989). New technologies can achieve up to 90 percent efficiency.

Another aspect of irrigation water demand management is to reduce overall crop water requirements. This can be accomplished through reduction of the acreage of irrigated cropland or through selection of crop types that are either drought tolerant or require less water. In some areas, application of water below yield-maximizing levels reduces overall demand for water and is still profitable.

Soil Water Management

Managing the quantity of water available to the plant is another component of water conservation. This entails the use of cultural and mechanical practices to enhance the water-holding capacity of soil and to increase the amount of water that reaches the root zone. These practices are applicable to both irrigated and dryland agriculture. Farmers can make more water available for crops by increasing water infiltration and soil moisture-holding capacity.

A number of water conservation practices are being used to improve soil moisture conditions. Furrow dikes trap precipitation within the rows, reducing runoff and increasing infiltration. Chiseling and subsoiling increase water infiltration and improve the plant-soil-moisture-air relationship. Reduced tillage practices improve the soil's water-holding capacity and increase infiltration in water-deficient areas. Contour farming, strip cropping, and terraces reduce runoff and increase infiltration. Field windbreaks reduce wind velocity over the field, reducing evaporation and increasing snow spreading over the field. Planting grasses or legumes in rotation with field crops increases infiltration, snow entrapment, and soil water-holding capacity. Mulching the field decreases evaporation losses. Pest management practices increase available water for crops by reducing weed competition. Nutrient management improves the efficiency of plant moisture utilization by ensuring healthy plants.

Government Initiatives

Water conservation is widely accepted as good public policy. Overall, there is significant legal authority for federal promotion of water conservation and a substantial level of federal support for water conservation programs. However, there is no unified approach across the federal government. The lack of a single mechanism to consolidate and coordinate programs may limit the effectiveness and efficiency of federal efforts to address water conservation issues.

Several statutes are central to the federal government's efforts to encourage and guide broad water conservation efforts in agriculture. One example is the Food, Agriculture, Conservation, and Trade Act of 1990. This act includes a number of programs to induce farmers and landowners to participate in soil and water conservation programs. Conservation easements, cost sharing, and other financial incentives are used to promote farming practices that conserve soil and water resources. In addition, the act includes measures to provide education and technical assistance for implementing water conservation and irrigation improvement practices.

A second example is the Reclamation Projects Authorization and Adjustment Act of 1992. This act encompasses a number of acts that together are expected to have a broad impact in the western United States. The act promotes adoption of improved water management through adoption of best management practices. Practices are to be technically and economically reasonable and not environmentally or socially unacceptable. A wide range of conservation activities are promoted, including development of water management plans, adjustments in the pricing of publicly supplied irrigation water, and adoption of water conserving practices and technology.

A third example is the Reclamation Reform Act of 1982. This act provides that the secretary of the interior shall encourage the full consideration and incorporation of prudent and responsible water conservation measures in the operations of nonfederal recipients of irrigation water from federal reclamation projects, where such measures are shown to be economically feasible.

USDA programs that assist voluntary installation and adoption of water conservation practices are the Agricultural Conservation Program, Great Plains Conservation Program, Small Watershed Program, Water Quality Incentive Program, and Colorado River Salinity Control Program. These programs provide financial assistance to producers for voluntarily implementing water conservation practices. Practices supported include windbreaks, conservation or protective cover, irrigation technology improvements, and subsoiling. In 1993, the Agricultural Conservation Program provided over $22 million for water conservation practices (USDA 1994a). Irrigation system efficiency increased from 48 to 64 percent for systems receiving assistance, conserving a total of 559,000 acre-feet of water.

One of the most powerful incentives for water conservation is irrigation water pricing. Publicly supplied irrigation water historically has been heavily subsidized to promote development. However, artificially low prices do not provide incentives to adopt more efficient practices. When the price of irrigation water is allowed to reflect demand and supply conditions, an optimal level of conservation is achieved. The higher prices associated with market pricing would reduce the demand for irrigation water and increase overall irrigation efficiency by reducing irrigation on marginal crops and promoting water-saving technologies and practices. The Reclamation Projects Authorization and Adjustment Act of 1992 requires price increases for water supplied by the Bureau of Reclamation to the Central Valley Project, the single largest bureau project in terms of acres served. However, significant institutional barriers, including diversity of state water laws and water management institutions and various institutional and administrative impediments to water market development, must be overcome before widespread pricing changes occur. As demand for high quality water increases, a greater emphasis will be placed on water conservation in agriculture in all parts of the country. The future success of U.S. agriculture depends on how well we manage our water resources.

—Marc O. Ribaudo

See also
Environmental Protection; Groundwater; Hydrology; Irrigation; Policy, Environmental; Water Use; Wetlands.

References
Jensen, Marvin E., and John D. Bredehoeft. "New Efficiencies in Water Use Vital for Nation." Pp. 18–27 in *Using Our Natural Resources: 1983 Yearbook of Agriculture*. Edited by Jack Hayes. Washington, DC: U.S. Department of Agriculture, 1983.
Martin, Guy R., Traci J. Stegemann, and Karen Donovan. *Water Conservation: The Federal Role*. Washington, DC: American Water Works Association, 1994.
U.S. Department of Agriculture. *Agricultural Conservation Program: 1993 Fiscal Year Statistical Summary*. Washington, DC: U.S. Department of Agriculture, Agricultural Stabilization and Conservation Service, 1994a.
———. *Agricultural Resources and Environmental Indicators*. Agricultural Handbook No. 705. Washington, DC: U.S. Department of Agriculture, Economic Research Service, 1994b.
———. *Field Office Technical Guide: Conservation Practices Phys-ical Effects*. Washington, DC: U.S. Department of Agriculture, Soil Conservation Service, 1992, sec. V A-1.
———. *1980 Appraisal Part I: Soil, Water, and Related Resources in the United States: Status, Condition, and Trends*. Washington, DC: U.S. Department of Agriculture, 1981.
———. *The Second RCA Appraisal: Soil, Water, and Related Resources on Nonfederal Land in the United States*. USDA Miscellaneous Publication No. 1482. Washington, DC: U.S. Department of Agriculture, 1989.
U.S. Geologic Survey. *National Water Summary 1983: Hydrologic Events and Issues*. USGS Water-Supply Paper No. 2250. Washington, DC: U.S. Government Printing Office, 1984.

Consumer-Goods Advertising

An image-driven tool to build brand-name identity, differentiation, and equity. Advertisements attempt to link product values with cultural values and thus generate a value-added component knows as sign value. This entry examines how national advertising campaigns use rural imagery and the meanings conveyed by such images. It concludes with concerns about advertisers' use of rural imagery in competitive advertising campaigns or "sign wars."

Rural Imagery in National Campaigns

What kinds of contemporary television advertisements come to mind when one thinks about images of farming? National consumer-goods television advertising is quite different from advertising in local markets, where farm images tend to be encoded as more mundane and less romanticized, especially if the product being advertised is used in the actual production process (e.g., feed, seed, or pesticides). In the 1980s and 1990s, the most familiar campaigns on behalf of agricultural producers included the glitzy generic campaigns for milk ("It does a body good"), pork ("The other white meat"), eggs ("The incredible edible egg"), beef ("Real food for real people"), and cotton ("Genuine cotton").

Like other campaigns for agricultural producers of basic commodities such as soybeans and potatoes, these campaigns feature virtually no farm imagery. Instead, they are devoted to constructing images of idealized consumers engaged in vital, healthy lifestyle relations. Since many of these campaigns are aimed at allaying fears of health risks associated with foods such as red meats and eggs, it makes sense that the focus would be on the consumer rather than the producer. Rural imagery crops up on consumer-goods advertisements that target demographic clusters likely to purchase products such as chewing tobacco, fishing lures, or automobile parts; but rural connotations also make their way into advertisements for cellular phones, cars, and cable television that seek to signify their symbolic opposite. Truck advertisements, however, are probably the most prone to use rural imagery, although they seem to prefer allusions to superindividuated, rugged, and nature-dominating ranchers over representations of farmers.

In the early 1980s, Goldman and Dickens (1983) examined farm imagery in consumer-goods advertising and concluded that agricultural and small-town imagery was constructed to justify a distinctively nonrural lifestyle, marked by ideologies characterized by leisure and private family and occupational spheres of life (Habermas 1970). Ironically, the same advertisements that stressed the past virtues of rural life also claimed to make these relations available once again via the consumption of the appropriate brand-name commodities. Advertising taps into a way of life that depicts relationships that are less formal, community-centered, less utilitarian, and signify honesty, trust, and goodness. Qualities of permanence, tradition, and interdependence are thus translated into meanings of authenticity and honesty. Drawing these connotations from a mythified past, advertisements routinely construct a visual nostalgia for a noncommodified and nonurban world. More than anything else, images of rurality in advertising connote the relative absence of impersonal market forces.

Meaning of Rural Imagery

The scene of golden wheat fields and giant harvesting machines is by now a stock image of prosperity and abundance. Although this scene represents the Heartland, it also has come to refer just as much to prior television representations as it does to any actual place or region. It has become commonplace for prominent images such as the glowing wheat fields or the lone cowboy to be recycled from previous media images. Hence, the meaning of the wheat field can just as easily be plugged into a commercial for beer, fast food, or a presidential candidate. The wheat field is a floating symbol of plenty that has been thoroughly divorced from any actual practice of farming. Similarly, although not uniquely a rural image, the sleepy, small-town barbershop of decades past (e.g., the television mythology of "Mayberry") has made its way into a range of consumer advertisements as a way of signifying a kinder, gentler place.

Another stock image that is still routinely invoked is the solitary farmer riding his tractor. This scene rarely has anything to do with farming whatsoever, but rather

has become a device used in cellular phone advertisements to indicate that the use of high-speed technologies is not antagonistic to an organic life lived outdoors and in nature. The individual farmer on his tractor not only works against the imagery of corporate farming; it also offers a reassuring symbol in the face of new technologies that threaten to eclipse both space and time. This is perhaps the most important point that can be made about the use of agrarian imagery in 1990s advertisements—it refers not to farming but to fears that consumers may have about corporate franchises and technologies that may leave us living in a world of "non-places," as Augé (1995) referred to the spaces of highways, franchises, airports, and supermarkets. Speed, as another French author, Virilio (1982), reminded us, has become the absolutely essential characteristic of all new computer technologies that are said to boost productivity and competitive efficiency in the emergent global economy. The phenomena of speed, instantaneity, and immediacy privileges places emphasis on time more than space, and with this comes a "loss of orientation." Nowhere is the accelerated circulation of meaning more evident than in advertising itself, as images turn over more and more quickly. But speed has thus far proved to be a socially and culturally destabilizing force. In this context, the imagery of farming offers a simplistic symbolic remedy to the accelerated transformation of social life.

Another usage with a similar purpose to the latter depicts the farmer and his wife as comic figures to dispel anxieties about the advent of the computer age. As computers become commodities marketed to consumers, this imagery has become predictable in advertisements such as those for Gateway computers, featuring a rustic Ma and Pa roadside stand from a previous era. Comically, we discover that they no longer can compete with Gateway prices. To carry out the theme, Gateway packaged its product in boxes that simulate the look of a Holstein cowhide. But the comic positioning of farmers goes beyond high tech. Playing on long-standing associations of farmers with taciturn dispositions, consumer-goods advertising for products such as Campbell's soup play out variations on the otherwise undemonstrative farmer erupting in staccato displays of desire for the processed food he consumes. In recent years, the comic figure of the farmer has turned toward postmodern representations in MTV-style advertising for products such as those of Pioneer electronics, with their depiction of images that blur and confuse. Given the flat, emotionless expressions of Grant Woods's "American Gothic" characters, it is not surprising to see the figure of the farmer modified and introduced as a postmodern set piece. Once again, in these ads the farmer is present not as a producer but as a consumer.

Rural imagery has been used to signify new beginnings, as in the well-known Saturn campaign featuring Spring Hill, Tennessee. These advertisements construct imagery of unpolluted nature, while observing the slow-moving and personal character of small-town life. This is consistent with themes observed in an earlier era of television advertising (Goldman and Dickens 1983). By dwelling on scenes of a green, pristine countryside at sunrise, along with horses and fences, Saturn attempts to situate itself as a new kind of industrial company in harmony with both nature and community. The amplified down-home character of Spring Hill signifies Saturn's own commitment to the solid social virtues of an earlier epoch. Public relations and community intersect when Saturn organizes a Saturn-owner reunion in Spring Hill. The advertisement opens with cars trekking in a line down a country road. Amid the craft fair imagery and barbecue lines, Saturn assembles images of a new kind of community of Saturn consumers joined with Saturn workers in Spring Hill. The name itself is perfectly chosen to suggest place, loaded as it is with bucolic imagery. The same style of small town representation was also prominent in the early 1990s in advertisements for Telecommunications Incorporated that focused on the ways in which cable television served to realize the Jeffersonian ideal of small-town democracy invigorated by well-informed citizens (Goldman and Papson 1996).

In a similar vein, the wave of nostalgia advertising that suffused the airwaves in recent years resurrected sleepy, soft-focus images of a rural heaven composed of big front porches and grandmas and grandpas, steering viewers to remember how good that lemonade tasted when it was fresh squeezed. It is not just old-timey products that advertise this way, but also artificial products that seek to wrap themselves in the values of moms, kitchens, and freshly made products. The country kitchen functions as the setting for a Country Crock Spread that relies on gauzy soft-focus techniques to simulate fraudulent memories of a time that may never have taken place for a product that is not made on a farm. In advertisements like those for a major automobile parts maker, nostalgia for rural relationships lends credence to the premise that the sponsor is part of stable and enduring relationships and ways of life. In a world that seems to be flying out of control, where instability of place and job has

come to define the character of our times, narratives of this sort convey a commitment to the stability of human relationships.

Rural Imagery and Sign Wars

Advertisers reduced rural life to something that can be used to mean a wide range of things—from nostalgia to authenticity. The ungrounded character of rural images becomes especially apparent when they become pawns in competing advertising strategies. In this sense, rural images become fodder for what Goldman and Papson (1996) called "sign wars"—battles between competitors that revolve around the images they associate with their parity products. This was exemplified in the early 1990s in an advertising contest between Ford and Chevy trucks centered around the name, and the citizens, of rural Ford County, Illinois.

There continues to be a relationship between the arrangement of rural images and the rapidity of technological and social change. Not surprisingly, advertisers have turned images of farm life and the countryside into nostalgia markers aimed at lessening a deepening sense of insecurity about a world where cultural values seem to be fractured and the conditions of stable, rewarding employment seem ever-more fleeting. Images of rurality still summon a vision of a world freed from the chains and straitjackets of commodified activities and relationships. More than ever, no matter how falsified, agrarian images are made to appeal to our anticommodity desires. As global capitalism turns more and more to communication technologies designed to conquer space and time, the imagery of farm life is no longer necessarily set against that of urban capitalist space; rather, this imagery acts as a proxy for the friendly corporate taming of technology in the context of still-a-place.

—Robert Goldman

See also
Consumerism; Marketing; Retail Industry; Signs.

References
Augé, Marc. *Non-places: Introduction to an Anthropology of Supermodernity.* London: Verso, 1995.
Goldman, Robert, and D. Dickens. "The Selling of Rural America." *Rural Sociology* 48, no. 4 (1983): 585–606.
Goldman, Robert, and S. Papson. *Sign Wars: The Cluttered Landscape of Advertising.* New York: Guilford Press, 1996.
Habermas, Jurgen. *Toward a Rational Society.* Boston: Beacon Press, 1970.
Virilio, Paul. *Speed and Politics.* New York: Semiotext(e), 1982.

Consumerism

A cultural pattern of people using purchased goods to satisfy wants and to mark social status, personal worth, and group identity. In a society that increasingly defines self-worth by the consumer goods owned, rural Americans—whose average consumption levels are lower than the urban Americans who figure so prominently in our national images of "the good life"—face some difficult dilemmas. Farm families are particularly challenged because the agrarian ethic of frugality and savings can be important in farm survival, but it also conflicts directly with status-oriented consumption aspirations. This entry explores personal definitions of success, alternatives to and disadvantages of consumerism, and variations in consumerism by generation, gender, region, and ethnic group.

Definitions of Personal Success

Because many rural families were highly self-sufficient in past generations, the contrast with today's consumption patterns seems sharper in many rural areas than in the city. However, most of the issues faced by rural dwellers are different only in degree, not in kind, from the struggles with consumption that urbanites face. The local community interacts with the national consumption norms, as seen on television and in movies, and can create its own series of expectations and values that for some areas bolsters an alternative to mainstream American consumerism. Anthropologists have argued that consumer tastes are constructed in the context of a larger political economy, and that to understand a particular local situation, issues of history, personal and family utility, social stratification, and political resistance are all important.

Since World War II, rising standards of living throughout the country have led to a shift in values and personal definitions of success. Spreading out from the industrial Northeast, a national middle-class ethic measures personal progress "on an ascending scale of expense: first, clothing and cosmetics required by the community for the mate hunt, then a car, a house, its appropriate furnishing and accouterments, then college for the kids, and finally surplus cash. At each step, ownership of property reveals a successful personality to oneself and others" (Baritz 1989, 106). This urban, middle-class definition of success conflicts with an agrarian definition of self-worth that historically emphasized property in land, personal achievement, self-improvement, respectability, hard work, and discipline (McNall and McNall 1983). Local groups develop a specific lifestyle that defines the fashion of the time and the success of the family or individual in meeting the approval of the group. Living the appropriate lifestyle establishes a claim to a particular social rank and determines future employment and marriage opportunities. As most Americans, rural and urban, have become more affluent in the post–World War II era, lifestyle has come increasingly to define personal success.

The urban and suburban consumption standards desired by many rural residents include houses with a comfortable amount of space and amenities such as carpet, appliances, and recreational equipment or vehicles. In some areas, certain types of cars and trucks mark social status, whereas in other communities families long for a vacation cabin, a fancy boat, or expensive vacations. For some regions, it is common for rural families to eat regularly in restaurants and shop in urban malls, but for other rural families these are longed-for luxuries. For still other families, such luxuries are considered inappropriate and spendthrift. In an interview conducted by the author, one Georgia woman said, "I've never been one to want, want, want" (Barlett 1993, 123). Such a person takes pride in frugally managing money, shopping for bargains, sewing clothes, canning food, and finding other ways of avoiding expenses so that family income can be used for other purposes. Although many farm families grow and preserve important components of their diets, the level of their purchases of food and clothing from stores is now very similar to that of nonfarm families.

Historical analysis of the emergence of a consumer culture in urban France, Germany, England, and China reveals that such an emphasis emerges when economies are expanding, when stratification becomes more fluid, and when gaps between social groups narrow. Merchandise becomes a means of personal and social self-definition. Such an emphasis on consumer products is found widely in rural societies today, and the spread of a consumer ethic into developing countries creates rural demands for goods and services that are very difficult for local economies to support.

Alternatives to Consumerism

The consumer ethic has spread widely throughout rural America, but it is not without challenge from alternative values. As illustrated by Jane Smiley's novel *A Thousand Acres,* the size of farm owned is important in many rural regions. In this ethic of property ownership, the size and sophistication of the operation can take precedence over the consumer goods or lifestyle of the farm family. Other farming traditions emphasize the farmer's craft and skill in producing food and fiber of high quality. Personal success comes from being the top butterfat producer in a county or having the highest soybean yield. Recently, some farmers have embraced alternative ways of farming and have taken pride in reducing chemical use and finding more sustainable methods of producing food. Such farmers may consciously choose to work their land less intensively and accept a somewhat lower income and less affluent lifestyle in order to accomplish a different goal of building a new farming tradition that is less harmful to the environment.

Another aspect of resistance to consumerism comes from families that value the nurturance and love that go into homemade food, clothing, entertainment, and decor. In an interview with the author, one Georgia farm woman said, "When I make a breakfast of grits and biscuits and sausage and my family leaves the table full, I feel proud. I have a sense of pride serving my family, but that's gone from America. Women today take the kids to McDonald's instead. Or buy a cupcake from the grocery. Not that that's a bad cupcake, but you can't have the same pride" (Barlett 1993, 162). Those families that hold to an anticonsumerist ethic teach their children that there are annual rhythms of saving during which treats are curtailed. Unlike their peers who can buy treats at school each day, these farm children come to accept that their family chooses to go without certain luxuries in order to invest in the farm. They learn to value family truck rides in the evening after supper "to look at the cows" rather than movies in town or fancy vacations. Their parents may chafe at the split upholstery in the living room or the rusty old car in the driveway, but their primary commitment is not to household consumption, but to farm continuity and business success.

As urban standards of decoration of the home have penetrated into rural areas, a number of much-welcome conveniences have made lives easier, especially for farm women. But consumerism also can displace some traditions in decor or household space. For example, some rural families have built predesigned homes similar to suburban houses available in many areas of the United States. These homes ignore the rural tradition of the big kitchen, in which cooking, farm planning, community networking, emotional support, and child care go on simultaneously. Fashion in home decor can lead to the devaluation of ethnic decorations or family heirlooms, a subtle component of disrespect for the diversity of our American heritage. Consumer standards also are affected by university extension services, which often promote a more homogeneous culture and may encourage purchased products over homemade ones. Home demonstration agents in the postwar South urged the consumption of new foods such as cottage cheese and peanut butter, while ignoring the calcium available in traditional greens, the protein available in field peas, and the cheaper sources of balanced nutrition in rice and beans. Some older farmers blame television for exposing children to new wants. One small-scale farmer said that for him, success is "doing what one does well," but his children measure success by having a "house and a car and a boat" (Barlett 1993, 137). School peers are another influence toward consumerism, as rural children keep up with urban children in designer jeans or sports shoes.

Disadvantages of Consumerism

For farm families, consumerism affects farm survival in difficult economic times. In ordinary years, expenses for a lavish lifestyle or such expenses as vehicles for children may be sustained by farm income, depending on the scale of farm. But in crisis years when losses are high, frugal families with a larger cushion of savings have an advantage. They may be able to cover losses more easily and still have sufficient cash flow to continue operation without renewed borrowing. Families that prefer a more modest lifestyle, and thereby avoid farm expansion and the use of hired hands, find that in crisis times their overhead is lower and they can get by with, as they would put it, a "tighter belt." Several studies have found that families that had tried to "keep up with the Joneses . . . to prove that one is 'making it'" (Bennett 1982, 419) were later at a disadvantage in the slump of the 1980s.

Similar disadvantages of consumerism can affect nonfarm families as well. When jobs are unstable, families benefit from a cushion of savings. Although they also benefit from the ability to keep up with an expected lifestyle and to take their place socially with a particular desired group, if that status is vulnerable to sudden changes in income, a more modest lifestyle can be better sustained until work is found again. Consumerism that is based on credit is particularly disadvantageous in hard times.

The emphasis on consumption as a marker of self-worth is lamented by some researchers who argue that it obscures the real sources of economic power and production by focusing on objects (Gartman 1986). Consumerism can be seen as part of the capitalist political economy in which worker exploitation and discontent are masked by a societal focus on lifestyle. But the increasing consumerism of rural America reflects as well the emergence of more fluid stratification and a somewhat more democratic order, especially when compared to the early eras of land barons, bonanza farms, and sharecropping. Although rural history varies greatly by region, in many parts of the United States there existed a period of sharp rural stratification in wealth in which consumption standards were very low for a significant portion of the population. Today's emphasis on consumerism reflects a softening of the rigidity of those boundaries and aspirations among a broader range of families that they might participate in a middle-class standard of living. At the same time, since the 1980s some rural areas have seen the rise of a new impoverished population; of course, other areas, such as the Lower Rio Grande Valley of Texas or areas of industrial agriculture in California, have continued to be home to extremely poor groups of landless agricultural workers, as well as more consumption-oriented property owners.

Generational and Gender Differences

Consumerism varies importantly by age and generation in many areas of the country. As one Georgia farm woman reported, "Young folks nowadays want a higher standard of living; they won't take it slow" (Barlett 1993, 135). Several middle-aged farmers remarked that their children were unwilling to begin married life at a lower standard of living than they had enjoyed in their parents' homes. The parents may have married and lived in a small apartment, but their children want to own a home, plus a television, VCR, washer, and dryer. Other young families are comfortable with sacrifices in standard of living in order to build up equity in the farm.

Education also affects consumer desires, often by comparison with the lifestyles provided by urban jobs. College-educated farmers may continue to maintain friendships with peers in business or professions and can sometimes struggle with a sense of "not making it" because their daily lives are not as affluent. Other farmers and rural residents, however, are clear that their consumption standards are lower, but they prefer the tradeoffs in high net worth or a more comfortable rural lifestyle. Critical to many rural families are the noneconomic rewards of a safe place to rear children, the opportunity to engage in work they enjoy, closeness to nature, connections with extended family and a family church, and the opportunity to "be my own boss" and operate a sophisticated business. These important values are rarely

extolled in the media and can lead rural families to feel their values are disdained by the larger mainstream culture. Some admit to feeling isolated and beleaguered. Particularly in situations in which children no longer plan to remain in farming, consumption standards can affect marital options and lifetime social ranking through their impact on the family's social status. In one Georgia case, a family that had struggled to make a living on a small farm, aided by part-time work off the farm, went into debt to buy new living room furniture when the teenage children began dating. The parents wanted to provide an attractive room "for courting," and this desire was not a vain gesture because it could have a major impact on their children's futures to be perceived by peers as "poor" rather than "comfortable."

Gender conflicts can occur regarding consumerism. Among farm families, the more common practice today for farm men to marry nonfarm women can bring into the farm decision making someone not familiar with the agrarian rhythms of savings and investment. Marital stress can result when women do not accept that the purchase of a sofa can be delayed but a combine cannot. Farm men also can feel the tension between being cash poor but land rich. In Wisconsin, operators of larger farms were more dissatisfied with their ability to provide an acceptable standard of living for their families (Wilkening and Gilbert 1987). In a Canadian study, Bennett (1982) emphasized the different needs of the farm and the household and noted that the ability of farm managers to balance such conflicting demands was an important part of farm family success.

Regional and Ethnic Differences

Region can play a part in variances in rural consumption patterns. Most obviously, diet, dress, and desired household items vary by locale. There is little desire for a snowmobile in rural Texas and more desire for a satellite dish in areas of poor television reception. In addition to these geographical differences, the overall attitude toward consumerism can vary. Bennett's (1982, 418–419) Canadian study reported that farmers took pride in living simply, regardless of their income. He found this anticonsumerist ethic "a kind of reverse snobbery." In the U.S. South, where sharecropping and harsh poverty were the norm for the majority of rural residents in the decades before the New Deal, families today struggle to overcome the association of rural life with poverty. Farmers in particular feel that their occupation is seen as a poor way to make a living and that they are expected to "live in a shack, have one pair of overalls and a broken down pickup truck" (Barlett 1993, 91), in the words of one Georgia farmer. A farm child who wears heavy work shoes to school may be embarrassed by the glances of his peers. Such a cultural context makes wearing the right shoes or having an attractive brick home an especially important status marker.

Ethnic differences, even in the same region, can affect consumerism. Salamon (1992) demonstrated that Illinois farmers of German origin often placed a primary value on family farm continuity. Standard of living and status competition over consumer items played a smaller role in the allocation of household resources. German families emphasized a frugal lifestyle, so that capital could be invested in the expansion of the enterprise, in hopes that children would be able to continue in farming. In contrast, families of British Isles origins often valued upward mobility and career success for their children more than farm continuity. Such goals also may have prescribed a period of frugality while children were educated toward good jobs off the farm. But a farmer also was judged by his willingness to take risks, borrow, and expand and not so much by his success in recruiting an heir to the farm. The more cosmopolitan orientation of some British Isles–origin farmers was reflected in different attitudes toward household consumption as well.

In conclusion, though the pressures of the consumer society on rural regions present conflicts and stresses, consumerism also adds a new degree of richness to the lives of rural families. Especially as cars and trucks allow isolated residents to engage in more social, religious, political, and civic activities, rural families can participate in the wider American culture in a more comprehensive way. Older farm families may have disdained the luxury of an annual vacation, citing the needs of crops and livestock, but those families that now do have an opportunity to see other regions—or even, other countries—bring a useful, new awareness back to the rural area. A family with a VCR has potential access to a range of experiences through videos and movies that can open a world of new ideas, experiences, and understandings. An opportunity to wear different kinds of clothes, hear different kinds of music, and eat different kinds of foods provides variety and dimension to the families that embrace these changes. Given that many of these opportunities come with a devaluation of family traditions, there are complex trade-offs in these consumption shifts. Especially with regard to larger homes, more elaborate furnishings, and the trappings of the consumer lifestyle in general, one can celebrate the greater affluence of America's rural regions but also lament the increased burden on global resources and the loss of local distinctiveness.

—*Peggy F. Barlett*

See also
Consumer-Goods Advertising; Marketing; Retail Industry; Values of Residents.
References
Baritz, Loren. *The Good Life: The Meaning of Success for the American Middle Class*. New York: Knopf, 1989.
Barlett, Peggy F. *American Dreams, Rural Realities: Family Farms in Crisis*. Chapel Hill: University of North Carolina Press, 1993.
———. "Status Aspirations and Lifestyle Influences on Farm Survival." Pp. 173–190 in *Household Strategies: Research in Rural Sociology and Development*. Vol. 5. Edited by D. C. Clay and H. K. Schwarzweller. Greenwich, CT: JAI Press, 1991.
Bennett, John. *Of Time and the Enterprise: North American Family Farm Management in a Context of Resource Marginality*. Minneapolis: University of Minnesota Press, 1982.
Collier, Jane. "From Co-owners to Co-workers: Changing Marital Relations in a Spanish Village." Bunting Institute Working Paper. Cambridge, MA: Radcliffe Research and Study Center, 1989.
Gallaher, Art, Jr. *Plainville: Fifteen Years Later*. New York: Columbia University Press, 1961.
Gartman, David. "Reification of Consumer Products: A General History Illustrated by the Case of the American Automobile." *Sociological Theory* 4 (1986): 167–185.
McNall, Scott G., and Sally Ann McNall. *Plains Families: Exploring Sociology through Social History*. New York: St. Martin's Press, 1983.
Mooney, Patrick H. *My Own Boss? Class, Rationality, and the Family Farm*. Boulder, CO: Westview Press, 1988.
Rutz, Henry J., and Benjamin S. Orlove. *The Social Economy of Consumption*. Monographs in Economic Anthropology, No. 6. Lanham, MD: University Press of America, 1989.
Salamon, Sonya. *Prairie Patrimony: Family, Farming, and Community in the Midwest*. Chapel Hill: University of North Carolina Press, 1992.
Salamon, Sonya, and K. Davis-Brown. "Middle-Range Farmers Persisting through the Agricultural Crisis." *Rural Sociology* 51 (1986): 503–512.
Wilkening, Eugene, and Jen Gilbert. "Family Farming in the United States." Pp. 271–301 in *Family Farming in Europe and America*. Edited by B. Galeski and E. Wilkening. Boulder, CO: Westview Press, 1987.

Cooperative State Research, Education, and Extension Service

A nationwide, university-based educational system that links research and educational resources and programs of the U.S. Department of Agriculture (USDA), the 1862 land-grant institutions, the 1890 historically Black land-grant institutions, Native American and Hispanic institutions, colleges of agriculture, experiment stations, and cooperative extension services to provide research-supported, knowledge-based educational programs throughout America. The Cooperative State Research, Education, and Extension Service (CSREES) attempts to provide educational services to a diverse audience in rural America. In addition to connections with each state's 1862 land-grant institution and the 16 historically Black 1890 land-grant institutions (including Tuskegee University), CSREES incorporated 29 Native American educational institutions, through passage of the 1994 Tribal College Act, and another 127 Hispanic-serving educational institutions into its outreach network. Within that network are contained 130 colleges of agriculture, 59 agricultural experiment stations, 57 cooperative extension services, 63 schools of forestry, 27 colleges of veterinary medicine, and 42 schools and colleges of family and consumer sciences. This entry traces the evolution of the cooperative extension system from its 1914 inception via the Smith-Lever Act through the restructuring brought about by the Department of Agriculture Reorganization Act of 1994.

The Smith-Lever Act

The Smith-Lever Act of 1914 established what has become the largest adult and youth education organization in the United States—the cooperative extension system of the Cooperative State Research, Education, and Extension Service. Extension programs currently are conducted in 3,150 counties by more than 17,000 professional educators who translate the results of USDA and land-grant university research and instruction efforts into readily understood, practical knowledge for distribution throughout America.

The extension system includes extension professionals located both at 1862 and 1890 land-grant institutions. The former colleges and universities were created in all 50 states, whereas the latter were established primarily in the South to address the needs of people of color. The 1994 Tribal Colleges Act is beginning to incorporate Native American professionals and programs in an expanded extension system better able to address the educational needs of all Americans.

The Smith-Lever Act was a significant piece of federal legislation that responded to the educational needs of the contemporary agricultural and rural populace. Several of its provisions set important precedents for subsequent federal legislation and appropriations. First, the act provided $10,000 annual appropriations to each state to conduct cooperative agricultural extension work. These funds gave national recognition and a stable, financial underpinning to the university dissemination efforts. Second, for the first time in the history of federal legislation the act

required matching funds by the states. This matching provision was copied in many subsequent acts and appropriations. Third, and most important, the legislation designated a county agent as integrator, demonstrator, and disseminator of research-based knowledge generated by the USDA and the land-grant colleges. The county agent became the cornerstone of this federal-state-local collaborative partnership, linking and closely binding the ties between the community and the college. The county agent concept evolved into a myriad of programs designed to meet the needs of rural and urban Americans.

Expansion of Responsibilities

During the extension's first four decades, most organizational attention was directed at the rural home. Agricultural agents worked with farmers to increase crop production, introduce new varieties and alternative crops, and develop marketing mechanisms. Home demonstration agents, later called home economists, introduced nutritional education programs to rural women through cooking and canning demonstrations, while also involving their children in organized youth activities led by volunteer 4-H leaders. The 4-H program targeted youths between ages 8 and 19 and has grown to the point where there are now nearly 6 million youths in both rural and urban areas actively participating in countless youth-led, and adult volunteer–assisted, programs. These range from the traditional rural topics of crop and livestock production to general topics of photography, pet care, health and safety, woodworking, and community development, all of which help to shape tomorrow's leaders.

County-based extension agents drew on the expertise of campus-based extension specialists to translate the work of their research colleagues into language that stimulated reader interest and transferred into practice. The campus-based specialists often traveled to the counties to give presentations, conduct on-farm demonstrations, and assist county agents on projects requiring closer collaboration between the community and the campus. During the late 1940s and early 1950s, extension enlarged its scope to address community and regional issues. Programs such as rural resource development, conservation, and public-policy education enabled the county agents to gather representative groups of community leaders to identify and address local concerns and issues. This was also the age of specialization within extension, with many agricultural agents and specialists gaining programmatic responsibilities for specific commodities.

Extension educators during the 1960s and 1970s

4-H programs, such as this one in Cass County, North Dakota, are operated by county-level Cooperative State Research, Extension, and Education Service agents.

began to address the interrelationships between humans and the environment, initially in reaction to the 1962 publication of Carson's *Silent Spring* and the attendant public outcry over the impact of pesticides on the environment. The issue hit even closer to home with Hightower's 1973 publication of *Hard Tomatoes, Hard Times,* which charged the land-grant system with favoring special interests and commodity groups and failing to deliver needed educational programs to the intended audience—the people of rural America. During this tumultuous period, extension consciously recruited people with social science backgrounds to complement the work of its agricultural sciences–trained staff.

Beginning in the 1950s, special congressional appropriations helped extension to transition into new programs and to serve new audiences. Since then, extension has built institutional capacity to provide educational outreach in the areas of farm safety, urban 4-H, integrated pest management, expanded food and nutrition education, and water quality.

The 1980s and 1990s have been a time of introspection for extension. Many internal reports (e.g., Dalgaard et al. 1988; Extension Committee on Organization and Policy 1987, 1995; USDA 1994) as well as external studies (e.g., Warner and Christenson 1984; Rasmussen 1989) encouraged the extension organization to redesign its structure and delivery mechanisms to better serve a rapidly changing society. Extension's *Framing the Future* report (Extension Committee on Organization and Policy 1995, 10) vividly captured the challenges confronting the organization as it nears its centennial anniversary: "Society is different today as a result of changes in values, ethics, community norms, family structures, and mobility; of aging and more diverse populations; of growing economic disparity; including the decline of the middle class; of a rural to urban shift; of a reduced sense of community; of the rise of a global economy and interdependence; of advances in science and technology; of concerns for environmental quality; and of political uncertainty. These trends oblige Extension to have a more diverse staff and faculty, to develop and deliver programs tailored to specific groups of learners, and to redefine programs, audiences, delivery methods, and operating structures to meet rapidly changing priority needs."

The Department of Agriculture Reorganization Act of 1994 ended the Extension Service's tenure as a standalone USDA agency. In October of that year the Extension Service was merged with the Cooperative State Research Service to create the Cooperative State Research, Education, and Extension Service. This merger was part of the Clinton administration's "reinventing government" initiative and Congress's "streamlining of USDA" and was estimated to save $2.5 billion, close 1,100 field offices, reduce staff by at least 7,500 employees, and eliminate 14 of the 43 USDA agencies. The avowed purpose of the reorganization was to better position the USDA for the twenty-first century. CSREES's creation was anticipated to stimulate the formation of new interdisciplinary teams that could better serve the educational needs of current and future audiences (CSREES 1995).

Extension recently made a conscious effort to shift attention away from specific programs and commodities affecting one particular group or organization and toward issues affecting a cross-section of local interests. This redirection placed greater emphasis on extension's public-policy education component as agents and specialists find themselves increasingly called on to facilitate the resolution of multiparty conflicts (Dale and Hahn 1994). A second trend has been the shift of extension activities from a county to a regional or area basis, largely as a result of economic and political factors. If this trend continues, geographic restructuring may include the transfer of campus-based specialists to regional offices. A third trend has been extension's embracing of computer and other new technologies to better serve its rural audiences. All extension agents and staff are connected by computer to instantaneously access information throughout the CSREES network and beyond. Virtually all extension offices also are interconnected via interactive communication technology, such as satellite dishes and downlink facilities, for improved educational delivery.

Will CSREES survive into the twenty-first century? The prognosis is positive, given the service's history of fairly rapid response to changing societal needs and circumstances. Extension in the future will probably resemble a system of equitable partnerships among public institutions of higher learning (the 1882, 1890, and 1994 land-grant institutions), public agencies, and the private sector working together to deliver timely and effective programs to all Americans—rural and urban.

—Emmett P. Fiske

See also

Careers in Agriculture; Government; History, Rural; Land-Grant Institutions, 1862; Land-Grant Institutions, 1890.

References

Carson, Rachel. *Silent Spring.* Cambridge, MA: Riverside Press, 1962.

Cooperative Extension System. *Building the Future: CES Strategic Planning for the 21st Century.* (October) Washington, DC: U.S. Department of Agriculture, Cooperative Extension System, 1994.

Dale, D. D., and A. J. Hahn, eds. *Public Issues Education: Increasing Competence in Resolving Public Issues.* Madison: University of Wisconsin, Extension, 1994.

Dalgaard, Kathleen, Michael Brazzel, Richard Liles, David R. Sanderson, and Ellen Taylor-Powell. *Issues Programming in Extension.* Washington, DC: Extension Committee on Organization and Policy/Extension Service–USDA and St. Paul: Minnesota Extension Service, 1988.

Extension Committee on Organization and Policy. *Extension in Transition: Bridging the Gap between Vision and Reality.* Blacksburg, VA: Virginia Cooperative Extension, 1987.

———. *Framing the Future: Strategic Framework for a System of Partnerships.* Urbana: University of Illinois, Cooperative Extension Service, 1995.

Fiske, Emmett P. "Controversial Issues as Opportunities: Extension's Effectiveness in Resolving Environmental Disputes." *Journal of Extension* 29 (fall 1991): 26–28.

———. "From Rolling Stones to Cornerstones: Anchoring Land-Grant Education in the Counties through the Smith-Lever Act of 1914." *Rural Sociologist* 9, no. 4 (1989): 7–14.

Hightower, Jim. *Hard Tomatoes, Hard Times: A Report of the Agribusiness Accountability Project on the Failure of America's Land-Grant College Complex.* Cambridge, MA: Schenkman, 1973.

Mayberry, B. D. *The Role of Tuskegee University in the Origin, Growth, and Development of the Negro Cooperative Extension System, 1881–1990.* Montgomery, AL: Brown Printing, 1989.

Prawl, Warren, Roger Medlin, and John Gross. *Adult and Continuing Education through the Cooperative Extension Service.* Columbia: University of Missouri Press, 1984.

Rasmussen, Wayne D. *Taking the University to the People: Seventy-Five Years of Cooperative Extension.* Ames: Iowa State University Press, 1989.

U.S. Department of Agriculture. Cooperative State Research, Education, and Extension Service. *Managing the Future: The CSREES Strategic Plan.* Washington, DC: U.S. Department of Agriculture, Office of Communications, 1995.

———. Extension Service. *Future Application of Communication Technology: Strategic Implementation Plan for the Cooperative Extension System.* Washington, DC: U.S. Department of Agriculture, Extension Service, Communication, Information, and Technology, 1992.

Warner, Paul D., and James A. Christenson. *The Cooperative Extension Service: A National Assessment.* Boulder, CO: Westview Press, 1984.

Cooperatives

User-owned, user-controlled businesses that distribute benefits to their users or patrons based on use. After an elaboration of this definition, this entry covers the following topics: principles, economic justification, legal aspects, and structure and scope, including major trade organizations. This entry focuses on cooperatives that have the common legal and financial structures characteristic of agricultural cooperatives. Mutual insurance companies (Hetherington 1991), credit unions (McLanahan and McLanahan 1990), and electric, telephone, and water associations also qualify as user-owned and -controlled organizations. However, their legal foundation, tax obligations, and equity structure are beyond the scope of this entry.

Cooperatives are a prime illustration of the American initiative of self-determination, independence, self-reliance, and self-help. They are a legal means for independent units to voluntarily form associations to achieve an important economic objective they could not achieve alone. These independent units may be individuals, companies, nonprofit organizations, or governmental units. Independence is maintained while simultaneously achieving the benefits of group and volume action.

Cooperatives are not nonprofit businesses. Nonprofit organizations can have no equity shares, and "no part of the income [can be] . . . distributed to its members, directors or officers" (Oleck and Stewart 1994, 10). Ownership in cooperatives can be traced to individuals, and income is distributed to these owners.

Principles

User control, user ownership, and user benefits are the contemporary principles on which cooperatives are built. If any one of these elements is missing, if an organization is not controlled or owned by its patrons, or if the benefits do not accrue to its patrons, it is not a cooperative. To these principles, value statements, promulgated by the International Cooperative Alliance, can be added. Cooperatives typically provide education about cooperatives to members, employers, and the general public; cooperate among cooperatives; and demonstrate concern for sustainable community development. But organizations adhering to the first three contemporary principles and not to the last three values would still be cooperatives because they are owned and controlled by users and benefits accrue to the users.

User Control. Cooperatives are controlled through boards of directors composed of, for the most part, members rather than by boards of professional managers. Cooperatives generally elect their boards and make other major decisions on a democratic or one-member, one-vote basis. Member voting proportional to patronage or investment also is possible in some states. Therefore, cooperatives are dependent not only on favorable economic environment and quality management, but also on the loyalty of knowledgeable members for patronage, ownership, support, and leadership. To help maintain member loyalty, cooperatives must develop policies that are fair and equitable so that one group of members does not subsidize another group.

User Benefits. Benefits can be returned in three ways. The first way is patronage refunds. Net income realized by the cooperative is returned to its members proportional to their patronage. A member with 2 percent of the business would receive 2 percent of the net income. Second, benefits sometimes are given to members immediately in the form of favorable prices—lower prices for supplies and services or higher prices for marketing products. A cooperative with this pricing policy may have little or no net income to distribute. Delayed payment marketing cooperatives pay all of their revenue less expenses to patrons; therefore their net income is zero. Third, benefits may accrue from access to supplies or market as in the rural electric cooperatives or a fruit farmer who has no other place to sell his or her fruit.

User Ownership. Patrons acquire ownership in cooperatives through retained patronage refunds, per unit capital retains, and, to a limited extent, direct investment. *Retained patronage refunds* are noncash allocations of net income allocated to members retained by the cooperative, resulting in an increase of member investment. *Per unit capital retains* are used by agricultural marketing cooperatives. They are a checkoff retained by the cooperative based on the quantity or value of products marketed. Say the patron receives a $40/ton payment for a product. The cooperative would, for example, withhold $4/ton and give the patron $36/ton in cash. Unit retains, $4/ton in this case, increase the members' investment in the cooperative. *Direct investments* are cash purchases of member certificates, common or preferred stock, or other forms of equity. In some traditional cooperatives this may

Nearly 100 bison producers formed the North American Bison Cooperative, which owns its own processing plant in New Rockford, North Dakota.

be as low as $1. The balance of needed equity is generated by one of the other two methods. Some agricultural processing cooperatives requiring considerable start-up capital establish higher minimum investments for each member, $13,950 in one case. Ownership in cooperatives is typically not permanent. Owners expect their equity to be redeemed in cash when their patronage ceases or on a rotation schedule.

Economic Justification

Waves of cooperative creation typically are associated with economic stress, exploitation, or ignored needs. For example, in 1896 an Iowa company raised the price of barbed wire 40 percent immediately after getting a monopoly. Affected farmers organized a cooperative to manufacture their own barbed wire. This cooperative saved farmers in that state over $5 million in one year. In the 1920s and 1930s, rural Americans were swallowed up in grime, drudgery, and grind for even the simplest of tasks. They witnessed the comfort and convenience of electricity enjoyed by their city counterparts. Investor-oriented utilities refused to supply electricity in rural areas. These utilities could not fathom such an effort ever paying off. But rural electric cooperatives, organized after enabling legislation and loan funds became available, made it happen. Electricity brought such a relief that one Tennessee farmer stood in his rural church with this witness: "The greatest thing on earth is the love of God in your heart, and the second greatest thing is to have electricity in your house" (Pence 1984, 2).

Cooperatives are created for the most part to correct market failures such as these. Market failure means that investor-oriented firms are either unwilling or unable to provide needed supplies, services, or market commodities for farmers and others at prices related to costs. Benefits captured by cooperatives arise from economies of size, profits from processing or marketing at the next level, improved market information, provision of missing services, assurance of supplies or markets, coordination, risk sharing and reduction, and provision of a competitive yardstick.

Strong, viable, and well-managed cooperatives are important to much of rural America because of low population densities. Declining rural population creates stress on institutional fabric with excess capacity and barriers to consolidation of local loyalties. Low population densities often create an environment where spatial monopolies are dominant, that is, where the size of the market will not support more than one business. Monopolies often extract excessive profits and/or have unnecessarily high operating costs. Also, many investor-oriented firms leave rural areas because of low returns, leaving affected businesses and communities without needed services. Rural America needs cooperatives to provide services other firms are unwilling to provide, generally because of low volume. Thus, cooperatives are a major solution to problems associated with the distinctive feature of rural America. They have the potential to enhance economic viability, to create a pool of trained leaders in rural areas, to establish esprit de corps in a community, and to maintain essential, private and public services. While serving member needs, cooperatives generate economic activity. As a by-product they create employment, pay taxes, and purchase supplies. For example, a new cooperative wet corn milling plant in a rural area will attract an estimated additional 3,200 people to the region and increase tax revenues by $4.5 million.

Cooperatives have an inherited public image of trust and a social conscience. In the main they deliver on that image. But cooperatives are not a panacea for declining rural areas. A board president of a cooperative that turned three local floundering businesses into profitable enterprises said, "As a cooperative it is not our business to keep towns going, but we're open to any opportunity to do [so]" (Miller 1996, 4).

Legal Underpinnings

State Law. Most cooperatives are charted under each state's special cooperative statute. As such they have limited liability, indefinite life, and other features similar to incorporated investor-oriented firms. Major differences are in control ("one member, one vote" as opposed to "one vote per share") and in how net income is distributed (return to members on basis of use versus dividends on basis of investment).

Federal Law. Individuals or organizations of any type that get together to acquire supplies and services are violating no federal law. But two or more businesses forming any kind of coalition to set prices on the goods or services they sell do violate federal antitrust laws. Exceptions to these laws have been passed where it was felt that market participants were at a disadvantage, as in labor and agriculture. The 1922 Capper-Volstead Act provides that cooperatives whose members are engaged in agriculture can organize marketing cooperatives without violating antitrust laws so long as one member has no more than one vote or dividends on equity are less than 8 percent, nonmember business is less than 50 percent, and prices are not enhanced unduly. The 1934 Cooperative Fishing Act provides equivalent protection for aquaculture cooperatives.

Tax laws provide for the single-tax treatment of qualifying patronage income. This avoids double-tax treatment of other corporations. Either the member or the cooperative, but not both, must report patronage-sourced income as taxable income. Income earned by consumer cooperatives is not taxable at all. Neither the cooperative nor the member have any tax obligation because patronage refunds are reductions in cost of consumer goods or services, not additional income.

Scope

There were an estimated 47,000 cooperatives in the United States in the mid-1990s. Most prominent were credit unions (12,559), housing (6,400), and agriculture (4,244). Membership was estimated at 100 million, but this figure is misleading because of double counting. Some farmers were members of more than ten cooperatives. Agricultural cooperatives accounted for $89 billion of the $100 billion in total cooperative business activity (unpublished data from the National Cooperative Business Association).

More is known of agricultural cooperatives because of the U.S. Department of Agriculture's (USDA) data collection efforts. The market share of these cooperatives is about 30 percent for all farm supplies and products marketed. It is highest for dairy (86 percent) on the marketing side and fertilizer (45 percent) on the supply side (Richardson annual). Differences in market share among the states ranges from 4 percent in Nevada and New Mexico to over 50 percent in some New England states (Cobia

1989). A few prominent brand names include Sunkist, Ocean Spray, Blue Diamond, and Welch. Cooperatives have a visible presence, if not a significant market share, in other industries. Among them are Associated Press, ACE Hardware, FTD Florists, and Best Western Motels.

There is a wave of interest among private companies, nonprofit organizations, and governmental units in forming various types of coalitions, many of them cooperatives. These coalitions are prompted by various efforts to share overhead expenses associated with equipment, services such as training, solid waste disposal, and health care insurance. Research, publications, and data on non-agricultural cooperatives are improving. The National Cooperative Business Association and the National Cooperative Bank, both of Washington, D.C., have the most complete documentation on these cooperatives. A center for cooperatives has been established for urban cooperatives at the University of the District of Columbia. In 1995, the mission of the Rural Business-Cooperative Service (formerly Agricultural Cooperative Service), USDA, was expanded from a focus on agricultural marketing and supply cooperatives to include all rural cooperatives. Cooperative development specialists, located in most state USDA rural development offices, provide information and support on a local level.

—*David W. Cobia*

See also
Agricultural and Resource Economics; Agricultural Law; Development, Community and Economic; Electrification; Value-Added Agriculture

References
Adams, Frank T., and Gary B. Hansen. *Putting Democracy to Work: A Practical Guide for Starting Worker-Owned Businesses.* Eugene, OR: Hulogosi Communications, 1987.
Cobia, David W., ed. *Cooperatives in Agriculture.* Englewood Cliffs, NJ: Prentice-Hall, 1989.
Egerstrom, Lee. *Make No Small Plans.* Rochester, MN: Lone Oak Press, 1994.
Hetherington, John A. C. *Mutual and Cooperative Enterprises: An Analysis of Customer-Owned Firms in the United States.* Charlottesville: University Press of Virginia, 1991.
McLanahan, Jack, and Connie McLanahan, eds. *Cooperative/Credit Union Directory and Reference.* Richmond, KY: Cooperative Alumni Association, 1990.
Miller, Patricia. "Keeping Main Street Alive." *Profiles* (CENEX LO'L Cooperative) (3d quarter 1996): 4.
Oleck, Howard L., and Martha E. Stewart. *Nonprofit Corporations, Organizations, and Associations.* 6th ed. Englewood Cliffs, NJ: Prentice-Hall, 1994.
Pence, Richard A. *The Next Greatest Thing.* Washington, DC: National Rural Electrical Cooperative Association, 1984.
Richardson, Ralph M., et al. *Farmer Cooperative Statistics.* RBS Report 4. Washington, DC: U.S. Department of Agriculture, annually.

Corn Industry

All activities from input supply, production, and processing to the delivery of finished food, feed, and industrial corn products to final users. This entry addresses the economic impacts of the corn industry, its supporting industries, its uses, the U.S. dominance in worldwide corn production, special challenges to the industry, and its future. Corn (maize) is the most valuable U.S. crop and is of major importance to the economy of the north-central United States. The Cornbelt ranges from Ohio to western Nebraska, and corn is the foundation of major livestock and corn-processing industries in the region. In 1996, U.S. production was valued at $27 billion dollars. Corn can be described as the backbone of the rural economy in Iowa, Illinois, and Indiana, parts of Missouri, Minnesota, South Dakota, Nebraska, and, to a lesser extent, parts of surrounding states. It touches the lives of every American and billions of other people who consume meat, dairy products, or foods made directly from corn.

Background

Today's corn (*Zea mais l.*) is descended from wild species in Mexico that provided food for Native Americans for centuries. One Native American word for corn means "that which sustains life." Major investments in research by land-grant universities, the U.S. Department of Agriculture (USDA), and private firms made corn an efficient converter of plant nutrients, water, and sunlight into a major element of the world's food chain. Research is transforming the crop into sources of energy and industrial raw materials for nonfood uses.

Most corn is a yellow dent type. The term *dent* refers to an indentation in the top of the kernel when it is physiologically mature. However, some consumers prefer other kinds of corn. In South America, a flint type is preferred. Flint varieties, when mature, have a hard, smooth top. Research shows that flint corn incurs less kernel breakage than dent varieties when handled repeatedly as the corn is moved into world markets. Its greater durability is offset by lower yields per unit of land than dent corn. For some food uses, white corn is preferred. Other types of corn are sweet corn and popcorn. Sweet corn is harvested when the kernels are immature, then canned, frozen, or sold in the ear.

Economic Impacts

Economic impacts of corn begin with industries that supply production inputs to farmers. To raise the crop, farmers purchase fuel, seed, fertilizer, herbicides, insecticides, farm machinery, trucks, parts and tires, repairs, and services, such as financing, insurance, and consultation on crop production problems. Each related industry has several stages. The seed industry includes research, conversion of research into commercial varieties, production and processing of seed, and financing, transporting, and marketing the finished product. At each stage, jobs are created and income is generated. The fertilizer, chemical, and farm machinery industries have similar stages. In addition, the farm machinery industry involves processing of steel, rubber, and other raw materials used in manufacturing. As income is generated in each related industry, additional dollars are spent in rural communities. Each dollar spent changes hands several times, creating a multiplier effect on earnings of nonfarm businesses.

After corn is harvested, a new chain of activities centers on delivery of corn to users at locations, times, and forms in which it is needed. Activities in this sector include drying, storage, domestic and foreign transportation, feeding of corn directly to livestock, and processing of part of the crop into manufactured livestock and poultry feeds and industrial and consumer products. Direct feeding of corn to livestock and poultry is the largest use. About 24 percent of the U.S. corn crop normally is exported, with 20 percent processed domestically. Most processed corn products are used in the United States, although a few are exported. Less than 1 percent of the crop is used for seed. The rest is held in reserve to help offset future shortfalls in production.

Historically a key element in the Native American diet, corn is now used for a variety of fuels and industrial products as well as a popular food source for people and animals.

Uses

Major food uses of corn include corn sweeteners, starch, meal, grits used in processed foods, corn flakes, chips, tacos, canned and frozen sweet corn, and corn oil for cooking and salad oils, dressings, and processed foods. Corn sweeteners grew from a small fraction of the U.S. caloric sweetener market to over 50 percent as a result of research that created liquid and crystalline high-fructose corn sweeteners. Fructose resembles sugars found in fruits. It is the leading sweetener in U.S. soft drinks and is widely used in other processed foods.

Corn is used to create industrial products, including adhesives, industrial absorbents, packaging materials, diapers, biodegradable garbage bags and table service, filters, and materials to clean oil spills. Research shows that corn has a promising potential as a carrier for agricultural chemicals and in the manufacturing of durable plastics. Corn is a major raw material in the

United States for manufacturing motor fuels and an oxygen-enhancing agent to meet the nation's clean air regulations. The corn-based fuel industry grew out of a Corn Utilization Research Center at Iowa State University in the 1930s and research at the USDA's regional laboratories. The Organization of Petroleum Exporting Countries' sharp increase in petroleum prices in the early 1970s and major tax incentives from the U.S. government and individual states also helped accelerate expansion in the 1980s and 1990s.

The largest use of corn is as feed for production of red meat, poultry, and dairy products. Expanding corn production permitted Americans to increase meat consumption since the 1970s. U.S. corn is the basis for livestock and poultry feeding industries in countries where feed supplies are limited. Japan, Taiwan, and Korea, for example, depend heavily on U.S. corn for meat production because of high population densities and limited availability of cropland. Corn also is a major ingredient in pet foods for American cats and dogs.

U.S. Dominance in Production

The United States is by far the world's largest producer of corn because of its highly fertile soils, abundant rainfall and irrigation water supplies, and a growing season long enough for the crop to reach maturity. A private enterprise economy where incentives for economic efficiency are passed to individual farmers, farm supply, and marketing firms and large investments in agricultural research and education helped to make the United States the leading producer of corn. Private enterprise and economic incentives created highly efficient input and marketing industries that provide essential inputs in large volumes during the brief planting season and can respond quickly to changing volumes to be conditioned, transported, exported, stored, or processed. Long-standing systems for extending research-based information to the private sector through the cooperative efforts of the USDA and state land-grant universities contributed strongly to the development of the corn industry. The United States usually produces 40 to 45 percent of the world's corn crop and accounts for 66 to 75 percent of global corn exports. Several other nations have rich soils but lack rainfall or have too short a growing season to grow corn in quantities produced in the United States. Other leading producers are China, Brazil, Mexico, France, Argentina, and South Africa.

Challenges

The corn industry faces vastly different challenges from many nonagricultural industries. Production is a biological process that can be interrupted or disrupted by weather, disease, insects, and other hazards beyond human control. In 1970, for example, after the hybrid seed industry shifted production to a female parent material that was male-sterile, the parent material and commercial varieties were attacked by disease, the Southern Corn Leaf Blight. This disease spread rapidly across the producing region, leaving disastrously low yields. The male-sterile corn was used to eliminate expensive hand labor in removing tassels from the plants. Detasseling prevented female plants from pollinating themselves with undesirable genetics. The industry responded quickly to the disease by producing seed the next winter in the Southern Hemisphere and in sub-tropical areas so that adequate supplies would be available for the next planting season.

Year-to-year variations in corn production caused by disease, adverse weather, or other factors outside the control of producers can cause huge fluctuations in corn prices. To manage price risks, futures and options markets are used widely in the corn industry to establish prices for crops delivered to the market at a future time. The Chicago Board of Trade futures market has been the world corn pricing center for over a century.

Another difference from nonagricultural industries is that one of corn's major inputs, land, has a fixed supply. World population expands at approximately 2 percent per year. Rising incomes increase meat and dairy consumption, thus raising the demand for corn. The industry is challenged to produce and process an expanding supply of corn for a growing population on an unchanging land base. At the same time, it must maintain soil productivity for future generations and avoid environmental degradation. The U.S. corn industry has made phenomenal strides in increasing corn production since hybrid seed was introduced in the 1930s. In 1969 (the year before the corn blight disaster), the average corn yield per acre was 85.9 bushels. By 1994, with continued public and private investment in research, the average yield had risen to 138.6 bushels per acre. Without large investments in research and huge increases in yields, U.S. and global food supplies would be much smaller and much more environmentally sensitive land would be tilled. Consumers around the world would face much higher food prices and a smaller variety of foods than they do today.

Other unique aspects of the corn industry involve seasonality. For high production, the Midwest crop must be planted between late April and the third week of May. Research shows that planting after this short window of opportunity seriously decreases production. That means 70 million or more acres of corn in the United States must be planted in one month. All related industries are on alert to meet this precise timing. During the harvest (late September to early November), other participants in the corn industry must be ready quickly to transport, receive, condition, and store a crop that totals nearly 400 million metric tons. Delays at any point may expose corn to devastating yield reductions from high winds, ear droppage, or possible molds and toxins if the crop is not dried quickly. Despite these challenges, the corn and related industries year after year provide U.S. and world consumers with an abundant supply of high-quality corn and corn products.

The Future

Scientists continue efforts to increase the productivity of corn plants. New research methods involve gene transplants to create corn with greater resistance to disease, pests, drought, and short growing seasons. This work helps corn production keep pace with growing world demand. New techniques enable plant breeders to create varieties with specific end-user characteristics. Corn with higher than normal oil content and specific oil characteristics is being developed. Other researchers develop corn with higher protein content and higher content of specific amino acids such as lysine. Others are searching for corn that will manufacture the nitrogen needed for its growth. If successful, that would reduce use of nitrogen fertilizer that can contaminate groundwater. Still other researchers are developing more efficient ways to harvest, transport, handle, condition, and process the crop. For the foreseeable future, corn will be vitally important to world consumers and the U.S. rural economy.

—*Robert N. Wisner*

See also
Biotechnology; Futures Markets; Grain Farming; Livestock Production; Marketing; Trade, International.

References
Food and Agriculture Organization. *Maize in Human Nutrition.* Rome: United Nations, 1992.
Johannessen, S., and C. A. Hastorf, eds. *Corn and Culture in the Prehistoric New World.* Boulder, CO: Westview Press, 1994.
Munro, E. "Corn Refining: An Essential Player in the U.S. Economy." *Corn Annual 1993.* Washington, DC: Corn Refiners Association, 1993.
U.S. Department of Agriculture, Economic Research Service. "Corn and the National Economy." *Corn.* Washington, DC: Corn Refiners Association, 25, no. 1, 1969.
Wallace, H. A., and W. L. Brown. *Corn and Its Early Fathers.* Rev. ed. Ames: Iowa State University Press, 1988.

Cowboys

People who ride horses and tend cattle or horses for pay. This entry examines cowboying as an occupation, cowboy clothing, and the cowboy and work. It addresses conflicting images of cowboys and cowboys in popular culture and rodeo and concludes with a discussion of modern cowboys.

Occupational Factors

Today cowboys most often work on cattle and/or horse ranches. From 1865 through the 1880s, however, thousands of cowboys herded cattle on long trail drives north from Texas. Also called cowhand, hand, waddie, or buckaroo, the cowboy works on horseback and dislikes any labor on foot. He has become an internationally recognized symbol of the American West. Rodeo competitors appropriated the term *cowboy,* but many such performers have no background in ranch work. Historically, cowboys have been men, but during the twentieth century a few cowgirls joined the ranks. Poet Georgie Sicking of Fallon, Nevada, worked much of her life as a salaried cowhand.

Modern usage of the term *cowboy,* first in hyphenated form, dates from the 1830s in Texas. Colonel John S. "Rip" Ford used the word *cow-boy* to describe the Texas border raider who drove off Mexican cattle during the 1830s. The term carried a tinge of wildness, of life at the fringes of law and civilization. After the American Civil War, westerners applied the term to ranch hands rather than cattle thieves.

Unlike the bold, dashing, romantic, heroic figure invented by pulp writers, the cowboy in reality was a poorly paid laborer engaged in difficult, dirty, dangerous work. In the 1870s, hands earned about $20 to $25 per month, plus "found" (food). During the 1880s, wages rose to $30 to $40. By the 1930s, wages still hovered around $45 a month. California buckaroo Dick Gibford (*American Cowboy* fall 1992) reported making $225 per month in 1966 "cowboyin' and breakin' horses." According to the *Wall Street Journal* (June 10, 1981), Arizona hands then earned about $500 per month, plus bed and board. The cow boss in charge of a ranch could make $1,150. Cow boss Jim Miller described cowboying as "still the lowest-paid job for what you have to know and do" (*Wall Street Journal,* June 10, 1981, p. 1). By the early 1990s cowboy wages had crept up to between $700 and $1,000 per month.

Contrary to B-western movie and pulp novel depictions, not all cowboys are White. Racial distribution of the rural labor force varies from place to place. On the northern ranges of Montana and Alberta, most hands are White. Hispanic cowboys (vaqueros) predominated on the ranges of Spanish California and eastern Oregon in the nineteenth century. Texas, Arizona, and New Mexico ranchers still hire many skilled vaqueros. African American cowboys figure prominently, especially on southern ranges. Native Americans work cattle and horses in Oklahoma, South Dakota, New Mexico, and elsewhere.

Clothing

Cowboy dress varies with climate and terrain. Early Texas cowboys borrowed large sombreros and other items of Mexican vaquero clothing. Beginning in the 1870s, John B.

Steer branding on round-up.

Stetson and other manufacturers made broad-brimmed beaver felt hats that offered welcome shade from the sun's strong rays. On southern ranges, some hands may favor a cooler straw hat made by Bailey or another manufacturer. Early cowboys wore durable wool or canvas pants. Blue denim jeans became part of the standard outfit after Levi Strauss began sewing his sturdy pants in the 1850s. Today Wrangler has replaced Levi's as the favorite jeans of rodeo and ranch folks. Trail hands up from Texas convinced Kansas boot makers to modify footwear to the cowboy's needs. They wanted high boot tops to keep out dirt and protect the lower leg. High heels keep the foot securely in the stirrup. Spurs dangle from the boot heels, adding a merry jingle and a measure of extra control over a horse. A bandanna ("wipe") protects the face against alkali dust when a hand rides "drag" behind a herd. A leather vest and leather chaps provide warmth and protection against thorns and cacti. The cowboy's leather chaps originated in the Mexican vaquero's *chaparreras*. His early spurs were big Chihuahuas from Mexico.

Like his dress, the cowboy's saddle and tack reflect strong Hispanic influence. The western stock saddle, with long stirrups, high cantle, and a large, sturdy horn, is modeled on the Mexican vaquero's saddle. Likewise the lariat (*la reata*), hackamore (*jáquima*), McCarty (*mecate*), and many other pieces of equipment come from Mexico. Like vaqueros and *charros* (gentlemen riders in Mexico), cowboys liked conchos, round shell-like silver decorations, on their chaps and other equipment.

Work

Trail drives and roundups occupied most hands during the nineteenth century. From 1865 to 1880, cowboys drove at least 3.5 million cattle from Texas to cattle towns in Kansas, Nebraska, and Wyoming. Herds generally ranged in size from 1,500 and 3,000 animals. The greatest number of herds traveled the Chisholm Trail to Abilene, Kansas. Working up to 20 hours a day, cowboys drove the animals from one watering place to the next. They had to guard against predators, straying cattle, and stampedes. The westward extension of railroads and quarantines against longhorns with fever-bearing ticks eliminated the long cattle drives. Epic drives and open-range herding gave way to transportation by large trucks and rail cars.

During the last century, youths, college graduates, immigrants, and others in search of adventure eagerly tried their hand at cowboying. Ranchers could impose restrictions on their hands, such as forbidding gambling and drinking. Ranchers could replace disgruntled cowboys quickly and easily. Cowboys made a few attempts to strike for better wages and conditions. These strikes failed owing to the political clout of wealthy ranchers and the surplus of hands on the range. By the late nineteenth century, much of the western range had been fenced or turned to crop production. Fencing reduced ranch labor needs. It also gave working hands another chore—stringing and tending fence. Cowboys also had to stoop to agricultural labor and put up hay for winter feed.

Conflicting Images

Ranch and rodeo cowboys often have generated unfavorable appraisals. When observed "hellin' 'round town," cowboys draw sharp criticism. Police records and contemporary press accounts well document the cowboy's penchant for gambling, drinking, and fighting. According to the *Topeka Commonwealth* (August 15, 1871), "The Texas cattle herder is a character, the like of which can be found nowhere else on earth. Of course he is unlearned and illiterate, with but few wants and meager ambition. His diet is principally navy plug and whiskey and the occupation dearest to his heart is gambling." In contrast, John Baumann (*Fortnightly Review* April 1, 1887) described the cowboy as "a loyal, long-enduring, hardworking fellow, grit to the backbone, and tough as whipcord; performing his arduous and often dangerous duties, and living his comfortless life, without a word of complaint about the many privations he has to undergo." Observers who watch hands sweating at work on the range, riding, roping, and branding, marvel at their strength, skill, courage, and hard work.

Like the carousing, cowboy gunplay has been exaggerated to titillate movie and pulp novel fans. A Colt revolver is too heavy and uncomfortable to pack all day. On trail drives or roundups, most cowboys leave their guns in the chuckwagon. Most hands are not particularly good shots; neither are sidearms very accurate. Some old-time cowboys did carry powerful and accurate carbines or rifles on their saddles. Self-conscious of their image, however, most nineteenth-century hands strapped on a six-shooter and perhaps flourished a carbine to add a macho touch to their photographs.

Popular Culture and Rodeo

During the 1880s, pulp novels, circuses, and wild west shows brought a stalwart, romantic cowboy hero to a nostalgic public. Although far removed from the drab truth of real cowboy life, the image of excitement, freedom, and drama continues to dominate popular accounts of the cattle frontier. The cowboy was and is the most mythologized of all rural folk.

As open-range ranching declined in the late nineteenth century, dude ranches opened employment opportunities for some cowhands. "Wrangling dudes," rather than horses and cattle, however, seems disgraceful to many cowboys. They disdainfully call the dude ranch cowboy a "savage," "dude puncher," or "dudolo" (a word play on gigolo). In the early twentieth century, rodeo competitors started calling themselves cowboys and cowgirls. As early as the 1880s, local boosters in North Platte, Nebraska (1882); Pecos, Texas (1883); and other towns recognized the appeal of "cowboy tournaments." From such beginnings grew the giant rodeos and stampedes at Cheyenne, Pendleton, Calgary, and elsewhere.

Today rodeo performers far outnumber working cowhands. Both groups preserve elements of traditional cowboy culture. Despite complaints from animal rights protesters, more spectators annually attend rodeos than professional football games. A few competitors, such as rough-stock rider Ty Murray, make it big. Like the ranch hand, however, many rodeo riders end the season with more bumps and bruises than money.

Cowboys have become internationally recognized icons in western art, folklore, literature, and films. Frederic Remington and Charles M. Russell inspired hundreds of later artists to depict cowboy life in paint and bronze. "Teddy Blue" Abbott, Andy Adams, Charlie Siringo, and hundreds more cowboys committed their often embellished memoirs to print. Ned Buntline's nickel and dime pulp literature led the way in romanticizing and glorifying cowboy heroes for a mass audience. The novels of Zane Grey, Louis L'Amour, and countless other pulp writers continue to sell well.

Since the mid-1980s, a cowboy authenticity movement has brought back real ranch and cowboy culture. Poets such as Wally McRae capture the problems and wonders of ranch life. Singers such as New Mexico's Michael Martin Murphey and Alberta's Ian Tyson bring old-time cowboy songs to a generation that had never heard them. Hat, tack, and saddle makers have revived the beauty and craft of cowboy material culture. Popular glossy magazines, such as *Cowboys and Indians* and *American Cowboy,* let readers vicariously ride the range.

Modern Life

At spring (and smaller fall) roundups, ranchers still employ extra hands. Cowboys scour the range and herd cattle to a central location. They separate animals by outfit, brand calves, castrate young bulls, dehorn some, and select those to be taken to market. Branding irons today may be heated by propane gas instead of buffalo chip or wood fires. With the heat, dust, and smoke, however, roundup looks much like it did a century or more ago.

The cowboy's low socioeconomic status limits his options for marriage and family life. Women, still relatively scarce in cattle country, usually marry ranchers or merchants, not poor, itinerant cowhands. Ranchers ("cowmen") own land and cattle; cowboys do not own land and seldom own cattle. Few hands can save enough of their meager wages to become ranchers themselves.

Given the low wages, men and women obviously do not cowboy to get rich. They like the natural beauty in which they work. They like to look at the world between a horse's ears. Many want to avoid the shackles and stress of modernity that fetter urbanites. Still independent, cowboys do nicely without office gossip, fax machines, and leaf blowers. Cowboys retain their own code of conduct. The cowboy believes in working hard and doing one's best. A top hand should be loyal, uncomplaining, helpful, and, if a male, chivalrous toward women. Good hands "ride for the brand," that is, they loyally support and defend their employer and his or her interests. Top hands require little, but they demand respect. If they do not get it, they do not protest; they quit. As in the nineteenth century, they go the extra mile to find a lost calf. Even though cowboys are fewer these days, the cowboy spirit remains alive and well.

—Richard W. Slatta

See also
Careers in Agriculture; Films, Rural; Folklore; History, Agricultural; Horse Industry; Ranching.
References
Dary, David. *Cowboy Culture: A Saga of Five Centuries.* New York: Knopf, 1981. Paperbound ed. Lawrence: University Press of Kansas, 1989.
Davis, Robert Murray. *Playing Cowboys: Low Culture and High Art in the Western.* Norman: University of Oklahoma Press, 1992.
Forbis, William H. *The Cowboys.* Rev. ed. Alexandria, VA: Time-Life Books, 1978.
Martin, Russell. *Cowboy: The Enduring Myth of the Wild West.* New York: Stewart, Tabori, and Chang, 1983.
Savage, William W., Jr. *The Cowboy Hero: His Image in American History and Culture.* Norman: University of Oklahoma Press, 1979.
Slatta, Richard W. *The Cowboy Encyclopedia.* Santa Barbara, CA: ABC-CLIO, 1994.
———. *Cowboys of the Americas.* New Haven, CT: Yale University Press, 1990.
Ward, Fay E. *The Cowboy at Work.* Norman: University of Oklahoma Press, 1987.
Westermeier, Clifford P., ed. *Trailing the Cowboy: His Life and Lore as Told by Frontier Journalists.* Caldwell, ID: Caxton Printers, 1955.

Crime

An act committed or omitted in violation of law. This entry briefly explores rural crime by way of comparisons to urban crime and pointed differences in the operations of the criminal justice system in rural America. The entry includes discussions of rurality, crime rates, fear of crime, the migration to rural areas of such violent groups as hate groups and youth gangs, rural-specific crime, and organized crime. Short overviews of law enforcement, the practice of law, and corrections are included.

Crime Rates

Rural America quickly is becoming a significant part of the crime experience in America. Rural areas often have been thought of as a shelter from the evils of inner-city crime. As a result of increased media coverage of inner-city crime and delinquency, crime has been studied primarily as an urban problem, with rural crime being perceived as insignificant. The rate of violent crime throughout the United States increased significantly between 1983 and 1993, but declined slightly between 1993 and 1995 (Bureau of Justice Statistics, 1997).

Rural crime rates remain slightly lower than urban rates. Crime is no longer just an urban problem. Some information on rural crime may not be totally representative since most rural areas frequently are governed by informal social controls. This decreases the amount of information gathered about violent crimes, especially interpersonal crimes such as domestic violence and child abuse.

There are noticeable differences between specific types of crime in rural areas and those in urban areas. Historically, rural crimes consisted primarily of property crimes, whereas urban crimes consisted of both property and violent crimes. The gap was greater for violent crimes. Crime rates for urban areas were higher than for rural areas for every offense. The most notable difference among all violent crimes was for murder, of which approximately 89 percent occurred in urban areas (Young 1990). However, in 1992 and 1993 the rate of violent crime in urban areas decreased, whereas for rural areas the rate rose slightly. The hypothesis is that the causes of violence in urban areas are beginning to "spill over" into the rural areas (McDonald, Wood, and Pflug 1996).

Another significant difference between urban and rural violent crimes is robbery. Urban areas experience robbery almost 53 times more often per 100,000 citizens than do rural areas. The rank order of offenses for property crimes are somewhat similar for urban and rural communities, with larceny as the most common crime and motor vehicle theft as the least common. McDonald et al. (1996) reported that rural residents are somewhat more vulnerable to property crimes than are urban residents. This is due, in part, to the greater distances that must be traveled by rural residents to purchase goods and services, leaving their households more susceptible to burglary and theft. Rural homes also are more isolated, making them less likely to be monitored by neighbors and impeding the mobilization of law enforcement officials.

Rural residents today do not perceive the crime rate to be increasing within their communities, even though rural crime rates have increased dramatically since 1960. The rural crime rate in 1960 for the nation was approximately 423 crimes per 100,000 rural residents. These rates had escalated 366 percent by 1989 to a yearly rate of about 1,974 crimes per 100,000 rural residents (U.S. Department of Justice 1990). During the same time, this increased rate was roughly equivalent to that of the more publicized 389 percent increase encountered by urban areas (Dunkelberger, Clayton, and Bachtel 1991). The arrest totals for rural areas increased by 2.6 percent from 1990 to 1991, with violent crime and property crime increasing 5.4 percent and 6.4 percent, respectively (U.S. Department of Justice 1993). Researchers now are speculating that disproportionately large increases in crime will occur in rural areas that experience rapid growth.

Recognizable differences also exist between crime victims in rural areas and urban areas. Elderly people in rural areas were victimized almost as frequently as other citizens, which is contrary to national studies that indicate the elderly population is victimized less frequently than other age groups (Donnermeyer 1982). Trends in rural crime also show that violent crimes such as homicide, rape, and assault are more likely to occur between acquaintances because of the nature of rural interaction.

Fear

Victimization and fear of crime are rural crime issues that are studied frequently. The most important factor relating to fear of crime among rural residents is the degree to which these residents view their neighbors as trustworthy and attentive to surrounding activity. Studies on fear of crime in rural areas generally conclude that, outside of violent street crime, rural residents share many of the same anxieties about crime as do urban residents (Weisheit, Falcone, and Wells 1994).

Rural residents are less likely than urban residents to use guns in the commission of their crimes, even though there is a greater likelihood that more rural than urban residents own guns. Gun ownership in rural areas is more than double that of urban areas. Approximately 27 percent of residents in large cities own some kind of gun, whereas more than 75 percent of rural residents are gun owners. Although most rural gun owners are hunters who use rifles, handgun ownership is still higher in rural areas (23 percent) than in urban areas (15 percent). Nevertheless, a 1990 report by the Bureau of Justice Statistics found that the rate of crimes committed using handguns was three times greater in urban areas (5.9 per 100,000) than in nonmetropolitan areas (1.7 per 100,000) (Weisheit et al. 1994).

Hate Groups

Closely related to the issue of violent crime is the prevalence of hate groups in rural areas. Hate groups and hate movements are by no means a recent feature of rural America. The infamous Ku Klux Klan began its intimidating efforts in rural Polaski, Tennessee, in 1865. Although much of the attention on hate activity in the recent past has been diverted to big cities, recruiting efforts in rural areas have been increasing steadily. This increase is due in part to the recent attention drawn to hate groups in these larger cities. Hate groups have a high potential for crime, especially violent crime. Rural residents find it easy to identify with members of these hate groups because of similar demographic characteristics. Rural hate groups usually are composed of average people with no interest in public attention for themselves or their cause. Their deep suspicion of government, combined with racism, anti-Semitism, and fundamentalist Christianity, is the main basis of many of these rural hate groups. These groups base their beliefs on distortions of existing rural values and emphasize religion, patriotism, and independence from government tyranny (Weisheit et al. 1994).

Youth Gangs and Juvenile Delinquency

Just as hate groups are motivated by ignorance and stereotyped attitudes, youth gangs are created by the need for a family, economic benefits, excitement, and a sense of power, which is provided by societal reactions to gangs' deviations. Joining a gang gives its members a sense of place and importance, consequently providing them with social relationships. Many young people are driven to join gangs because of their minority status, economic situations, and prevalence of gang activity in their neighborhoods. As a result of the prevalence of these youth gangs, the individuals who choose not to join a gang are constantly at risk of being victimized by members of the gangs. Thus, membership in a gang offers a sense of belonging and protection from rival gangs. It also promises reprisal if an attack does take place.

Traditional youth gangs only recently have come to the rural areas. The influx of gang activity is attributed mostly to out-migration from the northern urban areas, combined with readily available automobiles and an improved interstate highway system. Urban families that become aware that their children are involved in gang activities sometimes send their children to rural areas with the hope of precluding gang activity. However, exportation of gang members from urban to rural areas has caused many new youth gangs to be established.

Rural youths report less serious delinquent behavior than youths from urban areas. This could be credited partly to socially integrating factors such as family, church, and school, which are typically more influential in rural settings than are the various deviant influences found in urban areas. Rural juveniles are more integrated into society, commit less serious offenses, and have fewer court appearances than their urban counterparts. Another contributing factor to the lower number of reported incidents of delinquency in rural areas is informal social control. In most rural communities, residents know each other socially, leaving many incidents of juvenile delinquency to be handled by private citizens themselves rather than the authorities.

Rural-Specific Illegal Activities

Some crimes are specific to rural areas, such as agricultural crime and wildlife crime. Although these crimes may seem trivial compared to violent or property crime, they have a tremendous impact on the United States as a whole. The Uniform Crime Report (UCR) lists several items stolen each year as agricultural crimes. Each item's recovery rate also is documented. Among the items listed by UCR are theft of livestock, which accounts for approximately $20 million lost each year, and a recovery rate of 17 percent; $30 million lost each year to theft of agricultural equipment, supplies, and products from California farmers; and theft of timber and vandalism, which costs farmers in western Washington alone $1 million annually (Weisheit et al. 1994).

Wildlife crimes such as poaching or the taking of game or fish illegally are other growing concerns in rural areas. The U.S. Fish and Wildlife Service reported the 1990 value of wildlife shipments illegally entering and leaving the United States at more than $1 billion. Examples of replacement costs of such activities include an estimated $45 million annually for illegal harvesting of fish and wildlife in Illinois and more than $93 million each year on deer poaching in Pennsylvania alone (Weisheit et al. 1994).

Vice and Related Activities

Vice and organized crime are becoming features of the rural environment. Some of the same routes and expertise traditionally used for bootlegging and moonshining in rural areas are being used to transport other illegal merchandise, such as drugs and stolen auto parts. Small communities near major highways are experiencing increasing problems with prostitution, set up for truck drivers traveling these highways (Weisheit et al. 1994).

Law Enforcement

Components of the criminal justice system operate differently in rural communities than in urban areas. Rural culture has several features that have implications for rural policing and rural crime and that differentiate it from urban culture. Some of these features include informal social control, an aversion to sharing internal problems, and a mistrust of government and outsiders. Although such features seem to preclude rural jurisdictions working effectively with other police agencies, this is not the case. There has been a recent rise in the number of multijurisdictional drug task forces in rural areas, which demonstrates that these forces can work effectively together.

Law enforcement personnel found in rural areas differ from those in urban areas in that the sheriff is the elected officer in charge of apprehension and detention of all offenders. Because of the large areas that sheriffs oversee, deputies are hired to assist sheriffs in their duties. Compared to their urban counterparts, rural law enforcement officers generally work with lower budgets and less staff and equipment. Rural police prove to be more efficient than their urban counterparts and are more respected by the public. A 1991 Gallup poll found that 54 percent of urban residents reported having a great deal of respect for local police, whereas 61 percent of rural residents reported the same. The poll asked respondents about their perceptions of police brutality in the area. Approximately 59 percent of urban respondents felt there was police brutality in their area, whereas only 20 percent of rural residents perceived this. Past data have shown that rural departments, especially sheriffs, are more responsive to the community than their urban counterparts, who concentrate more on the dynamics of the police organization (Weisheit et al. 1994).

Practice of Law

The practice of law itself is unique to rural communities because of the small, close, personal networks that prevail there. As a result of these networks, attorneys in rural areas frequently face dilemmas, such as client confidentiality. The attorney-client relationship may be made complex by other social connections that attorneys and clients share, such as being members of the same church, having children on the same baseball team, or serving on common committees. Rural attorneys are more likely to provide more counseling for their clients than their urban counterparts. Rural courts tend to be more responsive to the surrounding community. They focus on outcomes when determining if justice has been served; urban courts focus more on processing cases and following proper procedures.

Corrections

Corrections is another aspect of the criminal justice system that varies between rural and urban areas. As with the other institutions of the criminal justice system, much of the research on the corrections component is focused on urban facilities, even though most jails are located in rural areas. The primary duty of the local sheriff is the operation of the county jail. Rural jails tend to operate under their estimated capacity, whereas urban jails more likely are overcrowded. Because of the low operating capacity, the fixed costs associated with maintaining a jail result in per inmate costs twice those of urban jails. Rural jails tend to be poorly staffed and underfunded, which probably accounts for higher rates of illness, homicide, and suicide within the jail. Nevertheless, economic conditions in rural areas induce rural citizens to continually lobby for the construction of prisons and jails in their

counties because of their economic benefits. Studies indicate that economic benefits come from payroll, construction, purchases from local businesses, and increased revenues from sales taxes and property taxes. Property values near prison facilities tend to increase since most prison officials seek to live nearby.

Rural America no longer can be considered a safe haven from the criminal activities of its urban complement. Although research indicates that rural crime rates are lower than urban crime rates, rural crime is on the rise. Organized crime, gang activity, and hate crimes are no longer unique to the urban setting. Nevertheless, little is known about the phenomenon of rural crime or that of rural policing. More comparisons must be done between rural and urban crime to better aid in the understanding of these processes. However, to appreciate and understand the phenomenon of rural crime, one also must understand how rural justice and rural crime vary across rural communities, not just how rural and urban areas differ (Weisheit et al. 1994).

—*Phyllis Gray-Ray, Melvin C. Ray, Terri L. Earnest, and Sandra Rutland*

See also
Agricultural Law; Domestic Violence; Marijuana; Policing.
References
Donnermeyer, John F. "Patterns of Criminal Victimization in a Rural Setting: The Case of Pike County, Indiana." Pp. 34–49 in *Rural Crime*. Edited by T. J. Carter, G. H. Phillips, J. F. Donnermeyer, and T. N. Wurschmidt. Totowa, NJ: Allenheld, Osmun, 1982.
Dunkelberger, John, Mark Clayton, and Douglas C. Bachtel. "Agricultural Crime in the South." In *Issues Facing Georgia*. 3, no. 5 (August 1991): 1–15. Athens: University of Georgia, Cooperative Extension Services, Extension Information Center.
Federal Bureau of Investigation. *Uniform Crime Reports: Crime in the United States, 1993*. Washington, DC: U.S. Government Printing Office, 1993.
McDonald, Thomas D., Robert A. Wood, and Melissa A. Pflug. *Rural Criminal Justice: Conditions, Constraints, and Challenges*. Salem, WI: Sheffield, 1996.
U.S. Department of Justice. *Bureau of Justice Statistics: National Crime Victimization Survey*. Washington, DC: U.S. Department of Justice, Office of Justice Programs, various issues.
———. *Crime in the U.S. 1992: Uniform Crime Reports*. Washington, DC: Federal Bureau of Investigation, 1993.
———. *Crime in the U.S.: Uniform Crime Reports*. Washington, DC: U.S. Government Printing Office, Federal Bureau of Investigation, 1990.
———. "Key Crime and Justice Facts at a Glance." http://www.ojp.usdoj.gov/bjs/glance.htm#Crime. Washington, DC: U.S. Department of Justice, April 28, 1997.
———. U.S. Department of Justice. *Juvenile Justice Bulletin*. Washington, DC: U.S. Department of Justice, Office of Justice Programs, Office of Juvenile Justice and Delinquency Programs, various issues.

Weisheit, Ralph A., David N. Falcone, and L. Edward Wells. *Rural Crime and Rural Policing.* Washington, DC: U.S. Department of Justice, National Institute of Justice, 1994.

Young, Thomas J. "Hate Groups in Rural America." *International Journal of Offender Therapy and Comparative Criminology* 34 (1990): 15–21.

Crop Surplus

The excess of production over quantity demanded at government-administered prices. The source of surplus stocks and the interaction between surplus stocks and market prices are discussed in this entry. In addition, a brief history of crop surpluses in the United States is covered, along with a summary of optimal levels of surplus stocks and who benefits from stocks.

Demand for Stocks

Part of total demand for any crop is the demand for stocks. This demand is largely composed of stocks purchased by processors and end users who want to ensure they have adequate reserves to meet their needs over the marketing year. Crop producers may carry reserves to provide seed for the next year, livestock feeders carry reserves to ensure against high feed prices at the end of the marketing year, and food processors carry reserves to ensure a continual flow of their product to the consumer. These reserves are considered to be normal or pipeline stocks that must remain in the system to ensure its normal operation.

Surpluses are stock levels that exceed the normal pipeline level. Surplus stocks can be held by private firms and individuals who speculate on increases in price caused by shortages in other parts of the world. The federal government can hold surplus stocks under the Commodity Credit Corporation (CCC). The CCC is a corporation in the U.S. Department of Agriculture (USDA) that is charged with carrying out the price support activities of the farm program by making loans to producers who pledge their crops in storage as collateral. The CCC takes possession of the crops in storage if the producers forfeit the stocks rather than repay the loans. CCC stock reserves are stored for use in subsequent years and released to the market when production is low and market prices would exceed a threshold level.

Sources

Agricultural crop production of wheat, feed grains, oilseeds, cotton, and rice is unique because only one crop is produced and harvested each year. As a result, supply is fixed at harvest time and prices are determined over the next 12 months as consumers draw down the supply. Weather in the United States and around the world provide random shocks to the supply of crops. As a result, the level of surplus stocks builds and declines over time.

The presence of crop surpluses acts as a depressant on market prices. As surplus stocks build, prices decrease, thus increasing the quantity demanded in the current year and reducing the quantity produced the next year. These reactions act to bring stocks to equilibrium levels. When supply is low, prices rise to ration consumption in a free market. Given sufficient freedom to react to prices, consumers and producers will reach an equilibrium price during each market period. Some interest groups in the United States believe the government should not be involved in holding stocks and that prices should be allowed to vary from year to year. Other interest groups hold that the government is the only entity that should hold stocks and that the stock policy should be used to ensure a stable supply of commodities at acceptable prices.

Prices

Agricultural prices are inversely related to the level of surpluses. The greater the level of surpluses, the lower the prices of crops, and when stock levels fall, prices increase. When looking at the relationship between prices and stocks, one must express stocks in terms of the normal quantity demanded; the stocks-to-use ratio is the relevant variable. As the stocks-to-use ratio declines, the level of surplus gets tighter, which causes prices to be more responsive to market news, and generally prices increase. When the stocks-to-use ratio increases, there are more than adequate stocks, so prices are less responsive and generally prices decline.

An examination of the stocks-to-use ratio for wheat since 1965 provides an example of how prices react to changes in the relative level of surplus stocks (Ray et al. 1994). During the 1965–1971 period, the stocks-to-use ratio averaged 54.5 percent and prices remained at about an average of $1.36/bushel. As a result of substantial increases in exports in 1972 and 1973, the stocks-to-use ratio declined to 17.2 percent and prices increased 190 percent to $3.95/bushel in 1973. In response to higher wheat prices in 1973 and 1974, U.S. wheat farmers increased 1975 wheat production 47 percent from the 1965–1971 average production level of 1,442 million bushels per year. The stocks-to-use ratio increased to 65 percent by 1976 as production continued to expand following the high prices in 1973, 1974, and 1975. This result points out an inherent problem with agricultural stocks, namely, that crop production continues to expand for several years after prices return to normal levels. One problem with unstable prices is that they cause farmers to overinvest in productive resources (e.g., land and machinery) when prices are abnormally high. These resources earn low rates of return when prices return to normal levels. These excess productive resources remain in production and add to the surplus situation in subsequent years.

The Holding of Stocks

Surplus stocks can be held by private firms or by the government. Economic theory holds that the benefits from private stock holding equal the cost of holding stocks, after price risk is adjusted for. This result comes about because firms invest in stocks as if they are any other risky investment and arbitrage (simultaneous purchase and sale of a commodity to profit from price difference) among speculators bid away excess profits beyond a return for risk in the long run. As a result, there are no excess profits to be gained from private businesses holding speculative stocks for a long period. Stocks necessary to meet humanitarian purposes during production shortfalls must be held by governments because private firms hold stocks only in the hope of profits. Humanitarian uses of stocks include sales at low prices, sales on long-term credit, barter of stocks for critical materials (e.g., tin, cobalt) under Public Law 480, and outright gifts from the U.S. government to countries experiencing crop shortages.

Stocks of grain are costly for governments to hold. The U.S. government rents storage from private grain companies when the CCC acquires stocks. In addition to storage costs of about $0.325 per bushel per year, the government must pay interest on the purchase cost of the grain at the prevailing interest rate for government bonds. Additional costs are accrued because grain can become old and go out of condition, thus forcing the rotation of stocks over time.

Proposals to establish world food reserves have been considered several times since the early 1970s, usually in conjunction with shortfalls in supplies. Such a reserve may be held in the form of grain or in cash, the former to be made available to countries forced to import grain in times of shortages and high prices. According to Eaton et al. (1976), to stabilize the world grain market, a reserve of 178 million metric tons would be required. This reserve would cover all possibilities of a shortage, but a smaller reserve of 58 million metric tons would cover 98 percent of the probable short falls over a 25-year period. Tweeten (1989) and Gardner (1979) reported the results of several studies to determine the optimal quantity of surplus stocks. A wheat reserve of 600 million bushels and a corn reserve of 40 million tons are thought to be sufficient to stabilize prices. A reserve of 600 million bushels of wheat is an intuitive answer to the optimal stock reserve question, given that U.S. wheat food demand ranged from 500 to 650 million bushels during the years these studies were completed (1970s and 1980s). As U.S. wheat food demand increased to about 800 million bushels in the 1990s, the optimal level of wheat stocks should be about 800 million bushels.

The question remains as to who gains more from the holding of stocks—consumers who gain stable prices or farmers who gain price supports. Economic theory shows that if the source of the instability in the market comes from demand, then consumers will benefit more than farmers from a program to stabilize stocks and prices (Tweeten 1989). However, if supply is the source of instability in the market, farmers will benefit at the consumers' expense from policy actions that manage surplus stocks to stabilize prices. In reality, instability in agricultural markets comes from both production and demand, so both groups benefit from a surplus stock management program.

Past Programs to Manage Stocks

The 1933 Agricultural Adjustment Act was the first farm program (Knutson et al. 1993). This act attempted to support prices through direct purchases of surplus stocks by the federal government and through management of production by the idling of cropland. Subsequent farm programs used a price support or loan rate mechanism to establish a minimum price and pull surplus stocks off the market. Several different supply control provisions, including set-asides, paid diversion programs, soil bank, and conservation reserve program, have been used to manage the production of grains and cotton. Surplus stocks were accumulated because the minimum support prices for these programs were set above equilibrium price levels for many years. To dispose of the surplus stocks, the CCC made some stocks available through food give-away programs, donated food to developing countries, and traded or sold food to importing countries under Public Law 480.

During the late 1970s, the attitude toward government holding of surplus stocks changed, in part because farmers were never pleased with the USDA when stocks were released and prices fell. A new farm program in 1977 established the farmer-owned reserve (FOR), which allowed farmers to place surplus stocks under a CCC loan for an extended time (up to four years). The CCC did not require payment of interest on the loan after the first year, and the government paid farmers to store their grain on farms or in commercial storage facilities. The FOR required that farmers repay their loans once price exceeded a threshold level. Under the FOR, surplus stock levels continued to build because market prices failed to exceed the threshold price. As a result, surplus stocks had to be released under a special program. In 1983, the secretary of agriculture announced the Payment in Kind (PIK) program to pay farmers a portion of their historical production, in the form of stocks under the FOR loan, in return for not planting part or all of their cropland.

The PIK program successfully reduced stocks, and subsequent droughts and floods brought stock-to-use ratios to all-time lows in 1996. The result was rapid increase in crop prices during the first four months of 1996 as markets reacted to weather and planting reports. The CCC did not hold sufficient stocks to be released into the 1996 stock deficit market, so prices continued to reach new highs and were more volatile than normal.

—*James W. Richardson*

See also
Agricultural Programs; Futures Markets; Grain Elevators; Marketing; Markets; Policy, Agricultural; Trade, International; Wheat Industry.
References
Eaton, D., W. S. Scott, J. Cohon, and C. ReVelle. "A Method to Size Rural Grain Reserves." In *Analysis of Grain Reserves*. ERS-634. Washington, DC: U.S. Department of Agriculture, Economic Research Service, 1976.
Gardner, B. L. *The Economics of Agricultural Policy*. New York: McGraw-Hill, 1990.
———. *Optimal Stockpiling of Grain*. Lexington, MA: Lexington Books, 1979.
Knutson, R. D., J. B. Penn, and W. T. Boehm. *Agricultural and Food Policy*. 3d ed. Englewood Cliffs, NJ: Prentice-Hall, 1994.
Knutson, R. D., J. W. Richardson, D. A. Klinefelter, C. P. Rosson, and E. G. Smith. *Policy Tools for U.S. Agriculture*. Bulletin B-1548 rev. College Station: Texas A&M University, Texas Agricultural Experiment Station, Agricultural and Food Policy Center, 1993.
Penson, J. B. Jr., O. Capps Jr., and C. Parr Rosson III. *Introduction to Agricultural Economics*. Upper Saddle River, NJ: Prentice-Hall, 1996.
Ray, D. E., S. P. Slinsky, R. M. Pendergrass, and R. L. White. *An Analytical Database of U.S. Agriculture, 1950 to 1992: The APAC Database*. AFPC Staff Paper No. 4-94. Knoxville: University of Tennessee, Agricultural Policy Analysis Center, 1994.
Tweeten, L. *Farm Policy Analysis*. Boulder, CO: Westview Press, 1989.

Cropping Systems

Designed arrangements of plant species that are produced for food and other human needs. This entry describes the history and development of managed agroecosystems, the natural resource use and environmental impact of these systems, and some promising alternatives for efficient future crop production. Economic and social implications of different approaches to farming are explored.

Historical Development

Organized agriculture, the conscious planting and harvesting of crops, and care of domestic animals, has been a vital part of human culture and society for about 10,000 years. Current systems of planting crops in rows were introduced as part of the industrial revolution a scant two centuries ago, while the intensive use of chemical fertilizers and pesticides began in the last half of this century (Plucknett and Smith 1990). Thus, the current agriculture and food system represents a short-term experiment, especially in terms of its impact on the environment.

When global human population and demand for food were low, human footprints had relatively minor impacts on the natural environment. Today's rapidly expanding human population, especially its use of scarce land and nonrenewable natural resources, is causing substantial changes in the earth's ecosystem that may have serious environmental implications for the future. In this historical context, it is not surprising that awareness of the finite nature of land and other natural resources is only now being transformed into genuine concern about the future of food systems and the survival of humans and other species.

Environmental Impact

Design of cropping systems involves the deliberate manipulation of natural environments and landscapes to provide food, feed, fiber, or raw materials for human or domestic animal use. Choice of species and planting systems has focused on maximizing the output of crops and income per unit of land, labor, or other scarce commodities. Until recently, the major emphasis was on short-term productivity and profits, increased food for a growing global population, and improved technology for predominant monoculture cropping systems. Today there is growing awareness of the finite supply of nonrenewable resources, the unintended off-farm effects of farming, and the long-term implications of increasing human population and its potential impact on the environment. Increased concern about the future has led to emerging concerns about the development of a sustainable agriculture (Harwood 1990).

Environmental implications of cropping systems begin with division of most agricultural regions according to political boundaries and private property lines that rarely correspond to natural features in the landscape (Jackson 1994). The section lines at each mile in the U.S. property grid system do not respect natural landforms; rectangular fields within those sections are designed to accommodate large mechanized equipment. Such political divisions and human-designated boundaries have led to labor- and machine-efficient cultivation techniques that direct tractors up and down slope, across wetlands and natural waterways, and parallel to field boundaries. The divisions have little respect for natural topography or for the landscape. An environmentally conscious farmer will design systems to include contour cropping to prevent soil erosion, place crops and pastures where they are most appropriate within the landscape, diversify crops within a farm and field to provide habitat for beneficial insects, and rotate crops to enhance soil fertility and reduce use of pesticides. Seeding waterways, planting shrubs and trees as filter strips along streams, and connecting noncultivated areas from one farm to the next to provide wildlife corridors are some methods used to lessen the negative environmental impact caused by human divisions of the landscape.

Management of Soil Nutrients and Pests

Soil management for cropping systems includes agriculturalists preparing land, planting and cultivating crops, and providing sufficient nutrients for crop production. A sophisticated process has evolved over the past 200 years to include farmers preparing land through plowing and disking, managing weeds with herbicides and cultivation, planting crops in rows with mechanized equipment, and applying chemical fertilizers to provide nutrients for extractive monoculture cereals or short-term rotations. Environmental impacts of this approach have included massive erosion of topsoil in some sites as a result of the action of wind and rainfall, loss of some pesticides and nutrients with water runoff during heavy rainfall events,

and soluble nutrients, pesticides, and breakdown products leaching through the soil profile and vadose zone into the groundwater. These are unintended effects of current cropping systems; they reduce profits by increasing input costs and cause larger-scale environmental degradation, whose costs eventually will be paid by society. Reduced tillage and increased residue from crops left on the soil surface can reduce runoff drastically, thus slowing the loss of soil, nutrients, and water. Band application of herbicides, coupled with timely cultivation, can reduce the economic and environmental costs of weed management. Careful soil testing and analysis can allow reduced nutrient application rates and less potential for contamination of the groundwater, especially by nitrates. No-till systems substantially reduce soil loss but often require increased use of pesticides, thus negating some environmental benefits. Such changes are being implemented by farmers for economic and environmental reasons (Karlen and Sharpley 1994).

Monoculture systems have contributed to environmental problems. Continual cropping of favored cereals (e.g., rice in lowland Asia and maize in central North America) has required increasing applications of fertilizers and pesticides to maintain productivity. These monocultures have received most of the attention of agricultural researchers concerned with increased productivity and of companies that provide fertilizers and pesticides. The Green Revolution promoted monocultures and use of improved technology to substantially increase cereal grain production in more productive lands, thus reducing the cost of food in some countries and helping to alleviate hunger.

However, from an ecological viewpoint, monoculture systems could be considered a short-term solution that allows farmers to dominate the natural environment for immediate production gains with a large investment of fossil fuel–based production inputs (Francis 1986). Too often this domination leads to farmers ignoring the models of biological cycling and efficiencies of resource use that occur in natural ecosystems. Crop rotations and multiple cropping systems provide benefits in soil fertility and pest protection. Use of green manure crops and animal manure or compost reduces the need for imported chemical fertilizers (Power 1990). External resources such as fertilizers have a high energy cost for production, transportation, and application to fields. They often become a source of nutrient pollution that reaches surface and groundwater systems. Learning from dominant natural ecosystems in each place can provide clues to the design of more complex cropping systems that make more efficient use of production resources (Jackson 1994).

Control of weeds, insects, plant pathogens (organisms that cause diseases), and nematodes in monoculture systems is complicated by accelerated evolution of pest biotypes or subspecies resistant to known pesticides. Although only a few dozen species resistant to pesticides had been identified up to about 1970, there are now reports of close to 1,000 known pests that are resistant to available products. There is no doubt about the efficacy of chemical pesticides applied at the right time if they can target an undesirable pest, yet farmers and industry are caught in a vicious circle that requires continual search for new products to control an accelerating array of undesirable species that limit production. The alternatives are to scout fields carefully and identify specific problems and to design an Integrated Pest Management program that combines the potentials of genetic resistance in crops, rotation of crop species, multiple cropping to provide diversity and homes for favorable predators, choice of planting dates and methods, and judicious use of chemical or biological pesticide where absolutely needed. Reduction of pesticide use can decrease costs to the producer and lessen the environmental impact of products arriving where they are not wanted. It also will slow the evolution of pest species to biotypes or strains that are resistant to known chemical and biological products (Bird et al. 1990; Liebman and Janke 1990).

Integration of crop and animal production systems provides another type of biological efficiency that cannot be realized in monoculture cropping. Use of crop residues for livestock grazing during winter months in the higher latitudes and primary reliance on forages and grazing provide low-cost feed sources and leaner meat compared with feedlot, grain-fed cattle. Livestock can harvest some fields and areas that are not easily farmed and can take advantage of feedstuffs such as low-quality hay or roughage that has little other value. Manure from grazing animals enhances the organic matter and fertility of the soil. Animal manure has become a difficult-to-handle waste product where animals are confined and concentrated; this by-product should be considered a valuable resource. The combination of crops and livestock provides a wider range of products for sale, thus buffering the variations in weather and prices that cause financial difficulties for farmers in most countries. These efficiencies of cropping system design contribute to profitability and to reductions of the negative environmental impact of many of today's prevalent cropping and animal raising practices. A well-designed and profitable farming operation reduces the incentive to plant monocultures of the most profitable crops in the short term and increases the flexibility to practice good stewardship of land and other natural resources for the long term.

Social Implications of Alternative Farming

Social dimensions of alternative cropping and farm decision strategies also affect the environmental impacts of these cropping systems in the long term. Concurrent with the growth in field size and scale of farming equipment have been an increase in size of properties owned or managed by each farmer and consequently a reduction in the rural population (Strange 1988). Larger farms and mechanization have brought greater labor production efficiencies to food production and released people to other growth sectors, such as industry. Although modern systems have increased the productivity per unit of labor, they have not necessarily improved rural quality of life for all involved in agriculture. They have increased production per unit of land in some cases but often have reduced productivity per unit of capital, fossil fuel–based inputs, and other scarce natural resources. Increased farm size has resulted in less field- and site-specific management and greater homogenization of production practices over larger land areas. As a result, there is less spatial diversity in the farmscape. Use of uniform practices across wide areas often results in fertilizer or pesticide applications that are less well tuned to specific nutrient or pest control needs in specific sites on the farm. Overapplication of these inputs can contribute to nutrient or chemical loss and reduction of water quality on the farm and downstream. These direct results of increased farm size can cause negative environmental consequences and loss of productive potential of the land.

Specialization and monoculture cropping systems on individual farms often have been accompanied by concurrent specialization in a larger farming region. As markets and infrastructure develop, new patterns become established; the agricultural industry matures in response to specific economic incentives and government support programs. Some crops begin to dominate the landscape. Examples are maize in the Platte River Valley of Nebraska and wheat in the northern Great Plains. The result is less diversity on each farm, less diversity in the watershed, less habitat for wildlife, and loss of connectivity of those areas that still provide cover. The only corridors left to conceal movement of larger animals are the stream courses, and even their value may be minimized by crop cultivation right up to the banks or heavy grazing by livestock if streams are not protected by fences.

In contrast, smaller farming units provide opportunity for careful placement of crops and design of cropping systems that better fit the topography and natural resources of the farm. Smaller equipment is more easily turned and can fit onto terraces or into smaller fields. The degree of involvement of the farmer with the land may be more intimate when there is greater daily contact with more fields on the farm, as compared to an operator who visits the fields infrequently because of working across a large area. Use of more uniform practices and greater reliance on chemical weed and insect control, in hopes that a single treatment will take care of the crop for an entire season, suggest there may be fewer trips to the field and infrequent scouting for problems as they occur. Jackson (1994) called this a reduction in eyes-to-acres ratio, a result of fewer people on the land and a homogenization of cultural practices across wide areas. The lack of contact or communication between a farmer and the soil also may lead to a sense of psychological distance from the critical natural resources and environment in which the farm operates and a further move toward farming as a business disconnected from natural cycles and processes. With increased farm size may come a separation of ownership from management of the farm; over 50 percent of land currently farmed in the Midwest is cultivated by nonowners. Moreover, with larger farms an increasing amount of the work is done by minimum- or low-wage employees and less by the farm manager. This further removes the people with a vested interest in the long-term quality of the soil and the farm from the work that is conducted there and may result in less careful management of critical resources such as crop residues and soil.

Specialization in fewer crops and enterprises and the move toward larger farms also have an impact on rural communities. When business operations increase in size, many of the inputs are likely to be purchased farther from home and distant markets are accessed more frequently. Not only are there fewer people to contribute to local business and infrastructure (e.g., schools, churches, and civic organizations), there also is more business that leaves the community. Each $1 spent in a rural community circulates three to five times before leaving that community. Although such economic details may appear at first glance to be disconnected to the health of the cropping systems and the surrounding natural environment, in reality they all are connected. Consolidation of farm-lands into larger tracts under control of fewer owners slowly signals the decline of rural communities. When such towns are no longer viable places to live, people leave for other places. This further removes the farmer and family from community and reduces even more the contact between people and their food supply.

Choice of crops and animals, design of cropping and crop/animal systems, decisions on input use, and destination of the harvest all affect the local community and the natural environment. The study of individual crops or components of the system in highly specialized, discipline-oriented research and education programs has worked against a needed understanding of the complexities of agro-ecosystems. Emerging programs that focus courses and student research on integrated systems, on agroforestry and agro-ecology, and on the viability of rural communities will help to establish the linkages between people and food production. New programs also will help to establish the needed understanding and respect of the realities of human dependence on a healthy natural environment.

—*Charles A. Francis*

See also
Agrichemical Use; Agriculture, Alternative; Agronomy; Mechanization; Pest Management; Tillage.
References
Bird, G. W., T. Edens, F. Drummond, and E. Gruden. "Design of Pest Management Systems for Sustainable Agriculture." Pp. 55–110. Chapter 3 in *Sustainable Agriculture in Temperate Zones*. Edited by C. A. Francis, C. B. Flora, and L. D. King. New York: John Wiley and Sons, 1990.
Francis, Charles A., ed. *Multiple Cropping Systems*. New York: Macmillan, 1986.
Harwood, R. R. "A History of Sustainable Agriculture." Chapter 1, pp. 3–19 in *Sustainable Agricultural Systems*. Edited by C. A. Edwards et al. Ankeny, IA: Soil and Water Conservation Society, 1990.
Jackson, Wes. *Becoming Native to This Place*. Lexington: University of Kentucky Press, 1994.
Karlen, D. L., and A. N. Sharpley. "Management Strategies for Sustainable Soil Fertility." Pp. 47–108. Chapter 3 in *Sustainable Agriculture Systems*. Edited by J. L. Hatfield and D. L. Karlen. Boca Raton, FL: Lewis Publishers, 1994.
Liebman, M., and R. R. Janke. "Sustainable Weed Management Practices." Pp. 111–143. Chapter 4 in *Sustainable Agriculture in Temperate Zones*. Edited by C. A. Francis, C. B. Flora, and L. D. King. New York: John Wiley and Sons, 1990.
Plucknett, D. L., and N. J. H. Smith. "Historical Perspectives on Multiple Cropping." Pp. 20–39. Chapter 2 in *Multiple Cropping Systems*. Edited by C. A. Francis. New York: Macmillan, 1986.
Power, J. F. "Legumes and Crop Rotations." Pp. 178–204. Chapter 6 in *Sustainable Agriculture in Temperate Zones*. Edited by C. A. Francis, C. B. Flora, and L. D. King. New York: John Wiley and Sons, 1990.
Strange, M. *Family Farming*. Lincoln: University of Nebraska Press, 1988.

Cultural Diversity

The presence of different groups in society, each retaining distinctive sets of attitudes, beliefs, customs, and lifestyles. This entry focuses on cultural diversity and patterns of interethnic group relations in rural America, with primary attention given to African Americans, Mexican Americans, and Native Americans. Key terms and concepts delineated are ethnic diversity, ethnic minority, multiculturalism, and interethnic group relations.

Ethnic Diversity

Many ethnic groups inhabit rural America. In addition to the three largest ethnic groups (African Americans, Mexican Americans, and Native Americans), a variety of other ethnic groups reside in rural America. For example, many Eskimos and Native Aleuts live in outlying rural villages in Alaska. Amish people are more highly concentrated in small rural enclaves of the Northeast and Midwest, especially in Pennsylvania and Ohio. The French Acadians (Cajuns) reside in southwest Louisiana and recently experienced a revival of their cultural heritage. Asian Americans, a highly diverse group of descendants from different Asian countries, are largely concentrated in the western and Northwest Pacific states. Chinese, Filipinos, and Japanese represent the largest Asian American groups. Many White ethnics of European ancestry (e.g., Italian, Polish, Russian, Czech, Hungarian, English, German, Irish, French, and Scottish) have experienced a cultural revival. All of these ethnic groups are important because collectively they form the social networks that make up the cultural fabric of America.

Ethnic Minority Groups and Inequality

An ethnic minority group is made up of people with a distinct social and cultural identity (e.g., nationality, language, and religion) who possess a relatively lower share of wealth, power, and economic opportunities and who are systematically subjected to social and economic discrimination based on ethnic and racial characteristics. Rural ethnic minorities differ in size, degree of wealth and power, socioeconomic status, national origin, cultural orientation, ethnic background, geographical location, and degree of acculturation and assimilation with the majority group. These differences can be traced to a wide range of historical, social, cultural, economic, and political factors that evolved from both intragroup and intergroup relations. Some scholars believe that in the future race or color no longer may be as dominant a factor in defining ethnic boundaries and relationships or in differentiating between minority and majority.

Interethnic Group Relations

In recent years, multiculturalism has been advocated as a model for intergroup relations because it emphasizes the sharing, recognition, and preservation of distinct cultural characteristics of different racial, ethnic, and religious groups within a society. According to the multiculturalism model, the cultural identity and traits of all rural ethnic minorities are worthy of preserving and sharing and play an important role in the cultural enrichment of rural America.

Interethnic group relations (e.g., Whites/African Americans, Whites/Native Americans, Whites/Mexican Americans, African Americans/Mexican Americans) may take one of two generic social forms: harmony or conflict. Mutual respect of different cultures, recognition of the rights of all groups, and common problems, interests, and goals may lead to interethnic harmony. Competition over scarce or valued resources, interpersonal and institutional racism, spatial invasions, political and economic domination and exploitation, protests from opposition groups, and cultural intolerance may lead to interethnic conflict. In the 1980s and 1990s, social changes, social forces, and social problems created the need for much intergroup dialogue and interaction.

Hate or resistance groups, such as the Ku Klux Klan and neo-Nazis, that advocate violence, racial separation, and White supremacy reside in some rural areas. Although their number, power, and influence have declined, they still pose a threat to ethnic harmony. However, even though many cultural traditions persist, the social and cultural fabric of rural America in the twenty-first century will look much different from that of the past.

African Americans

African Americans are the only ethnic minority group that is composed largely of descendants of slaves who were brought to America to provide labor for plantations, largely in the South. Approximately 5 million, or 17 percent of the total 30 million, African Americans reside in rural or nonmetropolitan areas, primarily in small towns, neighborhood settlements, and dispersed homesteads. In response to adverse economic conditions that have persistently plagued many rural areas, vast numbers of African Americans migrated to the city in search of a better quality of life. This trend created a series of issues concerning the life chances, economic opportunities, and quality of life of African Americans living in rural areas compared to those living in urban areas.

The racial desegregation of schools has been a major factor contributing to increased interaction between African Americans and other ethnic groups in rural areas. Although school desegregation contributed to overall improvement in the quality of education of African Americans, it also led to their loss of control over their schools and loss of freedom to teach their children about their history and cultural heritage as a part of the educational curriculum. Once the strong resistance to school desegregation was broken, many rural schools were desegregated with much less conflict than occurred in most urban areas. Busing was not a major issue in many rural areas because rural children always had been bused to school. Because of the dispersed housing pattern, the functions of neighborhood schools was not a serious issue in rural areas compared to urban areas. Nonetheless, the quality of education received by most rural African Americans continued to lag behind that of Whites, and competition for educational quality and control is still the source of much interethnic conflict.

Lack of employment opportunities and occupational mobility is a perennial problem plaguing many rural African Americans. Farming did not prove to be a rewarding occupation for most African Americans, who consequently migrated from rural farms to northern and western cities in search of a better quality of life. Historically, many African American farm laborers were displaced by mechanized agricultural technology. Moreover, the combination of shifting industrial activity and changing labor markets created a limited number of employment opportunities. African Americans often were hired in lower-level occupations in these industries. Also, racial discrimination in rural industries often increased racial and ethnic tension and conflict. Whereas the workplace served as a source of interethnic contact and interaction, rural ethnic communities remained largely segregated.

The increase in political education, awareness, and opportunities resulted in increased political participation among rural African Americans. In many small towns and communities, where they make up the majority of the population, African Americans have been elected to public offices such as mayor, school board member, constable, police juror, law enforcement officer, and alderman. In rural communities where African Americans make up less than 50 percent of the population, competition for public offices has been particularly fierce. However, in some areas new alliances and coalitions emerged

that transcend racial and ethnic boundaries. For example, in some rural communities African Americans and Whites formed coalitions to prevent environmental pollution resulting from industries dumping hazardous waste and contaminants near their community.

Native Americans

Native Americans are sometimes called First Americans because they were the first to inhabit what is now known as modern America, long before it was formed as a nation. Over a period of about 200 years, much of the Native American population was decimated by imported diseases and war by European settlers. Those who survived were pushed into the western and southwestern regions, and many were forced to reside on reservations or residential wards established for them by the government. In 1990, the majority of Native Americans (54 percent) lived on reservations, most of which were located in isolated rural areas (Hirschfelder and de Montano 1993). Currently, the largest concentration of the 1.9 million total Native American population of the United States resides in four southwestern states: Oklahoma, California, Arizona, and New Mexico. Sizable populations under 100,000 reside in North Carolina, Washington, and Texas (Meier and Ribera 1993).

A series of factors influenced interethnic relations with Native Americans. First, rural Native Americans continuously engaged in disputes with the government over control of land, natural resources, and socioeconomic policies. Second, issues pertaining to the termination of reservations created much intergroup conflict among Native Americans and between Native Americans and the government. Third, many Native Americans who waged a self-determination movement during the 1960s continued their struggle to reclaim and maintain their land rights, promote their economic well-being, and preserve their way of life. Fourth, attempts to assimilate Native Americans into the ethnic melting pot and the economic system of capitalism presented a continuing threat to the preservation of their cultural traditions. And fifth, many new rural economic developments on reservations, such as bingo parlors, lotteries, and casino gambling; the marketing of newly discovered natural resources (e.g., water, minerals, oil, gas, and coal); and environmental degradation threatened the traditional lifestyles and community solidarity of many Native Americans.

The majority of Native Americans who live on reservations live in poverty. In 1990, the unemployment rate for reservation Indians was 45 percent, compared to an average of 8 percent for the United States as a whole. This high rate of unemployment was due primarily to poor education, discrimination, and lack of industries on and near reservations. In 1990, more than 100 tribes in over 20 states had gambling operations that generated an estimated $2.5 billion a year (Hirschfelder and de Montano 1993). Although these new economic ventures provided a portion of the much-needed funds to improve economic conditions, such enterprises attracted people whose behavior sometimes clashed with local lifestyles. Crucial questions confronting Native Americans are how long they can maintain control of these economic enterprises and to what extent the profits will be used to improve the economic condition of the larger population.

Mexican Americans

Mexican Americans differ markedly from most other immigrant minorities. They are in close proximity to their homeland, they recently migrated from Mexico, and they are descendants of a twice-conquered people. Currently, Mexican Americans are the second largest and most rapidly growing minority and are concentrated in the southwestern states of New Mexico, Colorado, Arizona, California, and Texas. Most Mexican Americans are Catholic in religion, and a majority are mestizo in racial heritage. Mexican Americans constitute 61 percent of the Hispanic or Spanish-speaking population. Historically, Mexican Americans have been severely disadvantaged by poverty, inferior schools, language and cultural differences, employment as cheap migratory laborers, demographic concentration in the Southwest, selective rural-urban migration, and continuing heavy migration from Mexico.

A significant factor that influenced Mexican American interethnic relations in rural areas was the intermittent waves of heavy migration from Mexico that occurred in the post–World War II period. This period was marked by their drive to share in the social and economic opportunities that characterize the American dream while retaining their basic culture ethos. A major factor that gave impetus to this drive was *el movimiento,* or the cultural renaissance movement, which led to an increase in cultural awareness and identity among Mexican Americans.

Another important factor was Anglo American invasion of or migration into predominantly Mexican American populated areas of the Southwest, which resulted in the loss of Mexican American power and control over social, economic, and political institutions and the Mexican American way of life. Consequently, in some areas the Anglo population outnumbers the Mexican American population, which has been relegated to a minority position of second-class citizenship. The exploitation of the labor of Mexican American migratory workers by agricultural industries adversely affected Mexican American families by relegating them to jobs with poverty-level salaries and no health insurance, retirement pensions, or consideration for the quality of education of their children. In addition, the hiring of illegal Mexican immigrants by U.S. businesses and industries adversely impacted the socioeconomic status and quality of life of Mexican American families. Mexican American organizations have sprung up in many rural and urban areas in an attempt to promote and enhance the cultural identity, political power, and economic status of Mexican Americans.

—*Thomas J. Durant Jr.*

See also
African Americans; American Indians; Asian Pacific Americans; Culture; Ethnicity; Latinos; Migrant Farmworkers; Migration.
References
Chan, Sucheng. *Asian Americans: An Interpretive History.* Boston: Twayne, 1991.
Durant, Thomas J., Jr., and C. S. Knowlton. "Rural Ethnic Minorities: Adaptive Response to Inequality." Pp. 145–167 in *Rural U.S.A.: Persistence and Change.* Edited by T. R. Ford. Ames: Iowa State University Press, 1978.
Farley, John. *Minority-Majority Relations.* Englewood Cliffs, NJ: Prentice-Hall, 1995.
Gilbert, J., ed. "Minorities in Rural Society." *Rural Sociology* (Special issue) 56 (1991): 175—298.
Hawley, Amos, and Sara Mills Maize, eds. *Nonmetropolitan America in Transition.* Chapel Hill: University of North Carolina Press, 1981.
Hirschfelder, A., and M. Kreipe de Montano. *The Native American Almanac: A Portrait of Native America Today.* New York: Prentice Hall General Reference, 1993.
Kuvlesky, William P., Clark S. Knowlton, Thomas J. Durant Jr., and William. C. Payne. "Minorities." Pp. 103–123 in *Rural Society in the U.S.: Issues for the 1980s.* Edited by D. Dillman and D. Hobbs. Boulder, CO: Westview Press, 1982.
Lyson, Thomas A., and Willliam W. Falk, eds. *Forgotten Places: Uneven Development in Rural America.* Lawrence: University Press of Kansas, 1993.
Meier, Matt S., and Feliciano Ribera. *Mexican Americans/American Mexicans: From Conquistadors to Chicanos.* New York: Hill and Wang, 1993.
Rothman, J., ed. *Promoting Social Justice in the Multigroup Society.* New York: Association Press, 1971.
U.S. Bureau of the Census. *1990 Census of Population: Asians and Pacific Islanders in the U.S.* Washington, DC: U.S. Bureau of the Census, 1993.
———. *1990 Census of Population: Characteristics of American Indians by Tribe and Language.* Washington, DC: U.S. Bureau of the Census, 1994.
———. *1990 Census of Population: Characteristics of the Black Population.* Washington, DC: U.S. Bureau of Census, 1994.
———. *1990 Census of Population: Persons of Hispanic Origin in the U.S.* Washington, DC: U.S. Bureau of the Census, 1993.

Culture

The practices, objects, beliefs, and values that constitute a way of life for a people. Culture shapes what people do, think, feel, and believe. Culture also constrains people's options by inhibiting alternative ways of doing, thinking, or feeling. This entry describes some important cultural variables of rural American life: settlement patterns, architecture, speechways, foodways, community life, and rituals. Regional variation of cultural traits is emphasized.

Rural Life

To a traveler, rural communities today are culturally indistinguishable from the suburban communities that ring major cities. In both, the visitor finds the same fast-food restaurants, the same gas stations, the same motels and supermarkets, and similar housing subdivisions. Disk-jockey patter on rural radio stations is the identical packaged routine heard on the city stations. One sees pick-up trucks more frequently on the rural roads, however, and each driver waves, touches a cap or otherwise acknowledges a meeting, unlike the rather anonymous interactions of urban or suburban America. Other distinctive family, property, and community practices are recognized by rural Americans as unique to their locale and evidence of their ethnic heritage.

Rather than a single culture, rural America includes a diversity of cultures. Cultural variety emerged as a consequence of who settled in a place, during what historic period, and which unique social and physical environmental factors were encountered in the process. After the original settlement, various conjunctions of people, setting, and time occurred sequentially in a specific locale. A distinctive local culture emerged as a result of each conjunction leaving traces in local assumptions about proper behavior. Cultural practices that today are associated with a particular region were originated by agrarian groups spatially dispersed in remote locations. As people left rural places and migrated to nearby cities, they carried customs for preparing regional foods, for using regional materials domestically, and for adapting to regional climate and seasons. Thus, distinctive regional ways of life, patterns of kinship, cuisine, housing, rituals, governance, and language have roots in the cultures brought to an area by earlier rural inhabitants.

Ethnic Origin and Cultural Distinctiveness

Contemporary rural cultures are best understood through a look at their past. The Northeast, South, Midwest, Plains, Southwest, and West were each peopled uniquely, and particular ethnic groups rose to dominance. American Indians, the original rural inhabitants, accounted for the countryside encountered by initial settlers. Whether the aboriginal population lived in permanent settlements, as along the Mississippi or in the Southeast, or were nomads, as in the High Plains, speeded or slowed the inexorable spread of immigrants. European Americans' adaptation to the local ecology involved adoption of many American Indian cultural traits: names for places and species, indigenous foods, native medicinal plants, crops, transportation methods, and farming practices.

Diverse groups settled and interacted with the indigenous American Indians and the local ecology to produce distinctive regional rural cultures. From the early seventeenth until the mid-eighteenth century, four different waves of English-speaking settlers brought ways of life that affected regional cultures: Puritans from eastern England to Massachusetts; Royalist elite and indentured servants from southern England to Virginia; a largely Quaker movement from the north English and Welsh Midlands to the Delaware valley; and north Britons from the border areas and northern Irish to the Appalachian highlands. Migrants fanned out from these cores to the south and west. Racial minorities were used early in the South and far West to develop the local economy (African Americans as slaves or Chinese and Japanese as low-paid laborers) when labor was in short supply. In just 50 years during the mid-nineteenth century, the Midwest was settled through one of the most extraordinary transfers of land and people the world has known. Although the settlers were White and had Christianity, farming, and northern and western European peasant backgrounds in common, their cultural variety led to an ethnic mosaic. As a result of the Mexican-American War, Mexicans living in what is now the Southwest were granted citizenship. Their cultures interacted with those of Pueblos and other tribes to form a unique Southwest culture.

Settlement Patterns and Architecture

Community formation began when a rural region constituted the nation's frontier. Transportation difficulties and geographic dispersion related to terrain or government mandates, as, for example, the midwestern checkerboard settlement pattern, contributed to early rural communities maintaining a distinctive ethnic identity. In the Northeast, farmers traveled out to their land from villages. Town meetings became the basis of local government. Midwestern homesteaders lived on widely dispersed

Brian Zimmerman, 11, in front of his grandmother's store in Crabb, Texas, where he is the mayor—evidence that there is still a distinctive way of life in rural America.

provides river frontage to all, unlike river settlements elsewhere.

An enduring indicator of rural culture are built forms, called vernacular architecture. From the fieldstone barns, fences, and farmhouses of the mid-Atlantic region to the sod, wooden-frame, or brick houses and barns of the Midwest, rural peoples used traits from their culture of origin to shape native materials. For example, the shotgun house is a modest, popular domestic structure common along the Mississippi River and its tributaries. Although built by both Blacks and Whites, shotgun houses originated in the West Indies from a meshing of Caribbean Indian and African house forms with French structural components. Thus, the African American shotgun house emerged from the mixing of ingredients from multiple cultures. Similarly, the balloon farmhouse is unique to the rural Midwest. The small-town main street with imposing wooden façades hiding rather modest buildings was widely reproduced in American movies. The buildings of the mainstreet businesses are connected to one another and parallel a main road with perpendicular side streets on each side containing residences—a common pattern in the Midwest and West. Newer rural subdivisions do not follow the rectangular grid (derived from surveying of the Northwest ordinance), but use curved streets to provide the current priorities of privacy or ambiance.

Community Ways

Rural and small-town people possess a distinctive conception of place. Americans living in these places consistently believe that their small communities provide a supportive, quiet, neighborly, friendly, family-oriented, slow-paced, relatively egalitarian, and safe place to live. Rural peoples believe they share communities that provide an incomparable way of life that provide them control over their lives.

Everyone "knows everyone else" in small towns. Life there revolves around a core of social institutions: family, community, school, and church. Kin, neighbors, and friends meet one another at work, at church, on main street, at school, or at leisure activities such as high school basketball games. Daily life thus takes place among a cast of familiars whose social networks are overlapping rather than segregated. Children are considered to belong to the whole community. If a child misbehaves, a neighbor will have notified a parent with the news before the child reaches home. High school sporting events are occasions when the entire community turns out. Everyone is related

farms to assure their land claim. Midwestern village plans today reveal origins as central marketplaces. The governance of midwestern towns shows a historic dependence on volunteers for functions such as fire fighting. In the interior Plains, railroad companies platted trade-center towns to capture population and freight, but now many are ghost towns. Other settlement patterns, such as the plantations of the South and the great farms of the West and Southwest, were based on an agricultural system controlled by landed families that employed large numbers of enslaved or disfranchised minorities as laborers. County-level government emerged, controlled by the elite. A singular settlement pattern, the French long farm along the Mississippi, extended perpendicularly, rather than parallel, to the river. The form is exceedingly democratic: it to or knows someone on the team, in the band, or on the cheerleading squad. In addition to traditional football and basketball games, girls' volleyball and basketball now draw enthusiastic community support.

Rural traditions of cooperation, watchfulness, self-sufficiency, and volunteerism were originally forged on the frontier to sustain families, farms, and communities. Today rural men and women maintain self-sufficiency. They learn to fix equipment, have a familiarity with guns, use home remedies, and produce crafts to avoid travel or purchasing such services. Rural self-sufficiency carries over to valuing cooperative endeavors, whether to build a school, repair a church roof, or to deal with a village's economic decline. Similarly, rural communities support their own when natural or domestic crises strike. If a farmer dies before harvesting his fields, a child contracts leukemia and the family cannot pay its bills, or a home burns down, communities rally to raise funds or help families.

Communal traditions endure despite the diminished economic dominance of agriculture and the population changes that have transformed rural society. Whether reduced in size by out-migration or enlarged by newcomers, rural community mobilization occurs in times of crisis. Although the mass media superficially level rural and urban differences, the well-documented preference of rural people for rural life indicates a distinctive identity.

Speechways

Despite the potential homogenizing effects of television and radio, rural speechways vary distinctly. Rural dialects reveal the immigration history of a region. German, Dutch, and Scandinavian farmer-settlers of the Midwest in the nineteenth century evolved a dialect known by linguists as "Midlands" speech. Expressions such as "How's come" and "I want to go with" and the dropping of "to be" as in "The car needs washed" are Midlands traits. North-south distinctions are clear; southern Illinois speakers sound different from speakers in northern Illinois. Northerners say "faucet" and southerners say "spigot," a fruit's "pit" in the north is a "stone" in the south, and groceries that are "bagged" in the north are "sacked" in the south. Rural southerners answer, "Yes, ma'am" or "No, sir" and consider the plain answers of northerners to be rude. Rural peoples have mastered the art of commenting about behavior or events without committing themselves or offending neighbors, who must be faced on a daily basis. "He's real different" is a noncommittal phrase for a difficult or eccentric personality. Rural speechways resist homogenization because rural populations tend to be less mobile and less likely to obtain higher educations and more likely to value their distinctive speech patterns.

Foodways

Like language, regional cuisine resists homogenization and shows rural sources. Fowl, animals, fish, herbs, spices, vegetables, and fruits used by indigenous peoples were combined with ethnic foodways of immigrant populations to produce distinctive regional cuisines. Boiled and baked foods characterize New England, whereas fried, roasted, and grilled foods characterize southern and western cooking. Southern areas of the nation have spicier foods, the influence of indigenous peoples who originated in the Southwest. More general in distribution are two groups of foods: "mush" (a cornmeal porridge) and fruit pies. Mush, usually a breakfast food eaten either with milk or molasses or fried in a solidified state, was historically widespread from the South to New England. Although the corn base was borrowed from Indian cultures, mush is an American adaptation of the porridge dishes staple to European peasant cuisine. Today mush is typically served as hominy or grits in the South. The round fruit pie, a national favorite that led to the phrase "as American as apple pie" represents a borrowing by early Pennsylvania German settlers from British Isles neighbors that was carried west by pioneers. The form was adapted easily to local berries and other products. Breads were a staple of traditional American diets incorporating local or introduced grains. Distinctive breads associated with different regions were products of outdoor ovens among rural Pennsylvania Germans, French Canadians, Louisiana "Cajuns," and southwestern Indian tribes. Cities absorbed rural migrants and their cuisines as the nation urbanized. Boston baked beans, New England clam chowder, the crawfish dishes of New Orleans, the grits and ham of southerners, and the Thanksgiving menu all originated with rural cuisines.

Food is consumed distinctively in rural places. Rural people, particularly farmers, eat their largest meal, called "dinner," at midday and in the evening eat a lighter meal, called "supper." Food for winter traditionally was preserved by the canning or smoking of produce and meats. Rural households today typically use a freezer to store produce from the ubiquitous kitchen-garden and by law use the local meat locker to process home-raised meats. Garden produce and meats raised or hunted commonly are shared with kin or neighbors today as in the past.

Rituals

The American national holiday Thanksgiving originated in rural New England as a harvest celebration. Rural peoples' celebration of other national holidays use customs that reinforce a local identity. Fourth of July parades, for example, typically include the high school band, elementary school children on bikes, and service groups. A high school parade queen is crowned in honor of a local agricultural product, such as sweet corn, hogs, peaches, chilies, or cotton. The oldest man or woman, mothers of soldiers lost in national wars, and politicians wave from a local car dealer's convertible. Bystanders personally can greet most parade participants. Midwestern rural communities also celebrate annual "homecomings." These are organized by a community service group to induce return visits by out-migrants and simultaneously raise money for projects such as refurbishing a ballfield or remodeling the town hall. Churchwomen make salads and pies; men barbecue chicken, catfish, or steaks; and softball is played. Auctions are a common ritual to liquidate household goods, farm equipment, animals, houses, or farmland from estate settlements or farm retirements. Auctions of donated household or farm items also are held to raise community funds.

Rural people have rich social lives. Attitudes toward leisure reflect traditions of self-sufficiency. "We make our own" entertainment, they say. Saturday nights or Sunday afternoons teenagers gather at landmarks to have bridge parties, road parties, or cornfield parties. A bonfire is lit, cars hoods are sat on, and beer may be drunk. Small-town teenagers, whether in midwestern four-by-four pick-up trucks or in southwestern Hispanic "low-rider" cars, spend weekend evenings driving around to see and be seen "dragging main." Their parents and grandparents use card groups, such as euchre in the Midwest, as an excuse to socialize with friends or kin at home. Adult social gatherings typically are segregated by sex, with men and women clustering in different rooms. Similarly, sexual segregation occurs in the weekly gatherings of women's quilting groups and the male volunteer firemen's card groups at the fire station.

In the southern highlands of Kentucky or Tennessee, social get-togethers are likely to be accompanied by singing and the playing of fiddles, banjos, or dulcimers. People may not read music, but words and tunes pass from one generation to the next in an oral tradition. Among African Americans in the rural South, the blues and gospel music emerged from similar folk traditions. Rural music, crafts, and storytelling greatly influenced both popular and classical culture in America. Country music traces its roots to the folk music traditions of British Isles immigrants. It celebrates rural life, home place, the road, loneliness, family, loves, and friends in deceptively simple lyrics and tunes. Square dancing, clog dancing, the two-step, and other rural dance forms uniquely American are performed to renditions of original ethnic tunes continually recast by country musicians.

Rites of passages are excuses for community celebrations in rural areas. The entire community attends weddings, funerals, or graduations in part because everyone is related in some way to the main actors. Marriages are particularly important rituals. The community custom of *shivaree* is widely practiced in the rural Midwest. Friends or relatives of the newlyweds (on either the wedding night or during the honeymoon) devise practical jokes to interfere with conjugal relations. Male friends symbolically attempt to restore the newly married male to the fraternity of single men and failing that, make difficult the young couple's homecoming. Cowbells on the bed springs, a short-sheeted bed, or a kidnapping of the groom is associated with *shivaree*. Couples may find doorknobs greased, labels removed from cans, or plastic wrap covering the toilet on return from their honeymoon. These rituals typically are associated with loud noisemaking and are the grist of community gossip for weeks after at the local coffeehouse or at church services.

—*Sonya Salamon*

See also

African Americans; American Indians; Arts; Asian Pacific Americans; Cemeteries; Churches; Community Celebrations; Ethnicity; Folklore; Latinos; Music; Refugee Resettlement; Religion; Settlement Patterns; Values of Residents.

References

Brown, Linda Keller, and Kay Mussell, eds. *Ethnic and Regional Foodways in the United States.* Knoxville: University of Tennessee Press, 1984.

Cassidy, Frederic G. *The Dictionary of American Regional English.* Vols. 1–3. Cambridge, MA: Harvard University Press, 1985, 1991, 1996.

Fischer, David Hackett. *Albion's Seed: Four British Folkways in America.* New York: Oxford University Press, 1989.

Hummon, David. *Commonplaces: Community Ideology and Identity in American Culture.* Albany: State University of New York Press, 1990.

Salamon, Sonya. *Prairie Patrimony: Family, Farming, and Community in the Midwest.* Chapel Hill: University of North Carolina Press, 1992.

Tichi, Cecelia. *High Lonesome: The American Culture of Country Music.* Chapel Hill: University of North Carolina Press, 1994.

Yoder, Don. *Discovering American Folklife: Studies in Ethnic, Religious, and Regional Culture.* Ann Arbor, MI: UMI Research Press, 1990.

Dairy Farming

A specialized type of agricultural business in which fluid milk is the principal source of cash income. Dairy farming in rural America is placed in historical context from the first dairy animals that came with the original European settlers to the growth and development of the dairy industry over succeeding centuries. The location of milk production in the United States and reasons for changes during the twentieth century are presented. Sources of the great gains in productivity during the second half of the century are emphasized. Major issues facing dairy farmers at the end of the century conclude the discussion.

Introduction

Dairy farming is a very important type of American commercial agriculture. In 1992, gross sales of dairy products accounted for $17.8 billion of the $162.6 billion gross sales for all agricultural products. Dairy products accounted for 50 percent or more of total sales on about 100,000 of the nation's 1.9 million farms. Most dairy farmers specialize in milk production, and a large portion of the crops they produce are used to feed the dairy herd. In many cases, a substantial part of the concentrate feed needed to produce milk is purchased (U.S. Bureau of the Census 1994).

Historical Development

The first settlers who came to North America from Europe brought cattle with them as a source of meat and milk. Dairy animals were reported to have arrived in Jamestown, Virginia, in 1611 and at Plymouth Colony, Massachusetts, in 1624. Most families sought to have a cow as a source of milk and butter. Farming was largely a subsistence activity. Small surpluses of milk or butter were traded for other necessities like cloth, sugar, or tools. In the seventeenth century and well into the eighteenth, many families living in towns and villages kept a family cow and a horse in a barn in their backyard.

The settlers who pushed west across the Appalachians after the Revolutionary War took their livestock with them as they crossed each new frontier. When the first agricultural statistics were collected as part of the population census in 1850, there were 6.4 million dairy animals over two years of age reported in a country with 23 million people, or essentially one milk cow for every four people. The first regular shipment of milk by rail occurred in 1841 from Orange County, New York, to New York City. The first cheese factory was established at Oneida, New York, in 1851.

Most of the continental United States was settled by the second half of the nineteenth century. There were 76 million people and 16 million dairy cows in 1900, about one cow for every five people. Some specialization in dairy farming occurred with the advent of mechanical refrigeration in 1861 and commercial pasteurization machines in 1895. Cows were milked by hand. Yields averaged about 3,000 pounds of milk per cow per year.

Great advances were made in the dairy industry in the first half of the twentieth century. All-weather roads, telephones, and electrification changed life in rural America. Trucks and tractors replaced horsepower in the fields and on the roads. Milking machines replaced hand milking on dairy farms. Specialized dairy farms became more and more common. The practice of keeping a family cow was abandoned by most families quite rapidly after World War II. Production testing through Dairy Herd Improvement Associations was started in 1905 and continues today. Most farmers were members of cooperatives that bargained collectively for the sale of their milk or processed it into butter or cheese. Agricultural cooperatives were formed in larger numbers at the end of the nineteenth century to carry out many buying and selling

A dairy farmer supervises the milking process.

activities for farmers. Proving sires (bulls whose genetic characteristics are known through their offspring) and the use of artificial insemination to improve the genetic capacity of dairy animals was introduced in the 1930s. Substantial increases in knowledge about feeds and feeding were accumulated and extended through the Cooperative State Research, Education, and Extension Service, magazines like *Hoard's Dairyman,* agricultural newspapers, and radio.

As a result of these improvements in breeding, nutrition, management, and technology, average milk yields increased to 5,314 pounds per cow per year in 1950. Cow numbers peaked at about 24 million. With 151 million people in the United States, there was about one cow for every six people in the country. In 1950, most dairy farms had recently obtained electricity and milking machines. Bulk tanks were replacing the use of milk cans in the major dairy areas. With the advent of improved communication systems and all-weather roads, large numbers of these local cooperatives federated or merged into regional entities during the 1940s and 1950s.

In the 20 years between 1950 and 1970, a quiet agricultural revolution occurred across rural America. Farm numbers dropped from 5.4 million in 1950 to 2.7 million in 1969. Farm size increased rapidly, and mechanization became the general rule. Most of those who left farming found jobs in industry or in the growing service economy not far from their homes. The applications of science and technology in the dairy industry pushed average yields to 9,385 pounds of milk per cow per year, an increase of 80 percent in 20 years. Cow numbers declined from about 24 million to less than 14 million. Dairy surpluses became a public policy issue in the United States and nearly every developed nation in the Western world. Supply outran demand in the marketplace, and major efforts to manage supplies through a combination of market orders, price supports, and government programs were undertaken.

Much of the technology and the dairy systems used on farms in the 1990s were introduced and developed between 1950 and 1970. Loose housing (a housing system in which the herd is handled as a group except at milking time) and milking parlors were adopted widely by those expanding herd sizes. Around-the-barn pipeline systems became widespread in stall-barn operations. Mechanical systems to handle manure became the rule. A shift away from tower silos to horizontal storage began. Labor-saving technology was adopted in one form or another by those who remained in business. The vast majority of farms delivered grade A milk. The cream separator joined the milk can as a vestige of a bygone era.

Location of Production by Herd Size

Most of the specialization in dairy production occurred since World War II. In 1940 there were milk cows on 4.6 million of the 6.1 million farms counted by the census. At the end of 1994, every state reported some dairy farms, but there were a little less than 150,000 operations reporting at least one dairy cow. Of these, 54,360 had less than 30 cows. Essentially, 95,000 farms with 30 or more cows produced 95.2 percent of the national milk supply in 1994.

Nearly 39 percent of the national milk supply was produced on the 74,100 farms with 30 to 99 cows (see Table 1). Most of these farms produce all of the roughage and an important part of the concentrates consumed by their dairy herds. They are full-time commercial operations in which a large part of the labor is provided by farmers and their families. An average of 25–30 cows are handled per worker. Cows are typically housed in conventional stall or stanchion barns. Most replacement dairy calves used to replace older, less productive milk cows are raised by the operators. Manure is spread daily or on a regular basis on the cropland. The sale of milk and dairy animals provides most of the farm's cash.

Nearly 19 percent of the national milk supply was produced on the 14,600 farms with 100 to 199 cows. The number of farms of this size has grown quite rapidly since 1980; most of these units are expansions by dairy farmers who had smaller enterprises. Although some of these herds are milked in stall barns, most make use of milking parlors and some type of loose-housing facility. In most cases, farms of this size produce a large share of the feed the cows consume. An average of 35 cows is handled per worker.

The 6,900 farms with 200 cows or more produced 39.0 percent of the national milk supply in the mid-1990s. These larger dairy units are of increasing importance in all the dairy states and account for more than half of the milk produced in the South and West. Nearly all of these farms use loose-housing systems and automated milking parlors. Contracts for feed production, dairy cow replacement rearing, and many other services are common on units with 1,000 cows or more. Specialized crews often milk around the clock.

Location of Production by State and Region

Besides the substantial reductions in the number of farms milking cows during the twentieth century, major changes have occurred in the locations where dairying is centered. At the turn of the century, much of the nation's population was found east of the Mississippi River, and most of the cows were in the eastern half of the country as well. People moved steadily west and south, especially since 1960, and the dairy industry moved with them.

Wisconsin was the leading dairy state for much of the twentieth century, but California exceeded it in milk production in 1994 (see Table 2). The Northeast and the Great Lakes states of Wisconsin, Minnesota, and Michigan produce milk because cows are best able to convert the hay, pasture, and silage produced there into a useful, salable product. The numbers of people living nearby helped to provide a market for the milk and dairy products produced there, but climate and natural resources have had much to do with retaining the dairy industry in these states. Dairy production declined much more rapidly in the Corn Belt and South.

Notable growth in the amounts of milk produced on dry-lot dairies of 1,000 cows or more has taken place in the mountain and western states since 1980. These farms have advantages over more humid regions in handling manure, wastewater, odor problems, and disease and insect controls. As long as these operators can contract for or produce high-quality roughages, they have clear management advantages over producers in more humid regions. Still, over 70 percent of the nation's milk supply is produced in the eastern two-thirds of the country.

Sources of the Rapid Gains in Productivity

Average milk production per cow has increased from 5,300 pounds per cow in the 1950s to 16,100 in 1994. This remarkable increase in productivity is the joint result of many things, especially applications of science and technology and improved management. Great strides have

Table 1
Farms, Cows, and Production by Herd Size, U.S., 1994

Size of operation categorized by number of cows	Number of operations (as % of total)	Number of cows (as % of total)	Milk production (as % of total)
1–29	36.2	4.8	3.6
30–49	21.9	14.1	12.1
50–99	27.6	28.8	26.5
100–199	9.7	18.9	18.7
200 and over	4.6	33.4	39.0
U.S. totals	149,990 farms	9.5 million cows	153.6 billion pounds

Table 2
Milk Production: Rank Order by States, United States, 1899 and 1994

	1899			1994	
Rank	State	Percentage of total	Rank	State	Percentage of total
1	New York	10.6	1	California	16.2
2	Iowa	7.4	2	Wisconsin	14.6
3	Pennsylvania	6.7	3	New York	7.4
4	Wisconsin	6.5	4	Pennsylvania	6.7
5	Illinois	6.3	5	Minnesota	6.1
6	Ohio	5.9	6	Texas	4.1
7	Michigan	4.3	7	Michigan	3.6
8	Minnesota	4.2	8	Washington	3.4
9	Indiana	3.6	9	Ohio	2.9
10	Missouri	3.5	10	Iowa	2.6
11	Texas	3.4	11	Idaho	2.4
12	Kansas	3.4	12	New Mexico	2.2
	All others	34.2		All others	27.2

Source: National Agricultural Statistics Service, U.S. Department of Agriculture, Milk Production, February 1995.

been made in dairy nutrition; genetics and breeding; animal physiology; veterinary medicine; and the technology for milking, feeding, and materials handling.

Credit for tripling output per cow in a little over 40 years can be assigned to many causes. High on the list are the substantial improvements in the quality and quantity of feeds that are now available and the nutritional knowledge acquired by dairy farmers and their consultants. Balanced rations are possible because of forage testing, knowledge gained about what happens inside the rumen, and nutritional information obtained by scientists from thousands and thousands of experiments.

The dairy cow requires five major classes of nutrients: energy, protein, minerals, vitamins, and water. All five are essential for normal health and productivity. Next to water, the greatest need is for energy and protein. Dairy farmers determine the approximate quantity and quality of the energy and protein in the roughages and concentrates produced on their own farms. With this information, they purchase feed ingredients needed to mix a balanced ration that allows sustained high levels of production. Total mixed rations are an important reason for the increases in productivity.

Production testing and sire selection have dramatically improved the genetic potential of all the dairy breeds in this century. The identification of proven sires and the widespread use of these genes through artificial insemination has transformed commercial dairy production in a matter of decades. Undergirding these programs has been the willingness of dairy farmers to keep production records through Dairy Herd Improvement Cooperatives and to share these data with researchers and the cooperatives and private organizations that collect and distribute the semen. Concurrently, scientists have greatly increased the understanding of the anatomy and physiology of reproduction, the endocrine glands, and the ways in which hormones control and influence the cow and her behavior.

At the same time that nutritional and genetic advances have occurred, impressive progress has been made in solving herd health problems, developing disease prevention programs, and providing tools with which to operate and manage an increasingly complex dairy business. Records are fundamental to breeding efficiency, culling programs, and cash flow management. Dairy farmers must do an important part of the record keeping themselves but can also enlist paid professionals to assist them with production records, tax planning, and herd analysis.

Improved technology for dairy housing, milking, manure management, and feed production, storage, and handling contributed to increased productivity. The milking process remains a combination of art and science, but the ability to produce and deliver clean, low-somatic-cell-count milk is now available to every dairy farmer. The use of bulk tanks to store and refrigerate milk on farms and transport it to dairy plants for processing and distribution is only one of many ways in which advances in materials handling reduced labor requirements and human effort throughout the dairy industry.

In the final years of the twentieth century, scientific advances continue apace in the dairy industry. The use of embryo transplants to increase the number of offspring from individual donor cows is being practiced on some farms but is not a widespread commercial practice like artificial insemination. The use of bovine somatotropin (BST) has been cleared for general use by the Food and Drug Administration (FDA) after a substantial number of years of testing across the country. The use of genetically engineered products in food production is of concern to some consumers and remains a matter of public debate.

About 90 percent of the dairy animals in the United States at the end of the twentieth century are Holsteins and another 5 percent are Jerseys. Most dairy animals are not registered with a dairy cattle breed association and therefore are considered to fall into "grades." Nevertheless, the use of artificial insemination is so widespread among commercial dairymen that the genetic stock on most farms is essentially purebred if not registered. There is little crossing of breeds.

Issues Facing Dairy Farmers at the End of the Century

Public concerns about the environment have heightened at the end of this century. Most dairy farms are located relatively close to nonfarm neighbors. Farmers are becoming a minority even in rural communities. As a consequence, learning to live in harmony with one's neighbors and still spread manure and do regular farm work is of growing importance. Special concerns are associated with surface and underground water supplies. The handling of wastewater and applications of nitrogen and manure to cropland is critical. Stewardship of natural resources always has been an important concern of farmers. Finding acceptable agricultural practices that minimize the need for governmental regulation is of high priority.

Per capita consumption of all milk and dairy products has been declining in the 1980s and 1990s. Whereas consumption of cheese, yogurt, and low-fat milk increased, whole milk, butter, and ice cream face declining markets. Public concerns about the consumption of animal fats and cholesterol are reflected in dairy product sales. Dairy farmers authorized the collection of funds out of their milk receipts for dairy promotion programs at both the state and national levels. Emphasis is given to milk and dairy products as high-quality sources of calcium and protein and one of nature's "most perfect" foods.

In the second half of the twentieth century, the capacity to produce milk on farms has outrun effective demand in nearly every developed country in the Western world. Milk markets are increasingly regulated both because milk is a highly perishable product and because of needs to balance supplies with demand. International trade in dairy products is small relative to output because of barriers erected by individual countries to protect their markets and price support programs. For example, the North American Free Trade Agreement (NAFTA) exempts milk and dairy products from its terms and conditions. Finding ways to open world dairy markets to fair competition will be one of the key challenges for U.S. dairy farmers in the twenty-first century.

—Bernard F. Stanton

See also
Agricultural Programs; Animal Rights/Welfare; Biotechnology; Dairy Products; Livestock Production; Pasture.
References
Bath, Donald L., Frank N. Dickinson, H. Allen Tucker, and Robert D. Appleman. *Dairy Cattle: Principles, Practices, Problems, Profits*. 3d ed. Philadelphia: Lea and Febiger, 1985.
Church, David C. *Livestock Feeds and Feeding*. 3d ed. Englewood Cliffs, NJ: Prentice-Hall, 1991.
Ensminger, M. Eugene. *Animal Science*. 9th ed. Danville, IL: Interstate Publishers, 1991.
———. *Dairy Cattle Science*. 3d ed. Danville, IL: Interstate Publishers, 1993.
Perez, Agnes M. *Changing Structure of U.S. Dairy Farms*. Agricultural Economics Report 690, July. Washington, DC: U.S. Department of Agriculture, Economic Research Service, 1994.
Schmidt, Glen H., Lloyd D. VanVleck, and Michael F. Hutjens. *Principles of Dairy Science*. 2d ed. Englewood Cliffs, NJ: Prentice-Hall, 1988.
U.S. Bureau of the Census. *1992 Census of Agriculture, Volume 1. Geographic Area Series, Part 51. United States: Summary and State Data*. AC92-A-51. Washington, DC: U.S. Department of Commerce, Bureau of the Census, 1994.

Dairy Products

Foods made from milk. This entry discusses milk composition and the processing techniques by which dairy products are made. Some of these dairy products include fluid milk, cheese, frozen desserts, butter, dry milk, yogurt, condensed milk products, and by-products.

Introduction

Since the beginning of recorded history, humans have used the milk of mammals as a food source. In the early days, each family depended on its own animals for milk. Later, dairy farms and processing plants, known as creameries, were developed close to cities to pasteurize, package, and distribute milk. Dairy products in rural America consisted at first only of raw milk, cream, butter, and cheese. With the development of the dairy industry came improved processing and packaging methods and refrigeration.

Milk Composition and Quality

Cow's milk consists of water (87 percent), fat (3.9 percent), protein (3.2 percent), lactose (4.6 percent), and minerals (0.7 percent). These constituents vary with breed of cow, feed, stage of lactation, health and age of the animal, and environmental conditions.

The delicate, buttery flavor of dairy products is due in large part to the fat content. Milk protein, composed of two major fractions, caseins and whey proteins, is important in human nutrition. Lactose, or milk sugar, is essential for early brain development and gives milk its slightly sweet taste. Milk is an excellent source of calcium, phosphorus, and riboflavin, but a poor source of vitamin D. Consequently, vitamin D–fortified milk has been sold since the 1920s to prevent rickets in children. Because of milk's highly regarded nutritional status, it is often characterized as "nature's most nearly perfect food."

Prior to 1900, raw cow's milk generally was cooled only before consumption. Since then scientists have shown that diseases may be spread through milk that becomes contaminated by infected animals or by humans who are carriers of infectious diseases. Thus, to safeguard its quality, essentially all milk is pasteurized. Pasteurization is the process by which milk is heated to a certain temperature for a time to destroy all pathogens and most other bacteria.

Dairy products are subjected to a variety of laboratory tests to ensure public safety and meet composition standards. Mastitis is an inflammation of the cow's udder that results in the presence of somatic cells in milk. A high level of somatic cells (more than 750,000/milliliter [ml]) in milk is considered abnormal and should not be offered for human consumption. Improper treatment of mastitis with antibiotics may result in such medicines getting into the milk supply. Their presence is determined by a variety of sensitive and rapid tests that ensure a safe milk supply.

Dairy laboratories test both the raw milk and finished products for components such as fat and protein according to federal and state standards, which specify the level of fat required in certain dairy products. These tests are described in detail by Cunniff (1995) and are the basis for determining the purchase price of milk from the farmer.

Processing

Milk from the cow at approximately 34°C is cooled rapidly to 4.4°C or below to maintain quality. Cooled raw milk is hauled by tanker to dairy plants, where it is processed into milk products.

Separation. Centrifugal cream separators, introduced in 1890, use the force of gravity to separate the fat (cream) from the milk. Cream is added back to the milk stream to yield the desired fat content, or is used in other dairy products.

Homogenization. This process involves breaking the fat globules into small particles that form a stable emulsion in the milk. The fat globules do not rise by gravity to form a cream line. Today, most fluid milk products are homogenized.

A homogenizer is a high-pressure positive pump in which milk is forced through small passages under high pressure (14 to 17 MegaPascals [Mpa]) at velocities of approximately 180–245 meters/second (m/sec). The fat globules are broken up as a result of a combination of factors—shearing, impingement, distention, and cavitation. The fat globules in raw milk (1 to 15 [μm] in diameter) are reduced to 1 to 2 μm.

Pasteurization. The process of pasteurization, named after the French scientist Louis Pasteur, involves heating milk to kill pathogenic and most other organisms and to inactivate certain enzymes without greatly altering the flavor and nutritional content. The basic regulations are included in the Grade A Pasteurized Milk Ordinance, which has been adapted by most local and state jurisdictions.

Pasteurization may be done by batch or continuous-flow processes. In the batch process, each particle of milk must be heated to at least 62.8°C and held continuously at or above this temperature for at least 30 minutes. In the continuous process, the milk is heated to at least 71.7°C for at least 15 seconds. The latter is known as high-temperature, short-time pasteurization. Other continuous pasteurization processes using higher temperatures and shorter times, called ultrahigh temperature (UHT), are commercially employed. Following pasteurization, the product is cooled quickly to 7°C or less to prevent a cooked flavor.

Packaging. Milk packaging started when glass milk bottles were filled by hand and later by mechanical fillers. Plastic-coated paper milk cartons were introduced in 1932 and plastic milk containers in 1964. Milk packaging has progressed from the quart glass bottle to the half-gallon paper carton to the gallon plastic jug of today. Approximately 75 percent of fluid milk sold comes in such packages.

Aseptic packaging has developed in conjunction with high-temperature processing and has continued to make sterile milk and milk products a commercial reality worldwide. In the United States, UHT systems currently are processing fruit juices and some cream and ice cream mixes.

Fluid milk products include milk, reduced-fat milks, and cream. Fluid milk contains 3.25 percent fat as defined by the Code of Federal Regulations (1995). Also available are a range of reduced-fat milks such as 2.0 percent, 1.5 percent, 1.0 percent, and skim milk. Creams are defined as products that contain not less than 18 percent milk fat, such as whipping cream (36–40 percent milk fat) and table, coffee, or light cream (18–30 percent milk fat). Half-and-half, an alternative to cream, is a mixture of cream and milk (10.5–12 percent milk fat).

Cheese. Cheese making is based on the coagulation of casein from milk to produce curds and whey. Casein is precipitated by acidification, which can be accomplished by adding bacteria that produce lactic acid from lactose. There are over 400 cheese varieties; the composition of many is listed in Wong et al. (1988). Over 32 percent of the total milk supply in the United States is used to make cheese. The most popular cheeses are cheddar and Italian varieties. Cheddar cheese is made by inoculating pasteurized milk with a lactic acid culture and rennet to coagulate casein. The coagulated milk is cut into cubes and cooked to remove whey. The whey is drained, and the curd cubes are allowed to knit closely together by the cheddaring process. At the end of this process, the curd is milled into smaller cubes and salted. The salted cheese is pressed overnight for further whey removal and aged up to a year for flavor development. Other cheese varieties use different cultures and cooking times. In the case of mozzarella, heating the cheese curds develops the stringiness seen on pizza.

Frozen desserts are popular in the United States, especially ice cream, which was first sold in New York City in 1777. Ice cream consists of milk fat (8–20 percent) and nonfat milk solids (8–15 percent), with a total solids content of 36–43 percent. Dairy ingredients include milk; cream; butter; and condensed whole, nonfat, or dry milk. Sweeteners include a blend of cane or beet sugar and corn syrup solids. Stabilizers that improve the body of ice cream include gelatin, sodium alginate, sodium carboxymethyl cellulose, pectin, and guar gum. Emulsifiers such as lecithin, monoglycerides, diglycerides, and polysorbates incorporate air and improve the whipping properties. A mixture of these ingredients is pumped to a freezer, which whips the mix to incorporate air and freezes it to ice cream.

Other frozen desserts include frozen yogurt, sherbet, and mellorine-type products, parfaits, ice cream puddings, novelties, and water ice products. New reduced-, low-, and nonfat products and products containing low-calorie sweeteners are also on the market. Frozen desserts use 9.7 percent of the U.S. milk supply.

Butter contains over 80 percent milk fat with not more than 16 percent moisture. It was originally manufactured by churning farm-separated raw cream and had a relatively short shelf-life. Today a continuous operation with automatic controls is common. Per capita butter consumption has remained steady at 4 pounds for the past 20 years, using about 8 percent of the U.S. milk supply.

Dry milk is made by drum- or spray-drying to preserve milk in times of surplus. Approximately 5 percent of the milk supply is used for this product. Drying is preceded by concentrating milk in an evaporator. Drying takes place on a heated drum or by spraying milk under high pressure into a large stainless steel dryer, where it contacts heated air at approximately 200°C and evaporates to produce milk powder. Dry whole milk must be vacuum- or gas-packed to maintain quality during storage. Dry milk is a concentrated source of protein and lactose used in other manufactured food products. The moisture content for nonfat dry milk is 5 percent or less for standard grade and less than 3 percent for dry whole milk.

Yogurt is a fermented milk product that is increasingly consumed in the United States. Milk is fermented with *Lactobacillus delbrueckii bulgaricus* and *Streptococcus thermophilus* organisms that produce lactic acid and the characteristic yogurt flavor. Milk with 1–5 percent fat and 11–14 percent solid-nonfat is heated to about 82°C and kept at that temperature for 30 minutes, homogenized, cooled to 43–46°C, and inoculated with a 2 percent mixture of yogurt cultures. It is incubated at 43°C for three hours in a vat or in the final container and cooled and held at 4.4°C or lower. Fruit-flavored yogurts are common; 30 to 50 grams of fruit are placed in the bottom of the carton (sundae style) or mixed with the yogurt (Swiss style).

Condensed Milk Products. Evaporated milk contains at least 6.5 percent milk fat, 23 percent total milk solids, and 16.5 percent milk solids-nonfat. It is produced by condensing milk in a vacuum evaporator, packaging it in cans, and sterilizing it at 116–118°C for 15–20 minutes. It is subsequently cooled to room temperature within 15 minutes. Vitamins A and D and stabilizing salts, such as sodium citrate and disodium phosphate, may be added prior to sterilizing.

Sweetened condensed milk contains from 43 to 45 percent sugar, at least 8.5 percent milk fat, and 28 percent total milk solids. Condensed milk products are used widely in the manufacture of ice cream, baked goods, confectionery, and other food products.

By-products resulting from the separation or alteration of milk components are also of value. Lactose or milk sugar has about one-sixth the sweetening strength of sucrose and is used in infant formula, other processed foods, and pharmaceutical products. Casein is used to fortify flour, bread, and cereals and for glues and microbiological media. Many nondairy products such as coffee creamers, toppings, and icings use casein. Whey, the by-product of cheese making, is used widely as a dried or concentrated ingredient in other food products for its nutritive and functional value.

—*John G. Parsons*

See also
Agricultural Programs; Agro/Food System; Dairy Farming; Food Safety; Livestock Industry; Marketing; Markets; Nutrition; Policy, Food.
References
Code of Federal Regulations. Parts 100–169, 1 April. Washington, DC: Office of the Federal Register, National Archives and Records Administration, 1995.
Cunniff, P., ed. *Official Methods of Analysis of AOAC International.* 16th ed. Arlington, VA: Association of Official Analytical Chemists, 1995.
Grade A Pasteurized Milk Ordinance: 1993 Revisions. Publication no. 229, Washington, DC: U.S. Department of Health and Human Services, 1993.
Marshall, Robert, ed. *Standard Methods for the Examination of Dairy Products.* 16th ed. Washington, DC: American Public Health Association, 1992.
U.S. Department of Health and Human Services. *Milk Pasteurization Controls and Tests.* 2d ed. Rockville, MD: U.S. Department of Health and Human Services, Public Health Service, Food and Drug Administration, 1986.
Wong, Noble, Robert Jenness, Mark Keeney, and Elmer Marth. *Fundamentals of Dairy Chemistry.* 3d ed. New York: Van Nostrand Reinhold, 1988.

Decentralization

The dispersion or delegation of decision-making authority and management to more than one person or decision-making body; the undoing of the centralized control typical of federal governments and large businesses; and situations in which decision making and control over resource management, economic development, and the delivery of services is the prerogative of local citizens and agencies. Several key points will be covered in the following discussion. First, a distinction is made between industrial decentralization and the decentralization of federal authority. Second, the benefits of decentralization in rural areas are contrasted with the problems of centralized control. Third, because centralization and decentralization are not necessarily exclusive categories, examples of how the two work together in rural settings are explored. Finally, the future of decentralization is addressed in terms of its consequences for rural communities.

Federal Authority

Decentralization has traditionally been used to describe how federal governmental authority has been diffused. There are three major forms of decentralization of federal authority: deconcentration, devolution, and privatization. Deconcentration refers to the shift in workload from a central location to field offices. Many federal agencies, including the U.S. Department of Agriculture (USDA), have field offices. Rather than a true decentralization of power, deconcentration typically broadens the scope of federal authority. Although face-to-face meetings with field operators from these agencies give the impression of a government close to the people, the procedures that guide day-to-day activities are made in Washington, D.C. Devolution requires that authority be relinquished to local government officials. The goals of devolution are to create or strengthen independent local and regional governments. The mid-1990s law that provided block grants for welfare services to states and let state legislatures decide how to spend those dollars was an example of devolution. Privatization involves transferring government functions to nongovernmental institutions, such as community development corporations, credit associations, farmers' cooperatives, nonprofit organizations, and mutual aid societies.

Congressional legislators in the United States are attempting to devolve and privatize certain aspects of the federal bureaucracy in order to balance the federal budget and improve the delivery of important but costly services. As a consequence, in the future more planning, public services, and economic development efforts will be managed by government agencies and nongovernmental institutions at the state and local levels.

Industry

Major cities historically served as centers for business decision making. Except for agricultural production, most major businesses and nonfarm labor were located in cities. During the 1970s, rural economies grew as manufacturing firms relocated to rural areas. Industrial decentralization was the process of moving labor and decision making away from cities and centers of capital investment.

Not all rural areas and workers benefited from industrial decentralization. Most firms that relocated moved to exurbia, rural areas bordering metropolitan counties. These counties experienced job growth and in-migration. Many agriculturally dependent communities, particularly those in the Midwest, continued to decline. Although decentralization led to job growth in exurbia, it concentrated many young workers in low-wage jobs.

Centralization: Bad or Good?

Is centralized decision making and control a bad thing? Ritzer (1993, 12) is highly critical of overly centralized organizations. He points out that centralization leads to the "irrationality of rationality," or using standard procedures to deal with unique, nonstandard business and organizational problems.

Bureaucracies develop rules and regulations to achieve goals efficiently. These rules and regulations oftentimes identify the optimum means to achieve some goal or problem. Organizations gain control over day-to-day activities by formalizing rules and regulations. Workers need only follow standard procedures to be efficient. However, many highly centralized bureaucracies are often inefficient because of trained incapacity, red tape, alienation, and other organizational pathologies. Trained incapacity, or overconformity to rules, is one disturbing consequence of strict adherence to standard procedures. When faced with an unfamiliar situation or a situation with no guidelines, workers tend to treat the situation as though it fits existing guidelines, rather than to analyze the problem objectively and develop a unique solution. Trained incapacity leads to an inferior quality of work, and the organization's clients may ultimately become dissatisfied with the services they are getting.

Alienation, another disturbing consequence of over-centralization, also leads to inefficiency. Highly centralized organizations can be dehumanizing and alienating places to work because workers have little control over their day-to-day activities. Many employees who hold very specialized jobs have no real idea how their work contributes to the organization's overall goals. This detachment from their jobs can lead to low morale and poor-quality work.

Benefits

Proponents of decentralization claim that grassroots development programs and service delivery systems are more efficient and humane than those managed by federal bureaucrats. Development and service delivery programs are meant to enhance the social and economic conditions of communities, but centralized, federally run programs can fail to do so because of ignorance of local concerns, problems, and resources; a one-method-fits-all philosophy; and bureaucratic red tape.

Proponents argue that local citizens are better positioned to identify and address their development and service needs. They contend that community control leads to better relations between citizens and government officials, improves the managerial and technical skills of local citizens and government officials, and is more inclusive because minority groups within the community have more input concerning program goals and delivery of services. Community control, rather than centralized decision making, provides a better structure to deliver services and to coordinate various community development activities.

Achieving a Balance

Centralization and decentralization are not necessarily mutually exclusive categories. In reality, rural development programs and service delivery systems can be too demanding in their organizational requirements to be left totally to local communities. Local community efforts often are supported by funds and resources provided by state and federal agencies.

State programs help rural communities and businesses diversify and adapt to economic realities. Most state economies are deindustrializing; corporations in these states are moving their manufacturing plants to low-wage countries. Rather than let them pursue these industries, states encourage communities to build on their own competitive advantages, such as climate, proximity to markets, natural resource base, and workforce characteristics. State programs promote the business climates of rural communities and the strong work ethic of their citizens. They offer financial incentives to create new rural businesses, support the expansion of existing ones, and offer seed money for economic and technological innovations.

At the local level, decentralized planning efforts go by the names of "self-help," "street-level government," "community betterment programs," "community development corporations," and "business incubators." Self-help is a rural community betterment strategy that relies on the cooperation of local residents to enrich their own lives by improving their community's natural resources, facilities, service delivery systems, and job opportunities. In their pursuit of community betterment, citizens have created community development corporations and business incubators.

A community development corporation is a locally controlled, tax-exempt organization that operates self-help programs. They expand low-income housing; reduce illiteracy; improve the creditworthiness of minority families with local banks; and mobilize local, state, and federal resources for more jobs and higher incomes. Community development corporations seek grants from local, state, and federal governments and investments from the private sector.

Some community development corporations operate business incubators. Small businesses account for the largest amount of job growth in many regions of the United States, but because of the lack of capital, poor management, or poor marketing, new business ventures have a high failure rate. In some states, well over half of new businesses fail during the first four years. Local communities with business incubators have lowered that rate by providing businesses with rental space and operating services in the incubator's facilities. Services can be substantial—conference facilities, clerical assistance, custodial services, receptionist services, rental of equipment, and the like. Many incubators help new business owners develop management and marketing skills. Rural incubators are supported or operated by educational institutions, private organizations, town governments, and state agencies.

The Cooperative State Research, Education, and Extension Service

Some service delivery systems and rural development activities tap into local, state, and federal sources and thus cannot be seen as strictly centralized or decentralized. The USDA Cooperative State Research, Education, and Extension Service (CSREES) is organized along these lines. The general mission of the CSREES is to improve agriculture and strengthen families and their communities. In particular, extension agents disseminate information to farm operators and businesses to assist them in developing more efficient systems to produce and market agricultural products. Agents strengthen families, assist youth in acquiring life skills, and help communities resolve their development issues.

The structure of the CSREES varies slightly from state to state, but they commonly have a deconcentrated decision-making hierarchy in the state university system, usually through the departments of agriculture, home economics, or Cooperative Extension. CSREES offices are headed by deans, with associate deans, directors, and program managers as their assistants. Extension and program specialists, located on the university campuses or in regional offices, assist extension agents who are located in local (county) offices. Leadership and resources come from the local community. County governments often provide office space, clerical supplies, and other resources for extension agents. Local extension advisory boards provide recommendations and direction for and appraisals of extension services.

The Future of Decentralization in Rural America

Rural America is moving in contradictory directions. One direction leads to integration of industries. For example, livestock production and meatpacking are merging into a single industry. Many hog farmers are becoming subcontractors who supply a set number of hogs determined by a contract with an agribusiness conglomerate. This process takes some decision making away from individual farmers. Many rural communities are taking another direction by diversifying their economies through self-help, locally controlled activities. Ironically, both trends result from common social forces, particularly globalization and the emergence of the information superhighway.

Globalization is the process whereby people around the world are becoming more economically interdependent. For example, automobiles and computers may have been manufactured in the United States, but it is quite likely that over half of their parts were imported from Japan, Mexico, Singapore, or some other country. Economic activity is the pursuit of profit, and one way to achieve profit is to hire the cheapest labor regardless of national location.

Relocating industries, including agribusiness, to other countries leaves rural workers vulnerable to unemployment and income loss and marginalizes rural communities. In response, rural communities must either position themselves within the global marketplace through local development efforts or continue to wither away.

The impact of the information superhighway is much more ambiguous. Advances in telecommunications and computers allow many workers to live anywhere they wish, which amplifies the deconcentration of the labor force and exurbanization. However, these same technologies allow industry executives to regulate more efficiently the decisions of site managers without physically being at the sites.

Decentralization of decision-making authority, regardless of its form, has important implications for rural development, resource management, and service delivery systems. Rural America has many aspects. One set of aspects is economically vital and growing. Another set is stagnant and declining, suffering from poverty, environmental degradation, decaying infrastructures, and limited capacities to revitalize themselves. These problems cannot be overcome without federal assistance. A reorganization of federal policies toward rural America also may be in order. Many proponents of decentralization agree with these conclusions. They demand that federal bureaucrats recognize the diversity of rural communities and economies, assert that a one-method-fits-all approach will not work to reinvigorate these communities, and emphasize that the solutions to local problems will derive from grassroots, self-help initiatives supported by state and federal agencies.

—*Donald E. Arwood*

See also
Agro/Food System; Cooperative State Research, Education, and Extension Service; Development, Community and Economic; Future of Rural America; Government; Policy (various); Telecommunications; Trade, International; Urbanization.

References
Christenson, James A., and Cornelia B. Flora. "A Rural Policy Agenda for the 1990s." Pp. 333–337 in *Rural Policies for the 1990s*. Edited by C. B. Flora and J. A. Christenson. Boulder, CO: Westview Press, 1991.

Lapping, Mark B., Thomas L. Daniels, and John W. Walker. *Rural Planning and Development in the United States*. New York: Guilford Press, 1989.

Ritzer, George. *The McDonaldization of Society: An Investigation into the Changing Character of Contemporary Social Life.* Thousand Oaks, CA: Pine Forge Press, 1993.

Rondinelli, Dennis A., and G. Shabbir Cheema. "Implementing Decentralization Policies: An Introduction." Pp. 9–34 in *Decentralization and Development: Policy Implications in Developing Countries.* Edited by G. S. Cheema and D. A. Rondinelli. Beverly Hills, CA: Sage Publications, 1983.

Smith, Stewart N. "Six Ways States Can Spur Their Rural Economies." *Rural Development Perspectives* 4, no. 2 (1988): 8–14.

Weinberg, Mark L. "Business Incubators Give New Firms in Rural Areas a Head Start." *Rural Development Perspectives* 3, no. 2 (1987): 6–10.

Demography
See Rural Demography

Dental Health Care

The organization and provision of services to meet the preventative, acute, chronic, and long-term dental needs of a population. More than a quarter million trained professionals are dedicated to providing dental services to the U.S. public. The majority of them work in small, individually owned private practices. Although more than half of all dentists practice in major metropolitan areas, many practice in smaller communities scattered throughout rural America. Dental diseases are common in both urban and rural areas, and Americans spend more than $27 billion dollars annually on dental care. Many scientific and technical advances enabled the dental profession to make significant progress in combating dental disease over the past 40 years.

Rural residents most commonly face problems of access to care, poor diet and nutritional practice, inadequate insurance and financing mechanisms, and a lack of community water fluoridation. At the same time, many rural areas offer attractive alternatives to urban practice; focused efforts can result in successful recruitment of dentists. In rural areas, ethnic minorities and the poor are at greatest risk for dental health problems and neglect by employer-based insurance plans. Farmers and other self-employed workers are also typically disadvantaged with respect to dental insurance programs.

Care in America

U.S. dental care is delivered by a professionally trained workforce that includes more than 150,000 dentists, 100,000 dental hygienists, 200,000 dental assistants, and 60,000 dental laboratory technicians. Approximately 79 percent of the dentists are general practitioners who perform a full range of services for an average of 4,000 patients per year. Of the dental specialists, nearly half are either orthodontists (dentists who treat tooth and jaw alignment disorders) or oral and maxillofacial surgeons (dentists who specialize in surgical procedures involving the head, neck, teeth, jaws, and oral cavity). Other specialists include pediatric dentists (who treat children), periodontists (who treat diseases of the gums and other supporting tissues), prosthodontists (who focus on the replacement of missing teeth), endodontists (who treat disorders involving the dental pulp, the soft interior of the teeth), and oral pathologists (who work with oral cancers; genetic disorders; and head, neck, and oral disease identification). Public health dentists address the needs of broad segments of the public and communities. They study dental disease patterns and are concerned with disease prevention. Additional specialists focus on the elderly; practice forensic dentistry, pertaining to police, legal, or court proceedings; and repairing damaged and missing teeth.

Dentists are highly regarded as professionals and as trusted, ethical individuals. Approximately 68 percent of U.S. dentists are in solo practice. The average 1994 income of general practitioners who own practices was $117,610, according to the American Dental Association (1997). The vast majority of dentists are white males, but dental schools currently have high enrollments of females and ethnic minority students.

Of the many diseases humans face, those of the oral cavity are undoubtedly the most pervasive, not only in the United States but throughout the world. Chief among the many oral health problems are dental caries (cavities); periodontal disease (gum disease); oral cancers; and structural and functional problems that involve the teeth, mouth, head, neck, and skull. With proper oral hygiene or professional care, such problems can be prevented or managed effectively. However, the cost to treat and prevent dental disease is substantial. In the United States, where dental services are arguably the best in the world, annual expenditures for dental care topped $27 billion at the end of the 1980s. Despite scientific advances, cost control measures, and improved health status, dental care costs are expected to continue to escalate well into the next century.

These expenditures would undoubtedly be much higher were it not for numerous scientific and technical advances in dentistry over the latter part of the twentieth century. Educational, scientific, and technical discoveries had significant impacts on virtually all aspects of dental disease and oral health behaviors.

Community water fluoridation and fluoridated toothpastes, mouthwashes, and dietary supplements effectively reduced dental caries. Topical sealants further reduced the risk of caries in young children. Improved oral hygiene knowledge and practice and improved diets had broad impacts on the general population. The growth of dental insurance plans expanded access to care for many individuals. The widespread use of dental auxiliaries, improvement of dental management techniques, growth of small and large group practices in dentistry, and many technical improvements increased dentist productivity and thus, the amount of service available to U.S. residents. Increased numbers of minority and female dentists helped to open the dental care system to persons who might otherwise be reluctant to avail themselves of care.

Still, problems persist: dental caries declined since the 1940s, but nearly half of all school-age children still have some caries. On the average, in persons age 40 and older, more than 30 tooth surfaces are affected by caries. Diseases of the periodontal tissue affect nearly half of the adult population, and although gains were made in recent years, approximately 36 percent of persons over 65 lost all of their natural teeth. Oral cancers, often associated with tobacco use, remain a significant health problem and can lead to disfigurement and, in some cases, death.

Older Americans in particular represent a growing challenge to the dental profession. As overall health status improved, people live longer and have increased vulnerability to dental disease. Root caries, the development of carious lesions on the roots of teeth, was virtually unheard-of in the 1950s but is now seen with increasing frequency in dental offices. The administration of multiple medications to the elderly, a common occurrence, often precipitates conditions such as "dry-mouth" that, in turn, increase the risk of root caries and other oral health problems. Funding shortages in the 1990s have severely restricted epidemiological surveys and other public health research efforts, but there is every indication that dental disease (predominantly caries and periodontal disease) continues to compromise the health of the American people.

Care in Rural America

Although U.S. oral health is vastly better than it was 20 or 30 years ago, neither the public nor the profession can find satisfaction in current dental health statistics. Rural residents have particular cause for concern. The reader must exercise caution; generalizations, many of which cannot be substantiated, abound in reference to rural America. The Pine Ridge Reservation in South Dakota, the desert Southwest, and the Berkshires in Massachusetts, by way of illustration, are all rural, but have different populations, different social and economic systems, and thus different health and dental problems.

Demographic trends and other health system factors tend to exacerbate the lack of oral health and dental services for many persons living outside urban areas. Rural areas have slightly older populations, and these citizens are less likely to be covered by dental insurance. Dental care is likely to be less accessible and, in some instances, to be less comprehensive. Although it is not the rule, some rural (and, indeed, some urban) dentists find it difficult to keep current on new developments in dental materials and techniques, thereby denying their patients potential benefits from improvements in the profession. Rural citizens are less likely to have access to fluoridated water supplies, and areas of extreme poverty may have substandard

diets. When faced with dental emergencies (for example, severe injuries to the mouth), rural residents often drive further to reach a dental office or medical center than do people living in cities. Physicians and emergency medicine specialists generally are ill equipped to treat dental trauma. Oral surgeons may be several hours distant.

Rural dentists face problems of their own. They tend to be older than those in urban areas, have smaller practices, have greater difficulty recruiting highly skilled assistants and hygienists, and increasingly have difficulty competing with or participating in managed care systems.

Access to dental specialists for referral and consultation is a problem in many rural areas. Although 79 percent of the nation's dentists are general practitioners and are technically skilled in all aspects of dental care, many prefer to refer truly complex cases to specialists. However, when faced with having a patient travel 50 to 100 miles or more to an endodontist for a root canal or treating it themselves, they may handle the case rather than subject patients to long, painful delays in treatment.

Another aspect of the rural practitioner's isolation can be practicing without adequate backup for weekends and vacations. This sense of isolation extends to the rural practitioner's difficulty in obtaining continuing dental education. Advanced or continuing education, often dependent on dental school faculty and facilities, is usually offered in urban areas. This necessitates longer periods of absence from the practice than that experienced by the urban practitioner. Rural study clubs help dentists stay current but often do not provide the quality of programs frequently required by state agencies or associations for licensure or membership.

Recruiting dentists to small towns in rural areas, usually as young associates or as eventual replacements for retiring dentists, is sometimes difficult and may require more than a year of advance planning. Nonetheless, bridging practitioners in this manner is much easier and far more effective than recruiting dentists to practices that have been dormant for a year or more following the death or retirement of a dentist. Few young dentists are willing to risk establishing a solo practice in areas where residents have grown accustomed to seeking care elsewhere. The start-up costs to establish or retrofit such practices is high, ranging from $50,000 to $200,000, and young graduates, who often carry educational debts of $40,000 to $100,000, face enormous difficulties in obtaining financing. Spousal employment increasingly is an issue of concern to dentists who relocate. More and more dentists are married to trained professionals, and rural communities that represent exceptional practice opportunities for a dentist may not provide appropriate employment opportunities for the spouse.

Although rural residents face many dental health problems, they are not completely disadvantaged when compared to their urban counterparts. Diet and nutrition can be problematic in some areas, but most rural citizens have healthy diets and thus reduce their risk of certain dental diseases. Poverty and education must be considered when looking at diet and nutrition as factors associated with dental health. Fluoride supplements are available for those without fluoridated water supplies, and school health programs are often taken more seriously than in urban areas. Rural patients may find it easier to establish closer, long-term relationships with dental providers, and emergency care (for example, attention to a toothache in the middle of the night) is more readily available in many small towns than in large cities.

A fundamental aspect of access to care rests on the ability of rural areas to recruit dentists. Many young dentists and their families are drawn to rural communities that offer more attractive lifestyles than those found in highly urbanized cities. Outdoor recreational activities, slower-paced living, lower crime rates, a stronger sense of community, and community-based schools frequently are cited as advantages of smaller communities by dentists looking for new locations. Dentists drawn to rural communities for such reasons often become involved in community affairs and are more likely to be active participants in local and regional health-planning activities.

Disease prevention and control research is under way; however, neither significant breakthroughs nor the development of a caries vaccine are expected before the turn of the century. Technological advances in computerized communication (such as interactive television, distance education, the Internet, and World Wide Web systems) may help overcome some problems caused by the relative isolation of rural practitioners. These same developments may serve to extend dental expertise to rural medical clinics and remote communities. Direct care can only be provided by skilled practitioners, but consultative services extended to medical and other health care providers would be beneficial in certain circumstances.

Perhaps the most significant near-term developments will emerge in the arena of dental care financing. Managed care systems are making major inroads in dental care delivery in metropolitan and urbanized areas but have not had a significant impact in most rural communities. The elderly and rural poor are particularly at risk

with respect to most managed care programs, at least as they are structured in the mid-1990s. The cost of dental care is projected to escalate over the coming decade. Health care reform holds promise of improved service for all Americans. But, without adequate insurance mechanisms and measures to ensure the availability and acceptability of dental services, the gap in oral health quality will widen dramatically, with farmers and other self-employed workers, the elderly, and the rural poor (many of whom are ethnic minorities) disadvantaged most.

—*David O. Born*

See also
Health and Disease Epidemiology; Health Care; Nurses and Allied Health Professionals; Nutrition; Policy, Health Care.
References
American Dental Association. "Fact Sheet: Dentistry Today." http://www.ada.org/prac/careers/fs-dent.html. 1997.
Burt, Brian A., and Stephen A. Eklund, eds. *Dentistry, Dental Practice and the Community*. 4th ed. Philadelphia: W. B. Saunders Company, 1992.
Jong, Anthony W., ed. *Community Dental Health*. 3d ed. St. Louis: Mosby Year Book, 1993.

Dependence

Relying on others to meet one's needs due to socioeconomic limitations or personal inabilities in providing for oneself. The concept of dependence and, in particular, age-related dependence is examined in this entry. Differences in dependence levels are shown across U.S. regions, rural and urban areas, and racial groups. Several implications of dependence are suggested for rural development.

The Concept

Wimberley and Morris (1997, 25) broadly define dependence as a "dependent person, household, or community [that] relies on others for [meeting] social, physical, and/or economic needs." A dependent is generally unable to return goods or services in exchange for assistance. Children and the elderly are examples of socially dependent persons.

Dependence is a distinctive human resource issue for rural areas, although the concept is scarcely studied and poorly understood. Across large geographic areas and populations in the South, for example, dependence is intertwined with a poor quality of life. Current research suggests that devising and implementing effective rural development policies and programs must take the concept of dependence as well as education and unemployment into consideration. In the 1960s, the concept of dependence was used in studies of the changing composition of the population. Petersen (1961) classifies the population into three groups: dependent children below age 15, the active population at ages 15 to 64, and aged dependents 65 years old and over. Age-related dependence ratios are calculated by comparing the number of dependents in a specific age category per 100 persons of contributing or working age. Petersen uses these ratios to discuss changes in population over time (1880–1955) and in various geographic areas.

Petersen also discusses the usefulness of the concept of dependence and the contribution dependence ratios make to the traditional demographic tools of population pyramids and sex ratios. In summary, he notes that many of the observations about social behavior were false or incomplete in generalizing about populations in the absence of a full understanding of their demographic structure. This statement foreshadowed the importance of the concept of dependence as it is currently being developed in relationship to other variables, such as education, that traditionally are considered as useful indicators of social behavior.

Stockwell (1964), using the same age divisions, makes observations about the overall age distribution of the U.S. population, the changes in dependence over the time-period 1900–1960, and the usefulness of dependence ratios in making urban and rural comparisons. Both Petersen and Stockwell find the greatest utility in using dependence to further explicate the demographic structure of a selected population.

The importance of the concept of dependence is also found in contemporary texts. One of the most recent (Weeks 1996) points out that a parent must tend to children and that it is more difficult to be economically productive in a population in which the dependence ratio is high because of dependent children than one in which dependence is low. Furthermore, high youth dependence increases the need for school taxes, health services, and subsidized housing; results in less discretionary income for households; and results in fewer tax monies available for infrastructure such as roads and communications systems.

Following the early studies by Petersen and Stockwell in the 1960s, the concept of dependence has not been the focus of sustained research, and the literature on well-being virtually ignores dependence. Although many researchers examined population structure by percentages in various age categories, far less attention was given to dependence ratios. An exception is a study by Moland (1981) that examines farm and nonfarm nonmetropolitan population and African American populations based on 1950 and 1970 census data. In the tradition of Petersen and Stockwell, Moland uses dependence as a tool to examine the demographic structure and speculated on its connection to other changes in the population. Dependence was used primarily as a descriptive variable, and its relationship to other variables (for example, employment patterns) in the research was not explored.

In research on the nation's elder population and the southern Black Belt, Morris (1989, 1994) proposed the relationship of dependence to other quality of life measures. (The region within the South that contains a high concentration of African Americans is known as the Black Belt. The region stretches from Virginia through East Texas and up the Delta to Arkansas and Tennessee and covers 623 counties and parts of 11 states.) Additionally, she made a case to redefine youth dependents as those aged 17 and younger. This definition reflects a more socially meaningful division that recognizes the dependent state of most children through primary and secondary education. This change results in an enlarged youth category and a reduced active category as compared to earlier assessments. Further recognized is that all youths are not dependent and all elders have not necessarily retired. It is assumed, however, that the exceptions in one dependence age grouping tend to offset exceptions in another. Using these revised age categories, Wimberley and Morris (1993) examine age-related dependence by race in the United States, in the South, and across the Black Belt region using 1990 U.S. census data.

Dependence may be defined in a number of ways, but the advantage of using age-related measures of dependence is that this measure provides reliable, comparable data across regions and various subgroups of the population. As a baseline measure of dependence, age-related ratios serve as indicators of populations in need. As noted by Petersen (1961), the burden of dependence declines as the proportion of the active population increases. Conversely, high ratios of youth and elder dependence place increased demands on households, communities, and the population at large.

Regional, Nonmetropolitan, and Racial Levels
There are 62 dependents per 100 people of working age as calculated from the 1990 census: 20 are elder and 41 are youth dependents (numbers may vary slightly due to rounding). Thus, for every 100 people of working age—

Youth and elder dependents per 100 people aged 18 to 64

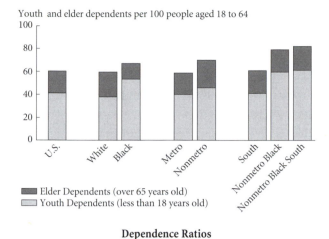

Dependence Ratios

Source: Calculated by Wimberley and Morris (1997) from 1990 U.S. Census.

though not necessarily working—there are 62 who are either too young to work or past the customary age for work (Wimberly and Morris 1996).

Although dependence is not uniform across census regions, nonmetropolitan areas, or racial groups, youth dependence generally runs at least twice that of elder dependence. Across regions, the elder dependence ratio is highest in the Northeast at 22 and lowest in the West at 18. In contrast, the Northeast's youth dependence ratio of 37 is the lowest for any region, whereas the Midwest and the West claim the highest youth dependence ratios at 43. Nonmetropolitan dependence varies across the country, but youth and elder dependence in nonmetro places generally is as much as five points higher than dependence in the population at large. When nonmetro dependence is compared with metropolitan dependence ratios, the difference grows even larger. In terms of how nonmetro families spend their resources, relatively more goes to provide for both the old and the young than is the case for metro families.

The South claims 45 percent of the U.S. nonmetropolitan population, and dependence in the South closely parallels the national pattern for nonmetro dependence. The Northeast yields the lowest total nonmetro dependence ratio of all regions. By implication, more nonmetro family income in the Northeast can go to needs other than childbearing and youth services.

The Midwest, with nearly one-third of the nation's nonmetro residents, has the highest nonmetro elder dependence at 28 and the highest total nonmetro dependence level of any region at 74. The lowest nonmetro elder dependence ratio exists for the West at 22. In contrast, western nonmetro youth dependence at 50 per 100 work-

ing adults is the highest of all regional levels of nonmetro youth dependence. This suggests a somewhat lower demand for elder services in the nonmetro West, in general, and a somewhat higher emphasis on the family- and community-based needs of the young.

African Americans—the nation's largest racial minority—have a higher total dependence level, 68 per 100, than the general population. Nonmetro Blacks, however, have an even higher total ratio of 80 dependents. And in the South, where over 90 percent of the nonmetro African Americans live, their total nonmetro dependence rises higher again to 83, with 62 youth and 21 elder dependents.

Outside the South, nonmetro total dependence for African Americans is quite low. Nonmetro dependence for elder African Americans is a low 7 per 100 in the Northeast and 8 per 100 in the West. In the Northeast, total dependence for African Americans in nonmetro areas was only 42. Partly because of lower life expectancies among Blacks, they have lower elder dependence than Whites. In regions other than the South, Black youth dependence ratios are in line with youth dependence for all populations. The South's high dependence level among nonmetro African Americans is the result of high youth dependence for Black children.

The region within the South that contains this high concentration of African Americans is known as the Black Belt. The region stretches from Virginia through east Texas and up the Delta to Arkansas and Tennessee, covering 623 counties and parts of 11 states.

Effect on Quality of Life and Rural Development
The impact of the interaction of region, nonmetro residence, and race is clearly illustrated in the South. The Black Belt South is the nation's largest region of poverty; high youth dependence contributes to the high prevalence of poverty in this rural area because household incomes are spread across a larger-than-average number of dependents. According to 1990 census information, poverty in the nonmetro Black Belt South affects 42 percent of the total population. The correlation between total, age-related dependence and poverty is notable and is quite strong in the southern Black Belt (Wimberley and Morris 1995).

Rural development efforts to improve the quality of life in such rural regions must take dependence into account. Although employment and higher incomes may take some individuals out of rural poverty, community services in nonmetro areas face greater demands than in metro areas because of the overall higher levels of non-metro dependence.

For example, the high dependence levels of the rural South make it doubtful that rural economic development programs or labor market development will be successful without human resource development to move people, families, and communities away from dependence. In many rural areas there are few jobs for those who can work. But even with sufficient jobs, many people are not employable because of dependence and other human resource conditions. To assist the working-age population to become employable, the dependence-related needs for day care, education, transportation, health services, and other rural human resource infrastructure needs must be taken into account.

Variations in youth and elder dependence from region to region require different perspectives on what constitutes basic human resource development for rural people and places. Therefore, the implications of dependence should be factored into the human resource side of rural development policies and programs.

—Libby V. Morris and Ronald C. Wimberley

See also

African Americans; Cultural Diversity; Development, Community and Economic; Inequality; Policy, Rural Development; Policy, Socioeconomic; Poverty; Quality of Life; Underemployment.

References

Moland, John, Jr. "The Black Population." Pp. 464–501 in *Nonmetropolitan America in Transition*. Edited by Amos H. Hawley and Sara M. Mazie. Chapel Hill: University of North Carolina Press, 1981.

Morris, Libby V. "Youth and Aged Dependency Ratios in the Black Belt: Influence on Education." Paper presented at the annual meeting of the American Society of Gerontology, Minneapolis, MN, November 1989.

———. "Dependence in the Rural South." *Southern Rural Sociology* 10, no. 1 (1994): 115–130.

Petersen, William. *Population*. New York: Macmillan, 1961.

Stockwell, Edward G. "Some Notes on the Changing Age Composition of the Population of the United States." *Rural Sociology* 29, no. 1 (1964): 67–74.

Weeks, John R. *Population*. 6th ed. Belmont, CA: Wadsworth, 1996.

Wimberley, Ronald C., and Libby V. Morris. "Black Belt Counties: A Challenge to the Land-Grant System." Pp. 63–74 in *Challenges in Agriculture and Rural Development*. Edited by Robert Zabawa, Ntam Baharanyi, and Walter Hill. Tuskegee, AL: Tuskegee University, 1993.

———. "Introducing Dependence into the Rural Development Equation." Paper presented at the meeting of the Rural Sociological Society, Arlington, VA, August 1995.

———. *The Reference Book on Regional Well-being: U.S. Regions, The Black Belt, Appalachia*. Mississippi State: Southern Rural Development Center, 1996.

———. *The Southern Black Belt: Dependence, Quality of Life, and Policy*. Nashville, TN: Center for Rural Studies, 1997.

Wimberley, Ronald C., Libby V. Morris, and Douglas C. Bachtel. "New Developments in the Black Belt: Dependence and Life Conditions." Pp. 77–84 in *New Directions in Local and Rural Development*. Edited by Ntam Baharanyi, Robert Zabawa, and Walter Hill. Tuskegee, AL: Tuskegee University, 1992.

Desert Landscapes

Geographic areas characterized by extreme climatic conditions, including very low precipitation and temperature extremes with great diurnal and seasonal variability.

Desert landscapes have been characterized as wastelands, as harsh and inhospitable wilderness. In contrast, rural areas are defined as areas that accommodate small to-moderate-sized communities and agricultural activities that require reliable precipitation and generally moderate temperatures. They frequently have been characterized as pastoral, sometimes rustic, country. Agricultural activities in rural desert landscapes tend to fall into two categories: irrigated farming and grazing.

Following a brief historical introduction, this entry addresses major actions and events that shaped the rural desert landscapes of the nineteenth and twentieth centuries. That era starts with the 1847 settlement of Mormons in what was at the time Mexican territory and that, via the Treaty of Guadalupe Hidalgo, became U.S. territory in 1848 and the territory of Utah in 1850. Other major actions and events include the expansion of irrigated agriculture, expansion of grazing following the Civil War, completion of the first transcontinental railroad in 1869 and of other lines that followed, and enactment of governmental programs intended to stimulate settlement and agricultural development of arid and semiarid areas of the West.

The First Rural Landscapes

The first rural landscapes in what is now the United States emerged in the desert Southwest more than 2,000 years ago, when hunting and foraging for food by indigenous peoples were replaced with a more sedentary lifestyle. This change in lifestyle was associated with the development of rudimentary forms of irrigation and the growing of food crops such as beans, corn, and squash. Accompanying this sedentary food production was the construction of more permanent forms of dwellings, the formation of hamlets and villages, and the evolution of community organizations. Communities were formed

The rugged terrain of the Arizona desert.

along desert rivers that provided water required to irrigate small farm plots and constituted the unifying matrix for the rural desert landscape.

From about A.D. 500 to 1,000, larger communities evolved and irrigation technology improved, incorporating systems of terraces and extensive canals to carry and distribute runoff from adjacent rivers. Dwellings and other structures within communities became more sophisticated. Masonry and mud-brick construction was intermingled with, and gradually replaced, earlier pithouses with roofs of brush and mud.

At the peak of development, about A.D. 900, a large communal, irrigated, agricultural complex of about 155,000 acres had been developed by the Hohokam people in an area that is now part of metropolitan Phoenix, Arizona. Included within this area were 300 miles of canals, some as much as 32 feet wide and 13 feet deep. Amid this canal network were approximately 80 Hohokam settlements. From about A.D. 1150 to 1450, for unknown reasons, the settlements steadily declined. Nevertheless, the imprint of that irrigation system on the landscape remained.

In the early 1800s, the Tohono O'Odham people restored and used part of that extensive Hohokam system. And in 1878, Mormon settlers in the area also recognized the potential of those abandoned canals and hired Pima Indians to restore parts of the system, which were again used to irrigate farm fields in the desert.

For much of the nineteenth century, the land west of the 100th meridian was known as the Great American Desert, a name given in 1819 by Major Stephen H. Long, who led several expeditions to the West. Long's desert, however, included lands to the east of the Rocky Mountains, an area later known as the Great Plains. Eventually, a distinction was made between areas that received between 10 and 20 inches of rain annually and those that received less than 10 inches. The higher rainfall areas, which included the Great Plains, were called grasslands, semiarid lands, or steppes. Areas that received 10 inches of rainfall or less annually were called deserts or arid lands. Nevertheless, in both arid and semiarid areas there can be significant variation in annual rainfall. Within the 48 contiguous states, deserts or arid lands now are defined as occurring primarily between the Rocky Mountains and the Pacific coastal mountain ranges. They include: the Great Basin Desert in southeastern Oregon, southern Idaho, and western Utah; the Mojave Desert in southeastern California, the southern tip of Nevada, and northwestern Arizona; the Sonora Desert in the southeastern corner of California and southern Arizona; and to the east of the Rocky Mountains, the Chihuahua Desert in southwestern Texas and southern New Mexico, extending up the Rio Grande valley.

Anglo Settlement

In 1847, Mormon settlers arrived in what would become the state of Utah. Their initial impact on the arid landscape was modest because their use of the land was oriented to provide shelter and food for subsistence and included development of irrigation systems for their farm fields. The primary comparable irrigated agriculture in the region at that time was the still-active communal system developed by the Spaniards and Indians in the early seventeenth century in the Rio Grande valley. As the Mormons spread their settlements in Arizona, along the Little Colorado, Gila, and San Pedro Rivers, and elsewhere, their proficiency in and the scale of irrigated agriculture increased substantially. Between 1850 and 1890, irrigated acres of Mormon lands increased from approximately 16,000 to 260,000 acres. Throughout the arid West, irrigated lands increased from approximately 3.5 million acres to approximately 7 million acres during the decade of the 1890s.

The stereotypical image of the American West is that of grazing lands and cattle, an image that, for the arid West, has some of its roots in the efforts of the Spanish Jesuits, who introduced cattle and horses into the southwestern United States from Mexico in the early eighteenth century. Initially however, there were many more sheep than cattle in the area, with the Navajo and Hopi Indians being among the first to raise sheep in that area. Although there were difficulties in sustaining cattle ranches in some areas because of Apache Indian raids from the

1830s through the early 1860s, eventually cattle greatly outnumbered sheep. After the Civil War, large herds of cattle were driven to Arizona and New Mexico from Texas. By the end of the nineteenth century, there was growing evidence of overgrazing in parts of the arid region, a trend that continued into the twentieth century.

The advent of the transcontinental railroad linking the East and West Coasts and traversing the arid portion of the country opened hitherto inaccessible markets for Mormon food products and the products of others who followed them. What had been small-scale subsistence agriculture became large-scale commodity agriculture. The first transcontinental railroad line, the Union Pacific Railway, linked Omaha, Nebraska, with Sacramento, California, via Promontory, Utah, in 1869. In 1881, Chicago and Los Angeles were connected by the Atchison, Topeka and Santa Fe Railway via a route through northern New Mexico and Arizona. The third transcontinental line, the Southern Pacific Railroad, was completed in 1883 and ran from New Orleans through Texas, southern New Mexico and Arizona, and on to Los Angeles. The Northern Pacific and Great Northern lines were completed in 1883 and 1893 respectively, and provided transcontinental connections from the northern Midwest to Montana, Idaho, Oregon, and Washington. Each line connected with others at their western, midwestern, or eastern destinations to complete links to East and West Coast cities. By 1893 at least five lines crossed the arid and semiarid regions of the West and provided access to markets for food products, both plant and animal, from in the arid and semiarid regions of the West. In addition, the location of the railroad lines influenced the location of rural communities as transshipment centers.

Settlement of the West was a topic of great interest to the U.S. Congress, as indicated by the Homestead Act of 1862 and similar acts that followed. The intention of these acts was to stimulate the occupation of lands presumed to be suitable for farming, a condition that did not always prevail. Nearly 500,000 farms were established between 1880 and 1900. The same concept was applied to arid lands when Congress enacted the Desert Land Act in 1877. That act was intended to promote irrigated agriculture and applied to all western states and territories except Colorado. It provided for individuals to acquire 640 acres of public land at an initial cost of 25 cents per acre, with an additional $1.00 per acre due after three years when proof was to be given that the land had been irrigated. Although more than 33 million acres were claimed, few were irrigated. The majority had been obtained in violation of the act, to be used by large corporations for grazing lands.

Failure of the Desert Land Act to provide the desired stimulus for the development of irrigated agriculture was readdressed in the Newlands Reclamation Act of 1902, which earmarked money from the sale of public lands in the 16 western states and territories to build dams and irrigation systems in the arid West. The first dam to be built was on the Salt River, east of Phoenix, Arizona, and was completed in 1911. Many more dams were to follow as the Bureau of Reclamation aggressively pursued the mandates of the Newlands Act and contributed to ever-expanding irrigation enterprises.

Contemporary Landscape Changes

The contemporary rural desert landscape is a product of this history that now includes the damming of most major rivers for irrigation and power generation. There are both historic and recent forces that continue to change the character and extent of these landscapes. Among the most notable are the ever-increasing demands for water brought on, in part, by the burgeoning cities, vacation communities, and suburbs and the resultant competition for water and land between urban growth and agriculture. Some of the highest rates of population growth in the country during the decade from 1981 to 1990 were found in arid land states, for example, Arizona, 37.2 percent; Nevada, 52.3 percent; New Mexico, 24.7 percent; and Utah, 18.4 percent. In addition to competition for land and water, other indicators of change include ground subsidence associated with the overdrawing of ground water to meet both agricultural and urban demands; the related loss of surface waters, riparian vegetation, and wildlife habitat in and along formerly perennially flowing desert streams; and, in some places, the advance of desertification, or the reduction of the biological potential of the land.

—*Ervin H. Zube*

See also
American Indians; History, Agricultural; Regional Diversity; Water Use.

References

Butzer, Karl W. "The Indian Legacy in the American West." Pp. 27–50 in *The Making of the American Landscape*. Edited by Michael P. Conzen. Boston: Unwin Hyman, 1990.

Council on Environmental Quality. *Desertification of the United States*. Washington, DC: U.S. Government Printing Office, 1981.

Hollon, W. Eugene. *The Great American Desert Then and Now*. Lincoln: University of Nebraska Press, 1975.

Lister, Robert H., and Florence C. Lister. *Those Who Came Before*. Tucson: University of Arizona Press, 1983.

Meinig, Donald W. *Southwest Three Peoples in Geographical Change 1600–1970*. New York: Oxford University Press, 1971.

Miller, Clyde A., II, Carol A. O'Connor, and Martha A. Sandweiss. *The Oxford History of the American West*. New York: Oxford University Press, 1994.

Westcoat, James L., Jr. "Challenging the Desert." Pp. 186–203 in *The Making of the American Landscape*. Edited by Michael P. Conzen. Boston: Unwin Hyman, 1990.

Worster, Donald. *Rivers of Empire: Water, Aridity and the Growth of the American West*. New York: Pantheon Books. 1985.

Development, Community and Economic

The mobilization of local resources (human, financial, physical, and social) to develop a more resilient, diverse, and innovative economy. This entry describes the social, political, and economic forces facing rural communities; examines why localities have become the primary site for community and economic development activities; evaluates the effectiveness of various strategies and tactics; and reviews some of the innovative rural, community-based efforts.

Introduction

Rural America has become much less dependent on agriculture as a source of income and jobs. Efforts to promote economic development now include tourism, small business development, downtown revitalization, business retention and expansion programs, and the creation of loan funds for microenterprises. Although the federal and state governments are actively involved in economic development, many rural communities are taking the initiative to create jobs and generate income.

Since the mid-1970s, political and economic changes transformed the context for community and economic development in rural America. The shift from a manufacturing to a service economy restructured the economic base of most communities, which contributed to greater inequality and poverty. The loss of manufacturing jobs may have a greater impact on rural than on urban areas because most rural communities do not have a strong enough service sector to support their local economy.

The farm sector experienced a severe crisis in the 1980s. Produced by a combination of declining land values and commodity prices and historically high interest rates and levels of debt, the farm crisis hurt many rural businesses dependent on the farm economy. A decline in the number of farms contributed to population loss and the demise of many key institutions that anchor rural communities. With fewer farms in the community, many of the retail and service establishments did not have a large enough market to support their businesses. Similarly, substitution of capital for labor in coal mines and timber mills reduced employment and supporting businesses in resource-dependent communities.

Globalization of the economy placed additional stress on businesses in rural areas. Rural areas were the beneficiaries of capital mobility in the 1960s as manufacturing plants moved their branches to low-cost rural areas, where wages are lower. Businesses continued the process of seeking low-cost areas of production in the 1980s by moving to areas in the world economy that have even lower wages. As a result, many rural communities began to experience the deindustrialization that had taken place in the urban centers of the Rust Belt in the previous decade. Many small firms in rural areas have not been able to take advantage of globalization because of transportation and communication barriers and difficulty in gaining access to credit and information about international markets. Deregulation of several key industries, such as transportation and banking, also placed rural areas at a disadvantage relative to urban areas. The loss of transportation links left many small towns isolated. Banking deregulation contributed to the capital shortage in many rural areas.

In addition to these structural changes, rural communities face major obstacles in their effort to promote economic development. First, most rural communities depend on only a few industries and are thus more vulnerable to bust-and-boom cycles. Second, the size or scale of rural communities makes it costly to provide public services and an infrastructure supportive of economic development. Many new businesses require business services and other forms of assistance that probably will not be available in small towns. Third, distance often places rural communities at a competitive disadvantage. Because of the high cost of transportation in some industries, many rural communities are not considered as possible sites for businesses.

The Community as the Site for Local Economic Activities

Local economic development became a central issue for rural communities in the 1990s. Many analysts would contend that it has become *the* policy issue facing local governments throughout the United States. Local government involvement in economic development activities is a relatively new phenomenon. Historically, economic development has been the responsibility of the federal and state governments. The federal government has a long history of contributing to local and regional development. Beginning in the 1950s, the federal government became involved in regional development by building the interstate highway system and by investing in the physical infrastructure (roads, streets, bridges, and other public works). During the 1960s, the federal government increased its role in economic development by stepping up federal aid to state and local governments.

Though the federal government's role changed in the late 1970s, the most radical change came in 1981. With the adoption of its New Federalism approach, the Reagan administration redirected the federal government's policy toward economic development. Rather than providing funds for local projects and physical infrastructure, federal policies under the Reagan administration emphasized national economic growth. The administration assumed that localities would be the ultimate beneficiaries of these policies.

New Federalism led to a substantial loss in federal aid to local communities. Communities no longer can count on the state or the federal government to raise revenues for them. At the same time, the federal and state governments mandate that local governments provide services that once were funded at higher levels. Consequently, local governments are asked to do more with less. For most local governments, attracting businesses to their community is seen as the best way to replace the lost revenue. Local governments adopted a wide variety of tax incentives and financial tools to encourage businesses to locate in their community on the assumption that any revenue lost through these practices would be made up through economic growth.

Rural communities have been relatively slow to enter the competition for jobs. In the past, economic development was seen by many leaders in rural communities as minimum maintenance at minimal cost. Low taxes and minimal governmental intervention was considered the most appropriate strategy by local officials. Responsibility for economic development was assigned to an individual, to the vagaries of the market, or in many cases, to larger governmental units at the state or federal levels. In recent years, rural governments became much more active in their effort to promote growth. Rural governments, however, often are hampered by their limited pool of expertise and access to key resources.

Debate exists as to whether communities are the appropriate level for economic development activities.

Some argue that encouraging local activities creates hypercompetition that only benefits businesses and results in a net loss for communities. In addition, the competition does not create new jobs but merely shifts them from one region or community to another. Others argue that economic development activities could more efficiently take place at the regional level if they were administered through regional development organizations or through the actions of multicommunity collaboration efforts. Yet an equitable system to distribute the costs and benefits across communities in regions does not exist. The case for community-based efforts is built on the premise that local people need to take control of the economic forces affecting their well-being. Community-based development efforts focus on initiatives that make use of local resources to generate jobs and income.

Strategies, Policies, Outcomes, and Impacts

The literature on local economic development focuses on three broad issues: adoption of policies and strategies, organization of activities, and the effectiveness of policies and strategies on outcomes and impacts. Adoption of policies and development efforts are influenced strongly by local economic conditions. Economically distressed communities are most likely to invest in efforts to generate jobs and income. Many economic development policies and tactics, however, require experience, expertise, and resources that may not be available in small towns.

The organizational structure for economic development influences adoption and effort. Having the local government serve as the lead actor in economic development and centralizing these efforts in a single agency or department facilitates the economic development process.

There is considerable debate in the literature regarding the effectiveness of locally based economic development activities. Research on this issue used case studies of business relocations, surveys of firms, and secondary data to examine the relationship between policy adoption and job, population, and income growth. Recent evidence suggests that some incentives such as tax policies do have an effect on growth. These local policies influence location decisions once a firm decides on the region in which it is going to locate and then considers the advantages and disadvantages of several localities.

There has been much less research examining the effects of various policies on community impacts, such as unemployment, poverty, or inequality. Summers et al. (1976) finds that attracting branch plants to rural areas had a negligible effect on unemployment or poverty rates.

One reason why industrial recruitment does not reduce unemployment or poverty is because the vast majority (approximately 80 percent) of the new jobs created are taken by in-migrants. Local residents may not have the skills or experience to take advantage of the new jobs created in their community, a situation often referred to as a skills mismatch. Racial and gender discrimination and the lack of available transportation and child care may serve as obstacles to the poor and underemployed in some rural communities.

Community-Based Growth

Because a growing number of rural communities chase after a declining number of firms willing to relocate in any particular year, there has been a shift in orientation toward local economic development among policymakers, researchers, and practitioners that emphasizes use and control of local resources to promote development. There is growing evidence that community-based economic efforts are increasing in frequency in the United States, particularly in distressed regions. Many accounts of these activities interpret them as a response to the economic restructuring that took place since the mid-1970s. Although an economic crisis or structural change in the local economy may be a precondition for grassroots efforts, it is not a sufficient condition.

A central characteristic of community-based economic development is that it relies primarily on local resources to stimulate demand. Grassroots efforts seek to minimize dependence on external organizations and institutions by promoting local ownership and control of resources (land, labor, and capital). Some refer to these grassroots efforts as economic development by the "bootstraps." This label implies, however, that communities use only local resources and become entirely self-sufficient from external organizations and resources. Few communities can implement such a strategy today.

Grassroots economic development strategies stand in stark contrast to traditional strategies that attempt to enhance the structural ties between communities and the larger society. Some argue that the increasing integration of communities into the national and international economy and society is inevitable, and efforts to reduce this dependency and integration will undermine the local economy. Grassroots economic development strategies are based on the assumption that these links with the larger society can be managed so as to increase benefits to the community.

Community-based development efforts simultane-ously contract and expand ties with the larger society. Contraction means that the community attempts to become self-reliant by reducing domination by outside corporations. The primary goal of contraction is to reduce external control over local resources. For example, land trusts, worker- and community-owned firms, and community development banks emphasize local control of resources. By taking control of these resources, communities may be able to reduce their vulnerability to sudden shifts in the economy or to decisions by nonlocal organizations and institutions. Expansion means that the community extends its economic activities to national and international markets. Trade, however, is conducted with decentralized firms based on principles of social responsibility. Many grassroots economic development efforts attempt to increase the demand for the goods produced and services provided locally. That is, community-based economic development efforts create a demand that produces local benefits and returns the created surplus to the local community.

Worker- and community-owned firms are examples of community-based strategies that promote local ownership and control of businesses. In many instances, branch plants that are being closed in rural communities are profitable, but they can be run more profitably at another site. Worker and community ownership provides a means to manage external linkages, but it is not based on a strategy to become autonomous. The economic decisions of the firm, however, are embedded in community needs as well as efficiency.

Another example is the establishment of community-oriented financial institutions, such as a community development bank. Most commercial financial institutions shift capital to the most profitable location or economic sector (taking risk into consideration), regardless of where the investors or savers are located. Rural communities generally do not lack capital, but capital belonging to community members is invested outside the community. Community development banks, however, limit their lending activities to ventures that benefit the locality. Investments are based on an evaluation of the social benefits and costs in the community. Community-oriented financial institutions may obtain a greater economic return by investing elsewhere, but they gain long-term benefits by making social investments in the community.

Community land trusts have been developed in many urban and rural communities in response to land speculation and the need for low-income housing. If land is permitted to operate as a commodity, the exchange value of land takes precedence over use value. As a result, land markets may not serve community or social needs. In many rural areas, the high cost of land locks out beginning farmers and poor people who seek to buy homes. Land trusts remove land from local markets and place it in the hands of communities rather than individuals.

Overall, these strategies to garner greater control over key factors of production attempt to shape development activities that will provide local benefits. Absentee ownership and control of these resources produce the type of underdevelopment that is characteristic of Third World economies. Community-based development strategies offer localities an alternative path of development.

Conclusion

Can rural communities survive the structural forces working against the development of a viable local economy? Community-based development can have an impact at the margins; it probably cannot replace all of the jobs and income being lost to the restructuring process. It does, however, produce a more resilient economy that will be in a better position to develop in the future. Long-term development may be possible if communities learn how to capitalize on local resources and to expand the local social capital. For many communities, this will require a different approach to local economic development—one that is participatory and inclusive. Unfortunately, participation is learned, and there are few other local institutions that promote participation. Thus, community-based development will require a comprehensive approach to economic development that links the economy to social institutions in the community.

Community-based development strategies can be more effective if they are supported with national and state policies and programs that address the specific disadvantages that rural communities face. These policies and programs need to recognize the changing structure of rural economies, particularly the shift from a dependence on natural resources to other types of economic activity. Rural policies should be comprehensive, recognizing the linkage between economic development, environmental quality, housing, health care, and other aspects of rural life.

—*Gary P. Green*

See also
Community; Community Celebrations; Cooperatives; Home-Based Work; Impact Assessment; Infrastructure; Manufacturing Industry; Policy, Rural Development; Regional Planning; Trade Areas; Value-Added Agriculture.

References
Bartik, Timothy J. *Who Benefits from State and Local Economic Development Policies?* Kalamazoo, MI: W. E. Upjohn Institute, 1991.

Bruyn, Severyn T., and James Meehan. *Beyond the Market and the State: New Directions in Community Development.* Philadelphia: Temple University Press, 1987.

Green, Gary P., Jan L. Flora, Cornelia B. Flora, and Frederick E. Schmidt. "Community-based Economic Development Projects Are Small but Valuable." *Rural Development Perspectives* 8 (1993): 8–15.

Gunn, Christopher, and Hazel Dayton Gunn. *Reclaiming Capital: Democratic Initiatives and Community Development.* Ithaca, NY: Cornell University Press, 1991.

Summers, Gene F. "Rural Community Development." *Annual Review of Sociology* 12 (1986): 341–371.

Summers, Gene F., Sharon D. Evans, Frank Clemente, E. M. Beck, and Jon Minkoff. *Industrial Invasion of Nonmetropolitan America: A Quarter Century of Experience.* New York: Praeger Publishers, 1976.

Wilkinson, Kenneth P. *The Community in Rural America.* New York: Greenwood Press, 1991.

Diversity
See Cultural Diversity; Regional Diversity

Division of Household Labor

The allocation of domestic chores within the home, specifically unpaid labor as performed by spouses. The division of household labor in rural homes traditionally has been highly segregated, such that wives perform the majority of chores and the more tedious tasks. Although recent studies support this allocation of labor, there is also evidence of a greater sharing of chores on the part of husbands. The conservative nature of rural attitudes, particularly those concerning family roles, is often cited as the reason for the segregation of household labor in rural homes.

The division of household labor attracted much attention among family researchers. One notable characteristic of this literature is the relative paucity of studies that sought to examine the division of household labor in the rural context. Although several researchers called for analyses of rural households in this regard (Dorfman and Heckert 1988; Hardesty and Bokemeier 1989), to date, few studies have focused on the division of household labor in rural households.

Among existing studies, most do note the uniqueness of marriages, marital interaction, and family structure in rural areas. For example, researchers suggested that rural wives are more likely to espouse traditional marital roles and adhere to more conservative norms as compared to their urban counterparts (Rosenblatt and Anderson 1981). Rural and urban areas overall maintain different ideals concerning marital interaction and marital roles. Hansen (1987) concluded that rural residents hold more conservative attitudes concerning social, familial, religious, and sexual issues.

Despite the stereotype of rural couples being very traditional (that is, almost exclusively patriarchal), several studies suggested that the nature of marital relations in rural communities is changing such that wives are becoming more influential in the decision-making processes within marriage (Dorfman and Hill 1986). Given that much of marital partners' influence in the decision-making processes is derived from their employment status, the increase in rural wives' participation in the paid labor force in recent years is likely to bring about marital roles and family structures that are more similar to those typically found in an urban setting (Bokemeier and Maurer 1987).

Household Labor among Rural Couples

The accompanying table presents an adaptation of a study performed by Lawrence et al. (1987), which compared couples from both rural and urban environments with regard to their respective divisions of household labor. There are several notable differences between the two types of couples. Among rural couples, wives are shown to perform 29.63 hours per week of household labor. Similar to recent nationally representative samples, rural wives perform almost three times as many hours of housework as their husbands (who report an average of 11.55 hours per week). Urban couples also display a rather skewed imbalance in the distribution of chores, yet the inequity is not as substantial. Among urban couples, wives report a weekly average of 24.62 hours per week, whereas husbands contribute the same amount of household labor as their rural counterparts (11.55 hours per week).

These findings can be interpreted in several ways. First, comparing rural and urban couples overall, rural couples clearly display a greater imbalance in the total household labor contributions of each spouse. Specifically, rural wives perform considerably more housework than their urban counterparts. Among husbands, rural/urban residence does not appear to significantly affect their respective levels of labor contributions in the home.

Mean Hours per Week Spent in Household Chores by Husbands and Wives, by Rural or Urban Residence

| Household Chore | Rural Couples | | Urban Couples | |
	Wives (N=220)	Husbands (N=220)	Wifes (N=220)	Husbands (N=220)
Food preparation	8.52	1.28	6.07	1.52
Dishwashing	3.27	0.35	2.57	0.46
Shopping	4.78	2.45	5.25	2.45
Housecleaning	5.37	0.35	3.85	0
Maintenance of home, yard, car, and pets	1.98	5.13	1.75	4.78
Care of clothing and household linens	2.33	0.23	2.33	0.12
Clothing construction	1.52	0.10	0.82	0.10
Management	1.87	1.63	2.10	1.52
Total household labor	29.63	11.55	24.62	11.55

Source: Adapted from Lawrence et al. 1987, Table III, p. 499.

Second, there are also notable differences in the segregation or sharing of individual tasks among couples in this study. Rural wives perform considerably more labor in the home than their husbands, but the distribution of their total labor time is different from that of their husbands. For example, four of the more onerous and repetitive chores—food preparation, dishwashing, housecleaning, and care of clothing and household linens—account for 65.8 percent of rural wives' total household labor contributions. Rural husbands, however, spend only 19.1 percent of their total housework time on the same four tasks. Among urban couples, wives spend about 60.2 percent of their total time in these four tasks, whereas husbands devote about 22.5 percent of their household labor contributions to these four chores. Relative to urban couples, rural couples display more traditional patterns of task allocation, both in terms of total time and task segregation.

Household Labor among Children

Within the gender role ideology explanation of the division of household labor, it is assumed that individuals' attitudes concerning gender roles, and particularly those within the context of marriage, substantially influence their own preferences of chore performance. Aside from evidence offered by studies of housework among adults, several researchers posit that such ideologies are established early in childhood (Blair 1992; Goodnow 1988). Several studies note that children's participation in household labor is similar to the gender-based patterns of chore allocation displayed by adults.

Lawrence and Wozniak (1987) find that rural boys spend approximately 6.4 hours per week in household tasks, whereas rural girls spend about 8.9 hours per week performing household chores. The tasks performed by rural children are also highly segregated (similar to patterns found among adults). Of the total time expended in household chores by rural girls, approximately 52.9 percent is spent on housecleaning, food preparation, dishwashing, or laundry. Rural boys, meanwhile, spend only 30.1 percent of their total housework time in the same four tasks. The presence of these patterns of chore allocation among children lends support to the contention of gender role ideology explanations.

Conclusion

Rural couples are often envisioned as being very conservative and traditional, particularly in terms of their marital roles. Results from the few studies that examined the division of household labor in rural households appear to support, at least partially, some of these stereotypes. Rural wives do report substantially greater amounts of time being spent in the performance of household chores, as compared to their husbands' total contributions. Further, the allocation of individual chores appears to be highly segregated among rural couples, such that wives spend the majority of their time in least desirable and most repetitive chores (such as cooking, cleaning, doing laundry). Evidence from studies of rural children's participation in household chores reveals similar patterns of chore allocation, thereby suggesting that the traditional division of household labor seen among married rural couples may have its origins in early childhood experiences.

At the same time, however, rural couples should not be viewed as being entirely conservative and traditional in their marital roles. Dorfman and Heckert (1988) suggest that the patterns of decision making among rural couples are becoming more similar to those displayed by their urban counterparts with respect to egalitarianism. Changes that occurred among the urban population in the United States since the 1960s that may potentially influence the allocation of chores (for example, higher rates of paid labor force participation by married women) are also evident among rural residents. Thus, decision-making processes among rural couples are more likely to be of a joint nature (involving input from both spouses) than to be solitary decisions (made by only one spouse). In all likelihood, the patterns of task allocation in rural households will become more and more similar to those displayed by the rest of the U.S. population as we approach the turn of the twenty-first century.

—*Sampson Lee Blair*

See also
Employment; Family; Home-Based Work; Labor Force; Marriage; Rural Women; Underemployment; Voluntarism; Work.

References
Blair, Sampson L. "Children's Participation in Household Labor: Child Socialization Versus the Need for Household Labor." *Journal of Youth and Adolescence* 21, no. 2 (1992): 241–258.

Bokemeier, Janet, and Richard Maurer. "Marital Quality and Conjugal Labor Involvement of Rural Couples." *Family Relations* 36, no. 4 (1987): 417–424.

Dorfman, Lorraine T., and D. Alex Heckert. "Egalitarianism in Retired Rural Couples: Household Tasks, Decision Making, and Leisure Activities." *Family Relations* 37, no. 1 (1988): 73–78.

Dorfman, Lorraine T., and Elizabeth A. Hill. "Rural Housewives and Retirement: Joint Decision-Making Matters." *Family Relations* 35, no. 4 (1986): 507–514.

Goodnow, Jacqueline J. "Children's Household Work: Its Nature and Functions." *Psychological Bulletin* 103, no.1 (1988): 5–26.

Hansen, Gary L. "The Effect of Community Size on Exchange Orientations in Marriage." *Rural Sociology* 52, no. 4 (1987): 501–509.

Hardesty, Constance, and Janet Bokemeier. "Finding Time and Making Do: Distribution of Household Labor in Nonmetropolitan Households." *Journal of Marriage and the Family* 51, no. 1 (1989): 253–267.

Lawrence, Frances C., Peggy S. Draughn, Grace E. Tasker, and Patricia H. Wozniak. "Sex Differences in Household Labor Time: A Comparison of Rural and Urban Couples." *Sex Roles* 17, nos. 9-10 (1987): 489–502.

Lawrence, Frances C. and Patricia H. Wozniak. "Rural Children's Time in Household Activities." *Psychological Reports* 61, no. 3 (1987): 927–937.

Rosenblatt, Paul C., and Roxanne M. Anderson. "Interaction in Farm Families: Tension and Stress." Pp. 147–166 in *The Family in Rural Society*. Edited by R. T. Coward and W. M. Smith, Jr. Boulder, CO: Westview Press, 1981.

Domestic Violence

The infliction of physical, sexual, and/or emotional injury on a member or members of one's family or household. Rural areas, although noted for somewhat lower crime rates in general, enjoy little, if any, respite from crimes of domestic violence. Characteristics of some rural communities, which may include geographic isolation, social isolation, greater conformity to conventional values and norms, and a lack of anonymity, are conditions that can exacerbate the problem. Victims of domestic violence who live in rural areas are faced with additional barriers. These range from a lower level of support services, including mental health counseling, shelters, and self-help groups, to the absence of a social infrastructure, including transportation, housing, child care, and employment opportunities. This entry examines current domestic violence rates, recent changes in state and federal domestic violence laws, social services available to victims of domestic violence, and correlates of domestic violence.

Rates

Estimates of child abuse range from a low of 500,000 to a high of 6.9 million cases per year in the United States. Approximately 2.5 million cases of child abuse are reported to authorities each year, and over one-half are substantiated (that is, accepted for further investigation and intervention). Almost all abuse is inflicted by family members; less than 5 percent of reported incidents are committed by someone outside the home. More than half of the victims are under the age of one and 90 percent are under five years of age. Homicide is the fourth-highest cause of death among children, with over 1,200 children dying from abuse-related causes each year. Age of the child, family income, and ethnicity are risk factors for child abuse. There is, however, no correlation between geographic location and incidence of child abuse. Children living in rural areas are as likely to be victims of child abuse as are their urban and suburban counterparts.

Estimates of intimate violence range from 572,000 to four million cases per year. On the average, women experience more than ten times as many incidents of violence by an intimate as men. The problem is so widespread that a woman has a higher probability of being assaulted by a partner in her own home than a law enforcement officer has of being attacked on the job. Additionally, intimate violence is rarely an isolated incident, but rather is cyclical in nature with each subsequent attack becoming more severe. Each year, 2,000 to 4,000 women are killed by their husbands or lovers, with over half of the murders of female spouses and partners committed by men after separation of the victim and perpetrator. Rates of violence committed by intimates are similar for women living in central cities, suburban areas, and rural locations. Residence in rural areas does not decrease the likelihood of experiencing intimate violence.

A lack of definitive data makes it difficult to measure accurately the incidence of elder abuse. According to a report by the U.S. House of Representatives Select Committee on Aging, at least 1.5 million elderly Americans are victims of abuse. It is estimated that fewer than 20 percent of cases are reported; underreporting is due to the isolation of the elderly from mainstream society and their fear that reporting the abuse will result in separation from family and possibly in nursing home placement. Women, especially those over age 75 who are physically or financially dependent on others for meeting their daily

needs, are most susceptible to abuse. Initial assumptions about elder abuse focused almost exclusively on adult children and caregivers as the primary perpetrators. Recent studies, however, indicate that of the approximately one million females age 65 and older who are victims of violence, roughly half are abused by a husband or male partner. There is no indication that elder abuse is less prevalent in rural areas than in urban or suburban areas.

Laws

Recent changes in state laws have made domestic violence an issue that must be addressed in both urban and rural communities. Congress passed the Child Abuse Prevention and Treatment Act in 1974, which created requirements that states had to implement in order to secure federal funding for child maltreatment programs. Requirements included the passage of child abuse and neglect laws and institution of procedures for reporting abuse, of procedures for investigations, and of training programs for protective services personnel. This legislation was amended in 1978, 1984, and 1988. As a result, each state has a child abuse and neglect reporting law requiring professionals such as medical personnel, school personnel, child care workers, social workers, and psychologists to report suspected cases of child abuse or neglect. Additionally, states either require or suggest that suspected cases of child abuse be reported by the general public. State laws require law enforcement officials to make arrests in spouse abuse cases if there is probable cause to conclude that an assault has taken place. The Older Americans Act of 1987 required state agencies on aging to assess the need for elder abuse prevention programs. Adult protective services workers in each state are mandated to conduct home investigations in suspected cases of elder abuse.

It cannot be assumed that laws are enforced and programs are implemented with the same degree of uniformity. Funding for these programs has always been limited; the budget cuts of the 1980s and 1990s meant that all programs are underfunded, but rural areas suffer from additional problems. The geographic isolation of some rural communities that fosters the myth that they are free from social problems, including domestic violence, poses serious issues for individuals in need of services. If domestic violence is not viewed as a significant problem, then training sessions for law enforcement officers and other professionals may be attended but will have little impact on their target populations.

Rural law enforcement personnel must address situations that range from handling traffic offenses to removing farm animals from roads to providing escorts for funerals; there is little incentive to specialize in domestic violence investigations. From a practical standpoint, many law enforcement officials who investigate domestic violence incidents must travel long distances without the reassurance that a backup officer is nearby, despite the fact that domestic violence calls are among the most lethal to law enforcement officials. Some rural judges who issue emergency protective orders are available only on a part-time basis and must cover large geographic areas. A victim, already apprehensive about requesting a protective order, may find the prospect of having to wait for the judge to issue the order too difficult to face.

Social Services

Low population density impacts social service delivery in rural areas. Many rural residents must travel to county seats or urban areas to receive services. Distance, combined with the attitude that incidents of domestic violence are really family problems that should remain in the family, makes it even more difficult to request or receive services. In child abuse cases, where investigation is mandatory, negative attitudes toward protective service agencies, which sometimes are viewed as arms of an intrusive government, may discourage the reporting of suspected abuse. When abuse is reported, service workers may need to travel several hours to investigate a case. If the child is thought to be in imminent danger, the worker must contact law enforcement officials to remove the child. This action may necessitate another lengthy trip. Some rural communities can provide little beyond investigative services. Resources such as community mental health centers, support groups, shelters, and education and prevention groups are unavailable. Even if these resources are available, distance and a lack of transportation may make them inaccessible.

The lack of anonymity that characterizes many rural communities impacts service delivery by law enforcement officials, court officials, or social service personnel. It is not unusual for clients and perpetrators to be known by service providers. In some instances, knowing that the police dispatcher who is called, the law enforcement official who responds to the call, the protective services worker who investigates a case, or the local mental health counselor who provides therapy to the family is a neighbor, a member of that client's Sunday school class or

civic organization, or perhaps even a relative is a sufficient deterrent to seeking help. Protecting the family name or saving the perpetrator from embarrassment may take precedence over the victim's safety. Although lack of anonymity affects all rural victims, it can be particularly difficult for individuals whose families constitute the influential forces in the community. Rural communities desperately need professionals such as physicians, lawyers, school personnel, and police officers, and these communities may make every effort to keep these individuals even if it means turning a blind eye to family problems such as domestic violence. Additionally, services such as spouse abuse shelters and safe houses, or chapters of self-help organizations such as Parents Anonymous, find it almost impossible to maintain anonymity.

Correlates

Economic conditions affect the need for services and the availability of these services. Although domestic violence cuts across all social classes, research indicates a relationship between economic instability and a number of social problems, including domestic violence. Whether in the form of plant closings, military base closings, or farm failures, economic crisis can be measured in increased rates of health problems, alcoholism, divorce, depression, anxiety, suicide, and abuse. Although some urban areas have been hit hard by a reduction in defense spending and manufacturing jobs, rural areas that depend on only one or a few facilities for the bulk of their jobs can be devastated by a plant or military base closing. This loss is compounded by a decrease in payroll taxes, property taxes, and in some instances, charitable contributions.

The farm crisis of the 1980s also had an impact on rural family life. The number of reported suicides in Iowa, for example, climbed to rates equal to that of the Depression; many other suicides were attributed to farm-related and hunting accidents. Although several of these suicides (some of which included family massacres) made the national newspapers, other violent incidents gained little attention but were indicative of the pressures felt by families. Statistics collected by the Iowa State Department of Human Services illustrate the impact of the farm crisis: "Despite a shrinking population, the number of cases of child abuse reported in Iowa went from nearly 15,000 to over 25,000 in 1987. . . . Reported cases of spouse abuse went from 1,620 in 1985 up to more than 4,500 in 1987" (Davidson 1990,97). The same economic conditions that precipitated personal and family crises drastically cut funding to agencies whose job was to help individuals handle these crisis situations. Funding for community mental health agencies, for example, was cut by almost one-third from 1980 to 1988.

Despite the fact that domestic violence is an age-old problem, services directed at the various types of domestic violence are relatively new. Laws protecting victims were not passed until the 1970s, and early services were poorly funded and understaffed. Funding was decreased during the 1980s when efforts to balance the federal budget took precedence over social problems such as domestic violence. Services that did develop were established and continue to be located for the most part in urban areas. Limited program budgets, minimal outreach efforts, and a lack of transportation make all but mandated services such as protective services investigations nearly inaccessible for most rural residents. Since it is highly unlikely that funding for domestic violence programs will increase in the near future, rural residents will receive increased services only if programs place greater emphasis on service delivery methods that emphasize outreach.

Twenty-four-hour hotlines with toll-free numbers can provide information and crisis counseling to all residents of a state. State coalitions that provide modest grants to fund local education efforts and support groups can make a small amount of money go a long way. Public service announcements can provide access to information about domestic violence for rural and urban residents alike. It is unlikely that domestic violence will ever be eliminated, but its effects can be diminished without pitting the needs of rural Americans against their urban counterparts.

—*Rosemarie Bogal-Allbritten*

See also
Crime; Family; Injuries; Marriage; Rural Women.
References
Bachman, Ronet. *Violence Against Women: A National Crime Victimization Survey Report.* Washington, DC: U.S. Department of Justice, Office of Justice Programs, Bureau of Justice Statistics, 1994.
Bogal-Allbritten, Rosemarie, and Lillian Rogers Daughaday. "Spouse Abuse Program Services: A Rural-Urban Comparison." *Human Services in the Rural Environment* 14 (Fall 1990): 6–10.
Davidson, Osha Gray. *Broken Heartland.* New York: Free Press, 1990.
Ginsburg, Leon H. *Social Work in Rural Communities.* 2d ed. Alexandria, VA: Council on Social Work Education, 1993.
Hampton, Robert L, Thomas P. Gulotta, Gerald R. Adams, Earl H. Potter III, and Roger P. Weissberg, eds. *Family Violence.* Newbury Park, CA: Sage Publications, 1993.
Wiehe, Vernon R. *Working with Child Abuse and Neglect.* Itasca, IL: F. E. Peacock, Publishers, 1992.

Drought

A deficiency of precipitation that results in a water shortage for some activity. This entry examines drought effects on farmers and communities, how early settlers adjusted to the drought hazard, the key role of the federal government in drought mitigation, and rural America's ability to cope with future droughts.

Effects

Drought is a natural element of climate; no region is immune to the drought hazard. The frequency of drought increases as one goes from east to west across the United States. One would expect the eastern and southern portions of the country to be the least vulnerable to drought, given their higher precipitation. Farmers and small businesses have had a mix of successes and failures in adapting to the drought hazard. Agriculturalists incorporated numerous methods to survive moderate droughts, particularly in semiarid regions. Small communities and farmers benefited from federal aid programs. Some researchers argue that despite these advances, rural America is still highly vulnerable to major droughts.

One problem in analyzing, assessing impacts, and delimiting drought areas is defining drought itself. What is considered a drought by a farmer whose crops withered during the summer may not be seen as a drought by a hydrologist. It follows that there can be many types of drought: agricultural, hydrologic, economic, and meteorological. To standardize measurement of drought magnitude, several indexes were developed. The Palmer Drought Severity Index is probably the best known. Despite attempts to define drought, confusion and uncertainty persist as to what defines a drought. Not surprisingly, the result has been individual and government uncertainty on when to undertake drought remediation efforts.

Drought can have wide-ranging impacts on farmers, communities, and the environment. Farmers experience decreased incomes from crop failure or reduction. Ranchers must find grazing land or purchase extra hay and feed for their cattle since drought will decrease available forage. North Dakota ranchers and farmers procured hay as far away as Colorado during the drought of 1988. Moisture deficiency frequently increases crop susceptibility to disease and pests. In addition, drought can hurt small rural communities. Not only do small towns often have limited water supplies, but local business people are strongly dependent on purchases from farmers and ranchers. As farm incomes plummet, local businesses generate less tax revenue, resulting in decreased funds for public services. In some cases, this domino effect can devastate rural areas.

A community's or farmer's vulnerability to drought can determine the extent of adverse drought effects. In many cases, rural people learned how to reduce their exposure to drought. Experience is perhaps the best teacher. In his study of Great Plains farmers, Saarinen (1966) found that drought perception varied according to the degree of aridity, amount of drought experience, type of farm operation, and personality differences. Farmers slow to adopt agricultural innovations were found to have a poorer understanding of the drought hazard or to underestimate drought frequency. Rural people's experience and innovation has lessened drought hazard's adverse consequences.

A general lack of preparedness and experience can magnify drought damage when it does occur. Drought in the 1960s caused water systems to fail in the Northeast. A 1986 drought in the Southeast severely stressed water systems, an area with relatively small water storage capacity. Farmers in more humid areas grow crops that are less drought resistant. The result can be cataclysmic losses. The 1988 drought reduced corn yields in the United States by 40 percent. Such an event-oriented learning process characterizes the history of drought adjustment and adaptation in the United States.

Early Responses

Native Americans either stored food for poor years or migrated to wetter areas. The early settlers of the Great Plains in the 1880s and 1890s brought their eastern preconceptions of drought and climate. A combination of boosterism, the myth of unending bounty, and the belief in climate amelioration moderated concerns about drought. The settlers soon faced severe drought in the early 1890s and realized that drought was a part of farming in semiarid regions, or for that matter, anywhere. A new emphasis on drought adjustment focused on creating an agricultural system that could be productive in even the worst droughts. Self-described experts propagated numerous dry-farming techniques, some of which were useful. However, faulty assumptions and poor science characterized many methods. A series of wet years in the 1920s, a renewed faith in the ability to overcome droughts, and good commodity prices resulted in record amounts of land under the plow by the 1930s.

Americans' perceptions and knowledge of drought have probably been more influenced by the Dust Bowl years of the 1930s than any other event. Ill defined, the Dust Bowl generally was considered to comprise the southern portion of the Great Plains (Texas and Oklahoma), and its greatest extent was in 1935–1936. Much of the rest of the country also experienced drought during the 1930s, but the stories of dust storms that required headlights during the middle of the day, fences covered by drifting sand, and the massive out-migration captured public and government attention. The enormous topsoil loss to wind erosion, continual crop failures, and widespread bankruptcies suggested that rural America had failed to adapt to drought and the semiarid environment. Climate was still considered to be the main culprit, but socioeconomic factors and poor technology were also given serious attention. The Dust Bowl experience probably had the greatest influence on the evolution of drought policy and adjustment techniques in the United States.

Some argued that a core cause of the Dust Bowl was not really drought but the economic system that put the farmers at risk in a marginal environment. Worster (1979, 5) says: "What brought them to the region was a social system, a set of values, an economic order . . . capitalism." Regardless of the socioeconomic cause, the Dust Bowl heralded a new era in drought management and relief.

The Federal Response

Beginning in the 1930s, the federal government took an increasing role in drought management and relief. The Agricultural Adjustment Administration and its successors provided direct financial relief to farmers during the Depression. The federal government created the Soil Erosion Service in 1933, later known as the Soil Conservation Service. Perhaps no other single federal program or organization had a greater impact on farmers' abilities to manage the drought hazard. Roosevelt's Prairie States Forestry Project (1934–1942) planted over 230,000 acres of shelterbelts in the Plains states, purportedly to reduce the effects of desiccating winds and periodic drought. The Bankhead-Jones Tenant Act of 1937 allowed federal purchase of nearly a million acres of marginal farmland for restoration to grassland. The Federal Crop Insurance Program had its beginnings in 1938. Federal agencies constructed water resource and irrigation projects. The list goes on. Conclusively, the Dust Bowl and its aftermath formalized the federal role in drought management and relief efforts.

The federal remedy seemed to make a difference during subsequent droughts. The southern plains drought of the 1950s actually affected a greater area than the 1930s drought. Yet the region did not return to the distressing, tragic conditions of two decades earlier (Hurt

1981). Federal agencies developed more programs. The Farm and Home Administration provided production emergency loans to some farmers for their annual crop production. The Soil Bank program allowed farmers to enter land, much of which was erosion- and drought-prone, into acreage reserves in 1956. Many farmers implemented technological adjustments developed under federal and state research efforts. Special tillage equipment and practices, fertilizer, irrigation, and drought-resistant grain helped to make farmers less vulnerable to drought.

Perhaps the best test of the socioeconomic and technological drought-mitigation efforts came during the extreme and widespread drought of 1988. The drought caused a 31 percent reduction in U.S. grain production. Total losses and costs of the 1988 drought topped $39 billion (Riebsame, Changnon, and Karl 1991). Rural communities and businesses saw income and sales decrease as the agricultural sector suffered. Major cities and small towns coped with dry wells and depleted rivers. Farmers received federal and state disaster aid. The Federal Crop Insurance Corporation provided $3 billion in payments, severely stressing its resources. Overall, federal and state response to the 1988 drought showed mixed results. One thing seemed clear—crisis management, rather than anticipatory planning, remained the norm.

Many innovative drought adjustments during 1988 came from those who suffered the most—farmers and rural communities. Farmers sold livestock or stored grain (prices are often higher during a drought) besides taking advantage of federal drought relief and crop insurance. Others used special tillage techniques to reduce erosion. Some farmers replanted their grain fields to hay forage crops. Others used the same fields for forage by placing livestock on fields of grain or row crops. Drought forced many farmers to diversify their operations. Refinancing of loans was common. Many farmers took advantage of the Conservation Reserve Program (CRP). The program allowed farmers to obtain payments if they retired highly erodible farmland for ten years and planted the land with grass or trees. Federal officials allowed farmers and ranchers to cut hay on a portion of their CRP lands during the drought. Farmers and ranchers became more flexible in their management decisions. The 1988 drought reinforced the tenet that local people may be the best source for effective drought adjustments.

Coping with Future Problems

Drought prediction seems the answer to farmers' annual crop selection dilemma. Borchert (1971) notes an apparent 21-year cycle of drought in the grassland region of the central United States. Researchers continue their efforts to unravel the many variables involved in climate prediction. As would be expected, the shorter the prediction interval, the more accurate the prediction. Unfortunately, most long-term climate predictions are still too spatially variable and unreliable to be of significant value in making economic decisions. However, progress has been made in estimating drought occurrence and timing. For example, the El Niño/Southern Oscillation may be a precursor of drought in some areas. Global warming has the possibility to obscure the prospect of reliable climate predictions even more. With time, the physical mechanics of climate and drought may be well enough understood to give area-specific, long-term predictions meaningful value.

Perhaps of greater worth to rural Americans is the current capacity to detect and monitor drought in its early stages. Early recognition of potential drought conditions can give policymakers and resource managers the extra time needed to adjust their management strategies. Information on soil moisture conditions can help farmers with planting and crop selection, seeding rate, fertilization, amount of irrigation, and harvest time decisions. Early drought warning systems can aid communities in decisions related to water storage in and release from reservoirs, implementation of water conservation measures, and obtainment of outside sources of water. Despite some disadvantages, the Palmer Drought Severity Index and other indexes can monitor potential drought conditions. The key is to provide reliable information as early as possible.

Despite the progress in developing drought-mitigation techniques, monitoring effects, and increasing awareness of the drought hazard, the United States remains vulnerable to drought. Although the ability to cope with mild-to-moderate droughts has improved significantly, the exposure to severe or extreme drought is still high. Continuing susceptibility to drought may, in part, be the result of a lack of planning. Researchers and officials continue to call for the development of a national drought plan. Regardless of their success or failure, drought will remain an enduring element of the rural American landscape.

—*David M. Diggs*

See also
Agronomy; Dryland Farming; Weather.
References
Borchert, John. "The Dust Bowl in the 1970s." *Annals of the Association of American Geographers* 61, no. 1 (1971): 1–22.

Hurt, R. Douglas. *The Dust Bowl: An Agricultural and Social History.* Chicago: Nelson-Hall, 1981.

Riebsame, William E. "The United States Great Plains." Pp. 561–575 in *The Earth as Transformed by Human Action: Global and Regional Changes in the Biosphere over the Past 300 Years.* Edited by B. L. Turner II, William C. Clark, Robert W. Kates, John Richards, Jessica T. Mathews, and William B. Meyer. New York: Cambridge University Press with Clark University, 1990.

Riebsame, William E., Stanley Changnon, Jr., and Thomas Karl. *Drought and Natural Resources Management in the United States: Impacts and Implications of the 1987–1989 Drought.* Boulder, CO: Westview Press, 1991.

Saarinen, Thomas. *Perception of the Drought Hazard on the Great Plains.* Research Paper no. 106. Chicago: University of Chicago, Department of Geography, 1966.

Wilhite, Donald. *Drought Assessment, Management, and Planning: Theory and Case Studies.* Dordrecht, Netherlands: Kluwer Academic Publishers, 1993.

Wilhite, Donald, and William Easterling, eds. *Planning for Drought: Toward a Reduction of Societal Vulnerability.* Boulder, CO: Westview Press, 1987.

Wilhite, Donald, and Michael H. Glantz. "Understanding the Drought Phenomenon: The Role of Definitions." Pp. 11–27 in *Planning for Drought: Toward a Reduction of Societal Vulnerability.* Edited by Donald Wilhite and William Easterling. Boulder, CO: Westview Press, 1987.

Worster, Donald. *Dust Bowl: The Southern Plains in the 1930s.* New York: Oxford University Press, 1979.

Dryland Farming

Cultivated agriculture in areas where potential water use by plants exceeds growing-season precipitation. Water deficiency is the primary limitation on plant production in dryland farming. Special farming practices are required to counteract soil water deficiency during the growing season. A particular farming region is not considered dryland just because it depends exclusively on natural precipitation. It is only considered dryland if water is the primary factor limiting production. The central U.S. Corn Belt is typical of an area that depends on natural precipitation but does not practice dryland farming. This entry discusses where dryland farming is practiced, gives a historical perspective, and describes necessary management strategies and sustainability.

Climate and Soil Zones

Dryland farming areas of North America are clustered within six geographic regions in the 17 western states of the United States and the 3 prairie provinces of Canada. These areas provide classic examples of the soil and climate regions where dryland farming is the norm. Annual precipitation ranges from 8 to 20 inches, but the percentage received as snow versus rainfall varies dramatically with latitude. North Dakota farmers, for example, are very concerned with trapping snow on their fields to conserve water, whereas Texas farmers receive so little snow that trapping it is not an issue. Precipitation effectiveness is greatly modified by the north-to-south temperature gradient. As temperature increases, the amount of water used by plants increases dramatically, and soil water-storage potential decreases.

Soils in dryland farming areas possess characteristics that are primarily a function of the climates they formed in and the grass vegetation that was growing on them in their native state. Principal soils of the Great Plains are classified as Mollisols, Entisols, Aridisols, Vertisols, and Ustalfs. The Mollisols are the most extensive soils in dryland areas and were formed under grass and forbs. They are characterized by dark-colored surface horizons high in organic matter and bases. Productivity (total plant material produced per year) of the soils always has been a function of the dry climate, long before planned management of the plains began. Soils in dryland areas are very unweathered compared to soils in areas with higher rainfall. This results in high fertility, especially for elements essential to plants like calcium, magnesium, and potassium. Because these soils were developed under prairie grass vegetation, they have a good organic matter supply in the surface soil. Unfortunately, this supply is easily depleted when the soils are placed under cultivation. Nitrogen is usually deficient after 30 years of cultivation, and farmers need to add nitrogen fertilizer to produce economic yields. In contrast, most of these soils are so well supplied with potassium that they will not need fertilizer potassium in the foreseeable future.

Historical Perspective

Early settlers of North America did not choose to farm in the areas where we now practice dryland farming because they thought they were deserts. To northern European immigrants, the prairies appeared barren and unproductive compared to their native lands. Farmers did not begin to realize until late in the nineteenth century that grain crops could be produced in these dry locations, and the earliest pioneer farmers did not recognize the many hazards that accompanied dryland farming and therefore often failed. Dryland farming research found solutions to many of the problems in the early twentieth century, and today 60 percent of the wheat involved in international trade comes from the drylands of North America. Hard red spring and winter wheats are the mainstay of the Great Plains dryland areas, and the soft white wheats are primary crops in the Pacific Northwest. These areas are referred to as the breadbasket of North America because of the large amount of wheat produced in them.

Dryland agriculture is highly dependent on precipitation from both snow and rainfall, which makes water conservation very important. Each small increment of precipitation is critical to production, and profit is highly related to efficient use of precipitation. For example, in eastern Colorado an additional inch of water above the initial yield threshold results in an additional 4.5 bushels per acre of wheat (Greb et al. 1974). The unpredictable climatic conditions always pose an additional large threat to farmers. Records in eastern Colorado show, for example, that the probability of receiving 75 percent or less of the average annual precipitation occurs about 25 percent of the time (Greb 1979). Economic fragility is an ever-present factor, and farmers must use cropping systems that can cope with this unpredictability. Dryland farms tend to have little enterprise diversity, with wheat being the primary cash crop. Whenever enterprise diversity is increased by producing crops other than wheat or by increasing livestock production, a more stable agricultural environment always results. Unfortunately, the cropping options are limited by plant adaptation and potential markets for the products.

Management Strategies

The change from the historically unstable agriculture to our modern productive systems started in the late 1930s. Duley and Russel (1939) were among the first to recognize that leaving crop residue cover on the soil surface during noncrop periods improved water capture, reduced evaporation, increased water retention, and decreased soil erosion. Although they did not recognize it at the time, their techniques also decreased soil stirring (cultivation), which indirectly had a positive effect on organic matter and nitrogen conservation. Water-storage efficiency in summer fallow (14-month time between wheat crops) increased from 19 percent in the 1916–1930 period to 33 percent with stubble mulch tillage in recent years. The additional water storage resulted from new production systems that maintained more residue cover on the soil surface with fewer tillage events. By 1970 improved water storage with no-till management made it possible to shift from a two-year wheat-fallow system to a three-year wheat-sorghum-fallow system in 16- to 19-inch rainfall zones.

Erosion potential in dryland farming areas has always been very high because of the small amount of vegetation produced by dryland crops and because the cropping practices used include large amounts of fallow time during which soils have no vegetative cover. The most common cropping system is the wheat-fallow system, in which winter wheat is grown for ten months and is then followed by a 14-month fallow period before the next wheat crop is planted. During the fallow period, the objective is to keep the fields weed free and to conserve as much of the total precipitation as possible. In areas where spring wheat is grown, the crop period is only three months, and the fallow period is 21 months long.

The fallow period opens the door for very serious erosion. Prior to the 1970s, weed control during fallow was done with tillage, which destroyed the residue left from the previous crop. Six or seven tillages during a 14-month fallow are not uncommon, and bare soil is quite likely to be present for several months out of the 14-month total. In cases in which crops are poor, the residue cover disappears even more quickly, and erosion possibilities are heightened. In dryland farming areas, agents of erosion such as wind and water are both prevalent. Erosion by water is potentially large, not because of long periods of rainfall but because the dryland farming areas receive much of their summer rain as highly intense thunderstorms. During these storms, rainfall intensity is greater than the soil's infiltration rate, and water runoff is large. Thus, water erosion is a problem even in very dry places. Erosion by wind can also occur after the wheat crop is planted because during the seedling establishment period, the soil is not covered by the small plant seedlings.

Residue cover on the soil surface is extremely effective in controlling erosion. Just 50 percent cover by residue decreases soil erosion by 70 percent. Management techniques ranging from cultivation timing to invention of sweep tillage machines helped farmers control erosion by leaving more crop residue on the soil surface throughout the fallow period and on into the wheat seedling stage. Using herbicides permits maintenance of even more residue cover because soils are not disturbed and residue is not destroyed by tillage machines, which further aids erosion control. Ultimate cover is obtained with no-till management, in which all weeds are controlled by herbicides and the soil is not disturbed except by the planting equipment. No-till provides the maximum control of soil erosion by wind or water.

Sustainability

Long-term viability and economic stability in dryland farming is achieved when farmers successfully integrate management factors ranging from water conservation to judicious fertilizer use for effective erosion control. The ability to withstand wide swings in climatic variation is linked directly to minimizing input costs and maximizing water conservation. Dryland farmers are usually very conservative in terms of machinery purchases and machinery maintenance. They learned that sustainablity results from keeping cash flow at a minimum for their operation, and this means as small a debt load as possible. Dryland farmers tend not to make short-term radical changes in their farming practices; they rely heavily on what they know sustained them in the past.

—*G. A. Peterson*

See also

Agronomy; Conservation, Soil; Cropping Systems; Grain Farming; Tillage; Wheat Industry.

References

Duley, Frank L. and Jouette C. Russel. "The Use of Crop Residues for Soil and Moisture Conservation." *Agronomy Journal* 31, no. 8 (1939): 703–709.

Greb, B. W. "Reducing Drought Effects on Croplands in the West-central Great Plains." U.S. Department of Agriculture Information Bulletin. no. 420. Washington, DC: Government Printing Office, 1979.

Greb, B. W., D. E. Smika, N. P. Woodruff, and C. J. Whitfield. "Summer Fallow in the Central Great Plains." *Summer Fallow in the Western United States.* Conservation Research Report no. 17, pp. 51–84. Washington, DC: U.S. Department of Agriculture, Agricultural Research Service, 1974.

Economic Development

See Development, Community and Economic; Policy, Rural Development

Economic Policy

See Policy, Economic

Education, Adult

The part-time participation of learners 17 years old and over in college courses, in-service training, developmental and basic education, and literacy programs. Adult education programs in our nation's rural areas have a long, distinctive history. Today, increasing numbers of rural adults participate in adult education, but ongoing barriers significantly inhibit their educational opportunities. Public policies have largely failed to address the difficulties of rural adult learners.

Organizations: A Historical Overview

Rural adult education projects emerged early in our nation's history. During the colonial period, farmers organized local and regional agricultural societies to increase production through an exchange of experiential knowledge at meetings and fairs. More highly organized voluntary organizations followed, such as farmer's institutes, the Grange, and the Farmer's Union, which also developed educational projects. The Land Grant Act of 1862 and the Hatch Act of 1887 provided, respectively, for land-grant universities and agricultural experiment stations, from which research was disseminated to farmers through printed materials, lectures, and exhibits. A notable example of early extension service, the Movable School of Agri-culture, was initiated at the Tuskegee Institute in 1906 by Booker T. Washington. A demonstration agent equipped with agricultural tools and exhibits traveled throughout the South in a mule-drawn wagon to upgrade farming and the standard of living among rural Black families (Goldenstein 1989).

Various dimensions of agricultural education (volunteerism, demonstration, and agriculture) were crystallized in 1914 through the Smith-Lever Act, which created the Cooperative Extension Service. At its inception, the Extension Service provided noncredit education in agriculture and home economics through land-grant universities and the U.S. Department of Agriculture (USDA). It expanded to include material on marketing, conservation, health, and community development. The Extension Service more recently shared research results directly with 40 million participants annually through field visits, workshops, courses, and conferences and with millions more through bulletins, correspondence, and the mass media. Although the Extension Service did not provide for general adult education, it set an example for the entire adult education field in statistics collecting and in-service training of professional and volunteer workers (Knowles 1977). By the mid-1990s, the Cooperative Extension Service employed 19,000 professional and paraprofessional staff assisted by three million volunteers.

Agricultural associations and institutions dominated adult education in rural America, but other educational programs and institutions attempted to meet the demand for knowledge among rural adults. In 1826, the American Lyceum was established by lecturer Josiah Holbrook along with his audience of farmers and mechanics in Millbury, Massachusetts. The lyceum movement popularized study groups, lecture series, and debates in thousands of small towns from Maine to Florida and through the Midwest. During the slack season of the agricultural

Adult education often involves specific vocational training, as in this workshop for apprentice cabinetmakers at the Tuskegee Institute in 1910.

year, vacation and "lay-by" schools allowed farm workers to study reading, arithmetic, citizenship, and domestic management. Outreach programs of these types were sponsored by the state, church societies, businesses, and individuals and may be seen as the rural precursors of Literacy Volunteers of America, Adult Basic Education projects, free universities, and in-service training programs.

Distance learning was initiated in 1873 with the introduction of correspondence courses through the Society to Encourage Studies at Home. The first established success of this type debuted in 1878 as the Chautauqua movement, which offered home-study courses and summer schools for adults. Today, communications technology enables rural adults to receive instruction off-campus by telephone, television, and computer. Students can view programs at home on broadcast television; watch videotaped courses in small groups at off-campus

sites; participate in live video courses via satellite transmission, viewing lecturers on monitors and speaking with them by telephone or over microphones; and receive, send, and discuss assignments through electronic mail.

Many institutions and agencies such as libraries, the mass media, and health and welfare agencies support adult education as one of their secondary functions. Of these, public libraries played a particularly important role in rural America, supporting self-education by providing materials, informational services, exhibits, and centers for community projects. Library service to rural areas was largely confined to the New England states during the nineteenth century (see DeGruyter 1980), but at the turn of the century, newly formed state library agencies undertook extension services in other rural areas, sending traveling libraries stocked with fiction books to deposit stations in small towns. The purpose of library services to rural adults was moral and cultural education. Following World War II, libraries were transformed from cultural sites to information agencies in response to the explosion of scientific and technological knowledge.

Participation

In 1991, 181 million adults entered or returned to the education process (National Center for Education Statistics 1994), indicating an emphasis on lifelong learning. No figures are available on the number of rural adult learners in 1991. However, in 1981, six million rural adults participated in adult education programs, constituting 28 percent of all adult learners in the United States at that time (National Center for Education Statistics 1982). These figures represent an increase of 34.4 percent in the number of rural adult learners between 1975 and 1981 (McCannon 1983). In-migration from suburban and urban areas accounts for some of the growth in the number of rural adults who reentered the educational system during that period, but changes in the rural economy, from the emergence of agribusiness to the impact of technological innovation, also increased the number of native rural adults reentering the classroom. Rural population increased since 1981, and it is very likely that the number of rural adult learners likewise rose.

Barriers to Participation

Adults in rural America today have many options from which to choose as they pursue their educational goals. However, they underuse programs, which indicates that even in the era of the information superhighway, ongoing barriers limit their access. Distance and higher costs continue to check the participation of rural adults, and cultural prohibitions act as deterrents. These barriers commonly are classified into three types: institutional, situational, and dispositional (Cross 1981). Traditional educational institutions often are located at a distance from rural communities and historically have not provided schedules that are convenient for rural adults or course offerings that are appropriate for them. In addition, financial support at colleges and universities is largely restricted to full-time students.

Situational barriers, which arise from personal living conditions as opposed to institutional practices, also check participation in education programs. Like their urban and suburban counterparts, rural adults struggle to find time for study, family, and jobs, but the extra travel time to distant educational sites magnifies the problem for rural adults. In a survey of educators and legislators, 79 percent of the respondents agreed or strongly agreed that distance from programs created excessive demands on student time and represented a significant barrier for rural adults (Easton 1991). The same majority believed that the high cost of adult education in rural communities inhibited access to educational opportunities. Services not only cost more in rural areas; they are also more scarce. Research indicates that the absence of academic and career counseling services particularly deters rural adults from continuing their education (McCannon 1983).

Attitudes and values peculiar to traditional rural culture may act as dispositional barriers. Rural women, for example, may be inhibited by a culture that does not value their educational ambitions (Marineau 1975). Similarly, traditional rural culture views education as a pursuit of children and adolescents rather than as a lifelong process. As a result, rural males of all ages tend to think they are too old for continuing education. Rural adults fear returning to the education system. Thus, the strongest dispositional barriers exist among rural adults with the direst educational needs—those with low levels of educational attainment and occupational skill (Sundet and Galbraith 1991). To some extent, rural adults must be persuaded that education will be to their advantage. Better public relations efforts, especially through the news media and peer support groups, are recommended.

Public Policy: Achieving Equity

Policymakers, researchers, and rural educators generally agree that federal policy has favored urban and suburban educational concerns. An early study of rural adult education (Landis and Willard 1933) concluded that rural citizens were systematically deprived of educational opportunities, and its authors recommended a national plan of redress.

The states hold primary responsibility for education, but where equity is an issue, the federal government has a legitimate stake.

The first comprehensive federal agenda to upgrade rural education in general was introduced in the 1980s, but earlier federal mandates did increase educational opportunities for rural adults. The Land Grant Act of 1862 established the land-grant university system; the Smith-Lever Act of 1914 established the Cooperative Extension Service; the Smith-Hughes Act of 1917 funded vocational education for youth and adults; the Adult Education Act of 1966 funded adult basic education and high school completion programs; and the Comprehensive Employment and Training Act of 1973 (CETA) provided short-term on-the-job training and basic skills instruction for the economically disadvantaged.

In 1982, Secretary of Education T. H. Bell announced the department's Rural Education Initiative, a set of objectives intended to provide a stronger voice for rural education and to rectify an imbalance in department efforts, which favored urban areas. At that time, Department of Education policy stipulated that rural youth and adults receive an equitable share of the department's information and assistance. Specifically, the department supported outreach and volunteer program development, expanded the database on education in rural areas, monitored eligibility and evaluation criteria to ensure equity for all Local Education Agencies (LEAs), and included rural institutions in demonstration and pilot projects.

In the early 1990s, rural education lost priority in the department as reforms were institutionalized, new priorities emerged, and staffs were reduced. During that time, the Federal Interagency Committee on Education's (FICE) subcommittee on rural education disbanded and the Department of Education's intergovernmental affairs liaison for rural education retired and was not replaced. For all practical purposes, federal policy regarding adult education in rural America is defunct, even though a recent survey of educators and legislators involved with rural issues found that at least 75 percent of the respondents believed that public policy should encourage lifelong learning. A similar majority of respondents believed that federal and state governments must commit themselves to adult literacy programs and provide more federal and state support for student loans and work-study programs for adult learners (Easton 1991). The unique character of rural adult education will remain a substantial issue for the nation's educators and policymakers in the years ahead.

— *Walter G. McIntire and Susan K. Woodward*

See also
Cooperative State Research, Education, and Extension Service; Education, Youth; Land-Grant Institutions, 1862 and 1890; Literacy; Refugee Resettlement.

References

Cross, K. P. *Adults as Learners: Increasing Participation and Facilitating Learning.* San Francisco: Jossey-Bass, 1981.

DeGruyter, Lisa. "The History and Development of Rural Public Libraries." *Library Trends* 28, no. 4 (1980): 513–523.

Easton, Stanley E. "Confronting Educational Barriers to Rural Adults: A 13-State Survey." *Journal of Research in Rural Education* 7, no. 2 (1991): 63–73.

Goldenstein, Erwin H. "Booker T. Washington and Cooperative Extension." *Negro Educational Review* 40, no. 2 (1989): 4–14.

Knowles, Malcolm. *The Adult Education Movement in the United States.* 2d ed. New York: Holt, Rinehart and Winston, 1977.

Landis, Benson Y., and John D. Willard. *Rural Adult Education.* New York: Macmillan, 1933.

Marineau, C. *Study of Barriers to Participation in Postsecondary Education as Perceived by Adults in West Central Minnesota.* ERIC Microfiche, ED 123 450, Morris, MN: Morris Learning Center, Office of Continuing Education and Regional Programs, December 1975.

McCannon, R. S. "Serving Rural Adult Learners." *New Directions for Continuing Education,* no. 20 (1983): 15–29.

National Center for Education Statistics. *Participation in Adult Education.* Washington, DC: U.S. Department of Education, Office of Educational Research and Improvement, 1982.

———. *Digest of Education Statistics.* Washington, DC: U.S. Department of Education, Office of Educational Research and Improvement, 1994.

Sundet, Paul A., and Michael W. Galbraith. "Adult Education as a Response to the Rural Crisis: Factors Governing Utility and Participation." *Journal of Research in Rural Education* 7, no. 2 (1991): 41–49.

Education, Special

The provision of educational services and support for students with disabilities in the public school system. This entry provides an overview of services for students with disabilities. It includes the forces leading up to the passage of federal legislation requiring access to appropriate educational programs. It describes the legal requirements of this federal legislation and discusses the effects of implementing the Individuals with Disabilities Education Act (IDEA) in rural schools and communities.

Services for Students with Disabilities: An Overview

Access to a public education designed to develop the abilities and potential of young people is both valued and taken for granted, yet it has not always been available for students who differ in their learning or their behavior. These students often are labeled according to their difference or deviation and either excluded from typical schooling or, in some cases, provided alternative kinds of educational opportunities. Special education for these students more often than not has meant separate or segregated education.

Concerned professionals in the early 1900s developed educational programs for students seen as exceptional or different. These programs usually were housed in separate facilities, often institutional settings for those with mental impairments or vision or hearing difficulties. Public schools were not required to serve these students, although some school districts did educate students with milder disabilities, in separate programs either within the schools or in separate special schools.

Educational programs for students with disabilities expanded from the 1950s through the 1970s. Three major forces affected services for students with disabilities during this time. First, parents of students with disabilities organized into advocacy groups to pressure legislative and policymaking bodies for equal access to educational opportunities for these students. Second, research conducted by professionals in both the medical and educational fields resulted in improved services for individuals with disabilities. Finally, as a result of several court decisions, schools were ordered to provide free public education for all school-age children with disabilities.

These combined efforts on behalf of students with disabilities came into focus in one comprehensive piece of legislation, the Education of the Handicapped Act, Public Law 94-142, which was passed by Congress in 1975. This law and its regulations required that all eligible students with disabilities, regardless of the severity of the disability, receive educational services designed specifically to meet their individual needs. This legislation was updated and renamed the Individuals with Disabilities Education Act (IDEA) in 1990. The change in the name of the law was significant because it reflected a focus on individuals rather than on the handicap or disability. Other changes expanded special education services to include workplace and training centers.

Students with disabilities were to receive related services such as special transportation, speech pathology, psychological services, and occupational and physical therapy. Students served under this law included those with the following disabilities: mental retardation, specific learning disabilities, serious emotional disturbances, speech or language impairments, vision loss, hearing loss, orthopedic and other health impairments, deafness or blindness, multiple disabilities, autism, and traumatic brain injury.

IDEA outlined four essential services that school districts must provide. Services must account for (1) nondiscriminatory and multidisciplinary assessment of educational needs; (2) parental involvement to develop each child's educational program; (3) education in the least restrictive environment; and (4) an individualized education plan (IEP). In the next section these four mandated provisions of IDEA are further explained.

Serving Students with Disabilities: Requirements of IDEA

The first provision of IDEA requires that school districts develop nondiscriminatory and multidisciplinary identification and assessment procedures. Assessment measures used to determine a student's eligibility for services need to be given in the child's primary language, and factors related to a student's cultural background must be considered during the assessment process. A comprehensive examination of the student's intellectual capability, school achievement, and social and adaptive behavior is often completed as part of this process. No single instrument may be used to determine eligibility for service; therefore a multidisciplinary team of professionals is required to complete the assessment. Individuals involved may include the school psychologist, speech and language specialists, special education and general education teachers, hearing and vision specialists, and the student's parents or legal guardians. The decision regarding the student's disability and educational needs comes from the multiple perspectives of this team.

The second provision stipulates that the student's parents play a critical role in identifying and developing educational services. Important parental rights guaranteed by IDEA include providing consent in writing for testing and for placement in special education, participating as members of the multidisciplinary team throughout the decision-making process, having access to all information and records regarding their child's program, and requesting a hearing if they cannot agree with the school district regarding the services provided for their child. These safeguards protect families and students with disabilities from possible inappropriate or harmful educational decisions.

The third provision of IDEA requires that students with disabilities be educated with their nondisabled peers whenever appropriate, rather than receive services in separate and often segregated settings. School districts must provide a range of services for students with disabilities to meet this provision. Options must range from consultative services provided in the general education classroom through more restrictive services that are provided in the student's home or hospital setting. A variety of specially trained personnel may be involved to provide services, depending on each student's individual needs. Decisions about where to provide services for students with disabilities are based on individual student needs and the requirement to provide services in settings with their nondisabled peers.

The fourth provision of IDEA requires that an individualized education plan (IEP) be developed for each student who qualifies for services under the requirements of the law. This plan, developed collaboratively by the multidisciplinary team (including the student's parents), serves as a blueprint to determine the actual services and programs that will be provided to the student. The IEP document contains information about the student's present level of functioning, annual goals, short-term instructional objectives, related services, percentage of time spent in general education, beginning and end dates of services, and a provision for an annual evaluation of the student's progress. The document is signed by the parents and educational personnel involved in providing services for that student.

Implementing IDEA in Rural Schools and Communities

How districts, particularly rural school districts, implement the requirement to serve students with disabilities varies depending on local conditions and issues. There is currently very limited information about services for students with disabilities in rural school districts. Helge (1984) published the results of a comprehensive survey that identified issues and problems rural school districts encountered when implementing the Education for the Handicapped Act, Public Law 94-142. She described the diversity and unique subcultures of rural school districts as major factors that both enhanced and challenged the provision of services for students with disabilities. These factors included characteristics such as varied topography (e.g., deserts, islands, mountain ranges, plains), economic diversity ranging from extreme poverty to wealthy resort communities, and variations in population density ranging from isolated ranches to small towns and clustered communities. Rural school districts experienced major problems regarding qualified staff recruitment and retention, resistance to change, the need for staff development, long distances between schools and services, cultural differences, geographic barriers, transportation and funding inadequacies, and difficulty serving students with low-incidence disabilities (for example, hearing and vision loss and multiple disabilities).

In a more recent discussion of services for special students in rural communities, Berkeley and Ludlow (1991) identified these same issues as continuing problems. They observed difficulties in personnel recruitment and retention and challenges in providing specific services for students with disabilities in rural schools. Critical to the success of students with disabilities in school programs is the quality and effectiveness of the educators who work with these students. Qualified teachers and other related professionals must be available to provide

the legally required programs for students with disabilities. Rural school administrators report that recruiting and retaining qualified special education personnel remains an ongoing dilemma. The shortage of special education personnel is a national need that is even more severe in rural school districts.

Simply preparing more teachers will not solve the problem, particularly in rural districts. Rural school districts must compete with urban school districts for an already limited number of specialized personnel, and many qualified special educators do not choose to relocate to small rural communities. Rural school districts often struggle with fewer fiscal resources, resulting in lower salaries and fewer classroom materials. These factors combine to serve as disincentives for recruiting educators to work with students with disabilities.

Rural school districts initiated several innovative strategies to recruit qualified educators. Many rural school districts advertise the benefits of working and living in rural communities in their recruitment materials. Benefits of teaching in rural schools include factors such as smaller class size, fewer discipline problems, opportunities to individualize instruction, and personal involvements with students. Involving parents in the development of programs for students with disabilities is sometimes easier for teachers since schools are often the center of rural communities.

Teachers who work in rural school districts are often from small, rural communities. Attempting to recruit graduates who have rural backgrounds is a strategy used regularly by rural school districts. Another recruitment idea that helps to attract and keep teachers in rural schools is something called "growing your own." Rural school districts work cooperatively with colleges and universities to bring teacher preparation programs directly to local communities. Using many of the new interactive technologies (such as two-way video and audio systems, computer conferencing via e-mail, satellite broadcasts), preparation programs can be delivered directly to very remote regions of the country. These technologies are used to update the knowledge and skills of educators already teaching in rural school districts, especially when access to institutions of higher education is difficult. Acquiring new skills and having opportunities to interact and share with other rural educators is an effective use of these new technologies.

Even with well-prepared educators in place, there are other dilemmas unique to rural environments with which rural school districts must grapple as they attempt to provide services for students with disabilities. Two aspects of rural service delivery are particularly challenging to school districts: serving students with low incidence disabilities and the legal requirement to provide related services to students (such as speech therapy, occupational therapy, physical therapy).

Students with low-incidence or very severe disabilities present particular challenges to rural school districts. Since there are usually very few of these students, a rural school district may attempt to serve only two or three students with multiple or severe disabilities. These students often require special adaptive equipment and medical care. Additionally, finding and funding specialized related service personnel is often a serious hardship for rural school districts. Districts that successfully serve these students often approach the problem from a systemwide perspective. Sharing itinerant teachers and specialists among several rural communities is one way rural schools address this challenge. When these students attend school in their own neighborhoods, local schools can combine strategies to assist them with their special programs, using community volunteers, peer support groups, itinerant support staff, and educators trained to work with a wide range of student abilities.

Although there are no easy solutions to the challenges of serving students with disabilities in rural schools, many innovative strategies are currently being implemented. Rural school districts are unique in their ability to creatively and resourcefully solve difficult problems. When students with disabilities are served in their local communities by caring individuals who are able to focus on each student's specific instructional needs, the goal of providing equal access and quality education programs can be achieved.

—*Joan P. Sebastian*

See also
Adolescents; Camps; Education, Youth; Policy, Socioeconomic.
References
Berkeley, Terry R., and Kay S. Bull. "Voices in Rural Special Education: Retrospectives, Prospectives, Possibilities." *Rural Special Education Quarterly* 14, no. 2 (1995): 10–16.
Berkeley, Terry R., and Barbara L. Ludlow. "Meeting the Needs of Special Student Populations in Rural Locales." Pp. 239–268 in *Rural Education Issues and Practices.* Edited by Alan J. DeYoung. New York and London: Garland, 1991.
Hardman, Michael L., Clifford J. Drew, and M. Winston Egan. *Human Exceptionality, Society School, and Family.* 4th ed. Boston: Allyn and Bacon, 1996.
Helge, Doris. "The State of the Art of Rural Special Education." *Journal of Exceptional Children* 50, no. 4 (1984): 294–305.
———, guest editor. "Special Topical Issue: Rural Special Education." *Journal of Exceptional Children* 50, no. 4 (1984): 293–369.
Joyce, Bonnie G., and Wilfred D. Wienke. "Preservice Competencies for Teachers of Students with Behavior Disorders in a Rural Setting." *Rural Special Education Quarterly* 9, no. 2 (1988): 4–9.
Lemke, June C. "Attracting and Retaining Special Educators in Rural and Small Schools: Issues and Solutions." *Rural Special Education Quarterly* 14, no. 2 (1995): 25–30.
Sebastian, Joan P. "Distance Teacher Education at the University of Utah: An Evolving Model." Pp. 33–45 in *Educational Issues in Utah: Governance, Legislation, Technology, and Finance.* Edited by P. F. Galvin and B. L. Johnson. Salt Lake City: Utah Education Policy Center, Graduate School of Education, University of Utah, 1995.
Sebastian, Joan, and J. McDonnell. "Rural Students with Low Incidence Disabilities: Recommended Practices for the Future." *Rural Special Education Quarterly* 14, no. 2 (1995): 31–38.

Education, Youth

The academic preparation of rural students in kindergarten through grade 12; elementary- and secondary-level instruction. This entry provides key information about the education of students in rural America: the number and location of students enrolled in elementary and secondary schools, their academic performance, and their post–high school careers.

Locating Rural Students

Rural students, even in this era of rampant urbanization, constitute a sizable portion of America's student body. In the early 1990s, there were an estimated 6.9 million students in rural areas, accounting for 16.7 percent of regular public school students. The 22,400 schools they attended constituted 28 percent of America's public elementary and secondary schools (Elder, 1994).

These students are found throughout the United States in a range of settings from isolated farms to villages and settlements on the fringe of urban concentrations of various sizes. Distinguishing between urban and nonurban locales is done in two ways by the Census Bureau. One approach defines urban and rural along a continuum by population size in a place, whereas the other makes population density distinctions by county type—metropolitan versus nonmetropolitan. The definitions are not equivalent. Rural pockets or places may be found within metropolitan counties, whereas a considerable number of urban centers exist in otherwise sparsely settled nonmetropolitan counties.

This interrelationship between these two ways of distinguishing between urban and rural is reflected in school designations as well. For example, 12 percent of

The quaint one-room schoolhouse, like this one in Larned, Kansas, was commonly used in rural areas well into the twentieth century. Such schools have given way to larger consolidated facilities that are able to offer a richer curriculum; still, rural schools tend to be much smaller than their urban counterparts.

schools in metropolitan counties are located in rural places. In the nonmetropolitan counties, just over half of the schools are actually in rural settings; the remainder are in the urban population concentrations located within these lightly populated counties. An awareness of these finer distinctions is critical when developing state and federal policies intended for rural schools and the students they serve. The following discussion is limited to the intersection of the two primary ways the federal government defines rural. Among the several states and within numerous federal, state, and private programs affecting rural issues, still other definitions may be found.

Although rural students are found in every state, the extent of their numbers and their proportion to the whole student population vary considerably. For example, Texas has the largest number of rural students (443,000), representing 12.9 percent of its student population. But although their enrollments are lower, 40 other states have higher proportions of students in rural settings. Overall,

proportions of students located in rural areas range from 3.5 percent in Connecticut to 47.1 percent in South Dakota.

Student Performance

Student population services in rural settings were commonly viewed as deficient a few decades ago. Improvement is the product of several converging forces. For over 100 years, extensive consolidation efforts drastically reduced the number both of rural schools and rural school districts. At the same time, states and districts continued to bring many of the latest innovations to remote and resource-strapped schools. Rural school personnel, for their part, traditionally approached their challenges creatively; the multigrade classroom is just one of many strategies devised to accommodate low enrollments.

Recent data from federal studies provide a new appreciation of what rural education can achieve. Prior to the 1980s, National Assessment of Educational Progress (NAEP) scores of students from what is termed "extreme rural" areas (generally, farming) fell below the national average. But by the 1980s, when the ongoing reform movement was launched, students from that population matched the average in every subject tested. These improved performance levels continue to be maintained. In another NAEP comparison, rural students scored higher than disadvantaged urban students, although they lagged behind advantaged urban students (National Center for Educational Statistics 1991a). In a test given to a large sample of eighth graders in the federal National Education Longitudinal Study of 1988, or NELS 88 (National Center for Educational Statistics 1991b), rural students (here encompassing a wide spectrum of all those in nonmetropolitan counties) met or exceeded the national average on every measure. As with the NAEP results, rural students scored above urban students but below those from suburban areas.

Two factors must be considered when interpreting these findings. First, there is considerable research suggesting that the positive elements of rural schooling, such as small classes, personal attention, and community ethos, may serve to offset the comparatively limited breadth of curricular offerings often dictated by low enrollments (Fowler and Walberg 1991). In this regard, the NELS findings showed that students in the smallest schools in general outperformed those from the largest ones. This is relevant to documenting school quality in rural America since very small schools abound there. Nearly three out of four rural elementary and secondary schools have less than 400 students, and almost 20 percent have less than 100 students (Elder 1994).

Second, there is abundant research literature showing conclusively that poverty, as measured by socioeconomic status and certain other factors, has a limiting effect on school performance. About one in five rural students (National Center for Educational Statistics 1991b) exhibit at least two risk factors such as having low family income, coming from a single-parent home, having parent(s) with little education, being home alone in excess of three hours a day, or having a sibling who dropped out of school. A larger proportion of urban students (26 percent) and a smaller proportion of suburban students (15 percent) are similarly at risk. Correlated with test results within each sector, these findings show that the greater the evidence of risk, the poorer the performance. Crippling poverty hampers the capacity of many rural schools to deliver services. It is not surprising that rural schools and districts took the lead in most of the 25 states where there has been school finance litigation. In 12 states, courts found school finance systems unconstitutional. Mandated remedies should generally benefit rural schools.

Preparing for Life after High School

National survey data (Marion et al. 1994) reveal what rural educators long have known: rural youth have fairly high dropout rates (although not the worst); they are less likely to gain an equivalency diploma later on; and those who remain in school tend less than their metropolitan counterparts to anticipate, prepare for, and enter postsecondary education programs. These are sobering findings because in today's economy as never before, future earnings are linked to education.

According to one national study (Kaufman and McMillan 1991), 7 percent of rural youth dropped out of school between the seventh and eighth grades, more than the suburban rate (5 percent), although below the urban rate (9 percent). In another national survey (Alsalam et al. 1992), 16 percent of rural sophomores dropped out, which was the same as the national average and the suburban rate; urban youth had a far higher rate (24.5 percent). Because these were not the same cohorts, the junior high and senior high school data cannot be added. Nevertheless, the findings suggest that perhaps more than one in five rural teenagers leave school before acquiring the minimal necessary skills to compete in today's demanding job market.

Location hampers the capacity of rural youths who left school early to later gain an education. Suitable programs are too few and too widely dispersed (Sherman 1992). As a result, rural dropouts are less likely than their metropolitan peers to find a place to obtain a high school equivalency diploma. This difficulty is reflected in one follow-up study that found that after six years, high school completion rates had risen only 6 percent for rural students, compared to 11 percent for suburban youth and 8 percent for urban youth (Alsalam et al. 1992).

Rural youths who remained in high school nevertheless had comparatively limited plans to further their education relative to their urban and suburban peers. One federal study (Marion et al. 1994) documented that rural seniors, compared to students in metropolitan areas, expected to conclude their education at lower levels and were more focused on work than on academic studies. With these attitudes, they tended to take fewer college-preparation courses (algebra, trigonometry, calculus, chemistry, and physics) and more courses in vocational and business fields (Pollard and O'Hare 1990). With lower aspirations and less preparation, fewer rural students (62 percent) compared to urban and suburban students (70.0 and 73.5 percent, respectively) enrolled in post–high school programs of study.

Researchers (Haller and Virkler 1992; McGranahan and Ghelfi 1991) suggest two reasons for this phenomenon: a lack of role models and a lack of employment opportunities. In a major national study, Pollard and O'Hare (1990) found that proportionately fewer rural seniors than nonrural seniors (12 and 19 percent, respectively) had college-educated parents (who tend to encourage their offspring to obtain a degree). More often than nonrural students, the rural students reported that their fathers wanted them to attend a trade school or to go directly into employment. Lower aspirations represent a realistic response to a local job market in which there are few opportunities to pursue professional or technical careers that require a college education.

Nevertheless, many rural youth did receive encouragement from home and school guidance counselors to continue their education after high school, and many did matriculate, although at lower rates than their metropolitan counterparts. Many rural youth did have professional ambitions but at lower rates than their nonrural peers. Nearly a quarter said they expected to hold a professional job by age 30, and 9 percent said they expected to be at high levels in their chosen professional career (Pollard and O'Hare 1990).

Of those who attended college, 36 percent completed four years of education, a rate that essentially matched that of urban youth but dipped below the 40 percent completion rate for suburban youth. When matching youth by socioeconomic status, nonrural advantage disappeared. In short, in terms of persistence in college, rural students demonstrate the capacity to succeed. Problems emerge, not as problems peculiar to location, but as handicapping conditions associated with poverty. When students having the same socioeconomic status are compared, performance is essentially the same regardless of location (Polland and O'Hare 1990).

Overall, rural schools succeed, sometimes in the face of severe challenges associated with isolation and lack of resources. However, the employment picture rural youth face after high school is bleak because today's economy is an urban economy. Low-skill, low-paying jobs remain in the countryside, whereas high-paying jobs are in the cities to which rural America's most talented youth are drawn. The metropolitan/nonmetropolitan pay distinction at one time was close to the difference in the cost of living. But by the mid-1980s, nonrural high school graduates earned 15 percent more in real terms, and college graduates in urban areas were enjoying a 30 percent advantage. To stem the tide of migration from the countryside, rural economic development and job creation must go hand in hand with any improvement in education opportunities. Until that is done, rural America will continue to train and educate its youth, only to see too many of them depart for urban areas (Polland and O'Hare 1990).

—*Joyce D. Stern*

See also
Adolescents; Education, Special; Educational Curriculum; Educational Facilities.

References
Alsalam, Nabeel, Laurence T. Ogle, Gayle T. Rogers, and Thomas M. Smith. *The Condition of Education 1992.* Washington, DC: U.S. Department of Education, National Center for Education Statistics, 1992.

Elder, William L. "Location and Characteristics of Rural Schools and School Districts." Pp. 13–19 in *The Condition of Education in Rural Schools.* Edited by Joyce D. Stern. Washington, DC: U.S. Department of Education, Office of Educational Research and Improvement, Programs for the Improvement of Practice, 1994.

Fowler, William J., and Herbert J. Walberg. "School Size, Characteristics, and Outcomes." *Educational Evaluation and Policy Analysis* 13, no. 2 (Summer 1991): 2.

Haller, Emil J., and S. J. Virkler. "Another Look at Rural-Urban Differences in Students' Educational Aspiration." Paper presented at the Rural Research Forum of the National Rural Education Association Meeting in Traverse City, MI, 1992.

Kaufman, Phillip, and Marilyn M. McMillan. *Dropout Rates in the United States: 1990.* Washington, DC: U.S. Department of Education, National Center for Education Statistics, 1991.

Marion, Scott F., Denise A. Mirochnik, Edward J. McCaul, and Walter McIntire. "Education and Work Experiences of Rural Youth." Pp. 61–68 in *The Condition of Education in Rural Schools.* Edited by Joyce D. Stern. Washington, DC: U.S. Department of Education, Office of Educational Research and Improvement, Programs for the Improvement of Practice, 1994.

McGranahan, David A., and Linda M. Ghelfi. "The Education Crisis and Rural Stagnation in the 1980s." *Education and Rural Economic Development: Strategies for the 1990s.* Washington, DC: U.S. Department of Agriculture, Economic Research Service, 1991.

National Center for Education Statistics. *Trends in Academic Progress.* Washington, DC: U.S. Department of Education, 1991a.

———. *The Tested Achievement of the National Education Longitudinal Study of the 1988 Eighth Grade Class.* Washington, DC: U.S. Department of Education, 1991b.

Pollard, Kelvin M., and William P. O'Hare. "Beyond High School: The Experience of Rural and Urban Youth in the 1980s." Staff working paper. Washington, DC: Population Reference Bureau, 1990.

Sherman, Arloc. *Falling by the Wayside: Children in Rural America.* Washington, DC: Children's Defense Fund, 1992.

Educational Curriculum

The content or subject matter taught in a school or similar setting. Basic concepts of curriculum and how it is differentiated from instruction are explored in this entry in order to demonstrate the uniqueness of the rural school curriculum. A discussion of the rural environment's influence on curriculum, rural curriculum innovations, and related issues follows.

Concepts

Considerable confusion exists about the difference between curriculum and instruction. Curriculum is considered the "what" of schooling, and instruction is the "how." Planned or structured learning cannot take place without both curriculum content and instructional methods. Some may argue that how subject matter is taught conveys its own message and becomes the hidden, and sometimes unintended, curriculum. For the moment, however, attention will be given to the intended content of rural education.

Rural schools and their urban counterparts provide a standard set of offerings common to all schools in the United States. The primary grades (kindergarten through the third or fourth grades) place a heavy emphasis on the basic skills of reading, language arts, mathematics, social studies, and science. These basic subjects are supplemented by special offerings of music, art, and physical education. In the middle years (grades five through eight), content takes precedence over skills. Integration of subject matter, such as mathematics with science or social studies with language arts, is usually present.

The secondary school is typically characterized by clearer divisions of subject matter. Subject areas break down further into discrete and separate offerings (for example, science offerings may include courses in biology, chemistry, and physics). Students follow schedules that divide their day into designated time blocks. Courses are taught by teachers specially trained in a particular content or specialization.

These general patterns of curriculum by levels exist across the country regardless of urban, suburban, or rural orientations and locations. However, because of some unique characteristics of rural settings, the content and methods of instruction can differ in many distinct ways.

Rural Differences

Caution is needed when suggesting that the rural curriculum is different from the urban one in part because of the strong emphasis on standardization of education in the United States. Yet, as state departments of education across the country attempt to ensure comparable education in all schools of their respective states, for a variety of reasons this does not always happen or is impossible to achieve. This results, in part, because of the intrinsic nature of rural schools including their isolation and limited fiscal resources.

An additional caution regarding statements about the rural education curriculum is the reality of diversity in rural schools. Rural conditions vary dramatically in the United States. There are significant differences in demographics, physical surroundings, cultural values, and historical background that contribute to the variety of practices and content in rural schools (Peshkin 1978). The content of mathematics and science may transcend these geographic and cultural differences. However, the content of social studies, language arts, and even reading will be influenced greatly by the region's culture and history.

Setting aside for the moment regional variation, the curriculum in rural areas seems to be influenced greatly by rural characteristics. These include social and political isolation; sparsity of population, human and fiscal resources, and technical expertise; limited numbers of and outdated school and community facilities; distance from major metropolitan areas; informal interpersonal and organizational relationships; small school enrollments; declining populations: importance of close and personal relationships; and public scrutiny of school matters (Carlson 1994).

Each of these characteristics influences the curriculum of rural schools in different ways. One visible influence on rural schools that is manifested in a variety of ways is the availability of fiscal resources. A traveler driving the secondary and back roads of the United States can observe from a distance the immediate impact of fiscal resources on rural schools. Facilities, playgrounds, and school yards are in clear need of repair and lack equipment or paved surfaces (Schmuck and Schmuck 1992).

Outside appearances do not always tell the full story, and schools that appear to be run-down can be graced with dedicated teachers and motivated students (Sher 1977). However, even the best of intentions and desires can be compromised by the lack of space for supplemental services (for example, health and special education), storage, special subjects (such as music, physical education, and art), inadequate or outdated or unavailable equipment and laboratories, and outdated or limited numbers of textbooks and library books (Gjelten 1978). There is probably no more visible way to determine the availability of curriculum resources for a school than to observe the number of microcomputers, their age and capacity, and the space for their use by students. Computer equipment often is limited, out of date, and lacking in peripherals (e.g., printers and modems). Much can be taught without computers, but as society moves rapidly toward a heavier reliance on the use of computer technology, a school's curriculum will be judged as inadequate without ample and up-to-date computer equipment.

Another technology affected by fiscal resources that plays an important role in making extensive curriculum offerings more available, particularly at the secondary school level and for academically gifted students, is the availability of distance learning technology. In more wealthy rural areas, secondary schools have courses taught with interactive television programs and video equipment. This technology permits rural schools to access a national network of special, advanced courses in literature, foreign language, science, and vocational technology offered by different institutions. Interactive television technology continues to grow and will provide courses that typically could not be offered in small, isolated rural areas because of too few students and distances between schools.

Limited fiscal resources, sparse populations, and social isolation handicap rural schools' ability to provide depth and breadth of curriculum offerings (Monk 1988). The result of these conditions is a lack of specially trained and knowledgeable personnel who can address the unique learning needs of students. Rural schools often lack teachers with in-depth training in certain areas of content (for example, science, mathematics, literature), which in turn, results in a more general presentation of curriculum content. Teachers often are asked to teach across many subject areas for which they have little or no preparation or background.

Distance and isolation makes it difficult for rural schools to provide special subjects (such as music, art, physical education) and support services (such as health care, counseling, school social worker). Geographic distances and physical barriers (such as mountains and streams) require specialists to travel great distances and serve many schools on a part-time basis. These support services are essential to ensure that special needs children can fully function and benefit from the curricular offerings of a school.

Rural Curricular Innovations

Rural schools creatively and imaginatively meet their challenges to accommodate the realities of rural places and provide curricula needed to prepare students for postsecondary educational programs and employment opportunities. Some rural schools and their communities capitalize on their strengths to minimize the impact of the delimiting conditions of rural places and their effect on curricular offerings. These strengths include a sense of neighborliness or community, a human scale that permits and values face-to-face interpersonal communications, respect for self-reliance and ingenuity, support for strong family and religious values, and an appreciation for informality and flexibility (Nachtigal 1982). Examples of rural schools and communities' efforts to increase curriculum options for their young people and adults include school cooperatives, school-based enterprises, and community-based learning.

Rural School Cooperatives. Some rural schools build on historical experience and recognition of the importance of cooperation to the well-being of people in rural areas by establishing programs that cross traditional boundaries among the school, community, and institutions such as social service agencies and higher education institutions. These cooperative arrangements take many forms and involve various combinations of organizations and individuals. Their purposes often grow out of local circumstances and the ingenuity of the people involved. Cooperatives may result in resource sharing, mutual problem solving, and creation of new and practical curricular options (Monk and Haller 1986). Learning opportunities may shift from the traditional classroom setting to places in the community or other organizations. Being flexible and meeting individual and unique needs are important to the success of rural school cooperative efforts. For example, vocational education offerings may be taught on-site in local businesses and manufacturing companies.

School-Based Development Enterprises. Rural schools in partnership with business leaders can play a central role in stimulating business enterprises by recognizing that communities often suffer from the lack of a viable economic and tax base of businesses and industries. This can take the form of the school serving as a potential business enterprise incubator and nurturing it to produce private, profit-making operations. Students in the school gain knowledge and practical experience by starting and operating a business that may result in postsecondary school employment. Fledgling business opportunities are unique to the communities and schools that spawn them. Some examples include formal wear boutiques, gift shops, T-shirt printing operations, pressure-washing firms, computer sales businesses, and cabinet shops.

From a school and curriculum point of view, the development of school-based enterprises provides an unlimited number of learning opportunities of a very practical nature. School business, mathematics, home economics, and industrial arts courses and curriculum can receive a major boost from business enterprise development. A side effect of school-based enterprises is the infusion of additional economic activity into the community. It provides products and services, which in turn, can provide an additional source of funds for a school system (Sher 1977).

Community-Based Learning. Many rural schools embark on efforts to link more tightly with their community members, parents, and different organizations by recognizing that the community is an untapped resource for curriculum learning. With the community as a focus, students and their teachers are encouraged to think of ways that knowledge and skills of the curriculum can be transmitted and applied through community-based activities. For example, history and written and oral expression may be taught and applied through historical reports of the community or on-going newsletters about the community's history and special events. Such efforts require that students find, read, and synthesize information from sources such as documents, community leaders, senior citizens, and state archives.

Another example is service learning projects. Students, along with a teacher-mentor and community members, propose service projects that will benefit the community and require skills and knowledge to successfully complete. Examples range from organizing after-school programs for elementary schoolchildren to establishing book discussion groups or providing home assistance to senior citizens. Whatever is chosen provides ample opportunity to test students' abilities and stimulates new areas of interest and further learning. Experiential opportunities demonstrate the relevance of a school's curriculum, provide payback to a community, provide students with a sense of place and connection to their community, and allow community members—often parents—to contribute directly to the learning of their students.

The intrinsic qualities of rural environments provide both opportunities for and serious constraints on educational curriculum for rural students. Rural schools will continue to be confronted with the reality of meeting national curricular standards, which are often modeled after those of highly respected suburban school districts, but with fewer fiscal and human resources. However, rural schools lead in curricular innovations, often driven by the necessity to conserve resources and maximize the positive virtues of smallness. This legacy and contrast will continue to be the rural school curriculum story until present disparities between urban and rural schools receive widespread national and state attention.

—*Robert V. Carlson*

See also
Education, Special; Education, Youth; Literacy; Music; Technology.
References
Carlson, Robert V. *A Case Study of the Impact of a State-Level Policy Designed to Improve Rural Schools in the State of Vermont.* Occasional Paper no. 36. Charleston, WV: Appalachia Educational Laboratory, February 1994.
Gjelten, Thomas. *Schooling in Isolated Communities.* Portland, ME: North Haven Project, 1978.
Keizer, Garrett. *No Place but Here: A Teacher's Vocation in a Rural Community.* New York: Viking Penguin, 1988.
Monk, David H. *Disparities in Curricular Offerings: Issues and Policy Alternatives for Small Rural Schools.* Paper prepared for the Appalachia Educational Laboratory. Ithaca, NY: Cornell University, Department of Education, February 1988.
Monk, David H., and Emil Haller. *Organizational Alternatives for Small Rural Schools.* Ithaca, NY: Cornell University, Department of Education, 1986.
Nachtigal, Paul M. *Rural Education: In Search of a Better Way.* Boulder, CO: Westview Press, 1982.
Peshkin, Alan. *Growing Up American: Schooling and the Survival of Community.* Chicago: University of Chicago Press, 1978.
Schmuck, Richard A., and Patricia A. Schmuck. *Small Districts, Big Problems: Making Schools Everybody's House.* Newbury Park, CA: Corwin Press, 1992.
Sher, Jonathan P., ed. *Education in Rural America: A Reassessment of Conventional Wisdom.* Boulder, CO: Westview Press, 1977.
Stern, Joyce D. *The Condition of Education in Rural Schools.* Washington, DC: U.S. Department of Education, Office of Educational Research and Improvement Programs for the Improvement of Practice, 1994.

Educational Facilities

The buildings, both permanent and mobile, that house the process of educating youth. This entry discusses the current conditions of rural facilities, including statistics, consolidation and cooperative options, multiple use issues, and technological advances. The entry also addresses the challenges faced by those utilizing rural educational facilities.

Current Conditions

Statistics. Rural school districts represent roughly two-thirds of all public school systems in the country.

They are responsible for educating between one-fourth and one-third of all students in the country. Rural school facilities come in many forms. The physical plant may be a one-room school, a larger building that houses students from many communities due to consolidation efforts popular in the 1970s, or a community building that can be converted into a school during the week. Most buildings are constructed of brick and concrete today, whereas in the past most were made of wood. Some rural schools are located in trailers. Of the facilities built or remodeled since 1984, 73 percent are specifically designed as one-room schools. Twenty percent of these were buildings that at one time were larger schools (*Rural Exchange* 1992).

At the turn of the century, over 200,000 one-room schools existed. These simple buildings represented the nation's commitment to education and were the center of community life. The country school continues to be a powerful cultural symbol. One-room schools, according to a National Education Association survey, have declined in number from 23,965 in 1960 to 837 in 1984 (Muse and Smith 1987). Most one-room school buildings built since 1980 are largely self-contained, newer, and structurally sound. The condition of older buildings still in use is frequently poor, and the cost of renovating them to meet modern health, safety, and Americans with Disabilities Act (ADA) regulations often is prohibitive. These older buildings often have poor insulation, wiring, and plumbing. Seventy-four percent of the existing one-room schools have been renovated or modified. According to a 1993 Nebraska school facilities study, 40 percent of administrators believed that their facilities impeded desired changes in instructional programming, and 55 percent of the buildings were not handicapped accessible. Generally, the smaller the school district, the higher the rate of inadequate buildings. Most buildings were between 40 and 90 years old and contained uncomfortable and obsolete classrooms (Pool 1993). Many of the one-room schools that were closed are preserved by historic societies and are documented in *Country School Legacy: A Collection of Histories of Schools* (Silt, CO, 1981), and in Leslie C. Swanson's *Rural One-Room Schools of Mid-America* (Moline, IL, 1976).

New schools based on the one-room model are being built. Many are private or parochial with ties to home schooling. Churches start the schools for students in the congregation and eventually expand to two or three classes. Many unique qualities of small schools have been recognized and are being revisited in this way. A 1988 survey found student satisfaction and attendance in general is better in smaller schools. This is even more true for students with low socioeconomic status and underachievers (Green and Stevens 1988).

Consolidation. Over the years, school consolidation often has been promoted as the answer to the financial problems of many small schools. School districts consolidated to economically justify a comprehensive school program. In many cases small schools were adversely affected by state funding formulas. A flat per-pupil rate resulted in rural schools being able to purchase fewer materials for student use. Research indicates that schools need between 300 and 500 students to break even when funds are distributed in this way (Planning and Research School Buildings Services 1984). The consolidation effort was a blow to many rural communities. Consolidation usually has low public support among the communities affected, and the costs of transportation outweighed most benefits. Savings were found in some areas such as personnel and energy costs. In one 1988 study, of six expenditure categories, only administration costs showed significant savings three years after consolidation (Streifel 1991).

Constraints of rural physical plants can be a challenge. The lack of libraries, gyms, and music rooms make smaller schools seem deficient. Vocational education is limited by facilities, but many students in rural areas are exposed to the work ethic early, and job training is completed in the home or community. Facilities for athletics and organized sports also may be limited. These needs often are met by using community buildings or outdoor classrooms.

Multiple Uses. In many instances, rural school buildings become the social centers of the community and serve multiple purposes. Buildings are centers for political activity, parties, Bible study, dances, films, funerals, voting, weddings, meetings, and classes for adult education. Students benefit from teachers who live in the community and the intense involvement of community members and parents. Most rural and one-room schools have citizen band radios and extra supplies in case of weather emergencies. Most teachers in rural areas are required to take emergency survival courses. These contingencies help the entire community in times of crisis.

Some rural schools coordinate community social services. Schools can provide recreation and health services for the community. Community partnerships are designed to combine resources to enrich all aspects of community education. Collaborative agreements with social service agencies are essential to providing adequate service in rural areas. Often the school is one of the largest economic enterprises in a community and becomes the only viable public service agency.

Alternative Service Delivery Models. In place of the all-or-nothing reorganization approach typically sought by state legislatures and departments of education, a range of alternative service delivery models emerged for rural schools. Schools may join in a consortium to pool finances, personnel, and building resources to address a common problem or initiative. These agreements can be formal or informal and variable in length and can solve one objective or many. Often state department of education personnel or university staff help with resources. Rural education cooperatives help to deliver needed services such as vocational training, special education, coaching, and music and art instruction by jointly hiring the staff needed. Cooperatives offer help in technology, centralized facilities, and sharing of resources. Mobile classrooms sent by cooperatives provide vans equipped with work space, assessment tools, and training activities for both teachers and students.

Three types of educational cooperatives may be used in a rural setting. First, agreements may be mandated by an external agency such as the state education association. Second, enabled arrangements can receive sponsorship by the state education association. And third, free-standing arrangements can be maintained solely by participating local education agencies. These agreements are needed especially to offer appropriate programming for special education students.

Transdisciplinary programming is used in cooperative arrangements to help alleviate rural school understaffing, particularly in remedial or special needs programming. Professionals from various disciplines may work together cooperatively and teach each other the skills and practices of their discipline so one member can carry out needed services. This role exchange or role release allows teachers, therapists, and parents to provide services that may be unavailable on a regular basis.

Technological Advances. Current technological advancements make distance education particularly useful to rural school facilities. Distance education is any form of instruction in which the learner is physically separated from the teacher. One of the most popular forms of distance education is the live, simultaneous transmission of a master teacher's lessons from a host classroom, studio, or multiple receiving site classroom in a distant location. This can include, but is not limited to, computer-assisted instruction (CAI), computer-managed instruction (CMI),

satellite television, and autographic teleteaching. These approaches to distance education provide many new types of learning in rural communities. Distance education has an increasing impact on rural schools by offering classes for which qualified staff are otherwise scarce, allowing for specialized classes with a very small student enrollment, and providing staff development. CAI and CMI enhance the mainstreaming and social opportunities for special needs students. Distance education and computer- or television-enhanced learning can be offered to the community and school through computer take-home programs or night classes at the school. Remote areas have the added challenge of inaccessible system relays for satellite or television reception. Remote areas use more videotaped programs for their teaching. Through the use of these independent study technologies, students become more self-reliant and independent in their learning.

Challenges

Transportation. Rural schools are by definition far from homes and other schools. Transportation costs become a major factor in decisions to keep one-room schools open, to consolidate, or to use collaboratives to provide services. Smaller schools may allow shorter bus rides for students than consolidated schools. Many students themselves drive to school at very young ages. Some districts with schools in remote areas pay parents isolation stipends to provide their children's transportation to school. Some parents believe they need to send their older students to larger schools in urban areas to receive a well-rounded education. The logistics of travel for athletics are also considerable. The length of travel time often makes it necessary to plan two or more events in a weekend, which claims a high percentage of a rural school's time, money, energy, and human resources. Some rural schools experimented with four-day school weeks with longer days to reduce transportation and energy costs. This resulted in lower student and teacher absenteeism but has not impacted student achievement scores.

Since it is difficult to reach many rural and remote school buildings, instruction often is delivered through learning modules or kits made by the teacher and distributed to parents, who deliver the instruction. This form of home schooling is supported by local school districts. Traveling book mobiles bring needed reference books to isolated homes and schools.

Transporting students during the day to other schools that offer different courses is another answer to reduced curriculum offerings. There is less need to maintain expensive, duplicate facilities such as cafeterias, industrial arts areas, and language and computer science laboratories. Nontraditional class periods that meet for longer hours with fewer classes during the day provide study and research time. More concentrated time with teachers in block scheduling works well for many students. Some schools use the school facility on Saturdays for classes.

Maintenance. Maintenance of rural schools is another challenge. Teachers are often responsible for their own building maintenance. This is sometimes supplemented with help from parents in the community. Other parent volunteer roles include teacher assistant, playground supervisor, hot lunch cook or server, or community-based education teacher.

Future of Rural Facilities

The future of rural school facilities seems to be a bright one. Much of the current research points to positive student outcomes in smaller schools. Restructuring led many school districts to recreate a country school atmosphere or to create schools within a school to enhance student growth. Many districts use the school facility as a community center or add health clinics and after-hours recreation programs. If the old African proverb "It takes a whole village to raise a child" is true, then a creative use of rural school facilities to help rural children may become a model for urban schools to emulate.

—*Jack T. Cole and Janaan Diemer*

See also

Computers; Education, Youth; Government; Sport; Technology; Telecommunications.

References

Green, Gary, and Wanda Stevens. "What Research Says about Small Schools." *Rural Educator* 10, no. 1 (1988): 9–14.

Muse, Ivan, and Ralph B. Smith, with Bruce Barker. *The One-Teacher School in the 1980s.* Fort Collins, CO: ERIC Clearinghouse on Rural Education and Small Schools, 1987.

Planning and Research School Buildings Services. *Small School/Large School Comparative Analysis.* Alberta, Canada: Planning and Research School Buildings Services, 1984.

Pool, Dennis L. "Nebraska School Facilities: Educational Adequacy of Structures and Their Funding." Paper presented at the Annual Rural and Small School Conference, Manhattan, KS, October 1993.

Rural Exchange (quarterly journal). Missoula, MT: University of Montana Press (Spring-Summer 1992).

Streifel, James, et al. "The Financial Effects of Consolidation." *Journal of Research in Rural Education* 7, no. 2 (1991): 13–20.

Elders

Adults age 65 or older. A brief profile of adults age 65 or older who live in rural America is provided and the state of knowledge about important aspects of growing old in a rural environment is summarized in this entry. The specific focus of the entry is on the social and economic characteristics of rural elders, their health status, family relations, and patterns of formal service utilization. The entry concludes with a brief comment on the primary conceptual frameworks used in rural gerontology.

One of the most dramatic demographic shifts occurring in the United States is the "graying of America." About one in four elders in the United States live in a sparsely populated or geographically remote rural area. In 1990, 26.3 percent of the overall elderly population, or 8.2 million elders, lived in rural community contexts (Coward et al. 1994).

Distribution

Rural elders live in a wide variety of topographical, environmental, social, and economic settings and comprise both long-term local residents and recent migrants. Although the term "rural" was once thought to be interchangeable with "farm," today the vast majority of older rural Americans do not live on farms or in farmlike settings (Krout 1986). In general, the nonmetropolitan population in the United States tends to be older than its metropolitan counterpart. Compared to metropolitan counties, a higher proportion of the nonmetropolitan population is age 65 or over (11.9 percent and 14.7 percent, respectively). In addition, elders living in nonmetropolitan areas tend to be concentrated in the oldest-old categories (that is, those aged 75 to 84 years and 85 and over) compared to their counterparts who live in metropolitan areas (Coward et al. 1994).

The age structure and racial/ethnic composition of the nonmetropolitan population varies considerably by geographic region. For example, 17.1 percent of the nonmetropolitan population in the west-north-central region of the United States is age 65 or older, whereas in the western mountain states, only 12.4 percent of the nonmetropolitan population is elderly. This regional variation is magnified when comparisons are made between states. For example, over one-fifth of the nonmetropolitan population of Florida (22.2 percent) is composed of persons aged 65 or older. In contrast, fewer than 1 in 20 (4.3 percent) nonmetropolitan residents of Alaska are aged 65 or older.

Because minority elders tend to be disproportionately located in urban areas, the population of rural elders at the national level tends to be less racially and ethnically diverse. Approximately 92 percent of the nonmetropolitan elderly population is White. Nonwhite rural elders, however, tend to be clustered in specific regions of the country. Consequently, the concentration of older rural African Americans in southeastern states, older rural Hispanics in southwestern states, and older rural Native Americans in western states makes issues of rural diversity more salient in these particular areas.

Personal Characteristics

The social and economic characteristics of older adults living in rural America tend to set them apart from their counterparts who reside in more urban and suburban settings, with rural elders generally being distinguished by greater vulnerability (Coward and Dwyer 1991). For example, elders from small towns and rural communities are more likely to live in poverty or on the verge of poverty (under 150 percent of the poverty level), compared to their counterparts who reside in more urban and suburban settings. Educational attainment also differs markedly by place of residence. Less than half of nonmetropolitan elders are high school graduates (46.7 percent), compared with 56.2 percent of metropolitan elders. Nonmetropolitan elders are also less likely to have attended college.

The relative economic disadvantage of elders in small communities is reflected in other aspects of their lives. Although the rate of home ownership is higher among elders in rural areas and small towns, the housing they occupy is disproportionately substandard and dilapidated (Bull and Bane 1992). Rural elders are less likely than their urban counterparts to have worked in a job that provides a pension plan. Consequently, the careers of men working in rural areas are less likely to end with retirement.

Health

There is substantial evidence in the gerontological literature that suggests elders living in rural America are in poorer health than their more urban and suburban counterparts (Coward and Dwyer 1991; Coward and Lee 1985). Such differences are not universal across all dimensions of health or among all subgroups of older rural adults. For example, nonfarm rural elders report the largest number of medical conditions and the most difficulty performing activities of daily living (such as bathing, dressing, getting to or using the toilet, shopping for groceries, preparing meals, and doing housework) com-pared to elders from other residential categories (worse even than inner-city elders). However, older farmers are among the most healthy segments of older persons in our society. This within-group variation should not detract from an appreciation of the overall poorer health of rural elders as a group. The better health of older farmers simply cannot counterbalance the prevailing poorer health of the much larger group of nonfarm elders.

Only a small number of studies attempted to determine whether these residential differences in health persist when the effects of other factors known to influence health are taken into account (such as income, race, gender, and age). The results have been mixed; in some comparisons, the introduction of other variables accounts for the residential differences that are observed, whereas in other cases they have not. Thus, for some differences in health, it is not residence in a particular setting per se that causes poor health. Rather, compositional differences in the populations that live in different settings account for the observed differences in health.

Nevertheless, place of residence is relevant to health care planners and advocates. Residence remains an important dimension of public policy planning for the aged because, ultimately, the location of health and human services must be thought of in geographic terms; services must be located in a particular place. At this most fundamental level, the distribution of need by geographic location is a critical consideration in health services planning despite the compositional differences that may be responsible for variation in health according to place of residence.

Family Relations

The family relations of elders who reside in small towns and rural communities are substantively different from their counterparts who live in more urban and suburban environments (Bull 1993). Rural elders are more apt to have a marital partner and, on average, to have more children. These are critical advantages because spouses and adult children are the primary family members with whom elders live and the principal source of aid and assistance for elders. On closer examination, the rural marital advantage is very pronounced only among younger-old women (those aged 65–69) and is much less prominent among men of all ages.

Although rural elders seem to be advantaged by having a larger number of adult children, this does not appear to translate into a greater propensity to reside with a child (Coward et al. 1993). In terms of the proximity of children to elderly parents, there is evidence of significant variability within the rural population. Elderly farm residents often have at least one very proximate child, most often a son, who participates in the farming operation and may eventually inherit it. Rural nonfarm elders, in contrast, are the least likely of any residential group to have proximate children, perhaps because younger people must often move to more urban areas in pursuit of educational and occupational opportunities. Given this pattern of geographic proximity, it is not surprising that farm and large-city elders report comparatively high rates of interaction with their children, whereas lower rates are observed among rural nonfarm and small-town elders.

Nevertheless, rural frail and disabled elders who require others' help to perform daily activities of living are more likely to be dependent exclusively on family members for such assistance, compared to older adults living in more urban and suburban settings. Although the greater reliance of rural elders on family members for support appears quite clear, the explanation for the behavior is not. Three possible explanations often are discussed. First, rural elders may be more reluctant than their urban counterparts to accept help from persons outside their kin network. Second, rural elders may be immersed in family networks characterized by more close-knit relationships and more durable feelings of filial responsibility and obligation. Third, rural elders may rely more on family care simply because they have access to a smaller number and narrower range of formal services. Although there are varying degrees of evidence for all three of these explanations, no one interpretation receives unreserved support.

Formal Service Utilization Patterns

There is substantial evidence that older residents of small towns and rural communities in general have access to a smaller number and narrower range of formal health and human services (Krout 1994; Rowles, Beaulieu, and Myers 1996). As a consequence, rural elders are less apt to receive formal services at any one point in time and are less apt to add a formal service provider to their caregiving network over time. These generalizations cannot be applied in every category, however. Research demonstrated, for example, that rural elders are more likely to attend a senior center than their urban and suburban counterparts. Similarly, recent research reported the greater availability and use of nursing home beds per capita among nonmetropolitan elders, especially those in small, thinly populated nonmetropolitan counties, com-

pared to older adults living in small, medium-sized, or large standard metropolitan statistical areas. The greatest deficiencies in rural social service systems for the elderly appear to be in the area of medical and community-based services for the frail and disabled, such as rehabilitative home health care services, hospices, adult day services, and respite care.

Two Conceptual Perspectives on Rural Gerontology

Many rural gerontologists envision residence in a sparsely populated, geographically remote area as a factor that can exacerbate other difficulties with which older people cope. Some scholars describe the double jeopardy of growing old and living in a rural setting. Others describe the triple jeopardy of growing old, living in a rural setting, and coping with a third condition or circumstance that places older people at risk of poor health or a lower quality of life (for example, poverty, the cumulative effects of a lifetime of discrimination, or a debilitating chronic illness). From this perspective, there is much that is not known about specific subgroups of rural elders (such as older rural Blacks, Latinos, and Native Americans; persons over the age of 85 who live in rural settings; older rural women; or rural elders living in poverty). Further research is needed on these important subgroups of rural elders.

Rural gerontology makes use of the concept of the person-environment fit. According to this conceptual framework, the degree to which an older person becomes disabled is a product of the interaction of their physical and mental functional capacities and the demands of the environment in which they live. Gerontologists traditionally emphasized strategies to alter or adapt the immediate environment of older adults (such as adding assistive devices such as hand rails, ramps, and specially designed doorknobs to homes). Rural gerontologists examine the degree to which the macro environment enhances or impedes the quality of life and effective functioning of older adults. Additional research is needed to identify the specific dimensions of life in rural America that most influence the lives of older adults.

—*Raymond T. Coward and Chuck W. Peek*

See also
Education, Adult; Health Care; Mental Health of Older Adults; Nursing Homes; Policy, Health Care; Policy, Socioeconomic; Public Services; Quality of Life; Rural Demography; Senior Centers.

References
Bull, C. Neil, ed. *Aging in Rural America*. Newbury Park, CA: Sage Publications, 1993.

Bull, C. Neil, and Share D. Bane, eds. *The Future of Aging in Rural America*. Kansas City: National Resource Center for Rural Elderly, University of Missouri at Kansas City, 1992.

Coward, Raymond T., and Jeffrey W. Dwyer. *Health Programs and Services for Elders in Rural America: A Review of the Life Circumstances and Formal Services That Affect the Health and Well-Being of Elders*. Kansas City: National Resource Center for Rural Elderly, University of Missouri at Kansas City, 1991.

Coward, Raymond T., and Gary R Lee, eds. *The Elderly in Rural Society: Every Fourth Elder*. New York: Springer Publishing Company, 1985.

Coward, Raymond T., C. Neil Bull, Gary Kukulka, and James M. Galliher, eds. *Health Services for Rural Elders*. New York: Springer Publishing Company, 1994.

Coward, Raymond T., Gary R. Lee, Jeffrey W. Dwyer, and Karen Seccombe. *Old and Alone in Rural America*. Washington, DC: American Association of Retired Persons, 1993.

Krout, John A. *The Aged in Rural America*. New York: Greenwood Press, 1986.

———, ed. *Providing Community Based Services to the Rural Elderly*. Newbury Park, CA: Sage Publications, 1994.

Rowles, Graham D., Joyce E. Beaulieu, and Wayne W. Myers, eds. *Long-Term Care for the Rural Elderly*. New York: Springer Publishing Company, 1996.

Electrification

The process of extending central station electric service through a network of transmission and distribution lines to make electricity readily available for use where needed. This entry describes the difficult task of electrifying the vast rural areas of the United States. It was accomplished by a unique partnership between the U.S. government and member-owned electric cooperatives, coupled with creative design and cost-cutting innovations. Today the combined cooperative utility system, with over 2 million miles of line serving 13 million connections (about 30 million people) in the most sparsely populated areas of the country, can be viewed as the nation's largest electric utility network. Cooperative rural electrification makes significant contributions to rural economic development, energy research, and international rural electrification.

Rural America's Dark Days

Continuous, dependable electric service is taken for granted today in the United States, even in the most remote areas. Yet, as recently as 60 years ago, tens of millions of rural people and 90 percent of the farm families lived without electric power. For rural people, these were the difficult years of the Great Depression. Many farm families, unable to scratch out a living, abandoned their farms to seek jobs elsewhere.

Those who remained yearned for the luxury of electricity so that they could discard the kerosene lamp, wood-stove, washboard, and outdoor privies. They needed electricity to have hot and cold running water and refrigerators like people living in the cities and to power milking machines, welders, grinders, and dozens of other productivity-improving farm machines.

The Rural Electrification Administration

Such were the conditions when Pres. Franklin D. Roosevelt signed Executive Order 7037 to create the Rural Electrification Administration (REA) under the authority of the Emergency Relief Appropriations Act of 1935. A year later, REA was made a permanent agency when Congress passed the Rural Electrification Act of 1936. It set in motion a partnership between the federal government and rural people that changed the face of rural America and greatly improve the living conditions and productive capability of farms and rural businesses.

The legislation authorized loan funds to implement the program. Existing electric utilities were challenged to carry out the task but showed little interest for anything except wiring the more densely populated areas. The REA, however, was committed to the area coverage principle, the goal of providing affordable, reliable, central station electric power to all farms and rural people, regardless of location. Morris Llewellyn Cooke, a progressive engineer who studied power distribution costs, was appointed to head the new agency and find innovative ways to make the program work.

Thus, from its very beginning, the electrification program was the product of creativity, innovation, experimentation, and a firm belief that great things happen when dedicated people work together for a common goal. REA administrator Cooke believed that electric utilities could be established and operated on much the same basis as the successful nonprofit, farmer-owned cooperatives. Rural people could be trained, with REA staff help, to oversee the management, construction, and operation of their member-owned rural electric cooperatives.

There were few patterns to follow. Those few farms that had electric service were usually close to existing utility lines running between cities and towns. There were some examples of small groups of farmers who formed cooperatives to buy electricity from utilities, and there were a few utility test lines that provided important information on feasibility and economics of farmstead electrification for future electric use projections.

One such test line was located at Red Wing, Minnesota. It consisted of about 6 miles of line to connect 20 farmsteads in a prosperous dairy community. A similar

Rural electric co-op workers repairing transmission lines.

Another segment of the REA staff was charged with developing ways to train electric cooperative managers, technical and administrative staff, and directors. A field organization was established to advise the fledgling electric cooperatives on everything from organization and engineering to rate structures and financial matters. The goal was for each electric cooperative quickly to become self-sustaining.

The program worked well, and the idea of using nonprofit cooperatives as the business entity to extend electric service was a success. That success, coupled with the pledge of area coverage, stimulated increased activity in the more remote, unelectrified areas. Men and women, potential future members, canvassed their neighborhoods and urged others to sign up and pay the five-dollar membership fee, to get electricity during the next phase of construction, or to organize a new electric co-op. Appliances often were purchased long before the lights came on. It was estimated that co-op members spent four dollars on appliances, electrical equipment, and wiring for each dollar spent on line construction.

Construction was slowed to a virtual halt when U.S. involvement in World War II demanded sacrifices. Electrification was recognized for its labor-saving role and for increased food and fiber production desperately needed for the war effort. "A one horsepower electric motor can do the work of eight men," read a poster that urged farmers to make effective use of electric power.

study was carried out in 1924 at the 8.4-mile Renner test line serving 17 farms (mostly dairy) near Sioux Falls, South Dakota. Both studies revealed that, given the opportunity, farmers would use increasing amounts of electricity profitably to increase production.

Cost-Cutting Innovations

Line construction and operation costs had to be kept to a minimum to make electricity affordable when a mile of line might serve only one or two consumers, compared to 20 or 30 for city electric systems. The REA engineering staff redesigned and standardized single-phase lines for rural utilities. Huge cost savings resulted from innovations and the redesign of virtually every aspect of electric utility operation. This included eliminating crossarms, increasing primary distribution voltages, extending distance between poles, implementing production line construction techniques, and having consumers read their own meters.

Postwar Electrification

Cooperatives' success in electrifying rural areas during the prewar years set the stage for expanded, dynamic postwar electrification efforts driven by the demand from farmers and returning veterans. At war's end, 43 percent of the farms in the United States remained unelectrified. The area coverage principle was more important than ever. Loan funds were made available through the REA to finance construction. There were major problems involving shortages of materials and trained staff. But by 1948, more than 40,000 consumers per month were connected to consumer-owned rural electric lines. By June 1949, more than 78 percent of U.S. farms received central station electric power; the remaining 22 percent were more difficult and costly and took considerably longer to electrify.

Rural Electrification Today

As a group, the electric cooperatives can be viewed as the nation's largest electric utility network. Nearly 900 rural electric distribution systems with a total of nearly 50,000 full-time employees provide power to nearly 13 million meters (farms, residences and businesses—about 30 million people) in 46 states. These electric cooperatives own and operate approximately 50 percent of the distribution line in the nation (over 2 million miles of line) but serve only about 10 percent of the nation's population. Rural electric lines extend into more than 2,600 of the nation's 3,128 counties, over difficult terrain including swamps, mountains, and deserts.

Nearly 90 percent of the cooperative connections are classified as residential (farm and nonfarm). In contrast, other segments of the utility industry enjoy a mix, about one-third each of industrial, commercial, and residential loads, which gives them more revenue and better load diversity, resulting in lower demand relative to revenue. Rural electric systems have an average density of only six consumers per mile of line compared to the average of 35 customers per mile of line for investor-owned utilities and about 48 people per mile of line for city-owned systems. Annual revenue from electricity sales for co-ops is about $7,000 per mile of line, compared to $59,000 per mile for investor-owned utilities and $72,000 for municipal utilities.

Because the nonprofit rural utilities are locally owned and controlled by the people they serve, they are uniquely qualified, and they are often called on to provide leadership and technical assistance in business development and other community services such as rural housing, rural water and sewer systems, telecommunications and home security systems, and economic development activities.

In spite of obstacles, by working together rural electric cooperatives have matured and evolved into a cohesive, important, and influential segment of the U.S. electric utility industry. Their success as a group has been enhanced by pooling their resources and efforts through service cooperatives such as generation and transmission cooperatives, statewide associations, purchasing and marketing organizations, financing cooperatives, and their national association.

Generation and Transmission Cooperatives

Building distribution systems was difficult, but securing the wholesale power to meet new demands for electricity was an even greater challenge. Initially, rural electric systems purchased wholesale power from many sources—investor-owned and municipal utilities and federal power sources such as the Tennessee Valley Authority and Bonneville Power Administration.

Ultimately, rural electric systems needed to develop their own power sources. They did this by forming generation and transmission (G&T) cooperatives to provide power to member utilities on a state or regional basis. Currently, rural electric systems generate 41 percent of their power needs through their G&Ts. The balance is purchased from investor-owned electric utilities (about 25 percent) and from federal power agencies and other public power sources (about 34 percent).

The 58 G&T cooperatives serve 750 member rural electric systems in 43 states. They generate about 5.6 percent of the nation's electricity. In 1994, G&Ts owned all or part of 142 operating plants. Of these, 79 were steam, 14 nuclear, 39 internal combustion, and 10 hydropower. Of the owned plant capacity, nearly 80 percent is coal-fired. As a group, these coal-fired generating plants are the cleanest in the industry, with 44 percent using modern flue gas scrubbers, compared to 20 percent for the industry nationwide.

From their early days, G&T cooperatives were active in technological development and were first, or among the first in many pioneering efforts, as suggested by the following examples. First, the United Power Association in Minnesota, in partnership with the U.S. government, constructed, successfully operated, and safely dismantled a small (23.8 megawatt) demonstration nuclear power plant. Additionally, the association demonstrated and tested a 200-kilowatt phosphoric acid fuel cell power plant for possible use with landfill gas. Second, the Alabama Electric Cooperative built and operates the nation's first compressed-air energy storage power plant to provide 110 megawatts of intermediate and peaking capacity. Third, the Basin Electric Power Co-op in North Dakota built and operates a plant that produces natural gas from lignite coal and uses the fines (finely crushed or powdered coal) from that coal to generate electric power. Fourth, Buckeye Power in Ohio was a leader in curtailing power costs by reducing demand with use of electronic controls to cycle the operation of residential water heaters and air conditioners. And fifth, Colorado-Ute Electric repowered and upgraded an obsolete 36 megawatt coal-fired plant to a highly efficient 110 megawatt circulating fluidized bed combustion power plant for a significant advance in clean coal technology.

Statewide and Service Organizations

Rural electric leaders throughout the country recognized the need for coordinated support, legislative efforts, and additional services that the individual electric systems could not do as well by themselves. They organized statewide associations to carry out these functions. Currently, there are 36 statewide organizations; 32 of these publish magazines that reach an estimated six million readers each month. There are 37 service organizations that member rural electric systems use to pool orders for purchasing electric materials and services.

The National Rural Electric Cooperative Association

The National Rural Electric Cooperative Association (NRECA), the national service organization for rural electric systems, grew since its formation in 1942 to an organization of more than 500 employees providing national representation, programs, and materials for its more than 1,000 member systems. NRECA was initially organized to assist member systems with national problems, including securing employee insurance at reasonable costs; protecting them against threatening wholesale power and legislative issues; and breaking the bottleneck for much needed line construction material.

NRECA now provides national leadership and member assistance in legislation, legal and regulatory issues, communications, energy policy, education, research, technology, conferences, insurance, and financial services. Its programs are financed by dues and fees for services. The NRECA headquarters is located in metropolitan Washington, D.C., at 4301 Wilson Boulevard, Arlington, Virginia 22203-1860. Two major publications of NRECA are *Rural Electrification Magazine,* published monthly, and *Electric Co-op Today,* a weekly news publication that reports on rural electric cooperatives.

Rural Electric Research

The creativity, innovation, and experimentation of the early days of rural electrification continues through NRECA's Rural Electric Research (RER) program. Funded by voluntary contributions from NRECA member systems, RER conducts comprehensive research and development projects to address the unique needs of rural electric systems. By pooling their research dollars, cooperatives conduct significant research far beyond the financial means of individual systems. As members of the utility industry's Electric Power Research Institute, they often leverage available funds as much as tenfold. RER's current annual budget for research is about $4.5 million.

Several hundred research projects have been funded, ranging from major 110-megawatt, compressed-air, energy storage, and fuel cell power plants to prepay

electric meters and new concepts in the delivery of electricity. New electricity application projects include agricultural electrical equipment, energy conservation and efficiency publications, and design and market development of closed loop/ground source (geothermal) heat pump systems and electric thermal storage heating equipment.

International Programs

On 1 November 1962, NRECA signed its first contract with the U.S. Agency for International Development (USAID). The purpose was to export the United States' model of rural electrification to developing countries. Since then, 250 electric cooperatives have been formed in 14 developing countries. Today those overseas cooperatives bring electricity to more than 34 million people.

NRECA currently provides technical and management assistance in 15 countries, creates cooperatives and other decentralized utilities, carries out extensive training programs, and introduces renewable energy programs (solar, wind, biomass, and hydropower). Its International Programs Division is totally self-supporting, with funding from service contracts with organizations such as USAID, World Bank, and overseas governments and cooperatives. In addition, the charitable arm of the organization, the NRECA International Foundation, is actively engaged in shipping donated electrical equipment and carrying out volunteer-assisted projects to electrify rural and remote areas of many countries. A sister cooperative program pairs utilities from the United States and overseas in a voluntary exchange of ideas, equipment, and training. The foundation funding comes from individual and corporate voluntary contributions.

The Rural Utility Service

Electric co-ops no longer need, and the REA no longer offers, many of the services provided during the program's formative years, but they still need the REA's stable source of loan funds. The Rural Utility Service (RUS) is a new agency created in the 1994 restructuring of the U.S. Department of Agriculture (USDA); the REA became the RUS. Its responsibilities were expanded to include rural water, sewer, electric, and telephone programs.

The RUS is now one of three agencies, along with rural housing and community development and rural business and co-op development, that make up the new Rural Economic and Community Development Administration. Co-ops are eligible for RUS loans to establish water and wastewater services for low-income areas to help resolve health and sanitation deficiencies. Wally Beyer, former manager of Verendrye Electric Co-op in Velva, North Dakota, was appointed the first RUS administrator.

National Rural Utilities Cooperative Finance Corporation (CFC)

Because of the need for additional funding to supplement the REA loan program, rural electric cooperatives developed and organized the National Rural Utilities Cooperative Finance Corporation (CFC) in 1969. CFC was organized as a cooperative, provides a source of private market financing, and offers a full range of financial services and programs to its more than 1,000 member systems and affiliates. The services include loan and loan guarantee programs and related short-term investment and equity and cash management services. CFC's strong membership support and diverse loan portfolio result in favorable ratings in the capital markets.

Related Nonprofit Service Organizations

Several additional nonprofit service organizations have an important role in the electrification and development of rural America. For example, the Banks for Cooperatives provide some loans to electric cooperatives. The National Rural Telecommunications Cooperative was formed to foster development and growth of satellite technology in rural America. The National Telephone Cooperative Association supports rural telephone cooperatives. The Western Fuels Association provides coal for consumer-owned utility power plants. The National Food and Energy Council specializes in agricultural electrical technologies and issues in support of member electric utilities. The Electric Power Research Institute pools research funding from all segments of the utility industry to carry out research of interest to its members. All of these organizations contribute to the success of the electric cooperative network (see Brown, Dahl, and Sparkman 1990).

—Lowell J. Endahl

See also
Cooperatives; Development, Community and Economic; History, Rural; Infrastructure; Public Services; Quality of Life; Technology.

Recommended Reading
Brown, J.C., Patrick Dahl, and Jennifer Sparkman, eds. *Rural Electric SOURCEBOOK*. Arlington, VA: National Rural Electric Cooperative Association, 1990.

Childs, Marquis W. *Yesterday Today and Tomorrow, the Farmer Takes a Hand*. Arlington, VA: National Rural Electric Cooperative Association, 1980.

Ellis, Clyde T. *A Giant Step*. New York: Random House, 1966.

Holum, Ken. *A Farmer Takes a Stand: Ken Holum's Story of Life on the Farm and Consumer Power*. Sioux Falls, SD: Center for Western Studies, Augustana College; and Hills, MN: Crescent Publishing, 1987.

McFate, K. L. *Energy in World Agriculture*. Vol. 3: *Electrical Energy in Agriculture*. New York: Elsevier Science Publishing, 1989.

National Rural Electric Cooperative Association (NRECA). *America's Rural Electric Story*. Arlington, VA: NRECA, 1985.

———. *International Programs*. Arlington, VA: NRECA, International Programs Division, 1994.

———. *Rural Electric Research: Year in Review*. Arlington, VA: NRECA, 1995.

Pence, Richard A., and Patrick Dahl, eds. *The Next Greatest Thing: 50th Anniversary Pictorial Review of Rural Electrification*. Arlington, VA: NRECA, 1984.

Rural Electrification Administration. *Rural Lines-USA: The Story of the Rural Electrification Administration's First Twenty-Five Years: 1935–1960*. Washington, DC: U.S. Department of Agriculture, REA, 1960.

Elevators
See Grain Elevators

Employment

The extent to which participants in the labor force have jobs. Rates of rural employment and underemployment differ from urban rates in the United States, and they vary by gender and race or ethnic group. The industries more prevalent in rural areas influence the structure of employment, the wages paid, and the perquisites received by rural workers. The recent trend toward deindustrialization of the U.S. economy and the declining ability of resource-based industries to provide rural employment probably will have important implications for the future.

Rates of employment, unemployment, and underemployment provide indicators of economic well-being, or conversely, economic distress. Generally, since the 1982 recession, rates of unemployment in nonmetropolitan America have been higher than those observed in metropolitan areas of the United States. Underemployment rates have also been higher in nonmetropolitan than in metropolitan areas. At the same time, it should be recognized that there are census rural/urban differences (as opposed to nonmetropolitan/metropolitan differences) and variations in employment, unemployment, and underemployment rates by both race and gender. Factors modifying either the demand or supply of labor affect the extent to which the labor force is employed, who is employed, who remains unemployed, and the quality of employment in terms of wages paid, perquisites offered, and hours of work.

The 1990 census documents that of the 42.7 million persons 16 years or older living in nonmetropolitan areas of the United States, 23.7 million are employed. The nonmetropolitan unemployment rate reported in the 1990 census was 6.9 percent. The nonmetropolitan labor force participation rate was 60.4 percent, based on total labor force estimates. In comparison, the rate of labor force participation in metropolitan areas was higher (66.7 percent) and the unemployment rate was lower (6.2 percent). However, the 1990 census also included rural/urban statistics. Labor force participation rates were lower in rural than urban areas, but the unemployment rate reported in the 1990 census for rural areas was 6.0 percent, lower than the 6.4 percent rate for U.S. urban areas (U.S. Bureau of the Census 1993).

The fact that differences exist depending on how places are classified is not surprising. What is important to note is that areas that are thought of as rural often have higher rates of unemployment and lower rates of labor force participation, especially compared to urban economies.

Variations by Race and Gender

Almost 70 percent of adult males and just over half (51.8 percent) of adult females in the nonmetropolitan United States reported participating in the labor force in the 1990 census. These rates are lower than in metropolitan areas, even when compared to the central cities (see Table 1). In metropolitan areas, unemployment rates are generally higher for adult males than for adult females. However, the unemployment rate for females in nonmetropolitan areas was slightly higher than for males (7.0 percent compared to 6.7 percent; see Table 1). Women in nonmetropolitan areas are also more likely to be economically underemployed than men, particularly in terms of earning poverty-level wages and being employed only on a part-time basis when full-time work is preferred.

Differences in labor force participation and unemployment rates by race or ethnic group are pronounced (see Table 1). Regardless of race or ethnic group, labor force participation rates are lower in nonmetropolitan than metropolitan areas, even in comparison to rates for the central cities. The lowest nonmetropolitan labor force participation rates are for Blacks (55.4 percent) and for American Indians, Eskimos, and Aleuts (56.4 percent). These groups are also most likely to be economically disadvantaged. The 1990 census shows that almost one in five (18.5 percent) nonmetropolitan labor force participants in the combined American Indian, Eskimo, and

Table 1
Labor Force Characteristics by Race, Ethnicity, and Gender

	Employment (number)	% in Labor Force	% Unemployed
Nonmetropolitan			
Male	13,094,213	69.6	6.7
Female	10,617,608	51.8	7.0
White	21,330,999	60.8	6.1
Black	1,592,453	55.4	13.6
American Indian, Eskimo, or Aleut	291,099	56.4	18.5
Asian or Pacific Islander	189,625	63.0	5.6
Hispanic origin	731,995	61.5	12.0
Metropolitan, in Central City			
Male	23,714,816	73.3	7.9
Female	11,873,734	57.0	7.5
White	25,323,753	65.2	5.7
Black	6,404,374	61.9	14.4
American Indian, Eskimo, or Aleut	192,720	65.9	13.2
Asian or Pacific Islander	1,556,088	65.3	6.1
Hispanic origin	4,559,694	66.5	11.3
Metropolitan, not in Central City			
Male	30,808,997	77.5	6.7
Female	25,561,834	59.1	5.0
White	49,582,809	67.8	4.5
Black	3,410,976	69.0	9.5
American Indian, Eskimo, or Aleut	245,134	67.6	9.9
Asian or Pacific Islander	1,665,873	70.3	4.6
Hispanic origin	3,689,827	70.2	8.9

Source: U.S. Bureau of the Census, *1990 Census of Population* (1990 CP-2-1), Tables 69–73.

Aleut population reported being unemployed. This compares to 13.6 percent unemployment in the Black population and 12.0 percent unemployment in the Hispanic population. As is shown in Table 1, nonmetropolitan unemployment rates in these populations are comparable to the high rates found in U.S. central cities. Underemployment is also more prevalent in these populations.

Sources of Employment

Rural areas have been negatively affected by the deindustrialization of the U.S. economy. Prior to the 1980s, rural areas were heavily dependent on growth in manufacturing to provide new jobs. However, since the 1980s, rural areas have lost significant numbers of manufacturing jobs that were not replaced by service sector jobs paying a wage comparable to the lost manufacturing jobs. Instead, in nonmetropolitan areas there has been growth

Table 2
Distribution of Employment, by Industry and Occupation

	Nonmetropolitan (%)	Metropolitan (%)
Industrial sector		
Agriculture	6.06	1.63
Forestry, fisheries	0.38	0.09
Mining	1.52	0.39
Construction	6.83	6.07
Manufacturing	20.92	16.82
Nondurables	9.20	6.37
Durables	11.72	10.45
Transportation, communications,		
other public utilities	6.19	7.32
Wholesale trade	3.25	4.67
Retail trade	16.78	16.84
Finance, insurance, real estate	4.66	7.62
Services	28.95	33.68
Public administration	4.46	4.86
Occupation category		
Managerial, professional, specialty	19.79	28.10
Technical, sales, administrative	25.83	33.26
Service	14.23	12.96
Farming, forestry, fishing	6.00	1.54
Precision production, craft, repair	13.44	10.78
Operators, fabricators, laborers	20.70	13.36

Source: U.S. Bureau of the Census, *1990 Census of Population* (1990 CP-2-1), Tables 34 and 35.

in lower-wage service industry jobs. The growth in high-wage service sector employment in the United States has been much more prevalent in metropolitan areas.

Differences in industry mix and occupational structure between nonmetropolitan and metropolitan areas are evident in Table 2. Nonmetropolitan areas are more dependent on employment in the resource-based industries (agriculture, forestry and fisheries, and mining). These jobs are often seasonal. Nonmetropolitan areas are also more dependent on manufacturing and less dependent on services, particularly finance, insurance, and real estate services and professional services. The latter industries pay higher average wages. The workforce in metropolitan areas is more likely to be employed in managerial, professional, and specialty occupations; in nonmetropolitan areas, other lower-wage, lower-skill occupations are more prevalent. Rural workers are also more likely to be concentrated in fewer occupations than urban workers, who face a more diverse occupational structure.

Workers employed in nonmetropolitan manufacturing and service industries are more likely to be underemployed than workers in corresponding industrial sectors in metropolitan areas. The higher rates of underemployment reflect the problem of unemployment as well as underemployment due to low wages or few hours of work. Nonmetropolitan workers in manufacturing are more likely to become unemployed than metropolitan employees. Nonmetropolitan workers in services are more likely to be underemployed than metropolitan service workers due to the conditions of work—either low-wage work or involuntary part-time employment.

Self-Employment and the Informal Economy

In addition to being employed in wage and salary jobs, rural residents are very often self-employed or working in the informal economy. Self-employment is particularly common in the traditional resource-related industries. The development of self-employment opportunities for rural areas has been suggested as a focus for rural development efforts. This focus is based on the view that many new rural employment opportunities have been generated by small enterprises, or microenterprises.

Many rural households also appear to participate in the informal economy. Jensen, Cornwell, and Findeis (1995) recently found that impoverished households in rural areas engage in a wide variety of informal work activities, including babysitting, raking leaves and rototilling, and selling agricultural produce locally. Informal work was found to contribute only a small amount of income to the family, but this income was perceived as being very important during periods of economic stress. Even among households not in poverty, such activities are relatively common in rural areas.

Informal economic activity is more common where formal employment opportunities are less available. The types of employment found in rural areas and better access to natural resources also may help to increase participation in the informal economy. Literature on the determinants of informal economic activity suggest that employment that is part-time, flexible, or related to the use of natural resources is more likely to foster development of informal economic activity.

Influential Factors

Given the spatial dispersion of rural areas and the problems that rural industries face in gaining access to output markets and, in some cases, access to inputs, rural employers tend to be disadvantaged in providing products at competitive prices. Some argue that access to a low-wage rural labor force is one reason industries locate in rural areas. The problem that this creates is a reliance on maintaining an underemployed rural workforce. Average wages are lower in rural areas, and the gap between rural and urban income earnings per worker widened in the past decade.

Industries in the United States have reduced their workforces to become more competitive with foreign producers. Rural America was negatively affected by the loss of many employers that provided local employment opportunities during the 1980s. In some cases, firms moved to lower-cost regions of the country where taxes were lower or tax incentives existed, labor unions were less prevalent, or local or state regulations were less onerous. In other cases, firms closed permanently because U.S. manufacturing was unable to compete effectively against foreign competitors, or companies moved outside the United States altogether. The low-cost labor that attracted industries to rural areas was perceived as being high-cost relative to the surplus labor that could be hired in other countries.

Rural areas in the United States lagged behind economically because the expanding service sector, which has served to soften the transition from a manufacturing to a service-based economy in urban areas, has not helped rural areas to as great an extent, at least since the 1980s. Rates of increase in service industry employment have been slower and new service jobs pay, on average, lower wages in rural than in urban areas.

Finally, concern continues over the ability of the resource-based industries to provide the same level of employment as in the past. For example, agricultural employment declined significantly during this century, both in terms of self-employment by farm families and hired farm workers. Although labor productivity in farming increased significantly over time, unemployment in rural communities will increase unless new jobs are created. The challenge for rural America is to create this new employment.

—Jill Findeis and Wan-Ling Hsu

See also
Careers in Agriculture; Development, Community and Economic; Division of Household Labor; Entrepreneurship; Home-Based Work; Labor Unions; Migrant Farm Workers; Underemployment; Work.

References
Bloomquist, Leonard E. "Local Labor Market Characteristics and the Occupational Concentrations of Different Sociodemographic Groups." *Rural Sociology* 55, no. 2 (1990): 199–213.
Findeis, Jill L. "Utilization of Rural Labor Resources." Pp. 49–68 in *Economic Adaptation: Alternatives for Nonmetropolitan Areas.* Edited by David Barkley. Boulder, CO: Westview Press, 1993.
Jensen, Leif, Gretchen T. Cornwell, and Jill L. Findeis. "Informal Work in Nonmetropolitan Pennsylvania," *Rural Sociology* 60, no. 1 (1995): 91–107.
Killian, M. S., L. E. Bloomquist, S. Pendleton, and David A. McGranahan, eds. *Symposium on Rural Labor Market Research Issues.* Staff Report AGES860721. Washington, DC: U.S. Department of Agriculture, Economic Research Service, 1986.
Lichter, Daniel T. "Measuring Underemployment in Rural Areas." *Rural Development Perspectives* 3 (February 1987): 11–14.
Lichter, Daniel T., Lionel J. Beaulieu, Jill L. Findeis, and Ray A. Teixeira. "Human Capital, Labor Supply, and Poverty in Rural America." Pp. 37–46 in Rural Sociological Society Task Force on Persistent Poverty, *Persistent Poverty in Rural America.* Boulder, CO: Westview Press, 1992.
Lichter, Daniel T., and Janice A. Costanzo. "Nonmetropolitan Underemployment and Labor Force Composition." *Rural Sociology* 52, no. 3 (1987): 329–344.
McGranahan, David A., and Linda M. Ghelfi. "The Education Crisis and Rural Stagnation in the 1980's." In *Education and Rural Economic Development: Strategies for the 1990's.* Washington, DC: U.S. Department of Agriculture, Economic Research Service,1991.
Smith, S. "Service Industries in the Rural Economy: The Role and Potential Contributions." Pp. 105–126 in *Economic Adaptation: Alternatives for Nonmetropolitan Areas.* Edited by David Barkley. Boulder, CO: Westview Press, 1993.
Tickamyer, Ann, and Janet Bokemeier. "Sex Differences in Labor-market Experiences." *Rural Sociology* 53, no. 2 (1988): 166–189.
Tienda, M. "Industrial Restructuring in Metropolitan and Nonmetropolitan Labor Markets: Implications for Equity and Efficiency." In *Symposium on Rural Labor Market Research Issues.* Staff Report AGES860721. Edited by M. S. Killian et al. Washington, DC: U.S. Department of Agriculture, Economic Research Service, 1986.
U.S. Bureau of the Census. *1990 Census of Population: Social and Economic Characteristics, United States.* 1990 CP-2-1. Washington, DC: U. S. Department of Commerce, Bureau of the Census, 1993.

Energy Conservation
See Conservation, Energy

Entrepreneurship
The process of creating new businesses in local economies. Whether rural economies are hostile to entrepreneurship (for example, markets are small, labor is lacking or unqualified, capital is scarce, infrastructure is wanting, business support services are inadequate, or discrimination against women and minorities is rampant) and are inferior to urban ones (for example, entrepreneurs fail more often, start businesses because employment prospects are poor, create fewer jobs, and operate less diversified businesses) are hotly debated issues. New business start-ups are of most concern. Social science literature shows most of these perceptions to be false.

This entry examines the contribution of entrepreneurs to rural economies, especially in new job creation, business start-ups, firm survival. and job retention. Characteristics of new businesses and entrepreneurs are discussed, along with the reasons for starting a new business and the problems encountered. The role of rural entrepreneurship in economic development is detailed, along with technical assistance efforts to aid small business. The entry concludes with an explanation for why so little accurate information about rural entrepreneurship exists.

Structure of Rural Economies

Like their urban counterparts, rural entrepreneurs contribute to job creation and new business start-ups as well as operating diversified enterprises. In rural North Dakota, 7,558 new businesses formed between 1980 and 1987, accounting for one-fourth of state employment and two-fifths of all businesses (Lin, Buss, and Popovich 1990). The industrial mix was nearly identical in rural and urban economies. New business survival and job retention rates are as high in rural as in urban areas, regardless of industrial sector. In Maine in the 1980s, rural and urban areas showed identical—90 percent—survival rates of businesses across industrial sectors (Buss and Lin 1990). Job survival rates were similar. Although intrastate urban/rural comparisons are similar, disparities exist across states. In Arkansas, for example, firms were only half as likely to survive as in Maine.

Rural economies are dominated by multiestablishment corporations. Rural corporations nationwide account for more than twice the net increase in jobs as do small independent firms (less than 100 employees). Small corporations (less than 100 employees) account for only one-fourth of new jobs created by corporations (Miller 1990).

Characteristics of New Business Entrepreneurs

Rural entrepreneurs starting new businesses have similar characteristics. Most rural entrepreneurs are in their mid-thirties, married, and college-trained and live substantially above the poverty line. Women are underrepresented but still start about 40 percent of new businesses. Women concentrate in retail sales more than do men and frequently operate businesses out of their homes because they often have family care responsibilities. Minorities, especially Native Americans and African Americans, are greatly underrepresented. Although African Americans constitute 40 percent of the population in Arkansas' Delta region, for example they start only 7 percent of new businesses.

Unemployed workers play an important role in rural economies and are similar to other entrepreneurs. Unemployed workers start about one in seven new businesses (Buss 1995). They are similar to other entrepreneurs demographically and start similar businesses.

About 5.7 million people derive their income from farms but do not necessarily live on them (Butler 1993). These farm entrepreneurs are typically White males, in their mid-thirties, and married. Farm entrepreneurs earn incomes at the national average, with very few unemployed or on welfare.

The majority of entrepreneurs in rural America started businesses because they had a good idea for a product or service or could not tolerate working for others. Negative reasons such as needing income, loss of job, or loss of another business are not nearly as important as positive motivations. Even for displaced workers, positive start-up motivations far outweigh negative ones.

Business Problems

Entrepreneurs face financing problems, especially taxes, inflation, and cash flow, when starting and operating businesses in rural economies. They may have difficulty finding qualified workers, usually because of out-migration to urban areas. Small markets are cited by many as a problem, but one-fifth of rural businesses in North Dakota, Iowa, Arkansas, Maine, and Michigan export goods and services, thus expanding market size.

Access to start-up capital is not a problem for most rural entrepreneurs. Two exceptions are women and displaced workers. But those who seek bank loans eventually succeed in obtaining financing. Only 3 percent of entrepreneurs in the five states previously mentioned sought, but were unable to obtain, a loan (Jordan and Buss 1995). Rural entrepreneurs borrowed $80,000 on average to start new businesses. Nine-tenths of rural entrepreneurs obtained bank loans from local banks, not from larger banks in big cities. Most entrepreneurs finance businesses through their own resources or by borrowing from friends. Venture and seed capital funds and equity financing are rare in rural areas. Much rural lending from all sources derives more from personal than from formal relationships.

Economic Development

Entrepreneurship is a centerpiece in most rural economic development strategies. Large businesses, although they dominate rural employment, are difficult to attract, are perceived to ignore local needs, and cause local economies to rely too heavily on one industry. Local entrepreneurs constitute an alternative; they are expected to need help. Like their urban counterparts, rural places offer training, especially during the early stages of business start-up. They provide technical assistance ranging from preparing business plans to solving personnel problems. Business development programs like small business incubators, industry associations or networks, worker cooperatives, and technology transfer programs are widely available. Businesses are financed with subsidies, low-interest loans or outright grants, market rate loans when access is a problem, loan guarantees, or seed or venture capital. Incentives are provided, including tax abatement, below-market land provision or facilities, free labor force training, and wage subsidies to targeted groups. Rural places offer favorable business climates and infrastructure, lower taxes, or low-cost space such as industrial parks. Finally, services can be provided by public institutions such as universities or community colleges. They also can be provided by nonprofit organizations, agricultural extension service private business organizations, independent professionals, or for-profit providers.

Even the remotest rural places offer entrepreneurs the full array of technical assistance, mostly on-site, but sometimes through telecommunications. But most rural entrepreneurs do not rely on technical assistance; they prefer self-help or informal networks of business associates, friends, or relatives instead. Lawyers and accountants are much more important than technical assistance providers. Most entrepreneurs are satisfied with the assistance provided, find it useful in their businesses, and recommend it to other entrepreneurs. Many entrepreneurs are unaware of services but report not needing assistance.

Myths about rural entrepreneurs persist because they have not been as well studied as their urban counterparts. Consequently, much information about rural entrepreneurs is assumed, often incorrectly. Existing studies tend to be single cases or anecdotes; were conducted during national recessions, especially in the late 1970s or early 1980s; or focused on isolated or atypical economies. There may be little agreement on what a rural or nonmetropolitan economy is. Finally, rural entrepreneurship studies may be based on faulty data. Uncertainty about rural entrepreneurship makes it a worthwhile study area.

—*Terry F. Buss and Laura C. Yancer*

See also
Cooperatives; Development, Community and Economic; Employment; Home-Based Work; Manufacturing Industry; Marketing; Retail Industry; Service Industries; Value-Added Agriculture.

References
Buss, Terry F. "Displaced Workers and Rural Entrepreneurship." *Economic Development Quarterly* 9 (February 1995): 12–24.
Buss, Terry F., and Xiannuan Lin. "Business Survival in Rural America: A Three-State Study." *Growth and Change* 21 (Summer 1990): 1–8.
Buss, Terry F., and Mark Popovich. "Exploding Myths about Rural Entrepreneurship." Proceedings of the 11th Annual Babson College Entrepreneurship Research Conference, Wellesley, MA. Center for Entrepreneurial Studies, Babson College, 1991. Pp. 350–386 in *Frontiers of Entrepreneurship Research*.
Buss, Terry F. and Mark G. Popovich. "Technical Assistance Services and Rural Business Start-ups." Pp. 152–161 in *Rural Development Strategies*. Edited by David W. Sears and J. Norman Reid. Chicago: Nelson-Hall, 1995.
Buss, Terry F., and Roger J. Vaughan. "Assessing the Accuracy of U.S. Department of Labor ES202 Files in Locating New Rural Businesses." *Journal of Government Information: An International Review of Policy, Issues, and Resources* 22, no. 5 (September 1995): 389–402.
Buss, Terry F., Mark G. Popovich, and David Gemmel. "Successful Entrepreneurs and the Problems in Starting New Businesses in Rural America: A Four-State Study." *Government and Policy* 9, no. 4 (1991): 371–381.
Butler, Margaret A. *The Farm Entrepreneurial Population, 1988–1990*. Washington, DC:, U.S. Department of Agriculture, Economic Research Service, 1993.
Jordan, Laura, and Terry F. Buss. "Who Gets Business Start-up Bank Loans in Rural America." Washington, DC: Corporation for Enterprise Development, 1995.
Lin, Xiannuan, Terry F. Buss, and Mark G. Popovich. "Rural Entrepreneurship Is Alive and Well." *Economic Development Quarterly* 4 (August 1990): 254–259.
Miller, James P. *Survival and Growth of Independent Firms and Corporate Affiliates in Metro and Nonmetro America*. Washington, DC: U.S. Department of Agriculture, Economic Research Service, 1990.

Environmental Protection

The maintenance of the surrounding environment to provide for the health, safety, and welfare of human communities and the protection of life on the planet. This entry addresses the regulation and management of rural environments as sources and sinks and as places vulnerable for conversion to other uses: the environment is the source of resources from which rural Americans make a living, and it is a sink for depositing waste. As populations grow and technology changes, the environment is in peril and, thus, in need of protection. Rural landscapes require careful planning to ensure sustained, regenerative resource use. These resources should not be degraded for future generations. Traditionally, rural residents were engaged in primary, resource-extracting activities, such as farming, ranching, mining, fishing, and forestry. Increasingly, rural residents use the environment for enjoyment, such as recreation and retirement. In addition, lands traditionally used for rural purposes are being converted to urban and suburban functions.

A Source of Resources

The essential elements of the environment are climate, earth, water, and living organisms. A good climate determines the feasibility and success of farming, ranching, and forestry because these activities depend on clean air, rainfall, and a propitious growing season. Because of the value of weather information to citizens, governments keep careful track and detailed records of temperature and precipitation data.

Although there has been much speculation about climate change, relatively little has been done to adjust rural activities in the United States to modify temperature. Vegetation modifies temperatures, and urban places are warmer than rural ones. As a result, rural land uses are beneficial and are likely to be promoted if concerns about global temperature increases. Even regionally, rural land uses can ameliorate the urban heat island effect.

Since the 1970s, air pollutants have been regulated. Point sources, such as those from smokestack emissions, are easier to regulate than those from nonpoint sources like vehicles. Urban and rural air pollution causes a variety of health problems and can damage crops. State agencies cooperate with the Environmental Protection Agency (EPA) to control harmful emissions.

The protection of Earth's resources has a longer history than air quality. In 1933, Congress enacted the Soil Conservation Act, which established the agency known initially as the Soil Erosion Service (until 1935), then the Soil Conservation Service (SCS, until 1994), and most recently the Natural Resource Conservation Service (NRCS). Part of the U.S. Department of Agriculture (USDA), the SCS helped to establish a nationwide system of conservation districts to control the erosion of soils by wind and water. The SCS and local conservation districts encouraged farmers to voluntarily adopt conservation plans. This voluntary system did not successfully curb erosion, so in 1985 Congress enacted new conservation measures in the Food Security Act. This law required farmers to follow a conservation plan to continue to receive federal agricultural subsidies. The law prevented farmers who plow highly erodible soils or wetlands from participating in federal agricultural programs. Through the Conservation Reserve Program, landowners received payments not to cultivate highly erodible lands.

Mining is an activity directly tied to the earth. Surface mining not only extracts minerals from the ground,

but also can destroy topsoil, wildlife habitat, and beautiful views. Because of such destruction, Congress passed the Surface Mining and Reclamation Act of 1977. This law and similar legislation by the states required that mining companies must follow landscape restoration plans and gain approval by federal and state agencies.

Water is another key component of rural environments. An ample water supply is necessary for farming, ranching, recreational activities, and retirement communities. The public and private agencies made substantial investments to bring water to semiarid and arid regions through intricate systems of reservoirs, canals, and groundwater pumps. Growing cities in the West frequently compete with farmers and ranchers for water supplies. Many western cities commonly engage in water ranching. The cities purchase rights to water controlled by rural residents. In other cases, ski resorts reduce water supplies through snow-making activities. In still other places, farmers and ranchers themselves diminish water supplies by pumping water from aquifers. As the competition for water increases, conservation will become a more important future issue.

There also can be too much water, as many rural communities periodically face flooding problems. As a result, governments have taken action to protect the safety and the health of citizens from flooding. The federal government requires landowners in flood-prone areas to carry flood insurance and local governments to adopt regulations for flood plains. Governments finance, construct, and sometimes manage flood-protection measures, such as levees. Environmentalists argue that structural measures are costly and can exacerbate flood problems. Natural, nonstructural alternatives, such as the preservation of wetlands and riparian areas, are an option to lessen the destructive aspects of flooding in ways compatible with the local ecology.

Plants and animals are other crucial components of rural America. Much of the western United States is in public ownership. The National Park Service is responsible for our most valuable natural wonders; the U.S. Forest Service (USFS) for timber and watershed lands; and the Bureau of Land Management (BLM) for rangelands, which are important for ranchers and miners. These lands contain valuable wildlife habitat and are subject to specific agency environmental protection requirements as well as provisions of the National Environmental Policy Act (NEPA) and the Endangered Species Act.

Congress enacted NEPA in 1969, and many states adopted their own environmental protection acts. NEPA requires federal agencies to assess the environmental consequences of their proposed actions and consider other possible actions. Federal agencies prepare environmental assessments and environmental impact statements, which detail the consequences of different options. They are available for review and comment by the public and state and local governments.

The USFS and BLM follow the principles of multiple use and sustained yield. These principles were first advanced in the United States by Gifford Pinchot in the nineteenth century. This utilitarian approach seeks to balance the use of USFS and BLM land for multiple purposes (such as timber harvesting, ranching, mining, watershed protection, recreation, and wildlife protection). The priority of uses is frequently the subject of intense debate in rural communities.

Increasingly, nongovernmental organizations are becoming more involved in environmental protection. Groups like the Nature Conservancy and the American Farmland Trust purchase property and protect it for its natural or agricultural values. Other organizations, like Trout Unlimited, Ducks Unlimited, and Pheasants Forever, work to protect fishing and hunting habitats.

Along the coasts, many rural communities depend on fishing. Fishery resources appear to be the most vulnerable of all our food sources. Because of concerns about the development of fragile coastlines, Congress passed the Coastal Zone Management Act of 1972. This act encouraged states next to the oceans, Great Lakes, and Gulf of Mexico to develop management plans. The states took various approaches to manage the coastal zone, with mixed results. For example, Washington State has one of the more ambitious programs. As a result of its Shorelines Management Act, all the shorelines of the state, including those along rivers and streams, are subject to regulation. Even so, the salmon population declined, and the fisheries industry is threatened. The shorelines law has not prevented this decline, perhaps because it was adopted after major damage occurred. Salmon continue to have significant economic and cultural value in Washington State and, as a result, efforts continue to restore their spawning routes.

A Sink for Wastes

In the past, the popular notion was that the environment was so vast it could assimilate all of the nation's wastes. Sewage and other wastes were dumped with little regard for the consequences to the land, water, or air. During the nineteenth century, the relationship between sewage and

disease became clear, and sanitary sewage systems were developed. The clean air and clear water legislation of the 1970s began to require the management of pollutants.

As with the clean air laws, clean water policy recognizes two types of pollutants: those from point sources, such as sewage treatment plants, and those from nonpoint sources, such as soil erosion. As in the case of air pollution, point sources have proven to be easier to manage than nonpoint sources. Wind and water erosion from farms, ranches, mines, and homes transports soils and with it frequently a variety of chemicals into rivers and streams. As a result, soil erosion is harmful both to the environment as a source and as a sink.

The federal government requires states to develop best management practices (BMPs) for the various activities that contribute as nonpoint sources of pollution. BMPs can be structural and nonstructural. BMPs reduce soil erosion; slow or reduce water runoff; or trap sediment and, in the process, reduce the annual loading of chemicals to surface water. Examples of BMPs include conservation tillage, field terraces and contours, filter strips, and grass waterways. Conservation tillage involves any tillage or planting system that covers at least 30 percent of the soil surface with residue after planting to reduce soil erosion. No-till, ridge-till, and mulch-till are forms of conservation tillage. Contour farming involves planting crops in rows across the slope. Constructed terraces shorten the length of slopes. A filter strip is a buffer area between the edge of a crop field and a stream or river. A grass waterway is a defined water runoff pathway covered by vegetation from the field to a water course.

The term "waste" can be controversial. For example, is animal manure a waste? Feedlots can affect water quality through the runoff of biodegradable organic matter, pathogenic organisms, and compounds of phosphorous and nitrogen. Similar problems result from strip mines, open pit mining, and mine tailings, because eroded soils from such areas can contain adsorbed metals. Such sediments and heavy metals can increase the acidity of water bodies. Because of the health consequences of animal manure and mine waste management, numerous measures have been undertaken to lessen the negative environmental consequences of such actions. Most measures involve strategies to retain the wastes on-site so they do not pollute surface or groundwater supplies.

Toxic wastes are subject to the most stringent regulations. A toxin is a substance that causes illness or death to living organisms when it is present in the body in relatively minute concentrations. With the Toxic Substances

Control Act, Congress required chemical toxicity testing. Other laws, such as the Resource Conservation and Recovery Act of 1976 and the Comprehensive Response, Compensation, and Liability Act of 1980, govern hazardous wastes handling during manufacture, transportation, treatment, storage, disposal, and clean-up.

Many rural communities face the prospect of becoming the proposed location for landfills and other waste sites. With less land available for such uses within metropolitan regions and with the controversy associated with siting such uses, sparsely populated areas are targeted as locations. Although economic benefits may be derived by rural communities from such facilities, there are also environmental costs. As a result, careful planning is necessary to assess who suffers and who benefits from waste disposal operations.

Preventing Unwise Land Conversion

The loss of productive farmland persists as an important issue in many parts of the United States and Canada. There has been considerable debate concerning the national rates of conversion and whether these rates constitute a serious problem, and this debate will no doubt continue. Meanwhile, in specific regions and in several states and provinces, the concern is high about loss of strategic farmlands—those areas with good soil and ample water that are close to markets. For example, in the Phoenix, Arizona, metropolitan region half the agricultural land went out of production since 1950, and a third of the citrus orchards have disappeared since 1970. The consequences of the loss of the desert and citrus orchards to the culture of the Southwest are staggering. The food security and ways of life of regions and nations depend on farmers and farmland.

The benefits of farmland protection include food production; the sustainability of rural communities; the preservation of national and regional heritages; the provision of open space; and the potential for several environmental amenities, including the retention of flood waters, the conservation of soil, and the enhancement of wildlife habitat. Unique farmlands (such as the cranberry bogs of New Jersey, orchards along the Niagara escarpment of Lake Ontario, and the citrus regions of the Sunbelt) provide a cornucopia of food varieties in the United States and Canada. Small-scale operations are often more viable for specialty crop production near growing cities. Such operations promote great economic opportunity within regions. Most unique farmland is located within or near metropolitan areas.

These lands are often the focus of intense debates pitting economically strapped farmers who wish to continue in agriculture but need cash against preservationists who value open space and recognize the long-term importance of good farmland. Such conflicts are unnecessary; farmland protection can benefit farmers and preservationists alike. In response, Congress passed the Farmland Protection Policy Act of 1981. Several states, notably Oregon, Illinois, Wisconsin, and Pennsylvania, also adopted laws to protect prime farmlands. To implement the federal law, the USDA designed the agricultural land evaluation and site assessment (LESA) system.

As urban and suburban uses convert prime farmlands and good forests, agricultural uses are forced to more fragile areas. Sometimes urban and suburban uses occur directly in environmentally sensitive areas. Sensitive areas are those that pose threats to human safety or to the environment, such as floodplains and earthquake zones. Environmentally sensitive areas also may contain special natural values such as a wetland or habitat for significant concentrations of flora or fauna. Areas that merit special attention because of the problem of critically low or declining resource supply or quality (such as farmlands, forests, or fisheries) also may be considered environmentally sensitive. Places with significant aesthetic, recreational, or historical values are sensitive. Finally, environmentally sensitive places include shorelines or riparian areas.

Governments at all levels have acted to protect environmentally sensitive areas. For example, in Washington State such areas can be identified by local governments. Once identified in local planning documents, they must be considered in the environmental review process required by state law. Wetlands receive protection by the federal government as a result of clean water and agricultural legislation.

In the past, land, water, and air were vast in North America. The continent was settled with little regard for the sustained use of natural resources. As populations increase, the limits to the resource supply become more clear. According to the World Watch Institute, three of the earth's natural limits already are slowing growth in world food production: the sustainable yield of oceanic fisheries, the amount of freshwater produced by the hydrological cycle, and the amount of fertilizer that existing crop varieties can use effectively. All three limits have profound implications for rural communities. World Watch president Lester Brown notes, "Nature's limits are beginning to impose themselves on the human agenda, initially at the local level, but also at the global level" (Brown et al. 1995, 5).

Fossil fuels, fertilizers, and technology masked these limits in the past. As soil erosion increased, so did farm productivity. The impact on the land of the technologies of the twentieth century is beginning to be recognized. As a result, the sustained use of resources is advocated to protect the environment. A regenerative approach would go further, acknowledging the environment as both a source and a sink and resulting in creative, inventive responses by human communities. In facing the growing urgency of environmental issues confronting rural communities, there is a need to heal, enhance, and manage the life-sustaining process of the planet and ensure the integrity of the landscape that connects cultural processes with natural phenomena.

—*Frederick Steiner*

See also
Conservation, Soil; Conservation, Water; Environmental Regulations; Groundwater; Land Stewardship; Policy, Environmental.
References
Arendt, Randall. *Rural by Design*. Chicago: APA Planners Press, 1994.
Brown, Lester R., et al., eds. *State of the World 1995*. New York: W. W. Norton, 1995.
Christensen, Brian, J. M. Montgomery, Richard S. Fawcett, and Dennis Tierney. *BMPs for: Water Quality*. West Lafayette, IN: Conservation Technology Information Center, n.d.
Lapping, Mark D., Thomas L. Daniels, and John W. Keller. *Rural Planning and Development in the United States*. New York: Guiford Press, 1989.
Ortolano, Leonard. *Environmental Planning and Decision Making*. New York: John Wiley and Sons, 1984.
Pielke, R. A., and R. Avissar. "Influence of Landscape Structure on Local and Regional Climate." *Landscape Ecology* 4, nos. 2 and 3 (1990): 133–155.
Sargent, Frederic O., Paul Lusk, José A. Rivera, and María Varela. *Rural Environmental Planning for Sustainable Communities*. Washington, DC: Island Press, 1991.
Steiner, Frederick R. *The Living Landscape: An Ecological Approach to Landscape Planning*. New York: McGraw-Hill, 1991.
———. *Soil Conservation in the United States*. Baltimore, MD: Johns Hopkins University Press, 1990.
Stokes, Samuel N., A. Elizabeth Watson, Genevieve P. Keller, and J. Timothy Keller. *Saving America's Countryside*. Baltimore, MD: Johns Hopkins University Press, 1989.
Westman, Walter. *Ecology, Impact Assessment, and Environmental Planning*. New York: John Wiley and Sons, 1985.

Environmental Regulations

Government rules, orders, and procedures dealing with the environment. This entry examines federal legislation on the environment that has profoundly affected rural America. Since the 1780s, a variety of legislation has been passed to regulate the environment. Three distinct periods can be distinguished: the age of disposition, the age of conservation, and the age of preservation. These policies have had positive and negative ramifications for rural America. Three criteria used to assess the impact of these policies are achievement of the intended goals, cost-effectiveness of achieving these goals, and public support for policies and programs.

The Age of Disposition

Environmental regulations during the first 100 years involved the disposition of federal lands. After the Revolutionary War, lands west of the original 13 states were ceded to the federal government. Additional land came under the control of the federal government through the purchase of the Louisiana Territory (1803) and the cession of Florida (1819), the annexation of Texas (1845), the Oregon Compromise (1846), the Mexican Treaty (1848), a purchase from Texas (1850), the Gadsden Purchase (1853), and the Alaskan Purchase (1867). This age was characterized by a series of legislative acts to facilitate development and settlement of federal land by transferring it to private ownership.

Natural resource regulations to open the West exemplify this period. The General Ordinance of 1785 mandated a survey of all federal lands to conform to a rectilinear system of townships based on true meridians. Through various acts and ordinances, public land was sold to individuals at auctions or through preemption for a minimum price ranging from $1.00 to $2.50 per acre. In return, individuals were expected to live on and develop the land.

A series of disposition policies gave lands to states for public purposes. For example, Section 16 of each township was given to states to be used for educational support. The Morrill Act of 1862 endowed agricultural and mechanical colleges in each state and established agricultural experimental stations. A series of Swamp Land Acts (1849, 1850, and 1860) granted lands to states to reclaim the land for development.

Other laws encouraged resource development and disposition. The Lode Law of 1866, the Placer Act of 1870, and particularly the Mineral Location Act of 1872 set the stage for exploration and exploitation by asserting the mineral land in the public domain was free and open for exploration and occupation by all citizens of the United States (Martin and Coie 1991). The Timber Cutting Act of 1878 allowed residents in some states to freely cut timber

The unintentional irony of this billboard's message highlights one of many environmental problems in rural America—the use of rural areas as dumping grounds for solid waste.

from public lands. Additional land was given to railroads to facilitate westward expansion.

Legislation passed during the age of disposition achieved the goal of nation building by settling large portions of territory and providing revenues to the new nation. Rural America grew at a rapid pace as farming, mining, and timber communities flourished. The policies successfully provided the raw materials needed for economic development. The public ideology of Manifest Destiny was supportive of the legislation. However, regulatory loopholes and unscrupulous tactics were used by more powerful economic interests to advance their own ends.

Exploitation of land and the depletion of timber and wildlife set the stage for the Transcendentalist movement. According to this philosophy, humans are the ultimate restorer of nature, and in turn, nature restores a humanity corrupted by civilization. Hence, preserving rural America's beauty restores humanity. The Transcendental-

ist movement advocated the superiority of rural agrarian existence over industrial life, and set the stage for a political movement for conservation.

The Age of Conservation

Environmental policies began to shift in the late 1800s toward an orientation of natural resource conservation and management. A progressive conservation philosophy used reservations to set aside public land for purposes other than disposition. The national park system began with a goal of setting aside lands for public enjoyment and use. Beginning in 1872 with Yellowstone, Congress designated certain regions as national parks. Other areas were later set aside, and when the National Park Service was established in 1916, 16 national parks already existed in rural America.

In 1882, the American Forestry Congress was created, initiating a new era of forest conservation. This movement grew out of a growing uneasiness over the future supply of natural resources such as timber and wildlife. The public feared a timber shortage because regulations allowed industry to freely exploit the nation's forests. The Forest Reserve Act of 1891 granted the president the right to establish forest reserves on public lands. Supreme Court decisions that public lands should be held in trust for all citizens gave Congress responsibility to determine how that trust was to be administered. The authority of the president to establish forest reserves was strengthened in 1897 with the passage of the Forest Management Act.

Forest reserves were limited to western states and territories until the early 1900s. Although there was a demonstrated need for forest reserves in eastern states, such a move required federal purchase of such lands from states. The federal government's authority to acquire land from states was challenged until the passage of the Weeks Act of 1911 and the Clarke-McNary Act of 1924 mandated the U.S. Forest Service to acquire forest lands.

Land was set aside for wildlife reserves. In 1892, the first wildlife refuge was established on Agognak Island, Alaska. The Migratory Bird Conservation Act of 1929 eased the way for the establishment of numerous waterfowl refuges.

Management of western lands was more controversial, pitting large ranch operations against smaller farm operations. The major areas of controversy centered on water and grazing rights. The Carey Act of 1894 provided grants of up to one million acres to each state for irrigation. However, research and capital were lacking, and complex local water customs prohibited certain types of water disbursement.

A wide range of policies was enacted to promote rural preservation and economic growth in other sectors of agricultural development. Conservation policies on rangeland attempted to settle heated rivalries of cattlemen and farmers competing for grazing rights or small homesteading. The Kincade Act (1904) promoted farm homesteading in Nebraska and served as a model for future settlement of the West. A system of leasing grazing land on the public domain was established to balance the rivalry.

In the 1920s, a series of droughts forced the abandonment of many homesteads in the arid West. The droughts, combined with overgrazing practices, took a heavy toll on public grazing lands. In an effort to conserve grazing lands in the public domain, the Taylor Grazing Act was passed in 1934. Grazing districts were established, and more stringent conservation management practices were instituted. The Taylor Grazing Act effectively closed settlement of remaining unreserved and unappropriated public lands.

Soil erosion became a public issue during the drought years of the 1930s, when up to 80 percent of the nation's farmland was eroding. The Soil Conservation Service, established in 1935, encouraged farmers and ranchers to determine local conservation districts and provided technical assistance to promote conservation activities. The rate of soil erosion was reduced, and by 1964, 92 percent of the nation's farmlands were in soil conservation districts.

Environmental regulations during the age of conservation were generally successful in fulfilling the goal of reserving lands for forests, wildlife sanctuaries, and public parks. The public was largely supportive of such measures. However, the system of reservation was wrought with conflicting interests between conservation and preservation. Conservation allowed for management activities in which resources could be harvested for public use, whereas preservation sought to curtail resource harvests.

Regulations affecting other areas of land management had varying success and did not always have full public support. This was particularly true of regulations of arid lands in the West. The most successful environmental regulations involved a grassroots organization and were exemplified by soil conservation districts and grazing districts. Although critics believed that some conservation measures were too costly and reserved too much public land, in retrospect it can be argued that not enough was done to conserve the rural American environment.

The Age of Preservation

The end of World War II ushered in a series of demographic and economic changes that shifted the goals of environmental regulation. The nation transformed from a predominantly rural population to an urban population, and a large portion acquired more disposable income and leisure time. This prompted an increase in outdoor recreation on public lands, which sometimes led to conflict and competition for resources. More important, the preservationist philosophy of the Transcendentalists reemerged with the rise of the environmental movement.

Environmental regulations of this time reflect a need to clarify the federal role. A series of commissions was created to review resource management activities.

This included the Outdoor Recreation Resources Review Commission; the Public Land Law Review Commission; the Commission on Marine Science, Engineering, and Resources; and the National Water Commission. Legislation primarily defined the authority and responsibility of federal agencies charged with managing public resources. Examples include the Fish and Wildlife Act of 1956, the Multiple-Use Sustained Yield Act of 1960, the Forest and Rangeland Renewable Resources Planning Act of 1974, the National Forest Management Act of 1976, the Federal Land Policy and Management Act of 1976, and the Coastal Zone Management Act of 1972. The Classification and Multiple Use Act of 1964 gave the secretary of the interior the responsibility to develop criteria to classify public lands for retention or disposal. Land was retained for a variety of uses, including livestock grazing, development of fish and wildlife, outdoor recreation, timber production, watershed protection, and preservation of public values.

The public became more aware of the environmental costs of industrial production, and the ensuing environmental movement influenced regulations. A major act during this period was the National Environmental Policy Act of 1969, which established the Environmental Protection Agency and promulgated numerous regulatory policies. As government responded to issues of pollution, its role shifted to allow federal agencies to formulate and enforce environmental policies independent of Congress. For example, the Water Quality Act of 1965 empowered the Federal Water Pollution Control Administration to establish standards to be implemented by the states. Previous attempts to force compliance with water safety standards had failed.

Environmental regulations during this time have often focused on urban and industrial issues. However, some regulations more directly affected rural America. Regulations and restrictions on the use of pesticides and other chemicals forced changes in farm operations. Groundwater quality issues that stem from agricultural runoff prompted regulations.

The goals of current environmental regulations during this period have not always been clear, thus making it difficult to measure their success. Regulations are costly and have not always received full public support. Interest group politics and concern over government intrusion dominated this period. These conditions make the assessment of the cost-effectiveness of these policies difficult.

The public lands will enter a new era of concern from society as it becomes more aware of the need to protect and preserve nature. At one time, national policy focused on the benefits of disposing of rural lands; now environmental sustainability and quality have become more important. As the nation approaches a new age of sustainability, environmental regulations will continue to be a source of conflict and change in rural America and society.

—*Duane A. Gill and DeMond S. Miller*

See also
Agricultural Law; Environmental Protection; Policy, Environmental.

References
Adams, David A. *Renewable Resource Policy: The Legal-Institutional Foundations.* Washington, DC: Island Press, 1993.
"Conservation." Title 15 *U.S. Code,* 1994 ed. Vols. 7 and 8. Washington, DC: Government Printing Office, 1995.
Department of the Interior, Federal Water Pollution Control Administration. *Guidelines for Establishing Water Quality Standards for Interstate Waters.* Washington, DC: Government Printing Office, 1967.
———. *Water Quality Standards: Questions and Answers.* Washington DC: Government Printing Office, 1967.
Gates, Paul. *A History of Public Land Law Development.* Washington, DC: Government Printing Office, 1968.
Martin, Guy, and Perkins Coie. *Natural Resources Overview.* Pp. 1–26 in *Natural Resources Law Handbook.* Edited by Donald Baur. Rockville, MD: Government Institutes, 1991.
McGinty, Kathleen A., Chair. *The National Environmental Policy Act: A Study of Its Effectiveness after Twenty-Five Years.* Washington, DC: Council on Environmental Quality, Executive Office of the President, 1997.
Micklin, Philip. "Water Quality: A Question of Standards." In *Congress and the Environment.* Edited by Richard A. Cooley and Geoffery Wandesforde-Smith. Seattle: University of Washington Press, 1970.
"Mineral Lands and Mining." Title 30, *U.S. Code,* 1994, ed. Vol. 16. Washington, DC: Government Printing Office, 1995.
Petulla, Joseph. *American Environmental History: The Exploitation and Conservation of Natural Resources.* San Francisco: Boyd and Fraser Publishing, 1977.
"Public Lands." Title 43 *U.S. Code,* 1994 ed. Vol. 24. Washington, DC: Government Printing Office, 1995.
Rosenbaum, Walter. *Environmental Politics and Policy.* 2d ed. Washington DC: Congressional Quarterly, 1991.

Epidemiology
See Health and Disease Epidemiology

Ethics
Either the normative, philosophical study of principles, rules, or standards that define moral rightness or wrongness or the actual moral practices of people. This entry discusses two related dimensions of ethics and rural America. The first is the ethics (or moral practices) of

people in rural America; the second is how the people of the United States morally ought to view and act toward rural America. These reflect the two different meanings of ethics noted above. Ethics in rural America pertains to the latter actual practices sense of the term. Ethical obligations concerning rural America should be understood in the former philosophical and normative sense of the term. Several prominent philosophers and analysts of rural America believe that there are some features of ethics in rural America that provide the basis for a normative assessment of what society ought to do for and to rural America (Comstock 1987). Many of these analysts believe that aspects of rural America ought to be secured, preserved, or protected because rural America is somehow ethically important.

Practices in Rural America

Description or explanation of the facts about ethics or moral life in rural America is more properly the domain of rural sociologists or anthropologists. However, some philosophical observations can be made about that moral life. The kinds of places that constitute rural America (farming, ranching, or mining communities, small towns and villages, and sparsely populated landscapes) may be precisely the kinds of contexts in which morality can be best practiced. These may be the kinds of places, and perhaps the only places, wherein the good life or the moral life can flourish. This idea rests on some contemporary philosophers having rediscovered ancient Greek ways of thinking about morality (MacIntyre 1984). According to the ancient Greeks and as typified in Aristotle's moral theory, the moral life functions best and sees its purest expression in smaller communities, which share a common culture, tradition, history, religion, or even set of adversities to surmount. The purity of this moral life consists in the strength of commitments to, or convictions about, the fundamental importance of being moral and the concomitant lack of any strong need for formal or legal enforcement or sanctions concerning the moral life. Thus, in small, homogeneous communities, beliefs about the moral life are an important part of the individual's and the community's self-identity. Given the history and sociology of rural America, especially the settlement of particular areas or communities throughout the nation by immigrants with common ethnic and religious backgrounds, it is to be expected that the moral life of those communities would tend to be purer and stronger than morality elsewhere. Whether this were ever true, or if it remains true, is a matter for much debate and

empirical investigation. This view, nevertheless, affects the judgments of some analysts, policymakers, and political and religious ideologues who wish to hold up rural America (or rather, particular aspects of rural America) as paradigms for the moral life or even the American way of life.

Related to the notion that morality tends to be purer in rural places is the idea that the kinds of work people do in rural America (farming and ranching, mining, and tending the store) is somehow also more ethical. Several agrarian philosophers maintain that there is something intrinsically ethical or moral about the simple life of farming and related vocations. Wendell Berry (1978), for example, maintained that the virtues or character traits that farming and rural community promote (e.g., self-reliance, sharing-in-community, and respect for nature) are those same excellences of character and community found in the Greek ideal of the moral life. Basic features of traditional farming and rural life represent ideals that all people ought to follow and may even constitute morality.

Both perspectives—rural life as morally purer, and farming and rural community as intrinsically virtuous— may have some basis in historical fact, although both perspectives also may be guilty of overromanticizing the moral quality of life in rural America in the early nineteenth century. Certain communities may have embodied and instilled virtue and moral convictions, but many throughout the land could hardly be praised for their records on race or gender relations or for how they treated outsiders. Not only did particular moral aberrations undoubtedly occur, but whole areas or communities may have engaged in practices that thoughtful people today and some of their own time and place would find morally unconscionable. The same is probably true today.

For whatever economic, sociological, or other reasons, the purity or completeness of ethics or morality in rural America at the present time probably does not differ significantly from ethics or morality in the larger urbanized society. In some places in rural America, the kinds of ethical beliefs or moral practices may even be worse than those of urban society, from a normative point of view. Granted, some of the objective indicators of immorality, such as crimes against persons and property, substance abuse, and racist, sexist, or other-motivated acts of violence, may be less visible in some areas of rural America. However, statistics can be misleading. It may be true that there is less total crime or fewer total acts of blatant immorality in rural areas, but conclusions about the relative morality or immorality of rural versus urban society must be based on per capita ratios. There is no a priori reason to regard rural America, either historically or at the present time, as any more or less ethical or moral than the rest of American society. Some would argue that rural America, or particular features of rural America, are deserving of special consideration by the larger society, nevertheless. These arguments are based on normative ethical considerations.

Obligations toward Rural America

The United States has had a long history of populism and agrarianism dating at least from Thomas Jefferson's time. Most agrarians and populists of the past tended to base their calls for protection or special treatment of rural communities or family farms on political or economic reasons. Some contemporary agrarians and populists use political and economic arguments to support their positions (Strange 1988). Others use normative, philosophical ethical arguments and principles to support their views. Three kinds of normative ethical arguments stand out: the equity argument, the moral specialness argument, and the sustainability argument.

According to the equity (alternatively called distributive justice) line of thinking, American society has an obligation to ensure that people in rural America, especially small family farmers, have a decent quality of life. This quality of life should be comparable in terms of rights and opportunities to that of nonrural people, mainly middle-class suburbanites. Pointing to larger socioeconomic systemic changes that have negatively affected small towns and farming communities, adherents of this view argue for special assistance for rural people (Thompson and Stout 1991). For example, rural community redevelopment monies or direct subsidies to smaller farms are required as a matter of social justice. Past public policies and the urban public's consumption preferences have caused injustices. They exacerbated the trend toward larger, highly industrialized farms and caused the diversion of commerce away from rural communities as a result of the interstate highway system. The larger society owes rural America some sort of compensatory special treatment as a matter of principle.

The moral specialness argument is essentially that discussed above, with a few variations. The major variation is the idea that family farms and their related rural communities or small towns are inherently ethical entities. The larger society has a moral obligation to protect, preserve, and save that way of life. This argument implies that morality requires people to give up their alienated or dehumanized urban and suburban ways and return to the country, assuming that is possible for 270 million people. Another variation on this theme is an aesthetic or cultural history idea. Rural America consists of many places of beauty and many places that represent or embody significant pieces of our national or cultural history. As such, the larger society should save or help preserve these places and the people who inhabit them, not so much for their intrinsic worth but because they provide meaningful experiences to others. Yet many people may never even see or experience those places directly.

The third and possibly most important argument for saving or preserving rural communities, small farms, or sparsely populated areas of this country is the sustainability position. Practicing sustainability is an ethical good because it fulfills moral responsibilities to future generations (Burkhardt 1989). Adherents of this view argue that preserving rural America as it is helps secure future food supplies for an ever-growing world population, provides recreational opportunities and a resource base for present and future people, and, most important, helps protect the environment as a whole. Sustainability proponents focus on protecting water recharge areas, wild areas, wetlands, and open landscapes and countrysides because these are home to the diversity of plant and animal species that are integral to the adequate functioning of the complete global ecosystem. Sustainability adherents differ concerning the relative values of open places, small communities, and especially farming, ranching, and mining operations with respect to the overall ethical goal of sustainability. All of these may fit, but only if specific changes are introduced into farming, ranching, and mining to make them more environmentally friendly.

Many critical points may be made about each of these three main arguments concerning why the larger society has ethical obligations to rural America. The overarching criticism is that the same principles or reasons that underlie the argument about saving or preserving rural America or some of its aspects can apply to urban places as well. The exception may be sustainability. Urban places, especially inner-city America, also have been damaged by trends in technology, transportation, and public policies. Equity may demand preferential treatment for people in those places as well. Analogously, certain places in urban America may have intrinsic moral value (in a moral quality-of-life sense), aesthetic value, or cultural history value. Neighborhoods in Boston, New York, or San Francisco; the Chicago lakeshore; the Baltimore harbor; and the Washington, D.C., monuments all have value. Sustainability appears to be the only value uniquely associated with preserving or securing rural America.

For sustainability to be the ethical reason behind helping rural America, however, rural America must be dehomogenized. Particular places, environments, and cultural practices, farming, foresting, ranching, mining, and new light-industrial activities must each be examined in terms of their contributions to maintaining or securing a livable environment for future generations. Any complete normative assessment of rural America demands specific ethical analyses and moral critiques of the particular places, communities, practices, and people who are found there.

—*Jeffrey Burkhardt*

See also
Land Stewardship; Religion; Theology of the Land; Values of Residents.
References
Berry, Wendell. *The Unsettling of America: Culture and Agriculture*. New York: Avon, 1978.
Burkhardt, Jeffrey. "The Morality behind Sustainability." *Journal of Agricultural Ethics* 2 (1989): 113–128.
Childs, Alan W., and Gary B. Melton, eds. *Rural Psychology*. New York: Plenum Press, 1983.
Comstock, Gary, ed. *Is There a Moral Obligation to Save the Family Farm?* Ames: Iowa State University Press, 1987.
Donagan, Alan. *The Theory of Morality*. Chicago: University of Chicago Press, 1977.
Hare, Richard M. *Moral Thinking: Its Levels, Method and Point*. Oxford, UK: Clarendon Press, 1981.
MacIntyre, Alasdair C. *After Virtue: A Study in Moral Theory*. 2d ed. Notre Dame, IN: University of Notre Dame Press, 1984.
Strange, Marty. *Family Farming: A New Economic Vision*. Lincoln: University of Nebraska Press, 1988.
Thompson, Paul, and William Stout, eds. *Beyond the Large Farm*. Boulder CO: Westview Press, 1991.
Wilkinson, Kenneth P. *The Community in Rural America*. New York: Greenwood, 1991.

Ethnicity

The perception of groups, concerning either themselves or others, that they are unique and that they have a special social and cultural heritage, received and passed on from one generation to the next. This entry addresses some of the early studies related to ethnicity, and examples of various ethnic groups are described. Ethnicity is a persistent aspect of many Americans' identities and continues to be a variable in the U.S. census. This persistence is related to several Old World and New World influences. Today's significance of ethnicity in rural America and its role for cohesion in a pluralist society are discussed.

Early Studies

The ethnic backgrounds of those who reside in America's countryside or in its small towns have never been the subject of a broadscale, comprehensive study or the object of intense investigation. Early social scientists considered race in studies of African Americans in the rural South, Hispanics in the Southwest, and American Indians. But Americans of European origins, the great majority of rural dwellers, were downplayed or ignored. Perhaps it was the dispersed conditions that led to the oversight. Unlike ethnic concentrations in large cities, national groups in the countryside were invisible and seldom seemed to be a social problem. The scattered circumstances led researchers to believe that successive generations would erode cultural attachments, and country folk rapidly would become mainstream Americans.

The latter assumption is correct to a great extent in regard to the nation's Atlantic and Old South states. Settled primarily by people of British Isles backgrounds in colonial times, the distinction between such originally diverse groups as Scots, English, and Welsh was blurred by intermarriage, and these became what later groups would call Old Americans, or Yankees. (Yet even in pre-Revolutionary times, some ethnic groups existed—various Germans in Pennsylvania, for example, whose way of life today is still distinct.)

The disregard for the rural national groups who came shortly before and in the decades after the Civil War has proven in recent years to have been a serious oversight. Several studies in states such as Texas, Missouri, Minnesota, and North Dakota show that the countryside in much of America was and is a mosaic of cultures. Insulated by geography, their distinctions never were erased. The Old Americans are there, but at the same time national enclaves highlight the geographic hinterlands. In some places, the Old Americans are islands of one culture, and national groups form the surrounding mass of inhabitants.

Examples of Ethnic Groups

Any review of rural ethnicity must make note of some highly visible, very enduring groups such as Hutterites in the Great Plains states and prairie provinces and the Pennsylvania Germans (for example, Amish, Dunkers, Mennonites) who now live in at least a dozen states from Ohio and Indiana to the West Coast. These Anabaptist groups have a relatively closed social system with an Old Country heritage of persecution and strong religious ties. They maintain their way of life through protective procedures such as distinctive garb, private schooling, pacifism, and marriage controls and sometimes through communal work or living arrangements.

These groups have been accurately classified as "extraordinary" (Kephart and Zellner 1991), but fully three-fourths of the U.S. landscape contains large numbers of what might be called "ordinary" groups. They are European in origin and routine in their religion and cultural ways: people from Slavic, Scandinavian, Mediterranean, and Germanic countries. These ethnic enclaves are found today especially in midwestern, south-central, and Pacific states, and isolated groups live elsewhere in America: Poles in New York, Pennsylvania, and Massachusetts; Germans in Pennsylvania, the Carolinas, and Georgia, and French in very durable settlements in Louisiana. Texas has an array of over a dozen intact ethnic regions.

A Persistent American Variable

The "What is your ancestry?" question used by the U.S. Census since 1980 for the first time provided a tool by which most of the nation's rural national groups can be identified. The resulting tabulations show the tendency for eastern and southern rural residents to blur the matter of ethnic origins; "American" is a frequent response. But from Texas northward, through Missouri, Oklahoma, and Colorado to the Canadian border, ancestry consciousness proliferates in ever more significant proportions. Oregon, California, and Washington contain their own special rural groups. They are not as numerous but are decidedly present. With rare exceptions, every national group listed in standard urban ethnic compilations has or had its rural counterpart.

Wherever the ethnic groups are, one factor of extreme importance stands out. The national groups, upon arrival in this new country, found themselves in a decidedly Anglo-American world. There was little of the classic western frontier. When they arrived, the European newcomers discovered in place about them, often in privileged positions, the grandchildren of the Old Americans—men and women whose roots went back to the early colonial period. These were the land agents, merchants, teachers, political figures, and gentry with American savvy and eastern financial ties.

This condition in itself led to several results. First, the ethnic bonds of the newcomers intensified. The newcomers previously were citizens of villages or provinces. In America they became Polish, Norwegian, and Italian. It was "we and the 'English.'" Second, the national church became much more significant than it had been in the past. It became the group's central rallying point. For the less numerous individuals with strong secular biases, newly founded associations became prime centers of national cohesion. The immigrants sometimes were not content with a type of pan-Lutheranism or American-brand Catholicism. Instead, synods, national parishes, and even whole new congregations arose. Third, an array of organizations like the Sons of Norway and Czech lodges dotted the American frontier. Politics, education, and business were controlled by the Yankees; the church and lodge were safe ethnic havens in the United States.

Old World and New World Influences

The Anglo-Americans' world did more than galvanize the immigrant groups' cultural forces. It became the pattern that shaped their Americanization processes. For much of the northern and central Midwest and for the far West, it was a Yankee pattern. In the Gulf and South Atlantic states, it reflected the traditions of the Old South. On arrival, the new Americans learned the ways of their adopted homeland, not just from textbooks but by imitating their American mentors. Through the ensuing decades, the groups became composites of Old Country heritage and New England or Old Southern traditions. Often the result was an amalgam of old and new values. A peasant work ethic was reinforced by Yankee Calvinist diligence; Old Country farming skills blossomed in a New World setting; Swiss newcomers excelled in dairy farming, Italians in wines, and Germans and Ukrainians from the steppes in grain farming. The political traditions of Europe dictated New World participation. Some felt at home among the Populists, some among the Socialists, some among the Democrats or Republicans. Some preferred a "King Man" or "Padrone" type of community organization; some were individualists; some retained their language and garb; some discarded the more outward features of the past.

The strangeness of the New World, combined with the condescending and sometimes hostile attitude of the Old Americans, led immigrants to seek the company of fellow countrymen who were already in residence in the various states. Ethnic enclaves or ghettos developed in the cities. The same phenomenon occurred in the country. The clustering of ethnic groups today is due, in most cases, to that early desire for security. Ethnic mosaics or "patchwork quilts" are frequent and quite accurate phrases used to describe the rural landscapes in many portions of America.

The initial choice of land for most immigrants was dictated by the time of arrival in this country, usually where homestead activity was taking place. At times the land selections were not propitious because they were submarginal or inappropriate to the group's prior experience. Some moved to more conducive terrain, and some abandoned rural settings altogether and settled in cities. Those who found their locations satisfactory remained, and it is their descendants who are most often the rural dwellers of today.

The Current Significance of Ethnicity in Rural America

Time in America meant gradual assimilation of the new nation's values. What remains today is a variety of national traits. More than any other single element, it is the religious heritage that persists. Besides the question of church affiliation, modern studies determined that the ethnic past still dictates other differences that frequently can be significant: voting patterns, birthrates, recreational practices, marriage patterns, land tenure, and ownership experience. Genetic characteristics contribute to the incidence of some diseases: alcoholism, diabetes, and multiple sclerosis. Some groups readily seek assistance from mental health services; others seek help only as a last resort. Farming practices vary: some are innovators; some prefer traditional ways; some are comfortable with mortgages and speculation; some excel in caution. Family styles certainly vary: some raise children to move far from the home in search of opportunity; others assume that their offspring will settle within arm's reach. The role of women differs considerably from group to group (Salamon 1992). No investigation of this feature of rural society today can afford to overlook the ethnic dimension.

An ethnic atlas of North Dakota (Sherman 1983) found almost 40 different national groups who took land in that state at one time or another. All had their identifiable portions of the prairie landscapes. Many were subdivisions of what might at first sight be considered a single group, yet they saw themselves as decidedly distinct, with their own history, dialect, religion, and special traditions. Six different kinds of German Russians appeared: Black Sea, Dobrudja, Volynian, Mennonite, Hutterite, and Volga. The German label also included Sudeten, Banat, Burgenland, Silesian, and Gallician settlers. Other national groups had less numerous but just as pronounced differences. Adaptation and assimilation in each group varied through the generations in sometimes substantial ways. If such differences occur in North Dakota, a student of the subject may be warned to watch for similar configurations elsewhere.

Casual observers and trained academicians have suggested a variety of differences for the nation as a whole. Germans, of whatever variety, tended to stay on the land; it was a way of life. British Isles and Irish farmers saw land as a commodity, an investment, and often as a speculative venture. Among the Scandinavians, Norwegians liked the prairies, whereas Finns liked the woods. Poles were less ready to accept American ways and often took farms that others passed by. Large-scale ranching was a matter for the British or Irish, whereas European immigrants preferred farming. Some groups built large barns, and small, utilitarian homes; others erected monumental homes and shortchanged the farm buildings. Some were dairy farmers; some were pork producers. Assessments such as these can be found in every part of America. These patterns occur with sufficient frequency to force the student of rural matters to look closely at the ethnic dimension in American life.

Ethnic Cohesion in a Pluralist Society

The question regularly arises, what remains of the ethnic component after intermarriages take place? No scholar has a satisfactory and universally applicable answer. There are those who believe that ethnicity does not necessarily disappear under these circumstances. If the national community is large enough, the offspring of mixed unions absorb the traditions no matter what confusion might exist in their lineage. Others suggest that in mixed-marriage families one ethnic tradition often predominates, and values and allegiances still point strongly in one prevailing direction. Given the growing number of mixed-ethnic marriages, this issue will increase in importance and deserve substantial analysis now and in the future.

For a substantial number of Americans, ethnicity is a matter of "roots." Thousands have found in the confusion of life a degree of certainty as they study their private ancestral heroes on both sides of the oceans. Additionally, ethnicity has proven to be "recreation." The relatively recent proliferation of ethnic celebrations that occur throughout the seasons (such as sauerkraut fests, polka festivals, smorgasbord days) highlights the diverse origins of inhabitants of the nation's countryside. Some have emerged into what can be classed as local industries—a German village in Texas, a Little Bohemia in Nebraska, a Hostefest in North Dakota, a New Holland in Michigan.

There are abundant signs that the ethnic dimension of America's hinterlands in one fashion or another is here to stay for a long time.

—*William C. Sherman*

See also

African Americans; American Indians; Asian Pacific Americans; Cultural Diversity; Culture; Inequality; Latinos.

References

Anderson, Charles. *White Protestant Americans.* Englewood Cliffs, NJ: Prentice-Hall, 1970.

Carmen, J. Neale. *Foreign-Language Units of Kansas: Historical Atlas and Statistics.* Lawrence: University of Kansas Press, 1962.

Holmquist, June Drenning, ed. *They Chose Minnesota: A Survey of the State's Ethnic Groups.* St. Paul: Minnesota Historical Society Press, 1981.

Kephart, William M., and William W. Zellner. *Extraordinary Groups: An Examination of Unconventional Life-Styles,* 4th ed. New York: St. Martin's Press, 1991.

Luebke, Frederick, ed. *Ethnicity on the Great Plains.* Lincoln: University of Nebraska Press, 1980.

Salamon, Sonya. *Prairie Patrimony: Family, Farming, and Community in the Midwest.* Chapel Hill: University of North Carolina Press, 1992.

Sherman, William. *Prairie Mosaic: An Ethnic Atlas of Rural North Dakota.* Fargo: North Dakota Institute for Regional Studies, 1983.

Thernstrom, Stephan, ed. *Harvard Encyclopedia of American Ethnic Groups.* Cambridge, MA: Harvard University Press, 1980.

Family

Two or more persons related by kinship or nonkinship ties who share emotional attachments and a variety of family roles and functions. Traditionally, social scientists and others regarded family as a group of persons related by blood or legal marriage, living together and cooperating economically and in child rearing. Hartman and Laird's (1983) definition of family recognizes two categories. One is the family of blood ties, living or dead, geographically close or distant, known or unknown, accessible or inaccessible, but in some way psychologically relevant. This category is the biologically rooted family of origin into which one is born, and it may include adopted family members and pretend relatives. The second category is the current family structure in which people choose to live. It consists of two or more people who make a commitment to share living space, develop close emotional ties, and share a variety of family roles and functions. It is this definition that will be used as the basis for this entry.

In rural America's ever-changing society, there is no typical family. There are many different types of families, such as nuclear, extended, single-parent, gay and lesbian, remarriage, dual-career, and communal. Families may be traditional, with two monogamous heterosexual parents and their children, with the husbands acting primarily as breadwinners and wives as homemakers. Conversely, they may also be nontraditional, wherein parental structure and roles are more diverse. This entry provides a demographic overview of the changing structure of rural farm families. It discusses the social and economic impact of the farm crisis on rural America, with emphasis on displaced farm families and poverty.

Varying Functions

Social scientists identify numerous and varying family functions consistent with the aforementioned definitions. Some basic functions of the family in an advanced industrial society such as the United States include the legitimation and regulation of mating and sexual relations, procreation and child rearing, emotional support and nurturing, economic support and household management, socialization of the family members into gender roles and other social roles valued by society and cultural groups, and the transmission of the culture.

The dynamics of families in rural America are not vastly different from families in urban America. There is an apparent convergence of urban and rural values and lifestyles (Lichter and Eggebeen 1992; Hennon and Brubaker 1988). Theoretical and empirical work on rural families tends to obscure differences between urban and rural families. However, some research attests to certain demographic and ecological factors, such as population, household composition, and family structure, that are unique to rural family life. These factors are shaped by the social and economic forces of residential mobility and poverty. The following provides a brief description of contemporary family life in rural America as it is influenced by social mobility and poverty.

Demographic Overview of Population and Household Composition

The U.S. Bureau of the Census (1992) defines urban and rural as type-of-area concepts rather than specific areas outlined on maps. The rural population consists of all persons in places with populations of 2,499 or less. It is predominantly White, with several other racial-ethnic groupings such as African American; American Indian, Eskimo, or Aleut; Japanese American; Filipino; Hawaiian; Korean; Vietnamese; Guamanian; Samoan; other Asian and Pacific Islanders; and others. In 1980, Whites made up 90.9 percent of rural inhabitants, African Americans 6.6 percent, and Native Americans and other racial-ethnic

Families perform many important social functions, one of the most important being the general transmission of culture to younger generations. A farm family in North Dakota sits down to dinner.

groups approximately 2.4 percent. In 1990, there was an increase in the percentage of White rural residents, but there were slight decreases in all of the other racial/ethnic groups. Whites inhabit approximately 93 percent of the housing units in rural America; African Americans about 5 percent; and American Indians, Eskimo, or Aleuts and others the remaining 2 percent.

In rural areas, the average number of persons per household and per family is minimal, and the percentage of rural households and families declined after 1980. The average number of persons per household in 1990 was 2.76, whereas the average number for rural families, at 3.16, was slightly larger. In 1980, rural families represented 27.3 percent of all families in the United States. In 1990, that percentage dropped to 23.0 percent. Families composed 78.2 percent of all rural households. The remaining 21.8 percent consisted of householders living alone (U.S. Bureau of the Census 1992).

The majority of the householders in rural areas in 1990 were married couples (66.9 percent), compared with 88.7 percent in 1980. Approximately 32 percent of those married couples had children under 18 years old. Female-headed families, with no husband present, constituted 8.2 percent of rural families, and 4.4 percent had children under age 18 (U.S. Bureau of the Census 1992).

Changing Structure

The demographics depict a changing family structure in rural America. Although married couples with one child remain the dominant family form, female-headed households have increased by 7 percent since 1980. The female-headed household is one of two demographic variables (i.e., racial/ethnic parentage and female-headed households) associated with poverty (Garrett, Ng'andu, and Ferron 1994). Female-headed families are likely to have incomes below the poverty level, which adversely affects the life chances of those who reside in them (McLaughlin and Sachs 1988).

Changing societal structure and economic conditions wrought changes in family life in rural America. The shift from a labor-intensive industrial society to a service industry of highly technological information systems is resulting in demand for skilled, specialized technical workers. The farming industry is declining because of high farming costs and increasing loss of farms. In the early years of this century, there was a dramatic rural-to-urban migration by young adults from farms to urban centers. More recently, society's changing social and economic structure resulted in a reversal of the earlier migration trends, as young families moved to rural and farm areas.

Lewis, Volk, and Duncan (1989) find changes in the ranking of reasons farming fathers gave for their young adult children leaving and returning home. In 1973, the primary reasons given for leaving home were, in order, to get married, establish their independence, and pursue their education. In 1983, however, education and marriage switched places: pursuit of educational training, establishment of independence, and marriage were given as reasons for children leaving the farm. The most frequently stated reason for young adult children returning home was having completed educational training. Other common reasons for returning home were employment problems, employment opportunities, and divorce.

Changing family structure, residential mobility, and poverty are inextricably bound in a network of socioeconomic relationships. Agricultural structure influences rural marriage behavior. Diversity and mobility are factors that contribute to both rural and urban families becoming less permanent and more transient.

Displaced Farm Families

The farm family has been seen as an enduring family type, bound to the farm and the land. Yet, the farm crisis of the 1980s displaced many of these families, forcing them off the farms and into the urban areas for work. In the 1980s, farmers were plagued by two key economic trends: the prices for both crops and livestock spiraled downward, and land values dropped drastically.

Persons most affected by the crisis and at greatest risk of forced displacement from farming were found to be the younger, better-educated, and large-scale operators who borrowed large amounts of capital during the 1970s to expand their operations (Bultena, Lasley, and Geller 1986). Other farmers, especially those who were older, well established, largely debt free, and employed in off-farm jobs, were relatively insulated from the farm crisis. Similarly, those farmers who did not borrow money to expand their operations because of limited capital, poor credit, or conservative thinking also were sheltered from the crisis.

Farm Loss

Loss of the family farm is comparable to any other major loss experienced through such life events as death or divorce. Loss of the family farm disrupts family functioning through loss of livelihood, social status, lifestyle, and often the family home. Emotional upheaval may accompany a farm foreclosure that, for some, may represent a loss of the family's past history and legacy for future generations. Thus, losing the family farm can cause great conflict between generations. The stress of displacement caused by the residential move is compounded by the farm family also experiencing (metaphorically) the loss of a job, a death in the family, and a divorce from the family (Jurich, Collins, and Griffin 1993).

Social Supports and Farm Loss

Unfortunately, due to limited availability of services, the lack of anonymity, and the alienation families can sometimes experience when using services in rural settings, most displaced farm families forgo needed mental health services. In times of trouble, extended family and neighbors can be primary sources of informal support. Families in trouble need such help (Wright and Rosenblatt 1987). Some studies found that rural families have more interaction and mutual assistance within their extended families than do urban families (Wilkening, Guerrero, and Ginsberg 1972). The insufficiency of the formal helping network and the inconsistencies of informal networks cause most displaced farm families to face stressors such as foreclosure and a subsequent decision to leave farming. Alcohol use has been reported among 12 to 18 percent of displaced farm families. Forty-nine percent reported becoming more physically violent, both in general and with family members and people outside their immediate family (Heffernan and Heffernan 1986). Consequently, marital problems that lead to divorce increase among troubled farm families. These precipitating factors contribute to poor coping strategies that may lead to murder or suicide. Wright and Rosenblatt (1987) provides an analysis of psychological and social forces that may limit support sought and received by families experiencing loss of the family farm. Community breakdown, fear of misfortune contagion, lack of tradition, and ceremony are a few of the many limitations. Family life education—programs and materials designed to assist families with marriage, parenting, and household management concerns—is one means to overcome the limitations and facilitate mutual support when farm families faced with farm loss require help.

Poverty

Despite the fact that the average net farm income in many states barely exceeds poverty levels, many people believe most farmers are making millions of dollars. The farm crisis made most Americans aware of the financial hardship of rural families and rural areas and how the decreased dependence on farming and other natural resource–based activities greatly contributed to increased levels of poverty in rural areas in the 1980s and 1990s.

Generally, poverty in the United States has been viewed as an urban problem (Lichter and Eggebeen 1992). U.S. poverty is associated primarily with the two demographic variables of ethnic parentage and female-headed households (Garrett, Ng'andu, and Ferron 1994). The aforementioned demographics indicate low percentages of rural habitation among racial/ethnic groupings and female-headed families. The combination of geographic isolation and these public perceptions of poverty with heavily weighted national statistics in favor of urban metropolitan areas led to the low visibility of rural poor (Lichter and Eggebeen 1992). The statistical reality, however, is that poverty rates in nonurban areas exceed those in urban areas. In 1990, U.S. census data showed 16.3 percent of the nonurban population was poor, compared with 12.7 percent in urban areas.

The view of poverty as an urban problem led to the perception that family structure and limited access to income cause disproportionate representation of poverty among racial/ethnic groups and female-headed families in urban areas. Regions dependent on natural resources or with large minority groups often have persistent pockets of rural poverty. Many poor rural families consist of two-parent, married-couple households with one or more workers. In 1993, the Rural Sociological Society Task Force on Persistent Poverty reported that the rural poor are more likely than the urban poor to be employed, but the low wages and lack of opportunities for full-time continued employment throughout the year perpetuates poverty among rural area inhabitants. Duncan (1994) averred that the focus on limited opportunity is supplemented by recognition that the work opportunities are affected adversely by political and cultural factors such as nondemocratic politics and oppressive plantation and sharecropping systems.

Rural family life, contrary to common beliefs, has never been an easy life. The work has been hard, has involved the whole family, and often has had only limited financial rewards. The farm crisis of the 1980s brought financial hardship and psychological distress for rural households. One of the more enduring impacts of the farm crisis may be the changed manner in which farmers make agricultural decisions (Bultena, Lasley, and Geller 1986). It also seems the crisis caused many farmers to seriously reconsider the long-held virtues of land ownership. In the future, more farm operators may pursue farm expansion through rental or lease arrangements rather than purchase. Innovation and risk-taking may be approached with more conservatism; farmers may be more reluctant to try new farming practices and technologies, especially when these entail substantial financial risk (Bultena, Lasley, and Geller 1986).

Despite financial hardships, psychological distress, and social upheaval, rural and farm families seek to live on the farm and in rural areas more for personal and social reasons than for economic reasons. They value the low crime rate, the closeness with the environment, and the informal support systems that a farm or rural setting offers (Wright and Rosenblatt 1987). Not only is this life valued by those who currently live in rural areas, but rurality and the tranquility associated with it are becoming a great commodity in a growing rural tourism industry.

*—Carolyn Junior Bryant
and Jacqueline M. Davis-Gines*

See also
Adolescents; Domestic Violence; Elders; Homelessness; Marriage; Policy, Socioeconomic; Poverty; Quality of Life; Rural Demography; Rural Women.
References
Bultena, Gordon, Paul Lasley, and Jack Geller. "The Farm Crisis: Patterns and Impacts of Financial Distress Among Iowa Farm Families." *Rural Sociology* 51, no. 4 (Winter 1986): 436–448.
Duncan, Cynthia M. Review of *Persistent Poverty in Rural America*, Rural Sociological Society Task Force on Persistent Poverty (Boulder, CO: Westview Press, 1993). *Contemporary Sociology* 23, no. 2 (March 1994): 264.
Garrett, Patricia, Nicolas Ng'andu, and John Ferron. "Is Rural Residency a Risk Factor for Childhood Poverty?" *Rural Sociology* 59, no. 1 (Spring 1992): 63–83.
Hartman, Ann, and Joan Laird. *Family-Centered Social Work Practice.* New York: Free Press, 1983.
Heffernan, William D., and Judith Bortner Heffernan. "Impact of the Farm Crisis on Rural Families and Communities." *Rural Sociologist* 6, no. 3 (May 1986): 160–170.
Hennon, Charles B., and Timothy H. Brubaker. "Rural Families: Characteristics and Conceptualization." In *Families in Rural America: Stress, Adaptation, and Revitalization.* Edited by Ramona Marotz-Baden, Charles B. Hennon, and Timothy H. Brubaker. St. Paul, MN: National Council on Family Relations, 1988.

Jurich, Anthony P., Olivia P. Collins, and Charles Griffin. "Coping with the Displaced Farm Family: The New Rural Migration." *Marriage and Family Review* 19, nos. 1–2 (1993): 77–98.

Lewis, Robert A., Robert J. Volk, and Stephen F. Duncan. "Stresses on Fathers and Family Relationships Related to Rural Youth Leaving and Returning Home." *Family Relations* 38, no. 2 (April 1989): 174–181.

Lichter, Daniel T., and David J. Eggebeen. "Child Poverty and the Changing Rural Family." *Rural Sociology* 57, no. 2 (Summer 1994): 151–172.

McLaughlin, Diane K., and Carolyn Sachs. "Poverty in Female-headed Households: Residential Differences." *Rural Sociology* 53, no. 3 (Fall 1988): 287–306.

U.S. Bureau of the Census. *1990 General Population Characteristics.* Washington, DC: Government Printing Office, 1992.

Wilkening, Eugene A., Sylvia Guerrero, and Spring Ginsberg. "Distance and Intergenerational Ties of Farm Families." *Sociological Quarterly* 13, no. 3 (Summer 1972): 383–396.

Wright, Sara E., and Paul C. Rosenblatt. "Isolation and Farm Loss: Why Neighbors May Not Be Supportive." *Family Relations* 36, no. 4 (October 1987): 391–395.

Farm Finance

The process of acquiring and using capital in agriculture. This entry addresses the sources of financing used by farmers: equity and debt funds. It examines several of the ways credit is used in the farm business and some of the investment decisions farm operators must make.

Sources

Any decision to expand or reorganize the farm business must involve an evaluation of the various means to obtain the capital resources. A farm operation requires two types of capital: investment capital and operating capital. Investment capital includes such items as machinery, equipment, land, and other durable inputs, whereas operating capital includes seed, chemicals, fertilizer, and other inventories and supplies.

The funds required to finance the investment and operating capital requirements of the farm business can be obtained from many sources but are usually classified into two basic categories: equity funds and debt funds. Equity funds are supplied by the owner(s) of the farm operation; they provide the backbone of any financing arrangement. Some people refer to equity funds as risk capital because, in the event of liquidation of the business, the holder of equity funds has the residual (last) claim on the liquidation proceeds after all other claims have been satisfied. Consequently, the equity capital holder bears the risk of any financial loss and also reaps the benefits of any profits or financial gains. In contrast, debt funds are provided by financial institutions or indi-

viduals with no ownership interest in the farm business. Debt funds usually carry a cash cost in the form of interest and have a first claim on net income or proceeds from liquidation.

A third method that can be used to gain control of investment capital items is that of renting or leasing. Operating leases are short-term, seasonal leasing arrangements whereby the lessee leases the equipment for a specified number of hours or days or on a per acre basis. Custom hiring is one form of an operating lease. In recent years, capital leases that involve a longer time commitment (such as three to five years) have become more popular for some machinery, equipment, and facility purchases. Renting or leasing a capital item such as machinery or land reduces the investment capital commitment of the farm operator, but it typically increases the cash flow and operating capital requirements.

Equity Sources of Funds. Since equity is the financial backbone of any business, acquiring or accumulating equity funds is essential for the successful farm operator. A farmer can accumulate equity through savings or acquire it through inheritance or marriage and other family arrangements. Alternatively, the farm operator may combine her or his equity capital with that of an outside investor or a family member, such as parents or a sibling, in some form of pooling arrangement to obtain a larger equity base, which then can be used to increase the size of the business and improve its efficiency through economies of size.

The most important source of equity funds is savings. Savings is the amount of income that is not consumed and is thus available for reinvestment in the farm business. The volume of savings can be increased not only by increasing farm income but also by reducing family expenditures and taxes. In many farm businesses, the primary method of increasing equity capital accumulation is through reduced consumption, particularly for young farmers. Another method to increase equity capital accumulation through savings is to obtain off-farm employment and substitute the earnings for farm income to meet consumption requirements.

Savings provides more than just equity funds that can be used to purchase assets. Savings indicates an ability to handle one's finances that will have an impact on the amount of credit or debt that can be obtained. It also indicates a willingness to forgo current consumption for the benefit of a higher level of income and standard of living in the future. Historically, farmers have had a higher savings rate than most people. Analysts have estimated that farmers save almost one-third of their income; that is, approximately one-third of their disposable income is reinvested in their farming operation.

A second important source of equity funds for many businesses is that of inheritances or gifts. For many young farm operators, accumulated savings will not provide an adequate financial base for a viable farm operation that has the potential for growth and expansion. One common way to augment savings is through gifts received from relatives and inheritances from parents. In most cases, accumulating equity funds through gifts and inheritances is part of an overall intergenerational transfer plan that has been developed to transfer the farm business as a going economic concern from the parents to the on-farm operating heir. In these situations, the operating heir typically has been active in the business for a number of years, and his or her acquisition of the farm at the death of the parents is a natural step in the transfer plan.

A third source of equity funds for the farm business comes from an investor—a doctor, lawyer, farmer, or spouse of a deceased farmer. Combining resources with an investor may not directly increase the equity funds of the farm operator, but it does increase the capital base and the size of the business available to manage. This increased size of operation may result in increased efficiency because of economies of size, increasing the income-generating capacity of the business and the accumulation of equity over time through higher savings. Thus, the benefits to the farm operator of using someone else's equity funds are primarily those of economies of size and future equity accumulation. In addition, the investor may be the only source of additional equity funds for beginning farmers who have no family members with sufficient resources to assist them in obtaining the critical mass of capital necessary to start farming. The investor also may play an important role in providing capital to agriculture through the rental market. This contribution occurs through the rental of real estate to operators who may not have adequate resources to purchase a similar tract of land.

Debt Sources of Funds. Although equity funds provide the financial backbone of any farm business, most farmers do not generate sufficient equity from savings or other sources to expand as rapidly as they desire. Thus, they are forced to use additional sources of funds in the form of debt or credit to expand their operations.

Farmers are served by a three-pronged credit market: the private sector, the cooperative sector, and government agencies. The private sector consists of such firms as commercial banks, merchants and dealers, insurance companies, finance companies, and individuals who make personal loans to farmers. For the most part, these financial institutions have been a dependable source of operating and investment capital for farmers and in many cases have developed specific lending programs for agricultural producers.

Although the private sector historically has been an important source of credit for farmers, at times it has had difficulty servicing agriculture because of the higher rates of interest that could be obtained making loans to nonagricultural businesses and because of the limited supply of funds that could be mobilized to loan to farm firms. Consequently, the cooperative credit system was developed to enable farmers to tap the national money markets. The cooperative credit system comprises the banks and associations of the Farm Credit System. The banks obtain funds by selling bonds on the national money markets to investors. The proceeds of the bond sales are then loaned to farmers or to grain-merchandising or input supply cooperatives. The entities of the Farm Credit System function as cooperatives and are owned and managed by the users of the system. The Farm Credit System has not only increased the availability of funds to farmers through access to national money markets, but it provided many new innovations in agricultural lending and stimulated the private sector to provide more efficient service to farmers.

The third component of the agricultural credit market includes the government agencies. The federal government provides funds to farmers through the Consolidated Farm Service Agency (CFSA) under two programs best known by their previous names: the Farmers Home Administration (FmHA) program and the Commodity Credit Corporation (CCC) program. In some states, state agencies also make loans to farmers, particularly beginning farmers. The primary purpose of the CFSA-FmHA program is to provide loans to farmers who cannot obtain funds from either the private or cooperative sectors. Consequently, the program provides funds for disaster situations and when risks are too high for the private or cooperative credit institutions. CFSA-CCC loans are part of the income and price support program of the U.S. Department of Agriculture (USDA). This program provides loans for grain storage as well as a combined operating loan–income support program to augment farmers' incomes by accepting the commodity as payment in full on the loan if commodity prices are below the loan value.

Use of Credit in the Farm Business

Credit is an important and necessary resource in nearly all commercial farm businesses. Credit is a somewhat unique resource in that it provides the opportunity to pay for the cost of using additional inputs and capital items from future earnings. Hence, the potential improvement in net farm income should be the determining factor in deciding whether or not to use credit in the farm business.

Credit can contribute to the improvement of net income of a farm operation in several ways. First, it can create and maintain an adequately sized business. In most farm operations, this means expanding the operation to obtain an acceptable level of income and to take advantage of economies of size. Credit can play an important role in acquiring the investment capital to expand the business as well as operating inputs to maintain a high volume of output.

Second, credit can increase the efficiency of the farm business. The use of credit may make it possible to substitute one resource for another (such as machinery for labor) as a means to reduce cost, improve timeliness, and increase the efficiency of the farm business. Credit may also be essential to increasing the intensity and timeliness of production by making it possible to obtain larger quantities of fertilizer and chemicals, better breeding stock, or more efficient machinery.

Third, credit can adjust the business to changing economic conditions. New technological developments or changing market conditions can mandate major changes in the farm business. For example, adopting confinement hog production technology or acquiring conservation tillage equipment or larger planting, harvesting, or power equipment may be essential to maintaining efficiency as prices decline and costs increase. Credit is a major resource that can assist in making these adjustments and changes.

Fourth, credit can help farmers meet seasonal and annual fluctuations in income and expenditures. Most farm operations have wide seasonal and annual fluctuations in expenditures and incomes. Cash inflows and outflows typically do not occur at the same time of the year, and cash deficits frequently occur from the planting to harvesting seasons. Using credit to match cash inflows and outflows is essential to efficient operation of the farm business if large cash reserves are not available.

Fifth, credit protects the business against adverse conditions. Weather, disease, and price are all uncertainties in the farm business. Good management can reduce the risk, but it is extremely difficult to eliminate all risks

in farming. Credit can play a major role in protecting the farm business from financial failure or liquidation when adverse conditions occur. Maintaining some credit in reserve that can be used in difficult situations, such as an equity margin in real estate that can be used for refinancing short-term obligations, may be an important method of protecting the farm business from unpredictable risks. Liability management (management of the structure and amount of the liabilities of the farm business) may be as important as asset management (diversification, flexible facilities, etc.) in protecting the farm business against the adverse financial consequences associated with risk.

And sixth, credit provides continuity for the farm business. The transfer of an ongoing farm business from one proprietor to another involves large quantities of capital. Without credit, many farm businesses would have to be liquidated during the transfer process because non-farm heirs frequently want their inheritance in cash and do not want to maintain ownership of farm real estate and other assets. In most cases, credit is essential for the successful intergenerational transfer of the business because the tax liability and claims by off-farm heirs erode the equity capital base, and either assets must be sold or credit used to replace the equity that has been lost in the transfer process.

Safe use of borrowed money is extremely important in a successful farm business. The creditworthiness of any farm depends on the risk-bearing ability of the operation, the returns that can be generated in the business, and the repayment capacity of the operation. Furthermore, farmers should be familiar with the legal documents involved in borrowing money, including the promissory note, the mortgage or security agreement and financing statement, and the installment contract. In addition, a farmer should understand the obligations he or she faces upon default, including foreclosure and bankruptcy procedures.

Investment Decisions

Capital investment decisions that involve the purchase of durable inputs, such as land, machinery, buildings, or equipment, are among the most important decisions undertaken by the farm manager. These decisions typically involve the commitment of large sums of money, and they will affect the farm operation over many years. Furthermore, the funds to purchase a capital item must be paid out immediately, whereas the income or benefits accrue over time. Because the benefits are based on future events and the ability to foresee the future is imperfect, considerable effort should be made to evaluate investment alternatives as thoroughly as possible. This evaluation may include analysis of the decision under alternative futures with respect to prices, productivity, and cost, because once the decision is made and an alternative is chosen, the direction and operation of the firm will be affected for a number of years.

Most capital investment projects can be classified as either output increasing or cost reducing. Investments such as new buildings, additional land, and more livestock generally are acquired to increase the volume of business. It is hoped that the added revenue will exceed added costs and that net profits will increase. In contrast, most machinery is acquired to replace manual labor or worn-out items whose repair costs are expected to be excessive. Thus, machinery has the general effect of reducing labor or repair costs without necessarily changing total output. Some investments will fall into both categories; that is, they may simultaneously increase output and reduce production costs. Some investments are neither output increasing nor cost reducing but nevertheless must be made for other reasons. For example, the owner of a large livestock operation may be required to invest in a new waste disposal system to comply with pollution control regulations. Although these types of forced investments must be made, a careful analysis is still needed to determine the particular type of system that should be installed.

There are four major steps involved in the evaluation of capital expenditure proposals. First, all possible profitable investment opportunities should be identified. This step should be taken to ensure that the most profitable—not just a profitable—investment is chosen. Second, the economic profitability and financial feasibility of the various possible investment opportunities should be evaluated. Assessing economic profitability involves determining the capital outlay required for each alternative and the earnings or benefits that will probably result from each alternative and comparing the outlay to the benefit stream. Evaluating financial feasibility involves a comparison of the cash inflows generated by the investment project with the principal and interest payments that are due on any borrowed funds used to purchase the capital item. Third, the decision should be reevaluated under different price and yield assumptions. Since the investment decision involves projections into the future and a major commitment over time, it is desirable to evaluate the economic profitability and financial feasibility of an investment alternative under different sets of future prices and productivity. And fourth, the choice of investment should be made based on the economic and financial evaluation as well as other factors that would influence the investment decision. As with any managerial decision, judgment must be combined with economic analysis to select the best option.

—*Michael D. Boehlje*

This entry is abstracted from Michael D. Boehlje and Vernon R. Eidman, *Farm Management.* New York: John Wiley and Sons, 1984. Reprinted by permission of John Wiley and Sons.

See also
Agricultural and Resource Economics; Bank Lending Practices; Financial Intermediaries; Foreclosure and Bankruptcy; Policy, Agricultural.

References
Barnard, Freddie, and Michael Boehlje. "Evaluating Financial Position, Performance, and Repayment Capacity for Agricultural Businesses." *Journal of the American Society of Farm Managers and Rural Appraisers* 59, no. 1 (1995): 73–79.
Barry, Peter J., Paul N. Ellinger, C. B. Baker, and John A. Hopkin. *Financial Management in Agriculture.* 5th ed. Danville, IL: Interstate Publishers, 1995.
Boehlje, Michael. "Evaluating Farm Financial Performance." *Journal of the American Society of Farm Managers and Rural Appraisers* 58, no. 1 (June 1994): 109–115.
Boehlje, Michael D., and Vernon R. Eidman. *Farm Management.* New York: John Wiley and Sons, 1984.
Brake, John R., and Emanuel Melichar. "Agricultural Finance and Capital Markets." Pp. 416–494 in *A Survey of Agricultural Economics Literature.* Vol. I: *Traditional Fields of Agricultural Economics, 1940s to 1970s.* Edited by Lee R. Martin. Minneapolis: University of Minnesota Press, 1977.
Harl, Neil E. *The Farm Debt Crisis of the 1980s.* Ames: Iowa State University Press, 1990.
Hopkin and Associates. *Transition in Agriculture: A Strategic Assessment of Agricultural Banking.* Washington, DC: American Bankers Association, 1986.
Hughes, Dean W., Stephen C. Gabriel, Peter J. Barry, and Michael D. Boehlje. *Financing the Agricultural Sector.* Boulder, CO: Westview Press, 1986.
Lee, Warren F., Michael D. Boehlje, Aaron G. Nelson, and William G. Murray. *Agricultural Finance.* 8th ed. Ames: Iowa State University Press, 1988.
van Horne, James C. *Financial Management and Policy.* 8th ed. Englewood Cliffs, NJ: Prentice-Hall, 1989.
Weston, J. Fred, and Eugene F. Brigham. *Essentials of Managerial Finance.* 10th ed. Fort Worth, TX: Dryden Press, 1993.

Farm Management

The process of managing business firms that produce primary agricultural products. Farm management involves applying the functions of planning, implementation, and control to the fields of production, marketing, and finance of farm businesses. This entry will address each of these steps in the farm management process.

A Farm's Life Cycle

U.S. and world agriculture is characterized by a wide range in the size and type of primary producing units. Some farms are owned by groups of individuals and hire most of the labor and management required. However, the great majority of farms in the United States are referred to as family farms. Family farms serve as a residence for the farm family and as a place of business. In addition, many of the family's leisure-time activities revolve around the farm, making it difficult to separate the business and way-of-life dimensions of farming on the typical family farm.

Because the individual entrepreneur dominates in the agricultural production sector, the typical farm firm exhibits a life cycle that parallels the life cycle of the operator. This is an important concept because a manager's goals or objectives may change over the life cycle of the individual and the firm. The first stage of the life cycle is that of entry, where the overall objective is to become a successfully established farm operator. The second stage is that of growth and survival. During this stage the manager acquires additional resources, attempts to increase efficiency, and consolidates any gains to ensure survival if difficult times are encountered. The third and final stage of the life cycle is that of exit or disinvestment. In this stage, the entrepreneur attempts to phase out the business and liquidates part of his or her assets or transfers ownership to the succeeding generation of managers.

Management Functions

The concepts of planning, implementation, and control provide a useful and meaningful delineation of farm management functions. Some of the important activities of each management function are listed in the table.

Planning. Planning is the most basic farm management function; it provides the mode of operation to accomplish the firm's objectives. Planning involves selecting a particular strategy or course of action from among alternative courses of action with the objective of obtaining the greatest satisfaction of the firm's goals. Thus, planning is deciding in advance what should be done, how each task should be accomplished, when the task should be done, and who will be responsible for completing the task.

The starting point for planning is to determine the goals and establish the constraints within which the firm will operate. Goals provide the basis for judging the desirability of alternative plans. Data on resource availabilities, including land, labor, and capital, and the restrictions imposed by the social, political, and economic environment are important in specifying the setting within which the firm must operate. Data on goals and restrictions provide the basis for proceeding with the planning process.

Two basic tools used in the planning process are budgets and written policy and procedure statements. A budget is a statement of expected results expressed in numerical terms. The development of expected annual cost and return budgets for specified enterprises, such as cattle or wheat, is a common activity of farm managers. Financial budgets, such as a cash flow budget, provide information on the expected cash inflows and cash outflows that will occur during the forthcoming production period.

In addition to budgets, policy and procedure statements can be useful as planning tools. Policy and procedure statements are used to guide or channel thinking and short-run or operational decision making. They can be used to ensure that the decisions will be consistent with and contribute to objectives. Policy and procedure statements can also be useful to communicate plans and courses of action to employees.

Because planning involves predictions with respect to future events, forecasting is an essential component of the planning process. Forecasting involves assessing the future and making provisions for it in the plan. In the development of enterprise budgets, for example, the farm manager must forecast not only the expected price of the products being turned out and the inputs being purchased off the farm but also the physical efficiency of the production process and the amount of product that will be forthcoming during the production period.

Implementation. The second major function of the manager is to implement the plan that has been developed in the planning process. This function involves acquiring the personnel and other resources necessary to get the tasks done, organizing the workload to complete the tasks on schedule, and actually supervising and directing the accomplishment of the various tasks. It involves organizing and directing the physical activities, whether they are performed by the farmers themselves or other employees.

Implementation of the farm plan requires the acquisition and coordination of the necessary land, labor, machinery, and capital resources. Acquisition of land through purchase alternatives, such as the mortgage or

Major Activities of Each Function of Farm Management

Planning	Implementation	Control
1. Determine and clarify goals and objectives.	1. Acquire and maintain land and other real estate.	1. Develop a system to measure production, marketing, and financial performance.
2. Forecast prices and production.	2. Acquire, train, and supervise the workforce.	2. Keep appropriate production, marketing, and financial records.
3. Establish the conditions and constraints within.	3. Acquire and maintain machinery and equipment services.	3. Compare actual record results with standards established in planning.
4. Develop an overall plan for the long run, intermediate run, and the current year.	4. Acquire capital, credit, and purchased inputs required by the plan.	4. Identify corrective actions needed, if any.
5. Specify policies and procedures.	5. Schedule tasks to be completed.	
6. Establish standards of performance.	6. Communicate with employees, neighbors, landlords, bankers, and others as required to carry out the plan.	
7. Anticipate future problems and develop contingency plans.		
8. Modify plans in light of control results.		

installment sale contract, must be evaluated. The alternative of leasing the land by using a cash or crop share lease is an important issue in implementing the production plan.

With respect to the labor resource, implementation requires the determination of whether full-time or part-time labor is required to complete the physical work. Obtaining information on prospective employees and choosing the right employee for the right job are important components of the implementation process. Once labor has been hired, coordinating their activities to produce the crops and livestock in a timely fashion, providing necessary training and opportunities for personal development of the workforce, and evaluating their performance and productivity are necessary.

Capital acquisition and management involve the determination of alternative sources of debt and equity funds and the terms available from these different sources. Evaluation of credit terms and credit instruments with respect to their cost and other advantages and disadvantages is part of the implementation process. Negotiation of credit terms and the timing of loan repayments are important components.

Acquisition of capital resources includes negotiating the purchase of, physically taking possession of, and having inputs (such as feed, seed, fertilizer, herbicides, machinery, and livestock) available when needed. Deciding on the brand and dealer for each input as well as negotiating the price and related terms is an important part of the implementation function.

Control. The control function involves measuring performance and correcting deviations from expected behavior to ensure the accomplishment of plans. Thus, control involves the traditional farm management activity of record keeping. Control is much broader, however, than simply keeping track of past performance through detailed historical records. The control function requires the farm manager to compare the actual outcome reported in the records to the projected budgets prepared during the planning process. Since the plans have been chosen by management to encompass the best means to accomplish the firm's objectives, deviations from plans as evidenced by the control system provide a warning that current performance may not accomplish the specified goals. If the control system is properly designed, this deviation between planned and actual performance should provide the manager with some indication of what might be the problem. Consequently, the manager with an adequate control system can detect problems early in their development and make appropriate corrections to ensure efficient satisfaction of the specific goals.

The basic control process involves establishing standards, measuring performance against these standards, and correcting deviations from standards and plans. Standards are the criteria against which actual performance can be measured and are derived from the goals that have been specified by the manager. Standards may be physical in nature and express such performance criteria as pigs weaned per litter, average daily gains, yield per acre, or pounds of pork or beef per hundred pounds of feed fed. Alternatively, they may be measured in financial terms such as rate of return on equity capital, production per dollar of expense, rate of capital turnover, debt to asset ratio, and production costs per acre.

The primary concept of control is to correct deviations between planned and actual performance so that the objectives of the firm can be most efficiently accomplished. A control system must, therefore, provide timely information that will enable management to make appropriate adjustments early enough in the production process to have an impact on performance.

Management Fields

To adequately perform the planning, implementation, and control functions within the farm firm, the manager must have analytical expertise and access to data in the fields or areas of production, marketing, and finance.

Production. The most obvious area of responsibility for the farm manager is that of production. Plans must be made and implemented with respect to the production system to be used for each crop and livestock enterprise. This involves selecting the combination and timing of inputs for each product. Enterprise-specific decisions (such as what insecticide or herbicide will provide the desired control or whether a silage or high-concentrate ration should be fed to the cattle) are typical production decisions. Selecting the type and size of tractor needed to prepare the ground and plant the crop in a timely fashion and deciding whether a confinement open-lot cattle-feeding facility will provide the lowest cost of gain (that is, the amount it costs to increase the weight of livestock and, thus, increase profit margins) are other examples of production decisions.

Marketing. The need for price and cost data to make adequate farm management decisions underscores the necessity for expertise in the second field of farm management, that of marketing. The ability to analyze the market and to reflect changing market expectations in production schedules, input purchasing, and product-selling strategies is an essential component of profitable farm management. Production scheduling decisions require the farmer to be acquainted with information on seasonal, cyclical, and trend movements in livestock and grain prices. Hence, the farmer must be aware of the supply and demand relationships for the particular product, the impact of consumer incomes and the availability of substitutes on product prices as suggested by income and cross-price elasticities of demand, and the expected response of other producers to current prices.

Such choices as which marketing channel to use, whether to sell cattle or hogs on a live-weight or grade and yield basis, and whether to sell grain at harvest or to dry and store it for sale at a later date are examples of marketing decisions that must be made by the farm manager. The evaluation of the profitability of alternative hedging strategies or the potential for contracting part of the corn or soybean crop for future delivery or contracting inputs such as livestock feed for future delivery also requires detailed analysis of market relationships and price expectations.

Finance. In addition to the information on production efficiency and market and price relationships, data must be obtained on resource availability for adequate farm management analysis. Except for the farmer's own labor and management resources, the acquisition of other productive inputs in farming such as land, machinery and equipment, and hired labor involves the outlay of money. Improving the farmer's labor and management skills through formal education requires the use of money for tuition and other expenses. Thus, the field of finance and financial management is an important area in which the farm manager must have expertise.

Finance involves decisions with respect to the acquisition of funds and the use of those funds to acquire the services of various resources. For example, purchasing real estate with various combinations of equity and debt funds requires a financial management decision. Leasing machinery as opposed to purchasing it and the repayment schedule that will be required to amortize the loan on machinery are important financial questions. The choice among alternative sources of funds, including the appropriate combination of debt and equity, requires detailed financial analysis, as does the comparison of the terms and interest rates offered by alternative financial institutions.

Financial management decisions involve such issues as organizing a business to withstand expected risk, holding cash reserves for unexpected contingencies, acquiring insurance policies for protection against property damage, and developing estate plans. For adequate financial analysis, the farm manager must be well enough acquainted with the concepts and procedures of cash flow to evaluate repayment capacity; must understand the phenomenon of present value analysis and the basis for discounting in investment analyses; and must have the ability to analyze financial statements, various tax management strategies, and alternative ways of organizing or incorporating the business.

In summary, production decisions involve basic questions as to what to produce, how to produce it, and which combinations of inputs and outputs to use. These decisions must be integrated with basic marketing decisions as to where, when, and how to buy and sell inputs and products. Finally, the what, where, when, and how of production and marketing decisions must be integrated with the financial decisions of where the funds will be obtained, with what terms they will be acquired, how they will be repaid, and for what purpose they will be used. Farm management involves the application of modern management concepts and principles to firms that produce and sell agricultural products. It is concerned with planning, implementation, and control of the production, marketing, and financing dimensions of the farm firm throughout the entry, growth, and exit stages of the firm's life cycle.

—*Michael D. Boehlje*

See also
Agricultural and Resource Economics; Agricultural Programs; Agriculture, Alternative; Cropping Systems; Farm Finance; Pest Management; Tillage.

References
Boehlje, Michael. "Concepts of Modern Agricultural Production." *Journal of the American Society of Farm Managers and Rural Appraisers* 59, no. 1 (1995): 36–38.
———. "Some Critical Farm Management Concepts." *Journal of the American Society of Farm Managers and Rural Appraisers* 57, no. 1 (May 1993): 4–9.
Boehlje, Michael D., and Vernon R. Eidman. *Farm Management.* New York: John Wiley and Sons, 1984.
Calkins, Peter H., and Dennis D. DiPietre. *Farm Business Management: Successful Decisions in a Changing Environment.* New York: Macmillan, 1983.
Harsh, Stephen B., Larry J. Connor, and Gerald D. Schwab. *Managing the Farm Business.* Englewood Cliffs, NJ: Prentice-Hall, 1981.
Kadlec, John E. *Farm Management: Decisions, Operation, Control.* Englewood Cliffs, NJ: Prentice-Hall, 1985.
Kay, Ronald D., and William M. Edwards. *Farm Management.* 3d ed. New York: McGraw-Hill, 1994.
Libbin, James D., Lowell B. Catlett, and Michael L. Jones. *Cash Flow Planning in Agriculture.* Ames: Iowa State University Press, 1994.

Farms

Tracts of land devoted to agricultural purposes. This entry describes types of farms and why there is an interest in the various types. A discussion of farm labor, capital, management, land ownership, residency, and dependency follows. The entry concludes with an evaluation of current farm trends.

Interest in Farm Types

Farms are defined by the federal government as any unit that has agricultural sales greater than $1,000 or has the potential for this level of sales. Given this broad definition, additional criteria are generally used to specify various types of farms. Research on farm types reflects an interest in the social organization of farming and calls attention to human relationships with the land and other natural resources. Farm types reflects policy choices made about basic societal issues such as land ownership and stewardship. Policymakers, social scientists, farm organizations, and rural advocacy groups focused much attention on farm types and their importance to rural communities. Research on farm types often addressed broad social issues affecting rural culture, such as class structure (who owns the land), stewardship (how natural resources are cared for), agricultural policy (what is needed to ensure the viability of family farms and protect the nation's food supply), and rural development (what types of farms are more likely to support local economic and social activities).

Because of the importance of farming to rural America and for consumers, much attention has focused on understanding farm changes. There have been two major threads of inquiry into the social and economic organization of farming. The first line of research documents changes in the number and size of farms. There is voluminous literature to document changes in the number of farms (USDA 1979, 1981). A second research thrust examines how farm types affect social and economic relationships within rural communities. This line of inquiry addresses questions about the social and economic organization of farming and the implications for rural culture and socioeconomic well-being of rural America (Albrecht and Murdock 1990; Buttel, Larson, and Gillespie 1990; and Strange 1988).

The debate about farm types and farm structure has a legacy dating back to the early years of the republic and has ebbed and flowed throughout agricultural history. After nearly 200 years of European rule, when the colonies achieved political independence from England, one of the most significant policy questions was what to do with the newly acquired, ungranted landholdings of the British Crown. The founders wrestled with the basic question of what type of farming would result in political stability and ensure economic and social growth for the new nation. There were two competing visions for rural America that were tied directly to landownership. Thomas Jefferson, the leading spokesman for liberal disposal of federal lands, argued for easy terms of credit to create a nation based upon independent family farms. Jefferson emphasized the political value of family farms

An example of the traditional American family farm. The difficulties of maintaining this type of farming have generated concern about the future of rural America.

and argued that farms worked by individuals who owned them would provide a seedbed for an agrarian democracy. Others, such as Alexander Hamilton, wanted to sell the land to the highest bidder to maximize federal revenues, use the proceeds to finance the newly created federal government, and invest in an infrastructure such as roads and seaports to support industry and commerce (Cochrane 1993; Kirkendall 1991).

Throughout the settlement period, subsequent land acts were liberalized as policies developed to create a nation of small, independent producers. The basic organizing principle of farming was not set forth in a single congressional act or law but emerged through a set of historical decisions about what type of agriculture was desirable. Family farms remained the basic organizing unit of the farm sector even though there was never complete agreement on what was meant by family farms.

Farming in colonial America generally meant subsistence agriculture. People raised food for their own family's consumption, and any surpluses were traded for other essentials. In this premarket economy, nearly every-

one was involved in farming and food production and preservation. This type of agriculture relied heavily on human and animal power with minimal use of machinery. Because of its labor-intensiveness and low productivity, food shortages and starvation were a common threat.

Although most farms in the colonial period were subsistence farms in which a wide variety of crops and livestock were produced, plantation agriculture patterned after the feudal landownership system in Europe took root in the colonies. In response to a growing export demand for tobacco and later cotton, the institution of slavery emerged. Throughout the colonial period, the two forms of agriculture coexisted: family farms in the New England states and plantations in the southern states. The internal strife between these two competing visions of agriculture was not resolved until after the Civil War, at which time slavery was abolished.

Farm Types Defined

According to the most recent agricultural census (1992), there are approximately 1.9 million farms in the United

States. Of these, 86 percent are classified as family- or individual-owned farms, 10 percent as partnerships, and 4 percent as corporate farms. Of those organized as corporations, 90 percent are considered family-held corporations. Given that some of the largest farms in the country, measured by either acres or gross farm sales, are organized as individual- or family-owned farms, a major shortcoming of the census data is that ownership structure does not provide much information about how they actually are operated or how farms changed.

Since 86 percent of the farms are classified by the census as individual- or family-owned (sole proprietorship), it is necessary to consider other dimensions in exploring farm types. One useful way to conceptualize farms is to ascertain who provides the majority of the labor, capital, management, and land. On family farms, the family provides the majority of the labor; provides the needed capital to finance the operation; is responsible for debts incurred; makes the day-to-day decisions about the farm; and owns some, although not necessarily all, of the land. Residency and dependence are two important additional dimensions of family farms. A strict definition of family farming requires that the family live on the farm and be dependent on the farm for a major portion of their income. Although there is not agreement on the relative importance of each of these dimensions, this operational definition provides a referent for comparing other types of farms.

Labor. The intent of government land disposal acts was to encourage a large number of small family-owned-and-operated farms. Both of these systems relied heavily on nonfamily labor. The proportion of labor provided by the farm family has been used widely as a measure of family farms. Hence, family farms often are defined as those in which the majority of labor is provided by the family, although this does not preclude the hiring of seasonal labor. Large-scale farm operations that hire the majority of labor, even though the family may provide the management of the farm, are categorized as larger than the family farm category.

Capital. The operator of a family farm is responsible for securing the farm's financing and repay its debts. In comparison to farms where partners or stockholders are able to offset farm losses with nonfarm income to reduce their tax liability, sometimes referred to as tax-loss farming, operators of family farms are responsible for the financial well-being of the farm. Other financing alternatives emerged as capital becomes a significant barrier for family farms. The key issue is not whether outside capital is used but whether the farm family is responsible for repaying the farm's debts.

Management. Management decisions are the responsibility of the farm operator on family farms. Where the farm operator surrenders managerial decisions to someone else, the farm no longer fits the historical definition of a family farm. As farmers enter into contractual arrangements with management firms or food processors who make the major decisions about the farm, the operator's role is reduced to providing labor and perhaps the equipment and facilities. These types of farms commonly are referred to as contract farms. Farmers often enter into these contractual arrangements by turning over the management of the farm in exchange for a guaranteed return on investment or profit as a way to secure capital or to reduce risk by receiving guaranteed prices. Contract farming emerged in the 1980s as a major force in swine and poultry production (Haroldson 1992; Heffernan 1984).

Landownership. A major tenet of the family farm system of agriculture was to ensure widespread ownership of land. A strict definition of family farms requires that the family own some, although not necessarily all, of the land it operates. Land ownership is an important factor differentiating family farms from other farm types. Even with liberal terms of purchase, many pioneer families could not afford to buy land. Land prices, unavailability of land for purchase, or lack of investment capital contributed to increases in sharecropping or tenant farming, in which the farm family does not own any land. Part-owned farms are those in which the farm family owns some land and rents or leases additional land from others. A relatively new variant of tenant farming, custom farming, emerged in some parts of the country. Custom farmers generally specialize in the production of only certain commodities and operate land that is owned by others. The custom farmer often provides the machinery, equipment, management, and other purchased inputs such as fertilizer and seed. Through high degrees of specialization and economies of scale, custom farmers typically farm large acreages and have multiple landlords.

Residency. The intent of the land disposal acts was twofold: to create a dispersed farming system and to foster the settlement of the interior of the continent. The family was often required to live on the land for a specified length of time to receive free or cheap land. Requiring recipients to live on the land as a condition of receiving public land was part of an explicit settlement policy. Residency is an important dimension when considering the social and economic impacts of farming on the viability of the local community. Living on the farm can be used to differentiate a family farm from an absentee-owned farm. In cases in which farmers live in the local community but not on their farms—technically not a family farm—the revenue generated by the sale of crops or livestock still remains in the community. However, when the farmer lives outside the community, the farm profits leave the community, which reduces the economic health of the community. This latter type of farm tenure is generally referred to as an absentee-owned farm.

There are growing concerns about certain forms of absentee ownership, especially outside investors and foreign investors. Several states regulate or prohibit outside investors and nonresident aliens from owning farmland (Haroldson 1992). There has been less concern about individual farmers continuing to own land even if they do not actively farm it or live on it. Retiring to the nearest town or perhaps retiring to another state, even though it results in absentee-ownership, has not been viewed as negatively as outside investors buying land. However, if concern is that outside ownership results in profits being siphoned out of the local community, then both types of absentee ownership may have equally detrimental effects.

Dependence. Dependence on the farm for a substantial part of one's income is an important consideration differentiating farm types. When the farm provides only a small portion of the total family income, the farm operator's primary occupation and identity may be its off-farm job. In extreme cases, the farm simply may be a diversion from routine activities, providing leisure time or recreation, and perhaps should be considered a hobby farm. In the case of family farms in which the family gains a majority of their income from the farm, their livelihood and way of life are closely associated with farming.

A major trend in farm types has been the movement toward more part-time farming. Many farm families have taken jobs off the farm because of persistent low prices, increased volatility in commodity prices, and associated risks in farming. Others have turned to off-farm jobs to provide supplemental income and benefits such as health insurance and retirement pensions. Currently about one-half of all farm operators work off the farm, and when the contributions of their spouses are considered, an even higher proportion of farms are part-time operations. As a result, the number of full-time family farms continues to decline. When both the husband and the wife work off the farm, it is appropriate to refer to them as dual-career farm

families. Because of the increase in the number of farm families holding multiple jobs, less free time is available for social and civic activities within the community. Many of the problems associated with dual-career families, such as diminished volunteerism, less community interaction, latchkey children, and less leisure-time activity have emerged among farm families.

Farm Types Reconsidered

Increased size and specialization in farming resulted in a decline among general farms (those that produced a mix of crops and livestock) and an increase in numbers of specialized farms (those that often produce a limited number of commodities). More and more, farms are denoted by the crops or livestock they produce, such as cash grain, dairy, swine, cattle, or vegetables. The higher levels of specialization and complexity along with growth in farm size has resulted in farming becoming a capital-intensive industrial process.

As farm size and specialization increased, the labor, capital, and management requirements exceeded what many farm families could provide. When a nonfamily, hired labor force is the major source of labor for the farm, the unit is likely to be viewed as a factory farm, a large-scale, industrial farm, or a corporate farm (Rodefeld 1982). Corporate farms can either be family or nonfamily owned. In some cases, farm families incorporated their farming operations to ease the transfer of the farm assets to their children. Other organizational forms adopted by family farms as they grew larger include partnerships among family members or with unrelated individuals. Intergenerational family farms denote those farms where two or more generations of family members farm together.

Most public concern surrounding nonfamily corporate farms pertains to threats to family farming's viability. As a result, several states regulate corporate farms by limiting the amount of land they can own (Haroldson 1992). In recent years, there has been a trend to link the farm sector with either the processing or supply sectors to achieve more coordination. Generally referred to as vertical integration, this arrangement occurs when a single firm owns multiple stages in the food system (for example, a manufacturing company that produces feed for its own livestock or slaughters its own livestock raised on its own farm). In vertically integrated companies, the farm is just one stage in the production process. Coordination is achieved through direct ownership of the farm rather than relying on contracts with individual farmers. These new farm types begin to blur the distinctions between a farm and factory and poses new challenges for discussing farm types.

As farming evolved, it redefined the occupation of farmer and had important consequences for farm families and rural communities. The changes in the business organization of farming resulting from new technologies, specialization, and coordination is redefining farming. What is less understood are the impacts of these changes on farm families, rural communities, and consumers. Understanding the linkages between farm types and community well-being was first studied by Goldschmidt (1978) over 50 years ago. Others such as Lobao (1990) and Buttel, Larson, and Gillespie (1990) subsequently explored various dimensions of farm changes on community well-being. Because farming provides the economic foundation for much of rural America, changes in farm types hold important social and economic implications for individuals, families, organizations, and communities.

—*Paul Lasley*

See also

Agriculture; Agriculture, Structure of; Farm Management; Landownership; Policy, Agricultural.

Recommended Reading

Albrecht, Don E., and Steve Murdock. *The Sociology of U.S. Agriculture: An Ecological Perspective.* Ames: Iowa State University Press, 1990.

Buttel, Frederick H., Olaf F. Larson, and Gilbert W. Gillespie, Jr. *The Sociology of Agriculture.* New York: Greenwood Press, 1990.

Cochrane, Willard W. *The Development of American Agriculture: A Historical Analysis,* 2d edition. Minneapolis: University of Minnesota Press, 1993.

Goldschmidt, Walter. *As You Sow.* Montclair, NJ: Allanheld, Osman and Company, 1978.

Haroldson, Keith D. "Two Issues in Corporate Agriculture: Anticorporate Farming Statues and Production Contracts." *Drake Law Review* 41, no. 3 (1992): 393–419.

Heffernan, William D. "Constraints in the U.S. Poultry Industry." Pp. 237–260 in *Research in Rural Sociology and Development.* Vol. 1, *Focus on Agriculture.* Edited by Harry K. Schwarzweller. Greenwich, CT: JAI Press, 1984: 237–260.

Kirkendall, Richard S. "A History of American Agriculture from Jefferson to Revolution to Crisis." Pp. I-14–I-25, Chapter 2, in *Social Science Agricultural Agenda and Strategies.* Edited by Glenn L. Johnson and James T. Bonnen. East Lansing: Michigan State University Press, 1991.

Lobao, Linda M. *Locality and Inequality: Farm and Industry Structure and Socioeconomic Conditions.* Albany: State University of New York Press, 1990.

Rodefeld, Richard D. "Who Will Own and Operate America's Farms?" Pp. 328–336, Chapter 32, in *Rural Society in the U.S.: Issues for the 1980s.* Edited by Don A. Dillman and Daryl J. Hobbs. Boulder, CO: Westview Press, 1982.

Strange, Marty. *Family Farming: A New Economic Vision.* Lincoln: University of Nebraska Press, 1988.

U.S. Department of Agriculture. *Structure Issues of American Agriculture.* Agricultural Economic Report 438, Economics, Statistics, and Cooperative Service. Washington, DC: U.S.Department of Agriculture, Government Printing Service, 1979.

———. *A Time to Choose: Summary Report on the Structure of Agriculture.* Washington, DC: U.S. Department of Agriculture, Government Printing Service, 1981.

Feedlots

Animal feeding operations, as defined by the Environmental Protection Agency (EPA) in 1976 as a result of the Clean Water Act of 1972; areas where animals are stabled or confined and fed or maintained for a total of 45 days per year or more in any 12-month period, and where crops, vegetation, forage growth, or postharvest residues are not sustained in the area of confinement during the normal growing season. The absence of vegetation is a visually determined criterion that integrates factors such as climate and soils and is also important because runoff is accelerated. Due to the bare surface, there is no plant evapotranspiration or nutrient uptake, and there is no vegetative filter. The time of concentration of runoff is very short so that peak runoff rate is high and carries much sediment (soil and manure particles). Operations with over 300 head of animals, if on a stream, or 1,000 head, if away from a stream, are considered a "concentrated animal feeding operation" (CAFO), which is considered a point source of pollution subject to state and federal regulations (U.S. Environmental Protection Agency 1993).

The major environmental issues connected with concentrated animal feeding operations such as feedlots are water quality, air quality, and sustainability of land and soil. Water supply and availability are problems in many places; it takes a well pumping continuously at 70 to 100 gallons/minute (gpm) to supply each 10,000 head of feedlot cattle with no downtime or wastage factors.

Water Pollution Abatement

A point source consists of a human-made conveyance structure for wastewater such as a pipe, ditch, or spillway. Items that are included in a point source are confinement buildings and feedlot surfaces. Slurry storage pits, stockpiles, and irrigation systems are included to the point of effluent release from the distribution device, but when the applied wastewater enters the soil, it reverts to a potential nonpoint source. Under the federal Clean Water Act of 1972, state and federal agencies regulate point sources. In major cattle-feeding states, tremendous progress has been made in controlling water pollution. Nonpoint sources consist of diffuse runoff from manure-treated cropland and pastures, rangeland, and forests. Nonpoint sources are subject largely to voluntary water quality management programs.

Runoff Control

Rainfall on an open feedlot surface produces runoff. About the first half-inch of moisture is absorbed (depending on ground slope, amount of manure, and antecedent moisture), and the remaining moisture runs off. That runoff is high in many constituents, including bacterial organisms, total solids, volatile solids, nutrients, and salts. It is about 10 to 20 times as strong as raw domestic sewage for most of these constituents. Therefore the runoff, along with other wastewater, has to be captured in runoff control structures until it can be recycled on land.

The design criterion for control of cattle feedlot runoff is the 25-year-frequency, 24-hour-duration storm, which varies from less than 3 inches to more than 10 inches per day. The Soil Conservation Service soil cover complex Curve No. 90 normally is used to convert the amount of rainfall to the predicted amount of runoff. For example, a 5-inch rainfall event will yield 3.8 inches of runoff, and a 7.5 inch storm will yield 6.3 inches of runoff.

Another component of the manure and wastewater storage volume is overflow cattle drinking/watering systems. Designs should also include additional capacity for sediment storage in the bottom of runoff holding ponds. Cattle feedlot operators need to de-water the runoff control structures by irrigating within three weeks after rainfall, if possible, unless they build additional storage capacity or design evaporation systems. It is difficult to efficiently treat organic solids in runoff retention ponds located near open feedlots because of intermittent loading. Runoff holding ponds are intended to provide short-term storage to allow for irrigation soon after rainfall.

Surface Management

Feedlot surface conditions are important from the standpoints of preventing muddy corrals in a dry climate and of controlling water and air pollution. Beef cattle feedlots use animal spacing (stocking density) of 100–400 square feet per head, depending on climate and size of cattle. Beef cattle excrete about 6 gallons of moisture per day per 1,000 pounds live-weight. At 400 square feet per head, this excretion rate amounts to an average of about 9 inches of moisture per year. At 200 square feet per head, moisture excretion is about 18 inches per year, and at 100 square feet per head, it rises to 36 inches per year. If cattle are given 600 square feet per head, moisture is nearly insignificant. However, where more area is available, the volume of runoff to be collected is greater, and dust is more likely to become a problem in summer months.

Moisture deficit (evaporation minus rainfall) is an important determinant in siting feedlots. In most cattle-feeding regions where open lots are used, evaporation exceeds rainfall (that is, moisture deficit) by 30 to 60 inches per year. Thus, additional moisture on a feedlot surface may not be a problem, but in more humid areas, there may be a tendency for lots to become muddy.

Managing the feedlot surface is very important for cattle performance and environmental protection. Manure needs to be harvested frequently. Not all of the manure should be collected. Rather, surface manure should be harvested and an undisturbed manure pack should be left. This will provide a surface seal or pad for the cattle to stand on, provide for rapid drainage from the feedlot surface, and prevent groundwater contamination. One should maintain good drainage with uniformly sloping pens, backfill and prevent wet spots, maintain the concrete aprons around feed bunks and water troughs, construct pens with 3–4 percent slope away from the feed bunk to the back of the pens, and build mounds where needed in flat pens. As much as 12 to 20 feet width of concrete apron behind the feed bunk should be in place. In a well-maintained feedlot, the cattle stand on the compacted/undisturbed manure layer above an interfacial layer of soil and moisture, with the higher-density soil just beneath. The interfacial layer provides an excellent seal that prevents infiltration, denitrifies nitrogen, and provides excellent drainage. A slice of a manure pack in a feedlot will show a black layer to be maintained over the clearly distinguished subsoil. There should be no ridges of manure beneath the fenceline that can trap water and provide a fly-breeding source.

As a standard of perfection, feedlot manure can be collected about once per month or two with a box scraper. This will improve drainage, maintain a good grade, and help as a dust control measure because there is less pulverized manure to create dust. The size of the manure sponge is reduced with frequent collection. This will maximize runoff and minimize absorption of water on a feedlot surface. This has implications with respect to odor. Odor intensity is stronger by 50 times or more from a wet feedlot than from a dry one.

Groundwater Pollution Control

Potential sources of groundwater contamination include the feedlot surface, if it is improperly managed; runoff retention ponds, which must be properly sealed; and land disposal areas, which should not be overloaded with manure or wastewater. Holding ponds must be built with proper soils engineering, testing, and placement and must meet both state and EPA requirements. Most states use a soil permeability criterion of 110^{-7} cubic meters/second (m^3/sec.), or 3.537×10^{-8} cubic feet/second (ft^3/sec.) with 1.0 to 1.5 feet of compacted clay to meet the permeability criteria. State regulations provide for separation distances between concentrated animal feeding facilities and water supply wells. For instance, a separation distance of 150 feet is the minimum state and EPA Region 6 requirement from feedlots in Texas.

Land Application of Manure and Wastewater

Land application of manure and wastewater is important from the standpoint of maintaining land and soil sustainability by managing annual nutrient balances and salt. Overfertilization of manure may cause the nitrates and phosphorus in the soil to build up, which may increase the potential for water quality impairments. In most instances, 10 tons per acre per year on irrigated cropland is an agronomic application rate that will not cause nitrate accumulation in the soil.

Every CAFO needs to have a nutrient management plan that takes into account both the amount of nitrogen and phosphorus produced in feedlot manure and crop acreage, yield, and nutrient composition. State Extension Services or commercial soil and water testing labs can supply soil test recommendations, based on the current soil nutrient status and crop nutrient uptake table, to use as a guide for nutrient planning. Runoff potential and leaching potential, as well as nutrient balance, should be taken into account when planning and conducting land application of manure and wastewater. Land area needs to be sufficient to achieve nutrient balance within a reasonable haul distance and away from streams: for irrigated cropland, about 2,250 irrigated acres for a 10,000-head feedlot with applications at an average of 10 tons per acre per year; for nonirrigated land, about twice that, or 4,500 acres. If feedlots do not have enough land, they must work with farmers to gain access to the prescribed amount of land. These acreage figures take into account a nitrogen balance but not a phosphorous balance. In areas with critical water quality problems, phosphorous concentrations in soils and dissolved phosphorous concentrations in streams may be a serious concern. In such cases, creating a phosphorous balance may require 100–500 percent more acreage for land application than creating a nitrogen balance would require, because plants take up less phosphorous than nitrogen and phosphorous can cause water quality problems (entriphication) in streams at much lower concentrations than nitrogen. The advice of a professional soil and plant scientist can be important in making these determinations.

It takes much less land for irrigation of the open-lot runoff because runoff can be applied at 4 to 6 inches per year. If annual average runoff yield from a feedlot is 4 inches per year, then about an acre of cropland per acre of feedlot drainage area is needed in an average year for runoff irrigation. More may be needed in humid climates.

Feedlot runoff typically is very high in total salinity and is in the medium range of soluble sodium. More irrigation water may be needed to manage salts and grow sufficient crops to take up the applied nutrients. Ideally, feedlots should have supplemental irrigation water available for dilution, adequate crop watering, or leaching as needed to properly manage the nutrients and salts.

Odor Control

Odors are an annoyance to people that affects their well-being. There are four quantifiable aspects of odor related to climate and to management of the feedlot surface: frequency, intensity (or concentration), duration, and offensiveness. In an open feedlot, odor intensity, duration, and offensiveness are partially controllable by managing manure moisture and reducing the inventory of manure and wastewater. Equipment and methods to measure the strength or intensity of an odor include a scentometer, butanol olfactometer, dynamic triangle forced-choice olfactometer, gas chromatography, chemical specific detectors, and electronic odor detectors (Sweeten 1995). For instance, on a dry open lot surface, the odor was less than 60 to 100 odor units (or dilutions to threshold). On a wet feedlot surface, the odor concentration went up to 2,000 to 3,000 dilutions to threshold (Tucker 1992). This indicates that the odor concentration produced from a wet feedlot surface would be 20 to 50 times greater than for a typically fairly dry feedlot surface.

Odor can be quantified and managed accordingly and the operation changed as necessary. Odor dissipates rapidly with distance except in atmospheric inversion situations. Feedlot sites that are downwind of neighbors by 1 mile or more avoid a valley situation that can limit dispersion and are favorable for odor dispersion.

Dust Control

Cattle stir up dust in early evenings in dry areas, which can create both a nuisance condition and the potential for traffic accidents. High-volume air samplers are used to measure total suspended particulate (TSP), and a PM-10 monitoring device is used to measure dust with less than 10-micron aerodynamic particle size. In California, average concentrations were 654 micrograms per cubic meter ($\mu g/m3$) average total suspended particulates at 25 feedlots (Elam et al. 1971). From research in 1987 at Texas A&M University, a mean of 412 $\mu g/m3$ was determined after monitoring three Texas feedlots on three different occasions (Sweeten et al. 1988). Feedlot dust can be partially controlled by harvesting manure frequently; increasing stocking density; sprinkling pens and alleys; and surfacing the alleys and pens with fly ash, which currently is being studied.

The main livestock waste management issues are surface and groundwater quality management; soil and land sustainability with respect to manure and effluent utilization for nutrient recycling; and air pollution control for odor and dust. Technologies have been developed that satisfy many of these environmental concerns and are largely compatible with improved management of cattle. Some states have strong regulatory programs. There is much happening in the livestock waste management area with respect to adoption of the best management practices to meet the requirements of state and federal agencies. It is time that all producers with CAFOs develop, adopt, and follow pollution prevention plans.

—*John M. Sweeten*

See also

Animal Rights/Welfare; Environmental Regulations; Livestock Industry; Livestock Production; Pasture; Ranching.

References

Albin, R. C., and G. B. Thompson. *Cattle Feeding: A Guide to Management*. 2d ed. Amarillo, TX: Trafton Printing, 1996.

Elam, C. J., J. W. Algeo, and T. Westing. *Measurement and Control of Feedlot Particulate Matter: Bulletin C: How to Control Feedlot Pollution*. Barkersville: California Cattle Feeders Associations. January 1971.

Sweeten, J. M. *Cattle Feedlot Waste Management Practices for Water and Air Pollution Control*. B-1671. College Station, TX: Texas Agricultural Extension Service, Texas A&M University, 1990.

Sweeten, J. M. "Odor Measurement Technology and Applications: A State-of-the-Art Review." Pp. 214–229 in *Proceedings, Seventh International Symposium on Agricultural and Food Processing Wastes (ISAFPW95), June 18–20, 1995*. Chicago, IL: American Society of Agricultural Engineers, 1995.

Sweeten, J. M., C. B. Parnell, R. S. Etheredge, and D. Osborne. "Dust Emissions in Cattle Feedlots." Pp. 557–578 in *Stress and Disease in Cattle*. Edited by J. L. Howard. Vol. 3, no. 3 of the Veterinary Clinics in North America: Food Animal Practice series. Philadelphia, PA: W. B. Saunders, November 1988.

Tucker, R. "Odour Measurements from Simulated Feedlot Pads." Pp. 103–121 in *Odour Update '92. Proceedings of a Workshop on Agricultural Odours*. MRC Report No. DAQ 64/24. Toowoomba, Queensland, Australia: Department of Primary Industries, 1992.

U.S. Environmental Protection Agency. 1993. "National Pollutant Discharge Elimination System General Permit and Reporting Requirements for Discharges from Concentrated Animal Feeding Operations." *Federal Register* (8 February 1993): 7610–7644.

Films, Rural

Major motion pictures in which natural and economic forces pose threats to the rural way of life or in which a nonurban backdrop forms a significant element. Rural America constitutes a significant element in about 5 percent of film. Films that belong to a specific genre draw from a selection of characters, story types, settings, situations, costumes, themes, and visual images shared by other films in that genre. Phases of genres include the naive primitive phase, the more complex classical phase, the revisionist phase, and the caricature or parodic phase. As a genre, rural film has passed through the naive primitive and classical phases and remains in the revisionist phase, with no films yet meeting the criteria of the parodic phase. Moving from the naïve through the revisionist genre phases are films about the plight of family farmers. From the 1936 *Plow That Broke the Plains* to the 1980s movies *Places in the Heart, Country,* and *The River,* a portrayal pattern emerges.

The developing genre of rural film has as a central theme the good rural family threatened by economic and natural forces beyond its ability to understand, much less control. Additional elements include the taciturn family spiritually linked to the land, strong women who assume leadership roles, and collective action that unites and celebrates the disenfranchised.

The Naive Primitive Phase

Breaking ground in several ways, the *Plow That Broke the Plains* (1936) intended to reveal the disaster the Dust Bowl wreaked upon the 400 million acres of prairie from the Dakotas to Texas. The film also revealed the human contribution to that disaster. Fifty years of history compressed into 28 minutes of film showed the natural prairie grazed, homesteaded, plowed, deeply plowed, planted an excessive amount of wheat in support of the war, then blown away by five rainless years. People who sought their fortunes "200 miles from water, 200 miles from town, but the land is new," as the film's narration intoned, were turned into homeless wanderers. The film's epilogue showed the U.S. Resettlement Administration transplanting 4,500 families to small farms; by 1935, 30,000 people a month abandoned their homes to drift west.

The *Plow That Broke the Plains* was the first motion picture completed by the U.S. Resettlement Administration. It was also the first motion picture placed in the congressional archives. Pare Lorentz, film critic and commentator, directed the film to Hollywood standards. Visuals and music carried the story, with only 700 words of dialogue in 2,700 feet of film. The characters were the people whose story was being told; no actors were employed for the film.

The film was widely acclaimed, endorsed by the Better Films Committee, the National Board of Review, and Pres. Franklin D. Roosevelt. It was accepted for the files of the Museum of Modern Art Film Library, but it was not accepted by commercial theaters. The film's running length was given as the reason for keeping the film off commercial screens. It was considered too long for a newsreel and too short for a feature, but Lorentz blamed the commercial producers' hatred of the New Deal for problems in putting *The Plow That Broke the Plains* before an audience.

One Hollywood producer was quoted as saying, "We resent many things the administration is doing. That is why the film never will be booked into our commercial theaters. We would not release your picture even if it were *Ben-Hur,* unless, of course, we happened to need the use of five submarines for a Navy picture" ("Dust-Storm Film" 1936, 22–23). The industry insisted that it was lack of market appeal rather than their own fear of government-subsidized competition that confined showing of *The Plow That Broke the Plains* to small independent exhibitors.

Of Mice and Men (1939) and *The Grapes of Wrath* (1940) reinforced the relationship between the Great Depression and rural life as an element of the rural film genre. They extended the genre by adding the issue of class structure, which would be transformed into one of collective action by the 1980s. *Of Mice and Men* emphasized, through the story George told Lenny, the ownership of land. In *The Grapes of Wrath* the Joad family, displaced from their farm, epitomized the spiritual strength, sense of community, and family values typical of cinematic farm families.

The Classical Phase

Salt of the Earth (1953) added the complexity that brought the genre into the second, classical phase by attributing to mine workers the qualities of the farm family—hardworking, close-knit families set against a harshly beautiful, larger-than-life landscape. The film shared much with *The Plow That Broke the Plains* and subsequent rural films. *Salt of the Earth* was a documentary. It used real people rather than actors to tell the story of striking mine workers. It faced distribution difficulties, not because Hollywood feared competition from government-subsidized films but because government feared ideological competition from blacklisted Hollywood exiles collaborating with the International Union of Mine, Mill, and Smelter Workers. The union had been expelled from the Congress of Industrial Organizations (CIO) in 1950 for being Communist-dominated.

The movie's intent was similar to that of *The Plow That Broke the Plains*. Producer Paul Jarrico and director Herbert Biberman wanted to create stories "drawn from the living experiences of people long ignored in Hollywood—the real working men and women of America" (Pallot 1995, 747). The silent wife seen in *The Plow That Broke the Plains* continued to toil alongside her husband, but here she gained a voice as she picketed in her husband's place when the mining company won an injunction forbidding the miners to picket.

Hollywood followed *Salt of the Earth* with safer fare. *Picnic* (1955) reinforced the sense of idyllic rural life by showing how a small Kansas town could be disrupted by an outsider. The outsider here embodied sexual temptation rather than the greed symbolized by bankers, who were outsiders to the farm ethic and were found in several subsequent films that together constituted the third phase of the rural film genre.

The Revisionist Phase

Collective action was established well beyond the hints found in *The Grapes of Wrath* as the genre entered the third phase with *Northern Lights* (1979), *Places in the Heart* (1984), *Country* (1984), and *The River* (1984). Although least known, the docudrama *Northern Lights* epitomized the rural film genre's revisionist phase. Like *The Plow That Broke the Plains*, *Northern Lights* set the family farm against the backdrop of the Great Depression. But nature was not the only enemy; economic institutions like banks and grain elevators conspired in the destruction of the independent farmer.

Northern Lights questioned and reinforced family

values by showing the ebb and flow of the Sorenson family, growing through marriage, the iron bond of family loyalty extending to the family into which a member has married. The bond among family members was typically expressed in deed more than in word, with the aging mother most silent of all. The family shrank as members died or moved away, becoming a metaphor for the dissolution of the family farm.

In one scene from the movie, the banker fastened his luxurious fur coat securely over his heart against the chill Dakota wind and against the wrath of his neighbors as he forecloses upon their farm. The young woman, like the women of *Salt of the Earth,* gained a voice, protesting the socioeconomic condition while demanding romance.

Ray Sorenson became increasingly disillusioned, perceiving the myth of rugged individualism as a hoax perpetrated upon the farmers to maintain economic power in the hands of a few. As an activist for the Nonpartisan League that united prairie farmers regardless of political party affiliation, he traveled from farm to farm achieving uneven success for the League. But the effect on the farm, managed by his brother, was consistent. The bank threatened foreclosure, and the grain elevators refused Sorenson's crops. The film ends on a note of poignant, hopeless optimism, showing Sorenson, now an old man in a nursing home, jumping rope to maintain his agility and strength for future battles.

Hollywood's offering *Days of Heaven* (1978), nearly contemporary with *Northern Lights,* represented a genre throwback reminiscent of *The Grapes of Wrath* and *Of Mice and Men* but one that contributed to the genre by incorporating biblical themes and reinforcing the notions of family fragmentation and reconfiguration. Migrant laborer Bill and his lover Abby masqueraded as brother and sister, enabling the farm owner to marry Abby. The three, plus Bill's sister Linda, became, briefly, a family. The wrath of Jehovah fell upon Bill and Abby, and the family disintegrated when their conspiracy was discovered. Although the threshing machines, locusts, and wheat fields were interchangeable with those of *Northern Lights,* *Days of Heaven* lacked the theme of collective action that had come to mark the genre.

Places in the Heart (1984), *Country* (1984), and *The River* (1984) popularized the genre, applying the formula that had evolved through *Northern Lights.* The differences between the settings were immaterial. *Places in the Heart* was set in Texas, *Country* in Iowa, and *The River* in Tennessee, but all three share screen-filling landscapes and battles with nature—oppressive sunshine and heat, torna-

does, and raging rivers. There is a Depression-era desolation to each of the films, although only *Places in the Heart* was set during the Depression. Only *Places in the Heart* made rural spirituality overt, opening with a montage of the entire community saying grace and closing with a communion service that unites the living and the dead in worship. The soundtrack featured familiar hymns.

Places in the Heart screenwriter/director Robert Benton said "there is an instinct . . . that we can't help creating families. I have spent all my life forming families" (Dworkin 1984, 29–33). The film quickly questioned the stereotype of the idyllic farm family, however, by revealing Edna's brother-in-law as a less-than-faithful husband and previewing the shattering of Edna's family by the shooting of her sheriff/husband.

Country shared *Places in the Heart*'s emphasis on religion, hymns, and family disintegration. Jewell's spiritual resources gave her strength to assume her position of leadership when she lost her husband, not through death but through psychological breakdown, as Gil became an abusive drunk.

Both *Places in the Heart* and *Country* celebrated matriarchal populism. The widowed Edna gathered representatives of the disenfranchised—Black itinerant Moze and blind Mr. Will—into her home and her family. Jewell organized her fellow farmers to fight farm foreclosures by the Farmers Home Administration (FmHA). In a demonstration scene reminiscent of *Salt of the Earth,* local farmers gathered round the auctioneer's truck chanting, "Don't sell! Don't sell!"

Unlike *Places in the Heart, Country* suggested, if not a happy ending, at least a reprieve for the farmers, adding to film credits a statement implying that protests like that at the Ivy farm forced the Reagan administration to place a moratorium on FmHA farm foreclosures. *Places in the Heart* offered no evidence to suggest Edna would survive the next season when Moze was forced by the Ku Klux Klan (KKK) to move on.

Even Mae took the reins of the farm in *The River* (1984) as her husband Tom fought the floods and buyout attacks on the farm by becoming "scab" labor in a distant foundry. Despite the hardships faced by the Garveys, director Mark Rydell moved away from the grim documentary style to provide a romantic vision of farm life described as "sugary" and "inauthentic" (Wall 1985, 105–106). The film's "affirmative view of life" appealed to Rydell, who described himself as "a celebrator of life and an enemy of cynicism" (Stern 1984, 19–20). The criticism of inauthenticity must have been particularly painful, considering that

Universal Studios bought 440 acres of land in Kingsport, Tennessee, to create a working farm as the movie set.

The collective action of *The River* took a nonpolitical turn when neighbors joined Tom's effort to hold back the flood with his tractor. *The River* is generally less political than its counterparts. *Places in the Heart* fought racism and sexism. *Country* protested against the FmHA. But *The River* lacked even a single bureaucrat from the U.S. Department of Agriculture (USDA).

The rural film genre has been dormant since 1985. Although *A River Runs Through It* placed religion and spirituality in the Montana rivers and rapids, thus visually recalling the genre, it did not address issues of rural life. There was no farm, real or imaginary, to which to cling; there was no attack by nature or economic forces; there was no collective action.

Rural-Related Film Genres

Westerns. With one notable exception, significant rural content is present in only 5 percent or fewer of films outside of the rural film genre. All of Western settings can be described as rural, yielding landscapes of the Great Plains, Rocky Mountains, and barren deserts dotted with cattle ranches, bunkhouses, and frontier towns. Identified as the "American genre," the Western appeared in 1903 with Edwin S. Porter's *The Great Train Robbery*. Westerns contain character types like cowboys; town marshals; Indians; dance hall girls; schoolmarms; cavalry officers; saloon keepers; Indian agents; gamblers; rustlers; and others identifiable by their costumes, props, behaviors, and situations.

The Great Train Robbery typified the primitive phase of the Western. The more complex classical phase was represented by the work of John Ford. Among Westerns, *High Noon* (1952), *The Wild Bunch* (1969), and *McCabe and Mrs. Miller* (1971) are cited as examples of the revisionist phase, whereas *Blazing Saddles* (1974) took irreverent aim at the conventions of the Western, bringing it into the parodic phase.

Action/Adventure Films. Within the genre of action/adventure films, the rural setting functions as a backdrop for the chase scenes, a place to get through or hide in as the film progresses from one point of conflict to the next, in 5 percent of the films. Of these, biker films account for 22 percent and trucker films for nearly 7 percent.

From 1954, when *The Wild One* was produced, through the 1980s, more than 70 biker films were made. Rarely sporting urban content, biker movies are described as "Westerns on wheels." Yet the protagonists in biker films are outlaws rebelling against civilization, whereas the protagonists in Westerns bring civilization to an untamed territory. Instead of highlighting sueded and fringed leather, chromed motorcycles are emphasized. Gang fights and gang rapes replace the gun duels at dawn that are characteristic of the Western. As Marlon Brando said in reflecting on *The Wild One*, "Instead of finding out why young people tend to bunch into groups that seek expression in violence, all we did was show the violence" (Sterns and Sterns 1992, 55–58).

Other Genres. Rural content is significant in 4 percent each of children's viewing and musicals. It drops to 3 percent of the mystery/suspense genre, 2 percent of science fiction/fantasy, and 1 percent of comedy. Fewer than 1 percent of documentaries (0.8 percent) and dramas (0.3 percent), the categories that spawned the rural film genre, offer significant rural content.

The rural backdrop is essential to many children's adventures, including four versions of *The Adventures of Huckleberry Finn* (1939, 1960, 1978, and 1993). They, with *The Adventures of Tom Sawyer* (1938) bring Mark Twain's bad boys of the Mississippi River to life. Other classic children's books with film adaptations set beyond the bounds of civilization include *The Adventures of Robinson Crusoe* (1952), *Swiss Family Robinson* (1960), and *Adventures of the Wilderness Family* (1975). Among musicals are the obligatory Westerns like *Can't Help Singing* (1944) and *Calamity Jane* (1953), a screen adaptation of *Oklahoma*.

In the mystery/suspense genre, the rural backdrop becomes an isolated location in which to terrorize victims. *The Desperate Hours* (1955) is only one example of a family imprisoned and tortured in their rural home, beyond reach or rescue, for the first 90 minutes of the 112-minute film. The rural law enforcement officer-turned-detective is another cliché of the genre, found in such films as *They Only Kill their Masters* (1972) and *Flashpoint* (1984).

Time travel and apocalyptic themes dominate among science fiction/fantasy films with rural backdrops. An example is *Cave Girl* (1985), in which scientific accident causes characters to reappear in prehistoric times. *Jurassic Park* (1993) brings prehistoric beings into a modern-day theme park. *The Day the Earth Caught Fire* (1962), *City Limits* (1985), *Lawless Land* (1988), and *The Handmaid's Tale* (1990) are among films addressing the reemergence of a rural nation following mass destruction resulting from uncontrolled scientific progress.

—Ann E. Preston

See also
Arts; History, Rural; Literature; Music; Theatrical Entertainment.
References
"Dust-Storm Film: U.S. Pictures Processes on Plains Leading to Tragedy." *Literary Digest* (16 May 1936): 22–23.
Dworkin, Susan. "An Epic of the American Soul." *Ms.* (October 1984): 29–33.
Lorentz, Pare. *The Plow That Broke the Plains.* Washington, DC: U.S. Resettlement Administration, 1936.
Pallot, James. *Movie Guide.* New York: Berkeley Publishing Group, 1995.
Pym, John, ed. *Time Out Film Guide,* 4th ed. New York: Penguin, 1995.
Stern, Gary. "The River Rolls On." *Horizon* (December 1984): 19–20.
Sterns, Jane, and Michael Sterns. *Encyclopedia of Popular Culture.* New York: Harper Perennial, 1992.
"They the People." *New Republic* (5 August 1936): 382–383.
Wall, James M. "Current Cinema." *Christian Century* (30 January 1985): 105–106.

Finance, Farm

See Farm Finance

Financial Intermediaries

Firms that channel funds and securities between savers and borrowers. The financial intermediaries serving agriculture provide the conduit for funds to flow from savers to borrowers in the amounts necessary to finance agricultural production, machinery, and equipment (known as non–real estate debt) and agricultural real estate. Although other entities are financed in rural America (such as municipalities, small nonagricultural businesses, and residential housing), only the intermediaries financing agricultural production and capital will be discussed here.

The four largest institutional suppliers of credit for agricultural production and capital are commercial banks, the Farm Credit System, the Consolidated Farm Service (formerly the Farmers Home Administration), and life insurance companies that lend only on farm real estate (see tables). The U.S. Department of Agriculture (USDA) reports that another major supplier of credit to agriculture for both real estate and non–real estate debt is as individuals and others. In 1992, more than one-fifth of the agricultural real estate and non–real estate debt to agriculture was supplied by individuals and others, including trade credit supplied by captive finance companies. Finally, the Commodity Credit Corporation made loans prior to the 1990s that were used to finance storage and drying facilities but currently does not make such loans. Each of these financial intermediaries is discussed in the sections that follow.

Commercial Banks

Commercial banks have historically been the largest institutional source of non–real estate farm loan funds and an important source of real estate farm loan funds. For years, the commercial banking system served rural America through a network of numerous independent institutions organized as "unit" organizations. In a unit-banking system, an individual bank maintains only one office or place of business. However, changes in bank branching laws resulted in a trend toward fewer, larger commercial banks that are part of multibank holding companies.

Rural banks in unit-banking states tended to be small and were limited in size by the amount of business in their respective communities. In the past, the laws of many states either prohibited or limited branch banking, which refers to multiple offices of a single firm. However, since the mid-1980s, restrictions on branching eased considerably in many states. Interstate branch-banking legislation was also passed by Congress and allows banks to purchase and operate banks in all states. The result was a trend toward fewer, but larger, commercial banking institutions.

During the late 1980s and the first half of the 1990s, there was a significant decline in the number of commercial banks in the United States and growth in size of those institutions that remain. This trend is expected to continue for the remainder of the decade. Some forecasters projected that the number of U.S. commercial banks will decline from almost 12,000 in 1990 to approximately 8,000 by the year 2000. Most of this restructuring will occur from mergers and acquisitions, not from the failure of commercial banks.

Although this decline in numbers and growth in size will result in somewhat fewer options for agricultural producers and local agribusinesses to borrow money, it is not expected to result in a dramatic decrease or serious problem of access to funds or capital markets. Larger commercial banking organizations may be able to provide a broader set of credit and financially related services to agricultural producers and agribusinesses than smaller unit banks.

The trend in the banking sector appears to be a move to a more focused business strategy that targets specific segments of the market with specific products

Table 1
Non–Real Estate Farm Debt (%)
(Excluding Operator Households and CCC Crop Loans),
31 December 1980, 1985, 1990, and 1992

	1980	1985	1990	1992
All commercial banks	39	44	49	52
Farm Credit System	26	18	16	16
Consolidated Farm Service				
(formerly Farmers Home Administration)	13	19	15	11
Individuals and others	22	19	20	21
Total	100	100	100	100

Source: U.S. Department of Agriculture. *Agricultural Income and Finance: Situation and Outlook Report.* U.S. Department of Agriculture, Economic Research Service, AIS-52, February 1994.

Table 2
Real Estate Farm Debt (%)
(Excluding Operator Households),
31 December 1980, 1985, 1990, and 1992

	1980	1985	1990	1992
All commercial banks	9	11	22	25
Farm Credit System	37	42	35	33
Consolidated Farm Service				
(formerly Farmers Home Administration)	8	10	10	8
Life Insurance Companies	13	11	13	12
Individuals and others	31	26	20	22
CCC storage and drying facilities loans	2	a	0	0
Total	100	100	100	100

[a]Less than 1 percent.

Source: U.S. Department of Agriculture. *Agricultural Income and Finance: Situation and Outlook Report,* U.S. Department of Agriculture, Economic Research Service, AIS-52, February 1994.

and services. The concept is to provide a broader set of products and services to a narrower market and to develop more complete financial relationships with fewer customers. The implication of this strategy for borrowers is that those who are targeted will receive more attention and have a broader array of products and services, but those who are not targeted will have fewer options and choices.

Farm Credit System

The Farm Credit System (FCS) is one example of a financial intermediary serving agriculture that was established as a result of past inadequacies in the financial markets in meeting the credit needs of agriculture. Its beginning dates back to 1916, when the Federal Land Banks (FLBs) were first established. The primary purpose of these banks was to make long-term agricultural loans secured by agricultural real estate. These institutions enabled pro-

ducers to obtain more favorable loan terms for land purchase and other real estate improvements than was the case with commercial banks. Later, associations were formed at the local level to deliver loan funds to producers. These associations were called Federal Land Bank Associations (FLBAs).

The Federal Intermediate Credit Banks (FICBs) were established in 1923 to provide a mechanism to which commercial banks and local finance corporations could either rediscount or sell their short- and intermediate-term agricultural loans (non–real estate debt) and thereby increase the flow of funds to producers. The FICBs in turn obtained their funds from the sale of fixed-term debentures in the national money markets.

Initially, FICBs were used very little by local financial institutions. Hence, a greatly enlarged credit program for agriculture was launched in 1933. The program created Production Credit Associations (PCAs), which in turn linked farmers with FICBs. It also established 13 Banks for Cooperatives to provide financing for farm cooperatives. All these organizations—Federal Land Banks, Federal Intermediate Credit Banks, and Banks for Cooperatives—were organized as cooperatives and were merged into the FCS. The FCS was then organized into 12 districts across the country.

During the "farm crisis" of the 1980s, the FCS experienced severe repayment problems in its loan portfolio. The result was implementation of major cost-cutting measures, including districtwide consolidations of PCAs and FLBAs, which was followed in several districts by mergers of PCAs with FLBAs into Agricultural Credit Associations (ACAs). An ACA provides both non–real estate and real estate loan funds to agricultural producers. At the district level, several FLBs merged with FICBs to form Farm Credit Banks (FCBs). The focus during the 1990s was on mergers involving the 12 Farm Credit System districts. Also, ten of the 12 district banks for cooperatives and the Central Bank for Cooperatives merged to form COBANK. This trend toward fewer but larger district banks will probably continue throughout the remainder of the 1990s.

The leaner, more streamlined organizational structure forced on the FCS by the difficulties of the 1980s will help it be a more cost-effective lender to agriculture for the remainder of the 1990s. The strength of the FCS in the 1990s should be its ability to handle very large loans cost-effectively; to provide a balanced package of short-, intermediate-, and long-term credit; and to provide expertise in agricultural lending. To gain cost-effectiveness with its

A bank in Bagley, Minnesota.

revised infrastructure, the FCS will probably expand its efforts to provide credit to larger farming operations. Consequently, the FCS may increase its market share of real estate and non–real estate loans from the levels seen in 1992. The increased share will no doubt come at the expense of commercial banks (see Tables 1 and 2).

Consolidated Farm Service

Consolidated Farm Service (CFS), formerly the Farmers Home Administration (FmHA), is a governmental lending organization operating under the auspices of the USDA. The bulk of the CFS lending in the past has been to young, beginning producers or others with limited resources who have the potential for ultimate success but who are unable to obtain sufficient financing from commercial sources. As these producers become better established, they are expected to use commercial sources of financing.

Under the authorization of the Farm and Rural Development Act of 1972, the CFS also guarantees qualified loans made by commercial banks and other private lenders. Loan terms are negotiated directly between the borrower and the lender. CFS guarantees up to 90 percent of the loan. In return, the commercial lender makes some concession on interest rates and makes loans to producers who would not otherwise be eligible for a loan from the commercial lender.

In the future, the market share of the CFS will probably be influenced more by social and political considerations than by economic conditions. The emphasis by commercial banks and the FCS on lending to large, commercial farming operations may result in reduced availability of credit for agricultural producers whose size or creditworthiness is less than acceptable for those lenders,

so the public sector may be asked to fill this gap. Social and political considerations will also strongly influence the amount and types of loans offered through CFS, which will no doubt decrease the authorization for direct loans and increase the authorization for guaranteed loans. Both direct and guaranteed loans provide credit to beginning farmers, farmers who cannot secure loan funds from commercial lenders, and farmers who are socially disadvantaged. The overall market share of the CFS is expected to erode over the next decade.

Life Insurance Companies

Life insurance companies are profit-oriented institutions whose principal financial activities are the sale of life insurance policies and payments of claims to policyholders. The long-run nature of their business requires that they accumulate and hold large reserves. These reserves generally are invested in a diversified portfolio of low-risk investments. Mortgages on agricultural real estate are one of these investment alternatives. Two problems are associated with mortgage loans on agricultural real estate from insurance companies. First, insurance companies often withdraw from agricultural lending during periods of tight money. Second, insurance companies generally restrict loans to larger or lower-risk borrowers.

Efforts to reduce per-dollar volume cost will result in an emphasis on lending to very large commercial farming operations and may result in fewer loans being made directly by employees of insurance companies and a greater number of loans purchased from other organizations, in particular commercial banks. The market share of the insurance companies is not expected to grow from its 1992 level of about 12 percent and may even decline slightly over the decade.

Individuals and Others

Trade credit represents an increasing source of non–real estate financing for producers in several areas of the United States. Trade credit arises from a merchandising transaction in which a loan originates with one of the participating parties. Generally, the originator is the seller of an agricultural input: feed, fuel, fertilizer, machinery, or a building.

The emphasis by commercial banks and the FCS on competing for the business of large agricultural operations may reduce the credit available for creditworthy customers who operate smaller operations. Captive finance companies that are subsidiaries of input suppliers appear to be an emerging supplier of credit for customers who operate smaller agricultural operations as well as some of the larger-volume borrowers.

These companies combine the sale and financing activities, much as automobile dealerships currently do. In many cases, these companies provide a form of collateral lending that requires less documentation and is more convenient for the borrower than applying for loan funds at conventional lenders. This approach is widely used in the farm machinery industry and is being used on an experimental basis or being studied by several seed, fertilizer, chemical, petroleum, and feed suppliers.

Finally, individuals finance a substantial portion of the agricultural real estate sold in the United States., either through contract sales or direct lending, particularly between family members. This practice is likely to continue in the foreseeable future.

—*Freddie L. Barnard*

See also
Agricultural and Resource Economics; Cooperatives; Decentralization; Farm Finance; Policy, Economic.
References
Barnard, Freddie L., Michael Boehlje, Julian H. Atkinson, and Kenneth A. Foster. "Financing Agriculture." *Indiana Agriculture 2000: A Strategic Perspective.* West Lafayette, IN: Department of Agricultural Economics, Purdue University, 1992.
Barry, Peter J., John A. Hopkin, and Chester B. Baker. *Financial Management in Agriculture.* 2d ed. Danville, IL: Interstate Printers and Publishers, 1979.
DeVuyst, Cheryl, David Lins, and Bruce Sherrick. "Financing Illinois Agriculture." *Illinois Agriculture, Agribusiness and the Rural Economy: Strategic Issues for the Next Century* (Special Publication 85, February). Edited by David A. Lins and Harold D. Guither. Urbana-Champaign: Department of Agricultural Economics, University of Illinois, 1994.
Kohl, David M. *Weighing the Variables: A Guide to Ag Credit Management.* Washington, DC: American Bankers Association, 1992.
Penson, John B., Jr., and David A. Lins. *Agricultural Finance: An Introduction to Micro and Macro Concepts.* Englewood Cliffs, NJ: Prentice-Hall, 1980.
U.S. Department of Agriculture. *Agricultural Income and Finance: Situation and Outlook Report.* USDA-ERS, AIS-52, February. Washington, DC: U.S. Department of Agriculture, Economic Research Service, 1994.

Folklore

Beliefs, customs, narratives, and other unofficial traditions that are passed on and shared by a group of people. Folklore has been described as "those materials in culture that circulate traditionally among members of any group in different versions, whether in oral form or by means of customary example, as well as the processes of traditional performance and communication" (Brunvand 1986, 9). The focus of this entry is on three main types of folklore: oral, customary, and material folk traditions. This tripartite division was proposed by American folklorist Jan Harold Brunvand (1986), and is widely accepted by professional folklorists and students of traditional life. Family folklore and the mystique of rural folklore also are discussed.

Oral Folklore

In some parts of the United States, folklore is still thought to be synonymous with oral tradition, owing to the large number of folkways preserved in speech or song: legends, folktales, myths, jokes, proverbs, riddles, rhymes, tongue twisters, lullabies, ballads, and work songs. Certain regions of the rural United States are believed to be unusually rich in oral folklore, including Appalachia, Cajun Louisiana, the Ozark Mountains, and the American Southwest. But in truth, rural folklore can be found wherever people have established agriculturally based communities, farms, ranches, or a country way of life. These folkways bind together the people of a rural area, often giving them a special sense of shared identity.

In the Great Plains region, for example, prairie farmers poke fun at themselves and the harsh realities of their own environment by the telling of "tall tales." These humorous stories typically deal with a wide range of natural phenomena: blizzards, droughts, dust storms, floods, hailstorms, and tornadoes. Nebraska folklorist Roger Welsch (1980) documented many of these tall tales in his volume *Shingling the Fog and Other Plains Lies.* He included stories about "strange critters," including aggressive hoop snakes, fleet-footed jackrabbits, and gigantic mosquitoes.

Oral folklore need not consist of stories or lengthy rhymes but can include short expressions or even single-word utterances. Folk speech often gives rise to a distinct but unofficial vocabulary that is readily understood by people who share a particular occupation (for example, truck farming) or who reside within a particular region (for example, the Florida Everglades). In the Colorado sugar beet country, the term "ditch rider" describes an individual who decides which irrigation farmers will be given a "head" of water and at what time.

Winfred Blevins (1993) amassed approximately 5,000 folk terms and expressions known to people throughout the western United States. The vast majority of these regional terms spring from the rural portions of the American West, including "borrow pit" (the ditch to the side of a road or highway), "fraidy hole" (a storm cellar), "nice kitty" (a skunk!), "sky farmer" (an agriculturalist in arid country with no access to any irrigation), and "wish book" (a mail-order catalog).

Customary Folklore

Although customary folklore may include oral-based information and expressions, it is distinguished by its emphasis on custom, belief, and actual practice. Customary folklore includes folk dances, folk dramas, folk games, folk gestures, life-cycle customs, seasonal celebrations, festivals, folk religion, and folk beliefs (or "superstitions"). Folk beliefs deal with nearly every aspect of human existence and encompass traditional phenomena such as folk medicine, weather-related beliefs, and even water witching.

Due to their geographic isolation and land-based way of life, rural people sometimes engaged in practices that were ridiculed by city folk. In the days before modern medical facilities and licensed physicians, rural folk relied on their own home remedies, herbal cures, and folk medical practices. Even today, many folkways persist in rural areas of the United States, especially in regions where there are identifiable ethnic populations. Wayland D. Hand (1976), in an edited volume on American folk medicine, provides considerable information about health-related folkways among Native Americans in California and the American Southwest; Mexican Americans in Texas and southern Arizona; Amish enclaves in Pennsylvania, Ohio, and Indiana; and a number of other ethnic groups.

Traditional weather-related beliefs (or weather lore) are especially common in rural areas where concerns with climatic conditions are tied to agricultural success and economic well-being. George D. Freier (1989), for example, collected and examined some 600 proverbs and folk beliefs pertaining to the weather. An expert in atmospheric physics, Freier concluded that a surprising number of these traditional beliefs withstood the test of time and thus have scientific validity.

Scholars Evon Z. Vogt and Ray Hyman, on the other hand, did not find the folk custom of water witching (or water dowsing) to be an empirically reliable technique. In their classic study, *Water Witching U.S.A.* (1979), they point out that water witching (i.e., the use of a forked stick to find underground water) is not confined to isolated geographic areas. Water witching is found among practitioners of all educational backgrounds and in cities and rural communities.

Material Folk Traditions

Folkways that result in handmade objects are known as material folk traditions. These are best represented by phenomena such as folk art, folk crafts, folk architecture, folk dress, and traditional foodways. When basic skills are passed on from one generation to the next in an informal manner, such skills also can be considered to fall within the realm of folk tradition: agricultural practices, gardening, animal husbandry, fishing, hunting, and trapping.

During the past century, professional folklorists directed their attention to collecting oral folklore and customary folklore in rural portions of the United States. In recent years, however, a growing number of studies documented material folk traditions. Many of these studies were inspired by Henry Glassie's ground-breaking 1968 work on material folk culture in the eastern United States and Michael Owen Jones's influential 1975 study, *The Hand Made Object and Its Maker*.

Few material objects typify and symbolize rural life as much as barns. Thus it is not surprising that several books have traced the history and distribution of barn types in various parts of the rural United States. Robert F. Ensminger (1992), for example, made an exhaustive study of the Pennsylvania barn. Even something as commonplace in the American Midwest as the corncrib received scholarly attention. Keith E. Roe (1988) traces the history of corncribs and examines their place in the folklife of countless rural Americans.

In studying material folk traditions, folklorists seldom lose sight of the human dimension. Handmade objects are interesting, but even more interesting are the people who preserve folk traditions and keep them alive. Professional folklorists work closely with informants who are intimately familiar with certain material folk traditions. In the course of their interviews and informal interaction, folklorists attempt to explain how and why certain traditions are maintained.

Folklorist Simon J. Bronner (1985) worked with several male chain carvers in southern Indiana. These men, who meticulously carved chains out of blocks of wood with pocketknives, were all retired. Despite living in towns and cities, they still had strong ties to their rural past. In documenting the material folk tradition of chain carving, Bronner soon discovered that he was also examining how elderly men coped with the rural-urban transition in their own lives. Thus, folklore often mirrors the forces of change, cultural adaptation, tradition, and cultural continuity.

Still another example of a study that examines the lives of rural folk and their folkways is Troyd A. Geist's *Faces of Identity, Hands of Skill* (1995). Geist profiles 15 North Dakota folk artists, many of whom have strong rural ties. The folk artists range from a Native American woman on the Fort Berthold Indian Reservation who continues the ancient gardening practices of her Mandan ancestors, to a Ukrainian American farm woman who weaves long stems of wheat into triangular house blessings. The Mandan woman proudly notes that she follows tradition by singing appropriate garden songs that ensure fertility. The Ukrainian woman hangs the finished wheat weavings in her kitchen to ensure a fruitful harvest and a prosperous year. Separated by completely different languages and cultural backgrounds, both women pursue agriculturally based folk traditions that are strikingly similar.

Family Folklore

In the mid-1970s, folklorists working with the Smithsonian Festival of American Folklife in Washington, D.C., interviewed more than 2,000 people from throughout the United States. The folklorists were interested especially in family-based traditions, including family stories, customs, expressions, and photography. Some of the material from this massive collection project resulted in a publication devoted exclusively to family folklore (Zeitlin, Kotkin, and Baker 1982). Although the Smithsonian's folklorists did not seek out rural folklore specifically, they did collect numerous family stories that dealt with rural and small-town life. The Smithsonian festival's researchers discovered many themes that ran through the family stories, regardless of the regional affiliation of the individual storytellers: heroes, rogues, mischief makers, survivors, innocents, migrations, lost fortunes, courtships, family foods, and supernatural happenings.

In terms of the "lost fortunes" theme, rural people often have a story in their family repertoire that begins, "We would be really rich today if only . . ." Other family stories, although widely distributed, may seem more difficult to categorize yet strike a responsive chord. Rural families from the Eastern Seaboard to the West Coast, for example, like to tell of a conservative grandfather or great-grandfather who preferred draft horses to tractors. Family storytellers frequently relate how this individual's first ride on a real tractor was not only memorable but also costly. The old-timer failed to use the brake as he headed toward the family barn, while yelling at the tractor, "Whoa! Whoa! Whoaaaaa!" Although told primarily for entertainment at family gatherings, such stories chronicle the impact of technological change on the lives of farm families and other country folk.

The Mystique of Rural Folklore

Folklore clearly occupies a prominent place in the lives of many rural Americans, but one must not fall into the trap of thinking that folklore is the domain of rural folk alone. One may find grizzled New England farmers who eagerly tell stories about chain-rattling spirits in an old graveyard but may just as easily hear young Chicago factory workers tell of a ghostly, long-haired hitchhiker who periodically appears on the freeway and then vanishes. The farmer in bib overalls who believes in water witching perhaps has his counterpart in the fashionably dressed businessman who alters his investment plans after perusing his daily horoscope. And the North Dakota farm woman who hangs handmade wheat weavings in her home to ensure prosperity may not be all that different from the female executive who refuses to take a room on the thirteenth floor of a posh Los Angeles hotel. Folk tradition comprises an important part of the cultural milieu of every human community, rural and urban, and thus folklore is an integral part of all our lives.

—*Timothy J. Kloberdanz*

See also
Barns; Culture; Ethnicity; Literature.
References
Blevins, Winfred. *Dictionary of the American West.* New York: Facts on File, 1993.
Bronner, Simon J. *Chain Carvers: Old Men Crafting Meaning.* Lexington: University Press of Kentucky, 1985.
Brunvand, Jan Harold. *The Study of American Folklore: An Introduction.* 3d ed. New York: W. W. Norton, 1986.
Ensminger, Robert F. *The Pennsylvania Barn: Its Origin, Evolution and Distribution in North America.* Baltimore, MD: Johns Hopkins University Press, 1992.
Freier, George D. *Weather Proverbs: How 600 Proverbs, Sayings and Poems Accurately Explain Our Weather.* Tucson, AZ: Fisher Books, 1989.
Geist, Troyd A. *Faces of Identity, Hands of Skill: Folk Arts in North Dakota.* Bismarck: North Dakota Council on the Arts, 1995.
Glassie, Henry. *Pattern in the Material Folk Culture of the Eastern United States.* Philadelphia: University of Pennsylvania Press, 1968.
Hand, Wayland D. *American Folk Medicine: A Symposium.* Berkeley: University of California Press, 1976.
Jones, Michael Owen. *The Hand Made Object and Its Maker.* Berkeley: University of California Press, 1975.
Roe, Keith E. *Corncribs in History, Folklife and Architecture.* Ames: Iowa State University Press, 1988.
Vogt, Evon Z., and Ray Hyman. *Water Witching U.S.A.* 2d ed. Chicago: University of Chicago Press, 1979.
Welsch, Roger. *Shingling the Fog and Other Plains Lies.* Lincoln: University of Nebraska Press, 1980.
Zeitlin, Steven J., Amy J. Kotkin, and Holly Cutting Baker. *A Celebration of American Family Folklore: Tales and Traditions from the Smithsonian Collection.* New York: Pantheon Books, 1982.

Food Policy
See Policy, Food

Food Safety

The relative likelihood that a particular food will not cause illness or long-term health problems. This entry examines food safety as a scientific processes and its meaning as interpreted through social and psychological processes. Issues pertaining to public concern and communication of food safety messages to consumers are addressed.

Safety as Determined by Scientific Processes

Food safety is one of the most difficult issues facing agriculture today. Fewer and fewer Americans understand agricultural production or have links with the food production system. Attention in recent years focused on a wide range of food safety issues such as the risks of pesticide residues in foods, paperboard milk containers leaching dioxin into milk, ceramic products leaching lead into food, salmonella bacteria in eggs causing outbreaks of illness, irradiated foods, *E. coli* in hamburgers, bovine spongiform encephalopathy (mad cow disease), antibiotics used in animals grown for consumption, possible carcinogenicity from color additives in food, and hormones given to cows to increase milk production.

Whereas it is common to hear that the United States has the safest food supply in the world, few understand or accept the idea of relative safety when applied to food. Society seems to demand total safety, meaning total freedom from risks. This persists in the face of the reality that no system, policy, or procedure can guarantee that all foods are safe for all individuals in society all of the time. Every single hamburger cannot be tested for bacterial contamination, nor can every single fruit be tested for pesticide residues. And even if it were possible to test every food item we purchase, who is to determine what a safe level of pesticide residue is? Who can guarantee that every single item we consume is prepared in a safe manner?

Today's science and technology make it possible to test for residues in parts per billion. But the question remains: is one part per billion of a particular chemical harmful? And how can we know for sure if it is? The answer, of course, is that evaluating food safety must be done in relative rather than absolute terms. Most scientists support a sixteenth-century axiom first advanced by Paracelsus that all substances are poisons—there is none that is not a poison; the right dose differentiates a poison and a remedy. Communicating this complex idea of the relative safety of the food supply is an important challenge facing the agriculture and the food production, processing, and distribution industry.

Part of this communication challenge rests with the different criteria consumers and scientists use to define what safe means. Not surprisingly, scientists often disagree with each other and with consumers. Scientists often disagree with each other because they make different assumptions about the toxicity of a substance or about consumer exposure to a substance. Although some argue that scientists disagreeing with each other is confusing for consumers, others point out that good science depends on scientists challenging each other's conclusions, assumptions, and methods. Only through disagreement and challenges can science make progress.

Scientists are sometimes frustrated with consumers because they may appear to be concerned with minor food risks while ignoring the significant ones. This attitude is aggravated when scientific conclusions and subsequent science-based recommendations are ignored in the face of a public outcry. New Jersey, for example, enacted a ban on serving partially cooked eggs in restaurants. The intent of this science-based ban was to prevent illnesses caused by Salmonella bacteria inside partially cooked eggs. However, the public did not agree. They protested and forced a reversal of the ban. Partially cooked eggs are now served in New Jersey restaurants despite the health risk.

Most experts agree that exposure to Salmonella bacteria puts millions of people at risk. Why then do people magnify the hazards that are slight, such as the risks posed by pesticide residues and shrug off risks that pose greater danger, such as eating partially cooked eggs? Scientists are often uncomfortable with how consumers determine what risks are important and what ones to ignore. However, if the public is to have a role in policymaking, risk assessment experts and policymakers must recognize the legitimacy of those factors that the public views as important in assessing and determining the level of acceptable risks.

Understanding Public Concern

Four issues are central to understanding the public's concern and evaluation of the food supply's safety. First, the criteria consumers use to evaluate risks are social and individual values rather than scientific assumptions

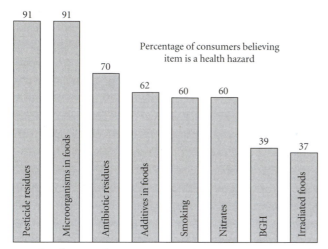

91 91 70 62 60 60 39 37

Percentage of consumers believing
item is a health hazard

Pesticide residues

Microorganisms in foods

Antibiotic residues

Additives in foods

Smoking

Nitrates

BGH

Irradiated foods

**Results of a Typical Consumer Survey Measuring Perceptions of
the Seriousness of Various Health Hazards**

Surveys of consumers typically show that concern about pesticide residues in
foods is near the top of the list, while threats that scientists consider important,
such as smoking, are usually lower on consumer lists.

about toxicity and exposure. Scientists, for example, consider such factors as how toxic the substance is, its prevalence in the food supply, and the amount of the substance people are likely to consume. Consumers, however, focus on very different factors.

Five factors are particularly important to understanding this first issue of consumer perceptions of food safety. The first relates to the nature of the risk exposure. Voluntary exposure to a hazard generally is perceived as safer than is involuntary exposure to the same hazard. For example, having both organically grown foods and conventionally grown foods (grown with pesticides) available to consumers provides a choice, making the consumption of conventionally grown or organically grown foods a voluntary decision. This may reduce the perception of risks of pesticide residues in conventionally grown foods.

A second factor that influences the perception of safety is whether a hazard is natural or manufactured. Naturally occurring risks, such as aflatoxin in peanut butter, tend to be accepted, as opposed to the same level of health risk from a manufactured chemical added to food as a preservative. A third factor, unknown risks, tend to be regarded as more risky than familiar risks. For example, *Salmonella*-caused illness (food poisoning) is familiar and is of much less concern than the unknown and less familiar risk posed by pesticide residues in food. This happens despite the fact that there are many documented cases of death and illness from *Salmonella* and no known cases of death or illness from pesticide residues in food.

A fourth factor affecting consumer perception of risk is morality. Risks that are perceived as trade-offs for monetary gain are generally perceived as less acceptable. For example, the use of antibiotics in poultry feed reduces the cost of poultry production. However, the public may view this drug-enhanced production as an irresponsible and potentially dangerous choice made only to increase the profits of the poultry industry. A fifth factor is that consumers tend to ascribe more hazard to situations in which there is someone to blame. Thus, the risks from a naturally occurring hazard such as glycoalkaloids in potatoes are of much less concern for many consumers than is the same risk posed by adding a manufactured chemical to foods.

A second issue central to the public's evaluation of food safety is that the trust and credibility of the food industry and agriculture is declining. This can be linked with the food industry's past success in convincing the American public to trust that the food system will deliver safe foods. Consequently, every breach of the system, every little problem that catches the public's attention, calls that trust into question. Trust and credibility are built over long periods of time but can be lost instantly. Several recent cases caused the American public to question the safety of the food supply. Examples include using Alar in apple production and the *E. coli*–contaminated hamburgers that resulted in children's deaths. Other cases that caused consumers to question food supply safety have been the use of artificial bovine growth hormone (BGH) in dairy cows and the occurrence of bovine spongiform encephalopathy (BSE), also known as mad cow disease, in Great Britain. Although scientists say that neither BSE nor BGH actually threatens the safety of the food supply, the perception among consumers is less positive.

A third issue is that the public has limited information about how pragmatic science works. Science education in this country focuses on seductive topics such as black holes in space, the exciting underwater world of the polar ice cap, and other scientific delights. Little has been done to help the public really understand how science works and how it impacts their daily lives. For example, although scientists continue to study microbial and chemical contamination in food, the public has limited information on which to base an informed decision about food safety. Little information is available to the public to build understanding of the range of safeguards currently in place to protect the food supply or advances being made to understand causes of various diseases such as cancer. Little information is available to help the public understand the major activities under way to prevent importing of animals with diseases such as BSE. A greater understanding of these activities would help consumers put various risks into a broader perspective and deepen their understanding of the food production, processing, and distribution system.

The fourth issue concerns the media, who share the blame for consumer attention and concern for minor risks. Much can be said about the mass media's role in fostering many of today's agricultural industry problems. Safety violations within the food industry must be brought to the consumer's attention, but there is disagreement regarding how the media should convey this type of information. Disagreement also exists concerning the media's ability to educate consumers. However, one of the media's important roles is to call attention to significant problems, not to solve them. The media face difficulties in describing and reporting risk situations. They may exaggerate hazards or fail to help consumers put individual risks in perspective.

Communicating Meaningful Messages to Consumers

Consumers want to reduce the complex technical, scientific risk assessment tasks to simple dichotomies: Is a product safe or not safe, or should a product be used or not used? Risk-assessment scientists also simplify complex questions, but generally in terms of probabilities of risk. The public is not trained to think in terms of probabilities, and scientists cannot say that a particular food or the food supply is absolutely safe without talking about relative safety. Although the temptation may be to develop persuasive communication messages, a careful examination suggests that persuasive strategies are dangerous at best and catastrophic under some circumstances. Messages to convince consumers that the American food supply is the safest in the world are meaningless. Only one food-related death reported by the media can challenge the integrity of the food supply by showing that the food is not absolutely safe. What the industry must do is build a long-term understanding of the nature of risk, and the safeguards in place to protect the food supply from unnecessary health hazards.

Farmers and the food processing and distribution industry face difficult challenges. Food safety and the public's perception of the safety of the food supply have reached crisis levels in recent years. Consumers are no longer satisfied to be told that the United States has the safest food supply in the world. They need to understand what that means and know that every effort is being made to make the food supply safer. How the industry deals with this challenge will play a key role in determining the character of the food production, processing, and distribution industry in the future.

—*Clifford W. Scherer*

See also
Agro/Food System; Biotechnology; Nutrition; Pest Management; Policy, Food.
References
Allen, F. W. "Towards a Holistic Appreciation of Risk: The Challenge of Communicators and Policy Makers." *Science, Technology, and Human Values* 2, nos. 3 and 4 (1987): 138–143.
Covello, V. T., D. von Winterfeld, and P. Slovic. "Risk Communication: A Review of the Literature." *Risk Abstracts* 3, no. 4 (1986): 171–182.
Fiorino, D. J. "Citizen Participation and Environmental Risk: A Survey of Institutional Mechanisms." *Science, Technology, and Human Values* 15, no. 2 (1990) 226–243.
Krimsky, S., and D. Golding, eds. *Social Theories of Risk*. London, UK: Praeger, 1992.
Mazur, A. *The Dynamics of Technical Controversy*. Washington, DC: Communications Press, 1981.
Ruckelshaus, W. D. "Science, Risk, and Public Policy." *Science*. (September 1983): 1026–1028.
Sandman, P. M. "Risk Communication: Facing Public Outrage." *EPA Journal* 13, no. 9 (1987): 21–22.
Scherer, C. W. "Strategies for Communicating Risks to the Public." *Food Technology* (October 1991).
Winter, C. K., J. Seiber, and C. F. Nuckton. *Chemicals in the Human Food Chain*. New York: Van Nostrand Reinhold, 1990.

Foreclosure and Bankruptcy

Foreclosure: a termination of all rights of the mortgagor or his or her grantee in the property encumbered by a mortgage. Bankruptcy: the state or condition of being unable to pay one's debts as they are, or become, due (equitable definition of insolvency) or when debts exceed assets (bankruptcy definition of insolvency). This entry discusses foreclosure, bankruptcy, types of bankruptcies, redemption, bankruptcy trends during this century, penny auctions, and sheriff's sales.

Foreclosure

Foreclosure is a process by which a mortgagor of real or personal property or other owner of property subject to a lien is deprived of his or her interest in that property. A foreclosure is a legal proceeding in which a mortgagee either takes title to or forces the sale of the mortgagor's property in satisfaction of a debt. A foreclosure sale involves selling mortgaged property to obtain satisfaction of the mortgage out of the proceeds, whether authorized by a decree of the court or by a power of sale contained in the mortgage. If proceeds from the sale fail to pay the debt in full, the mortgagee may obtain a deficiency judgment. There are no current national or state data series giving the number of farm or rural foreclosures.

Types of Bankruptcies

Bankruptcy occurs when individuals' or businesses' financial circumstances deteriorate to the point that they are entitled to take the benefit of the federal bankruptcy laws, which provide for the orderly handling of unpaid debt held by creditors. The bankruptcy code contains five operative chapters (7, 9, 11, 12, and 13) under which bankruptcy petitions may be filed with the bankruptcy courts. All petitions except Chapter 9, which applies exclusively to municipalities, may be used by farmers. Chapter 7 provides for straight bankruptcy in the form of a liquidation proceeding and involves the collection and distribution of all the bankrupt's nonexempt assets by a trustee appointed or approved by the court in the manner provided by the code. It accounts for a majority of all bankruptcies, and most cases are personal and not business.

The debtor rehabilitation provisions of the code (Chapters 11, 12, and 13) differ, however, from the Chapter 7 straight bankruptcy because the debtor looks to rehabilitation and reorganization rather than liquidation, and the creditors look to future earnings of the bankrupt, rather than property held by the bankrupt, to satisfy their claims. Chapter 11 involves an individual or business reorganization, with most cases being the latter. A plan under Chapter 13 involves the full or partial repayment of debts while assets are shielded from creditor action; it involves reorganization or adjustment of debts of an individual with regular income or a business. Historically, most Chapter 13 cases have involved nonbusiness petitioners. Individuals most commonly file under Chapters 7 or 13.

Chapter 12, the Family Farmer Bankruptcy Act of 1986 (P.L. 99-554), was enacted in response to the farm financial crisis of the 1980s and became effective on 26 November 1986. It involves the adjustment of debts of a family farm (as defined in the code) with regular income and makes available to farmers the equivalent of a Chapter 13 repayment program. Chapter 12 cases are classified as business bankruptcies.

Chapter 12 modifies the normal Chapter 11 bankruptcy procedure by permitting farmers to submit a reorganization plan directly to the bankruptcy court, with no review by creditors. Because creditors cannot reject the debt repayment plan developed under Chapter 12, farmers can reduce the amount owed, extend the payment period, and lower the interest rate to current market levels, or a rate even lower, on existing loans. The writedown of secured debt is limited to fair current market value of the underlying land or other asset, which can be less than the original loan value.

This chapter gives family farmers in financial stress considerable power to demand concessions from lenders relative to Chapter 11. Under Chapter 11, where farmers typically filed before Chapter 12 became effective, creditors have the right to block the debtor's plan and force liquidation. The availability of Chapter 12 to certain farmers encourages creditors to negotiate debt restructuring arrangements outside bankruptcy. Chapter 12 originally was to expire on 1 October 1993, but it was extended for five years until 1 October 1998 (P.L. 103-65).

Redemption

An important concept related to foreclosure and bankruptcy is redemption, which exists only in Chapter 7 and not in the other bankruptcy chapters. It is the right of a debtor and sometimes of a debtor's other creditors to repurchase from a buyer at a forced sale property of the debtor that was seized and sold in satisfaction of a judgment or other claim against the debtor. This right usually is limited to forced sales of real property. Redemption is also a bankruptcy term for extinguishing a lien on exempt property by making a cash payment equal to the value of the property. The redemption period is the time during which a defaulted mortgage, land contract, deed of trust, and so forth, can be redeemed. Such a period is commonly provided for by state statute.

Bankruptcy in the First Half of the Twentieth Century

Twice in the twentieth century were concerns about farmer bankruptcies heightened. The first involves an extended period from 1920 through the Great Depression of the 1930s. The U.S. economy generally prospered during the first two decades of this century. The agricultural sector was also generally prosperous, with the 1910–1914 period often being regarded as the golden age of American agriculture (with the subsequent parity price formula being based on these years), which was then followed by a boom during World War I.

After 1920, however, commodity prices collapsed. Sharply lower incomes left many farmers, who had borrowed to finance land acquisition and improvements before 1920, unable to repay their loans. Loan losses, in turn, caused the failure of many banks in commodity-producing regions. The number of banks fell sharply, particularly in the Midwest and South. These problems continued or were intensified by the general economic collapse in 1929 leading to the Great Depression and by widespread adverse weather problems affecting agriculture in the 1930s. Changes in farmland prices illustrate the magnitude of the economic forces at work. Nominal farmland prices fell from a post–World War I high of $69 per acre in 1920 to a Great Depression low of $30 per acre in 1933. Per acre farmland values then slowly increased in most subsequent years, but it was 1951 before the $74 per acre value exceeded that of 1920.

There were 6.41 million farms as defined by the census in 1910 and 12,001 farmer bankruptcies during the 1910–1919 period; but this figure jumped to 51,863 between 1920 and 1929. The all-time-high single-year farmer bankruptcy total was registered in 1925, when 7,872 farmers filed for bankruptcy, a rate of 12.2 per 10,000 farms based on 6.47 million farms. There were 37,634 farmer bankruptcies from 1930 to 1939, with 28,280 of these occurring during the 1930–1935 period.

The farm financial crisis of the Great Depression left some long-lasting impressions, including the accounts of the migration of rural residents from the Midwest, South, and Great Plains to the cities of the region and to the Pacific states in search of better work opportunities. They also include scenes of multiple auctions of farms and farm assets in numerous rural settings, as foreclosures and bankruptcies took their toll. (An auction is a public sale during which items are sold one by one by an auctioneer, each item going to the last and highest in a series of competing bidders.) Foreclosed farms and their assets were auctioned to the highest bidder at numerous sheriff's sales under the auspices of the courts and carried out by the local sheriffs as agents of the court.

Local farmers and rural residents held penny auctions in a significant number of instances to counter what they considered to be unjust foreclosures caused by low farm prices resulting from forces beyond their control. A penny auction is a collusion by farmers and local residents to offer or purchase a foreclosed farm at auction for only a few cents on the dollar, thus rendering the entire action untenable for the foreclosing parties, since they recover little or nothing from the auction. Noncooperating bidders often were threatened with violence to win their compliance with the scheme. Such action could result in the farm's not being sold. The intended outcome

was to force the lender into an accommodation that would enable the farm family to remain on the farm.

Bankruptcy in the Second Half of the Twentieth Century

The second episode of concern about farmer bankruptcies in this century came during the 1980s, 50 years after the Great Depression, when there were 2.44 million farms and a much differently structured industry. The economic climate of the 1970s encouraged farmers to expand production and benefit from export opportunities and strong commodity prices, farm income, and farmland values. High rates of inflation and low real interest rates further encouraged investment in farmland. Generous credit from various sources helped finance the expansion. A considerable number of farmers took on too much debt and became quite vulnerable to sudden shifts in economic forces.

Economic conditions reversed in the early 1980s, when export markets contracted and input prices and interest rates rose. Monetary policies designed to reduce inflation prompted interest rates to rise to unprecedented levels in the early 1980s. The financial stress turned to crisis when declines in farm commodity prices, income, and land values (the largest asset, used to secure much of the debt) made it difficult for some farmers to service their debts. These economic changes, not an overall lack of efficiency, produced the most severe financial stress for the U.S. farm sector since the 1930s. The farm sector experience during the 1980s was less a problem of income than a problem of absorbing large capital losses.

There are no farmer bankruptcy data for the crucial 1981–1986 period that covered the farm financial crisis period. Bankruptcy statistics specifying a filer's occupation, including farmer, were recorded by the Administrative Office of the U.S. Courts until October 1979. Under the Bankruptcy Reform Act of 1978 (P.L. 95-598), these data were no longer reported. The only exception is quarterly data on those who filed for bankruptcy protection under Chapter 12. Some 16,251 Chapter 12 bankruptcies were filed from the date of its implementation on 26 November 1986 to 30 June 1994. There were 4,812 Chapter 12 bankruptcies filed during the year ending 30 June 1987, for a bankruptcy rate of 21.7 per 10,000 farms based on 2.2 million farms (and this excludes the Chapter 7, 11, and 13 farmer bankruptcies filed that year, for which no data exist). This is the highest annual bankruptcy rate recorded, eclipsing the previous high in 1925. However, the 1987 rate probably includes all the farmers who had waited for the new legislation to take effect; the rates in subsequent years are influenced by the generous writedown-of-debt provisions of Chapter 12.

Indicators of Farm Financial Stress

Total farm numbers fell from about six million in 1945 to about two million today, causing concern through time about the loss of a way of life. However, there is no available evidence to verify that increased farmer foreclosures and bankruptcies are key leading indicators of farm sector financial stress. Rather, foreclosures and bankruptcies are only a subset of the complex phenomenon of farm business exit and entry. Large numbers of farm foreclosures and bankruptcies thus do not necessarily translate to a decline in farm numbers. Farm foreclosures and bankruptcies did not prevent farm numbers from peaking at 6.8 million in 1935 during the Great Depression. In part, this phenomenon resulted from the growth of quasi-commercial subsistence farms rather than from favorable economic returns on the farm. Still, the net outflow of people from farming began in earnest during the post–World War II prosperity rather than during a period of financial stress. By contrast, the foreclosures and bankruptcies of the 1980s occurred in the midst of a long decline in farm numbers, setting off a particularly acute wave of concern.

—*Jerome M. Stam and Ron L. Durst*

See also
Agricultural Law; Financial Intermediaries.
References
Alston, Lee J. "Farm Foreclosures in the United States during the Interwar Period." *Journal of Economic History* 43, no. 4 (1983): 885–903.
Bankruptcy Code Rules and Terms. St. Paul, MN: West Publishing, 1995.
Black, Henry Campbell. *Black's Law Dictionary.* 6th ed. St. Paul, MN: West Publishing, 1990.
Shephard, Lawrence, and Robert A. Collins. "Why Do Farmers Fail? Farm Bankruptcies 1910–78." *American Journal of Agricultural Economics* 64, no. 4 (1982): 609–615.
Stam, Jerome M., Steven R. Koenig, Susan E. Bentley, and H. Frederick Gale, Jr. *Farm Financial Stress, Farm Exits, and Public Sector Assistance to the Farm Sector in the 1980's.* Agricultural Economic Report no. 645 (April). Washington, DC: U.S. Department of Agriculture, Economic Research Service, 1991.
Wickens, David L. *Farmer Bankruptcies, 1898–1935.* Circular no. 414 (September). Washington, DC: U.S. Department of Agriculture, 1936.
Wilson, Robert B. "Chapter 12: Family Farm Reorganization." *Journal of Agricultural Taxation and Law* 8, no. 4 (1987): 299–310.

Forest Products

Items made of solid wood (for example, lumber and furniture), wood fibers and particles (for example, paper and particle board), chemicals derived from wood (for example, rayon and industrial chemicals), and nonwood products (for example, bark mulch, maple syrup, and Christmas trees). This entry discusses the importance of forest products and describes examples of wood and wood-based products, specialty forest products, and forest by-products.

Economic Importance

Forest products are an important part of the economic and industrial framework of the United States. The activities associated with harvesting and processing forest products often form the major manufacturing base in most parts of rural America. These direct manufacturing activities alone employ over 1.8 million workers with a payroll of about $39 billion. However, the full economic impact of forest products can only be assessed by adding to these figures all those individuals involved in the transportation, distribution, and marketing of forest products and the allied businesses associated with the forest products manufacturing industries.

Since colonial times, forest products have been and still are an indispensable part of American life. These products of the forests, which range from lumber to build houses and furniture to fiber for newspaper and magazines to chemicals for commercial, industrial, and pharmaceutical uses, form the very core of American social and economic structures and standard of living. A typical person in the United States uses hundreds of individual wood and wood-based products every day. In many cases, peole use the products without ever realizing that the products are wood or wood-based in origin and, therefore, derived from the forests.

The American appetite for wood products is the highest in the world. The annual consumption of all forms of wood and wood products in the United States is over 2.4 cubic meters (84.9 cubic feet) per person. For other developed nations, the consumption is 1.2 cubic meters (42.4 cubic feet) per person; the average for the world is only 0.7 cubic meters (24.8 cubic feet).

Forest products can be divided into two major groups: timber or wood and wood-based products and specialty forest products. Forest products are produced throughout the United States. However, most operations tend to be concentrated in rural areas, reflecting the close connection between the products and the source of the raw material—wood and other materials coming from the forests.

Wood and Wood-Based Products

Wood and wood-based products are the largest and most important group of forest products and the ones that significantly impact the U.S. economy and standard of living. For a better understanding of their extent and diversity, these products can be conveniently subdivided into three segments: solid wood products, particle and fiber products, and chemically derived products.

Solid Wood Products. When people think of wood products, this is the segment that typically comes to mind. These are the traditional wood products, those steeped in the history of civilization and the development of nations. For ease of understanding, the solid wood products can be classified into four major groups.

The first group is the round wood products, those shaped like the stem of the tree itself. This includes products such as poles (for example, utility poles and barn poles), pilings, posts, logs (both saw logs and veneer logs), and pulpwood. These products and those in the next group are commonly called the primary forest products.

Sawn wood products such as lumber, railroad ties, sawn posts, and timbers constitute the second group. These are traditionally considered as products of the sawmill and are produced from the conversion of sawn logs. The annual consumption of lumber in the United States is over 45 billion board feet of softwood lumber and over 10 billion board feet of hardwood lumber. (A board foot is a volume of wood 1 foot long by 12 inches wide by 1 inch thick or its equivalent.) The annual per capita consumption of all lumber in the United States is over 220 board feet. The terms hardwoods and softwoods refer to the class of the trees from which the lumber is produced and not to the hardness or softness of the wood. Softwood lumber comes from those trees that are botanically classified as gymnosperms and whose leaves are usually needlelike, such as the pines, firs, and cedars. Hardwood lumber comes from those trees botanically classified as angiosperms, which have broad leaves, such as the oaks, maples, and poplars.

The third group is the broad category of manufactured wood products. This group contains the traditional wood-based products such as houses, furniture, cabinets, and flooring. It includes all the toy and novelty items made from wood and specialty products such as toothpicks, spools, and bowls. Less obvious are the numerous commercial and industrial products such as pallets, boxes, crates, forms and templates, and manufacturing components. For example, in pallets alone, the United States produces about 450 million wooden pallets each year for use in the handling and distribution of food and other consumer and industrial products. Treated wood products also are included in this group. Examples include lumber, railroad ties, and poles that are injected with chemicals under pressure to prevent deterioration from decay and insect attack, thus prolonging their useful or service life.

The fourth group is veneer and plywood. Veneers are thin sheets of wood sliced or peeled from logs. Veneers are used as the decorative layer of panels for furniture and cabinets and to make plywood. Plywood is usually made from an odd number of sheets of veneer glued together face to face with the grain of the alternating plies turned at a 90-degree angle to each other. Plywood is used primarily in building construction, manufacturing of other wood products, and paneling.

Fiber and Particle Products. The second segment includes wood products manufactured from particles of wood or the basic wood fibers themselves. The most common products of this group are the traditional pulp, paper, and paper-derived products. To make pulp, wood is chemically and mechanically reduced to its basic elemental fiber, and the pulp, in turn, is used to produce the entire spectrum of paper and paperboard products. These range from standard writing paper, magazines, and newspapers to paper products, such as napkins, cardboard, bags, sanitary paper products, and paperboard cartons. The per capita consumption of paper and paperboard products in the United States is about 700 pounds per year.

Fiber boards constitute the other component of the wood fiber–based products. There are three major types of fiberboards: hardboard, insulation board, and medium density fiberboard (MF). Hardboard is used in various manufactured products, building construction, and some consumer products such as pegboard. Insulation board is used in building construction and as ceiling tile. MF is used as a corestock in furniture and cabinets.

Particleboards are the other part of this product segment. They are generally classified into two categories, industrial and structural. Industrial particleboards are used in applications such as shelving, floor underlayment, and corestock in furniture and cabinets. These traditionally go under the name of particleboards. The structural particleboards are typically called waferboard (an older product) or oriented strand board (OSB)—the newer product). Structural particleboards usually are made from larger wood particles or flakes than industrial particleboards. Structural particleboards are used in roof, wall, and floor sheathing.

These products, based on wood particles and fibers, are sometimes called engineered wood products. The concept involves reducing wood to a particle or fiber form and then putting this material together again to form a new product designed to have a particular set of properties that make it perform well in specific applications. Structural particleboards and parallel strand lumber are two examples of these new classes of wood products.

Chemically Derived Products. The third segment of the wood products grouping is the chemically-derived products. In this case, wood is a chemical raw material. It is not just sawn or machined but reduced to its basic chemical elements, which are then reconstituted in some other chemical form to create an entirely different product. Wood is a lignocellulosic material, and the cellulose fraction can be used for diverse products such as chemical feed stocks, industrial solvents, rayon fibers and films, lacquers, thickeners, and alcohols. The lignin fraction yields phenols, vanillin, adhesives, fuels, foams, and thermoplastic materials.

Specialty Products

Although timber or wood is the major product of the forest, other specialty forest products are also important to the industry, especially in rural America. There are five general categories of these specialty products.

Decorative Materials. These are products of the forests used by florists, decorators, artists, and craft artisans. The materials used include such items as leafy materials, pinecones, holly, pine boughs, berries, vines, and bark. Christmas trees are also a part of this category. Over 45 million Christmas trees are harvested each year in the United States.

Edible Products. The edible products that come from the forests include wild honey, nuts, fruits and berries, mushrooms, and maple syrup. Some of these products, like maple syrup and some nuts, have become traditions in the United States.

Medicinal or Pharmaceutical Materials. U.S. forests produce numerous plants and trees that are reported to have medicinal or pharmaceutical properties. Some of these include balsam gum, ginseng, witch hazel, and sassafras.

Naval Stores. The oleoresin from southern yellow pine trees has long been tapped for the production of naval stores. The pitch or resin produced is refined into rosin and turpentine. Today, however, most of these materials are commercially produced as by-products of pulp mills rather than by tapping pine trees.

Soil Conditioners and Mulches. Bark, sawdust, wood chips, and pine needles (called pine straw) have been used as both soil conditioners and mulches around plants. Hardwood and softwood bark has become the major mulch material available in truckload bulk and in bag quantities.

By-Products

The residues generated in the production of wood products have in themselves become products. Sawdust is pulped and used to produce paper products. It is refined and used as fillers and extenders in other materials like plastics and adhesives. It is used in floor sweeping compounds and fuel. Solid wood pieces usually are chipped for pulping or particle boards manufacture or used as a fuel.

Many wood products manufacturing operations use the residue of other wood products operations as part of their own production. For example, in the southern United States, over one-third of the production of pulp for paper and paper products is derived from the wood residue of other wood products manufacturing operations, primarily sawmills.

—*Fred M. Lamb*

See also
Foresters; Forestry Industry; Forests; Sawmilling; Trees.
References
Panshin, Alexis J., E. S. Harrar, James S. Bethel, and W. J. Baker. *Forest Products*. New York: McGraw-Hill, 1962.
Perlin, John. *A Forest Journey: The Role of Wood in the Development of Civilization*. Cambridge, MA: Harvard University Press, 1991.
U.S. Department of Agriculture. *Special Forest Products for Profit: Suggestions for Rural Areas Development*, Agriculture Information Bulletin No. 278. Washington, DC: Government Printing Office, 1963.
Youngquist, Waldemar G., and Herbert O. Fleischer. *Wood in American Life, 1776–2076*. Madison, WI: Forest Products Research Society, 1977.
Youngs, R. L. "Every Age, the Age of Wood." *Interdisciplinary Science Review* 7, no. 3 (1982): 211–219.

Foresters

Managers of the trees, soil, and other plants found in the forest to produce timber, wildlife habitat, recreational opportunities, and scenic beauty. Foresters use professional and scientific expertise to manage forest resources in the service of the landowners or forest managers. This entry lists the forest ownership types and associated management goals. Professional and technical skills needed for foresters are described, and major forestry occupations are listed.

Nonindustrial Private Forests

Most of the nation's forests, about 424 million acres, are privately owned. Much of this forest is in small parcels, commonly referred to as nonindustrial private forests, owned by individuals or families who expect a variety of benefits and results from their land. Foresters help landowners plan long-term development, use, and protection of their forests and look after their day-to-day management and practical needs. Foresters create an inventory of the type, amount, and location of the timber and other valuable forest resources on the property. When landowners decide to sell timber, foresters estimate the approximate worth of the trees and arrange for their sale. The forester works with loggers and road builders to represent the landowner in making sure the harvest and extraction of the trees does not damage soils, creekbeds, or vistas important to the landowner. The forester is challenged to build a close relationship with forest owners; to be sensitive to their needs and desires; and to understand the various economic, social, and political factors that influence how forests are managed.

Industrial Private Forests

About 71 million acres of private forests are owned and managed by forest-products companies. Foresters help these companies grow timber that can be milled for wood, pulp, paper, and other products. The companies manage their forests using technology and practices that maximize production of high-quality timber on a sustained basis. Typically, individual companies that process timber are small, employing fewer than 50 people. But some firms are very large, employ thousands of people, and rank among the nation's leading manufacturers. The use of increased technology and the need for companies to stay competitive has pushed the industry toward larger and fewer companies, but small and large companies are located throughout the nation, especially in rural areas.

Foresters help plan the removal of timber so that the remaining trees will produce a new or improving forest. They also supervise the planting and growing of new trees. They prepare the land for planting using controlled burns, bulldozers, tractors, or herbicides. They select the types of young trees or seeds to be planted and then monitor their growth.

Public Forests

Public forests comprise about 313 million acres. They provide timber; recreation; wildlife habitat; and water and forage for horses, cattle, and sheep. Many foresters work for federal, state, county, and municipal governments. They manage public forests and parks and work with private landowners to protect and manage forestland outside of the public domain.

Many factors influence the nation's forests: continuously increasing demands for forest products, a growing population seeking more and new forms of recreation, a need for more clean water, and the expansion of urban and rural development adjacent to forest (Grey and Gregory 1989). Interest in and debate over various conflicting uses of public lands makes the forester's job very challenging. Political decisions may or may not be compatible with planned forest resource management strategies and natural resource capabilities. Legal challenges to public forest management plans are increasing, which often curtails vegetation management until the lawsuits are settled. Meanwhile, fuels continue to build up as trees die from insects and diseases. Thus, curtailing forest management can lead to devastating conditions like large wildfires and widespread insect infestations.

Foresters are required to continuously assess changes in the forest. They use photographs from airplanes and satellites to map large forest areas and to monitor changes in forest condition and land use. For example, when a tree disease or forest insect is found, foresters will use aerial photography to measure the extent of the infestation and monitor its spread over time. Although foresters sometimes work in the office, they often work outdoors in all kinds of weather. The work can be physically demanding and require travel to isolated areas. Some foresters work very long hours fighting fires or walking long distances to the job location.

Global Implications

Management of the nation's forests has global implications. Technology and forest management practices are regularly shared internationally. The ease of world travel encourages more international visitors to go to American forests for recreation and research. World trade influences the marketing and consumption of U.S. forest products. The world environment is affected by public and private influence on and management of the nearly 737 million acres of forest in the United States. Air quality and global temperature are affected by the nation's forests. Shifting production and availability of forest

Management of fire danger and wildfires is just one part of the forester's complex job.

products has significant international economic and environmental implications.

Educational Requirements for Forestry Careers

Forestry is a science that involves the management of forest resources in an increasingly complex world. A bachelor of science degree in forestry or a related forest resource curriculum is the minimum educational requirement for professional careers in forestry. To qualify as a forester, a person typically has a four-year degree from a college that offers professional forestry education. In the federal government, a combination of experience and appropriate education may occasionally substitute for a professional forestry degree, but this is very rare today because of the competition for jobs and general reduction in the number of government employees. Some states have mandatory licensing or registration requirements for professional foresters. These states require a four-year degree in forestry, a specific quantity of field experience, and the successful completion of an examination.

College curriculums for foresters and disciplines related to forestry, like ecology, hydrology, wildlife biology, entomology, soil science, and landscape architecture, stress science, mathematics, communications skills, computer science, and technical forestry courses. Courses in forest economics and business management are very useful. In addition, most schools encourage students to seek summer jobs that provide experience in forestry or conservation work. Forest management requires a broad knowledge of the natural environment and a good understanding of policy issues and the increasingly numerous and complex environmental regulations that affect many forestry-related activities. Social issues and political demands have critical effects on general forest management on public and private lands.

Foresters in highly specialized disciplines or who wish to teach or perform specialized research generally must have master's and doctoral degrees. Today, many experienced professional foresters who wish to advance in agencies and organizations return to school to complete a master's degree. As competition for jobs continues to increase, advanced degrees in forestry and related disciplines and public administration are becoming more important in acquiring positions.

Forestry Occupations

Working as a forester appeals to many people because of the variety of professions that may be pursued in the public and private sector. There are between 20,000 and 30,000 forestry professionals active today. Most entry-level positions, whether with federal, state, or local governments, private industry, or forestry consulting groups, require a considerable amount of outdoor work in rural areas. For those with an associate's degrees or technican's certification, salaries start from $14,000 to $16,000 per year. In professional positions, graduates with a bachelor's degree start at roughly $18,000 to $20,000 per year.

There are opportunities for career advancement for people who choose to remain in rural areas. Some people choose to move to urban areas where company and government headquarters are often located in order to advance their careers. Others choose careers in urban forestry and never work in rural areas. There are also international opportunities.

Some people choose to become consulting foresters and serve rural communities or travel to various locations advising state and local governments, private landowners, private industry, and other forestry consulting groups, in the United States and internationally. Careers in forestry are personally rewarding, provide opportunities to make positive contributions to the environment, meet the needs of people, and help conserve forest resources for future generations.

The Society of American Foresters is the official agency for accrediting professional forestry and recognizing forest technical educational programs in the United States. For a list of forestry schools presently accredited or recognized by this organization, write to Society of American Foresters, 5400 Grosvenor Lane, Bethesda, MD 20814.

—*Melody S. Mobley*

See also
Forest Products; Forestry Industry; Forests; Parks; Sawmilling; Trees; Wilderness.
References
Grey, Gene, and Gregory Smith. *So You Want to Be in Forestry*. Bethesda, MD: American Forestry Association and Society of American Foresters, 1989.
Careers in Forestry. Miscellaneous publication no. 249 (revised March 1967). Washington, DC: U.S. Department of Agriculture, Forest Service, 1967.
"Careers in Natural Resources: New Directions in an Evolving Science." *Journal of Forestry* 92, no. 3 (March 1994): 28–29, 31–32.
Leopold, Aldo. *A Sand County Almanac*. New York: Oxford University Press, 1949.
Society of American Foresters. *Task Force Report on Sustaining Long-Term Forest Health and Productivity*. Bethesda, MD: Society of American Foresters, 1993.

Forestry Industry

That part of the economy involving the extraction and manufacturing of wood-based products, including pulp and paper. In what follows, four facets of the industry in the United States are discussed. The first section identifies the kinds of firms and employment trends in the industry. An important question to be addressed about this industry is the extent to which it is dominated by oligopolies—a few large firms that compete by increasing advertising and introducing new product lines rather than by lowering prices. Section two deals with industrial concentration trends. Section three focuses on the important historical shift from labor- to capital-intensive forms of production within the industry. Why communities dependent on the forestry industry have unusually high rates of poverty is the subject of section four.

Firms and Employment in the Industry

Industry firms (see Figure 1) can be classified by stages of the production process. Stages one through three, here-

after designated as primary production activities, include the most central work in the industry: logging, milling, producing paper, and making wood-based chemicals. Secondary manufacturing of finished goods, such as printed material, furniture making, and home building, are classified as stage four activities. Firms specializing in wholesaling and retailing are included in stage five. By the late 1980s, the sum of activities by these firms amounted to 5 percent ($185.8 billion) of the nation's gross national product.

A recent estimate suggests that firms in stages one through three of the production process employ 1.6 million workers, about 9 percent of the total manufacturing employment in the country (Haynes 1990). Fifty-two percent of the work in the industry, or more than 800,000 jobs, consists of harvesting and processing logs into raw materials. More advanced production, such as furniture manufacturing and the chemical coating of high-grade paper, represents just under one-half of all manufacturing in the industry. However, these jobs have higher skill require-

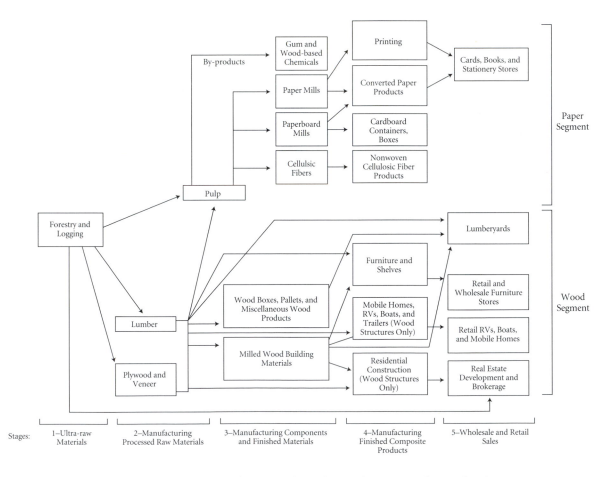

Figure 1. Kinds of Firms and Their Interrelationships in the Forest Products Industries

Source: Adapted from D'Aveni and Illinitch 1992.

ments and offer both more pay and greater employment stability.

Both the number of firms and workers in each stage of wood-based manufacturing have generally declined, whereas the volume of goods produced continued to grow, albeit unsteadily. Changes in interest rates for home mortgages, the overproduction of pulp and paper products, an oversupply of commercial office space, and increasingly important environmental restrictions on access to public forests for the preservation of old-growth forests and endangered species are among the reasons for volatility in the industry.

Between 1958 and 1986, major changes, including the sharp restructuring of employment in the industry, occurred for firms in primary production activities, defined above as Stages 1 through 3 (see Figure 1). The sharp restructuring of employment in the industry is especially noteworthy. By 1986 the volume of expenditures in the industry regained strength with a substantially reduced workforce. Plant managers shifted production to more automated milling and pulping operations in an attempt to recover from a major profit squeeze caused by the combined effects of higher energy costs after the energy crises of the 1970s and high wages.

Shaw (1993) documents the pronounced restructuring of employment among firms located in the Pacific Northwest. Since 1980, the region has lost over 200 sawmills and 105 panel plants owned by major corporations such as Louisiana Pacific, Weyerhaeuser, International Paper, and Boise Cascade. To compensate for the energy-crisis-induced profit squeeze, firms reinvested capital in newer, more efficient industrial plants in the South and Northeast.

Capital disinvestment in the Pacific Northwest forest industries since the mid-1970s conflicted with conventional wisdom. Although most people think of the forestry industry as primarily occurring in the West, the actual growth is more pronounced east of the Mississippi, in both the North and South. As early as 1982, only 20 percent of national forestry industry employment was located in the West (Haynes 1990). Although the industry is a relatively important employer in that region, until trees on privately owned western forestland mature, the future of the industry, will most likely be linked to the newer plants and younger forests in the South, plus parts of Maine, Pennsylvania, and Wisconsin. Nearly 40 percent of the total employment in the industry is in the South, the nation's wood basket.

Industrial Concentration Trends

Although the industry may present a highly competitive environment for its more than 4,000 firms, it increasingly has the problems of an older industry in an advanced stage of the production cycle. A relatively small number of transnational firms play a dominant role in the production and sale of products, leaving a residual market for a large number of companies. Between 1972 and 1987, for example, the 20 largest paper mills increased their share of the total value of shipments from 66 to 78 percent. A similar trend is evident for veneer and plywood production. The 20 largest pulp mills controlled 99 percent of the value of shipments annually from 1972 to 1987 (U.S. Bureau of the Census 1992).

Another tendency that points toward a concentrated structure involves the integrated production capacity of the large new industries. Of the top 15 forestry industries, virtually none reported all their sales in 1992 within either the paper, pulp, and packaging industries or within the wood and building products sector (Shaw 1993). Boise Cascade reported 49 percent of its 1992 sales in paper-related production, whereas 32 percent of sales involved wood and building products. International Paper reported that 54 percent of its sales in 1992 involved paper products, whereas 10 percent involved wood and building products. Only a few of the largest companies, such as Stone Container, Consolidated Paper, and Westvaco, reported 90 percent or more of their sales in paper production.

The most competitive conditions in the industry are in stages one and two, with a large concentration of firms comparable in size and wage levels (see Figure 1). The percentage of value for shipments controlled by the 20 largest commercial loggers declined from 45 percent in 1972 to 33 percent by 1987. Similarly, the 20 largest saw and planing mills controlled 36 percent of the value for shipments in 1977 and 21 percent in 1987 (U.S. Bureau of the Census 1992).

It remains to be seen whether deconcentration within stages one and two will continue into the twenty-first century. As noted, a shift in capital investment into larger, energy-efficient milling operations occurred during the 1980s. Carroll (1995) predicts that capital-intensive logging practices, such as helicopter logging, will be more likely in the future. This innovation reduces both soil compaction from log skidders (haulers) with rubber tires and the need for as many unpaved logging roads, which are a source of stream siltation from soil erosion. Whether smaller firms in the industry can afford this

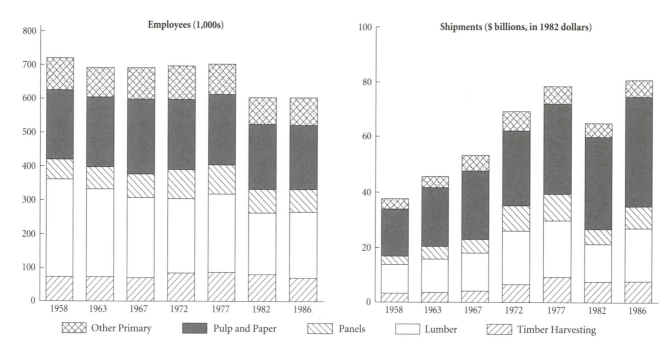

Figure 2. Employment and Value of Shipments in the Primary Timber Processing Industries, by Industry, 1958–1986

Source: U.S. Census 1990.

technology or the wages demanded by highly trained workers remains to be seen.

From Labor-Intensive to Capital-Intensive Production

Until the 1930s, labor-intensive production methods dominated the primary processing industries. Logging camps that swept the nation from east to west during the nineteenth and early twentieth centuries, leaving cutover areas and ghost towns in their wake, embodied these methods. Large numbers of skilled and unskilled males found physically demanding, dangerous work in highly exploitative, company-owned logging camps. Working 12-hour days, crews felled, delimbed, bucked (sectioned), and drove logs to lumber and pulp mills by rivers.

Even before World War II, the shift from labor- to capital-intensive primary production was well under way. The development of West Coast gyppo (subcontractors) logging was an important first step in the transition. According to Carroll (1995), timber felling, bucking, and skidding operations—tasks whose results were readily measured—came to be the domain of gyppo loggers immediately following World War I. The practice permitted mill owners to acquire more capital by externalizing harvesting and hauling costs. That gyppo logging came into existence as the militant International Workers of the

World gained widespread popularity in the logging camps of the Northwest, the center of the industry at the time, in all likelihood was not coincidental.

Technological developments before and during World War I added momentum to the growth of gyppo logging. The internal combustion engine, used to truck logs to mills and, by the 1930s, chain saws gave independent gyppos greater productive capacity. Caterpillar tractors derived from the World War I tank increased the ability of the gyppos to haul logs from areas far from roads. Thus, even before World War II, the processing industry was on the way to converting labor-intensive logging into a system of production based on small-scale capital.

World War II and the postwar baby boom provided added incentives to increase the productivity of workers in forests and mills. Producers could not meet the growing demand for lumber and paper with their traditional methods. Production was limited, in part, by a shrinking supply of workers caused by rural-to-urban migration and restrictive immigration quotas. The few remaining rural workers could demand high wages, and employers faced an added price squeeze as a result of New Deal legislation in 1938 that required payment for workmen's compensation insurance.

Consequently, the advent of gyppo logging using

Like other natural resource industries, forestry is a delicate balance of environmental preservation and maximum utilization of trees for products such as paper, furniture, and building materials.

chain saw harvesting technology was only the first in a series of technological development in the industry. Aided by a growing network of forestry schools, engineering labs, and government research units, the industry adopted a series of harvesting and wood-processing techniques leading to what has been called "no foot on the ground, no hand on the tree" harvesting technology (Vail 1989, 370). Drive-to-tree feller bunchers, incendiary devices such as napalm to thin forests, chain flailers for rapid delimbing, mobile high-lead yarding equipment, and helicopters came to play important roles in an increasingly automated industry.

Poverty in Local Economies

Surprisingly little research exists on the social consequences of wood-based products firms squeezing labor from production to continue operating at a profit. However, there is evidence to suggest that communities dependent on the forestry industry have higher levels of poverty than other rural areas (Rural Sociological Society Task Force 1993). Whether poverty is a direct result of job losses triggered by firms automating to protect profits and forestry workers refusing to relocate remains one of the significant issues in this literature.

Recent theoretical work suggest three possible reasons why extractive economies have more poverty (see Rural Sociological Society Task Force 1993). First, as already indicated, the industry contains milling, pulping, and paper production sectors that are highly concentrated. Oligopolies in these sectors tend to be multiregional; profits from production flow toward metropolitan headquarters and to geographically dispersed capital investors. Declining numbers of jobs in rural branch plants affect income levels in the community. However, the equipment and supplies for the plants come from outside, and the processing of logs, pulp, or lumber rarely occurs at the site of extraction or milling. Fewer industrial jobs throughout the nation limit options for rural unemployed forestry industry workers, and their local employment options are also limited. Moreover, the workers and their families remain deeply committed to their occupations and communities (Carroll 1995).

A second explanation involves rational underinvestment in human capital. Residents in communities dependent on the forestry industry, especially places with primary production firms, are unwilling or financially unable to support adequate public schools. The problem is partly the result of forest industry branch plant managers powerful enough to keep their industrial property underassessed and thus to avoid most local taxes. This shifts the tax burden for local services such as schools onto low-wage earners in the community. Add to this residents' relatively low expectations about the return from high educational attainment, and these communities tend to foster underinvestment in human capital with poor schools, limited actual prospects for realizing a high return from school achievements, and high rates of school dropouts.

A third possible explanation for higher rates of poverty within local extractive economies focuses on a possible acceleration in the rate of job losses in forestry industries and the growth of rural poverty stemming from environmental concerns. Growing public interest in old-growth forest preservation and the protection of biodiversity could stimulate what environmental sociologists call planned scarcity. The shortage of wood supplies would be a result of state action on public forest land in response to an increasingly powerful environmental social movement.

Market analysts recognize a similar possibility in Canada, where one can also find growing interest in forest land preservation. Nearly 90 percent of Canadian forests are on public land. Unless forestry-dependent communities that find themselves without access to harvestable forest resources because of planned scarcity are able to develop alternative sources of employment, there could be a positive relationship between growing interest in forest preservation and rates of rural poverty.

—*Craig R. Humphrey*

See also
Forest Products; Foresters; Forests; Natural Resource Economics; Sawmilling.

References
Carroll, Matthew S. *Community and the Northwestern Logger: Continuities and Changes in the Era of the Spotted Owl.* Boulder, CO: Westview Press, 1995.
D'Aveni, Richard A., and Anne Y. Ilinitch. "Complex Patterns of Vertical Integration in the Forest Products Industry: Systematic and Bankruptcy Risks." *Academy of Management Journal* 35 (1992): 596–625.
Haynes, Richard W. *An Analysis of the Timber Situation in the United States: 1989–2040.* U.S. Department of Agriculture General Technical Report RM-199. Washington, DC: U.S. Department of Agriculture, Forest Service, 1990.
Rural Sociological Society Task Force on Persistent Rural Poverty. *Persistent Poverty in Rural America.* Boulder, CO: Westview Press, 1993.
Shaw, Carol A. "Outlook Mixed for Forest Products Industry." *Standard and Poor's Industrial Surveys* (5 August 1993): B75–B85.
U.S. Bureau of the Census. *1987 Census of Manufacturing: Subject Series: Concentration Ratios in Manufacturing.* MC87-S-6. Washington, DC: U.S. Government Printing Office, 1992.
Vail, David. "How to Tell the Forest from the Trees: A Comparison of Recent Technological Innovations in Logging Systems in Sweden and Maine." *Technology and Society* 11 (1989): 347–376.

Forests

Complex plant communities including trees, shrubs, annual plants, soils, and a variety of animal life. Forests provide many benefits ranging from timber to scenery. Their composition is influenced by their location and climate, and their distribution varies widely across the United States. Forests are a product of the land, and the management goals of the landowners determine the uses of the forest. This entry describes the multiple benefits of forests. It examines forest types and their relationship to landownership and, finally, how forests affect rural America.

More Than Trees

Forests provide many benefits for rural America. Timber growing and processing provides jobs linked directly to timber, the most obvious physical product of the land. Leasing land for hunting and other forms of recreation benefits rural landowners and local businesses such as gas stations and restaurants. Forests can provide a basis for nature-based tourism, which benefits rural communities through local businesses. Finally, forests provide recreation opportunities for local residents and the feelings of peace and tranquility usually associated with rural America.

Forests offer much more than trees. They provide timber, wildlife, water, recreation, scenery, and many other products, including some as obscure as nuts, mushrooms, and various herbs and medicinal plants. Regardless of the product, all forests have one thing in common—land. Land is the basis of the forest, and its location, quality, and ownership help to shape its use. It is sometimes said that land remains in forests because it is not good for anything else. Its distance is too far from population centers to use for commercial or industrial purposes, and it is either inaccessible or not of sufficient quality to be used for agricultural purposes. As a result, forests are associated with rural America. However, the amount of forested land has decreased in the United States. As rural areas have developed, land has been converted from forest to more profitable uses. This conversion generally helps communities economically, but it changes their character considerably. Fortunately, the decrease in the amount of forest slowed, perhaps to the point of stabilizing, in recent years.

Types and Landownership

Forests and the patterns of landownership are factors that play a major role in shaping rural communities. The U.S. Forest Service conducts periodic forest surveys to collect data about forestland and landownership, tree species and sizes, and quantities of timber that have been removed (primarily harvested) or died. The surveys track and monitor changes in forest condition and forestland characteristics. These surveys focus on land and timber. No attempts are made to inventory wildlife, recreation, or other forest products. The results of the survey are valuable to researchers and are published both in detailed and summary form. Several publications are devoted to each state. Data presented here are from the most recent summary publication (Powell et al. 1994; see table).

Western forests are primarily coniferous, made up mostly of pines, firs, spruces, and hemlock. Eastern and midwestern forests tend to have more variety, containing hardwoods such as oaks, hickory, maple, beech, and aspen. The forests may be made up predominantly of a mixture of hardwood species, hardwoods and conifers, or predominantly conifers. The most common conifers in the East and Midwest are pines, although spruce, fir, and other conifers can be found in these areas. In general, trees are larger in the West than in the Midwest and East.

About one-third of the land area in the United States is forested, but forested land is not distributed evenly across the country. The Northeast, for example, an area often associated with large cities and many people, is 67 percent forested. The Pacific Northwest, which is often thought of in terms of its forests, is 47 percent forested. Forestland in the United States is distributed roughly such that the East has the highest percentage of forestland and the Pacific Northwest ranks second. The north central and south central United States rank third. Other areas have less forested land, and the Great Plains area, which is about 2 percent forested, ranks last. The most heavily forested state is Maine (89 percent), and the least

Unreserved Forest Land (%) by Ownership Class and Region (1992)

| Region | Ownership Category | | | |
	National Forest	Other Public	Forest Industry	Nonindustrial Private
Northeast	3	8	15	74
North central	9	19	5	66
Southeast	6	6	19	70
South central	5	4	19	72
Great Plains	24	6	1	70
East total	6	8	15	71
Intermountain	48	23	2	27
Alaska	6	69	0	25
Pacific Northwest	38	16	22	25
Pacific Southwest	36	11	10	44
West total	29	38	5	28
U.S. total	17	22	10	51

Source: Powell et al. 1994.

heavily forested state is North Dakota (1 percent). Some states with large populations are about as heavily forested as some rural states. New York, for example, is 62 percent forested, and South Carolina is 64 percent forested.

Forest landownership plays a crucial role in the development of rural areas. Ownership patterns are not constant across the United States. The forest survey classifies timberland ownership into four main categories: national forest, other public (e.g., state-owned or community-owned), forest industry, and nonindustrial private.

Most (67 percent) of the forestland in the western United States is in public ownership, and much of this land is classified as national forest. In general, public landownership is associated with large blocks of forested land and a set of management goals that presumably have society's best interest at heart. In the East, however, most (86 percent) of the land is in private ownership. Much of this land is owned by the forest industry, which, as with any industry, comprises firms whose principal objective is profit maximization. These are probably the most intensively managed lands. However, the vast majority of forestland (71 percent) in the eastern and midwestern United States is owned by nonindustrial private forest landowners. This ownership category is the most diverse; these lands often consist of fairly small blocks of forest interspersed with agricultural lands.

Nonindustrial private lands make up such a large part of the forestland ownership in most of the United States that they play a significant role in the development of rural America and in rural economies. The term "nonindustrial" is really a misnomer. It is defined as a "class of private lands where the owner does not operate wood-using plants" (Powell et al. 1994, 119). Thus, nonindustrial means that the land is not used by the forest industry, but these lands can be owned by farmers, other private individuals, industry-based owners who are not in the forest industry, or any other type of landowner who does not fit into the other ownership classes. Insurance companies often own large amounts of forestland, which is managed to provide income for pension funds. Farmers and other private individuals, however, often own forestland for reasons that have little to do with income or profits. Many of these individuals own land because they inherited it, and they wish to keep the land in the family. Thus, the objectives of landowners in this category vary considerably and, as a result, the level of management of these lands also varies considerably.

Effect on Rural America

Landownership plays an important role in the development of rural areas. If most forested lands in a region are in public ownership, these lands will probably be managed for a multitude of uses. Many people associate public lands with parks and recreation areas. The Bureau of Land Management, National Park Service, U.S. Forest Service, and many state and municipal forest landowners make a considerable amount of land available for public recreation. Hiking, camping, sightseeing, canoeing, hunting, fishing, and similar activities are associated with these lands. These activities attract local townspeople as well as tourists. The types and numbers of tourists determine the nature and extent of development of the rural communities. In cases in which the attraction is highly unusual or unique (for example, the redwoods in California or Yellowstone National Park), rural economies depend on tourism as their mainstay. Stores, motels, and other services are oriented toward the visitor as well as the resident. Money flows into these areas from the visitors.

Much of the public lands are used to produce timber. In the early part of the century, when the United States was developing, timber was needed to fuel economic growth and development. Much timber has been and still is produced on public lands. In 1991, three billion cubic feet, or 18 percent of all timber, was harvested from public lands. Where timber production is significant, rural areas develop a profitable industry around the planting, care, and harvesting of timber and the production of timber-based products. Jobs created directly by this activity include tree planting, timber management,

logging, and lumber and paper manufacturing. Towns often grow around a sawmill. Many towns in the northwestern United States are based on a timber production economy that , in turn, is based largely on a supply of timber from public lands. These areas tend to be self-sustaining unless they are shaken by an outside influence. For example, the spotted owl has altered the course of some rural areas in the Pacific Northwest. Efforts to protect this endangered species affected the supply of timber on which these areas depend for their livelihood.

In areas where the forest industry owns a significant amount of forestland, timber-related jobs and businesses are part of the structure of rural communities. Timber on these lands is managed intensively, and the trees are often planted in rows as tree plantations. Pine plantations are common in the southern United States. Although some think tree plantations are the firm's primary source of profits, this is often not the case. Forest industry landowners often own sawmills or paper mills and usually are involved with some type of large-scale wood processing. Firms often treat their mills as their primary source of profits and their timberlands as a sort of insurance policy that guarantees a reliable source of raw material for the mills. Their lands are managed intensively and efficiently; the landowners are adamant about replanting their lands. Although timber is the primary product of these lands, many forest industry landowners, particularly in the South, are actively involved with leasing their lands for hunting. Thus, rural areas with forests may have timber production–related jobs as part of their economy and obtain the recreational and monetary benefits associated with hunting.

Nonindustrial private forest landowners are the most diverse group. Rural communities reflect the attitudes of these landowners, which range from opposition to trespassing to an open welcome to fee use only. These landowners may produce timber, firewood, or other forest products, which affects the local economy by adding to its production base. They may lease land to hunters or other recreationists, thereby affecting the tourism base of local communities. They may provide recreation for local residents, or they may not produce anything or allow anyone to use their land, in which case they provide benefits primarily for themselves.

As a group, nonindustrial private forest landowners tend to have poorly stocked lands; the lands produce timber well below their capacity. Most of these lands are not managed intensively. For example, the forest industry owns about 14 percent of the timberland in the United

States but produced 33 percent of the timber in 1991. Nonindustrial private forest landowners own about 59 percent of the timberland but produced 49 percent of the timber in 1991.

Forests affect rural America in many ways. They support a variety of plants and animals. Their ownership and the changing priorities of society are the primary determinants of their use. The uses of the forests help shape the development, growth, and economies of nearby rural communities.

—Allan Marsinko, William Zawacki,
and Don Roach II

See also
Forest Products, Foresters, Forest Industry; Parks; Trees; Wilderness.

References
Adams, M. A., and R. W. McLellan. *Use of Nonindustrial Private Land for Public Recreation: An Annotated Bibliography.* Clemson, SC: Clemson University, U.S. Department of Agriculture, Soil Conservation Service and Department of Parks, Recreation, and Tourism Management, n.d.

Dana, Samuel T., and Sally K. Fairfax. *Forest and Range Policy.* New York: McGraw-Hill, 1980.

Davis, Richard C., ed. *Encyclopedia of American Forest and Conservation History.* 2 vols. New York: Macmillan, 1983.

Fahl, Ronald J. *North American Forest and Conservation History: A Bibliography.* Santa Barbara, CA: Forest History Society, 1977. Computerized database updated annually by Forest History Society, Durham, NC.

Holland, Israel I., G. L. Rolfe, and David A. Anderson. *Forests and Forestry.* Danville, IL: Interstate Publishers, 1990.

Powell, Douglas S., Joanne L. Faulkner, David R. Darr, Zhiliang Zhu, and Douglas W. MacCleery. *Forest Resources of the United States, 1992.* General Technical Report RM-234. Washington, DC: U.S. Forest Service, 1994.

Royer, Jack P., and Christopher D. Risbrudt, eds. *Nonindustrial Private Forests: A Review of Economic and Policy Studies.* Durham, NC: School of Forestry and Environmental Studies, Duke University, 1983.

Stuckey, G. L., Jr., D. C. Guynn, Jr., Allan P. Marsinko, W. M. Smathers, Jr. "Forest Industry Hunt-Lease Programs in the Southern United States: 1989." Pp. 104–109 in *Proceedings from the 46th Annual Conference of the Southeastern Association of Fish and Wildlife Agencies,* 25–28 October, Corpus Christi, Texas. Edited by Arnold G. Eversole. 1992.

Thomas, Margaret G., and David R. Schumann. *Income Opportunities in Special Forest Products.* Agriculture Information Bulletin no. 666. Washington, DC: U.S. Department of Agriculture, Forest Service, 1993.

Williams, Michael. *Americans and Their Forests: A Historical Geography.* Cambridge, MA: Cambridge University Press, 1989.

Fringe Benefits
Forms of compensation offered to workers as supplements to wages. Employers in rural areas offered numerous benefits in addition to monetary wages because farms and mining towns were relatively isolated. Farm employers provided in-kind benefits with values that at times nearly matched the cash payments they paid to workers. In mining districts, employers often rented housing to workers and sold goods to them at company stores. Because the isolation of farms and mining regions declined with the spread of automobiles and highways, the range of fringe benefits provided in rural areas is now similar to the typical fringe benefits offered in urban employment.

Farm Perquisites
In the early 1900s, farm employers offered a wide range of fringe benefits to farm laborers who were employed throughout the year. Farmers offered their workers room, board, and laundry services, either in their own homes or in buildings on their properties. Laborers and tenants with families often were provided with dwellings on the farm property, foodstuffs produced on the farm, and fuel. Many were given garden plots and were allowed to use the employer's farm tools or livestock to perform various tasks. The value of these perquisites was substantial. A 1925 U.S. Department of Agriculture (USDA) study showed that the value of average monthly perquisites ranged from 28 percent of the total value of the employment package (cash plus market value of perquisites) in New England to 45 percent in the South (Alston and Ferrie 1985).

For good workers who had an extended relationship with their farm employer, the perquisites in the South often extended beyond the provision of goods and shelter to a form of paternalism. When trouble occurred, many long-time Black tenants in the South turned to their landlords for help. Landlords sent for doctors when workers were ill. If someone was jailed, the employer often paid the fine, provided a lawyer, or used his or her influence to have the tenant released. Some employers and landlords provided workers with food and shelter during old age.

There are several economic rationales for the widespread use of in-kind benefits. First, before automobiles were widely available, the distances between farms and the relatively small number of workers on each farm made it costly for an independent to provide many of these benefits. Second, farmers often found it less expensive to offer perquisites than to pay enough additional cash for workers to buy the services in the market. The cost per person of feeding and sheltering people was often much lower for the family when they also fed and sheltered their workers. Third, farmers could monitor the behavior and diets of their workers by providing these benefits and thus could potentially improve the labor productivity of their farms. Finally, the provision of paternal benefits and the development of long-term relationships in rural living often aided farmers in keeping valued workers from moving to other places. Such benefits were not easily traded in markets and were not always easily established with other employers.

Recently, some economic historians have argued that the strong paternalistic relationships on southern plantations were important factors in determining the timing and nature of social welfare programs between the 1930s and the 1960s. Southern plantation owners pushed southern leaders and committee chairmen in the U.S. Congress to block or change social security and unemployment insurance legislation during the 1930s. The southern plantation owners apparently feared that federal social insurance programs would break down their paternal relationships with tenants and farm workers and cause a stream of out-migration from the South. As southern farming became mechanized and personal transport improved, however, the plantation owners themselves lost interest in the paternal relations, and their opposition to federal programs declined.

Company Towns

The provision of food, shelter, and medical treatment took another form in the company towns that developed in the mining and lumber industries of the early 1900s. Employers in these settings owned the housing and stores and often provided a company doctor. The situation differed from farming because the employer paid a wage to the workers and then charged them for rent, goods bought at the store, and a hospital fee for the use of the doctor. Some employers helped establish benefit funds for the families of workers injured or killed in accidents.

Coal company towns grew up near mines in more remote, less settled locations, like southern Appalachia and the Rocky Mountains. The quality of life varied from towns that were squalid pits to model towns with decent housing, subsidized schools, and recreation centers. Life tended to be better in newer, larger towns in less mountainous areas because the costs of providing better services were lower.

The common view is that employers established company towns to exploit a monopoly on store goods and housing. The story seems plausible at first because there was only one store in many towns, and the company owned all the housing. However, the monopoly story does not withstand more careful scrutiny. The mines in company towns competed for labor in regional labor markets with hundreds of mines. When the miners chose among mines, they considered not only the wages and safety, but also the town's reputation for quality of housing, rents, and store prices. As a result, rents tended to be low. When companies charged higher rents or offered lower-quality housing they typically were forced by the market competition to pay higher wages. Wages adjusted partially to offset higher company store prices. Miners also used collective action through unions and strikes to improve wages, rents, and store prices.

The regional labor markets did not work perfectly. Miners faced some costs in moving from town to town; therefore, they did not move in response to small changes in prices. Conditions worsened during coal busts, especially in the late 1920s and early 1930s. The competition among employers across mines and across industries meant that workers found coal mining to be a reasonable alternative to jobs in other industries during boom periods. When conditions in the industry worsened during the 1920s and 1930s, however, large numbers of workers left coal mining for other industries.

The union-busting image of coal company towns stems in part from the nature of the housing leases. The leases made housing contingent on employment, allowed less notice for eviction, and allowed the company control over visitors. Many companies claimed that they rarely enforced the leases, and they often deferred rental payments when work was slow or the tenant was sick or injured. However, some companies used the clauses to keep union men out and to evict workers when they struck. The evictions and the presence of company guards at times contributed to the greater incidence of violent strikes in company towns.

Union busting, however, was not the primary reason for company towns. Fear of unionization was common to all employers, but company towns existed largely in areas isolated from other industrial and agricultural activity. The isolation gave both workers and employers reasons to seek company housing. By renting, workers could avoid being tied to a single mine and could eliminate the risk of capital loss on a house in a town dependent on a highly fluctuating industry. Employers had incentives to own the housing to avoid giving independent contractors a local monopoly position. An independent could freely exploit the monopoly at the expense of the employer, who was forced to pay higher wages to compete for workers in the regional labor market. Employers eliminated this wealth transfer by owning the housing themselves. As mining regions became less isolated and automobiles and roads improved, the number of independents who would provide services rose, and the company town diminished in significance.

Company stores have been probably the most reviled and misunderstood of economic institutions in songs, stories, and serious scholarly works. The most common charge against the company store was that company store prices were exorbitant. Because pricing practices varied across stores and across goods within stores, many studies that rely on scattered evidence on a few prices at a few stores have been highly misleading. Careful studies by the U.S. Coal Commission in 1921, the U.S. Immigration Commission in 1908, and the Illinois Bureau of Labor Statistics in 1885 suggest that at most company stores the prices were similar to and sometimes even lower than those at nearby independent stores. Store prices were higher at more isolated mines, but part of the higher prices could be attributed to the higher costs of transporting the goods to inconvenient locations. Further, there is some evidence that the higher prices were partially offset by the payment of higher wages at these mines.

Another common charge was that miners were paid entirely in scrip and on payday "owed their souls to the company store." Scrip was a convenience because it allowed workers to draw on their wages as they earned them. The use of scrip did not imply that miners became debt peons. Evidence from government reports and archival sources shows that miners received a significant proportion of their earnings in cash, that these proportions varied widely for individual miners, and that relatively few miners were in debt. The cash payments miners received on payday reflected what miners had left over after paying for rent, some food expenses, and a variety of other expenses. Most people, even today, would be left with approximately the same percentage in cash after paying their rent and other bills. Few miners were in debt to the store on payday because employers rarely gave more scrip than the miner had already earned. The companies feared that the miner would leave without repaying the scrip or working off the debt.

The negative image of the company town stems in part from nonmaterial factors. In a larger city, workers might have become angered with their employer over working conditions, their landlord over rent, the local merchant for price gouging, and the local politician for inadequate garbage collection or police service. In an urban setting the workers' dissatisfactions could be diffused over several independent entities. In the company town, the employer was landlord, merchant, and politician rolled into one. The employer therefore became the focal point of discontent over any and all aspects of life. Since the company town was private property, employers could prevent trespassers and maintain political control over the town. Workers feared the abuse of this power and the violation of their personal freedom. Violence erupted when these fears were realized in some situations in which miners struck for higher wages or better conditions. In consequence, all aspects of the company town, material and nonmaterial, stood indicted.

The fringe benefits on farms and in mining camps were part of an overall employment package. In urban areas, many of these benefits were offered by independent sources. In order to attract new workers or keep current workers from moving, farm and mine employers had to provide many parts of the employment package that urban employers did not, largely because the isolation of these rural areas meant that there were few or no independents who could effectively offer housing, board, and other benefits.

—*Price V. Fishback*

See also
Agricultural Law; Employment; Insurance; Workers' Compensation.
References
Allen, James B. *The Company Town in the American West*. Norman: University of Oklahoma Press, 1966.
Alston, Lee, and Joseph Ferrie. "Labor Costs, Paternalism, and Loyalty in Southern Agriculture: A Constraint on the Growth of the Welfare State." *Journal of Economic History* 45 (March 1985): 95–118.
———. "Paternalism in Agricultural Labor Contracts in the U.S. South: Implications for the Growth of the Welfare State." *American Economic Review* 83 (September 1993): 852–876.
Brandes, Stuart D. *American Welfare Capitalism, 1880–1940*. Chicago: University of Chicago Press, 1976.
Fishback, Price. *Soft Coal, Hard Choices: The Economic Welfare of Bituminous Coal Miners, 1890–1930*. New York: Oxford University Press, 1992.
Shifflett, Crandall. *Coal Towns: Life, Work, and Culture in Company Towns of Southern Appalachia, 1880–1960*. Knoxville: University of Tennessee Press, 1991.

Fruit Industry
See Temperate Fruit Industry

Future of Rural America

The complex, diverse influences that will result in multiple societal outcomes for America's rural areas. This entry provides an overview of rural diversity and change and the views Americans in general may hold about rural populations. It offers a redefinition of the role of agriculture. The agricultural dominance of the past is being replaced by macro population, economic, social, and cultural forces occurring at both the national and international levels. The "baby boom" effect and the impact of persistent pockets of poverty are described.

Diversity and Change

An understanding of rural America's future should be rooted in knowledge of the complexity and diversity of existing rural society rather than reliance on misconceptions or myths about rural life. The 1995 National Rural Conference on "Understanding Rural America" examined six distinct categories of rural counties. The categories, based on each county's dominant economic activity, included farming, manufacturing, service, retirement destination, federal land, and persistent poverty counties. The diversity implied by this classification runs contrary to the prevailing view that rural America is an agrarian society—it depicts a rural America rich in its variety of economic types. In reality, only 9 percent of the U.S. rural population lives in farming counties. Rural America has less to do with farming than conventional wisdom would lead one to believe.

The complexity and diversity of rural America are not limited only to rural economic institutions. Rural America can be viewed appropriately in terms of the substantial variety in cultural and social forms; rural differences abound in ethnic, racial, religious, community, social class, linguistic, and political dimensions. An understanding of the prospects for the future of rural America thus should not be limited by oversimplified notions of rural life but should reflect the current complex and diverse reality. Given this perspective, even the most conservative assumption about the future of rural America must anticipate many different rural Americas.

Visualizing the Population

At one level, ruralness is dealing with the density and distribution of populations. One method of grasping the spatial distribution is to imagine a map of the United States on which dots are used to represent people. The resulting dot density map would reveal areas of population concentration and sparseness—a visualization of urban and rural areas. This image highlights the massive population concentration along the great urban corridor that begins with Boston and extends south through New York City to the area around Washington, D.C. Also highlighted would be the other population concentrations such as those of Chicago, Los Angeles, Atlanta, Houston, Miami, and the other urban centers. From this view, the conception of America would tend to engender an urban-centered, or perhaps urban-dominated, perspective. Since only one in four Americans are classified as rural, the vast majority of map dots would depict urban areas. The tendency toward urban-centered or urban-dominated perceptions extends beyond population matters to other institutional areas and, consequently, can obscure a broad understanding of the future of rural America.

Rural America is often treated as a minor and declining part of American society. Neither of these views is correct. Rural America is currently, and will be for the foreseeable future, a major part of American society and will continue to increase in absolute, if not relative, size. Although farm numbers and farm labor figures historically have declined, the size of the rural population has either increased or remained stable during each decade of the twentieth century. Nonfarming rural populations have grown sufficiently to offset farm-related losses. The confusion arises from growth rate differences in rural and urban America; the rural areas have not grown as rapidly as the urban centers. However, rural populations do continue to increase in absolute terms and grew more rapidly during the last decade than they did earlier in this century. The trend is for continued growth, with the rate of increase more closely approximating that of the urban centers.

Returning to the dot density map, one can imagine that all the dots representing urban dwellers are eliminated and only the rural dots remain. The resulting image would improve visualization of a rural America unencumbered by the visual dominance of the much larger urban population. Surprisingly, the two maps are very similar, indicating that the spatial distribution of rural populations approximates that of the total population. A major reason is that large concentrations of rural populations live along the edges of urban places. Rural and urban places often blend one into the other in ways that diminish traditional differences.

A fundamental societal change will be the transition from a society dominated by urban-centered forces and lifestyles to one that attempts to merge the strengths of both rural and urban life. Population growth along the edge of rural and urban America can be attributed to a motivation to combine desirable aspects of both rural and urban lifestyles while minimizing the undesirable features. The increasing interconnectedness of the rural and urban lifestyles provides the context for anticipating the future and suggests that both will be shaped by similar influences and may experience common or related trends.

Redefining the Role of Agriculture

Large-scale American agriculture is well positioned to prosper in the context of the forces of growing world markets, open competitions, decentralization, and technological reliance. The convergence in America of superior expertise, excellent natural resources, favorable climate, and strong technological orientation results in a strong position in the world markets. Contrary to the assumptions of those who tend to overestimate modern agriculture's negative impact on the environment and sustainability, American agriculture will probably maintain high productivity and develop technological solutions to these problems. Scientific and technological advances in genetic engineering, information-based farming systems, and improvements in food processing and transportation will keep American agriculture highly productive and decrease impacts on the environment and energy supplies. In addition, American expertise in processing, transportation, and marketing will be used in international production to further magnify the impact of American agriculture.

Ironically, while American agriculture expands as an industry, the future of rural America will become increasingly defined not by agriculture, but by its non-agricultural character. The century-long trend of having fewer farms with increasing total farm acreage will continue. The rural population will evolve into a dual system in which a small minority is engaged in agriculture, whereas the vast majority (about 95 percent) is involved in diverse economic enterprises. The larger of the two rural economies will be distinct, unconnected, and independent from agriculture. Rural development strategies based on increasing agricultural production will be of limited promise since the success or failure of agriculture will have little appreciable direct effect on the well-being of the majority of rural people. Instead, the economic success of most rural Americans will be tied to macro urban, national, and international circumstances.

The Baby Boom Effect

Rather than agriculture, the single most dramatic influence on the near future of rural America will most likely be the aging of the "baby boom" generation (those born between 1946 and 1964). The baby boom generation is the largest, most successful, wealthiest, best educated, and most self-indulgent cohort in the demographic history of the United States. Members of this generation are demanding consumers whose loyalties and lifestyles change often. This generation will invest a substantial part of its wealth in rural America. The oldest of the 75 to 80 million baby boomers are just now reaching 50 years of age. For the next 20 to 30 years, the majority of the generation will experience its greatest occupational success, highest income, greatest reduction in parenting obligations, and greatest amount of discretionary time. Never before has there been a group of individuals entering their peak mature years who collectively hold such substantial resources. Many will pursue lifestyle avenues that will involve an expenditure of their resources in rural settings. An attempt to combine the positive lifestyle features of rural and urban living is a have-it-all strategy consistent with this generation's history.

As baby boomers move into their peak mature years, they will follow a number of paths, some of which will result in the expenditure of considerable resources in rural settings. These lifestyles include increased use of rural America for entertainment and recreation, migration from urban and suburban neighborhoods to rural-urban edge communities, the development of dual residency with both rural and urban homes, and the establishment of urban estates by the very wealthy. Each of these will be examined below.

First, modern communication technology has made what was once thought of as predominantly urban entertainment universally available. Movies, theaters, sporting events, libraries, art galleries, and lectures are becoming available to rural America through satellite and Internet access; the urban advantage in these arenas is diminishing. However, there are whole ranges of valued activities that require substantial allocations of land, which is available primarily in rural settings. Activities such as boating, hiking, skiing, hunting, fishing, and golfing require space. Baby boomers who "want it all" will find rural settings where both types of entertainment and recreation can be most effectively experienced.

Second, housing needs and desires for baby boomers will change as they move from their child-rearing to their mature years. Two general types of transitions in the pattern of home ownership will greatly impact rural America. The baby boom generation will achieve success in combining the advantage of rural and urban life through migration to or establishment of rural, urban-edge communities or through the dual ownership of both rural and urban residences. The first adaptation will most likely involve the sale of homes built for or located in neighborhoods characterized by families with children. A desire to have new housing consistent with their age-related lifestyle interests, especially recreation and entertainment, will be a major motivating force.

The second adaptation is to have both rural and urban residences. The ownership of a second home, a vacation home, a condominium, or time-share arrangement exemplifies this adaptation. In the future, dual rural-urban home ownership will blur the concept of primary and secondary residences. The rural residence will probably be viewed as the primary homestead.

Third, this dual residence adaptation can take on a grand scale with the very wealthy. The desire to hold and enjoy large estates has occurred among the powerful and wealthy in many societies. In American history, for example, the wealthy often displayed their wealth through the purchase and development of large rural estates. There are many individuals within the baby boom generation who acquired great wealth through investments, high technology, manufacturing, and entertainment who will opt to translate their wealth into a modern form of the rural estate. One significant consideration is that the actual number of wealthy individuals able to expend such resources will peak during the next 25 years. The prospect for developments of large estates exceeds, at least in numbers, the period of the previous generation.

The bulk of the baby boom generation ultimately will enter the retirement years. Because of their great numbers, retirement needs and caring for the elderly will inevitably emerge as major American industries. The demands for housing, health care, security and safety, and recreation will become major forces shaping both rural and urban America. The ability of society to remain sufficiently productive and care for such a large aging population is a widely recognized challenge.

Persistent Pockets of Poverty

Poverty will continue as a problem in specific locations. Since the Great Depression of the 1930s, rural poverty shifted from a subsistence-level poverty based on small farms and farm labor to one based on governmental support. Large concentrations of rural poverty in Appalachia, the Mississippi Delta, and along the Texas border will continue into the future. Primarily through governmental transfer payments, these locations developed social and economic structures that are detached from productive economic enterprises. Such locations are not positioned collectively to take advantage of growing opportunities because of a lack of competitiveness. These high-poverty areas generally will not be attractive for baby boom generation migration and investment.

One can expect many rural communities to grow and prosper, while others decline or disappear altogether. Few communities will succeed as trade centers for agricultural areas. However, communities that evolve to meet the needs and desires of the maturing and aging baby boom generation can thrive. Communities located near the edge of rural and urban areas will have the special advantage of proximity, allowing a more effective blending of rural and urban lifestyles. Communities that bring together a cluster of lifestyle products and services in a geographic center will flourish. Growth communities will combine amenities such as housing design for a maturing population, excellent recreation and entertainment opportunities, superior health services, and security and safety. Rural America's diversity and complexity will provide a variety of opportunities to meet these needs, and a rural community's ability to meet needs will determine its future success or failure.

—*Arthur G. Cosby*

See also
Agriculture, Structure of; Poverty; Rural Demography.
References
Castle, Emery N. "The Social Scientist and Rural America." Awards ceremony presentation of the Rural Sociological Society, August 1995.

Heffernan, William D. "Confidence and Courage in the Next 50 Years." *Rural Sociology* 54, no. 2 (1989): 149–168.

Howell, F. M., Y. Tung, and C. W. Harper. *The Social Cost of Growing-up in Rural America: A Study of Rural Development and Social Change during the Twentieth Century*. Mississippi State: Social Science Research Center, Mississippi State University, October 1995.

Jahr, D. "Rural Concerns and the National Policy Environment." *American Journal of Agricultural Economics* 70 (1988): 1078–1084.

Johnson, K. M., and C. L. Beale. "The Rural Rebound Revisited." *American Demographics* 17, no. 7 (July 1995): 46–55.

Miller, L. A. "The Urban Underclass and the Rural Poor." In *Survey of Social Science: Sociology Series*. Edited by Frank N. Magill. Pasadena, CA: Salem Press, 1994.

Mitchell, Susan. *The Official Guide to the Generations: Who They Are, How They Live, What They Think*. Ithaca, NY: New Strategist Publications, 1995.

1995 National Rural Conference. "Understanding Rural America." Agriculture Information Bulletin no. 710. Washington, DC: February 1995.

Wimberly, R. C. "Policy Perspectives on Social, Agricultural, and Rural Sustainability." *Rural Sociology* 58 (1993): 1–29.

Futures Markets

Markets in which prices are established for commodities that will be delivered at a future date. Standardized contracts are traded in the futures markets. These contracts may call for the delivery of a commodity or its value in cash for a year or more in the future. Futures markets provide a way to transfer the price risk of holding or producing a commodity to those who try to profit from price changes in the commodity. To the extent that futures markets facilitate the transfer of unwanted price risk in producing commodities, futures markets provide a way to stabilize income in rural areas. Futures markets also provide estimates of the likely future value of commodities. The price information provided by futures markets can lead to more efficient resource use in the commodity's production and processing. Thus, the futures markets are important in the economic development of rural areas.

How They Work

The futures market is a market in which prices are determined for commodities that will be delivered at some time in the future. In the futures market, standardized contracts are traded rather than the commodity itself. The futures contract is a commitment to deliver or receive a specified quantity and quality of a commodity (or its value) some time in the future. If the futures contract is held until it matures, the contract seller is obligated to deliver the commodity, and the buyer is obligated to accept delivery. However, delivery is not the ultimate disposition of most futures contracts traded since they can be offset anytime before they mature by reversing the initial transaction. For instance, a futures contract buyer can sell the contract anytime before it matures, and a seller can buy back the contract before maturity. Profits or losses in the futures market result from the difference at which the futures contract is originally bought (or sold) and later sold (or purchased).

The price of the futures contract is determined by public auction at commodity futures exchanges. Futures exchanges are generally organized as nonprofit organizations, providing a mechanism for the buyers and sellers of futures contracts to trade. The exchanges have highly developed systems of self-regulation and trade monitoring to protect trader interest. In addition to self-regulation, the Commodity Futures Trading Commission (CFTC), a federal government agency, regulates and monitors exchange activities to enforce federal laws affecting market integrity and trade interest. As of 1990, there were 14 futures exchanges in the United States, most located in Chicago or New York.

Most futures market participants trade through brokerage companies. These companies own seats or the rights to trade on the futures market exchange. The futures trader places an order to buy or sell a futures contact through the broker and is charged a commission for the service. Orders are executed on the floor of the exchange through a public auction process matching buyers and sellers.

Futures trading is not new. The development of organized futures markets dates back to the early 1800s in the United States. Farmers and merchants in the Chicago area began to sell corn time contracts calling for the delivery of corn at a future date and for an agreed-upon price. As soon as the forward contract became an accepted way to do business, contracts could be bought and sold many times before delivery of the corn to the ultimate holder of the contract. This provided a way for those who wished to speculate on corn prices to profit by buying contracts at a low price and attempting to sell them to a corn user at a higher price. Contract trading took place in public squares or on street corners until the Chicago Board of Trade was organized in 1848. The Board of Trade has operated continually since that time and is the oldest of all U.S. futures exchanges.

The early development of futures markets centered on agricultural commodities. Almost all major agricultural commodities have futures contracts. Agricultural commodities dominated futures trading activity until the 1980s. Futures market trade in financial instruments, such as treasury bills and foreign currencies, have since eclipsed agricultural futures in trade volume.

Market Participants

Two basic groups are interested in using futures markets: speculators and hedgers. Speculators enter in the futures market to establish a price for a commodity that they neither own nor have committed for production. They have no intention to deliver or accept delivery of the traded commodity. Speculators simply trade to make a profit from price-level changes.

Hedgers establish prices for commodities they do own or have committed to produce and will be delivering or receiving sometime in the future. Hedging is the opposite of market speculation. Hedging is accomplished by placing an offsetting position in the futures market from that held in the cash market. For instance, a hedger of a commodity that is being produced sells futures contracts to establish a price. The hedger sells because this is the opposite of purchasing inputs in the cash market to produce the commodity. When the product is produced and actually ready to be delivered in the cash market, the hedger buys futures contracts to nullify or offset the previous futures contract sale. The purchase of futures contracts can also be viewed as taking an opposite position in the futures contract from that taken in the cash market sale of the production. The cash market and futures market prices must come close together at or near the futures contract delivery time due to the possibility of delivery on the futures contract. Thus, any of the hedger's profits or losses in the futures market will be offset by profits or losses in the cash market. The hedging process works as a balancing scale; when profits in one market go down, the profit in the other market goes up, thereby putting the actual net price received by the hedger back to the one set originally.

As an example, consider a corn producer who sells a December corn futures contract at $3.00/bushel in June to establish a harvest price. If the cash corn price and futures price were $2.50 per bushel at harvest, the producer would sell corn on the local market for $2.50 and buy the futures contract back at $2.50. The producer would then receive $2.50 in the cash market and a $.50 profit in the futures market to net $3.00 per bushel for the corn.

If, however, both cash and futures prices were $3.50 per bushel at harvest, the producer would sell corn on the local market for $3.50. But the producer now must buy the futures contract back at a higher price than the original selling price, resulting in a futures market loss of $.50 per bushel. The result is that the net corn price received by the producer is still $3.00 per bushel.

Hedgers may also "forward price" through the futures market production inputs that they must buy later in the cash market. For instance, a livestock producer who must buy corn for feed can hedge the needed corn's purchase price by buying futures contracts. When the corn is actually purchased, the futures contract can be sold. If corn prices increase, a profit will be made in the futures market to offset the higher cash corn price the livestock feeder must pay. If prices decline, a lower price will be paid for the corn, but a loss will be incurred in the futures market. Any production input with a futures market can be hedged. Production inputs traded on futures markets range from fertilizers to interest rates.

Speculators, as compared to hedgers, have no product to deliver or accept. If they sell a contract in the futures market, they must later buy a contract to offset the prior sale (in the same way the production hedger does). But when speculators offset their contracts, they have no product to sell on the cash market to offset losses or profits in the futures market. They profit only to the extent they are able to guess which direction the market is headed. To make a profit, speculators in the futures market must be able to buy or offset at a price lower than the price at which they first sold, or they must sell at a price higher than that at which they originally bought.

Hedging is a method of reducing price risk by establishing a price in advance of a commodity's delivery. Speculating is a way to increase risk because speculators take on the price risk associated with commodities they do not own. Thus, futures markets exist to transfer risk from those who do not want it (hedgers) to those who want to speculate on price changes.

Futures market speculators usually lose money. However, since futures market trading provides tremendous financial leverage, it is attractive to those seeking the possibilities of very large returns. The leverage provided speculators is a result of margin trading. Margin is a form of good faith money that must be deposited on the exchange when a trade is enacted. Margin is usually a small fraction of the total contract value, most often about 10 percent. A futures contract trader can speculate on price changes of a commodity for a mere fraction of the total value of the underlying commodity as compared to buying the commodity outright for speculation.

To have an efficient commodity futures market, both speculators and hedgers are required. However, many more speculators are needed than hedgers. The large number of speculators as compared to hedgers is a result of the need to get in and out of the market when participants desire. In order to attract a large number of speculators to a market, there must be price risk. Commodities that have heavy price regulation or prices that do not often fluctuate because of market structure are not good candidates for a futures market.

The Role of Futures in the Rural Economy

Futures markets participants in rural economies are usually associated with the production, merchandizing, or processing of agricultural goods. Direct agricultural producer use of futures markets is relatively small. The complexity of the markets and margin requirements are most often cited as reasons for low producer participation. However, producers may be participants and thus beneficiaries of futures in indirect ways.

Grain elevators or merchants routinely make forward contracts available to producers of their commodities by using the futures markets. The producer of a forward cash contracted commodity benefits by ultimately transferring risk to the futures market speculator. The producer is better able to plan production, secure financing, and stabilize income. Merchants are able to handle larger commodity supplies than if they had to accept the associated price risk. The example may be expanded to include input suppliers and lenders. Thus, producer use of the futures markets is not confined to the small numbers directly involved in futures trading themselves.

The resultant use of futures is a more efficient production and processing sector for the commodity. The profit margins required by the merchandizing and processing sectors may be reduced as efficiencies are increased and risks reduced. Smaller processing margins should mean either reduced prices for consumers or higher prices for producers. In either case, the aggregate effect is to allow agricultural areas to fully and efficiently use resources.

—John C. McKissick

See also

Agricultural and Resource Economics; Agricultural Prices; Agro/Food System; Corn Industry; Grain Elevators; Wheat Industry.

References

Blank, Steven C., Colin A. Carter, and Brian H. Schmiesing. *Futures and Options Markets: Trading in Commodities and Financials*. Englewood Cliffs, NJ: Prentice-Hall, 1991.

Chicago Board of Trade. *Commodity Trading Manual*. Chicago: Chicago Board of Trade, 1989.

Chicago Mercantile Exchange. *A Self-Study Guide to Hedging with Livestock Futures*. Chicago: Chicago Mercantile Exchange, 1986.

Edwards, Franklin R., and Cindy W. Ma. *Futures and Options*. New York: McGraw-Hill, 1992.

Hieronymus, Thomas A. *Economics of Futures Trade for Commercial and Personal Profit*. New York: Commodity Research Bureau, 1971.

Leuthold, Raymond M., Joan C. Junkus, and Jean E. Cordier. *The Theory and Practice of Futures Markets*. Lexington: Lexington Books, 1989.

Purcell, Wayne D. *Agricultural Futures and Options*. New York: Macmillan, 1991.

Schwager, Jack D. *A Complete Guide to the Futures Market*. New York: John Wiley and Sons, 1984.

Gambling

The activity of playing betting games for monetary rewards. American rural communities increasingly use recreational gambling as a vehicle for tourism and economic development. The gaming industry spread beyond traditional urban locales and into rural America, and now casino gambling is common in rural communities, on Native American reservation lands, and on riverboats. Communities saw gaming as a means to obtain substantial economic benefits, but negative social, economic, institutional, and environmental impacts also accompanied many of the new gaming developments in rural America.

The last decade of the twentieth century saw the proliferation of gambling across America in rural and urban communities, on Indian reservations, and on riverboats along major waterways. The rapid spread of legalized gambling, supported by the gaming industry, indicates increasing public acceptance of recreational betting and a relaxation of moral sanctions against gambling activities. Gaming development is proclaimed as a painless strategy for community revitalization and economic prosperity. Local and state governments see gaming as a way to add new money to public budgets without increasing individual taxes. This is particularly attractive for rural communities that already rely on tourists or lack other growth options. The spread of gaming across America made recreational gambling easily accessible for much of the population but also stimulated concerns about the potential negative impacts of gambling. The future will introduce even more questions about the role of gambling in American society and the consequences of gaming development for rural people and places.

The Proliferation of Gaming Opportunities

The American experience with legalized gambling can be traced to early colonial-era lotteries, the proceeds of which supported public works projects, schools, and local development initiatives. Gambling was common in places like mining boomtowns during the country's western expansion, but the spread of crime and increasing moral outrage eventually led to the abolition of most gambling activities. The return of casinos to Nevada in 1931, the emergence of state-sponsored lotteries in the 1960s, and the opening of casinos in Atlantic City in 1978 ushered in a new period of tolerance. By 1995, 48 states, excluding Utah and Hawaii, had some form of legal betting operations (casinos, lotteries, pari-mutuel racing, bingo, and card rooms); many states allowed more than one type of gambling. In 1991, gamblers placed bets totaling about $300 billion; by 1995, gamblers wagered nearly $400 billion a year. Nevada and New Jersey continue to lead the nation in wagering and revenues, but Mississippi and Illinois (riverboat casinos), Connecticut (Native American reservation gaming), and Colorado (rural community casinos), contribute substantial amounts to the gambling total as well. Industry experts predict strong growth into the future, as gambling becomes one of the most popular and fastest-growing leisure and tourist activities in America.

The spread of gambling beyond cities into rural areas began with the opening of casinos in Deadwood, South Dakota, in 1989, and continued with the development of gambling in three Colorado mountain towns, Black Hawk, Central City, and Cripple Creek, in 1991. Each of the four new gaming communities was a former boom-and-bust gold mining town surviving in the 1980s primarily on seasonal tourism and limited mining activ-

Shooting Star Casino in Mahnomen, Minnesota.

ity. Gaming was invoked ostensibly as a way to save these communities from becoming ghost towns and to stabilize the seasonal economy. At about the same time, efforts were under way in midwestern states to institute riverboat gambling; Iowa had the first riverboat casino in 1991, and other states along the Mississippi River and other major waterways opened riverboats later. Native American gaming followed as a result of the Indian Gaming Regulatory Act of 1988. States with legalized gambling contracted with tribes residing within their borders to allow casino development on reservation lands.

The new rural gaming initiatives are characterized by three common themes. First, gaming is consistently promoted as an economic stimulus and revitalization measure for small or rural communities suffering depression and stagnant economies. Proponents claim that gaming development will add jobs, improve personal and community wealth, provide new revenue sources, and reduce local taxes. Second, gambling is rationalized as a new type of entertainment tourism, which is seen to impose minimal social or cultural disruptions on a host community. Gambling by tourists is expected to introduce new money into a locale and region without destroying attractive and valuable elements of community life. Third, gaming development is seen as a way to provide extra resources for underfunded social and community welfare programs, including education and historic preservation. Entertaining tourists is not enough; all campaigns in favor of gambling dedicate some portion of tax revenues to social causes.

With proposals for gaming development under consideration across the country, citizens and government leaders have questioned the viability of continued indus-

try expansion and evaluated the impacts of gaming on individuals and communities. A coherent body of knowledge about gaming impacts is emerging, and parallels across settings are becoming evident.

Riverboat Gaming

Six midwestern states allowed riverboat gambling, and several dozen floating casinos were in operation by 1995. Each state places different limits on types of games available, allowable betting or loss amounts, and boat location (cruising on the river or simply floating at a dock). Competition between the states encouraged some early dislocations as boats pulled anchor and moved to states where tax rates, betting limits, and hours of operation were more favorable. Analyses of riverboat gaming conclude that this type of gaming operation appears to bring new service sector jobs to communities, but since the boats are geographically constrained, they rarely stimulate increased business activity in commercial zones of a town. In addition, although more tourists visit the communities with riverboat casinos, they come primarily to gamble, not to participate in other local entertainments or to shop in local businesses. Leaders and citizens in communities with riverboat gaming report concern about increases in street crime near the docks; land speculation for expanded patron parking areas; crimes such as drunken driving, fraud, and theft; and problem gambling among visiting and local players.

Native American Gaming

The 1988 Indian Gaming Regulatory Act allowed states with gaming to enter into compacts with Native American tribes in their borders to expand gaming development to local reservations. Tribes may provide the same types of games of chance offered elsewhere in that state. The development of one large casino on each reservation is common, although questions about what constitutes a reservation and who is a tribal member are hotly debated. Large reservation casinos have proven particularly lucrative near well-populated cities in the East and Midwest, but even more remote reservations in the West have had economic success operating casinos. Tribal governments often require that casinos be staffed by tribe members, although professional casino corporations are sometimes contracted to provide initial set-up, staffing, and operations assistance. Reports confirm that casino gambling provides tribes with substantial revenue for reservation projects; moreover, this revenue is usually exempt from state taxation. There has been little public domain research about reservation gaming, and assessing positive and negative community consequences is difficult. Rural counties surrounding gaming reservations report positive economic gains from tourism but question the social costs of crime that may accompany the developments.

Gaming in Rural Western Casino Towns

The gaming communities of Colorado and South Dakota share similar historic circumstances and comparable outcomes from gaming development. Gambling is limited to the commercial zones in each town, maximum bets are limited, and gaming revenues are partially earmarked for historic preservation. Although the gaming proposals were intended to favor development of small, locally owned casinos, property speculation, consolidations, and competition made it virtually impossible for smaller businesses and casino owners to compete against large, well-financed, external casino-hotel corporations. Local residents who could sell or lease property for casinos or parking profited with the gaming developments, but those who rented shops were displaced. Since the strongest proponents of gaming—local business leaders—tended to hold positions of governance in the communities seeking gaming, conflicts over self-interest versus community interest were common during the establishment of gaming.

In the western gaming towns, significant economic gains in the form of property sales, tax revenues, and gaming proceeds accrued to individuals, local governments, gaming entrepreneurs, and the states of Colorado and South Dakota. Substantial social, political, and environmental costs also were documented. Many historic buildings were gutted for reconstruction as casinos; hillsides and open spaces were reconfigured as parking areas. Demands on local governments increased, and citizens found it difficult to conduct normal business and community activities. Automobile and bus traffic increased dramatically, and with thousands of new visitors a day, criminal offenses and arrests increased, particularly for drinking and driving violations, assaults, and thefts. Community conflict escalated when residents felt local leaders were unresponsive to their concerns about rapid growth; recall elections were common.

The casino developments in South Dakota and Colorado exhibited patterns typical of those in Atlantic City and other rapid-growth rural communities. Large, externally driven gaming developments were introduced to save a community from suspected decline, thus creating a new situation of dependency for local residents. Although many of the growth issues common to other boomtowns result from incoming resident populations, the gaming towns have been primarily affected by an influx of day tourists. The same type of basic services are needed to accommodate the needs of either new residents or tourists. Town or city governments must upgrade and improve local services and infrastructure prior to receiving financial benefits from the new industry, and this creates long-term public debt. The new gaming towns replicate this pattern since redevelopment beyond the casino zone for the benefit of the community as a whole has been slow to materialize. New hotels, gas stations, groceries, businesses, varied entertainments, and other community services were rarely evident even five years after gaming was introduced. Some casino owners have been quite generous, however, in contributing to local programs and needs.

The new casino developments of South Dakota and Colorado provide several lessons for other communities considering casino gaming as an economic development strategy. Campaigns in favor of gaming typically are waged on the basis of values, not comparative data. Promoters tend to minimize the risk of negative social impacts and elevate the potential for economic gains. Since a portion of tax revenues from gaming accrue to the state, the state becomes a tacit partner in the promotion and dispersion of the casino industry, raising issues about whether governments should advocate activities that encourage citizens to engage in potentially risky behavior. The current approach of allowing unrestricted, free-market competition for casino development in rural communities results in growth that favors corporate casino management, excludes small businesses, and subdues the cultural or historic authenticity of rural places. To the extent that the casino industry is successful in replicating the profitable model of all-inclusive gambling resorts (creating hotel, restaurant, entertainment, and gaming complexes typical to Las Vegas), communities will suffer the effects of colonization by gaming corporations, to the detriment of unique rural qualities.

The Future of Rural Gaming

Continuing economic constraints and recessionary times are likely to encourage more gaming proposals in the future. Since several mega-casinos will open in major American cities in the next few years, casino promoters in rural areas will continue to encourage adoption of gaming as a way to maintain a competitive position in the tourist economy. If the elections of 1992 and 1994 were any indication, the outcomes are not guaranteed. Colorado voters rejected four constitutional amendments proposing gambling for about two dozen other towns in 1992, passing only an initiative that required a local vote before gaming could be implemented. Casino owners' efforts to increase betting limits in Deadwood, South Dakota, also were rejected. In the 1994 elections, citizens of Colorado, Florida, and Wyoming denied new initiatives for casino betting, but video gambling and lotteries were approved in South Dakota and New Mexico, and slot machines were approved for Missouri riverboats.

Large-scale community projects such as gaming development deserve greater systematic study than is usually provided by media, policymakers, or citizens. The rhetoric of despair employed in the pro-gaming proposals, combined with a lack of contextual and comparative analyses, should give pause to communities considering these types of development. Relevant data about employment, crime, business transfers, local revenues and expenditures, personal and community health, and other social and economic indicators often are conspicuously absent from debates about the merits of gaming. Nonetheless, the future could bring further loosening of restrictions against entertainment gambling, increased efforts to elevate betting limits and extend the number of games offered, continued pressure from gaming industry promoters, and greater consolidation of small operations. The overwhelming rationale for expanding gaming opportunities will be the demand for more revenue to address short-term needs. Rural communities debating the merits of gaming must consider whether that growth option is responsive to all residents and to the integrity of place and whether the benefits of gaming outweigh the associated costs.

—*Patricia A. Stokowski*

See also
American Indians; Development, Community and Economic.
References
Abt, Vicki, James F. Smith, and Eugene Martin Christiansen. *The Business of Risk: Commercial Gambling in Mainstream America.* Lawrence: University Press of Kansas, 1985.
Dombrink, John, and William N. Thompson. *The Last Resort: Success and Failure in Campaigns for Casinos.* Reno: University of Nevada Press, 1990.
Eadington, William R., ed. *Gambling and Society: Interdisciplinary Studies on the Subject of Gambling.* Springfield, IL: Charles C. Thomas, 1976.
Long, Patrick, Jo Clark, and Derek Liston. *Win, Lose, or Draw? Gambling with America's Small Towns.* Washington, DC: Aspen Institute, 1994.
Rubenstein, J. "Casino Gambling in Atlantic City: Issues of Development and Redevelopment." *Annals of the American Academy of Political and Social Science* 474 (July 1984): 61–71.
Stokowski, Patricia A. "Undesirable Lag Effects in Tourist Destination Development: A Colorado Case Study." *Journal of Travel Research* 32, no. 2 (1993): 35–41.
———. *Riches and Regrets: Betting on Gambling in Two Colorado Mountain Towns.* Niwot, CO: University Press of Colorado, 1996.

Games

An exercise of voluntary control systems in which there is an opposition between forces and that is confined by a procedure and rules in order to produce a predictable outcome. People play games for fun and enjoyment as a part of their daily lives, in whatever setting they live. They also participate in games at social gatherings where the games are an integral part of the socialization process.

Characteristics

Games have been an important part of rural culture since this country was formed and even before its settlement. These activities were not necessarily team games, which required more participants, but individual or small group games played by individuals, families, several families from adjoining farms, or groups within small communities. People often speak of "playing a game" or "game play," which further emphasizes the relationship between games and recreational activities.

Games are repeatable because of their systematic pattern and their predictable outcomes. Play, however, is less systematic and is open-ended with respect to outcomes. In a game, the participant's voluntary control over procedures has been subordinated in anticipation of, but without guarantee for, a given goal. Sports are games (for example, baseball and basketball games) in which players follow rules more closely than in more informal games. The specificity of the rules depends on the level at which the sporting event is being played.

Very early games were noted in early written records, and information is also provided by archaeologists studying artifacts and graphics from vase paintings and tomb murals that show ancient people playing games. Artifacts include board games from as early as 2600 B.C. and game equipment found throughout the ancient world. Shakespeare mentions nearly 50 different games and sports in his plays, including blindman's bluff, chess, dice, hide-and-seek, leapfrog, and shovelboard (shuffleboard). Many of these games are still familiar today, although perhaps in slightly different forms.

Games occur as a regular part of daily life, but they also serve as an integral part of the socialization process at social gatherings. Here a group of children participate in a potato sack race.

Games were introduced into many nations and cultures at various periods of history as a result of commerce, war, exploration, and education.

Sometimes it is difficult to draw a distinct line between games and sport; for example, archery and shooting are often referred to as both games and sports in the literature. In rural areas today, bales of hay and archery targets are often seen in farmyards or along a wooded fringe of home sites. The people who use these targets may be merely sharpening their skills for hunting or competition or playing a game with other members of the family or friends.

Shooting is another pastime in rural areas; although it is related primarily to hunting, it can also provide much enjoyment. There are specific shooting games in which one can participate. For example, turkey shoots were social events in rural communities in the eighteenth and nineteenth centuries. Although they were highly competitive, they had an atmosphere of gamesmanship about them.

Many old games have been passed from one generation to another without the participants' writing them down or codifying the rules. The fewer the rules, the greater the chance for innovative play and spin-off of other games from the basic game (for example, from hide-and-seek came kick-the-can and run-my-good-sheep-run). New games may be made up or the rules changed to meet new situations that the players encounter. Innovation was particularly important in rural areas where equipment may not have been available or where not enough people were present to make up full teams.

Rural Children

Games are useful tools for promoting enjoyable interaction between people from a variety of backgrounds. Games can be used in many situations; it would be difficult or impossible to compile a complete listing of games. They occupy all or part of the time at parties, church or school gatherings, family affairs, social organization meetings, or camps. Games, songs, and stunts at meetings held by churches, 4-H, Future Farmers of America (FFA), or similar groups consist of starters, stretchers, socializers, and signatures. Starters are used as people gather for a meeting. They are mixers to get people acquainted, warmed up, and enthusiastic about the meeting. Stretchers give people a chance to move around between more formal parts of a program. Socializers are used during the social period or the main portion of the meeting. Signatures bring the meeting to an appropriate and definite close.

Rural schools with a mix of grades one through eight were places in rural culture where children learned most of their games, primarily from older children as well as from their peers. Schools provided a greater opportunity to mix with several age groups. Younger, less skilled children were guided by older children or brought into a game to even the sides. More than urban schools, rural schools used games as part of the educational process.

Rural children can also play games during the walk to and from school. Because schoolmates traveled several miles to school, playing chase, tag, or guessing games along the way helped to make the walk go faster and be more enjoyable. Rolling a tire or a hoop could be considered a solitary game, and rural children often enjoyed this pastime on the way to school. Children played a variety of solitary games. When there were no other children on a farm to play with, children used their imaginations to create things to do, many of which could be considered games to provide fun for the child. The child could practice an aspect of a game, like shooting marbles in a pot, circle, or line; compete against an imaginary opponent; play mumblety-peg with a jackknife to see how high a score can be generated; or shoot baskets and imagine making different moves and shots to win a championship game.

Farm children played games involving horses or other animals. Horse games using poles, barrels, or flags are popular at horse shows and local fairs. Practice or participation in a game with another family member or friends is less important than having fun in a favorite activity. Catching small pigs or calves can be fun. Horseshoes is a game that uses equipment from a farm animal and is more popular in rural communities than in urban settings. Community horseshoe teams often compete with teams from other areas.

Card games have been around for centuries and are still a favorite in both urban and rural settings. Cards may be one of the most universal games played throughout the world because they have been passed on by each generation. Card games are learned most frequently from parents or grandparents in a family setting. Games like cribbage or war can be played with as few as two players, whereas many types of solitaire are played by only one person. Card parties are a favorite rural social activity.

Social Games

Social gatherings in rural areas were opportunities for games. The families of a "threshing round" gathered to plan the schedule for threshing grain at the various farms and meetings after the harvest to settle accounts. These provided opportunities for children's games like apple dunking, sack races, pony races, hayrides, kissing games, and flashlight tag. Men played poker or checkers, had shooting contests, or told stories. Women prepared food, played cards, and watched over the children. The evenings frequently ended with a dance, and different types of dances or games revolved around music.

The "play party" is a distinctive game-dance combination that occurred in early American history. In some communities, dancing was frowned upon, so people developed the play party, in which words of a song gave direction for the action or movement of the group. Young and old participated in games that involved dance movements but, because they were not dances per se, were acceptable in the community. There are ways to get around the mores of a community to have fun.

Game playing starts at a very young age, with games such as London Bridge, here-we-go-'round-the-mulberry-bush, and stoop-tag. These games progress through the teenage years and adulthood into bridge, poker, and various ball games. Some games are played throughout most of adult life until age or lack of interest causes a change in game patterns. There is also a sequence of times for games throughout the year. Children drop one game and take up another as the seasons change every year. Marbles for boys and jacks or hopscotch for the girls led the games in the spring. These were followed by softball, kite flying, hoop and tire rolling, and jump rope.

There is no lack of games available to people in rural areas because of the rich heritage of games passed from generation to generation. Although many games originated centuries ago, there is room for innovative gamesmanship today. Much of the attention to new games is currently directed toward higher-level technology and mechanical games, but these are not "the only games in town." The old favorites still are interesting and inviting for both children who are just beginning to play games and the parents and older siblings who enjoy teaching old games to children.

—*Robert D. Espeseth*

See also
Culture; Recreational Activities; Sport.
References
Avedon, Elliott M., and Brian Sutton-Smith. *The Study of Games.* New York: John Wiley and Sons, 1971.
Carlson, Reynold Edgar, Theodore R. Deppe, and Janet R. MacLean. *Recreation in American Life.* Belmont, CA: Wadsworth Publishing, 1972.
Ellis, Michael J. *Why People Play.* Englewood Cliffs, NJ: Prentice-Hall, 1973.
Huizinga, Johan. *Homo Ludens: A Study of the Play Element in Culture.* Boston, MA: Beacon Press, 1955.
Meyer, Harold D., and Charles K. Brightbill. *Community Recreation.* Boston, MA: D.C. Heath, 1951.
Newell, William Wells. *Games and Songs of American Children.* New York: Dover Publications, 1963.
Rader, Benjamin G. *American Sports—from the Age of Folk Games to the Age of Televised Sports.* 2d ed. Englewood Cliffs, NJ: Prentice-Hall, 1990.
Regnier, E. H. *Fun at the Meeting Place.* Revised. ORPR 14. Urbana-Champaign: University of Illinois Cooperative Extension Service, 1969.
Tillman, Albert A. *The Program Book for Recreation Professionals.* Palo Alto, CA: Mayfield Publishing, 1973.

Government

A social institution concerned with establishing consent and exercising control, power, and authority over public functions. Government depends heavily on citizen participation and citizen-based political and administrative leadership. The major challenges include enhancing administrative capacity, controlling political influence, meeting budgetary and fiscal needs, and providing high-quality and efficient public services.

The Northwest Ordinance of 1787

Rural local government is based on the principles outlined in the Northwest Ordinance of 1787, which provides for the organization of counties, townships, special districts, and school districts. When local governments were first established in the United States, they were designed to provide administrative services and government to a largely rural, agricultural population. In this light, many of the nation's founders, particularly Thomas Jefferson, articulated the view that the foundation of democratic government rested on the yeoman farmer's involvement in and commitment to local government.

The Northwest Ordinance of 1787 underscored the commitment of the struggling new republic to foster citizen-based governments in the new territories. The ordinance established that the new territories would be federal and democratic in orientation, that government would be decentralized to the local level, and that the administration of government services would remain under local citizen control. This far-reaching piece of legislation created the institutional model of U.S. rural local government, with townships, counties, court systems, public education, public works, and law enforcement, that survives nearly intact today. Although deviations from the model of the Northwest Ordinance can be found in Louisiana and some of the original colonies, these deviations serve as incomplete exceptions to the rule of citizen-controlled and decentralized local rural government.

The political structure, administrative apparatus, functions, programs, policies, and politics of rural governments vary widely from one rural area to another despite the common origins of much of the nation's rural government institutions. It is this diversity that provides the strength and adaptability of rural governments in the United States, and it has kept rural government relevant to the needs of its citizenry. Conversely, this diversity makes it exceptionally difficult for rural governments to band together and exercise political power comparable to that wielded by the larger urban and metropolitan governments.

Rural governments have not been subjected to the intense scrutiny that metropolitan and urban governments receive. The last intensive review of this subject is Clyde Snider's *Local Government in Rural America,* originally published in 1957. The political science and public management academic communities tend to overlook rural governments as a separate field of study and treat it as urban government writ small.

Rural Governmental Structure

Geography, history, and pragmatism are the three factors that most influence how rural governments organize themselves. One commonality for rural governments is the establishment of a county government. With the exceptions of Connecticut and Rhode Island, all states possess this governmental structure. In 1992, there were 3,043 counties in the United States, of which approximately two-thirds were considered rural by the General Accounting Office. Nearly all rural counties exercise some form of judicial, taxation, and law enforcement functions. Most rural county governments are the depository for land records and vital statistics, build county roads and bridges, and provide numerous public health and social welfare services.

A style of county courthouse typical in the rural Midwest; this one in DeSmet, South Dakota, serves Kingsbury County.

In some states, particularly in the South and West, the rural county is the only form of local government. In other states, the county may share some duties and responsibilities with smaller units of government such as townships, boroughs, or districts. In all cases, however, the county's legal power and standing are circumscribed by the state. Because of Dillon's Rule (*Merriam v. Moody's Executors* 1868), counties are considered administrative arms of the state and have only those powers expressly delegated by the state or necessarily implied to discharge the powers expressly delegated. Rural counties, in other words, must petition the state legislature for specific grants of additional authority to respond to the changing needs of their citizens.

The township is a common form of rural governmental structure found in the Midwest and Northeast. This form of government is less common in the West because the population density was often too low to support this form of governmental structure. Historically, many townships were founded primarily as a mechanism to support public education. Today, however, the scope of America's 16,666 township governments varies dramatically, even within states. Some rural townships still support a public school system, roads, water and sewers, public safety, and park systems. Most township governments, however, atrophied as county, regional, and state governments grew in size and complexity and assumed the duties of the township officers. Many townships lost their identities as partial or complete townships were incorporated into neighboring and growing municipalities.

The biggest structural change occurring in rural government is the proliferation of special districts that provide single administrative services like rural electrifi-cation, soil conservation, mosquito control, airports, mental health, special education, fire protection, and emergency services. These districts have increased dramatically since the 1940s. There were less than 8,300 special districts in 1942; but by 1992 they numbered more than 33,000 (including urban special districts). Special districts often provide the only mechanism through which basic services can be reasonably and efficiently provided to rural areas. Since these districts are service- and problem-oriented, their boundaries often transcend the traditional political boundaries of the counties and townships.

In stunning contrast to the growth in special districts is the collapse in the number of school districts in the United States. School districts numbered more than 108,000 in 1942, but by 1982, consolidations reduced the number to less than 15,000, a number that remained relatively stable through the second half of the twentieth century. Throughout the nation, depopulation in rural areas and the need or legal necessity to provide the full range of educational programs and equal educational opportunities to children in rural areas forced the merger or extinction of more than 80 percent of the nation's school districts.

Organizational Structure

One of the most prevalent features of rural government in America is the extent to which organizational structures have been decentralized and kept formally under popular control. Rural counties, for example, will elect not only their legislative bodies (such as county commissions) but a broad range of other posts that would commonly be considered purely administrative. Rural counties in Florida, for example, elect their sheriff, tax collector, property appraiser, and county clerk. In other states, the rural county may hold elections for such positions as the school superintendent, county treasurer, county surveyor, county coroner, and county engineer.

Throughout rural America, administrative and policy functions often are closely intertwined to the point that governance and administration are difficult to separate. In many rural counties, the county commissioner and other elected county officials are expected to fill simultaneously legislative, executive, and administrative roles. The multilevel autonomy of the individual officeholder means that each officeholder is in a struggle for control of resources and policy, and neither appointed nor elected officials are able to administer properly in their own spheres of influence.

Complicating matters further is the prevalent practice in rural governmental units of constituting numerous citizen boards and commissions to address specific administrative issues. The intent is to depolitize many administrative issues and remove points of friction among various elected officials. However, the result is often a heightened level of conflict and diffusion of responsibility. The mandates of these boards and commissions may include topics such as historic preservation, specific public building site location, zoning, economic development, and juvenile justice task forces. Rural boards and commissions almost always are staffed by citizen volunteers, and appointments are often made for political purposes. The single-function boards and commissions add another level of politics, another check on government, and an expanded accessibility to government by concerned citizens.

Because rural public administration is staffed by citizen politicians, it often lacks the administrative capacity to perform its roles and responsibilities. Nationally, about 23 percent of all counties have a council administrator form of government, in which an administrator is appoint by the elected council/commission and carries out the policies of the legislative body. Among the approximately 1,600 counties with populations of less than 50,000, only 181 (or 11 percent) have the commissioner/manager form of government. This form of government is most heavily concentrated in a handful of states, including Florida, Idaho, Michigan, Nevada, North Carolina, and Virginia. In rural townships, professional administration/management is even less prevalent.

Administrative Capacity

In accordance with the original intention of the national founders, the prevailing pattern of public administration throughout much of rural America is still characterized by citizen politicians and citizen involvement in rural governance. In the 1990s, however, the problem was to determine how nonprofessionalized government can execute the increased service responsibilities that state and national governments have placed upon them. Rural governments tend to have fewer financial resources, less expertise, an absence of economies of scale, higher citizen expectations, and increasing state and federal mandates for public services. Political conflict increases in such an environment, and it becomes increasingly difficult to achieve the community consensus upon which the democratic model rests.

Within rural counties and townships, the lack of administrative capacity poses serious challenges, and the shortage of professional managerial expertise handicaps rural governments in their ability to plan and manage a wide range of services in the most economical, effective, and responsive manner. Well-meaning and committed but untrained commissioners or township supervisors often lack the wherewithal to make the appropriate judgments on technical issues such as building rural public works; delivering effective medical service; planning for natural disasters; planning for land use; and accommodating and responding to burgeoning community crises such as domestic abuse, AIDS, drug enforcement, crime, and the needs of the elderly. In short, many rural governments still rely on institutions designed for the frontier vision of the eighteenth and nineteenth centuries rather than facing the responsibilities of the present and planning for the issues of the future.

Politics

Politics in rural areas is becoming more similar to local politics in other parts of the United States, and rural government is losing its distinctive political character. Nevertheless, there are still distinct differences in political campaigning, party structure, and political involvement in rural areas.

Rural-based political campaigns tend to rely more heavily on personal contact and traditional door-to-door campaigning than is the case in other parts of the United States. This differentiation, however, is becoming less pronounced for several reasons. First, the expansion of cable television to rural areas made it possible for campaigns in rural areas to be conducted heavily through the electronic media so that face-to-face campaigning is less essential. Second, the replacement of small-town, Main Street America with regional commercial centers changed the locus of political campaigning to the regional malls. Third and most important, rural power in state legislative districts has been considerably diluted in recent decades following the U.S. Supreme Court's one-person, one-vote decisions. These decisions enhanced the political power of urbanized areas in the state decision-making processes about districting. A result of this shift in political power at the state level is that rural areas often are attached to more densely populated districts so that rural-based interests became marginal in the political process. Thus, many state legislators and other district-based officials have a rural constituency, but that rural-based interest may be a relatively small component of the interests of the full district.

Rural-based county- and township-level political organization parallels the structure of local party organizations in more densely populated areas. These party structures tend to be more informal, and the level of interparty competition tends to be somewhat lower than is found in more urbanized areas. Rural counties have countywide party organizations with county committees and often district- or precinct-level structures. These committees focus on the recruitment, selection, and advancement of promising political candidates for county elected posts and for advancement to state legislative office. Because of the reduced level of interparty competition in the past, rural parties and their candidates fared reasonably well and often achieved influential positions in state government through the powers of incumbency and seniority. As term limits become a more accepted practice, rural areas find their advantage to be diminishing as seniority becomes less relevant.

Political participation rates, voter turnout, and party identification in rural areas are becoming more similar to those found in more densely populated areas. With the exception of the southeast, rural America tends to support Republican Party candidates more than the nation as a whole. The disproportionate predilection toward the Republican Party nearly disappears when the heavily Democratic cities are removed from consideration. Rural areas, in other words, are not significantly more partisan than suburban or nonmetropolitan regions.

Levels of voter turnout tend to be somewhat higher in rural areas compared to other regions in the nation. However, much of the difference in voter turnout in rural areas may be due to variables such as the prevalence of longer-term residency, higher age profiles, demographics associated with a civic culture, and relatively large fixed wealth. The associative factors rather than ruralism itself may explain much of the comparatively heightened level of political participation in rural areas.

Taxation and Financial Pressures

One of the most unheralded phenomena in rural government in America has been the concerted push by regional, state, and the national governments to equalize service delivery and the provision of public services among urban and rural areas. For rural government this has meant an enormous expansion of government responsibility beyond its traditional domain. Deinstitutionalization of mental health services, expansion of special education programs, strengthening of environmental protection and solid waste disposal regulations, expanded clean air and water provisions, uniform jail standards, and newly implemented growth management and planning requirements are a few of the new special services required by other units of government of counties, special districts, and school districts in rural areas.

This expansion and the national standardization of public services have placed enormous new burdens on rural governments. First, many rural governmental officials deeply resent the intrusion on their autonomy implied by these proliferating intergovernmental mandates. Second, intergovernmental support to rural local governments, particularly by the federal government, declined just as the need for services increased. Third, the aging demographic profile of many rural counties and the relatively high concentration of poverty in many rural counties increases the demand for many human services and reduces the revenue capacity upon which a rural government can draw. Fourth, the value added by traditional rural economies, particularly property values, has not kept pace with local, rural fiscal demands. These factors combine to mean that the level of fiscal burdens on taxpayers to support local governments in rural areas is higher than in metropolitan areas.

Challenges

The paradox for government in rural areas is that the environment in which rural governments operate changed dramatically in recent decades, but governmental institutions and administrative structure have been frozen in the patterns established in the nineteenth century. Rural no longer means remote, and rural life choices no longer imply minimal government and substandard levels of service. Rural residents now demand from their elected officials, and are often entitled by state or federal law to receive, a proliferating menu of local public services. Simultaneously, citizens in rural areas are often adamantly opposed to increases in administrative staffing, professionalism in administrative structures, distant and bigger government, and higher levels of taxation. Thus, the squeeze between citizen needs and governmental resources in rural governments is exceptionally brutal, and significant change, reforms, and innovations in rural government cannot be avoided much longer.

—Jim Seroka

See also
Leadership; Policing; Policy, Socioeconomic; Politics; Public Services; Regional Planning.

References

Bryan, Frank. *Politics in the Rural States: People, Parties and Processes.* Boulder, CO: Westview Press, 1981.

Cigler, Beverly. "The Special Problems of Rural County Governments." Pp. 89–106 in *County Governments in an Era of Change.* Edited by David Berman. Westport, CT: Greenwood Press, 1993.

Johnson, Kenneth M., John P. Pelissero, David B. Holian, and Michael T. Maly. "Local Government Fiscal Burden in Non-metropolitan America." *Rural Sociology* 60, no. 3 (Fall 1995): 381–398.

Phillips, Willard, and Barton D. Russell. *Rural Government: A Time of Change.* Washington, DC: U.S. Department of Agriculture, 1982.

Reeder, Richard. *Rural and Urban Government Fiscal Trends 1977–1982.* Washington, DC: U.S. Department of Agriculture, 1988.

Reeder, Richard, and Anicca A. Jansen. *Rural Governments—Poor Counties 1962–1987.* Washington, DC: U.S. Department of Agriculture, 1995.

Seroka, Jim. *Rural Public Administration: Problems and Prospects.* Westport, CT: Greenwood Press, 1986.

Snider, Clyde. *Local Government in Rural America.* New York: Appleton-Century-Crofts, 1957; reprint, Westport, CT: Greenwood Press, 1974.

Grain Elevators

Facilities that buy grain from farmers; grade, condition, and store grain for periods of time; and sell and ship grain to export markets or to end users for manufacture into animal feed, food for human consumption, or industrial products. Most grain elevators are located in grain-producing areas. A few are located at export ports and at terminal locations, including Chicago, Minneapolis, Kansas City, and Wichita. This entry focuses on those grain elevators located in grain-producing areas in rural America. It describes the functions and the changing role of the local grain elevator system in rural America.

The System

Most U.S. grain harvests last only three or four months. Wheat harvest begins in Texas in late May and usually is completed in the northern Wheat Belt in late July or early August. Corn and soybeans are typically harvested in September and October. Consumption, however, occurs throughout the year. Much of the consumption takes place at locations distant from the production points. Thus, a marketing and distribution system is required to accumulate, condition, store, and transport the grain to consumption areas throughout the entire year. Most grains are sold by farmers to nearby grain elevators. The grain elevators store the grain and sell it to end users throughout the year.

In the mid-1800s, a grain elevator system developed so that farmers would be required to haul the grain no more than 5–6 miles. This was about the maximum round-trip distance to grain elevators that horses pulling wagonloads of grain could travel to and return home with purchased supplies within one day. Competition for a producer's grain was limited to the two or three elevators located in nearby towns.

These early grain elevators purchased grain and almost immediately sold it for delivery by a railroad to a large terminal market. The terminal elevators accumulated, stored, graded, and sold the grain to end users. All of the early local grain elevators were located on a railroad line because railroads were the only available mode to transport grains to distant markets. The grain elevator was the source of supplies used in agricultural production, including feed, twine, rope, farm equipment, harnesses, and animal health supplies. The elevator was the main source of coal for heating and kerosene for lighting. Many elevators also sold clothing, small hardware, cooking stoves and utensils, and canning and food supplies.

The early elevators were owned by large grain companies, local partnerships, or sole proprietors. Farmers perceived that they were not treated fairly by the private sector elevators and often blamed the grain companies and railroads for their deteriorating financial plight. Some farmers argued that cooperative buying and selling would enable them to achieve economies of scale by buying inputs and consumer goods and selling outputs. Moreover, cooperatives would enable farmers to bypass middlemen who were perceived as engaged in unethical business practices. The first cooperative grain elevators were formed in the Midwest around 1850. By 1900, numerous farmer-owned cooperative elevators had been established in the Midwest. Those cooperatives provided competition to the privately owned elevator in the same town and some competition to those located in nearby towns.

In the early days, grain elevators earned most of their revenue from buying and selling grain and from selling farm and household supplies. They also earned a small amount of revenue by storing grain, but their storage income was small because the early elevators were small, wooden houses that could store only very limited amounts of grain. During the mid- to late 1950s, federal government price support programs withheld grain from the market to raise prices to farmers. Before the 1950s, "ever-normal granary" supplies (the supplies farmers held as part of federal programs to maintain farmers' incomes and a national food supply) were stored largely

Grain elevator in DeSmet, South Dakota.

on farms. In contrast, most of the increase in government-stored grain during the mid- to late 1950s was stored in local grain elevators. This rapid increase in government-stored grain resulted in a major expansion of grain elevator storage capacity, mostly in upright concrete silos. Elevator storage capacity continued to increase during the 1970s and 1980s. Total grain elevator storage capacity increased from about 5.0 billion bushels in 1961 to 8.5 billion bushels in 1993. Over 53 percent of the 8.5-billion-bushel capacity is located in Illinois, Iowa, Texas, Kansas, and Nebraska. Over half of the 3.5-billion increase in capacity from 1961 to 1993 is located in Iowa, Illinois, and Nebraska. At harvest time in the Corn Belt, many grain elevators also store corn outside, usually on a concrete or asphalt pad. Cold temperatures during the winter keep this corn from deteriorating. However, these outside piles of corn must be moved to market by February before the weather turns warm.

A Typical Grain Elevator

Grain elevators range in size from 500,000 bushels to several million bushels of storage capacity. A typical plant is constructed of poured concrete or steel. A scale for weighing grain is placed in a driveway or other readily accessible position. Elevators have one or more pits below ground level into which the grain is dumped from trucks or tractor-wagon combinations. The grain is transferred from the receiving pits to storage bins by a series of belts. Vertical belts typically have V-shaped buckets to lift grain to the top of the elevator. Grain is moved to the different parts of the elevator by electrically operated machinery and by gravity. The storage bins may be equipped with spouts and a weighing scale to load grain into railroad cars and trucks.

Changing Ownership Patterns

During the 1960s and 1970s, the railroad system serving most of the grain elevators in the Corn and Wheat Belts fell into despair. Branch lines deteriorated to the extent that trains with new 100-ton covered hopper cars derailed on a daily basis. Most of the railroad companies earned little or no profit, and several lost huge amounts of money and bordered on bankruptcy. As a result, many branch lines were abandoned. The rail and ties were taken up and salvaged, and the rights-of-way were sold or turned back to the adjoining landowners or converted to trails. Grain elevators without rail service attempted to regain access to rail service by consolidating or merging with nearby elevator companies that continued to have rail service. Most of the elevators that lost their rail lines continue to be operated but not as independent operations. Rather, many are now part of a multilocation company or cooperative. In some areas, up to 20 elevators merged or consolidated and are operated under one management. Only a very small number of elevators have been dismantled or are unused. Rather, most remain in operation, with several locations under the control of one management group.

As branch rail lines were abandoned, almost all new storage facility investments were made at grain elevator locations with rail service. Today, many grain elevators on rail lines have up to 20 million bushels of grain storage, can load 100-car unit trains, and provide official weights and grades. These very modern facilities enable the grain elevator to bypass the terminal markets and ship grain directly to domestic end users, to export ports, and directly into Mexico. Bypassing terminal elevators reduces transportation and handling costs. These savings are usually shared by farmers, consumers, grain processors, and transportation companies. Thus, grain elevator management must have access to up-to-date world and local information on market prices and supplies to successfully operate in the national and global markets.

The capital requirements of large, modern unit-train loading elevators often can be raised only by farmer-owned cooperatives (unit-trains refer to a set of 54 grain cars going to the same destination). Thus, in many dense grain-producing areas of the Corn and Wheat Belts that rely heavily on unit-train rail transportation, cooperatives became the dominant type of organization owning and operating grain elevators. Sole proprietor–operated elevators exist mainly in areas of less dense production and in those areas located close to grain processors or barge terminals that ship grain down navigable rivers. In these latter two cases, trucks are likely to be the dominant mode of grain transport. Significantly less capital is required for these truck-based grain elevators.

Many local cooperative grain elevators jointly own regional grain marketing cooperatives and grain processing cooperatives. For example, Iowa grain cooperatives own Agri Industries, a grain marketing cooperative, which itself owns barges, rail cars, and barge-loading elevators on the upper Mississippi River. Agri Industries, in

a partnership with Cargill, also owns Agri Grain Marketing, a grain-merchandising firm. Iowa cooperatives also own a large share of AGP, a large soybean-processing cooperative, as well as smaller grain-marketing cooperatives. Cooperative grain elevators in other states also own regional grain-marketing and -processing cooperatives and have partnerships with other large grain firms.

Risk Management
Grain elevator management typically uses the futures market to hedge grain it owns in storage but has not yet sold. Management also uses the futures market basis to establish the prices bid to farmers and to decide when to sell the grain held in storage. Basis is defined as the difference between the most recent futures contract and the cash price that the elevator bids for grain on a specific day. Elevators profit as the basis becomes smaller on owned grain stored in the elevator. When the expected basis change and the spreads between the futures contract months are large enough to guarantee a reasonable return for holding the grain, the operator generally will keep the grain in storage and hedge it on the futures market. A profitable spread covers the costs of interest, based on the value of the stored grain, the amount of borrowed capital in the business, insurance, cost of storage, shrinkage, and quality deterioration. The basis also protects the grain elevator from the risk of grain price fluctuations. The grain elevator with hedged grain faces only the risk of changes in the relationship between the futures price and the local cash price. Handling margins and basis improvement income are major sources of revenue for most grain elevators.

Changing Roles
The grain elevator industry is continuing to undergo major change. Computerization, biotechnology, and satellites circling the globe have major impacts on grain elevator operations. Biotechnology created grains with differentiated qualities that must not be comingled with other types of grains. Differentiated quality grains include those with high protein or oil content or elevated or decreased levels of different kinds of fats and amino acids, each of which have high values in specific markets. Identifying and maintaining the identities of these differentiated qualities requires computerized testing equipment, many storage bins, and access to many new emerging markets.

Grain elevators have become major sources of high-technology inputs to and services for agricultural production. Elevators increasingly provide fertilizer, herbicides, and pesticides and application services customized to specific field conditions by using information relayed from globe-circling satellites. The margins on these inputs and charges for application services are a large source of income for grain elevators. Elevators have evolved from small facilities serving a horse-powered agriculture during the mid-1800s and early 1900s to large, very sophisticated operations buying grain from and selling supplies to large sophisticated farming operations. They are major players in national and global markets for generic and quality differentiated grains.

—C. Phillip Baumel

See also

Agrichemical Industry; Futures Markets; Grain Farming; Marketing; Trade, International; Transportation Industry.

References

Baumel, C. Phillip, Thomas P. Dunka, Dennis R. Lifferth, and John J. Miller. *An Economic Analysis of Alternative Grain Transportation Systems: A Case Study.* National Technical Information Service, PB 224 819 (November), Springfield, VA, 1973.

Chicago Board of Trade. *GRAINS, Production, Processing and Marketing.* Chicago: Chicago Board of Trade, 1982.

Lasley, Paul, C. Phillip Baumel, Ron Deiter, and Pat Hipple. "Strengthening Ethics within Agricultural Cooperatives." Ames: Department of Sociology, Iowa State University, unpublished report.

U.S. Department of Agriculture. *Agricultural Statistics, 1961.* Washington, DC: U.S. Department of Agriculture, 1961.

———. *Grain Stocks.* (January). Washington, DC: U.S. Department of Agriculture, National Agricultural Statistics Service, 1961.

———. *Grain Stocks.* (January). Washington, DC: U.S. Department of Agriculture, National Agricultural Statistics Service, 1994.

Grain Farming

The economically profitable and environmentally benign propagation of any small-grain or coarse-grain cereal crop that is intended for human or animal consumption.

Changes in Twentieth-Century Agriculture

More dramatic changes in grain farming occurred in twentieth-century America than in the entire time since the dawn of agriculture 10,000 years ago in the Fertile Crescent. At the turn of this century, agriculture was slightly above subsistence levels. One farmer produced enough to feed seven people. Farmers of the early 1900s constituted nearly 50 percent of the population and depended on animal power for fieldwork. By 1940, the farm population declined to 25 percent of the nation's population. As tractors replaced horses and mules for power, oat and barley acreage declined. After World War II, cheap nitrogen fertilizers replaced manures and legumes that were used in rotation to provide nitrogen for succeeding crops.

Tremendous yield increases were observed with genetic improvements of field crops and management techniques. Hybrid corn replaced open-pollinated corn varieties during the late 1940s and 1950s; hybrid grain sorghum was accepted by farmers in the 1960s; and semidwarf wheat varieties were developed in the 1970s. Increased petroleum prices during the energy shortage of the 1970s caused farmers to reduce the number of tillage operations but increased their dependence on chemical pesticides. In the 1980s and 1990s, farmers became more concerned with soil and water conservation issues. Government farm programs required farmers to maintain adequate crop residue levels to reduce soil erosion. Farmers currently make up less than 2 percent of the population, and they rely on tractors with 100- to 300-horsepower engines at costs of $80,000 to $100,000. Today, each farmer produces enough to feed more than 100 people.

Mechanization, Tillage, and Soil Erosion

After World War I, the use of mechanical power spread across the country, but many people resisted this movement and predicted that various evils would befall agriculture and the nation (Pinches 1960). Farmers were already using corn planters and grain drills pulled by draft animals. The first usable tractors were generally small, with 10- to 30-horsepower engines, and were priced at $500 to $1,200. They were used mainly for plowing, which could be done faster than with animal power. By 1940, more than half the farmers in Iowa and Illinois had tractors. The farm population declined over time, and farm size increased, as did output. As tractors became larger, tillage implements became larger to cover more acres per hour.

It had been axiomatic for decades that good farmers had croplands devoid of all plant residue prior to planting. Farmers thought their fields needed to be clean-tilled (that is, plowed, disked, and harrowed repeatedly) to obtain maximum yields. Fall plowing after row crop harvest was a standard tillage practice most farmers used to help spread the workload and avoid the inconvenience of spring plowing, which often led to lower grain yields. Unfortunately, fall-plowed fields were left unprotected during the winter and spring months. Wind and water

A wheat threshing crew in western Kansas in the late 1880s.

eroded millions of tons of topsoil from these bare soils before the row crop, which was planted in the spring, could cover and protect them. Soil erosion became a national problem that threatened soil productivity. Studies in Kansas showed that for every inch of topsoil lot, organic matter decreased and wheat yields were reduced nearly 2 bushels per acre (Havlin et al. 1995).

Conservation Tillage Systems

High fuel prices of the 1970s, concern for environmental problems, and government restrictions on crop residue levels provided the impetus for conservation tillage systems that required fewer tillage operations and used implements that disturbed the soil less, leaving more residues on the surface and thereby reducing soil erosion. For row crops, these systems included no-till, minimum-till, and ridge-till. No-till systems have no tillage operations prior to planting or throughout the year; minimum-till systems have only one or two light tillage operations. With ridge-till systems, ridges are formed by cultivation between rows of the existing crop. They are untouched after harvest until the following spring when a planter with a special attachment scrapes residue and the top one or two inches of the ridge into the space between rows. Seed is placed into the scraped area of the ridge, and ridges are rebuilt by cultivation during the growing season. Conservation tillage systems for row crops are suited best for rotations with soybeans or other crops that produce less residue but can be used in continuous systems.

Wheat-Cropping Systems and Conservation Tillage

In semiarid areas, the wheat harvest is followed by a fallow period in which the land is left idle for more than a year until the next fall planting season. This practice was used to rebuild valuable subsoil moisture. Fallowed fields were clean-tilled to limit weed growth. However, it was discovered that excessive soil moisture was lost with each tillage operation during the summer fallow period. Tillage implements were developed, such as the V-blade plow and chisel plow, that left considerable residues. The V-blade tilled 2–5 inches under the soil surface, cutting off weed roots but leaving wheat residues standing. These implements reduced soil moisture loss and erosion. Later, low doses of residual herbicides applied after wheat harvest replaced most tillage operations to control weeds and conserved more soil moisture.

Agricultural researchers and farmers concluded that combining herbicides with conservation tillage systems resulted in such appreciable soil moisture savings that the fallow period could be shortened and a row crop (such as grain sorghum, corn, or sunflowers) could be planted in the spring. Farmers could grow two crops in three years, compared to two wheat crops in four years with the wheat-fallow system. This new wheat–row crop–fallow-cropping system had a greater water use efficiency (that is, more total grain produced per inch of water) than the wheat-fallow system. Wheat yields remained the same as with wheat-fallow, but farmers harvested an additional crop.

Surprisingly, many farmers resisted adopting the wheat–row crop–fallow system. The government farm programs of the 1980s and 1990s created disincentives for farmers to switch cropping systems. Farmers were encouraged to reduce their wheat acreage, for which they received a deficiency payment on a preestablished farm yield base that was the difference between the current market price of wheat and the target price established by the U.S. Department of Agriculture (USDA). Wheat prices

A farmer using a combine to harvest wheat in 1990.

per bushel that farmers received were notoriously low compared to the cost of production, and farmers were satisfied with the deficiency payments from the government and felt no need to switch cropping systems. However, some farmers saw enough flexibility in the government farm programs and an opportunity to increase farm profits while maintaining and sustaining soil productivity. The wheat–row crop–fallow-cropping system slowly replaced the wheat-fallow system.

Pest Problems with Conservation Tillage Systems

Wheat is grown continuously in much of the Great Plains. Farmers abandoned plowing the wheat straw under after harvest; instead, they use disking and field cultivator operations that leave more residue on the soil surface. This proved effective in reducing erosion and having more available soil moisture at planting time, but foliar diseases proliferated, causing grain yield losses. Two important wheat fungal diseases, tan spot and speckled leaf blotch, are able to oversummer in the straw and infect seedlings in the fall. Foliar fungicide applications in the spring have not been economically feasible for dryland wheat because of its low yield potential and the fungicide's cost. Fungicides have become feasible with irrigated wheat and its potential for greater yields.

As tillage is eliminated to reduce erosion and conserve soil moisture, pest problems generally increase, causing more use of chemical pesticides. Triazine herbicides, such as atrazine, became the mainstays against weeds in corn and grain sorghum production, whereas sulfonylurea herbicides (e.g., Glean and Ally) are used extensively in wheat production. Public concern for water quality and food quality and safety resulted in restrictions on chemical use. Farmers responded by using one-half-rate applications instead of the full, recommended rates and banding herbicides over the seed zone. Crop rotations were reintroduced to disrupt weed, disease, and insect cycles that build up; they also allow farmers to use a cadre of pesticides with different modes of action, a strategy to slow down the development of resistant pest populations. Using disease- and insect-resistant crop varieties is another important management tool to reduce pesticide dependence.

Genetic Improvements in Crop Varieties

Pests have always plagued crops, resulting in losses in yield and quality. Private and public plant breeders developed hybrids and varieties with better disease and insect resistance, subsequently increasing grain yields. One of the first major improvements in corn was the development of resistance to stalk rots, which increased stalk strength, resulting in better plant standability and ease of harvest. Breeders selected for corn leaf canopies with more erect leaves instead of wide, drooping leaves to allow more light penetration and to increase plant photosynthetic capacity. Development of corn and grain sorghum hybrids increased grain yields 50 to 75 percent over those of open-pollinated varieties. Average U.S. corn yields in 1900 were 28 bushels per acre; they reached a record 138 bushels per acre in 1994.

Breeding improvements in hard red winter wheat have not matched those of corn, with yield increases of only 0.25 bushels per acre per year since the early 1900s (Cox et al. 1988). In 1900, the average U.S. wheat yield was a meager 12 bushels per acre, whereas by the 1990s, average yields had increased to 38 bushels per acre. The introduction of stiffer-strawed, semidwarf wheat varieties increased yields by 10 to 20 percent over those of tall, standard type varieties. These shorter varieties increased plant standability and improved the grain-to-stover ratio. Considerable efforts have been made to develop earlier-maturing wheat varieties with better heat and drought resistance and the ability to avoid or tolerate stresses during grain formation.

Increased Fertilizer Use

As grain farmers became more specialized, with fewer livestock, there was little need for crop rotations that included grassy meadows, small grains such as oat and barley, or forage legumes. Although legumes were included in rotations to provide nitrogen to succeeding crops, inexpensive nitrogen fertilizer rapidly replaced them. There was an inverse relationship between increased nitrogen fertilizer use and legume seed production. Nitrogen fertilizers resulted in dramatic crop yield increases, allowed improved varieties to demonstrate their genetic superiority, and increased crop water use efficiencies.

In 1960, 2.7 million tons of nitrogen fertilizer were used, and the amount increased to more than 11 million tons by 1990 (Hargett and Berry 1990). Ammoniacal sources, including anhydrous ammonia and urea, are the most common forms of nitrogen fertilizer. They are developed through the Haber-Bosch process, in which hydrogen and nitrogen gases react to form ammonia (Tisdale et al. 1993). Generally, gaseous forms of nitrogen fertilizers are applied with tillage equipment, and liquid and dry forms are either broadcast over the field prior to planting or applied with the planter in a band near the seed. Broadcast-applied liquid and dry fertilizers are incorporated into the soil surface with tillage equipment or left on the surface in no-tillage systems. Longtime no-till farmers noticed an increased nutrient concentration or stratification in the upper few inches of the soil surface.

As soils are mined of plant nutrients through farming, they eventually become deficient in phosphorus and potassium if fertilizers containing these nutrients are not applied. Phosphorus was one of the first nutrients shown to give a yield response when applied to soils with low phosphorus levels. Farmers commonly observe a return of $3 to $5 for every $1 spent on fertilizers. With reduced use of animal manures and with the enactment of the Clean Air Act, deposition of sulfur has been substantially reduced, increasing the incidence of sulfur deficiency in the soil. Depending on the region, many micronutrients deficiencies are also observed.

—*James P. Shroyer*

See also

Agrichemical Use; Agricultural Programs; Agriculture; Mechanization; Tillage; Wheat Industry.

References

Beale, Calvin. "A Demographic Perspective on the Farm Population." Pp. 162–170 in *A Taste of the Country: A Collection of Calvin Beale's Writings.* Edited by Peter A. Morrison. University Park: Pennsylvania State University Press and RAND Corporation, 1990.

Cox, T. S., J. P. Shroyer, Liu Ben-Hui, R. G. Sears, and T. J. Martin. "Genetic Improvement in Agronomic Traits of Hard Red Winter Wheat Cultivars from 1919 to 1987." *Crop Science* 28, no. 5 (September–October 1988): 756–760.

Hargett, N. L., and J. T. Berry. *Commercial Fertilizers 1990.* TVA Bulletin Y-216. Muscle Shoals, AL: Tennessee Valley Authority, National Fertilizer and Environmental Research Center, 1990.

Havlin, John, Alan Schlegel, Kevin C. Dhuyvetter, James P. Shroyer, Hans Kok, and Dallas Peterson. *Enhancing Agricultural Profitability and Sustainability: Great Plains Dryland Conservation Technologies.* S-81. Manhattan: Kansas State University, Cooperative Extension Service, 1995.

Pinches, Harold E. "Revolution in Agriculture." Pp. 1–10 in *Power to Produce: 1960 Yearbook of Agriculture.* Washington, DC: U.S. Department of Agriculture, 1960.

Tisdale, Samuel L., Werner L. Nelson, James D. Beaton, and John L. Havlin. *Soil Fertility and Fertilizers.* 5th ed. New York: Macmillan, 1993.

Greenhouses

Modified environmental units, which include cold frames, hotcaps, shade houses, mist rooms, and saran houses, designed to provide optimum growing conditions to produce horticultural crops year-round or during the early growing season.

Design and Type

The structural design and size of greenhouses vary depending on individual tastes, available space, building materials, climatic conditions, and intended use. Hobby greenhouses are usually small, often attached to the south side of an existing building. Educational greenhouses are built by public or private schools for classroom instruction and laboratory exercises in seed germination, cutting propagation, plant identification, and cultural practices. A conservatory or display greenhouse maintains and displays many exotic plant species native to various ecological regions of the world. Institutions like land-grant universities, the U.S. Department of Agriculture (USDA), seed companies, and pharmaceutical laboratories have research greenhouses where new varieties, uses, and biological functions of plants are investigated. Commercial greenhouses grow plants for wholesale or retail markets. With few exceptions, commercial greenhouses in rural communities are usually small businesses run by families.

Retail greenhouses raise small quantities of many different crops, whereas wholesale greenhouses focus on volume production of a few species. Cut flowers, potted plants, foliage plants, bedding plants, and herbaceous perennials typically are grown in commercial greenhouses.

Greenhouses can be used to raise freshwater and saltwater fish species (aquaculture greenhouses) and mushrooms (mushroom houses). Hydroponic greenhouses grow plants in nutriculture systems containing no natural soils. Growth chambers and phytotrons used in plant-related research provide the environmental conditions that are more precisely controlled than those in conventional greenhouses.

Construction

Factors like environmental modification, maintenance, accessibility, nearness to market, and potential future expansion must be considered for proper greenhouse location. Greenhouses usually are built on a south-facing slope to maximize sunlight entry during the winter. A windbreak planting may be established on the greenhouse's north side to reduce wind speed, thus reducing excessive heat loss.

If plants are grown on ground beds, the soil should have deep, loose characteristics with good drainage, a high nutrient-holding capacity, good buffering characteristics, and no toxic compounds. A well-drained soil will reduce chances for disease development. Leveled ground is desirable for ease of moving carts and other equipment.

Greenhouses should have access to a reliable source of good water with a neutral pH and low salinity. Building layout on a proper site will accommodate future facility expansion. Greenhouse ridges should be oriented east-to-west in northern latitudes for maximum light penetration. For southern locations, the orientation can be any direction. Greenhouses must be built to withstand forces created by wind (wind load) and snow (snow load) as well as weights created by the superstructure (dead load) and living plants, such as flower baskets, tomatoes, and cucumbers hung from the ceiling (live load).

Greenhouses are constructed with transparent or translucent glazing materials that allow a maximum entry of sunlight into the growing area. For several centuries, greenhouses traditionally were built with wood frames and covered with glass panes, as the name "glasshouses" implies. Glass panes allowed good light transmission and were long-lasting but lost heat and were prone to hail damage. Since the invention of plastics, an increasing number of greenhouses are covered with synthetic polymer materials, such as polyethylene film, fiberglass, plexiglass, polyvinyl chloride, polycarbonate sheets, or other rigid plastic panels.

At the turn of the twentieth century, the Gothic-arch style and standard-peak greenhouses were popular. Today, greenhouses are arc-shaped, easy to construct, and well suited for plastic covers. They are constructed with metal frames of galvanized steel or aluminum that are stronger and more durable than the wooden frames.

A greenhouse range is formed by gutter-connecting several individual Quonset greenhouses. Gutter-connected greenhouses have no internal side walls and are well-suited for mass production and automation. They are more labor- and energy-efficient than the freestanding greenhouses. Contiguous greenhouses are gutter-connected houses in which the internal sidewalls are intact, separating the range into individual compartments. Localized control for temperature and pest problems may be easier with contiguous greenhouses than with the regular greenhouse range.

Polyethylene films are extensively used for individual Quonset houses or gutter-connected modified Quonset houses. They are usually covered with double layers of air-inflated polyethylene film. The air-inflation retains heat and reduces tearing caused by high winds. Corrugated fiberglass reinforced plastic (FRP) sheets, which transmit diffused lights, are well-suited for carnation and other cut flower greenhouses. Whereas FRP itself has low thermal transmission, heat loss from a fiberglass-covered greenhouse is greater than that from the plastic film–covered greenhouse. The more expensive rigid plastic panels, such as acrylic (Plexiglas) or polycarbonate sheets, are durable and minimize conduction heat loss from the greenhouse.

Crops Grown

More than 85 percent of American greenhouses are used to grow floricultural crops, consisting of cut flowers, flowering potted plants, foliage plants, and bedding plants. Major cut flowers are roses, chrysanthemums, carnations, gladiolus, and alstroemeria. Locally grown cut flowers have a longer keeping quality; however, a large portion of cut flowers purchased in the United States is imported. Chrysanthemums, poinsettias, azaleas, Easter lilies, and African violets are important potted flowering plants. Unlike cut flowers, almost all potted flowering plants sold in America are supplied by domestic growers. Florida, Texas, and southern California produce many of the foliage plants purchased in the United States. However, local greenhouses in any region can easily propagate and grow a variety of foliage plants with minimum production costs. Bedding plants are usually flowering annuals grown from seeds. The public demand for bedding plants for landscaping has increased steadily.

The use of herbaceous perennials in private and public gardens has become very popular. Once established, they are easily maintained with little attention for irrigation or winter protection. An inexpensive greenhouse can be used for seed germination and the culture of young plants. Since many of the herbaceous perennials used in landscaping require vernalization (a wintering process) for shoot growth and flower initiation, they are often kept in a greenhouse with little heating during the dormant period. Fully grown plants are usually hardened off outdoors before they are marketed. There is a growing interest in the collection and use of native plant materials well adapted to the local climate. This may create to a new demand for more localized greenhouses.

Less than 10 percent of American greenhouse area is used to produce vegetables, herbs, and other edible crops, mainly because of the availability of fresh produce from southern states and Mexico during the winter months. This is in contrast to the European or Oriental countries, where more than 65 percent of greenhouse space is devoted to vegetables. In recent years, hydroponic production of certain vegetables like tomatoes, cucumbers, and lettuce has risen in the United States. Most of the edible crops grown in greenhouses are not exposed to pesticides, thanks to the effective use of biological pest control measures. However, organic production of edible crops in the greenhouse requires much more attention, because of the difficulty in using organic fertilizer in an intensive production system.

Local greenhouses grow various ornamental woody plants and fruit trees. These plants are propagated by seeds, cuttings, or grafting, which can be done inside a greenhouse during the winter months. Mature seedlings, rooted cuttings, and grafted plants are nurtured inside a greenhouse until they reach certain sizes and are then transferred to a sheltered outdoor area to harden off. For cutting propagation, a humidity control house with misting system is required. Certain ornamental trees like palm; Norfolk island pine; rubber tree; and fruit trees like orange, grapefruit, and pomegranate can also be grown in the greenhouse year-round.

Environmental Control

Although a greenhouse collects much solar energy during the day, it must be heated during the night because of conduction heat loss through the glazing material. The heat loss at night varies by the type of superstructure, cover material, and the temperature differential between the interior and exterior of the greenhouse. Greenhouses can be heated with coal, wood, heating oil, kerosene, natural gas, propane, or electricity. The best fuel source is based on the cost and type of equipment used, heat value, combustion efficiency, and availability of heating fuel. Heating systems can be centralized, localized, fan-and-jet system, or solar.

Greenhouses must be cooled during the summer to maintain optimum temperature. They can be cooled by natural ventilation, but a more controlled temperature can be achieved by an evaporative cooling system, such as the pad-and-fan evaporative cooling system. This system can lower the greenhouse temperature to about the wet-bulb temperature (a function of relative humidity). The higher the relative humidity, the higher the wet-bulb temperature. Therefore, the evaporative cooling system works best in the western part of the United States where relative humidity is low. For a small hobby greenhouse, a packaged cooling unit (swamp cooler) may be used. The fog cooling system has gained a popularity in the 1990s since it does not require an installation of evaporative pads.

Plant Culture

A growing medium or root substrate functions as an anchor and provides water, oxygen, and nutrients to plants. An ideal growing medium at any time should be composed of 50 percent solids, 25 percent water, and 25 percent air on a volume basis. Natural soils are often amended with sand, peat, perlite, vermiculite, or organic matter to improve porosity, water retention, and nutrient-holding characteristics. The soil-less or peatlite mixes are prepared with peat mixed with various proportions of perlite and vermiculite.

One of the most important factors affecting the success of plant production is the availability of good water. Water that contains high level of salts (>1.3 millimho/centimeter electrical conductivity) should not be used for irrigation. Frequently, the analysis of irrigation water can tell what levels of additional macronutrients and micronutrients are needed to make a completely balanced nutrient solution.

Many formulations of macronutrients (nitrogen, phosphorus, potassium, calcium, manganese, sulfur) and micronutrients (boron, chloride, copper, iron, manganese, molybdenum, zinc) are commercially sold. Depending on solubility, fertilizers can be applied when soil is mixed, dry-applied to grown plants, or dissolved in water and applied as solution. The use of organic fertilizers for greenhouse crops is possible when plants are grown on natural soil that harbors nutrient ions for an extended period of time.

There are two different objectives for lighting: first, to enhance photosynthesis by increasing light intensity, and second, to regulate day length for flower induction for short day plants. For northern greenhouses, artificial light supplementation may increase crop yield from 20 to 30 percent. Greenhouse crops like tomatoes, cucumbers, carnations, and roses benefit from supplemental lighting.

Inside air-tight commercial greenhouse ranges, plants may experience a suboptimal level of carbon dioxide (CO_2), resulting in reduced photosynthesis. Actively growing plants in tight houses can quickly lower CO_2 concentrations below the ambient level (less than 300 parts per million [ppm]) during the day. The CO_2 concentration can reach levels well above 400 ppm at night because of active plant respiration. After sunrise, plants resume photosynthetic activity, eventually using up the CO_2 inside the greenhouse if no ventilation is on. Fresh air is needed during the day when plants actively fix CO_2 into carbohydrates. Increased levels of CO_2 enhance crop yields up to 40 percent. For small greenhouses where there is a plenty of air draft, the cost-effectiveness of the carbon dioxide enrichment is debatable.

Healthy plants can be produced without the use of

much pesticide if greenhouses are maintained under good sanitary conditions and the sources of insect pests and disease organisms are excluded. Since many pathogenic bacteria and fungi are soil-borne, the growing media may need to be routinely steam-sterilized for continued use. To prevent disease, many crops are grown in containers filled with sterile media such as commercial potting mixes. For insect pest control, certain beneficial predators like ladybugs, lacewings, and parasitic wasps can be successfully used. Integrated pest management programs use all available strategies of prevention, exclusion, biological control, and chemical application to bring about the best, most cost-effective results.

Economics

Greenhouse production is one of the most intensive agricultural production systems. It is intensive in terms of capital investment, labor requirement, water and chemical use, and amounts of gross income generated per unit area. The average gross income per square foot of growing area is about $10. Thus, an acre of greenhouse, which is usually run by a family, can produce an annual gross revenue of about $300,000. Since the input for unit area is also high, net income will depend on managerial ability and market availability.

Greenhouse production costs are divided into overhead fixed costs, semifixed costs, and direct costs. Fixed costs are the expenses that are permanent regardless of crops grown (for example, depreciation, interest, repairs and maintenance, property tax, and insurance). Semifixed expenses, or overhead variable costs, are expenses that usually increase as production increases but are not directly related to the number of units produced (for example, office supplies, telephone, manager's salary, heating fuel, electricity, water and sewer, business travels, equipment operation, advertising). Direct costs (or variable expenses) are the expenses that fluctuate depending on the size and kind of crops grown (for example, expenses to purchase seed or cutting material, growing media, fertilizer, pesticides, containers and labels, telephone calls for marketing, and packaging).

In a typical greenhouse, about one-third of the total production costs is for labor, followed by marketing costs, direct costs, and heating costs. Although the fixed costs are difficult to reduce, there is some flexibility for reducing variable costs by management decisions. The total production costs for an average greenhouse usually range from $3 to $8 per square foot of growing area, depending on the crops grown.

The market channels for various greenhouse products changed considerably during the 1980s and 1990s. Whereas earlier flower markets consisted of florist shops, increasing number of flowers are now sold through mass-market outlets like grocery stores, K Mart, and Wal-Mart stores. Plant shops like local nurseries continue to sell locally grown or shipped-in potted plants for landscape use. Greenhouses are usually built to satisfy the needs of customers who want fresh products that are more reliable.

Most family-run greenhouses grow small quantities of many different species for a retail market, whereas the large commercial greenhouses specialize in volume production of a few selected species. The current trend is that more consumers buy flowers and landscape plants from large merchandizing stores. These stores purchase many plants from a small number of specialized growers on contract. Even some retail growers may need a mass-market outlet for leftover products that did not move through retail stores. The idea of using direct marketing or selling at farmer's markets for locally grown flowers, vegetables, herbs, and fruits is a relatively new development. Locally built community greenhouses may play an important role in supplying seasonal and off-season products to these viable direct markets.

Roles in the Rural Community

Flowers and ornamental plants grown by a greenhouse are usually consumed within the community, ultimately beautifying the region and providing a pleasant living environment for the residents. Well-landscaped streets and parks decorated with flowering plants enhance the quality of living for that community. People working on a community project have a strong sense of pride and belonging. Beautified streets, recreation areas, and public parks attract out-of-town visitors. A community-run greenhouse can be the inexpensive source of plant materials to be used on a seasonal basis for public buildings and community centers.

Out-of-season vegetables and other edible plants can be produced with a minimum amount of capital investment. Tomatoes, European cucumbers, and lettuce can be grown with hydroponic culture systems to maximize yield and reduce production costs and can be produced organically. Organic soils often contain beneficial microorganisms that maintain a balanced fungistatic activity essential for symbiotic relations between them. Mushroom houses also use organic composts for spore germination and fungal growth. Growing system sustainability can be realized when solar energy is collected as heated water during the day and used as a source heat exchanger at night. For organic production, a greenhouse may be screened to prevent pest entry into the growing structure. The exposed cooling pad areas where the insect pests are easily introduced can be screened with fabric materials to filter out unwanted pests while allowing air entry.

Many outdoor-grown plants can be sheltered in a greenhouse through the winter and reestablished during the growing season. Garden plants like potted roses, geraniums, street trees, and tropical plants can be maintained inside a greenhouse. Greenhouses can be used to care for house plants while homeowners are away. Greenhouse businesses have been formed to maintain interior plantscapes. These operations routinely condition unhealthy plants from home environment and reuse and can be extremely beneficial as rural community projects.

A conservatory with well-maintained decorative and flowering plants is an ideal place for recreational and cultural events. Community organizations like garden clubs, nature groups, and park boards can attach greenhouses to offices. Community greenhouses that grow and maintain exotic plants can be added to childrens' facilities. A greenhouse attached to a retirement community or nursing home serves a therapeutic purpose. Horticultural therapy greenhouses can be supported by the community or nonprofit organization and should be constructed with low benches and wide walkways for wheelchair and handicapped accessibility. Concerts, wedding ceremonies, craft shows, pet shows, and other volunteer activities are held in the community greenhouses. Such greenhouses are decorated with unusual plants like blooming orchids, bromeliads, ferns, palm trees, or cacti that provide the visitors with relaxation and a feeling of being in an exotic place.

—*Chiwon W. Lee*

See also
Agriculture, Hydroponic; Horticulture; Temperate Fruit Industry; Vegetable Industry.
References
Ball, Vic. *Ball Red Book*. 15th ed. Reston, VA: Reston Publishing, 1991.
Boodley, James W. *The Commercial Greenhouse*. 2d ed. Albany, NY: Delmar Publishers, 1997.
Langhans, Robert W. *Greenhouse Management*. 3d ed. Ithaca, NY: Halcyon Press of Ithaca, 1990.
Nelson, Paul V. *Greenhouse Operation and Management*. 4th ed. Englewood Cliffs, NJ: Prentice-Hall, 1991.
Reed, D. W. *A Grower's Guide to Water, Media and Nutrition*. Batavia, IL: Grower Talks Bookshelf, 1996.

Groundwater

The subsurface water occupying the void space in geologic material. The quality of subsurface water in the saturated region (aquifer) is used to define its potential use. Approximately 90 percent of the inhabitants of rural America depend on groundwater as their major source of water. This contrasts with the nearly 50 percent of the population of the nation as a whole that relies on groundwater. As such, the quality and quantity of groundwater is extremely important to the majority of the nation's inhabitants.

In recent years, numerous laws, legislation, policies, and agencies have been established to ensure the continued availability and quality of groundwater. Efforts are under way to clean or stabilize the environmental problems caused by past environmentally detrimental activities and to ensure new ones are not created. Ongoing efforts seek to better define the quantity and quality of water throughout the country and any deviations in them. And efforts continue to develop new technologies and equipment to clean low-quality groundwater so that it may be productively used.

Aquifers

An aquifer is the saturated soil-rock-water complex where usable water resides in the subsurface. The top of the saturated region is the water table. The ability of a subsurface material to store water and effectively yield it to a well are indicated by the values of the porosity and permeability of the geologic material. The permeability of the aquifer material describes how easily water flows through the material. The permeability of sand can be up to one million times greater than that of clay. As a result, water flows very slowly in a clay formation relative to a sand one. This makes clay a poor material for an effective aquifer as it will not release the water it contains in a reasonable time.

The location and composition of the subsurface materials can often be very complex, like that of the geologic material one observes in mountains and road cuts. Each of the subsurface materials has its own porosity and permeability characteristics. Thus aquifers are often irregular in their horizontal location and thickness.

Because of continued digging and well boring over the years, the locations of producing wells are known, and from them, the structure of the aquifer is inferred. From this information, one sometimes finds that wells nearly adjacent but at different depths may be pumping water from different aquifers. When a number of wells have been drilled in similar terrain, local drillers often have a good idea where to drill and at what depth they will intersect the water table. Where the terrain is more complex and there are fewer existing productive wells, the location to drill and depth of water are more questionable.

Many local and federal government water agencies have maps and information on the location and quality of aquifers throughout the United States. These exist mainly for areas where there is current habitation. Very rural areas are often either not covered or covered with very rough detail. To help bridge this gap, local water agencies can be contacted about local aquifer information and how to obtain it.

Water Quality

All groundwater contains some chemicals. The particular chemicals present and their concentrations vary considerably. Salts are found to some degree in all natural water. These are picked up largely in the movement of water over the land and through the soil. Salt concentration can vary from 20 parts per million (ppm) for water from a spring to 300,000 ppm for brine. Various water uses have their own quality requirements. Water that is unfit to drink may be suited for use in industrial operations. Water is measured in terms of chemical, physical, biological, and radiological constituents to quantify its quality. These values are compared against established water quality criteria to determine its suitability for use as drinking water or for irrigation, industrial, recreation, and other purposes.

The physical properties examined when groundwater is tested include temperature, color, turbidity, odor, and taste. Biological testing is done mainly to detect the presence of coliform bacteria. These are hardy bacteria found in the intestines of warm-blooded animals and unpolluted soil. Their presence suggests a pathway back to the feces of humans or animals. If such a path exists, very harmful organisms from sick animals may also be present in the water. The ratio of the number of fecal coliform bacteria to fecal streptococci bacteria in a water sample often is used to distinguish whether the sources of bacteria are mainly from humans or from other warm-blooded animals.

The multitude of agencies and organizations that collect water quality data share their data so that more is known about groundwater quality throughout the United States. Baseline water quality data exist for much of the country. Deviation in these current levels can be and is used to fine polluters or others who cause a degradation of groundwater quality either directly or indirectly.

Wells

Access to groundwater is typically by wells. Wells that are less than 15 meters (49.2 feet) in depth often are constructed by digging, driving, boring, or jetting. Deeper wells are constructed either by a cable tool method or by rotary drilling (Todd 1980).

In all cases, wells should be protected from surface drainage of polluted water entering them. In addition, they must be sealed so polluted water cannot enter the wells at various depths from subsurface sources of polluted water. Failure to adequately seal and protect wells are major causes of water pollution.

Many wells are fitted with instruments so that the water level can be monitored. Other wells are used to monitor water level and quality (for example, chemical concentrates), which may fluctuate because of several factors. Among these are land use; local pumping rate; surrounding area water withdrawals; and natural and artificial recharge, farming operations, and industrial operations.

Contamination Sources

One major source of groundwater pollution is leakage from underground storage tanks used to store petrochemicals and other chemicals. Over time the older steel tanks deteriorate because of moisture and soil chemicals and in many cases experience leaks. In urban settings, those that can be identified are being replaced by fiberglass and coated metal tanks with associated monitoring equipment. One major problem in rural areas is the close proximity of tanks to wells used for domestic water on farms and ranches. The potential exists for pollution of drinking water and the occurrence of associated health problems.

Excess fertilizer use results in fertilizer being carried away in runoff water, drain water, and percolating water. In some cases, the fertilizer-rich percolating water makes its way to the aquifer, and fertilizer residues are found in drinking water.

Although newer pesticides are designed to break down into benign residuals, it is possible to have groundwater contamination in certain environments where the water table is near the surface and the soils have high permeability. Many older pesticides still move in the subsurface and continue to pollute groundwater.

In the case of some mines, the water pH from the runoff tailing piles comes close to that of acid. Contact of acidic water with soil can release toxic trace metals, and aquifers can be polluted by such water. Hardrock mining activities, such as constructing tunnels and fracturing rock, also can disturb the subsurface flow net and allow pollutants to enter the aquifer.

Septic tanks are the main means of sewage disposal from houses in rural settings. In general, they do an excellent job with no threat to the groundwater. There are situations, however, in which pollution problems can occur. If septic tanks are not pumped periodically, scum and sludge can accumulate, overflow into the drain field, and clog the flow paths. This can result in an overflow of liquid into the tile field, which can potentially leak into a water well if it is not well sealed. If the soils in the area have a high permeability and the water table is shallow, the liquid residue from the septic tank may not have adequate time to interact with the soil and its bacteria before intersecting the aquifer. In addition, the disposal of toxic materials into the house plumbing system can place those chemicals into the liquid of the drain field, which moves to the aquifer.

Groundwater Mining

Some western states adopted legislation to address the groundwater mining issue. The intent is to decrease groundwater level decline by limiting irrigation withdrawals. As competition for limited water supplies increases, water becomes a valued commodity. The value of water for irrigation cannot compete with its value for industrial and municipal supplies. The competition for water available to agriculture and declining water supplies resulted in an increase in agricultural water use efficiency. Laws have been changed to ease water supply reallocation to nonagricultural users and to increase local and state involvement in water resources management.

Recharge

Aquifers are recharged by the movement of water from the surface. The natural form of this movement is percolation through the soil of infiltrated water from precipitation, snowmelt, streamflow, and pond water. Aquifers can be artificially recharged in several ways, including water spreading and recharge through pits and wells. The idea behind surface water spreading is to increase both the time for infiltration and the wetted surface area. The well recharge or injection method involves operating an existing water well in reverse, that is, by pumping water into the ground. A primary consideration in all forms of artificial recharge is whether it will increase detrimental impacts on aquifer water quality. The recharge water may be high in salts or other chemicals that will degrade the quality of the existing groundwater. The recharge method may bypass or decrease the travel time through the cleaning processes in the soil (breakdown by bacteria, absorption, and chemical reactions).

Monitoring

Monitoring groundwater levels and checking chemical quality are ongoing activities in all of the states and involve many agencies. Coordinating and sharing data allow for a better understanding of baseline data and deviations from them. Several large information systems are being loaded with groundwater data and made available for access through computer terminals in many of the offices of groups, agencies, universities, and organizations working with water resources. The public can often access this information through local federal offices within the U.S. Department of Agriculture (USDA), the Environmental Protection Agency (EPA), and the U.S. Geological Survey.

Cleaning

Research activities since World War II have determined different means to remove various pollutants from water. Many of these techniques are used by the commercial market and are available to the public. Thus, there are many types of equipment available to remove or reduce water chemicals to safe levels. Water with chemical concentrations too high for specific uses can have these concentrations reduced so that the water can be used for the purpose sought.

Pollution Potential Prediction

Several schemes have been developed and used to predict the vulnerability of groundwater to pollution from various pollutant sources. LaGrand (1983) developed an empirical point-count system that uses factors such as water table depth, sorption above the water table, permeability, water table gradient, and horizontal distance to arrive at vulnerability for a specific situation.

The approach has been expanded by the National Water Well Association and the EPA into a system called DRASTIC, which evaluates the groundwater pollution potential of specific geohydrologic settings. DRASTIC has been further modified by the USDA Soil Conservation Service to be more site-specific and useful as a planning tool. The modification, called System for Early Evaluation of Pollution Potential of Agricultural Groundwater Environments (SEEPPAGE), focuses on the vadose zone and the uppermost saturated zone. The system allows users to compare the relative risks of groundwater contamination among various sites and to select the most favorable site.

Numerous other models and automated systems are available that describe and predict the relationships between various pollutants, geohydrologic settings, and the contamination of groundwater. Many agricultural, university, and water resource field offices offer the use of these models to alleviate existing or potential pollution problems.

Water Protection Policy

Many states are developing and expanding legislation, regulations, and programs to protect groundwater. This is especially important because of the difficulty and expense of cleaning contaminated aquifers, providing alternative water supplies, or adding more water treatment processes to existing treatment systems. Local, state, and federal agencies work together and share information to better detect water pollution activities. Polluters are identified and fined or prosecuted, and the pollution activity is stopped.

The federal government currently is attempting to orchestrate amendments to the various water resources protection laws and regulations to allow them to be interpreted with less adverse impact on the states and citizens. A watershed management program is addressed in the Clean Water Act, and a strong source-protection program is addressed in the Safe Drinking Water Act. Any state wishing to undertake watershed management under the Clean Water Act and include groundwater under the goals for source protection would meet the requirements of the Safe Drinking Water Act. The majority of states completed statewide nonpoint-source assessment and management plans and state clean water strategies with EPA approval. These define the present nonpoint source problems and how they will be reduced in the future.

Anyone constructing new facilities or generating wastes must develop a plan to handle wastes so they will not adversely impact the quality of water resources. The legislation, laws, and regulations are intended to cause individuals, companies, and government to minimize or eliminate pollution from their activities initially rather than engage in costly cleanup after it has occurred.

—*William O. Rasmussen*

See also
Conservation, Water; Environmental Protection; Hydrology; Irrigation; Water Use.
References
Fairchild, Deborah M., ed. *Groundwater Quality and Agricultural Practices.* Chelsea, MI: Lewis, 1987.
LaGrand, H. E. *A Standardized System for Evaluating Waste Disposal Sites.* 2d ed. Worthington, OH: National Water Well Association, 1983.
Sun, Ren Jen, and John B. Weeks. *Bibliography of Regional Aquifer-System Analysis Program of the U.S. Geological Survey, 1978–91.* Water-Resources Investigations Report 91-4122. Reston, VA: U.S. Geological Survey, 1991.
Todd, David Keith. *Groundwater Hydrology.* New York: John Wiley, 1980.
U..S. Department of Agriculture, Soil Conservation Service. *SEEPPAGE: A System for Early Evaluation of the Pollution Potential of Agricultural Groundwater Environments.* Engineering Geology Technical Note 5. Chester, PA: Northeastern National Technical Center, 1988.
———. *Design and Construction Guidelines for Considering Seepage from Agricultural Waste Storage Ponds and Treatment Lagoons.* Technical Note 716. Ft. Worth, TX: Southern National Technical Center, 1990.
———. *ENG—Agricultural Waste Management Field Handbook—Part 651.* Document no. AWMFH-1. Washington DC: U.S. Department of Agriculture, Soil Conservation Service, 1992.
U.S. Environmental Protection Agency. *National Water Quality Inventory.* Report EPA 440-4-90-003. Washington, DC: EPA, Office of Water, 1990.
———. *Risk Assessment, Management and Communication of Drinking Water Contamination.* Report EPA 625-4-89-024. Washington, DC: EPA, Office of Water, 1990.
U.S. Geological Survey. *National Water Summary 1987.* Water Supply Paper 2350. Denver, CO: USGS, 1990.

Health and Disease Epidemiology

The study of the distribution and determinants of health and disease in a population. This entry compares rural and urban health statistics and highlights health problems and high-risk groups of particular relevance to rural communities. Comparisons of fundamental measures of population health reveal no glaring differences between rural and nonrural U.S. residents. Rural populations experience slightly lower annual mortality than their nonrural counterparts but generally report somewhat greater occurrences of chronic health problems. After taking into account the age, race, and gender differences between rural and nonrural populations, the overall mortality rate for nonmetropolitan statistical areas is still 4 percent lower than that in metropolitan areas (U.S. Congress 1990).

There are, however, specific types of mortality (including infant mortality and deaths from injury) for which rural residents have comparatively higher mortality rates. Residents outside metropolitan statistical areas consistently report more chronic disease and disability than do residents of metropolitan areas, although the incidence of acute health problems appears to be quite similar (U.S. Congress, 1990). In addition, there are several specific health conditions of concern to rural populations because demographic, occupational, and environmental risk factors for these problems are most often found in rural areas.

Mortality

Mortality statistics indicate that there would be approximately 34 fewer deaths per year for a typical group of 100,000 U.S. rural residents than in a same-size group of U.S. metropolitan area residents whose age, sex, and race

composition was identical to the rural group (U.S. Congress 1990). These age-, sex-, and race-adjusted mortality rates for rural residents are lower than those for metropolitan area residents for most specific causes of death except accidents. Adjusted death rates among rural residents in 1980 were 31 per 100,000 for motor vehicle accidents and 29 per 100,000 for non-motor-vehicle-related accidents, whereas the comparable rates for metropolitan statistical area residents were 21 per 100,000 and 22 per 100,000, respectively (U.S. Congress 1990).

Available national data show no marked differences in fetal, neonatal, or infant mortality rates between metropolitan and nonmetropolitan statistical areas (McManus and Newacheck 1989). However, data from Florida document higher infant mortality rates in counties that are both outside metropolitan statistical areas and whose largest town has a population of less than 10,000 than in larger counties. Discrepancies in infant mortality appear to stem from differences in infant birth weights and maternal prenatal care use across urban and rural communities. However, other studies found persistent rural-urban mortality differences within groups of infants born at similar birth weights (Baker and Kotelchuck 1989), which implicates access to and use of prenatal care as the prime reason for differential rural-urban infant mortality. At the other end of the age spectrum, there has been little comparison of mortality data between rural and nonrural elderly. However, there is comparative information on morbidity (that is, indicators of disease and disability) in this age group.

Morbidity

Overall, residents outside metropolitan statistical areas report incidences of acute health problems (short-term illness or injury) similar to those of metropolitan area residents. Data from 1986 show the number of acute illness episodes per 100 residents in metropolitan and nonmetropolitan areas to be almost identical at 173 (U.S. Congress 1990). (Recurrent episodes of acute illness are counted separately, so each person, on average, may have more than one occurrence.) The frequency of nonfatal accidental injury in nonmetropolitan areas is lower than that seen in metropolitan areas. However, residents outside metropolitan areas on average report greater disability resulting from these accidents (U.S. Congress 1990). This, coupled with the relatively higher rural area fatal accident rate, suggests that, although somewhat less common, accidents in rural areas tend to be more severe. Agricultural accidents are one type of rural area accident, as will be discussed further later, and children under age 15 account for up to one-quarter of farm injuries in some states (Schenker, Lopez, and Wintermute 1995). With respect to the more typical acute childhood illnesses, respiratory conditions are the most common problem reported in both rural and nonrural communities. Slightly higher rates for these conditions are reported in metropolitan statistical areas than in nonmetropolitan areas—131.4 and 124.9 occurrences per 100 persons under 21 years of age, respectively (McManus and Newacheck 1989). However, a study of urban and rural communities in southwestern West Virginia found no significant difference in the impact of childhood respiratory illness across communities.

Although mortality and acute condition occurrence rates are generally similar across rural and urban populations, notable differences in both the occurrence and severity of chronic disease (long-duration illness typically more prevalent in older age groups) do exist. The prevalence of many common, serious, chronic conditions, including heart disease, hypertension, diabetes, and arthritis, is greater in nonmetropolitan areas than in urban areas (U.S. Congress 1990). Almost 47 percent of rural residents (defined here as residents of counties in nonmetropolitan statistical areas that have less than 20,000 urban residents) report at least one chronic condition of some kind, compared to approximately 40 percent of the residents in nonrural areas (Braden and Beauregard 1995). Of all the major chronic conditions, only cancer appears to occur less frequently in rural populations than in urban populations (Howe, Keller, and Lehherr 1993). However, rural residents with cancer tend to be diagnosed with more advanced disease and hence have less favorable outcomes than their urban counterparts. Last, although

there is a common perception that rural residents have fewer mental health problems than city dwellers, available data on mental illness in rural populations is, unfortunately, still quite lacking (Wagonfeld 1990).

Self-Rated Health and Health-Related Quality of Life

In addition to measuring morbidity and mortality, the impact of disease in populations can also be gauged by how individuals rate their own health status and the extent to which they report that health problems limit their quality of life. In 1987, 28 percent of the U.S. rural population (again, defined as all residents of nonmetropolitan statistical area counties that have less than 50,000 urban residents) reported their health status to be either fair or poor (as opposed to good or excellent). This did not compare favorably with residents of nonrural areas; between 19 and 22 percent of these residents classified themselves as being in only fair or poor health (Braden and Beauregard 1994). National data also show a greater proportion of rural residents reporting health-related limitations on physical activity (36 percent) and mobility or self-care activities (26 percent) than nonrural residents (Braden and Beauregard 1994). However, one study of Kentucky residents that adjusted for differences in gender, race, marital status, education, age, and income found that discrepancies in health-related quality of life seen across metropolitan and nonmetropolitan statistical areas prior to adjustment were no longer statistically significant after adjustment (Mainous and Kohrs 1995).

Groups at Special Risk and Health Problems of Special Interest

Although descriptive statistics on mortality, morbidity, and health-related quality of life give a valid overview of the epidemiology of health and disease in rural populations, it is important to note that rural populations are in themselves quite varied. As such, we can expect there to be considerable differences in health and disease across subgroups within any rural community. For example, elderly rural residents living on farms have notably lower rates of activity limitation than rural elderly living in nonfarm settings (Cutler and Coward 1988). Also, since lower socioeconomic status is generally associated with poorer outcomes on virtually every known measure of health status, it is not surprising that rural residents of lower socioeconomic status are at greater risk of adverse health events than rural residents of higher socioeconomic status. For example, the prevalence of both binocular and monocular blindness in one isolated rural community was found to be twice U.S. national rates. Within this community, education level and employment status, both markers of socioeconomic status, were strongly associated with impaired vision. Those who had not completed high school had five times greater odds and those currently unemployed had three times greater odds of impaired vision, compared, respectively, to those who graduated from high school and those currently employed.

Epidemiologists commonly compare health statistics across individuals' occupational classifications in order to highlight possible workplace risks. Two of the four job classifications with the highest fatal occupational injury rates (rates that range from 20 to 28 fatalities per 100,000 workers per year and that are ten times greater than those for the next highest occupational categories) are occupations set predominantly in rural areas: mining and agriculture/forestry/fishing. These occupations also rank high with respect to disabling occupational injury. Agricultural work has also been repeatedly cited as an occupation that appears to pose certain specific health risks. For example, farmers are at increased risk for early hearing loss and, although they exhibit lower all-cause mortality than the general population, farmers have higher rates of non-smoking-related cancers at numerous sites (Blair and Zahm 1993).

In addition to personal characteristics that affect health, like socioeconomic status or occupation, factors related to biological agents themselves and to the surrounding environment are also important when assessing population health. Rural residents, especially farm-dwelling rural residents, have greater risk of zoonotic diseases (diseases caused by infectious agents common to both animals and humans) than other segments of the population. The environment in which rural residents live increases their exposure to other health hazards such as pesticides (Blair and Zahm 1993), agricultural organic dusts, or nitrates in well water. These exposures may translate into a variety of health risks. For example, rural residence, and in particular well-water use, was associated with increased risk of Parkinson's disease in one study, whereas parental residence in counties with high agricultural productivity was associated with increased risk of their infants being born with congenital limb reductions.

Health problems at present characterized as urban health issues can be, or can quickly become, significant in rural areas as well. Syphilis and human immunodeficiency virus (HIV) are two examples. Syphilis was considered an urban problem in North Carolina during the early 1980s, but by the mid-1990s, syphilis rates in counties outside of metropolitan statistical areas in North Carolina surpassed those in metropolitan area counties. Although the U.S. HIV epidemic began in urban centers in California and New York, instances of return migration of HIV-infected individuals from cities to their rural hometowns were anecdotally documented as early as 1989. Incidence rates of acquired immune deficiency syndrome (AIDS) in nonmetropolitan counties in North Carolina, which have been steadily increasing since the epidemic began, were in 1992 approximately equal to the rates in the state's urban areas in 1989. Also in North Carolina, a survey of HIV-infected patients seen in various clinics at a large teaching hospital found that almost half of those living in rural areas reported rural residency at the time they believe they became infected.

—Craig J. Newschaffer

See also
Addiction; Elders; Food Safety; Health Care; Injuries; Policy, Health Care; Quality of Life.
References
Baker, S., and M. Kotelchuck. "Birthweight-specific Mortality: Important Inequities Remain." *Journal of Rural Health* 5, no. 2 (April 1989): 155–170.
Blair, Aaron, and Sheila Hoar Zahm. "Patterns of Pesticide Use among Farmers: Implications for Epidemiologic Research." *Epidemiology* 4, no. 1 (January 1993): 55–62.
Braden, Jill, and Karen Beauregard. "Health Status and Access to Care of Rural and Urban Populations." *National Medical Expenditure Survey Research Findings* 18. Agency for Health Care Policy and Research pub. no. 94-0031. Rockville, MD: U.S. Department of Health and Human Services. Public Health Service, Agency for Health Care Policy and Research, Center for General Health Services Intermural Research, 1995.
Cutler S., and R. Coward. "Residence Differences in the Health Status of Elders." *Journal of Rural Health* 4, no. 3 (October 1988): 11–26.
Howe, Holly L., Jane E. Keller, and Melinda Lehherr. "Relation between Population Density and Cancer Incidence, Illinois, 1986–1990." *American Journal of Epidemiology* 138, no. 1 (July 1993): 29–36.
Mainous, Arch G., and Francis P. Kohrs. "A Comparison of Health Status between Rural and Urban Adults." *Journal of Community Health* 20, no. 5 (October 1995): 423–431.
McManus, Margaret A., and Paul W. Newacheck. "Rural Maternal, Child and Adolescent Health." *Health Services Research* 23 (1989): 807–846.
Schenker, Marc B., Ricardo Lopez, and Garen Wintermute. "Farm-related Fatalities among Children in California, 1980 to 1989." *American Journal of Public Health* 85, no. 1 (January 1995): 89–92.
U.S. Congress, Office of Technology Assessment. *Health Care in Rural America*, OTA-H-434 (September). Washington, DC: U.S. Government Printing Office, 1990.
Wagonfeld, M. O. "Mental Health and Rural America: A Decade Review." *Journal of Rural Health* 6, no. 4 (October 1990): 507–522.

Health Care

The organization and provision of services meeting the preventative, acute, chronic, and long-term health-related needs of a population. This entry covers the following subjects: changes in the industry, the distribution and adequacy of rural providers, the use of nonphysician providers, the viability of rural hospitals, and the future of rural health care delivery systems.

Changes in the Industry

As the pace quickens toward the twenty-first century, significant change is being experienced in many, if not most industries. However, few industries are changing faster than health care. Since the 1960s, there has been an explosion of medical technology that is reshaping the way medicine is practiced in the United States and throughout the world. Equally important are changes in the way medical care is being financed and delivered. With the introduction of Medicare in the 1960s, the federal government not only became a major financing agency for health care but in many ways became the leading force in health care policy reformation.

An example of Medicare's influence occurred in 1983 when the Health Care Financing Administration (that is, Medicare) changed its payment methodology to providers from cost-based reimbursement to prospective payment. With this shift, health care providers no longer received payment for services based upon the costs of treating an individual patient. Rather, they received a fixed average cost for treatment of a specific diagnosis (known as adiagnostic related group, or DRG). With the introduction of a fixed payment, the incentive to control resource utilization was now placed on the health care provider organizations. Although prospective payment was introduced only in 1983, by the end of the 1980s most private insurance companies followed suit by introducing some form of prospective payment in their own reimbursement methodologies.

The influence of Medicare in the development and modification of health policy for the future cannot be overstated. This is especially true because the leading edge of the disproportionately large baby boom cohort will be eligible for Medicare benefits in less than 15 years.

Another leading force of change in the health care industry is the introduction and proliferation of managed care organizations. With the advent of managed care in all its varieties (such as health maintenance organizations, preferred provider organizations, and independent practice associations), provider organizations assume a

Dr. Lee Mizrahi and the rest of the staff of a free clinic for migrant workers pose in a field near Delano, California.

much greater level of financial risk in medical service delivery. This risk is greatest when provider organizations, usually health maintenance organizations, accept a fixed capitated payment for each plan subscriber (usually known as a "per member per month" payment). Provider risk is assumed in less restrictive plans in which physicians and other providers discount their services to insurers in return for these plans encouraging their members to use providers who offer discounts.

As these industry changes occur, the impact of these changes on rural areas and the ability of rural health care delivery systems to adapt is often left out of the national discussion. The following discussion examines some of the more salient characteristics and issues surrounding rural health delivery systems. Specifically, the discussion focuses on the distribution and adequacy of health care providers in rural areas, the viability of small rural hospitals, and what the future may hold for rural health care delivery systems.

Distribution and Adequacy of Rural Providers

Concern about having an adequate supply of health professionals in rural areas is not new. The supply of primary care physicians (general practitioners, family physicians, general internists, general pediatricians, and sometimes obstetrician/gynecologists) has been of specific concern. In 1978, the federal government designated 1,209 health professional shortage areas (HPSAs) nationwide. These are contiguous geographic service areas (usually counties) with a population-to-primary-care-physician ratio of 3,500 to 1 or greater. In 1978, of the 1,209 designated shortage areas, 73 percent were located in nonmetropolitan areas. In spite of the large increases in the physician supply since 1978, the number of shortage areas has been increasing, and the distribution of these shortage areas has remained rather stable. In 1986 there were 1,611 designated HPSAs, of which 73 percent were located in nonmetropolitan areas; and in 1994 there were 2,514 designated HPSAs, of which 71 percent were located in nonmetropolitan areas (Ricketts 1995).

Although the maldistribution of primary care physicians is generally recognized, there has been considerable debate regarding potential solutions. In the late 1960s and early 1970s, programs such as the National Health Service Corps (NHSC) and area health education centers (AHEC) were established to address these concerns. The NHSC programs provided both scholarships for medical students and educational loan repayment for medical graduates in return for a specified number of years of service in shortage areas and those designated as underserved areas. The AHEC programs offered medical students rural rotations and clerkships to encourage the establishment of a rural practice.

However, some suggested that the market would correct the maldistribution itself. In the early 1980s, the Graduate Medical Education National Advisory Committee (GMENAC) issued a report that many interpreted as a prediction of a national oversupply of physicians; it was thought that, as a result, physicians would diffuse into rural areas and lessen the maldistribution (DHHS 1981). Today, there is little evidence that the market will correct the maldistribution of primary care physicians. Although the number of physicians increased substantially, the distribution of physicians remained relatively unchanged. Between 1970 and 1993, metropolitan areas experienced a 121.6 percent increase in physician supply, whereas nonmetropolitan areas witnessed only a 73.3 percent increase (Ricketts 1995). Although significant distributional differences remain and the rate of increase is still less than experienced by metropolitan areas, nonmetropolitan areas have experienced substantial growth in physician supply.

Use of Nonphysician Providers

Because of the chronic physician shortages in rural areas documented above, the use of nonphysician providers is helping to fill a widening void left by physicians unwilling or unable to initiate or sustain a rural practice. Physician assistants, nurse practitioners, and certified nurse midwives constitute a growing class of nonphysician providers. These professions were developed to expand the availability of primary health care services and improve access to services for medically underserved areas.

Although they continue to serve a supplemental function to physicians, the role of nonphysician providers today is increasingly instrumental in providing direct primary care services. Nonphysician providers can substitute for physicians in as many as 60 to 90 percent of primary care functions (Office of Technology Assessment 1986; Osterweis and Garfinkel 1993) at a lower cost. Further, with the largest specialty area among rural physicians being family practice, the potential impact of these nonphysician providers on rural health care is substantial.

The objective of increasing the diffusion and use of nonphysician providers into rural underserved areas has been apparent in several policies and programs. The National Health Service Corps offers loan repayment and scholarships for nonphysician providers. The Rural Health Clinics Act of 1977 provides rural clinics located in shortage areas with enhanced reimbursement for service to Medicaid and Medicare beneficiaries if a nonphysician provider is employed in the rural clinic. Additionally, the Health Care Financing Administration established programs that provide greater flexibility for rural hospitals through the use of nonphysician providers (e.g., the Essential Access Community Hospital program and the Medical Assistance Facility program).

Unfortunately, the recruitment of nonphysician providers to rural locations is somewhat hampered by some well-founded barriers. These include state and federal regulations that obstruct direct reimbursement, prescriptive authority, excessive malpractice and liability premiums for some specialties, gate-keeping behavior among organized medicine, and a lack of understanding about the capabilities of nonphysician providers. Consequently, the use of nonphysician providers in rural areas slowed. In 1984 approximately 18 percent of nurse practitioners were practicing in nonmetropolitan areas, compared with 12 percent in 1988. Greater reductions were found among physician assistants, where the percentage working in nonmetropolitan areas declined from 30 percent in 1985 to 13 percent in 1990 (National Rural Health Association 1992).

Viability of Rural Hospitals

There is little question that the hospital is the hub of the health care delivery system in rural communities. However, besides serving as the focal point for health care delivery, rural hospitals are often important providers of social services; serve as an important asset in the recruitment of new businesses to the community; and are themselves often one of the largest employers in the community. In every sense of the word, rural hospitals are institutional and economic anchors in their community. Unfortunately, the viability of many rural hospitals has been steadily eroding.

Since the early 1980s, rural hospitals failed in unprecedented numbers. Between 1980 and 1983, an average of 12 rural hospitals closed each year. However, between 1984 and 1986 that annual average increased to 25, and by the end of the decade (1987 to 1989) an average of 42 rural hospitals closed annually. More recently, the number of closures slowed and stabilized with an average of 25 between 1990 and 1993 (AHA 1992).

Some reductions in hospital use are a function of the technological changes in medicine. Many procedures that were routinely performed in the hospital are now performed in an outpatient setting, which affects both rural and urban hospitals. However, the magnitude of these changes appear disproportionately to affect rural hospitals. For example, between 1980 and 1990 rural hospital admissions declined 37 percent, while outpatient visits increased 36 percent. During the same period of time, urban hospitals admissions declined only 6 percent, while outpatient visits increased 52 percent (AHA 1992).

Similar trends are found for other hospitals statistics as well. Between 1980 and 1990, rural facilities experienced a reduction of 17 percent of their certified beds and a 16 percent decrease in occupancy rates; overall, there was a 14 percent reduction in the number of rural hospitals. Although a similar trend was noted by urban hospitals, the magnitude of loss was much less. Between 1980 and 1990, urban facilities experienced a 2 percent loss of certified beds, an 11 percent decrease in their occupancy rate, and an overall 1 percent loss in the number of urban hospitals (AHA 1992).

Another significant factor affecting rural hospitals is the population loss and declining rural economy in many parts of the United States. Like any business, hospitals are not immune to the demographic shifts experienced by many rural communities. Although the total rural population increased by 4.2 percent between 1980 and 1990, more than 50 percent of all rural counties lost population during that period. Especially hard-hit were the Great Plains and Western mining states (U.S. Department of Agriculture 1991). Many of these rural communities continue to struggle to adjust to these demographic shifts that left them with fewer residents, a smaller service area, a disproportionate number of elderly residents,

and a greater percentage of poor and uninsured residents. The results of these shifts challenged many, if not all, of the local service sectors. Main street businesses continue to close, local school districts consolidate, houses of worship close, and most youth that are not tied to the land leave after graduating from high school.

A final factor affecting rural hospitals is a phenomenon known in the marketing literature as "outshopping," which is the process of bypassing the opportunity to use local services for and choosing similar services in larger urban markets. Outshopping primarily occurs as a result of perceptions that bypassing local services results in better quality or lower prices.

Several studies examined the loss of market share among rural providers to urban facilities. Hart, Rosenblatt, and Amundson (1989) examine the loss of rural hospital market shares to urban facilities in Washington, Montana, Alaska, and Idaho and found the loss ranged from a high of 60 percent to a low of 40 percent. These loss figures are relatively low compared with recent insurance claims data made available through the North Dakota Health Care Data Act. In an examination of 85 percent of all hospital insurance claims originating from rural areas, only 26 percent of rural residents were discharged from small rural hospitals. Rather, 23 percent were discharged from larger rural referral centers, and 51 percent were discharged from large urban hospitals. Finally, when examining rural physician services, Ludtke, Geller, and Hart. (1990) found that rural physicians lost, on average, 40 percent of their patient base to urban physicians.

The tremendous loss of market share experienced by rural health care providers seriously undermines the economic viability of these services. Studies suggested that those most likely to use nonlocal providers are younger and better insured (Ludtke et al. 1989). The consequence of selective outshopping for medical services is that rural facilities find their patient base predominantly filled with elderly Medicare beneficiaries. Additionally, because of the downturn in the rural economy throughout much of the 1980s, the percentage of indigent and uninsured care provided in rural areas significantly increased.

The Future of Rural Health Care Delivery Systems

It is clear that the future will bring more rural hospital closures and difficulties in recruiting and retaining health care professionals. However, with rural residents composing approximately one-fourth of the nation's population, there will always be a need for rural health care delivery systems, and they will not disappear. Rural health care delivery systems must change and adapt to this new environment. Two areas that hold promise for rural communities are the development of rural health care networks and the development of telemedicine.

Rural Health Networks. The idea of establishing rural health networks is not new, but it is changing. For many years, rural hospitals came together under the organizational umbrella of a rural hospital alliance, cooperative, or network. Members of these organizations often found efficiencies of participation in areas such as joint purchasing, joint marketing, and common political advocacy; However, the common feature of these organizational structures was the homogeneity of its members (i.e., rural hospitals).

More recently, there has been significant interest and activity in the development of vertically integrated networks. Unlike previous rural health networks, these vertically integrated networks are characterized by their heterogeneity of participants (i.e., rural clinics and hospitals, urban providers, and nursing homes). Consequently, when autonomous organizations agree to form a vertically integrated network, access to a broad range of services for residents in the service area increases. As various providers affiliate with the network, the actual service area increases as well; the community expands and is redefined.

Telemedicine. Telemedicine is the practice of health care delivery, diagnosis, consultation, treatment, and transfer of medical data and education using interactive audio, visual, and data communications. Today, many rural health experts view telemedicine as a critical tool for the direct care of rural patients and for the development of rural health systems. Telemedicine affords rural residents ready access to medical specialists and subspecialists without the inconvenience of traveling to urban centers.

The most sophisticated, costly telemedicine projects use interactive two-way video technology, whereby medical specialists in urban settings can see, hear, and examine rural patients who are referred by their local physician. This technology is commonly used by rural physicians to consult with urban specialists without the patient being present. Other telemedicine projects use modern telecommunications technologies to digitize and forward radiologic film (X-rays), cardiac strips, and other diagnostic data for review by urban specialists.

Although still in its infancy, telemedicine technology has the potential to address several chronic problems that plague rural health care delivery systems. It provides rural patients with access to services unavailable locally; decreases outshopping behavior; reduces feelings of isolation among rural physicians; and helps create a collaborative environment between rural providers and their urban colleagues.

—*Jack M. Geller*

See also

Addiction; Dental Health Care; Health and Disease Epidemiology; Mental Health; Mental Health of Older Adults; Nurses and Allied Health Professionals; Policy, Health Care.

References

AHA (American Hospital Association). *AHA Hospital Statistics: A Comprehensive Summary of U.S. Hospitals, 1991–92 Edition.* Chicago: American Hospital Association, 1992.

Hart, G. L., R. A. Rosenblatt, and B. A. Amundson. *Rural Hospital Utilization: Who Stays and Who Goes?* WAMI Rural Health Research Center working paper series, March 1989.

Ludtke, R. L., J. M. Geller, and J. P. Hart. "Rural Physicians' Market Share Retention." *Journal of Hospital Marketing* 4, no. 2 (1990): 105–117.

Ludtke, R. L., J. M. Geller, J. P. Hart, and K. M. Fickenscher. "The Relationship between Site, Access Variables, and Loss of Local Clientele." Paper presented at the National Rural Health Association, May 1989.

National Rural Health Association. *Study of Models To Meet Rural Health Care Needs through Mobilization of Health Professions Education and Services Resources.* Vol. 1. Washington, DC: Health Resources Services Administration, 1992.

Office of Technology Assessment. *Nurse Practitioners, Physician Assistants, and Certified Nurse Midwives: A Policy Analysis.* Washington, DC: U.S. Government Printing Office, 1986.

Osterweis, M., and S. Garfinkel. "The Roles of Physician Assistants and Nurse Practitioners in Primary Care: An Overview." In *The Roles of Physician Assistants and Nurse Practitioners in Primary Care.* Edited by D. K. Clawson and M. Osterweis. Washington, DC: Association of Academic Health Centers, 1993.

Ricketts, T. C. "Meeting the Workforce Needs of Rural Areas." Paper presented for the User Liaison Program, Agency for Health Care Policy and Research, Charlottesville, VA, May 1995.

U.S. Department of Agriculture. *Rural Conditions and Trends.* Washington, DC: U.S. Department of Agriculture, Economic Research Service, spring 1991.

U.S. Department of Health and Human Services, Office of Graduate Medical Education. *Report of the Graduate Medical Education National Advisory Committee (GMENAC) to the Secretary of the Department of Health and Human Services.* Vol. 1: *Summary Report.* DHHS pub. no. (HRA) 81-651. Washington, DC: U.S. Government Printing Office, 1981.

History, Agricultural

The social, economic, political, cultural, and technological developments in American agriculture. This entry provides an overview of the most significant developments in American agriculture from colonial times to the present.

The Colonial Period

Since the establishment of the Jamestown settlement in Virginia nearly 400 years ago, American agriculture evolved in seemingly contradictory ways. It became an increasingly commercialized, technologically sophisticated, and highly capitalized business. At the same time, agriculture went from being virtually a universal enterprise to one practiced by only a relative handful of people and from being the mainspring of the American economy to a peripheral economic enterprise. As agriculture became modernized and peripheralized, farm life became decreasingly unique and distinct from life off the farm.

The English North American colonists in the seventeenth and eighteenth centuries created an agricultural system that combined elements of both the Old and the New Worlds. From Europe, they brought notions of private property and a market system; sophisticated tools such as plows and harrows and water- and wind-powered mills; domesticated animals such as sheep, swine, cattle, and horses; and small grains and other crops that were important parts of their diets. In America they prepared their fields as the Indians did, by girdling trees and burning underbrush; built log cabins; erected worm fencing that did not require nails; grazed their animals unsupervised in the forest, learned to farm the abundant land extensively; and adopted such Indian crops as corn and tobacco.

American agriculture in the seventeenth century assumed some of the characteristics it continues to display today. Although most European farmers lived in nucleated agricultural villages, most colonial Americans lived on individual farmsteads. One of the consequences of this decision was a heavy dependence on family labor; another was a heightened sense of individualism and personal freedom. The colonists also demonstrated a decidedly commercial bent. Although they attempted to minimize risk by maintaining maximum self-sufficiency, they were alert and responsive to commercial opportunities wherever those might appear.

Their openness to innovation, the possibilities of the environment, the attractions of the market, and British economic policies embodied in the mercantile system conjoined to create vital regional agricultural economies by the early eighteenth century. In the Middle Atlantic and New England colonies, farmers produced livestock and foodstuffs for home consumption and export, especially to the sugar colonies in the West Indies. The colonies in the Chesapeake Bay region produced tobacco for export to England and Europe, which also served as destinations for rice and indigo from South Carolina.

The need for nonfamily agricultural labor, which was especially intense in the southern colonies, led to the large-scale importation of indentured servants from Europe and later slaves from Africa. Slave importation became particularly pronounced during a period of high prosperity that began about 1740 and continued until the Revolution. During that period, 125,000 Africans were imported into the colonies. In combination with the impressive natural increase of the slave population, these importations meant that by 1776, 20 percent of the colonists were slaves of African birth or descent, and most worked as agricultural laborers.

The agricultural population expanded so rapidly that by 1750 there were severe land shortages in long-settled coastal areas, resulting in rising social conflict between the landless and landed and debtors and creditors and increasing interest in western lands. The British tried to prevent colonial settlement west of the Appalachian Mountains with the Proclamation of 1763, but when the colonies declared independence in 1776, settlers began to flood into the West. The Treaty of Paris, which ended the War of the American Revolution in 1783, gave the new nation title to a vast potential agricultural empire south of the Great Lakes and east of the Mississippi River. This domain was progressively expanded, most significantly by the Louisiana Purchase in 1803 and the acquisition of the Oregon country and the Mexican cession territories in the 1840s.

1800–1870

Between 1800 and 1860, agriculture rapidly expanded over the area between the Mississippi and the Appalachians. This expansion was facilitated by improvements in water transportation, especially the introduction of steamboats on the western river system before the War of 1812 and the completion of the Erie Canal in 1825 and by the introduction of railroads in the 1840s and 1850s. Breaking the power of most major Indian groups during the Revolution and the War of 1812 allowed their removal from lands coveted by White farmers. Government maintenance of an orderly but permissive method of surveying and disposing of public lands, culminating in the Homestead Act of 1862, which essentially gave land away to farmers who met minimal conditions, also spread settlement. Most important in stimulating expansion, however, was high demand for American agricultural products in

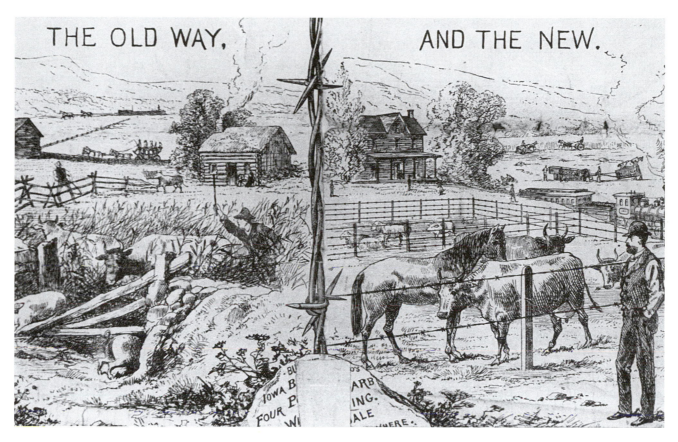

THE OLD WAY,   AND THE NEW.

A tongue-in-cheek view of the importance for American agriculture of the introduction of barbed wire.

growing urban centers in the United States and in Europe. The product most coveted was cotton, which became a feasible crop in most of the South as a result of Eli Whitney's invention of the cotton gin in 1793. Between 1800 and 1860, cotton production rose from 73,000 to 3,841,000 bales. Cotton constituted 7 percent of the value of American exports in 1800 and 57.5 percent in 1860. Although cotton dominated American exports, products such as pork, beef, and wheat fed American urbanites.

This was also a period in which farmers became more self-conscious, founding newspapers, agricultural societies, and local fairs. Their self-regard partially reflected enhanced social status. The early nineteenth century represented the high point for Jeffersonian agrarianism, which held that farming was the most legitimate and beneficial of occupations and that farmers were the most moral and patriotic of citizens.

The Civil War was significant for agriculture in both the North and the South. In the North, the war saw rapid progress in mechanization, especially with the widespread adoption of the reaper to harvest small grains. During the war the government initiated a national agricultural policy designed to professionalize farmers and make them more scientifically and technically sophisticated. As part of this effort, in 1862, Congress made the U.S. Department of Agriculture (USDA)—mainly a scientific agency in its early years—an independent government department. In 1889 the USDA achieved cabinet status. Also in 1862, Congress passed the Morrill Land-Grant College Act, encouraging the states to create colleges to discover and teach the scientific principles of agriculture. This legislation was supplemented by the Hatch Act (1887), which provided states with funds to conduct agricultural research, and the Smith-Lever Act (1914), which created an extension service to disseminate research results to farmers.

The Civil War revolutionized southern agriculture by destroying the slave labor system on which commercial production depended and by severely disrupting the credit and marketing system. Slavery was replaced by a variety of free labor arrangements, the most important of which was sharecropping, under which landowners and laborers divided the crop. A new credit and marketing structure called the crop-lien system developed, under which merchants lent materials to farmers who pledged their unplanted crops as collateral. Under these devices cotton production recovered and even expanded, but southern agriculture remained relatively impoverished until after World War II.

1870–1899

Agriculture underwent the most dramatic expansion in its history between 1870 and 1900, as the number of farms, acreage in farms, and production volume of most major crops more than doubled. Expansion was especially dramatic on the Great Plains, where the extension of railroads, confinement of Indians on reservations, development of new farming techniques, and strong European demand for American wheat and beef conjoined to bring rapid settlement.

Farmers in the late nineteenth century became increasingly commercial in response to market opportunities and to a flood of seductive consumer goods. Increasingly, urban media and retailers such as Montgomery Ward and Sears and Roebuck shaped rural tastes and spread an urban culture that became stronger over the ensuing century. This cultural hegemony shaped social and economic behavior. The growing tendency of commentators to judge the lives of rural women by urban standards of domesticity was a clear sign of this trend, as was the tendency to stigmatize rural people as "hicks" and "yokels," dramatically revising the perspective of Jeffersonian agrarians.

Urban hegemony caused some unease among farmers, but much more disturbing were economic challenges such as the growing difficulty of securing credit, price manipulation by middlemen, and uncontrollable market fluctuations. A succession of agrarian protest movements—the Grange, the Farmers Alliance, and the Populist Party—arose between 1870 and 1895, all promising to control or do away with middlemen, especially by developing cooperative enterprises, inflating prices, and helping farmers market more effectively. None succeeded in controlling government, but their very existence testified to the reality that farmers were the most consistently dissatisfied group of the period.

1900 to the Present

Farmers' economic problems eased substantially after 1900. Farm prices rose at a much faster rate than did the general price level, allowing some farmers to mechanize by adopting tractors and most to improve their material standards of living. Especially attractive to farm families were automobiles, which broadened rural horizons and enriched rural social lives.

The 1900–1920 period was one of intense urban preoccupation with reforming rural social and economic deficiencies. The Country Life Movement encouraged a restructuring of rural society, especially through consolidation of schools and enrichment of the curriculum, as well as movement of the agricultural economy to a higher level of organization, efficiency, and sophistication. Rural people were generally resistant to this outside interference, but many of the goals of the Country Life Movement were at least partially realized in ensuing decades.

Agricultural prices hit unprecedented highs during and immediately after World War I before plummeting in 1920. Margins were tight throughout the decade of the 1920s, leading to large-scale rural-urban migration and putting a premium on the achievement of economies of scale, especially through mechanization. Between 1920 and 1930, the number of tractors on farms rose from 246,000 to 920,000.

Most farmers suffered severely during the Great Depression, which began in 1929. In 1932 gross farm income was only 40 percent of what it had been three years earlier. Indebted farmers faced a liquidity crisis in which hundreds of thousands lost farms. Social services could not be supported, and rural people strove for maximum self-sufficiency by "living at home." Hard times rekindled agrarian protest, as farmers joined the Farmers Holiday Association and other radical groups. Adding to the difficulties of farmers on the Great Plains was a drought that helped create the Dust Bowl phenomenon.

The serious crises of rural America were addressed by Pres. Franklin D. Roosevelt's interventionist New Deal program. The federal government refinanced farm mortgages and became the major farm lender in the country. Federal crop loans put a floor under prices, and subsidies raised farm incomes. Government crop insurance diminished weather risk. In the Dust Bowl, conservation programs addressed problems of erosion, and federal welfare and resettlement programs helped the most desperate victims of dust and depression. By creating the Rural Electrification Administration, the government helped wipe out one of the major differences between rural and urban living. Government programs helped raise incomes and diminish price risk, but they were not totally positive. They made agriculture second only to defense in level of subsidization among American industries, and they disproportionately benefited the largest, richest, and most efficient commodity producers. In the South, they lavished benefits on landlords who used government money to replace sharecroppers with machines.

The New Deal diminished price risk, and the spread and elaboration of mechanization and the chemical revolution after World War II mitigated production risk. Farms were ever more highly capitalized, and farmers were increasingly sophisticated businessmen and efficient producers. A tight cost-price squeeze put a premium on the achievement of economies of scale, with the result that farm numbers dwindled and farm sizes rose. In 1940 there were still about 6,000,000 farms in the country, but by 1991 there were only about 2,100,000. Of these, only 40,000 were considered economically significant. Farm depopulation was dramatic. From 31,000,000 in 1940, the farm population shrank to under 5,000,000 in 1990.

For a brief period in the 1970s, the increasing efficiency of farmers was seemingly rewarded by high prices and rapidly rising land values. Crop shortfalls in much of the world, the liberalization of trade with the Soviet Union and China, and dollar devaluation by the Nixon administration conjoined to push bread and feed grain prices sharply higher. Prosperity was intense but short-lived, and beginning in 1979, farmers were caught between falling prices and rising interest rates. The 1980s witnessed a farm depression as severe, in some ways, as that 50 years earlier. This depression saw the rise of a new protest group, the American Agriculture Movement, and a debt crisis that was especially severe for young farmers, but it failed to alter the direction of agriculture toward greater productive efficiency and technical sophistication.

As farm people moved from overwhelming majority to tiny minority, their lives were transformed. Today, their material expectations, life experiences, and education levels are less different from those of urban people than has ever been the case before. Once major and defining, the differences between life on the farm and life off the farm have been so obliterated by such forces as education, technology, and urban cultural hegemony as to become trivial.

—*David B. Danbom*

See also

Agriculture, Structure of; History, Rural; Mechanization; Policy, Agricultural.

References

Benedict, Murray R. *Farm Policies of the United States, 1790–1950: A Study of Their Origins and Development.* New York: Twentieth Century Fund, 1953.

Bidwell, Percy Wells, and John I. Falconer. *History of Agriculture in the Northern United States, 1620–1860.* New York: Peter Smith, 1941.

Danbom, David B. *"Born in the Country": A History of Rural America.* Baltimore. MD: Johns Hopkins University Press, 1995.

Daniel, Pete. *Breaking the Land: The Transformation of Cotton, Tobacco, and Rice Cultures since 1880.* Urbana: University of Illinois Press, 1985.

Fite, Gilbert C. *American Farmers: The New Minority.* Bloomington: Indiana University Press, 1981.

Gray, Lewis Cecil. *History of Agriculture in the Southern United States to 1860.* Gloucester, MA: Peter Smith, 1958.

Hurt, R. Douglas. *American Agriculture: A Brief History.* Ames: Iowa State University Press, 1994.

Russell, Howard S. *A Long, Deep Furrow: Three Centuries of Farming in New England.* Hanover, NH: University Press of New England, 1982.

Schlebecker, John T. *Whereby We Thrive: A History of American Farming, 1607–1972.* Ames: Iowa State University Press, 1975.

Shover, John T. *First Majority—Last Minority: The Transforming of Rural Life in America.* DeKalb: Northern Illinois University Press, 1976.

History, Rural

The historical narrative of life in rural America and the historical study of rural American society. Rural history holds importance in general American history for two reasons: the predominance of rural life in earlier generations and the imprint of rural culture on American life. Rural history, often studied in the United States in the context of the frontier and settlement, comprises a rich narrative of cultures and institutions. Central to this story, however, is the decline of rural culture in America with urbanization and commercialization.

The Rural Frontier

In 1893, the historian Frederick Jackson Turner noted the statistical closing of the American frontier era of free land and stated his famous frontier thesis. Turner not only recounted the rural history of the United States to that time but also set down interpretations that shaped the study of rural history for generations to come. Turner said that the experience of pioneering shaped the American character. He also said that the frontier went through definite stages of rural development. The frontier first wrought a reversion to the primitive, after which came a succession of frontier types that brought higher levels of enterprise and complexity. The frontier cattleman was one type; he was succeeded by the pioneer farmer, who in turn gave way to the equipped farmer. The process led eventually to town making, urbanization, and industrialization.

The Turner thesis is an example of American exceptionalism, the belief that the American experience is unique. It would be possible to study the rural development of the United States as part of world trends, but little of that has been done. Instead, rural American historians

Pioneers in their covered wagon settling Loup Valley, Nebraska.

traditionally focused on the United States. This gave a peculiar intellectual importance to rural history, even in an urbanizing country.

Rural Movements and Regions

Rural history provides important threads in the political history of the United States. It is notable that at least since Bacon's Rebellion in Virginia in 1676, agrarian radicalism has been recurrent. The most celebrated agrarian movement was the Populist crusade. The Populist movement, which originated in organizations known as farmer's alliances during the 1880s and organized politically in the 1890s, was strong in the southern and western states. It sought both to remedy the disadvantageous economic and social position of farmers and to pursue broadly democratic reforms. Historical opinion about the Populists is divided: some say that they were progressive reformers, others that they were strident reactionaries. Prior to the Populists, the Patrons of Husbandry, or Grange, organized farmers politically in the Midwest, and subsequent to the Populists, the Nonpartisan League revived agrarian insurgency on the northern plains.

These are merely the best-known farm movements in a history of many such movements that continue into the present.

Rural history in such a vast nation as the United States is influenced by concerns of the discrete sections (Turner's term), or regions (the term more favored in the twentieth century). Prior to the Civil War, the sectional distinction that loomed largest was between the slave-holding South and the free-labor North, a distinction hinging on agricultural labor (one of the few subjects in rural history that attracted the attention of Marxist historians). Within the South, however, rural historians have since shown there were profound differences between the plantation South and the more yeomanly backcountry. Subsequent to the Civil War, other regions differentiated and evolved their own distinctive rural societies. The South, with the rise of sharecropping, remained defined by the social limitations of its labor system. The Corn Belt complex of feed grains and livestock distinguished the Midwest. The Great Plains were characterized first by extensive ranching and then by extensive grain farming. These and other regions were articulated and their rural identities bolstered by intellectuals such as Allen Tate (spokesperson for the literary Southern Agrarians) and Walter P. Webb (the leading historian of the Great Plains).

Industrialization and Rural Decline

Throughout all regions of the country, the rise of industrialization and rural-urban migration both fed on and shaped rural development. According to the Jeffersonian tradition, farmers are the pillars of society and the source of public virtue. By the late nineteenth century, however, farmers had to adjust to industrialization. They welcomed such labor-saving devices as binders and windmills, but they also felt victimized by monopolistic business interests and sensed that their public standing was diminished. Even as the frontier expanded in the West, carving out new farms, the migration of farm folk to cities commenced. Concern over this and the potential of farmers to feed the nation in the future led to the Country Life Movement in the early twentieth century. Urban reformers sought to transform rural life, making it more rewarding and more productive.

Nevertheless, the country became ever more urban and less rural. Whereas in 1860 the United States had a population that was 80 percent rural (living on farms or in towns of less than 2,500 residents), in 1900 it was only 39 percent rural, and farmers produced only 20 percent of the nation's income. Farmers were definitely a minority in the twentieth century. In 1940, 23 percent of the population still lived on farms, but in 1970, less than 5 percent did so, and 20 years later, less than 3 percent. The rural-urban migration not only fed industrialization but also brought about social change in the nation's cities. The Great Migration of Blacks from the sharecropping South to the industrial cities of the Northeast and Midwest is arguably the most significant demographic movement in American history. The so-called Okie migration of displaced farmers from the South and the southern plains to California, commencing during the 1930s, introduced southern-agrarian culture to the West Coast. The more America urbanized, the less self-sufficient were its remaining farmers. Post–World War II farm families, in particular, abandoned efforts to supply the necessities of life for themselves and devoted their labors to production for urban and export markets. Farmers were by this time fully integrated, economically and socially, into American urban culture.

For some historians, the distinction between urban and rural lost its importance. Scholars writing from the perspectives of central place theory (a geographic conception) or dependence theory (an economic construct) emphasize the influence that the metropolis always exerted on the countryside.

Certainly, nostalgia for the rural past should not obscure the profound human problems peculiar to the nation's rural history. The rural society of the antebellum South exploited Blacks held in bondage; even after emancipation, southern sharecropping, coupled with the onerous crop-lien system of credit, oppressed poor Black and White farmers alike. Elsewhere, popular belief placed great faith in the so-called agricultural ladder. It was supposed that young would-be farmers could make their start as farm laborers; graduate to greater autonomy as tenant farmers; and finally, having made their stakes, buy their own farms or move west and take up homesteads. Unfortunately, the agricultural ladder seldom worked so beneficently. It took considerable capital to develop a supposedly free homestead. Farm laborers' wages were so poor and agricultural depressions so frequent that farm folk were as likely to move down the ladder as up it. During the Great Depression, the Resettlement Administration (later the Farm Security Administration), a federal agency, sought to resettle oppressed farmers in model communities, without notable success. Overall, the rural history of the United States is marred by chronic economic distress.

Gender and Ethnic Considerations

In writings since the 1970s, feminist historians upset many of the assumptions of Turnerian rural history and provided a more complete picture of rural life. Historians of farm women pointed out that from colonial until recent times, farm women were constrained by patriarchy. Although it remains debatable the degree to which their hard lots were the product of patriarchy and the degree to which they simply were overworked owing to the depressed circumstances of their farms, it is certain that farm work was differentiated according to gender. Generally, men were expected to produce for the market economy, whereas women were responsible for the household sphere. This sphere might be broadly defined, however, making women influential in rural history in three ways. First, they managed their own households. Second, they performed domestic production for the market. Through management of poultry and manufacture of butter, for instance, they provided relatively constant sources of cash income that moderated the fluctuations of crops and livestock. Third, although barred from some public roles, they emerged prominent in the matters of religion, education, and charitable endeavor. In more recent years, large numbers of farm women adapted to the end of farm self-sufficiency by taking urban employment, once again providing stable incomes that help to safeguard the fortunes of the family farm.

General trends notwithstanding, as the literature of the new social history written since the 1960s has shown, a wealth of ethnic variations are evident in American rural history. The patterns of agricultural settlement, whether through chain migration or through organized colonization, often crystallized on ethnic lines. This commenced in colonial times but was particularly evident during settlement of the Great Plains, when land companies organized colonies of Germans, German-Russians, Swedes, Norwegians, Czechs, Eastern European Jews, free Blacks, and other ethnic groups. Ethnic concentration in particular agricultural regions continued to recent times with such examples as Japanese and Filipino prominence in horticultural industries on the West Coast. Moreover, certain ethnic groups predominated in certain types of agricultural labor. Most significantly, and especially since World War II, immigrant Mexican laborers filled labor needs in the American West, from the fruit and vegetable industries of California to the beef and sugar beet industries of the Great Plains.

Rural Institutions and Structures

Rural culture required rural institutions, such as the common country schools and the country-town Main Street, along with churches, farm and ethnic associations, threshing rings, and purely social organizations. Local schools not only educated children but also served as social centers for adults and meeting places for school programs, literary societies, and play parties. Local merchants not only provided goods but also extended credit, and Main Street, through the institution of Saturday night trading, was a locus of social activity. Such rural institutions inevitably declined with urbanization and rural depopulation, and their functions were assumed by urban and, in many cases, federally organized agencies. Through school consolidation, a reform that commenced early in the twentieth century, farm children were brought into town school systems. The automobile made it possible to bypass local merchants and shop in regional centers. The Cooperative Extension Service, beginning in 1914, organized 4-H and home demonstration units; the Rural Electrification Administration, beginning in 1935, assisted rural electric cooperatives; and the Soil Conservation Service, commencing in the same year, organized

soil and water conservation districts. Few examples of purely rural institutions remain today.

Rural culture left distinctive marks on the landscape in the form of material culture, the built environment. Cultural geographers trace the origins of material cultures to their cultural hearths—French, English, Dutch, and Spanish colonial house types, for instance—and also trace the impact of the local environment on vernacular architecture. The frontier log cabin, for instance, that stereotypical dwelling of Turner's American pioneers, derived from European origins but assumed different forms on the New England frontier, in the southern backcountry, and in the American West. Use of earthen materials might be a perpetuation of cultural heritage—as with adobe in the Hispanic Southwest or with rammed earth among Eastern European immigrants—or it might be an adaptation to environment, as with simple sod houses on the plains. Other, functional structures integral to rural life—Pennsylvania ramp barns, New England stone walls, Midwestern corncribs—whether still functional or not, serve as continuing reminders of rural history on the landscape.

—*Thomas Isern*

See also
Agriculture, Structure of; Culture; Ethnicity; History, Agricultural; Landownership; Rural Women; Settlement Patterns; Social Movements; Town-Country Relations; Urbanization.
References
Billington, Ray Allen. *Westward Expansion: A History of the American Frontier*. 5th ed. New York: Macmillan, 1982.
Danbom, David B. *"Born in the Country": A History of Rural America*. Baltimore, MD: Johns Hopkins University Press, 1995.
Dorman, Robert L. *Revolt of the Provinces: The Regionalist Movement in America, 1920–1945*. Chapel Hill: University of North Carolina Press, 1993.
Fink, Deborah. *Agrarian Women: Wives and Mothers in Rural Nebraska, 1880–1940*. Chapel Hill: University of North Carolina Press, 1992.
Fite, Gilbert C. *American Farmers: The New Minority*. Bloomington: Indiana University Press, 1981.
Fuller, Wayne E. *The Old Country School: The Story of Rural Education in the Middle West*. Chicago: University of Chicago Press, 1982.
Hayter, Earl W. *The Troubled Farmer, 1850–1900: Rural Adjustment to Industrialism*. DeKalb: Northern Illinois University Press, 1968.
Hurt, R. Douglas. *American Agriculture: A Brief History*. Ames: Iowa State University Press, 1994.
Isern, Thomas D. *Bull Threshers and Bindlestiffs: Harvesting and Threshing on the North American Plains*. Lawrence: University Press of Kansas, 1990.
Noble, Allen G. *Wood, Brick, and Stone: The North American Settlement Landscape*. 2 vols. Amherst: University of Massachusetts Press, 1984.

Home Economics

Academic discipline concerned with the well-being of individuals and families. Home economics has played a major role in the well-being of families in rural America since the late 1800s. Programs have been made possible through the Morrill Act of 1862 that established the land-grant universities, the Morrill Act of 1890 that established the historically Black land-grant institutions, the Smith-Lever Act of 1914 that established the Cooperative Extension Service, and the 1917 Smith-Hughes Act that established vocational education programs. In addition, the 1984 Carl D. Perkins Act reflected societal changes in vocational education. This entry emphasizes the contributions made by the historically Black land-grant colleges and universities (or 1890s institutions) and the Cooperative Extension Service to rural America. Home economics programs in these two institutions arguably have served rural areas to a greater extent than similar programs in other academic and vocational institutions.

The Morrill Act of 1890

The Morrill Act of 1862 established the land-grant colleges and universities. Black people were not specifically excluded from the land-grant institutions established by the Morrill Act of 1862, but the slavery and, later, segregation of that era virtually eliminated Blacks from enrolling in those colleges and universities. Congress passed the second Morrill Act in 1890, thereby providing equal educational access for Black students and equal opportunities for Black residents in rural America to receive information. There are 17 1890s colleges and universities; most are located in rural areas and have served rural families with unrecognized dedication and diligence. The 1890s institutions continue to provide outstanding programs, extending far beyond racial boundaries, for all rural families and individuals.

The earliest home economics program on record offered through the 1890s institutions was the domestic science program at Southern University, located in Baton Rouge, Louisiana. As with all early home economics programs, its mission was to improve the quality of life by teaching the basic concepts of home living, food preparation, sewing, and housekeeping skills. Other 1890s schools quickly introduced home economics programs, including the pioneer schools of University of Arkansas at Pine Bluff; Virginia State University; Alabama A&M; Alcorn State University in Lorman, Mississippi; Kentucky State University; and Prairie View A&M in Prairie View,

Texas. By 1925, most 1890s institutions offered home economics–related subjects. The name of domestic science changed to home economics in the early 1900s, and the content of the courses gradually changed from service-oriented homemaking skills to an emphasis on food and nutrition, child development and family relations, clothing and textiles, and teacher training.

The 1890s institutions' programs in rural areas have a long history of applied research projects. Food and nutrition studies and clothing/fabric durability studies were among the first research projects. Today, research at the 1890s colleges and universities continues with a focus on improving the quality of life for rural families. For instance, research at Alabama A&M studied the clothing, nutritional, and housing status of rural elderly people in Alabama. Health practices and housing issues of rural residents continues to be the research focus of home economics programs at several 1890s universities. Prairie View A&M recently studied patterns of living in disadvantaged families and the quality of food, clothing, and shelter among southern rural elderly. At the University of Maine at Eastern Shore, researchers studied the factors affecting learning and cognitive development of children in rural and urban areas. Contributions of Alcorn State University home economics researchers included developing alternative uses of catfish and crawfish, thus contributing to these industries in Mississippi, and assessing the basic human needs of low-income rural families. Research at North Carolina A&T examined marketing and economic problems related to textile products and their use by rural families and issues related to adequate housing. Tuskegee University studied the effect of environmental pollutants on the quality of food products grown by limited-resource farmers. Home economics researchers at Tuskegee concluded that rural nutrition problems continue to worsen, whereas some urban nutrition problems may be improving.

Most of the 1890 home economics extension programs were begun in 1972 or thereafter. This legislation authorized direct funding to the 1890s institutions and has been well used to develop outstanding programs to serve rural America. Some examples of programs include Lincoln University's nutrition education programs in collaboration with the Missouri Gerontology Institute and Kentucky State University's Extension Program, which serves rural individuals who are hard to reach, unreached, or have limited resources and skills to improve the quality of their lives. The University of Arkansas at Pine Bluff addressed the needs of adolescent parents and introduced home maintenance and improvement programs. The Home Economics Extension at Alcorn University focused on the needs of low-income and limited-resource families through programs ranging from teaching money management to child development and helping families deal with high-stress situations such as drug abuse.

Contributions through Vocational Education

The first federal vocational education legislation was passed in 1917. The mission of vocational education, to prepare people for work, has not changed for 68 years. However, the nature of work and the composition of the workforce has changed. Thus, groups that traditionally have been underserved in vocational programs were to be especially sought out and served through provisions in the Carl D. Perkins Vocational Education Act of 1984.

Kister, Smith, and Hughes (1985) provide an overview of programs that have significance for rural areas. Education for parenting, especially pregnant teenagers, has been a major emphasis. Programs to raise self-esteem and career exploration possibilities have been offered to youth from economically deprived areas. Adult family life programs, held in migrant housing centers, Indian reservations, senior citizen centers, and mobile classrooms, offered information on topics ranging from prevention of child abuse to low-cost meal planning and preparation.

The Carl D. Perkins Vocational Education Act of 1984 brought many opportunities and programs to rural areas to overcome sex bias. Examples include the Nontraditional Training Program, which prepares single parents and homemakers in Florida for groundsperson and line worker positions with utility and cable television companies; the Reentry Women program, which provided training, employment, and support services to displaced homemakers in Wisconsin; and a teen self-sufficiency program, which provides employability and life-management skills, vocational education, child care, and transportation to Wisconsin teen parents.

Contributions through the Cooperative Extension Service

The Smith-Lever Act, passed in 1914, authorized Cooperative Extension work in agriculture and home economics. Food and nutrition and safety and health have historically been a major emphasis of home economics extension. During World War I, the Extension Service was designated as the chief food production agency of the nation. The home demonstration agents (i.e., home economists in the Extension Service) were called upon to assist the United States in providing its food supply.

The home demonstration agents made another significant contribution to the nation when they gave demonstrations that were effective in emergency mass feeding during the influenza epidemic in 1917–1918. During the drought and Great Depression of the 1930s, home demonstration agents established canning kitchens in thousands of communities. The Red Cross supplied cans, and the home economists presented home-canning instruction programs. During the 1930s, clothing renovation and alteration and recreational and cultural activities that could be provided with few financial resources were also taught.

During World War II, the extension home demonstration agents in Hawaii performed an extraordinary service for the war-torn islands. They taught homeowners how to ventilate blacked-out rooms, how to conserve food and find substitutes for unobtainable foods, how to make emergency use of coconuts, and how to comply with possible evacuation orders. At the request of the military officers, they taught mess sergeants to prepare island foods and showed soldiers how to subsist in a tropical jungle by living off the land.

Cooperative Extension Service continued to provide rural Americans with information to improve their health through better nutrition. The Expanded Food and Nutrition Education Program (EFNEP), first established in 1968, continued to be a popular program throughout the 1970s and 1980s.

A program targeted at limited resource families, Operation Ship Shape, taught people in Iowa to handle their own home repairs. The program concentrated on helping women, especially single parents, to overcome the idea that home repair was "man's work" and to develop confidence in their ability to maintain their homes.

Extension Home Economics moved from a skill-oriented approach toward an issues/concepts informational method in the 1970s and 1980s. The decision-making process, rather than the solution of specific problems, became the focus. Programs began to show the multidisciplinary approach needed to deal with contemporary issues. For example, education about pesticides covered the care of clothes worn during application, laundry safety, and textile research for protective clothes.

Contemporary home economics programs in the Cooperative Extension Service focus on interdisciplinary health and safety programs. For example, the Cooperative

Extension Service in Georgia has an important role in designing community health organizational structures in rural areas through its Community Wellness program.

Kansas Extension offers a program to educate individuals about cardiovascular risk reduction. Colorado Extension, in cooperation with the American Heart Association, conducts workshops in rural communities to reduce cholesterol levels and develop a readiness to change health behaviors. Puerto Rico's health education program resulted in almost 25,000 persons adopting dietary practices to reduce the incidence of chronic diseases associated with nutrition. North Carolina's Community Health Advocacy Program contributes to rural health by providing health information and resources, promoting health-related agency cooperation, and educating about individual health issues.

Contributions through Research and Service Home Economics programs at private and public higher education institutions have been conducting rural research programs and applied service projects. For example, Texas Tech University has consistently been a leader in home economics research and applied programs. Regenerating Rural America: The Y.E.S. (Youth Exchanging with Seniors) Project was initiated in 1990. Its goal is to promote intergenerational relationships between youth and seniors. Young people receive training related to the aging process, provide services to older people, and in turn, provide an opportunity for older people to share their wisdom with the younger generation.

Texas Tech home economists have also been leaders in nutrition education. *Education for Self-Responsibility IV: Nutrition Education Curriculum Guide*, consisting of three volumes for prekindergarten through Grade 12, was developed by the Home Economics Curriculum Center at Texas Tech to incorporate nutrition education principles into each academic subject matter area.

Rural older adults have been the subjects of several research projects. A comparison of informal support systems of rural and urban adults found that illness prompted more assistance giving and receiving for rural older adults than urban older adults (Scott and Roberto 1987). The morale of older rural widows and widowers was studied. Results indicated that when widows and widowers lack the necessary skills and resources to maintain a satisfactory lifestyle or to function competently in their new roles after the loss of their spouse, their morale is negatively affected (Scott and Kivett 1985).

Since the late 1800s, home economists have served rural families by providing research and practical infor-

mation. As the needs changed, so too have the home economists' programs. At one time, rural families needed specific survival skills, such as how to produce and preserve food. Today, the focus is on health education and delivery of health-related services to rural America. Once known as domestic science, the name of home economics is changing throughout America to portray more clearly its contemporary programs; human environmental sciences, family and consumer sciences, and human development are frequently used titles. In spite of these changes, the mission of home economics remains the same: to improve the quality of life for families and individuals.

—Harriett Light, with Melanie Gardner

See also
Education, Youth; Family; Food Safety; Housing; Land-Grant Institutions, 1862 and 1890; Nutrition; Policy, Food; Quality of Life.

References
Alstad, George, and Jan Everly Friedson. *The Cooperative Extension Service in Hawaii, 1928–1981.* Honolulu: University of Hawaii, College of Tropical Agriculture and Human Resources, 1982.

Cobb, Brian, and David E. Kingbury. "The Special Provisions of the Perkins Act." *Vocational Education Journal* (May 1985): 33–34.

Fahm, Esther Glover. "Home Economics—Our Roots, Our Present, Our Future." In *Historically Black Land-Grant Institutions and the Development of Agriculture and Home Economics.* Edited by Leedell Neyland. Tallahassee: Florida A&M University Foundation, 1990.

Hooten, Elizabeth, Susan Raferty, Vee McCord, and Warren McCord. *Alabama County Health Councils Handbook.* Auburn, AL: Auburn University, Alabama Cooperative Extension Service, 1992.

Jenkins, Susan. "Community Wellness: A Group Empowerment Model for Rural America." *Journal of Health Care for the Poor and Underserved* 1, no. 4 (1991): 388–404.

Kister, Joanna, Joanna Smith, and Ruth P. Hughes. "Planning New Directions for Consumer and Homemaking Education." *Vocational Education Journal* 60, no. 4 (May 1985): 36–37.

Neyland, Leedell, ed., with special assistance from Esther Glover Fahm. *Historically Black Land-Grant Institutions and the Development of Agriculture and Home Economics 1890–1990.* Tallahassee: Florida A&M University Foundation, 1990.

Sanders, H. C. *The Cooperative Extension Service.* Englewood Cliffs, NJ: Prentice-Hall, 1966.

Schwieder, Dorothy. *75 Years of Service: Cooperative Extension in Iowa.* Ames: Iowa State University, 1993.

Scott, Jean Pearson. "Differences in the Morale of Older, Rural Widows and Widowers." *International Journal of Aging and Human Development* 21, no. 2 (1985): 121–136.

Scott, Jean Person, and Vira R. Kivett. "Differences in the Morale of Older, Rural Widows and Widowers." *International Journal of Aging and Human Development* 21, no. 2 (1985): 121–136.

Scott, Jean Pearson, and Karen A. Roberto. "Informal Supports of Older Adults: A Rural-Urban Comparison." *Family Relations* 36, no. 4 (October 1987): 444–448.

Home-Based Work

The variety of employment statuses, including employees who work for one company at home, self-employed business owners who operate from their homes, and independent contractors who may work from home for several companies. The term "cottage industry" refers to paid production organized in and around workers' homes. "Sweated labor," more commonly used to describe early twentieth-century industrial work in urban and rural areas, indicated the intensity of production organized under exploitative piece rates and designed to extract maximum labor from the homeworker. It is only the location of work that links these categories of employment. Homework in historical and contemporary contexts, particularly rural settings, is addressed in this entry.

Historical Background

Aspects of all paid labor are regulated by law, but only homework done as an employee in certain industries is prohibited by federal and state laws. In 1938, the Fair Labor Standards Act (FLSA) prohibited employee homework in ladies' garment, jewelry, knitted outerwear, and several apparel-related industries after long campaigns by social reformers publicized the abuses and exploitation of women and children in tenement sweatshops. Prior to implementation of the FLSA, homework was prevalent in a vast array of industries, including cigar rolling, shoe binding, hat making, flower arranging, food processing, and button making.

Although the reformers' campaign focused on urban, often immigrant, homeworkers, many women and children in rural areas also engaged in homework. Merchants in the United States started most homeworking in rural areas because they wished to avoid the regulations and wages imposed by urban craft guilds. Poverty and underemployment in rural areas attracted merchants seeking an available, low-wage labor force. During colonial times, many homeworkers in the rural Northeast were textile producers or processors involved in fiber spinning, weaving, and carding of fibers. As textile production mechanized and relocated to factories, employers put out hat braiding, palm-leaf weaving, and button and shoe making to rural homeworkers. In the early 1800s, merchants relied on rural homeworkers for products ranging from hats, shingles, shoes, paper, and woodenware to food items such as butter, grain products, and produce. Many low-income rural households, particularly farm families, depended at least in part on the income earned from home-based work, especially when several members of the household participated.

Recent Developments

Industrial homework reappeared in the public view in the early 1980s as homeworkers in New York, Wisconsin, and Vermont spoke out to defend their jobs in the knitted outerwear industry. Public hearings followed at the state and federal levels as elected officials rediscovered homeworking and sweatshops in much the same way earlier leaders rediscovered poverty in the early 1960s. The surprise, however, was not only in the contemporary existence of homeworking but in the variety of occupations that people performed in their homes for pay. In addition to garment construction and knitted outerwear, researchers found electronics and computer chip assembly work, automotive assembly work, shoe making, clerical work, computer programming, insurance claim filing, craft work, toy assembly, and production of jewelry and jewelry boxes. Contemporary homeworking occurs in many industries not mentioned or regulated by the FLSA. As a result of these hearings and the Reagan administration's focus on deregulation, bans on homeworking in five industries previously regulated by the FLSA were replaced with a certification program. The U.S. Department of Labor issues permits to businesses that require employers to pay minimum wage to homeworkers. The certification program attempted to regulate the conditions of home-based work. Enforcement continues to be a problem because of the low numbers of officials available to inspect employers and homeworkers and because homework is still largely invisible; payment of minimum wage becomes the worker's responsibility under the piece rate. The majority of home-based wage workers today are women, with the exception of professional or white-collar homeworking, which seems to be fairly evenly divided between male and female workers.

Prevalence of Homeworkers

It is challenging to estimate the numbers of home-based wage workers in the United States using available aggregate data. Kraut (1988) uses the 1980 census data to estimate 750,000 white-collar, nonfarm homeworkers; using Bureau of Labor Statistics data for 1985, Christensen (1989) and Silver (1989) estimated 1.9 million homeworkers, of whom 953,000 were full-time homeworkers. Using the same data, Silver estimated 501,151 of the 1.9 million homeworkers were rural, nonfarm residents. These data all have limitations, such as not counting second jobs that are home-based or undercounting workers engaged in illegal forms of homework. The latter category encompasses 50,000 workers in New York City and 40,000 workers in Los Angeles alone. Silver concluded that the number of homeworkers of all types in the United States remained fairly constant during the 1980s, with small increases in the rural, nonfarm, home-based workforce.

Industrial homework has long been viewed sociologically, albeit incorrectly, as an obsolete form of production that was eliminated by more efficient forms of standardized mass production. However, the diversity of firms that subcontract labor and other production seems to be increasing. Christensen (1989) reports on a 1986 Bureau of National Affairs survey of 441 firms. She found that of two-thirds of those firms using subcontracts for production or administrative work, 13 percent increased the number of such contracts between 1980 and 1985. In rural New York, Dangler (1989) found 67 firms located between Rochester and Utica that employed homeworkers, most of whom were subcontracted by major companies such as IBM, Ford, Magnavox, Kodak, and Squibb.

Christensen (1989) conducted the first national survey on women and home-based work. One-half of the 14,000 respondents were homeworkers in clerical fields such as typing, legal and medical transcription, data entry, insurance rating, bookkeeping, and word processing. Among these respondents, the typical white-collar homeworker was self-employed and married, paid hourly or by the piece, and was covered by her husband's health insurance. Notably, the reasons the clerical workers had for working at home were not driven by technology; rather, they perceived homework as one way to meet their needs to increase cash flow and care for their families. Although technological developments may increase workers' opportunities to work from home, it seems that values and preferences for flexible schedules, less commuting, and greater control over one's work environment play strong roles in the trend toward home-based work.

Costs and Benefits of Homework

Employers and workers engage in home-based work for some of the same reasons: homeworking saves money. For employers, whether they use independent contractors or employees who work at home, the savings are substantial. They save on space, utilities, wages, and benefits. Employers are often concerned about quality control and productivity when workers are not subject to immediate supervision and seek ways to monitor the quality and quantity of production by homeworkers. Often, employers pay workers on a piece rate, so that only approved final products are remunerated. Employers also benefit by having a flexible labor force, the size of which can vary with need. Instead of dealing with hiring and layoffs, many homeworkers have unstable contracts that allow employers to shrink or expand the labor pool as needed. In many cases, employers pay lower wages and cover fewer or no benefits, including pensions, medical insurance, unemployment, or worker's compensation for people working at home. Many of these costs are transferred to the worker.

Many workers report savings by working at home; they report fewer expenses for clothing, meals, transportation, and child care than when they work outside the home. In addition, home-based workers perceive flexibility as one of the main advantages. Many homeworkers are women with young children, disabled persons, or rural residents, individuals for whom full-time work outside the home may be difficult. The flexibility to arrange work hours around other responsibilities, such as child care, farming, or other employment, along with greater autonomy and control over work, is often mentioned as the main advantage of working at home.

Workers experience disadvantages in home-based employment as well. Several of the overhead costs saved by employers, such as health insurance, Social Security, and pensions, are borne by workers. Because of the costs involved, many homeworkers are not covered. Proponents assert that homeworking is a good option for women with dependent children, yet many homeworkers with children report paying for child care or working when children are sleeping. On average, however, homeworkers have lower expenses for childcare than do on-site workers. Autonomy and flexibility seem to characterize homework only to the extent that the worker is able to separate paid work from the unpaid home and family work of the household. This often presents a greater challenge to women, who bear much of the responsibility for children, housework, and family care work, and may be accentuated among homeworkers in rural contexts in which the gendered division of labor is more traditional. Additionally, some homeworkers cite isolation as a disadvantage because of the lack of social interaction with coworkers. This may be significant in that home-based workers are at a disadvantage when firms consider people for advancement; the lack of participation and presence in the formal work environment can negatively affect the home-based worker.

Problems with Homework

Some social problems have been observed as a result of the resurgence of home-based work. Department of Labor officials increasingly observe child labor in the garment districts of major cities and in the agricultural belts of rural areas. There are wage and hour violations often associated with home-based work, especially when employers pay for work finished, not for hours worked. The presence of unstable work such as low-paying home-based work exacerbates conditions already disproportionately present in rural areas, such as the numbers of working poor and under- and uninsured workers. Home-based business owners tend to earn lower incomes and lack insurance coverage, making this work option attractive in diminishing rural households where there is another, higher income, and employer-provided benefits. Since employers often are motivated to use homeworkers to avoid unionization, this employment practice further undermines the competitiveness of labor, specifically rural labor forces.

Another problem observed in home-based work is employers' use of labor status misclassification. According to FLSA regulations, homeworkers are employees, unless they can show that they are self-employed. These regulations are broadly defined and leave loopholes that allow some employers to classify home-based employees as independent contractors, thus avoiding obligations such as minimum wages, maximum hours, and social and health insurance coverage. The judicial system applies a test of economic reality to determine whether a worker is an employee or an independent contractor. This test is comprised of five criteria: independent control over one's business life, control over profits and losses, investment of risk capital, control over the permanency of contracts, and the extent of skill contributed by the individual to the business. Misclassifying home-based workers allows employers to reap the benefits of having employees without fulfilling their responsibilities.

In spite of these problems, some rural areas encourage home-based employment in an effort to boost local economies. In the Midwest during the 1980s, a small garment company was started that relied solely on home-based workers. This was hailed as a local success, an example of rural entrepreneurship. By the late 1980s, the company was sued by the Department of Labor for egregious violations of fair labor standards and was ordered to pay back wages. There are other, more positive examples of home-based employment that served as incubators of family businesses or as sources of additional household income that have not exploited rural workers. Increasing job options in constrained labor markets is admirable and should be supported, but cau-

tion should be exercised in regard to developing jobs that do not provide a living wage, leave workers uninsured, or otherwise take advantage of the weaker position of rural job-seekers.

—*Christina Gringeri*

See also
Employment; Fringe Benefits; Insurance; Labor Force; Underemployment; Work.
References
Beach, Betty. "The Family Context of Home Shoe Work." Pp.130–146 in *Homework: Historical and Contemporary Perspectives on Paid Labor at Home*. Edited by Eileen Boris and Cynthia R. Daniels. Urbana and Chicago: University of Illinois Press, 1989.
Boris, Eileen. *Home to Work: Motherhood and the Politics of Industrial Homework in the United States*. New York: Cambridge University Press, 1994.
Christensen, Kathleen. "Home-based Clerical Work: No Simple Truth, No Single Reality." Pp. 183–197 in *Homework: Historical and Contemporary Perspectives on Paid Labor at Home*. Edited by Eileen Boris and Cynthia R. Daniels. Urbana and Chicago: University of Illinois Press, 1989.
Costello, Cynthia B. "The Clerical Homework Program at the Wisconsin Physicians Service Insurance Corporation." Pp. 198–214 in *Homework: Historical and Contemporary Perspectives on Paid Labor at Home*. Edited by Eileen Boris and Cynthia R. Daniels. Urbana and Chicago: University of Illinois Press, 1989.
Dangler, Jamie Faracellia. "Electronic Subassemblers in Central New York: Nontraditional Homeworkers in a Nontraditional Homework Industry." Pp. 147–164 in *Homework: Historical and Contemporary Perspectives on Paid Labor at Home*. Edited by Eileen Boris and Cynthia R. Daniels. Urbana and Chicago: University of Illinois Press, 1989.
Gringeri, Christina. "Inscribing Gender in Rural Development: Industrial Homework in Two Midwestern Communities." *Rural Sociology* 58, no. 1 (1993): 30–52.
———. "Assembling 'Genuine GM Parts': Rural Homeworkers and Economic Development." *Economic Development Quarterly* 8, no. 2 (1994): 147–157.
———. *Getting By: Women Homeworkers and Rural Economic Development*. Lawrence: University Press of Kansas, 1994.
Kraut, Robert E. "Homework: What Is It and Who Does It?" Pp. 30–48 in *The New Era of Home-based Work*. Edited by Kathleen E. Christensen. Boulder, CO: Westview Press, 1988.
Silver, Hilary. "The Demand for Homework: Evidence from the U.S. Census." Pp. 103–129 in *Homework: Historical and Contemporary Perspectives on Paid Labor at Home*. Edited by Eileen Boris and Cynthia R. Daniels. Urbana and Chicago: University of Illinois Press, 1989.

Homelessness

The condition of being without a home. The lack of awareness of rural homelessness in the United States occurs in part because rural homelessness looks different than its urban counterpart. Rural homeless are less visible; they more often live in abandoned facilities or doubled up with family or friends than on the street or in shelters. The numbers of rural homeless have increased, with recent estimates of between two and five homeless persons per 1,000 rural population. Rural homelessness more often is attributed to local economic conditions, such as the farm crisis, and less often to personal difficulties, such as alcohol and drug abuse. Rural homeless are younger, better educated, and residentially more stable than their urban counterparts. Whereas a relatively high percentage of rural counties report some services for homeless persons, most lack intensive housing and job supports necessary to address the roots of the problem.

Research Literature

Since Michael Harrington drew public attention to American urban poverty, rural poverty has been largely ignored. Although the rates of poverty in rural parts of the United States are as high as those in central cities, the image of rural Appalachia is all but forgotten, and rural poverty and homelessness became almost invisible to the public and to policy analysis. The "urban only" myth of homelessness survives in part due to lack of academic research on the topic. A 1990 volume on homelessness in 14 states, all with sizable rural populations, almost totally ignored rural homelessness. Only one report indexed the term "rural," whereas the others, at best, only acknowledged that rural and small-town homelessness has risen and, at worst, asserted that homelessness is an urban problem (Momeni 1990). Most researchers who note that homelessness is not exclusively an urban phenomenon give no further attention to the topic. Many studies that purport to offer rural data in reality focus on homelessness in small cities in rural states.

Rural homelessness is, no doubt, difficult to study. That difficulty is exacerbated by lower absolute numbers of rural homeless; lower use of public services because of factors such as a greater likelihood that the rural poor live in a two-parent family (and thus are ineligible for programs such as Aid to Families with Dependent Children [AFDC]); scarcity of social services and shelter programs; and greater reliance on relatives, friends, and self-help strategies. In addition, despite higher poverty rates, rural and small-town residents, including social service personnel, tend to deny the presence of homeless persons in their communities.

Causes

Some causes of rural homelessness mirror those in urban centers, whereas others derive from circumstances unique to the rural areas. Rising family instability, depression, suicide, teen pregnancy, and alcohol and drug abuse have been documented in rural areas. A higher percentage of rural homelessness is attributable to economic reasons. The 1980s farm crisis rippled throughout rural communities and caused farm debt and foreclosures, small business failures, and displacement of entire families to larger commercial centers; increased unemployment and underemployment; and in general led to lower salaries, a rising cost of living, program cutbacks, and a shortage of adequate local housing. During the farm crisis, these problems began to occur on a scale that overwhelmed the traditional local support network of friends and family, resulting in increasing rural homelessness.

Shortage of low-cost housing reached crisis proportions in some rural areas. Difficult economic times provide few resources to refurbish old homes or build new ones. Some counties refuse government assistance for low-income housing for fear that homeless people might be attracted to the area. Infringement of urban dwellers who purchased second homes contributed to housing shortages and inflation in rural areas and forced locals into substandard housing.

The primacy of economic causes of rural homelessness was substantiated in a 1990 Ohio study (First, Rife, and Toomey 1994) in which over 60 percent of the rural respondents cited unemployment, eviction, cessation of government benefits, or disaster as the primary reason for their homelessness. Family conflict and dissolution was cited by about 30 percent, whereas individual problems, such as alcohol and drug abuse, were noted by only 5 percent as a cause of their homelessness.

Defining and Counting the Homeless

Media-constructed images of homelessness, limited to persons on the streets or in shelters, dominate popular understandings and academic study of homelessness. This narrow conceptualization is inadequate for the study of homelessness in urban areas and fails more profoundly when used as a guide to examine the phenomenon in rural areas. Rural areas have comparatively few people on the streets and usually do not have shelters. Instead, rural homeless are found in abandoned houses and cars or move in with family or friends.

A four-part continuum, which provides a more useful framework to examine rural homelessness, was constructed to study homelessness in Iowa (Wright and Wright 1993). The continuum, based on the amount, permanency, and adequacy of shelter, includes (1) "on-the-street" homeless who live on the streets without even nominal shelter; (2) "quasi-homeless" who live in cars, tents, abandoned buildings, and other makeshift arrangements; (3) "sheltered homeless" who reside in facilities designed to house individuals or families in need of a temporary residence; and (4) "doubling up" homeless who live with a family member or friend not by choice but because without such support they would be without home or shelter.

Baseline data provided by a 1985 study of homelessness in 16 randomly selected rural Ohio counties estimated that there were 0.24 homeless persons per 1,000 residents in rural counties (Fitchen 1992). Since then, service providers and advocacy groups observed increasing numbers of rural homeless (Patton 1987; Segal 1989; First, Rife, and Toomey 1994). A 1990 study of 21 randomly selected rural counties in Ohio located 919 homeless adults, approximately two persons per 1,000 population (First, Rife, and Toomey 1994). A 1992 Iowa study defined 13 counties with no town larger than 2,500 persons as rural. Seven counties with less than 20 persons per square mile, but with one or more towns with populations between 2,500 and 4,300, were identified as semirural. Social service and education personnel identified 449 persons (3.98 per thousand) in rural counties and 475 persons (7.48 per thousand) in semirural counties as fitting into the four homeless categories.

On the Street. The literally homeless are rare in rural areas. On-the-street rural homeless have been found to make up from 0 to about 5 percent of the total. Rural counties in Iowa reported no "on-the-street" homeless, but in semirural counties they constituted 1.5 percent of the total reported homeless. About 4.2 percent of the homeless identified in the 1990 Ohio studies were on the street.

Quasi-Homeless. In the 1992 Iowa study, 3.6 percent of the rural and 21.1 percent of the semirural homeless lived in quasi-homeless conditions. Just over 10.3 percent of the homeless identified in the 1990 Ohio study were living in cars or other limited shelter.

Sheltered. Rural areas have relatively few shelters. A late-1980s Missouri study (Frank and Streeter 1987) asserted that persons displaced by the rural economic crisis did not use shelters but instead found employment in town, got help from family and friends, or joined a migrant labor stream. Eleven percent of the reported homeless in the rural and 47.1 percent of those in semirural counties of Iowa were in shelters or transitional housing. The 1990 Ohio study found that 39 percent of the homeless lived in missions, shelters, and inexpensive motels and hotels.

Doubling-Up. Over 85 percent of the homeless in the rural counties of Iowa in 1992 were living with relatives and friends. In the semirural areas, doubled-up dropped to 30.3 percent of the total, perhaps reflective of a different distribution of the homeless or possibly indicative that reporting personnel in the larger towns are less aware of persons living with relatives and friends. Over 46 percent of the homeless identified in Ohio in 1990 were doubled-up. Doubling-up is becoming more difficult in many rural areas because of newly implemented housing regulations that may require eviction and termination of public assistance for violation of overcrowding laws. In addition, financially strapped households are less able to support additional people.

Characteristics of Rural Homeless

Although rural and urban homeless share many characteristics, they differ in some important ways. Rural persons are homeless for shorter duration, have fewer debilitating personal problems (Hoover and Carter 1991), and are more likely to have been permanent or long-term (more than one year) residents of the area in which they live. They are younger, disproportionately of minority racial and ethnic heritage, more likely to be single women or mothers with children, more highly educated, and less likely to be disabled than their urban counterparts.

Studies of rural homelessness consistently found relatively high levels of employment, particularly among young families, but lack of sufficient income to provide secure housing. Almost one-third of the 1990 Ohio homeless had worked for pay during the previous month, about 14 percent full time, and only 38 percent cited welfare as their main source of income (First, Rife, and Toomey 1994). Generally, rural poor families receive fewer welfare benefits and more often live in states that do not provide AFDC for two-parent families. Young women who have limited skills or cannot work due to child-care responsibilities constitute a large segment of the rural homeless population and tend to be employed in lower-level jobs than comparable women in urban and suburban areas.

Many displaced rural workers become travelers who crisscross the country following rumors of good jobs. Typically, they have limited financial resources and barely adequate means of transportation and thus often become stranded in rural communities because of vehicle breakdown, the need for medical attention, or a lack of financial resources to go further. Some studies have identified "new hermits" as part of the rural homeless mix. These are people returning to the land and Vietnam veterans who find it easier to drop out than to cope (Frank and Streeter 1987).

Short- and Long-Term Solutions

Conditions faced by homeless persons are worse in rural than in urban areas, and short-term services that address the immediate needs of homeless persons are less consistently available. Shortage of affordable housing is more acute in rural areas. Rural citizens are less likely to be tolerant of unconventional behavior and are likely to resent and shun mentally ill or other unconventional persons who drift in. And it is more difficult to deliver specialized services, including education, in sparsely populated areas.

Despite these difficulties, over half of the rural county social service providers reported availability of day care, low-rent housing, health programs, clothing assistance, meals, counseling, housing assistance, church programs, and in-school support. A higher percentage of the rural counties reported availability of special transportation and teachers trained to identify the needs of homeless children. Rural communities were less likely to report shelters, alternative schools, teen parenting programs, or Big Brothers/Big Sisters programs in the county (Wright and Wright 1993). Such short-term solutions primarily address the symptoms of homelessness. The more complex task of actually reducing the occurrence of homelessness in rural areas will involve providing dependable, affordable housing, jobs with adequate salaries, and general revitalization of rural economies.

—*Susan E. Wright and R. Dean Wright*

See also
Employment; Policy, Socioeconomic; Poverty; Social Class; Underemployment.

References

First, Richard J., John C. Rife, and Beverly G. Toomey. "Homelessness in Rural Areas: Causes, Patterns, and Trends." *Social Work* 39, no.1 (1994): 97–108.

Fitchen, Janet M. "On the Edge of Homelessness: Rural Poverty and Housing Insecurity." *Rural Sociology* 57, no. 2 (1992): 173–193.

Frank, Robert, and Calvin Streeter. "Bitter Harvest: The Question of Homelessness in Rural America." Pp. 36–45 in *Social Work in Rural Areas: The Past, Charting the Future, Acclaiming a Decade of Achievement: Proceedings of the 10th National Institute of Rural Areas.* Edited by A. Summers, J. Schriver, P. Sundet, and R. Meinert. Columbia: University of Missouri at Columbia, School of Social Work, 1987.

Helge, Doris. "Educating the Homeless in Rural and Small School District Settings." Pp. 212–231 in *Educating Homeless Children and Adolescents: Evaluating Policy and Practice.* Edited by James H. Stronge. Newbury Park, MA: Sage, 1992.

Hoover, Greg A., and M. V. Carter. "The Invisible Homeless: Nonurban Homeless in Appalachian East Tennessee." *Rural Sociologist* 11, no. 4 (Fall 1991): 3–12.

Momeni, Jamshid, ed. *Homelessness in the United States: State Surveys.* New York: Praeger, 1990.

Patton, Larry. *The Rural Homeless.* Washington, DC: Health Resources and Services Administration, 1987.

Segal, E. "Homelessness in a Small Community: A Demographic Profile." *Social Work Research and Abstracts* 25, no. 4 (1989): 27–30.

Wright, R. Dean, and Susan E. Wright. *Homeless Children and Adults in Iowa: Addressing Issues and Options in Education, Services and the Community.* Des Moines: State of Iowa, Department of Education, 1993.

Horse Industry

The aggregate of individuals, firms, and farms engaged in breeding, raising, training, and using horses. This entry provides an overview of the ways horse ownership and use affects the rural economy. It addresses the meaning of expenditures for horse ownership, maintenance, and use for the rural economy; the impact of major racing and show facilities; and the effects of tourism associated with horse shows, racing, and events. It shows the relative importance of horses and equine activities as a component of the rural economy by identifying the major ways horses induce expenditures and create jobs.

Introduction

Horses are an integral part of life in rural America. The consequences of horse farms, pastures, fencing, and buildings for the aesthetic appeal of the countryside should not be underestimated. Horse production, training, and events make major contributions to the rural economy. Nearly every U.S. county has horse farms, show or performance facilities, and organizations. Many have a regular schedule of equine activities. Breeding and sales, racing, pleasure riding, showing, and other endeavors are significant sources of income, employment, and recreation. Various segments of the horse industry are associated with diverse clusters of institutions, professions, and activities. Each horse breed and type of competition has unique organizational arrangements for registration, competition, and recognition.

The importance of the horse industry in rural America is difficult to document because statistical information is generally not available. Some equine census

Owners with their brood mare and her new foal.

information is collected by animal health authorities on an occasional basis for disease management purposes. State veterinarians monitor horse populations, but intensive surveys are done only in the case of disease outbreaks that require complete coverage of inoculations in a specified area.

Following the decline in horses on farms in the 1950s, detailed enumeration of this class of livestock by the National Agricultural Statistics Service was stopped. The Census of Agriculture does continue to report the number of horses on farms every five years, but most horses are not on the units producing food animals or crops enumerated by the National Agricultural Statistics Service. Horses are not considered a food or fiber commodity, so the main sources of estimates are in the private sector. Some national breed associations maintain accurate records and ease the registration of young horses. Other listings are rendered less useful by registration of horses in several related breed associations and by fee structures that discourage registration of every foal. The U.S. Equine Marketing Association (1992) issues the only annual state-level horse population estimates by breed. We estimate that 4 percent of American households own at least one horse.

Horse Organizations and Events

There is no general horse association in rural America. Instead, the American horse industry is best understood as a loosely connected aggregate of breeds and related associations that support an annual cycle of competitions and recognition in each state, region, and the nation. Organizations and associations provide the framework for owners, riders, horses, and spectators to come together. Most state associations have connections to regional or national organizations that register animals, sanction events, and organize championship competitions.

The horse industry tends to be segmented by breed, locality, and activity. Breeds represent the major divisions in communication and association among horse owners. For the horse owner, a breed defines a reference group for information sharing, a potential market for sales or breeding services, and a context for display and use of a valued possession. Breed-specific organizations focus their efforts on the promotion of one breed of horse.

Locality-based organizations usually involve users of different breeds of horse. Similarly, activity-based organizations are formed for those whose common interest is a horse sport. Many horse owners, however, belong to a combination of organizations. They might belong to a particular activity association such as one for barrel racing, as well as an organization promoting a specific breed such as the quarter horse.

Equine events can be divided loosely into two broad classifications: general events and breed-specific events. In general events, many horses of various breeds participate in the activities. Separate classes are held for each breed at a show, or more than one breed can perform the desired activity, as with jumping. In breed-specific events, only the animals of one breed participate. The fees for breed shows may be higher than for general events, and participating animals are required to have papers showing they are purebred. Many owners never compete in shows or participate in special activities with their horses. Casual horse ownership and use are a widespread and significant aspect of the horse industry in rural America.

The wide diversity in the location and scale of horse activities and uses is an important feature of rural America's horse industry. The more activities that exist, the greater the need for horses that can perform the specific activities. As an activity grows in popularity, so does its impact on the rural economy. Greater numbers of horses draw bigger crowds, thereby increasing tourism and expenditures by outsiders and residents in a locality. The economic effect is carried throughout the community and region, as activities create demand for services, clothes, equipment, facilities, and horse production.

Components of Economic Impact

Horses have impacts on the rural economy through the service businesses they support; breeding fees and sales; spectator and participant travel and entertainment expenses away from home; and the largest category, care and maintenance. Owners buy feed, materials, and services for horses every day. Their purchases represent demand for facilities, farm products, suppliers, and a variety of technicians and professionals. Horse care and maintenance are central mechanisms by which the economic impacts of horse ownership are transmitted.

Care and Maintenance. Broadway et al. (1994) developed cost estimates for the care and maintenance of racehorses, show horses, and casual-use recreational horses. The average annual cost of keeping an Alabama racing horse in training was estimated to be $15,390 in 1990. The estimated average annual cost of keeping a show horse was $11,005. The high levels of expenditures for each set of animals reflect the more intense level of care and maintenance required to keep them in proper condition. These estimates of typical owner outlays are based on Alabama data but probably approximate or are somewhat lower than expenditure patterns in other parts of the country.

Horses used for purposes other than showing or racing are classified as recreational-use horses. They cost their owners about $3,140 annually per horse for care and maintenance. These costs include feed, housing, shoes, equipment, medicine, veterinary care, insurance, and other outlays. Expenditure levels for these animals reflect lower care and maintenance needs associated with horses not actively showing, racing, or competing in other events. Although the study did not estimate separate budgets for breeding stock, expenses for these animals probably approximate those of a recreational horse.

Impacts of Racing. The racing industry has five major sets of income flows: (1) pari-mutuel takeout (that portion of the amount wagered that is not returned to bettors) goes to the track and state and local governments; (2) purses go to racehorse owners and jockeys; (3) training fees and other compensation go to trainers, grooms, and jockeys; (4) income from the sale of yearlings and stallion breeding services goes to breeding farm owners and employees; and (5) throughout the process, professionals and firms receive money from services to support horse maintenance and use.

In addition to pari-mutuel takeout, tax revenue impact includes real estate tax, sales tax, and license fees and the direct tax impacts of the employment expenditures, business expenditures, and horse owner outlays. Some states (e.g., Kentucky) collect taxes on breeding fees and the sale value of horses, racing and otherwise, and others levy a specific pari-mutuel tax to support regulatory activities at the track and other purposes. The rest of the tax revenue is generated by the actual operation of the track. Combined revenue to state and local governments, in taxes and support of regulatory activities, can be as low as 3 percent of the handle, but sometimes can be higher (for example, 5 percent in Texas).

Admissions, the pari-mutuel handle (live racing and simulcasting), and concession receipts represent the main sources of income for the track, although some of this money may flow to out-of-state management or ownership. The economic impact on the locality and region centers on monetary flows to individuals and businesses. These are chiefly reflected in employment at the track and in a variety of direct expenditures. Professional fees and other services represent an aggregate of expenditures that includes legal costs, advertising, and various items associated with operation and maintenance of the track. These flow to local firms and individuals and are a major source of the track's impact on individuals.

Stakes, purses, and winnings represent the direct flow of revenue to jockeys, owners, and breeders from horse racing. Losses and winnings from wagering represent a significant redistribution of income within the local community. One study estimates that about a quarter of the stakes and purses flow to residents of a state (Broadway et al. 1994). This figure underscores the significant interstate connections of horse racing. Horses, owners, and trainers from other states often collect most of the purses, but they spend considerable time and money in the locality doing so.

An extensive array of breeding and boarding farms raise the next generation of racing horses. These farms are particularly labor intensive, representing significant direct contributions through wages to the local economy. Much of the attention to the economic impact of horses is directed to the racing industry, but other horse uses have much more pervasive effects on rural life.

Shows and Other Spectator Events. Shows are competitions in which prizes are awarded based on body conformation, groomed appearance, physical capabilities, and behavioral performance of the horse and rider. Horses and owners accumulate points for participation and achievement that can lead to state, regional, national, and sometimes international recognition. Certified judges award place standings and points based on relevant criteria.

Shows provide an opportunity for horse owners, trainers, breeders, and riders to exhibit their animals. Shows stimulate interest in breeding stock and training procedures because winning horses and trainers command higher sale prices and breeding fees. Additionally, shows provide spectator entertainment, though admission is not usually charged for smaller or local shows. Regional and area shows that attract many overnight visitors to a community can represent a significant economic injection into a locale.

Showing is a very important component of the horse industry and has a significant impact on rural America's economy. On average, owners of active show horses spent $1,495 on annual travel and related expenses during horse shows in Alabama in 1989 (Broadway et al. 1994). The estimate includes expenditures for fuel, food, and lodging for the persons traveling with the horse, stall fees, and registration fees for the horse. Horse shows and competitions create demand for clothing, tack, and other accoutrements. Large cities with indoor show arenas particularly benefit from tourism and other economic activity generated by large horse shows. Spectator outlays, participant expenditures, and other monetary flow are considerable when visitors number in the thousands.

Besides the on-site expenditures, shows generate a substantial amount of tourism income to the area. This economic activity results from spectators and participants traveling from out of town, renting motel rooms, and purchasing meals and other goods during the shows. Polo, dressage, schooling shows, open shows, trail rides, rodeos, and other events produce significant benefits to the hosting localities. Traveling owners and horses require additional housing expenses. Some spectators travel long distances to view the activities.

Rodeos, polo matches, cutting events, barrel racing, trail rides, field trials, equestrian events, and other activities also make identifiable contributions to America's rural economy. The impacts are concentrated in the community that hosts the event. Most of an event's economic impact on a local economy is derived from the spectators because there are typically many more spectators than contestants. Spectators generate economic activity through admission fees, concessions, and souvenirs. Farriers, stock handlers, veterinarians, and other providers receive income for services that support rodeo events.

Out-of-state horses stabled in a locale represent a significant economic impact to the area. This impact stems from the purchase of food and lodging for personnel accompanying the horses and services and supplies for the horses. For example, each out-of-state horse stabled at the track or show ground may generate revenues that average $90 per day. Visiting horses have important direct tourism impacts because horses, riders, trainers, service providers, and vendors all require food and lodging. Though a small facility with a short program may attract relatively few horses, the total impact can be large.

The number of jobs associated with horse breeding, raising, and care is related to the intensity of use. Race horses require approximately one employee per 12 horses; show animals require approximately one employee for 20 horses; but animals maintained for recreational use and breeding use employ, on average, approximately one individual for every 100 horses.

Employment impacts may tend to the lower end of the range because owners and unpaid family members provide labor for the many single or small sets of animals held by recreational users. Total employment associated with horses also includes racetrack or arena employees, regulatory staff, trainers, other care and maintenance employees, and a variety of self-employed individuals who provide services to horses. Some jobs, for example, show staff, are also created during large events.

Employment in the horse industry generates additional employment in other industries. This idea is described by an employment multiplier. Trenchi and Flick (1982) estimate the employment multiplier for the livestock industry to be 1.74. Simply conceived, this means that every job created in the livestock sector creates a total of 1.74 jobs throughout the economy. This multiplier applies mainly to the relatively small component of breeding farm employment. Most other horse-related jobs are in the service sector, which tends to have lower employment multipliers.

Economic impacts reflect the immediate injection of monetary flows through the purchase of goods and services by equestrians, tracks, major show arenas, and visitors. Income flows also can be shown to generate additional economic activity; this is labeled the "multiplier effect." The estimated income multiplier for the horse industry is 2.9 (Trenchi and Flick 1982). This means that every $1 transaction in the horse industry results in $2.90 of total economic activity.

Conclusion

Horses have significant links to the agricultural sector and the larger economy. According to a national study by the accounting firm of Peat, Marwick, and Mitchell (1987), about 16 percent of the U.S. agricultural and agribusiness gross economic product comes from the horse industry. Horse production and maintenance create demand for oats, corn, clover, alfalfa, hay, and other farm products. Straw and wood shavings for bedding also are farm-based commodities used by horse owners.

Across rural America, a widespread and diverse set of households owns one or two horses for casual use. Although they do not make the same level of investment as more intensive users, these horse owners demand a significant amount of services and products to ensure their animals' health and well-being. Spending by horse owners, breeders, and trainers for buildings, fencing, and equipment clearly helps to bolster the rural economy. Although the horse population may be small in a state, the impacts are magnified due to the high value of the animals and the connections to racing, shows, and events.

*—Joseph J. Molnar, Cynthia A. McCall,
Regina Broadway, and Robert M. Pendergrass*

See also

Agriculture, Structure of; Animal Rights/Welfare; Community Celebrations; Cowboys; Livestock Industry; Pasture; Ranching; Recreational Activities.

References

Broadway, Regina D., Joseph J. Molnar, Cynthia A. McCall, and Robert M. Pendergrass. *Organization, Impacts, and Prospects for the Breeding and Raising of Horses in Alabama.* Bulletin 623. Auburn: Alabama Agricultural Experiment Station, 1994.

Peat, Marwick, and Mitchell. *The Economic Impact of the U.S. Horse Industry.* Washington, DC: American Horse Council, 1987.

Trenchi, Peter, III, and W. A. Flick. *An Input-Output Model of Alabama's Economy: Understanding Forestry's Role.* Bulletin no. 534. Auburn: Alabama Agricultural Experiment Station, 1982.

U.S. Equine Marketing Association. *Information on the Alabama Horse Market.* Silver Spring, MD: U.S. Equine Marketing Association, 1992.

Horticulture

The science, technology, and art of producing and utilizing garden crops, such as fruits, vegetables, ornamental and landscape plants, herbs and spices, and medicinal plants. Horticulture is part of our daily life in relation to food, medicine, recreation, enjoyment, and enhancement of the environment. It is a large industry with large numbers of commercial enterprises (such as farms, orchards, vineyards, nurseries, processing plants, and marketing companies); home gardens, orchards, lawns, landscaped private and public golf courses, parks, and other recreational areas. Most people in rural America are engaged in horticulture on a full-time or part-time employment or on a leisure-time, amateur basis. About 40 percent (by weight) of the food consumed in the United States consists of horticultural products (fresh and processed fruits, nuts, vegetables, and herbs and spices), which are very important sources of vitamins, minerals, and dietary fiber. The thousands of plants grown for ornamental purposes contribute greatly to the quality of life in rural America. The following aspects of horticulture are briefly discussed in this entry: economic impact, classification, horticultural food crops, and nonfood roles of horticulture for humans.

Economic Impact

Horticulture represented about 15 percent of total agricultural receipts in the United States in 1993. The estimated farm gate value of horticultural crops was $26.5 billion ($4.9 billion for greenhouse and nursery crops, $9.8 billion for fruits and nuts, and $11.8 billion for vegetables); their estimated retail-level value was $97 billion. Hundreds of thousands of jobs in rural America are dependent upon the horticultural industries (including production, processing, and marketing of fruits and vegetables; production, distribution, and sale of ornamentals; and landscape design, implementation, and maintenance). Careers in horticulture include teacher, researcher, plant breeder, seed producer, nursery manager, horticultural adviser, extension specialist, consultant, horticultural therapist, landscape horticulturist, park supervisor, botanic garden curator, quality assurance manager, production manager, fresh produce marketer, and pest control adviser.

The United States was a net exporter (in dollar value) of vegetables and melons ($2.5 billion exports versus $2.1 billion imports) and a net importer (in quantity) of fruits (4.9 billion pounds exports versus 10.4 billion pounds imports) in 1993. Bananas represent about 75 percent of the fruit imports.

Classification of Crops

Horticultural crops typically are classified into three major categories: edible, industrial, and ornamental crops. First, edible crops are subdivided as fruits, nuts, vegetables, herbs and spices, and beverage crops. Fruits, along with selected examples, include temperate fruits (apple, pear, apricot, cherry, nectarine, peach, plum, strawberry, and cane berries), subtropical fruits (avocado, grapefruit, orange, lemon, lime, and mandarin), and tropical fruits (banana, mango, papaya, and pineapple). Nuts include temperate nuts (almond, filbert, pecan, and pistachio) and tropical nuts (Brazil nut, cashew, and macadamia). Vegetables include root vegetables (potato, onion, garlic, and sweet potato), leafy and stem vegetables (asparagus, cabbage, celery, lettuce, and spinach), floral vegetables (artichoke, cauliflower, and broccoli), immature-fruit vegetables (cucumber, summer squash, lima beans, snap beans, peas, pepper, and sweet corn), mature-fruit vegetables (cantaloupe, honeydew melon, watermelon, pumpkin, winter squash, and tomato), and other vegetables (mushrooms and other edible fungi). Herbs and spices include basil, thyme, oregano, mint, and cinnamon. Beverage crops include cacao, coffee, and tea.

Second, industrial crops are subdivided as medicinal plants (mandrake and chamomile), oil seeds (jojoba and oil palm), and extractives and resins (scotch pine and rubber). And third, ornamental crops are subdivided as landscape (nursery) plants and flower, bedding, and foliage plants. Landscape (nursery) plants include lawn and turf, ground covers and vines, evergreen shrubs and trees, and deciduous shrubs and trees. Flower, bedding, and foliage plants include annuals (petunia, marigold, and sweet pea), biennials (foxglove and sweet william), and perennials (rose, shasta daily, and salvia).

Food Crops

Contribution of Fruits and Vegetables to Human Nutrition.

Fruits and vegetables contribute about 91 percent of vitamin C, 48 percent of vitamin A, 27 percent of vitamin B_6, 17 percent of thiamin (B_1), and 15 percent of niacin (B_3) in the U.S. diet, as well as 26 percent of magnesium, 19 percent of iron, and 9 percent of calories that Americans consume. Legume vegetables (beans, peas, cowpeas), potatoes, and tree nuts contribute about 5 percent of the per capita availability of proteins in the United States. Other important nutrients supplied by fruits and vegetables include folacin, riboflavin, zinc, calcium, potassium, and phosphorus. Green and yellow vegetables are rich in carotenoids and other antioxidants.

Trends in Consumption of Fresh Fruits and Vegetables.

Consumers' concerns about diet and nutrition, health and safety, and quality and freshness influence their food consumption patterns. Per capita consumption of fruits and vegetables in the United States continues an upward trend; in 1993, it was 280 pounds of fruits and 421 pounds of vegetables and melons per person. Health and nutrition experts recommend eating at least five servings of fresh fruits and vegetables per day. The number of fresh intact and cut produce items available to consumers and the year-round supply of most of these products have increased during the past few years. This trend is expected to continue in the future.

Quality of Fresh Fruits and Vegetables. Consumers judge quality of fresh fruits and vegetables on the basis of appearance, including freshness and firmness at the time of initial purchase. Subsequent purchases depend on the consumer's satisfaction in terms of flavor or eating quality of the product. Consumers also are concerned about the nutritional quality and safety of fresh fruits and vegetables. Grade standards have been developed to identify the degrees of quality in the various commodities and thereby aid in establishing their usability and value. These standards provide a common language for trading among sellers and buyers. However, the U.S. standards for grades of fresh fruits and vegetables are voluntary except when their use is required by buyers or industry marketing orders.

Production Systems for Edible Crops. California produces about 35 and 44 percent in quantity of the U.S. total vegetable production and fruit and nut production, respectively. Florida, the second-largest producer of horticultural crops, produces 13 percent of vegetables and 31 percent of fruits, mostly citrus. The remainder of U.S. fruit and vegetable production is distributed among all other states, primarily Washington, Arizona, Texas, Michigan, New York, Idaho, Oregon, Wisconsin, Hawaii, and Georgia. The challenge to producers of horticultural crops is how to maintain high productivity of good-quality crops while protecting the environment and preserving natural resources. Increasingly producers are reducing their use of water (by employing more efficient irrigation methods), chemical fertilizers (by improving application methods and timing), and pesticides (by using integrated pest management procedures). These trends toward more sustainable production systems are relevant for small and large farms as well as for the home garden.

Marketing Systems for Edible Crops. Orderly marketing of fresh fruits and vegetables involves their transport between production area and consumption point, which may be a few miles or several thousand miles away. Short-term or long-term storage also may be used to regulate the quantity of some commodities reaching the markets. The main marketing channels for fresh produce in the United States are (1) food service establishments, restaurants, and institutions (such as schools, hospitals, prisons); (2) retail food stores through distribution centers and wholesale markets; and (3) direct producer-to-consumer sales (such as roadside stands, farmer's markets, pick-your-own operations). Organically produced fruits and vegetables represent about 1 percent of the total produce in the average retail store. They are distributed mostly through direct marketing operations and health food stores.

Nonfood Roles of Horticulture for Humans

Plants as Healers. Throughout history all human cultures have used various parts of plants growing in their environment for medicine. Even today, many medicines contain plant extracts or synthetic versions of them. For example, aspirin's active ingredient is found in willow bark, and digitalis is found in foxglove. Isolating and using only the active ingredients, however, also may increase their side effects because the plant's own balancing chemicals are not used.

Humans have always been dependent on plants for physical survival, not only for food but also for medicine and fiber (for example, building materials, clothing, floor mats, and baskets). Recently, researchers also began to document social, psychological, emotional, and perhaps even spiritual effects of plants on humans. For example, psycho-physiological effects of plants on humans include lowered blood pressure and heart rates, less need for pain medication following operations, shorter hospital stays, and fewer postoperative complications. Gardens specifically designed for Alzheimer's care facilities result in much calmer behavior and many fewer outbreaks of frustration among patients. Furthermore, horticultural therapists include gardening in therapeutic programs for psychiatric and physical rehabilitation patients and for prisoner rehabilitation programs.

The mechanisms of these psycho-physiological effects of plant-human interaction are far from being understood. One hypothesis is that from an evolutionary perspective, we are closely related to our food-gathering ancestors. Humans evolved and learned to survive in an environment of plants and still may respond instinctively to the survival value vegetation had for our ancestors. Another hypothesis is that horticultural activities, especially the production process, increase people's awareness of and participation in life cycles of plants, which in turn makes them more aware of their own physiology, cycles, and rhythms, and may also lead to a feeling of connectedness to the greater environment. A third hypothesis is that horticultural activities, especially gardening, give people a sense of control over their environment, a sense of responsibility to other living things, an opportunity to nurture in a nonthreatening environment, and an opportunity to experience success. These elements, in turn, lead to a greater sense of value for oneself and to reduced stress levels.

Plants in Living Environments. Recognition of people's general attraction to plants stimulated much growth in the nursery industry and in landscape design and architecture. Most supermarket chains carry fresh flowers and flowering plants, making those items more readily available to consumers on a daily basis. A greater variety of houseplants and garden plants are sold at nurseries and at most large drugstores and hardware stores. Landscape designers and architects increasingly are called upon to develop interior and exterior gardens for office complexes, hospitals, apartment complexes, hotels and convention centers, and retirement facilities. They also are called upon to design parks, recreational areas, golf courses, and playgrounds. Plants are used extensively to beautify the environment and to modify our environments for greater living comfort and efficiency. In addition to providing the oxygen needed for survival, plants provide summer shade, fire protection, windbreaks, privacy, and soil erosion prevention.

Plants, Art, and Rituals. Cultures from prehistoric times gave symbolic meanings to plants and used plant materials in ceremonies, rituals, and art. Clusters of different kinds of pollen found in the grave of a Neanderthal suggest flowers may have been part of the funeral process of early human ancestors. Egyptian pharaonic tomb murals painted 2,500 to 4,500 years ago portray numerous varieties and uses of plants. Public buildings and churches built during the last millennium exhibit plants in paintings and in carvings (for example, ceiling plaster designs, cornices, and capitals). Leonardo da Vinci believed fundamental truths of nature could be found by studying plant structures.

Plants themselves are often the material with which artists express themselves. Examples include bonsai, topiary, and flower arranging and design. Landscape designers often consider their creations artistic expressions.

Today plants play an increasingly prominent role in celebrations, ceremonies, and rituals. Flowers are given for births, birthdays, Valentine's Day, Mother's Day and to cheer people when they are ill, to apologize, to welcome people, and to bid them farewell at their funeral. Conifer trees and poinsettias are decorations for the winter holidays; spring holidays feature lilies. And what are school proms, weddings, and other formal occasions without corsages and boutonnieres?

Conclusion

Horticulture has always and will continue to be an integral part of people's lives on many different levels. As its diverse applications become better understood and appreciated, the horticultural industry will have an increasingly positive economic impact, creating more business and employment opportunities. Horticulture is bound to play a vital role in efforts to preserve and improve the total living environment.

—*Adel A. Kader and Aileen A. Kader*

See also
Agriculture, Hydroponic; Greenhouses; Temperate Fruit Industry; Vegetable Industry; Wine Industry.

References
Brickell, Christopher, Elvin McDonald, and Trevor Cole, eds. *The American Horticultural Society Encyclopedia of Gardening.* New York: Dorling Kindersley, 1993.

Francis, Mark, Patricia Lindsey, and Jay Stone Rice, eds. *The Healing Dimensions of People-Plant Relations.* Davis, CA: Center for Design Research, 1994.

Janick, Jules. *Horticultural Science.* 4th ed. New York: W. H. Freeman, 1986.

Kader, Adel, ed. *Postharvest Technology of Horticultural Crops.* 2d ed. Oakland: University of California, Division of Agriculture and Natural Resources, 1992.

Preece, John, and Paul Read. *The Biology of Horticulture: An Introductory Textbook.* New York: John Wiley and Sons, 1993.

Relf, Diane, ed. *The Role of Horticulture in Human Well-Being and Social Development.* Portland, OR: Timber Press, 1992.

Housing

Shelter for people. This entry discusses how rural housing is defined, characteristics of the housing inventory, and new housing. Common indicators of housing quality and affordability measures are examined. Finally, financing of housing and the issue of homelessness are explored. Housing in rural areas tend to be newer, single-family dwellings and are more likely to be owned than rented. Rural housing quality has steadily improved, although rural owners are still more likely than urban owners to have severe plumbing, heating, and upkeep problems. Urban owners are more likely to make improvements and alterations than rural owners. There is a long history of concern about the availability and cost of financing of housing in rural markets. Although housing appears more affordable in rural areas, quality may be lower in part due to the lack of regulations.

Definitions

A clear, simple definition of what constitutes rural housing does not exist. Yet the definition of rural housing is critical to any discussion of the topic. Urban/metropolitan areas can be defined using several criteria; rural/nonmetropolitan areas are defined by exclusion. Depending on the data presented, this entry uses either a rural or nonmetropolitan area to describe the location of housing outside metropolitan areas. Based on the Census Bureau definition of urban and rural areas, rural housing is that located in a geographic area not classified as urban. Urban housing comprises all housing units in urbanized areas and in places of 2,500 or more inhabitants outside urbanized areas. An urbanized area comprises an incorporated place and adjacent densely settled (1.6 or more people per acre) surrounding area that together have a minimum population of 50,000. To be considered a metropolitan area, an area must include a city of 50,000 people or an urbanized land area of at least 50,000 population with a total metropolitan population of at least 100,000. To be classified as a farm unit, occupied housing units must report sales of agricultural products of at least $1,000 during the 12-month period prior to the data collection.

Rural areas have unique characteristics that require consideration in the development of programs and policies to address housing needs. Although the majority of rural Americans are well housed, there are many for whom housing is inadequate or unaffordable. Rural America is diverse in its needs and problems. Concerns of special groups such as the homeless, Native Americans, and migrant farm workers require special attention.

In 1993, approximately 24 percent of the nation's housing units were located outside metropolitan areas. Of these, about 7 percent were farm households. The number of rural housing units outside urbanized areas was 29 percent in 1993. Using a broader definition of rural, Dolbeare (1995) reports that 38 percent of all occupied housing units are in rural areas. Close to half of the 36.4 million rural units, as defined by Dolbeare, were located in the rural portions of metropolitan areas. The South had both the largest number of residents and the highest proportion who lived in rural areas, 43.6 percent. The Midwest, however, was home to a larger proportion of the nation's population residing on farms than any other region in the country.

Characteristics

According to the 1993 American Housing Survey, about 80 percent of all rural households owned homes, compared with 59 percent of urban households. About 86 percent of rural farm households owned homes. Thus, policies that support home ownership are comparatively more important to rural residents.

Manufactured housing, which as these examples attest has come a long way since the early days of trailers, plays an important role in providing affordable housing in rural areas.

The predominant housing structure type in rural areas is single-family detached, as compared with multi-family structures. About 15 percent of rural housing units are mobile homes, compared with 2 percent of urban housing units. However, more urban owners lived in single-family homes than rural owners (89 percent and 83 percent, respectively). Rural renters are more likely than urban renters to live in single-family units (60 percent and 29 percent, respectively). Rural housing is newer than urban housing. The median age of urban housing was 30 years, compared with 21 years for rural housing. In 1993, the median value of rural homes was $73,407, which is 78 percent of the median value of urban homes ($93,098). The ratio of home value to income is similar in rural (2.1) and urban areas (2.4).

New Housing

New housing units account for approximately 10 percent of the housing stock each year. Although rural housing is newer than urban housing, 78.7 percent of all new units in 1993 were built in metropolitan areas. The average and median sales prices of new homes are higher in metropolitan areas than in nonmetropolitan areas. In 1993, the average new home price in nonmetropolitan areas was $109,400 and the median new home price was $96,500, whereas the average new home price in metropolitan areas was $151,900 and the median price was $129,400. Homes located outside metropolitan areas were smaller, with an average square footage of 1,860 compared with 2,160 in metropolitan areas; they were less likely to have central air conditioning; and they had fewer bathrooms. The average price per square foot was $53.80 in nonmetropolitan areas, compared with $56.15 in metropolitan areas.

Quality

Although physical conditions have traditionally been worse in rural areas than in urban areas, there has been some improvement. Agricultural laborers, especially migrant farm workers, may be subject to some of the worst housing conditions in rural areas. A measure used to assess housing quality has been the lack of complete plumbing facilities. The 1993 American Housing Survey (AHS) revealed that less than 2 percent of both rural and urban housing units do not have complete plumbing facilities. Also, there was a slight difference between urban and rural in the AHS indicator of overall physical adequacy of the units. Therefore, the housing quality problems of the 1930s and 1940s—lack of plumbing and crowding—have been solved for the majority of the population in the 1990s. Although 8 percent of households were still living in physically inadequate housing in 1991, the rural-urban differences in quality have been greatly reduced.

Rural owners were more likely than urban owners to have severe plumbing problems or moderate heating and upkeep problems. Rural renters were more likely than urban renters to have severe plumbing problems and moderate heating problems. Renters were more likely than owners to have these physical housing problems.

Rural households were less likely to have access to public sewers than urban households and were more likely to use septic tanks, cesspools, or chemical toilets than urban households. Whereas 94 percent of urban households used public sewers, only 31 percent of rural households did so. A public system or private company provided water to 96 percent of urban households compared with only 56 percent of rural households. Wells were the primary source of water for 41 percent of rural households.

Of rural households, 96 percent reported there were no problems such as crime, noise, traffic, litter or housing deterioration, poor services, and undesirable commercial, institutional or industrial facilities in their neighborhood, compared with 98 percent of urban households. However, 43 percent of rural households ranked their neighborhood as best compared with 29 percent of urban households.

Urban owners were more likely than rural owners to make improvements and alterations to their units. Additions were made by 12 percent of urban owners, compared with 9 percent of rural owners. Kitchen remodeling was undertaken by 8.9 percent of urban owners and 6.8 percent of rural owners, and bathroom remodeling was performed by 10.7 percent of urban and 8.5 percent of rural owners.

Affordability

Affordable housing has been a concern for the last decade as housing costs rose faster than family incomes. With increased attention to affordability, many policymakers emphasize rent-to-income ratios and rising average house prices relative to median income. However, it is more important to examine household income in relation to adequate housing. There are two critical factors to note. First, average new housing, on the whole, exceeds adequacy standards and should be expected to be affordable by everyone. Second, many households pay an acceptable percentage of income for housing but receive severely inadequate housing for the amount paid. Stone (1993) suggested an approach to affordability that includes household size and income along with nonshelter needs. This calculation method does not increase the extent of the affordability problem but rather changes its distribution. Twenty-one percent of rural households and 31 percent of urban households paid more than 30 percent of income for housing. A comparison of monthly housing costs as a percentage of current income indicates that urban housing residents had slightly higher housing cost burdens than rural households. The median metropolitan owner with a mortgage spent 22 percent of income on housing, compared with 20 percent for the median nonmetropolitan owner. Renters paid a higher proportion of their incomes for housing than owners. All renters paid about 29 percent of income for housing, compared with 26 percent for rural renters.

Regulations affecting housing costs and the impact on affordability in urban areas has been studied, and a direct relationship has been found between the cost of housing and regulatory systems. Regulations are less prevalent in rural areas, and as a result received little research consideration. However, underregulation may result in poor-quality housing and lack of protection for the money invested.

Financing

The provision of housing depends on the availability and cost of capital. There is a long history of special concern about rural financial markets. Research indicates that residential financing is less available and more costly in rural areas than in urban areas. A factor contributing to the major role that manufactured housing plays in rural areas is the availability of financing. Most manufactured homes are placed through dealers who offer financing. There have been major changes in capital markets in the recent past. A key question is how national is the mortgage market today. Availability or lack of financing may be a local rather than national phenomenon.

Congressional concern that rural households wishing to purchase homes face private sector loan funds shortages resulted in special programs to finance rural housing. One program influencing the quality and availability of housing in rural areas is the Consolidated Farm Service (CFS) program, formerly a part of the Farmers Home Administration (FmHA). CFS loan programs are directed to very low, low-, and moderate-income borrowers. Families can obtain financing for modest homes in nonmetropolitan areas. CFS also provides funding for some rural rental housing. Another source of funding for residential mortgages is the Farm Credit System, which makes loans for farms and modestly priced rural housing.

Other federal financing assistance includes Federal Housing Administration (FHA) mortgages and Veterans Administration (VA) mortgages. Of all owned mortgaged housing units in 1993 in rural areas, 2.6 percent received CFS financing assistance, 8.3 percent received FHA assistance, and 4.5 percent received VA assistance. This compares with urban areas, in which 0.5 percent received CFS assistance, 17.1 percent received FHA assistance, and 7.8 percent received VA assistance. Thus, federal programs for rural areas play only a small role in residential financing of single-family homes. However, government sponsored enterprises such as the Federal National Mortgage Association and Federal Home Loan Mortgage Corporation may have leading roles in the future.

Financing methods varied for new housing by location. Nonmetropolitan housing was purchased with cash

28 percent of the time, compared with 9 percent for metropolitan purchases. Conventional financing was used for 64 percent of nonmetropolitan purchases, compared with 74 percent of metropolitan purchases. Government-sponsored financing (FHA, VA, and CFS) was used for 19 percent of metropolitan housing mortgages, compared with 8 percent in nonmetropolitan areas.

Homelessness

Although definitions of homelessness vary, homelessness is substantial in nonmetropolitan areas, even when only those people seeking shelter and services are counted. It has been estimated that about 12.3 percent of the national homeless population is located in nonmetropolitan areas. The rural homeless are more difficult to count than the urban homeless since they are hidden in such places as vacation campsites and shacks. Native Americans and migrant farm workers represent a significant portion of the homeless population in nonmetropolitan areas. Family conflict, especially domestic violence, is a major factor in homelessness in rural areas. However, characteristics of the homeless population vary greatly from location to location.

Homelessness provides an example of extreme problems of quality, affordability, and service issues. In the future, policymakers must be willing to accept responsibility for developing programs, policies, and regulations to deal with these critical housing needs.

—*Anne L. Sweaney and Carol B. Meeks*

See Also
Homelessness.
References
Bureau of the Census. *Characteristics of New Housing: 1992.* Bureau of the Census, Current Construction Reports, Series C25. Washington, DC: U.S. Government Printing Office, 1993.

Dacquel, Laami T., and Donald C. Dahmann. *Residents of Farms and Rural Areas: 1991.* Bureau of the Census, Current Population Reports, P20-472. Washington, DC: U.S. Government Printing Office, 1993.

Dolbeare, Cushing N. "Conditions and Trends in Rural Housing: A Home in the Country: The Housing Challenges Facing Rural America." Fannie Mae Office of Housing Research. 30 October 1995.

Housing Assistance Council. *Rural Homelessness: A Review of the Literature.* Washington, DC: Housing Assistance Council, December 1991.

Meeks, Carol B. "Rural Housing: Status and Issues." MIT Center for Real Estate Development. HP no. 19. Cambridge, MA: Massachusetts Institute of Technology, Center for Real Estate Development, 1988.

Stone, Michael E. *Shelter Poverty.* Philadelphia, PA: Temple University Press, 1993.

Tin, Jan S. *Housing Characteristics of Rural Households: 1991.* Bureau of the Census Current Housing Reports, Series H121/93-5. Washington, DC: U.S. Government Printing Office, 1993.

U.S. Department of Agriculture. *Focusing on the Needs of the Rural Homeless.* Washington, DC: Rural Housing Service, 1996.

Ziebarth, Ann C., and Carol B. Meeks. "Public Policy and Financing for Rural Housing." *Advancing the Consumer Interest* (forthcoming).

Hydrology

The study of water as it moves through the earth, atmosphere, and oceans, particularly how land uses influence the processes through which precipitation (atmospheric deposition of rain, snow, and ice) becomes groundwater and stream flow. Hydrologic processes are varied, and the manner in which they operate varies also, depending upon climatic, geologic, ecological, and land-use conditions. They operate over space, that is, across the landscape, in areas that are defined by topography and the pattern of stream flow. This entry presents the watershed concept, discusses how rural land use affects hydrologic processes, and presents ecoregions as a means to categorize rural landscapes on hydrological grounds.

The Watershed Concept

For any point on any stream, an area can be defined that is uphill of that point. Since water runs downhill, this is the region from which water is gathered to that point on that stream. This region is known as the watershed or drainage basin of that stream. Watersheds vary in size from less than an acre for a small farm pond to over one million square miles for the Amazon River, with the world's largest watershed, and the Mississippi River, the dominant river of North America, which drains lands from the Continental Divide at the crest of the Rocky Mountains in the West to the crest of the Appalachian Mountains in the East.

Watersheds are organized hierarchically over the landscape with reference to tributaries. For example, the Gallatin River in Montana is a tributary of the Yellowstone River, which is a tributary of the Missouri River, which is a tributary of the Mississippi. Thus, the Gallatin watershed is a subset of the Yellowstone watershed, which is a subset of the Missouri watershed, which is a subset of the Mississippi watershed.

Rural Land Use and Hydrologic Processes

The quantity and quality of water running in any stream or river can be attributed primarily to the balance

Dams like this one on the Colorado River in Glen Canyon, Arizona, are responsible for a large part of the power generated in the United States.

between precipitation and evaporation on the one hand and land use within the watershed on the other. Thus, rivers carry more water during the wet season or following a major storm or snowmelt event than during the dry season or a short-term drought.

Land use intervenes between precipitation and stream flow. For example, a rainstorm that produces a gentle rise of clear water when that river's watershed is predominantly forest, pasture, and wetlands may produce a muddy flood when it has been coverted to cropland. The reason for this lies in how the land surface, and particularly its vegetation cover, responds to rainfall and runoff. In a forest or well-maintained pasture, most rain falls on tree leaves or needles or blades of grass. As much as 35 percent of it then reevaporates in a process called interception and thus never reaches the ground. But on a field of row crops, such as cotton, corn, or soybeans, most of it falls on bare ground, except when the crops are at their fullest growth in late summer. Thus, little is intercepted, and a greater quantity of water reaches the ground surface.

Once water reaches the ground in the forest or pas-

ture, most of it seeps into the soil, in a process called infiltration, because (1) the downward force of the raindrops has been dissipated by leaves; (2) roots provide convenient avenues for infiltration; and (3) fallen leaves, low-lying plants, and living and dead blades of grass cover the ground, creating a high-friction obstacle course for water running downhill over the soil surface. On a plowed field, in contrast, much of the rainfall impacts the soil directly, creating tiny rain-splash craters in the soil. Sparser roots provide fewer avenues for infiltration, with many holes already closed by particles deposited by rain splash. The lack of plant matter covering the ground then allows uninfiltrated water to run unimpeded over the soil surface in the erosive process called overland flow. In this way soil is carried downhill in sheets; in small channels called rills; and, in extreme cases, in rapidly developing gullies.

These seemingly subtle differences in hydrologic processes at the micro level actually produce major differences in water quantity and quality at the larger scale of watersheds. In a predominantly forested watershed, less than 1 percent of precipitation becomes surface runoff, and soil erosion is negligible. In pasture, runoff is typically a moderate 6 percent and erosion less than 0.1 tons/acre/year. In a cornfield, runoff can be greater than 40 percent of precipitation, and erosion is often over 10 tons/acre/year and is sometimes as high as 50 tons. On bare fallow ground or construction sites, runoff can reach 50 percent and erosion 70 tons. These differences determine whether rapid runoff will cause a river to create a major flood filled with damaging sediment following a rainstorm, or whether the rainfall will be dissipated by evaporation and transpiration (the evaporation of water by plant leaves) and by high rates of infiltration to the soil, which releases its water slowly, either through subsoil flow or percolation to groundwater. Thus, streams and rivers whose watersheds are composed mainly of dense vegetation, especially natural vegetation, tend to have more stable water flows and lower concentrations of sediment and nutrients than streams whose watersheds are predominantly composed of intensive agricultural or urbanized land. Yet even in an urban or agricultural watershed, wetlands and riparian (streamside) vegetation can alleviate some of the pollution that agriculture, forestry, mining, and urbanization generate.

This excessive delivery of sediment and nutrients and sometimes pesticides to streams and rivers is called nonpoint source pollution, in contrast to the point-source pollutants that are delivered to waterways directly by factory or sewer pipes. Nonpoint pollution's primary impacts are on aquatic ecology, although human health issues can also arise. Excessive sediment from soil erosion can smother fish-spawning grounds. Nitrogen and phosphorus from fertilizer runoff, in a process called eutrophication, can cause algae blooms and subsequent oxygen depletion when the algae decay. Excessive nitrates in drinking water have been associated with blue-baby syndrome and gastric cancer. Pesticides are toxic in high concentrations and may be carcinogenic in low concentrations. These problems of nonpoint pollution are widespread in rural America.

The Ecoregion Concept

Differences in watershed characteristics have been captured and mapped for the conterminous 48 states using the concept of ecoregions. Ecoregions identify areas of relatively homogeneous ecological systems based on patterns of land use, land-surface form, potential natural vegetation, and soils. Land use is the key variable in defining an ecoregion since it captures much of the variation in the other three. For example, steep, wet areas with thin mountain soils tend to support forests and thus a land use of timber production or outdoor recreation. Flatter, moist areas tend to support agriculture, with the type dependent upon climatic and soil characteristics.

Ecoregions do not correspond to watersheds. Rather, they delineate land areas that, because of their land use and other characteristics, tend to have streams with similar water quality. For example, the Western, Central, and Eastern Corn Belt Plains ecoregions generally contain streams with great problems of nonpoint source pollution, largely from agriculture but exacerbated by urban and industrial pollutants and river channelization and navigation improvements. These streams run with high sediment, nutrient, and organic loads that limit the quantity and diversity of aquatic plants and animals that can live there. These problems are also evident in the central California valley, northern Piedmont (which contains the lower reaches of the Susquehanna and Potomac Rivers that drain into Chesapeake Bay), and several ecoregions in the Great Plains.

In contrast to these problem areas, favorable land use patterns create good water quality in forested and pastured areas, even in the Midwest. The Ozarks ecoregion is renowned for its clear streams and lakes filled with game fish, as are the northern Minnesota wetlands, northern lakes and forests, and north central hardwood forests ecoregions where abundant wetlands act to further alleviate any agricultural runoff problems. Good water quality also predominates in much of the Northeast and Appalachians, particularly the Northeastern Highlands, Northern Appalachian Plateau and Uplands, North-Central Appalachians, Blue Ridge Mountains, Central Appalachian Ridges and Valleys, and Central Appalachians ecoregions, except where pollutants delivered from localized urban, industrial, and mining activities have taken their toll. Parts of these ecoregions recently improved water quality through control of urban and industrial pollutants and an increase in forest cover. The forested, mountainous ecoregions of the Pacific Northwest (Coast Range, Cascades, Sierra Nevada, Eastern Cascades Slopes and Foothills, Northern Rockies, Montana Valley and Foothill Prairies, Middle Rockies, Wasatch and Uinta Mountains, and Southern Rockies) provide the pristine trout and salmon streams that Norman MacLean immortalized in his short novel and movie *A River Runs through It*. However, many of these streams are threatened by clear-cut forestry practices, mining, and dam construction. Much of the South provides an intermediate case where interspersed agriculture, commercial forestry, natural forests, and streamside wetlands combined with substantial dam construction and river engineering create a mosaic with great local variation in hydrologic conditions and water quality.

In summary, hydrologic conditions (the flow regime of streams and rivers, water quality, and associated aquatic habitats) vary greatly across rural America and are dependent largely on patterns of land use in the watersheds that delineate the rural landscape. Reductions have been made in the export of pollutants from industries and city sewers (point-source pollutants), but certain regions of rural America suffer from generally poor hydrologic conditions. Where agriculture and other land uses that systematically remove vegetation cover lead to soil erosion and sedimentation or expose water flows to toxic chemicals and excessive nutrients, nonpoint pollution has degraded the operation of hydrologic processes.

—*Christopher L. Lant*

See also

Conservation, Water; Environmental Protection; Groundwater; Irrigation; Water Use; Wetlands.

References

Clark, E. H., II, J. A. Haverkamp, and W. Chapman. *Eroding Soils: The Off-Farm Impacts.* Washington, DC: Conservation Foundation, 1985.

Doppelt, B., M. Scurlock, C. Frissell, and J. Karr. *Entering the Watershed: A New Approach to Save America's River Ecosystems.* Covelo, CA: Pacific Rivers Council, 1993.

Dunne, T., and L. B. Leopold . *Water in Environmental Planning.* New York: W. H. Freeman, 1978.

Karr, J. R., and D. R. Dudley. "Ecological Perspective on Water Quality Goals." *Environmental Management* 5, no. 1 (1981): 55–68.

Karr, J. R., L. A. Toth, and D. R. Dudley. "Fish Communities of Midwestern Rivers: A History of Degradation." *Bioscience* 35, no. 2 (February 1985): 90–95.

Omernik, J. M. "Ecoregions of the Conterminous United States." *Annals of the Association of American Geographers* 77, no. 1 (1987): 118–125.

U.S. Geological Survey. *National Water Summary 1990–91: Hydrologic Events and Stream Water Quality.* Washington, DC: USGS, 1993. (Also see subsequent publications as they are released.)

Impact Assessment

An evaluation of the consequences of an intervention. Interventions examined by impact assessment may be a specific project, such as the construction of a power plant, or a government policy or program. The evaluation of the consequences may be ex ante (that is, conducted before the implementation of the project or program) or ex post (that is, conducted after the project or program has been completed). Among the key dimensions of impact assessment are environmental impact assessment, social impact assessment, economic and fiscal impact assessment, and demographic impact assessment. Closely related concepts include technology assessment and risk assessment. This entry reviews key dimensions of impact assessment and describes the steps in an assessment. The related topics of technology assessment, risk assessment, public consultation, and environmental sustainability also are briefly discussed. Also examined is the growing interest in strategic environmental assessment (that is, application of impact assessment principles at policy and program levels) and in assessment of cumulative impacts.

Key Dimensions

Environmental impact assessment (EIA) can have several meanings. In its most narrow sense, EIA is the exercise of identifying, predicting, and evaluating the environmental impacts of a proposed project in order to prepare an environmental impact statement as required by law or policy. Typically, the term *environment* is taken to include the human environment as well as the biophysical environment, although many discussions of EIA emphasize the latter. To the extent that the human environment is included, EIA can be considered to include social impact assessment.

Although the impacts of human activities on the natural environment had been observed for centuries, official requirements that these effects be taken into account in project planning began with the National Environmental Policy Act (NEPA) of 1969. Signed into law by President Richard Nixon on 1 January 1970, the NEPA required that proponents of development projects that involved U.S. federal land, federal tax dollars, or federal jurisdictions file an environmental impact statement detailing the impacts of the proposed project, as well as project alternatives, on the physical, cultural, and human environments. During the years that followed, many state governments enacted similar legislation, calling for studies of the environmental impacts of development projects. Many nations around the world established a variety of processes to incorporate environmental impact assessment into planning and policy making.

Social impact assessment (SIA) is a methodology for examining social change or potential social change arising from development projects or processes that are external to the social group. The social impacts, also sometimes termed *socioeconomic impacts,* of development can be defined broadly to include (1) economic impacts (including changes in local employment, business activity, earnings, and income); (2) demographic impacts (changes in the size, distribution, and composition of the population); (3) public service impacts (changes in the demand for, and availability of, public services and facilities); (4) fiscal impacts (changes in revenues and costs among local government jurisdictions); and (5) social impacts (changes in the patterns of interaction, formal and informal relationships resulting from such interactions, and perceptions of such relationships among various groups in a social setting). Many discussions of social impacts emphasize only the latter group of effects (that is, changes in patterns of interaction, relationships, and perceptions).

Steps

The steps of an environmental impact assessment include (1) describing the proposed action, (2) defining the affected environment, (3) determining possible impacts, and (4) reporting the results. In describing the proposed action, the assessment should give attention to how the project will relate to various environmental dimensions. For example, development of a new mine may entail development of access corridors; surface mining and reclamation may affect a substantial acreage of wildlife habitat and suggest a potential for contamination of surface and underground water sources; and the construction and operation of the facility may lead to the in-migration of several hundred workers and their families.

Defining the affected environment is the second major step in EIA. The geographic scope of the assessment may differ, depending on the type of environmental resources being considered. For example, in regard to possible effects on flora and fauna, the focus will probably be on the areas physically affected, directly or indirectly, by the project (that is, the areas within or immediately adjacent to the mine site, access routes, and/or sites of project-related residential development). The assessment of water quality effects would be focused on the portion of the watershed downstream from the project facilities, whereas the socioeconomic analysis would be directed toward the communities where most of the project-related population would be expected to live.

To describe the affected environment in adequate detail, a variety of baseline studies may be required. The purpose of baseline studies is to describe and quantify ecosystem components and the ecological, economic, and social systems that link them before the project or program begins. For example, baseline studies may be undertaken to supplement existing information with regard to the plant and animal species found in the affected area and their relative abundance. Similar information will be needed regarding the social environment (for example, number of inhabitants, population trends). Whereas impact analysts will obtain these data from secondary sources (for example, periodic censuses) when possible, special studies may be needed to supplement the secondary information.

The projects and policies subjected to EIA often are complex, potentially affecting many dimensions of the biophysical and human environment. As a result, scoping usually is recommended early in the assessment process in order to focus the EIA on key impacts and issues. The scoping process typically involves meetings with groups of key stakeholders to identify their concerns related to the project. In addition to these interactions, the assessment team may utilize methods such as an impact assessment matrix to identify those environmental or social components that could be affected significantly by the development.

Once the relevant impacts have been identified, the next step in EIA is to forecast or predict the nature and magnitude of each. Impact prediction or forecasting typically uses a variety of models that have been developed by the respective disciplines to relate project stimuli to various environmental effects. For example, computerized economic-demographic assessment models often are used to relate the number of new project-related jobs to resulting changes in the population of nearby communities.

After impacts are projected, analysts are able to compare the relative importance of the various environmental effects. The potential extent, duration, and magnitude of the effects are factors that often are considered in evaluation of the importance of the projected impacts. Extent often refers to the size of the area affected. Typical ratings may be local (within or directly adjacent to the project area), regional, state, national, or international. In some cases, estimates of the surface area or the population affected are provided. Duration of impact refers to the ability of an ecosystem, or valued ecosystem component, to recover from the impact; generally this is measured as a time interval. For example, duration of impacts could be rated as short (less than one year), medium (one to ten years), and long term (more than ten years). Magnitude refers to the percentage of a population or resource that may be affected by an impact.

A final step in EIA is to develop a plan to mitigate or manage the impacts deemed to be important and to monitor environmental and social effects as the project proceeds. The term *impact mitigation* came into widespread use following its inclusion in the NEPA. Although the initial tendency was to view mitigation in a narrow context of reducing or eliminating negative impacts, many practitioners now believe that a broader and more comprehensive approach is desirable. *Impact management* is a term that came into widespread use, with mitigation seen as a more narrow term. Impact management encompasses measures that enhance a project's local benefits. It uses approaches that provide various forms of compensation to local interests and actions that reduce or eliminate negative effects.

Impact monitoring systems have become recognized as being virtually essential to effective impact management. The primary purpose of a monitoring system is to provide accurate and timely information for decision makers involved in impact management activities. Such information enables project officials and community leaders to periodically reassess community needs and revise associated mitigation plans. It also may serve as the basis for developing revised impact projections. Thus, at any given time the monitoring system should allow policymakers to evaluate the effectiveness of impact management activities while providing the information needed to guide future mitigation efforts.

Technology Assessment

Technology assessment can be defined as a class of policy studies that systematically examines the effects on society that occur when a technology is introduced, extended, or modified. Technology assessment emphasizes those unintended, indirect, or delayed consequences; it ultimately comprises a systems approach to the management of technology, reaching beyond technological and industrial aspects into societal and environmental domains. To the extent that much impact assessment addresses the effects of technological changes, technology assessment and impact assessment overlap. The two approaches can be distinguished, however, in that impact assessment encompasses other forms of future-directed policy analyses that differ from technology assessment.

Risk Assessment

The essence of EIA is prediction, and prediction necessarily entails uncertainties. The uncertainties associated with impact assessment lead to a desire to alert decision makers to the possibility of serious adverse effects where the distribution of probabilities of occurrence or severity do not form a statistically normal distribution. Risk assessment offers methods for making uncertainties explicit in the communication of scientific analysis to policy and decision makers. Risk assessment, as it evolved in the United States, has been narrower and more tightly focused than environmental impact assessment. Risk assessments generally are associated with regulatory legislation, such as the Pure Food and Drug Act. However, the methods of risk assessment can be applied more generally to the process of characterizing the potential adverse effects of exposure to environmental hazards.

Public Consultation

Public consultation has become an integral component of impact assessment. Public consultation is a systematic process that provides citizens and organizations with easily accessible opportunities to become informed about a proposal and to register their views about it to planners and decision makers. The goal of public consultation is that, as a result of a mutual education process, the final proposal will be technically sound, economically attractive to residents and the proponent, generally understood and accepted by most of those affected, and thus politically viable. In many cases, public perceptions and concerns about physical impacts cause more problems than the physical impacts themselves; public consultation can help to manage these public perceptions and concerns.

Public consultation is generally most effective if it is initiated early in the development process. As noted previously, meetings with key stakeholder groups are central to the EIA scoping process. In addition, involvement of key interest groups early in the development process may allow for changes in the project design that may help alleviate concerns. Once the impact prediction phase of the EIA has been completed, public input may prove useful in assessment of the importance of various project effects and in development of impact mitigation measures and a monitoring plan. Finally, stakeholder groups may be invited to assist in implementing the mitigation and monitoring plan.

Environmental Sustainability

Environmental sustainability (ES) has become a major consideration in resource management, and hence in environmental assessments. ES has been defined as the maintenance of natural capital, which means the nonliquidation of environmental assets. On the output side, ES means that wastes should be kept within the assimilative capacity of the local environment without impairing its future waste absorption capacity. On the input side, for renewable resources ES means keeping their harvest rates within the regenerative capacity of the natural systems that generate them. Quasi-ES can be achieved for nonrenewables by depleting them at a rate at which renewable substitutes or other sustained income from investments elsewhere are developed by human intervention.

With increased recognition of the importance of impact assessments has come intensified interest in education, training, and professional development for impact assessment practitioners. Education and training in EIA principles, procedures, and analytical methods are offered as part of many university curricula. In addition, a variety of specialized short courses have been developed, often targeted toward practicing professionals. The need of practitioners for professional development and networking opportunities has led to the development of a professional association for impact assessment practitioners, the International Association for Impact Assessment (IAIA).

The founding of the IAIA in 1981 provided an international forum for people interested in research and the practice of EIA, SIA, technology assessment, and risk assessment. Since 1982, the IAIA has published a journal titled *Impact Assessment* (originally *Impact Assessment Bulletin*), which provides an outlet for both scholarly articles and professional practice contributions and for reviews of recent books and major research monographs. The IAIA now has members in more than 90 countries, and attendance at a recent annual conference exceeded 600.

Strategic Environmental Assessment

Although the requirement for EIA for proposed projects became thoroughly institutionalized in the United States, concerns emerged that project EIA may occur too late in the planning process to ensure that all the relevant alternatives and impacts are considered adequately. As a result, increased emphasis is being placed on the application of EIA to policies, plans, and programs of government agencies. Those who advocate applying EIA at the policy and program level point out that alternative approaches, cumulative impacts, synergistic effects (which may be cross-sectoral in nature), ancillary impacts, and regional or global impacts may all be better assessed initially at the policy, planning, or program level rather than at the project level. When EIA analysis is applied at these levels, it often is referred to as strategic environmental assessment. The principal application of strategic environmental assessment in the United States has been in the preparation of programmatic environmental impact statements. Generally, these are prepared for groups of actions that are related geographically or have similarities of project type, timing, media, or technological character.

Related to the growing interest in strategic environmental assessment is concern that greater attention be given to cumulative impacts. Project EIA often results in failure to take account of the potential for combined effects of two or more (independent or related) developments and the possible indirect or secondary effects. A further concern is that activities characterized by minor, but collectively significant, impacts usually fall outside the scope of environmental assessment. For example, the impacts of drilling one oil well may be minor, but development of 50 wells in a relatively restricted area may have substantial effects. On the international scale, global problems of diminished biodiversity, buildup of carbon dioxide, depletion of the stratospheric ozone layer, and acid rain can be cited as significant cumulative impact problems.

—*F. Larry Leistritz*

See also
Development, Community and Economic; Environmental Protection; Mining Industry; Municipal Solid Waste Management; Petroleum Industry; Policy, Environmental; Regional Planning; River Engineering; Urbanization; Wetlands.
References
Goodland, R., and H. E. Daly. "Three Steps toward Global Environmental Sustainability." *Rome (SID) Development* 2 (1992): 35–41.
Jain, Ravinder K., L .V. Urban, G. S. Stacey, and H. E. Balbach. *Environmental Assessment.* New York: McGraw-Hill, 1993.
Leistritz, F. Larry, and Steven H. Murdock. *The Socioeconomic Impact of Resource Development: Methods for Assessment.* Boulder, CO: Westview Press, 1981.
Ortolono, Leonard. *Environmental Planning and Decision Making.* New York: John Wiley and Sons, 1984.
Porter, Alan L., A. T. Roper, T. W. Mason, F. A. Rossini, and J. Banks. *Forecasting and Management of Technology.* New York: John Wiley and Sons, 1991.

Income

Money acquired from employment or from entrepreneurial activities of an individual's labor and capital resources. Income issues have been and continue to be important in rural America. In general, urban residents earn more income than rural residents, especially small and part-time farmers. The gap between urban and rural incomes narrowed during the 1970s but widened again during the 1980s and 1990s. The income gap is offset by higher wealth, primarily accumulated through land and other assets, among some of the rural population. Income for farm producers and individuals in rural America, just like their urban and suburban counterparts, represents the lifeblood of economic well-being. Income provides for the purchase of goods and services for the farm and rural family, capital for the agriculture and rural business enterprise, and the financial safety net for unexpected family emergencies and retirement. No issue, other than property rights associated with use of land in rural areas, may be of greater concern to rural families. This entry examines rural farm and nonfarm incomes since 1930, governmental attempts to bolster rural residents' incomes, and the effects of changes in the structure of agriculture on their incomes. Rural residents' incomes are compared with their wealth.

The Setting

Income concerns in agriculture and rural America have been widespread since the 1930s. Agriculture was a major economic sector in rural America during this time, and income for farm families averaged only about 50 percent of income levels for nonfarm families. Low incomes encouraged those involved in agriculture to seek employment in other occupations. The number of farms declined by over 50 percent between 1930 and 1970. However, mechanization and improved crop and livestock production technologies more than offset the migration of people from agriculture. Surpluses of agricultural commodities remained, resulting in rural farm incomes, specifically from agriculture, that remained substantially below nonfarm income until the 1970s.

Government

A historical perspective indicates that income problems in rural America in agriculture started about the same time as the Great Depression. Actually, the depression in agriculture preceded the depression in the general economy. Although the U.S. government had not been involved directly in maintaining the income of the farm sector in America prior to this time, the government became meaningfully involved soon thereafter.

A series of policy actions by the federal government resulted in numerous pieces of legislation to bolster the income of American farmers and consequently of rural America. The programs adopted by Congress to bolster farm incomes can be grouped into two primary categories: production controls and price and income support. These programs were the cornerstone of U.S. farm policy from the 1930s through the 1970s, and significant remnants remain today. The general philosophy of the price and income support policy was to maintain commodity prices, most times above market levels, although commodity surpluses remained. Government costs skyrocketed because, although people left the agricultural sector, production increases outpaced demand increase as a result of further mechanization and production technologies. This, in turn, led to the need for production controls, and a vicious cycle started.

A Transformation

From the mid-1960s through the 1970s, a change in income levels in rural America began to appear. For the first time, farm income levels rose to about 70 percent of nonfarm income levels. Different individuals cite different reasons for this change. In reality, the transformation in income levels probably occurred for a combination of reasons. In the mid-1960s, the government began a long-term trend to lower price support levels to world market levels or lower. The phase-in of this change was completed in the 1970s. U.S. farmers were forced to compete under global conditions. This brought about the need for another migration of people and resources out of the agricultural sector, but it also resulted in higher incomes for those who remained. In addition, global conditions favored U.S. producers. First, weather conditions drastically reduced supplies in some sections of the world. U.S. secretary of agriculture Earl Butz encouraged farm producers to "plant from fence row to fence row" to cover these shortages and capture economic gains. Second, world populations continued to grow above the U.S. average and demand for agricultural crops was strong. Third, in many countries incomes of the population increased, which raised the demand for U.S. products.

Another adjustment that helped ease income pressure in agriculture and rural America was the further out-migration of workers, owners, operators, and tenants who depended on agriculture as their primary source for income. Two outcomes of the out-migration during this period were that total farm income, although not rising briskly, was distributed among fewer people and those who left agriculture for employment in other fields were earning higher incomes. Many of these individuals continued to maintain their homes in the rural communities rather than move to urban or suburban areas. From 1970 through 1979, rural population grew from approximately 53.8 million to 55 million. The farm population fell during that same period from 9.7 million to 7.5 million. The increase in rural population during this period is significant. Not only was it a conscious decision for those displaced from economic activity associated with farming to remain in rural America, but it also meant that people were leaving urban and suburban areas for rural locations.

Why did they leave urban and suburban centers? There were many reasons, including quality-of-life concerns, crime, family values, and congestion. Although these urban and suburban inhabitants changed the location where they lived, most did not change employment.

They brought higher than typical incomes to their new communities, which implies that rural America benefited in terms of income.

A final reason for the transformation of America's rural communities was technological transformation. Although infrastructure in rural America typically lags behind that of urban areas, by the late 1970s significant improvements in rural areas were present. These advances included highways and telecommunications improvements. In modern jargon, rural America joined the twentieth century.

Transformation Outcomes

The results of the transformation that took place in the late 1970s were distributed among the rural population still engaged in agricultural production activities and those living in rural areas but not directly engaged in agricultural production activities. Implications of the changes were distinct. Data from 1993 indicate that average farm operator household income was slightly more than $40,000. Average U.S. household income for the same year was about $41,400. Unlike the pre-1965 figures, income levels between nonmetropolitan and metropolitan regions were very similar. However, if the farm operator income levels are separated into classifications of farms with more than $50,000 of sales and those with less than $50,000 in sales, the income levels, as well as the source of incomes, diverged. Farms with more than $50,000 in sales had an average farm operator income level of almost $55,000, about 50 percent of which was derived from farm income. Farms with less than $50,000 in sales had an average farm operator income of approximately $35,000, none of which was derived from farm income. In terms of income, larger farms had incomes higher than the U.S. average and smaller farms had income lower than the U.S. average.

The income problem in agriculture may no longer be a decades-old problem of farm producers making less than the general population; however, that conclusion depends upon individual perspective. The income quandary for large producers may be based on year-to-year variability in crop and livestock production and prices. For smaller producers, income levels have improved to about 80 percent of the national average, but that income is earned from nonproduction activities. The share of self-employment income from the farm, cash rent, and wages of household members from farm activities is negative. The economic lifeblood of the small producers remains in nonfarm jobs.

What can be understood about nonfarm jobs? Earnings from nonfarm jobs in real dollars (inflation removed with a base of 1991) has remained relatively flat since 1970. There has been very little growth in real off-farm earnings. Not only has growth been relatively flat, but also the earnings gap in real dollars between employed individuals in metropolitan and nonmetropolitan areas has widened since the mid-1970s. During the 1970s, the non-metropolitan-to-metropolitan earnings ratio steadily closed from about 76 percent to 81 percent. During the 1980s through the early portion of 1990, the gap began to widen again, and in 1991 it stood at 73.5 percent. Real earnings in metro areas are increasing at a faster pace than nonmetropolitan areas.

What is the implication of this information? On average, nonmetropolitan residents are better off in America, with incomes more comparable to urban and suburban residents. Individually, income gains in rural or nonmetropolitan areas accrued to farm operators and, to a much smaller extent, to those employed in nonfarm jobs. The benefits to farm operators have been concentrated among those with sales greater than $50,000, and smaller farm operators are still confronted with a significant income difference.

Individuals living in nonmetropolitan areas dependent upon nonfarm income will face financial challenges much like those of their urban and suburban neighbors. Income will be heavily dependent on national economic events and public-policy decisions. Rural residents with significant income off the farm will not be exempt from business cycles, business failures, interest rate fluctuations, slower growth in government expenditures, downsizing, recessions, and other economic events. The challenges to maintaining an adequate standard of living will be extraordinary.

The Great Debate

A degree of friction remains between urban and rural residents regarding income levels. Urban residents often claim the cost of living in metropolitan areas is greater than rural areas; rural residents claim just the opposite. Both are accurate in their assessments. Some aspects of living in urban America are more expensive than in rural areas. The opposite is also true. In general, data indicates it is more expensive to live in urban areas than rural areas. The subject is great for philosophical debates. There are some aspects of living that are clearly more costly in urban areas (for example, housing) and other costs are greater in rural areas (for example, food and apparel).

Wealth: The Forgotten Factor

It would be inappropriate to conclude a discussion about income and the economic well-being of people without raising the issue of wealth—that is, the accumulation of all one's property and assets. There is an old saying that farmers are cash poor but asset rich. Aggregate data support this concept. In a 1992 Federal Reserve System summary of wealth, in which dollar values were based on constant 1989 dollars, the average value of net worth (assets minus liabilities) for all families in the United States was $183,700. The median was $47,200, indicating a skewness, or unequal distribution, with most families clustered on the lower end and a small proportion stretching out on the top end. A very limited number of families have great sums of wealth. The same trends also are present in data for families involved in farming, fishing, and forestry. The average net worth of these families is $322,300, with a median of $107,300. Individuals earning income from enterprises associated with rural America have a much higher net worth, both from an average and median statistical base, than the typical family in the United States. A more accurate measure of economic well-being than income alone is a combination of income and wealth. From this perspective, many families residing in rural areas are among the wealthiest not only in the United States but also in the world.

—*Rodney L. Clouser*

See also
Agricultural Prices; Policy, Economic; Poverty.
References
Board of Governors of the Federal Reserve System. *Federal Reserve Bulletin* 78, no. 1 (January 1992): 1–18.
Bureau of Economic and Business Research. *Florida Statistical Abstract: 1994.* Gainesville: University of Florida Press.
Clouser, Rodney L., et al. "Agriculture and Economic Change in Florida: Facts, Issues, and Options." Circular 888. Gainesville: Florida Cooperative Extension Service, 1990.
Danziger, Sheldon, and Peter Gottschalk, ed. *Uneven Tides: Rising Inequality in America.* New York: Russell Sage Foundation, 1993.
Knutson, Ronald D., J. B. Penn, and William T. Boehm. *Agricultural and Food Policy.* Englewood Cliffs, NJ: Prentice-Hall, 1983.
Lankford, Philip M. *Regional Incomes in the United States, 1929–1967: Level, Distribution, Stability, and Growth.* Chicago: University of Chicago, Department of Geography, 1972.
Osberg, Lars. *Economic Inequality in the United States.* Armonk, NY: Sharpe, 1984.
U.S. Bureau of the Census. *Statistical Abstract of the United States: 1992.* 112th ed. Washington, DC: U.S. Government Printing Office, 1992.
U.S. Department of Agriculture. *Rural Conditions and Trends.* Washington, DC: U.S. Department of Agriculture, Economic Research Service, various issues.
———. "Structural Characteristics of Farm and Ranch Business." Washington, DC: U.S. Department of Agriculture, Economic Research Service, Rural Economy Division, n.d. Mimeograph.

Inequality

The unequal distribution of socioeconomic resources, such as wealth, prestige, and power, in a given population. This entry highlights the lower socioeconomic standing of minorities and women in rural areas and provides an overview of the explanations for this pattern. The entry presents data from the 1990 census to illustrate the degree of socioeconomic inequality in these areas and discusses various forms of discrimination that rural minority groups and women have experienced. The entry concludes with an overview of the contemporary policy climate affecting the conditions of these groups.

Explanations

Rural areas historically lagged behind socioeconomically compared to urban places. Yet certain segments of the rural population, minorities and women, fared even worse socioeconomically. Various explanations are used to explain the lagging socioeconomic fortunes of minorities and women in nonmetropolitan settings. For instance, individual-level or human capital explanations identify the limited human capital stock of disadvantaged groups as the key factor accounting for their low socioeconomic position. Accordingly, minorities tend to have certain demographic (for example, young average ages) and human capital (for example, lower educational levels) characteristics that limit their earnings position in the labor market. Similarly, women have narrower labor market experiences as a result of greater labor market instability, which reduces their earnings potential.

Structural explanations, such as regional restructuring, uneven development, and dual labor market perspectives, focus attention on labor market attributes. During the 1970s and 1980s, many industrial jobs moved from the traditional industrial centers in the Northeast and Midwest to the southern and western portions of the country. The Sun Belt's abundant, cheaper workforce and relative lack of unions influenced the Rust Belt to Sun Belt movement. However, in the competition for incoming jobs, rural communities of the region—home to the overwhelming majority of the nation's rural minorities—tended to attract jobs in lagging industries. Leaders of rural communities, faced with high levels of unemployment, used lucrative incentive packages in their attempts to entice businesses to relocate to their communities. Industrialists had the upper hand and were able to obtain the most favorable incentive packages. Rural sociologists questioned the long-term commitment of these employers to rural communities because the presence of large, cheap labor supplies in other parts of the country and abroad served to draw jobs away from these places. Thus, inequities exist between urban and rural settings in the quality of jobs available.

Minorities and women participate disproportionately in the least attractive segment of the labor market. Labor markets are divided into primary and secondary segments. The primary segment of the labor market represents the better jobs characterized by more favorable pay scales, opportunities for upward mobility, attractive health and benefit packages, and stable, secure employment. The secondary segment of the labor market, in contrast, represents low-paying, seasonal, insecure jobs with limited, if any, health and benefit packages. Whereas majority group workers are overrepresented in the primary labor market, minorities and women are overrepresented in the secondary labor market. These groups are particularly vulnerable because the least attractive jobs are the ones that make their way into rural communities. Within this context, minorities and women are more likely to find employment in the secondary labor market. In the competition for jobs, minorities and women often are situated at the end of the hiring queue, where they may be the last to be hired and, when economic strains occur, the first to be fired.

Rural settings have unique historical legacies reflecting strained interethnic relations, which complicate matters for disadvantaged groups. The roots of the subordinate and subjugated position of many of the nation's minority groups lie in rural areas. The plantation image associated with slavery, the loss of Mexican American lands to the Southwest Whites, and the forceful movement and genocide leveled against Native Americans all invoke rural impressions. People in rural areas, characterized by greater homogeneity, tend to be less tolerant of those who are different from themselves. Human ecologists note that rural labor markets are more likely to reward workers on the basis of ascribed statuses (such as gender, race, and ethnicity) than do industrialized labor markets in urban settings. Minorities and women are likely to experience greater forms of inequality under such conditions in rural areas than in urban areas.

Rural Disparities

Demographers commonly use the gini-coefficient to measure how evenly an area's income is distributed across income categories. The gini-coefficient ranges on a continuum from 0 (when the area's income is evenly distributed across income categories) to 1 (when the area's income falls into only one income category). Analysis based on the nation's 3,141 counties shows a greater prevalence of income inequality among nonmetropolitan counties than among metropolitan counties. Nonmetropolitan counties average a higher level of income inequality (average gini-coefficient of 0.3888) compared to their metropolitan counterparts (0.3786).

In a proportionate sense, nonmetropolitan counties are almost three times more likely than metropolitan counties to be among the 100 counties with the highest levels of income inequality, whereas metropolitan counties are more than twice as prone to be among the 100 counties with the lowest inequality levels. Counties with the highest levels of inequality are concentrated in areas that have been characterized as persistent poverty counties, most of which are predominantly nonmetropolitan and minority. Clusters of high-inequality counties are located along the Texas-Mexico border, Arkansas-Missouri Ozark region, Mississippi Delta, Appalachian region, and Arizona–New Mexico reservation areas. The greatest nonmetropolitan-metropolitan gap in level of inequality occurs in the South, where nonmetropolitan counties have an average gini-coefficient of 0.4115 compared to an average of 0.3881 among metropolitan counties. Of the 100 counties in the United States with the highest levels of inequality, 73 are nonmetropolitan counties in the South.

Low Status among Rural Minorities and Women

Three measures often are used to indicate socioeconomic status: a group's unemployment rate, median income level, and percentage of families with incomes below the poverty threshold. Census data indicate that nonmetropolitan minorities fare worse socioeconomically not only compared to nonmetropolitan Whites, but also compared to their metropolitan ethnic counterparts. The unemployment rates of nonmetropolitan minority groups were two to three times higher in 1990 (American Indians, Eskimos, and Aleut, 18.5 percent unemployed; African Americans, 13.6 percent; Latinos, 12.0 percent) than that of nonmetropolitan Whites.

Minority families located in nonmetropolitan areas exhibit the lowest income levels (ranging from a low median family income of $15,935 among African Americans to a high of $19,369 among Latinos) and highest rates of family poverty (ranging from a low poverty rate of 29.0 percent among Latinos to a high of 35.5 percent among African Americans). Moreover, the median family income of minorities is, on average, only about 55 percent (African American families) to 66 percent (Latino families) that of nonmetropolitan White families, whereas nonmetropolitan minority families are approximately three times as likely as nonmetropolitan White families to be in poverty.

Nonmetropolitan minorities also lag behind socioeconomically compared to their metropolitan peers, with the greatest differentiations involving American Indians, Eskimos, and Aleuts. Nonmetropolitan members of this group have unemployment and poverty rates that are about 1.6 times higher and a median family income that is only two-thirds that of their metropolitan counterparts.

Distinct gender differences are apparent, even though women have comparable unemployment rates as men. Women's unemployment rate (6.0 percent) in metropolitan settings is somewhat lower than that of men's (6.3 percent) and the rates for men and women in nonmetropolitan areas are the same (7.0 percent). In contrast, women fare significantly worse with respect to earnings and poverty. For instance, the median income of year-round, full-time women workers in metropolitan and nonmetropolitan areas is only about two-thirds that of their male counterparts. Similarly, families with female householders are significantly more likely to be in poverty than married-couple families, 6.5 times in the case of metropolitan areas and 4.6 times in the case of nonmetropolitan settings. However, nonmetropolitan women lag behind their metropolitan peers in each of the socioeconomic indicators: unemployment rate (7.0 percent for nonmetropolitan women versus 6.0 percent for metropolitan women), median income of year-round full-time workers ($15,307 and $20,660, respectively), and percentage of families with female householders in poverty (39.3 percent and 29.2 percent, respectively).

These rates and averages do not take into account the composition and regional differences between the various groups. Thus, these unemployment, income, and poverty gaps may simply reflect group differences in education, age, nativity, regional distribution, and other pertinent characteristics. Direct standardization is one way to adjust group rates and averages for such variations. Supplementary analysis using this method suggests that

ethnic, gender, and type of place (metropolitan/non-metropolitan) socioeconomic differentials, although less pronounced in some cases, persist, even after group variations in composition are adjusted for. This analysis uses unemployment, wage, and poverty data for the population 25 to 64 years of age who are high school graduates (with no college education) from the 1990 Public Use Microdata Samples.

The results indicate, for example, that even if all ethnic groups in metropolitan and nonmetropolitan areas had the same age-gender-nativity-regional profiles as metropolitan Whites, nonmetropolitan minorities would continue to fare worse socioeconomically compared to nonmetropolitan Whites and their metropolitan peers. In addition, if men and women in both types of areas were assumed to have the same age-ethnic-nativity-regional characteristics as metropolitan men, women, particularly those in nonmetropolitan areas, would continue to have lower median wages and higher poverty rates.

The results of these analyses do not provide direct measures of the amount of discrimination that minorities and women experience; they only identify the residual group differences in socioeconomic outcomes that cannot be explained by those group compositional and regional differences that were taken into account. These findings are consistent with those from other research pointing to race, ethnic, and gender discrimination in labor markets and institutions.

Labor Market Discrimination

Using similar residual approaches as those just discussed, extant research suggests that minority group members experience earnings discrimination in the marketplace, with the level of discrimination referred to as the "cost of being a minority worker." The findings of these studies indicate that African Americans, as a group, face the most discrimination. However, the labor market earnings literature neglects nonmetropolitan areas. All too often, studies assume that minority group status attainment and discrimination processes within nonmetropolitan and metropolitan settings are similar.

Whereas several studies control for nonmetropolitan and metropolitan residence, few examine the interaction of place of residence and various factors on ethnic and gender socioeconomic inequities and discrimination. This body of research has been based predominantly on African Americans. Research that focused on discrimination in a more direct fashion, such as audit studies, is based primarily in urban settings.

Institutional Discrimination

Evidence indicates that rural minorities are subjected to discrimination at the institutional level. A substantial amount of research has documented the underrepresentation of groups such as the poor, minorities, and women in the delivery of services from land-grant universities and extension-based programs. Users of these services have been disproportionately White farmers with larger operations. Although African Americans have had Black land-grant institutes (the 1890 land-grant schools) to address the plight of African American rural residents, other rural minority groups, such as Latinos, have lacked this institutional structure.

Rural-based policies to deal with the problems of rural minorities historically have failed to treat such groups fairly. For instance, the U.S. Commission on Civil Rights' report of 1982, *The Decline of Black Farming in America,* documented African Americans' high level of the need for Farmers Home Administration credit programs and the low level of participation of African Americans in these programs. The report criticized the U.S. Department of Agriculture and the Farmers Home Administration for their failure to "integrate civil rights goals into program objectives and to use enforcement mechanisms to ensure that black farmers are provided equal opportunities in farm credit programs" (U.S. Commission on Civil Rights 1982, iv). Farmworkers, especially migrant farmworkers, have been exempted historically from employment policies such as minimum-wage laws, workers' compensation, and collective bargaining. Although farmworkers have made some scattered gains in work-related legislation, they continue to lag behind other occupational groups in improving their working conditions.

Contemporary Policy Climate

A variety of broad policies have attempted to improve the social and economic conditions of minority groups and women. Policies related to the provision of equal opportunities and the protection of the civil rights of minorities and women have succeeded to varying degrees, especially in the case of women. President Lyndon Johnson's War on Poverty programs helped reduce poverty in the 1970s. However, efforts to reduce spending on social programs and limit equal opportunity mandates in the 1980s and 1990s jeopardized those gains.

The poor, minorities, welfare mothers, and immigrants today increasingly have been viewed as the source of many of the nation's economic ills. A variety of policy initiatives have been undertaken with these groups in mind. Examples include California's Proposition 187 and Civil Rights Initiative, the Republican Party's Contract with America, and the *Hopwood* v. *Texas* (1996) case ruling against the consideration of race and ethnicity in university admissions. California's Proposition 187 (1994) was to make illegal aliens ineligible for public social and health care services and school education at the elementary, secondary, and postsecondary levels. Under California's Civil Rights Initiative (1996), the state would be unable to discriminateagainst or grant preferential treatment to any individual or group on the basis of race, sex, color, ethnicity, or national origin in the operation of public employment, education, or contracting. The Contract with America was the Republican Party's 1994 promise to restore American's faith in government through a series of legislative acts and reforms, governmental downsizing, and tax reductions. Such policy initiatives, while not intended solely for rural areas, have the potential to worsen the social and economic standing of rural minorities.

—Rogelio Saenz, Cynthia M. Cready,
and Clyde S. Greenlees

See also
Land Reform; Policy, Socioeconomic.
References
Allen-Smith, Joyce E. "Special Issue: Blacks in Rural America." *Review of Black Political Economy* 22, no. 4 (1994): 7–202.
Cotton, Barbara. "The 1890 Land-Grant Colleges: A Centennial View." *Agricultural History* 65, no. 2 (1991): 1–172.
Falk, William W., and Thomas A. Lyson. *High Tech, Low Tech, No Tech: Recent Occupational and Industrial Changes in the South.* Albany: State University of New York Press, 1988.
Jensen, Leif, and Marta Tienda. "Nonmetropolitan Minority Families in the United States: Trends in Racial and Ethnic Economic Stratification, 1959–1986." *Rural Sociology* 54, no. 4 (Winter 1989): 509–532.
Lyson, Thomas A. *Two Sides of the Sunbelt: The Growing Divergence between the Rural and Urban South.* New York: Praeger, 1989.
Lyson, Thomas A., and William W. Falk, eds. *Forgotten Places: Uneven Development in Rural America.* Lawrence: University Press of Kansas, 1993.
Rural Sociological Society. Task Force on Persistent Rural Poverty. *Persistent Poverty in Rural America.* Boulder, CO: Westview Press, 1993.
Tickamyer, Ann R., and Cynthia M. Duncan. "Poverty and Opportunity Structure in Rural America." *Annual Review of Sociology* 16 (1990): 67–86.
Tolbert, Charles M., and Thomas A. Lyson. "Earnings Inequality in the Nonmetropolitan United States: 1967–1990." *Rural Sociology* 57, no. 4 (Winter 1992): 494–511.
U.S. Commission on Civil Rights. *The Decline of Black Farming in America: A Report of the United States Commission on Civil Rights.* Washington, DC: U.S. Commission on Civil Rights, 1982.
Warner, Paul D., and James A. Christenson. *The Cooperative Extension Service: A National Assessment.* Boulder, CO: Westview Press, 1984.

Infrastructure

The basic facilities and services of a community or society. Infrastructure includes the transportation and communication systems, power plants, waterworks, waste disposal, police and fire protection systems, schools, prisons, and post offices. Some writings extend this definition of infrastructure to include public housing, industrial parks, and information technology. The infrastructure of rural America serves rural people by facilitating access to opportunity and choice, whether markets for local businesses or jobs, education, and personal consumption for local households. Rural infrastructure links the rural community to the metropolitan core area of its region. Its critically important role demands a host of supporting institutions—economic, social, and governmental—among which state and local governments play an increasingly important role. The physical infrastructure of an area is a necessary, but not a sufficient, condition for an area's economic growth and viability. This entry describes the importance of the physical and economic infrastructure in rural areas and explains the role of governmental spending and investment in maintaining this infrastructure.

Physical and Economic

Much of the building of the nation's physical infrastructure happened piecemeal. Only the influence of national defense immediately after World War II brought together the necessary support for a massive unified effort in transportation infrastructure investment: the building of the interstate highway system. This was a long-term program that affected the economic well-being of population and industry in both rural and urban areas. Establishment of the interstate highway system was followed by a second unifying influence in transportation infrastructure: the work of the Federal Aeronautics Administration in planning for and implementing a system of air transportation nodes, centered on metropolitan core areas remarkably similar in their economic structures. The two unifying federal accomplishments in transportation systems planning solidified the central role of the two dozen or so high-order distribution and producer services centers of the U.S. economy. These centers now serve as the core areas of their respective economic regions.

The commuting area, the daily journey to work of an urban-centered workforce, is referred to as the labor market area (LMA). It is the basic building block in a "bottom-up" approach to regional economic organization. Figure 1 summarizes the key concepts introduced for the study of regional infrastructure investment within this

framework. The economic activities that occur within a region account for a corresponding differentiation of their role in regional economic organization. Concentration of high-order producer services and infrastructure (e.g., communications, transportation, energy systems, and a region's major educational and research institutions and technology-intensive manufacturing) characterize the economy of the metropolitan core area, usually the largest and most densely populated labor market area in its economic region. Beyond the core area lie other LMAs. These include most, if not all, economic regions; other highly urbanized metropolitan LMAs; nonmetropolitan LMAs serving as multicounty shopping and service centers; and the most sparsely populated LMAs of small towns and open-country settlement. Rural and nonmetropolitan LMAs are the most numerous in each economic region, but not in total population and economic activity. They include the overspill areas bordering the core area, as well as the most distant, natural resource–based peripheral areas.

The economic base of an area is formed by the export-producing activities of the resident populations. These include the goods and services produced by local businesses, governments, and households and the activities that cater to visitors purchasing locally—available goods and services that bring new dollars into the community. The components of an area's economic base vary from one part of the area to another and from one time period to the next. Interarea trade is the lifeblood of each local economy.

The differentiation of economic activity by location and the corresponding differences in the economic base of labor market areas correlate with the differentiation by location of regional infrastructure. Both the center and periphery have the basic infrastructure for commodity and people transportation and energy production. The center, however, has the high-order infrastructure of

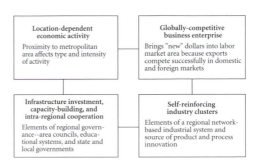

Figure 1. Regional Economic Organization for State and Local Infrastructure Investment

The Cheyenne River diversion ditch in West Fargo, North Dakota, channeled flood waters around the city during the 1997 Red River Valley flood.

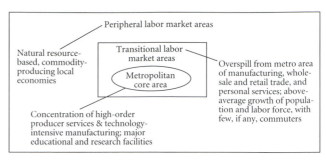

Figure 2. Elements of a Working Model for Targeting State and Local Infrastructure Investment

communications, transportation, education, health care, and producer services. The overspill of manufacturing and producer services industries into the surrounding countryside attracts a growing labor force that, in turn, supports a gradually increasing number and variety of consumer-oriented businesses, especially retail trade and personal services. The peripheral labor market areas adapt to their more remote locations by exploiting the gifts of nature, which become the principal means, when coupled with price-competitive production technologies, of acquiring income from outside sources for the purchase of their many imported goods and services.

Having well-targeted infrastructure investment calls for a special understanding of the linkage between a region's economic base and its economic performance. The value of product disbursements, for example, vary by industry and location from one part of a region to another. They are high value added in the metropolitan core area, low in the rural periphery. They correlate closely with levels of industry investment per worker. Where expected profits are high, with little risk of failure, investment and production follow, along with jobs that generate above-average earnings. The location of the production activity in an economic region, whether in the core area, the periphery, or somewhere in between, has much to do with the earnings of its labor and capital resources and the region's long-term viability.

Figure 2 illustrates the linkages among the four fundamental elements of state and local infrastructure investment planning. Location-dependent economic activity refers to its proximity to a metropolitan core area and the spatial-economic organization of the production of goods and services in a region. Its type and intensity are the first order of determinants of the economic viability of any regional industrial system. New research findings confirm earlier insights that the most strategic relationships among firms in network systems serving global markets often are local because of the importance of timeliness and face-to-face communication for rapid product development. State and local infrastructure investment thus provides the immediate environment for successful, globally competitive, export-producing enterprise to support both the rural community and activities in the metropolitan core area that seek access to the low-cost suppliers in the rural areas.

Still missing is readily accessible information on the critical elements of the local economic base and their problems and prospects for future growth and development. Easy access to such regional information helps identify the community economic base, target community services, build core competencies, modify legacy systems, and make policy choices, all requirements for successful local and state governance underlying infrastructure investments that effectively serve rural areas and their residents. Thus, on the eve of the twenty-first century, as rural areas become even more differentiated in population and economic base than ever before, the infrastructure requirements that of the local economy also differ, depending on location within the larger regional economy and linkages with the metropolitan core area and its markets and infrastructure.

Government Spending and Investment

Total government spending includes intergovernmental transfers and direct outlays for operations and physical capital. Capital spending in the 1986–1987 fiscal year (FY)

Table 1
Total Capital Outlays for Specified Activities, by Type of Government, FY 1986–1987 to FY 1990–1991 (in $ billion)

	Total		Federal		State		Local	
	1986–87	1990–91	1986–87	1990–91	1986–87	1990–91	1986–87	1990–91
Selected federal programs	83.1	79.2	83.1	79.2	0.0	0.0	0.0	0.0
Education services	18.2	28.1	0.0	0.1	6.0	6.9	12.2	21.0
Social services and income maintenance	6.4	7.8	2.9	3.0	1.6	2.1	1.9	2.7
Transportation	33.0	43.0	1.0	1.4	21.5	27.4	10.5	14.2
Public safety	5.0	7.4	0.4	0.5	1.9	3.2	2.7	3.8
Environment and housing	24.7	31.5	7.9	9.4	2.0	3.0	14.7	19.2
Government administration	3.5	5.2	0.4	0.7	1.0	1.3	2.2	3.2
General expenditures not elsewhere classified	5.8	7.9	1.1	1.3	1.2	1.5	3.5	5.2
Other expenditure	15.4	17.0	0.0	0.0	2.1	2.5	13.3	14.5
Total	195.2	227.2	96.9	95.6	37.3	47.9	61.1	83.7

Sources: U.S. Bureau of the Census, *Government Finances in 1986–87*, Series GF-87/5 (Washington, DC: U.S. Government Printing Office, 1988); and U.S. Bureau of the Census, *Government Finances in 1990–91*, Series GF-91/5 (Washington, DC: U.S. Government Printing Office, 1993).

Table 2
Total Capital Outlays for Specified Activities, by Type of Government, 1986–1987 to 1990–1991 (percentages)

	Total		Federal		State		Local	
	1986–87	1990–91	1986–87	1990–91	1986–87	1990–91	1986–87	1990–91
Selected federal programs	23.1	18.7	23.1	18.7	0.0	0.0	0.0	0.0
Education services	7.5	8.4	0.0	0.5	9.7	8.5	7.3	9.0
Social services and income maintenance	3.2	2.6	4.6	3.5	1.8	1.5	3.9	3.9
Transportation	50.0	51.2	16.7	15.6	65.2	68.5	38.9	40.6
Public safety	8.1	8.4	8.0	6.3	11.2	12.3	6.9	7.2
Environment and housing	16.7	22.8	8.4	14.9	18.2	20.0	34.2	32.0
Government administration	8.0	8.1	4.4	4.4	7.7	6.8	10.0	10.7
General expenditures not elsewhere classified	9.5	6.2	4.6	1.6	7.1	7.1	17.5	19.3
Other (utility; liquor store)	22.3	21.0	0.0	0.0	26.3	25.0	22.2	20.1
Total	15.6	13.9	16.9	13.6	14.8	13.5	14.2	14.5

Sources: U.S. Bureau of the Census, *Government Finances in 1986–87*, Series GF-87/5 (Washington, DC: U.S. Government Printing Office, 1988); and U.S. Bureau of the Census, *Government Finances in 1990–91*, Series GF-91/5 (Washington, DC: U.S. Government Printing Office, 1993).

increased from $195 billion to $227 billion, but its share of all government spending, which increased from $1.8 trillion to $2.4 trillion, dropped from 11 percent to 10 percent. Federal spending dropped from 63 percent to 62 percent of the total. Its capital spending dropped even more, from 50 percent to 42 percent of the total capital spending. Thus, state and local governments were left with an increased share of governmental capital spending.

Table 1 focuses only on the capital outlays for the physical infrastructure of rural and urban America and their growth and change over the four-year period from FY (fiscal year) 1986–1987 to FY 1990–1991. Sharp reductions in capital outlays for national defense and the postal service accounted for the absolute decline in federal government capital outlays during this period. State and local government capital outlays increased from $98.4 billion to $131.6 billion, a 34 percent increase. Federal government capital spending for the same items

increased from $112.1 billion to $146 billion, a 30 percent increase, slightly less than the overall increase in direct spending. However, intergovernmental outlays of the federal government increased by 44 percent, from $111.4 billion to $160.1 billion, during the same period. Thus, the present-day changes in the financing of government functions were already under way in the 1980s.

Table 2 focuses on the shares of total direct spending among governmental activities accounted for by capital outlays at each governmental level in the two periods. Whereas total capital outlays as a percent of all spending declined for both federal and state governments, it increased for local governments. However, share increases, representing budgetary reallocations, occurred for selected activities at all government levels. At the federal level, the environment and housing share increased from 8.4 percent to 14.9 percent. It increased for state government but declined for local government. At the state level, the transportation share increased from 65.2 percent to 68.5 percent. It increased for local government but declined for the federal government.

The changing sources of funding fail to show the corresponding changes in the criteria for identifying and selecting high-priority infrastructure investment projects. The restructuring of the nation's economy and the accompanying changes in industry location and population distribution, especially in rural regions, leave many roads, bridges, and other facilities largely unused, but nonetheless maintained in top-notch condition. State and local infrastructure planning efforts remain piecemeal and uncoordinated. There still is no clear consensus about the implications of these changes on the varying local demands for the many different kinds of infrastructure investments that most clearly affect the well-being of rural residents and their local economic base. An understanding of the role of infrastructure in rural America is incomplete and therefore without some corresponding appreciation of the economic geography of rural America. This can serve as a guide to sort the infrastructure requirements of different rural areas, located varying distances from metropolitan areas, and performing varying roles in a region's economy.

Many, but not all, rural areas now face continuing disinvestment in rural infrastructure as farm numbers fall. In some areas, however, falling farm numbers foreshadow a new wave of local infrastructure investments. These investments now link local manufacturing establishments with product markets and input supply sources in the metropolitan core area. They also connect with the individual households in the local labor market area. They include producer services, such as banking, finance, management, and accounting, and new forms of transportation and communication that further facilitate the linkage functions of local infrastructure. The new technologies, global in scope, yet local in consequences, radically change the mix of infrastructure investments now sought for rural areas.

Finally, the new infrastructure serves to bring metropolitan area residents to rural areas with important recreation amenities and attractions as seasonal visitors. Some build or buy second homes or even establish permanent residency. They contribute to an expanding local business economy; they may engage in a common effort with other metropolitan area residents to conserve the nearby agricultural areas vulnerable to soil and wind erosion; they may confront local residents with new land-extensive efforts to preserve natural habitats for existing wildlife populations. Meanwhile, the overspill of population and industry from the metropolitan core area to its urbanized periphery continues, adding to the mounting costs of the new infrastructure demanded by the increasingly powerful suburban constituencies. Thus, the question of infrastructure investment in rural areas and its adequacy is complicated by the diverse and contrasting patterns of regional population growth and change.

—Wilbur R. Maki

See also

Decentralization; Development, Community and Economic; Electrification; Government; Municipal Solid Waste Management; River Engineering; Technology; Telecommunications.

References

Advisory Commission on Intergovernmental Relations. *Financing Physical Infrastructure.* Report A-97. Washington, DC: U.S. Government Printing Office, 1984.

Congressional Budget Office. *Public Works Infrastructure: Policy Considerations for the 1980s.* Washington, DC: U.S. Government Printing Office, 1983.

———. *Federal Policies for Infrastructure Management.* Washington, DC: U.S. Government Printing Office, 1986.

Hussain, A., W. Maki, D. Olson, and D. Braslau. "The Changing Structure of the Transportation Sector: An Input-Output Analysis." Staff Paper Series P93-22. St. Paul: University of Minnesota, Department of Agricultural and Applied Economics, 1993.

U.S. Congress. Senate. Joint Economic Committee. *Deteriorating Infrastructure in Urban and Rural Areas: Hearings before the Subcommittee on Economic Growth and Stabilization of the Joint Economic Committee Congress of the United States.* 96th Cong., 1st sess., 18 June and 30 August 1979.

———. Committee on Environment and Public Works. *Rural Transportation Issues: Hearings before the Subcommittee on Water Resources, Transportation, and Infrastructure of the Committee on Environment and Public Works.* 101st Cong., 2d sess., 20 August 1990 (Boise, Idaho).

Injuries

Physical damage to the human body resulting from exposure to agents or conditions that exceed human tolerance. Injuries are a major health problem and touch residents of rural America just as they do urban residents. Although rural America has its idyllic qualities, immunity from injuries is not one of them. This entry focuses on unintentional injury in rural America, as opposed to intentional injury, such as homicide or suicide. Agricultural injuries are very common and, being unique to rural America, are discussed in depth. Outdoor recreational injuries, motor vehicle injuries, injury prevention programs (also known as intervention), obstacles to intervention, and organizations and agencies involved in intervention activities are discussed as well.

Agricultural

Agriculture is one of rural America's chief industries. According to the National Safety Council, agriculture is the most dangerous industry in the United States based on work death rate (work-related deaths per 100,000 workers). Agricultural deaths totaled 1,100 in 1993, for a work death rate of 35. There were an estimated 130,000 injuries resulting in death, permanent disability, or temporary disability beyond the day of the accident. By comparison, mining and construction, which along with agriculture historically have had the highest work death rates, had fatalities of 200 and 1,300 and rates of 33 and 22, respectively, in 1993. The total work fatalities for all U.S. industries combined was 9,100, and the rate was 8.

Agriculture as an industry includes production agriculture (consisting primarily of farms, ranches, and orchards—farming for short) and various agricultural services. It also includes forestry and fishing, but excludes logging operations and agribusinesses such as commercial grain elevators and chemical dealers. Farming accounts for the vast majority of agricultural fatalities and nonfatal injuries. Several unique characteristics and situations result in high death rates.

Farms are both homes and work sites. Besides living on the farm, many farm family members of all ages actively work there. As a result, family members, hired farmworkers, and visitors are exposed to farm hazards. Men, women, and children are all victims of farm injuries. It is estimated that between 175 and 300 children die each year as a result of farmwork or work site–related accidents. Victims range in age from less than 1 year old to people in their 90s. When the term *farmer* is used to refer to a victim, it may mean any farm family member, farmworker, or visitor.

Tractors and other farm machines are involved in the majority of fatal farm injuries. Tractor rollover (when the tractor turns over on top of the operator) is the single most common fatal farm injury event in the nation. Tractor rollovers kill nearly 200 people every year. Tractor rollovers can occur for a variety of reasons: operation on steep slopes, improper hitching, hidden holes or obstacles, driving too near a ditch or stream bank, operation at improper speeds and resulting loss of control, collisions with motor vehicles, or other such incidents. Another common fatal event is tractor runover, when a person is run over by the wheel of a tractor. This results from falling off the tractor, being an unseen bystander, or starting the tractor from the ground. Sometimes a victim is run over by the trailing implement instead of the tractor itself.

Encounters with other machinery account for numerous fatalities and serious injuries. Farm machines are designed to grab, compress, crush, chop, or process materials. Unintended contact with moving machine components can result in a person's hand, arm, leg, or entire body being pulled in or entangled in the machine, causing serious injuries such as mutilations, impalements, amputations, or death. Other machine-related injuries result from a person being crushed beneath falling machinery or being struck by flying objects from machines.

A variety of structures may be found on farms, and these are sometimes involved in injuries. Falls from tall structures such as silos or grain bins, from the roofs or second floors of buildings, or from ladders used for maintenance and construction result in many injuries. Some structures are confined spaces—those with limited access not designed for continuous human occupation. On farms these include liquid manure storage structures, grain and feed bins, and silos. Atmospheric hazards in confined spaces include toxic gases or lack of oxygen. Manure produces toxic gases, especially when the stored manure is agitated prior to pumping. Silo gas may be produced for about three weeks after filling as a result of the fermentation process. Some silos are designed to be oxygen limiting and thus do not have enough oxygen to support life. The hazard in grain or feed bins is entrapment and potential engulfment and suffocation by free-flowing contents. Exposure to any of these hazards can result in serious injury or death.

On livestock farms, contact with animals frequently results in injury. Bulls, boars, stallions, and other male animals can be very aggressive toward humans, especially when with female animals, and cause serious or fatal injury. Female animals with newly born offspring will be very protective and can cause serious injury. Most farm animals are docile, but even during normal handling, it is common for animals to kick, unintentionally step on feet or toes, or pin a person against a wall or stall.

Farmers undertake a variety of diverse tasks, including the construction and repair of structures and machinery, earth moving, hauling, plumbing and wiring, chemical application, and wood cutting. Contact with the tools and machines, such as chain saws, hand and power tools, and materials, can result in injury. Farmers may be exposed to, and injured by, chemicals as a result of improper use or mechanical failure of application equipment. They face injury from such diverse hazards as falling trees, electrical wiring, and bodies of water. Since they use motor vehicles for farm-related work, such as hauling supplies or traveling to meet with bankers and accountants, they face injury from motor vehicle crashes. Farmers suffer various musculoskeletal injuries and cumulative trauma disorders from such jobs as lifting heavy objects and stooping to milk cows.

Recreational

Recreational injuries are a problem in rural America. Many outdoor recreational activities take place in rural areas. All-terrain vehicles (ATVs) are commonly used, both for work and recreation, but thousands of people have been killed or injured from rollovers or collisions. From 1982 to 1989, there were 1,346 ATV-related fatalities; in 1988 alone, there were an estimated 62,800 ATV-related injuries treated in hospital emergency departments. Snowmobiles are an off-road vehicle common in northern climates, and accidents involving snowmobiles include collisions with fixed objects such as trees or fences, with cars, or with each other. Hunting is an activity conducted in rural areas, and gunshot wounds and falls from tree stands are the common ways in which hunters are injured or killed. Water sports such as swimming and boating are common rural activities that may result in injury or death from drowning or collisions.

Motor Vehicle

Motor vehicle injuries are common in rural America. Although just 32 percent of all motor vehicle crashes (causing injury or property damage) occur in rural areas, 65 percent of all motor vehicle fatalities occur in rural areas. There were 27,400 motor vehicle fatalities in rural areas in 1993. Rural areas include state and interstate highways as well as county and local roads, and speeds are higher on such roads than in urban streets. Rural areas account for 69 percent of fatal collisions with other vehicles, 67 percent of fatal collisions with fixed objects, and 45 percent of all pedestrian fatalities.

Prevention Programs and Obstacles to Intervention

Injuries are preventable. Three basic strategies are used to prevent injuries in rural America as well as in the rest of the country: (1) hazard control engineering, (2) safety education to persuade voluntary behavior change, and (3) regulation enforcement to require behavior change. First, improved design of vehicles, equipment, and transportation systems can eliminate hazards that make injury prevention less dependent on individuals' behaviors. For example, some country highways have many tight curves. Crash prevention on these highways is dependent on the vehicle operators' ability to decrease their speeds and properly negotiate the curves. However, elimination of the curves reduces the potential hazard of drivers losing control and driving off of the road. Airbags and seat belts reduce the potential injury if a crash does occur. Second, safety education can help people to operate equipment or perform tasks more safely. For example, some hazards cannot be eliminated, are difficult to eliminate, or are cost prohibitive to eliminate. Pulling into an opposite lane to pass slow-moving vehicles on country highways presents a safety hazard. Converting these highways into four-lane roads would be cost prohibitive. Instead, people must be trained to pass other vehicles safely. Third, appropriate safety regulations can be developed. Existing regulations already require people to participate in driver's training prior to licensure, store gasoline in proper containers, and use safety devises such as vehicle lights.

Several factors make injury prevention more difficult in rural areas. First, the geographic dispersion of rural residents makes it difficult to hold meetings, carry out inspections, or conduct other activities that can lead to injury reduction. Second, regulation enforcement is not always feasible in rural areas. It is difficult for a government agency to conduct hazard inspections on the nation's 2 million farms. Third, most states have limited numbers of government employees charged with the responsibility for farm safety, and many states have no such employees. Fourth, farming is a very independent type of business. Farmers' traditional independence makes it difficult to convince them to make accident-reducing changes. Many farmers perceive that injuries are an expected part of farming.

Organizations and Agencies Involved in Intervention

Many organizations and agencies assist communities to promote injury prevention in rural areas. Voluntary organizations prominent in farm injury prevention include the National Institute for Farm Safety, the American Society of Agricultural Engineers, the National Safety Council, and Farm Safety 4 Just Kids. Public agencies involved in rural injury prevention include the U.S. Department of Agriculture Cooperative State Research, Education, and Extension Service, with offices in almost every county in the nation, and the National Institute of Occupational Safety and Health, part of the U.S. Centers for Disease Control and Injury Prevention. These organizations, or their members, work with farmers and other rural residents and with local physicians, nurses, teachers, public health personnel, and farm organizations to prevent or reduce the number of injuries on farms and in rural areas.

Other organizations active in rural injury prevention include the National Farm Medicine Center in Wisconsin, the New York Center for Agricultural Medicine and Health, the Institute for Agricultural Medicine at the University of Iowa, and the Breaking New Ground Resource Center at Purdue University. State departments of natural resources actively have promoted injury prevention for recreational activities such as hunting, boating, and snowmobiling. State and federal departments of transportation are active in motor vehicle crash prevention.

—Mark A. Purschwitz

See also

Food Safety; Health and Disease Epidemiology; Health Care; Workers' Compensation.

References

Baker, Susan, Brian O'Neill, Marvin Ginsburg, and Guohua Li. *The Injury Fact Book.* 2d ed. New York: Oxford University Press, 1992.

Murphy, Dennis. *Safety and Health for Production Agriculture.* St. Joseph, MI: American Society of Agricultural Engineers, 1992.

National Academy of Sciences. *Injury in America.* Washington, DC: National Academy Press, 1985.

National 4-H Council. *4-H ATV Rider Handbook.* Chevy Chase, MD: National 4-H Council, 1990.

National Safety Council. *Accident Facts, 1994 Edition.* Itasca, IL: National Safety Council, 1994.

Purschwitz, Mark, and William. Field. "Scope and Magnitude of Injuries in the Agricultural Workplace." *American Journal of Industrial Medicine* 18 (1990): 179–192.

Insurance

A way to manage financial risk through transfer of the risk to an insurance company in exchange for payment of a premium. This entry discusses risk management as the basis of insurance programs. Various types of insurance are described, including health, disability, life, homeowners, auto, liability, credit, crop, and flood or earthquake.

Risk Management

Risk management is a foundation of successful financial management. A carefully planned risk management strategy can save a family money and mental anguish.

There are five steps in handling risk, whether it is the risk of getting cancer or the risk of hail damaging a crop. The first step rural residents typically take is to identify the risks to which they are exposed. They consider health (for example, illness, disability, or death), property they own (for example, automobiles and barns), and activities they do (for example, farming and travel). They consider the perils to which they or others might be exposed (for example, personal liability, water hazards, or flooding). The second step is to evaluate potential losses and consider the financial impact of each risk identified in the first step. They think about the number of times they might be exposed to the risk in a year and the potential dollar cost of that loss. Some losses are easier to guess than others. It is not crucial that estimates be exact from a financial standpoint, but they need to determine the potential magnitude of the various losses. Step three is to select risk management strategies. It is important to understand the ways to manage risk and to consciously decide which to use. The four strategies are risk avoidance, risk reduction, risk acceptance, and transfer of risk.

Sometimes risk simply can be avoided. For example, a person avoids the risk of horse riding injuries by not riding horses. Although avoidance is a valuable strategy and can be used in some cases, it is not always realistic. Risk can be reduced in some cases when the likelihood that it will occur, or the size of the loss if it does, is decreased. For example, the potential for injury is reduced when farm equipment safety precautions are followed. Likewise, rural residents can take lessons before skiing and install smoke detectors. Risk acceptance, in which a person pays for losses that occur, can be done when the loss is small or inexpensive or when everyone is exposed to the risk and the cost is predictable. This strategy should be used only when a person can truly afford the potential risk and should be a conscious decision rather than something that happens because there was no risk management plan. Finally, rural residents may purchase insurance and transfer the risk of loss to the insurance company. In exchange for a premium, which is based on the potential for loss, the potential cost, and the company's cost to offer the insurance, the company takes the financial risk. Often, a combination of strategies offers the best protection. For example, people may pay a deductible on health insurance, thus accepting part of the potential loss while transferring the catastrophic loss. People also refrain from smoking and exercise regularly, resulting in less chance of illness. They plan, avoiding a risk management strategy of risk acceptance by default.

This family has managed to save some of their furniture from the fire that may claim their house. Rural dwellers face particular danger from fire because their homes may be at a considerable distance from a fire station.

The fourth step is to implement the plan. After making a plan, rural residents may put it into action. They comparison shop, making sure to compare the same coverage with each provider and determine that the insurance companies are economically viable and likely to be in business for a long time. They take a list of the specific coverage needed. References such as *Best's Insurance Report* or *Consumer Reports* may be used to develop a list of features for coverage. For example, in October 1993 *Consumer Reports* published an article on homeowner's insurance that contained a worksheet for determining the amount of coverage needed. Local cooperative extension offices, state bureaus of insurance, and local libraries may offer information. Rural residents must select an insurance professional available in the community to help with coverage and necessary changes over time. They look for a person with whom they are comfortable asking questions and who answers clearly. And they should establish a savings account to provide the necessary funds for the risks they assume, including deductibles and copayments. Although it is unreasonable for most people to

have enough savings to cover all the possible losses, they must be careful to include sufficient funds in case they experience more than one loss in a short period.

The fifth step is to evaluate the plan. After putting a risk management plan into effect, rural residents should evaluate it occasionally or when life changes occur, such as marriage, divorce, birth or death, moves, major purchases, or job changes. Even if no changes occur, insurance plans should be evaluated at least every five years. Many people buy insurance and forget about it, resulting in too much or too little coverage. Others comparison shop for homeowner's and automobile coverage every year. There are rarely financial advantages in staying with the same company for many years.

Types

Many types of insurance are available, including insurance to protect one's health, home, automobile, crops, loans, and even a pet.

Health. One of the most important types of coverage for most rural families is health insurance. It is expensive because health care costs continue to climb. Since group coverage is much cheaper, many families obtain coverage through their employers. Self-employed families, such as farmers, often buy coverage as part of a group of similarly self-employed families. It is important to select coverage that will pay for the large, catastrophic losses. The maximum limits for major medical coverage should be checked, whether they are yearly or lifetime. Most people need a minimum of $1 million lifetime coverage. Those who cannot afford as much coverage as they wish select coverage for major medical expense. They reduce the premium by accepting a higher deductible, purchasing co-insurance (agreeing to pay a percentage of the cost while the company pays a percentage), or paying for routine, expected care, such as an annual physical. Policies that cover only specific illnesses (such as cancer) or injuries should be avoided. There is no way to know what will happen in the future, so the best coverage is that which pays in a variety of situations.

Indemnity income policies, or those that pay certain dollar amounts for each day a person is in the hospital, are tremendously expensive for the coverage provided. An emergency fund would be a better source of funds. Policyholders should understand the coverage and keep up with changes in policies. Today many citizens have managed care plans that restrict physicians, hospitals, laboratories, and other care providers. Policyholders should know what steps are required to get approval to access care so the insurance will pay and to avoid waiting periods for preexisting conditions when coverage is switched. They must recognize that insurance companies may each define preexisting conditions (and other terms) differently and that they may change the definition over time.

Disability. People of working age are more likely to become disabled than to die, and a disabled person can be a greater financial burden to the family. Insurance policies typically cover 50 to 70 percent of predisability pay. The best protection is provided in policies that pay if a person cannot perform his or her regular job. Many policies reduce payments by any sum received from social security. Policies vary in the time they will pay; the best coverage lasts until eligibility for retirement benefits. One should reduce the cost of coverage by waiting as long as possible before receiving benefits. Most policies begin paying 30, 60, or 90 days after disability.

Life. When considering life insurance, one should anticipate the financial loss caused by the person's death rather than the emotional loss—that is, what it would cost to pay someone else to do the things that the family

member did. Thus, the income provider needs coverage, as does the service provider (the homemaker). The amount of coverage needed varies with the obligations. Large debts, potential of taxes due, needs for income immediately after death, care of dependents, coverage of final medical and funeral expenses, and other bills should be considered. As debts are repaid, children become independent, and savings increase, the need for life insurance decreases. Life insurance is available in many forms, some of which combine risk management with investment. Insurance shoppers must compare the costs, risks, and rewards of each policy.

Homeowner's. All rural residents need some form of homeowner's or renter's insurance. Renters must recognize that the landlord's insurance covers only the structure, not their belongings in it. Homeowner's insurance also provides liability coverage. This insurance is available in several different forms, which often are referred to with letters and numbers (for example, HO-1 Basic). An "all risk" policy provides the most coverage. Replacement value coverage is more expensive but assures enough money to buy a new item. Depreciation value insurance will pay only what the used item was worth when lost. Owners need to keep coverage current with community building costs. Home insurance costs vary considerably across the country and are influenced by such factors as how far the property is located from the fire department.

It may be necessary to purchase special riders or floaters for some property. Barns and other outbuildings may require additions to the basic policy. Policies typically limit coverage for items such as jewelry, guns, antiques, silver, artwork, collectibles, furs, photographic equipment, and computers. Farm owners may receive special protection for damage done to or by animals they own through their homeowner's policies. When cattle get in the highway and a motorist strikes them, the owner may face not only the loss of the animals, but also the expense of the damaged car or injured person.

Auto. Most states require automobile insurance through one of two systems: no fault and tort. In no-fault states, each driver is responsible for his or her damages and injuries. There is no determination of fault in most cases. However, in tort states the party "at fault" is responsible for damages and injuries. Premium costs are influenced by a wide range of factors, including the coverage provided; the value and type of vehicle; the driver's gender, age, marital status, and driving record; and the use of the vehicle. Insurance costs must be checked when a person is shopping for an automobile. According to Tobias

(1993), one should choose the highest deductible that is affordable and only the coverage needed. Comprehensive and collision coverage may not make sense for a vehicle that is not worth much.

Liability. Many citizens find a need for more liability coverage than they can obtain through their homeowner's and automobile insurance. Umbrella liability coverage may be purchased to obtain that coverage.

Credit. Some creditors offer credit life or credit disability insurance. This insurance is available to ensure that debts are repaid if the policyholder dies or is disabled. The easily accessible coverage offered by lenders often is very expensive for the protection it provides. Many consumers raise their automobile costs unnecessarily by including this coverage in their loans and rolling one loan into another when they purchase another vehicle before completing payments on the first vehicle.

Crop. Farmers who participate in government programs usually are required to purchase crop insurance. Some is available through the government, and other insurance is available through private insurance companies. Close attention must be paid to the changing requirements for this form of insurance.

Flood or Earthquake. Those who live in an area prone to floods may be eligible to purchase government-backed flood insurance. Most private insurance policies do not cover this peril. In areas susceptible to earthquakes, homeowners may purchase insurance from private companies as an addition to basic coverage.

—*Irene E. Leech*

See also
Agricultural Law; Health Care; Housing; Workers' Compensation.
References
Bamford, Janet, Jeff Blyskal, E. Card, and A. Jacobson. *The Consumer Reports Money Book*. New York: Consumer Reports Books, 1992.
Fleisher, Beverly. *Agricultural Risk Management*. Boulder, CO: Lynne Rienner, 1990.
Gardner, Robert J., Robert B. Caplan, Barbara J. Raasch, and Charles L. Ratner. *Ernst and Young's Personal Financial Planning Guide: Take Control of Your Future and Unlock the Door to Financial Security*. New York: John Wiley and Sons, 1995.
Garman, E. Thomas, and Raymond E. Forgue. *Personal Finance*. 4th ed. Boston: Houghton Mifflin, 1994.
Goldman, Jordan E., and Sonny Bloch. *Everyone's Money Book*. Chicago: Dearborn Financial, 1994.
Golonka, Nancy. *How to Protect What's Yours*. Washington, DC: Acropolis Books and the Insurance Information Institute, 1983.
"Homeowners Insurance." *Consumer Reports* 58, no. 10 (October 1993): 627–635.
Rejda, George E. *Principles of Risk Management and Insurance*. Glenview, IL: Scott, Foresman, 1982.
Tobias, Andrew. *Auto Insurance Alert*. New York: Simon and Schuster, 1993.
Williams, C. Arthur, Jr. *Principles of Risk Management and Insurance*. Malvern, PA: American Institute for Property and Liability Underwriters, 1981.

Intergenerational Land Transfer

The passing of ownership and control of land from one generation to the next, typically through family relationships. This entry emphasizes the strong values held by agricultural families regarding intergenerational family continuity, examines typical stages in the transfer process, and recognizes transfer as a major developmental life stressor. Successful family coping techniques are examined, followed by a summary of estate planning strategies.

The Values of Inheritance

The transfer of a family farming operation from one generation to the next is a complicated, long-term process that involves successful negotiation of a wide array of personal, family, farm management, and financial factors. The steps of such a transfer occur over a period of many years in stages that must accommodate the needs and interests of both a younger, entering generation and an older, retiring generation.

Family farming is vitally linked with the intergenerational transfer of land. The U.S. Department of Agriculture estimated that there were 2,090,700 farms in the United States in 1993 (Kabacher and Oliveira 1995). Farmers owned and rented 919 million acres of land, averaging 440 acres per farm. The manner in which those farms are operated and organized varies widely. They may be organized as individual operations, partnerships, corporations, or cooperatives, with the vast majority (91 percent) operated by individuals. However, individually owned farms have the smallest acreage and gross sales. In landownership, the majority of farmers (55 percent) owned all the land they operated. These full-ownership farms had the smallest number of acres and the smallest gross sales. Part-owner operations, farming a combination of self-owned and rented land, accounted for 36 percent of the farms but farmed 59 percent of total acres and produced 58 percent of total sales. Only 8 percent rented all their land.

Farming traditionally has been an inherited occupation. Most farm families want to bring members of the next generation into the business in some manner leading to transfer of ownership. The desire to pass the farm to the next generation is a commonly held value when compared to other family businesses. Farm families have been described on a continuum from yeoman to entre-

Farm families frequently consider farming more of a way of life than just an occupation and have a strong desire to pass on land like this West Virginia farm from one generation to the next.

preneurial on the basis of their goals. The major goals of yeoman farmers include passing along the farm and the trade of farming to a child. In contrast, the primary goal of entrepreneurial farms is to optimize profit, with intergenerational transfer of low importance. The primary reason that two-generation farms exist is to transfer the business gradually from one generation to the next.

For the generation contemplating entry into farming, career choice clearly is related not only to experience and involvement in parents' farm operations, but also to less tangible family relationship factors such as emotional indebtedness and family loyalties. This interweaving of financial, experiential, and family relationship factors creates powerful bonds across generational boundaries and the potential for conflict and disagreement as well.

The concept of developmental stake has been used to explain the differing levels of commitment that parents and children have to their relationship. In many urban families, parents might be considered to have more stake in the intergenerational relationship than their children, based on factors such as values about carrying on traditions, involvement with children, and support in later years. In many farm families, a high symmetry exists between parents' and children's stake in the parent-child relationship and their stake in the continuity of the farm. The farm serves as a connecting point for generational interests.

Understanding this intergenerational interdependence requires understanding the interests of several generations interacting at differing points in their developmental life cycles. Issues of the older, retiring generation include assurance of financial status as they transfer assets, change in identity and self-image, control of and involvement in the farming operation, location of residence, and source of supportive care and family contact. For the younger generation, given the high financial cost of farm start-up related to the costs of capital, inheritance may offer the only doorway into farming as a career. For younger families, transfer decisions may occur when they are likely to be considering expansion of the operation, the building of a residence to allow for growing children, a willingness to take on risks in return for future profits, and a desire to be more heavily involved in management decisions and ownership. The prevalent interests of one generation may be much different from those of the other generation at any particular point in time. For these families, it makes little sense to ask whether farming is a way of life or a business; it is both, intricately interwoven.

Stages

Farm retirement and intergenerational asset transfer are generally a twice-in-a-lifetime experience, once as a young entering farmer and once as a retiring farmer. Marotz-Baden, Keating, and Munro (1995) described farm retirement as occurring in three stages. During the first stage, the farmer begins to reduce farm labor input, transferring responsibility for labor to the next generation. This provides an opportunity for hands-on experience and limited day-to-day decision making for younger members of the family, while freeing time for the older generation to focus on production, financial, and marketing decisions. During the next stage, the younger generation takes more responsibility for the longer-term management decisions that will provide the basis for their long-term career status. In the final stage, the older generation transfers the actual ownership of physical assets, such as machinery, farmstead, and land.

A Major Life Stressor

Given the complicated nature of intergenerational farm transfer, the lack of understanding of the process by many farm and legal consultants, and the great implications for the lives of the people involved, transfer can be a major source of stress and conflict. Farming is a high-stress occupation involving long hours of work, seasonal variations in demands and income, lack of boundaries between work and family life, high accident rates, high levels of capitalization, and a sense of high involvement in government paperwork and regulation. Transfer decisions bring

together a number of critical role transitions at one time that may involve conflicting interests. The strong socialization of children to enter farming and the occupational implications for them make farm transfer a major source of potential family conflict.

The involvement of more than one child may be a complicating factor in farm transfer. Bringing one additional household into an operation may place demands on the farm's income potential. Multiple children wishing to enter the operation may place stress on the operation and require major expansion. Often families may select one child who is socialized to become the recipient of the farm. This may create sibling conflicts and complicate the estate planning for parents who wish to treat each of their children fairly and equally. Their wish may become quite complicated when one child remains on the farm, providing not only major amounts of involvement and labor but also daily family support for parents while siblings living at greater distances have little or no farm involvement. Generally, the child receiving the farm is a son. However, it is becoming more common that daughters remain involved as an operator. Sex-role expectations, relationships with in-laws, and even situations in which transfer arrangements may extend to include long-term hired employees are all opportunities for complications and added stress.

Coping Strategies

In a survey of farm families involved in transfers, Russell et al. (1985) identified five primary coping strategies helpful with transfer-related stress: discussion, expression of anger, farm management, individual coping, and professional counseling. In general, these techniques reflect the basic values associated with rural America: self-reliance (using individual coping techniques for personal stress), family (using open discussion about feelings, opinions, and ideas among family members to better understand needs and negotiate conflicts), and community (using professionals as consultants and advisers and relying on professional agriculture-related organizations for education and information about approaches to transfer). Lastly, the expression of anger was a frequent response, especially when the younger generation believed it had little control over critical decisions. However, anger was rated quite low in terms of helpfulness. The younger generation, especially daughters-in-law, expressed the greatest amount of stress, probably as a result of they had less control over critical decisions and had fewer resources.

The transfer of a family farm operation to the next generation is a major stressor for all family members, with different effects on each member. Open discussion, considered very helpful in the decision-making process, is vital in identifying the interests of all family members involved in the transfer process. However, open discussion may increase stress, highlight conflict, and be quite difficult for families. At such times, the assistance of an informed facilitator with special knowledge of the intergenerational transfer process and conflict resolution may be of great assistance. Even in cases in which the heirs do not agree with transfer decisions, it may prevent continued conflict in the receiving generation if the parents have clearly and specifically stated their wishes and rationale for their decisions to their heirs.

Estate Planning

Since the 1970s, significant changes have occurred in estate planning of farm transfers. First, dramatic reductions in land values and sharp drops in the federal estate tax burden have reduced federal estate tax liabilities. Whereas there has been some recovery in recent years, land values generally are at or below their pre-1981 levels. Under present law, in most instances federal estate tax is not a concern until the estate size exceeds $600,000.

Another significant development in farm and ranch estate planning concerns the role of the wife. In the past, it was common for all farm property to be titled in the husband's name. Today, estate value is far more likely to be balanced between husband and wife, recognizing the right of the wife to share in family income and property ownership.

There also seems to be a much wider recognition that estate planning requires a team approach, not only among professionals such as attorneys, accountants, financial advisers, and trust officers, but also among the individuals planning the transfer as well as their heirs. It may be helpful to identify estate transfer objectives pertaining to the parents together, the parents individually, the on-farm heirs, and the off-farm heirs.

Estate planning goals typically include minimizing federal transfer tax liabilities, minimizing the cost of probate such as attorney fees and court costs, and conserving property during life and after death in relation to the wishes of the family. The primary goal must be reflective of each individual family's interests in establishing the next generation in the operation and maintaining a set of values and concerns about how that transfer happens.

Methods

Many states impose a state-level inheritance and/or estate tax. When a person dies without a will or trust, or with a will or trust that fails to dispose of all of the person's property, state statutes specify the disposition of property after the death of such person. For other estates, the disposition is determined according to a properly executed and valid will. Property may be transferred via gifts made during life. In general, a gift is subject to taxation at fair market value. When the gift involves a present interest in property (outright and with no strings attached), each individual may transfer, free of gift tax, $10,000 per person per year to as many people as desired. The advantages of lifetime giving include the possibility of moving property into the hands of family members who are in lower income brackets and the possibility of transferring the family business to successors.

Trusts place in the hands of a trustee management the control and legal title of property for the benefit of specified beneficiaries according to directions spelled out in the trust instrument. The most commonly used trust is the revocable living trust, in which the grantor retains the right to amend, modify, or revoke the trust until death, at which point the trust becomes irrevocable. Trusts may be set up as a joint trust for both spouses or as an individual trust. A trust also may be irrevocable; the grantor relinquishes all control and power upon creation of the trust. Asset-sheltering trusts are designed to make the grantor eligible for public assistance benefits such as long-term care in nursing facilities. Testamentary trusts are trusts that become effective at death. They may protect the interests of minor children or disabled heirs in the event of a parent's death. A marital deduction trust may serve to protect the interests of a surviving spouse.

Implications for Those Working with Farm Families

Nearly one-third of all family farms are controlled by farmers reaching retirement age. Compared to the general population, farm operators have an older age structure, with 47 percent aged 55 or older compared to only 22 percent of all self-employed workers in nonagricultural industries. It is estimated that over 500,000 farmers will retire in the 1990s, outpacing new entrants two to one. With the tight profit margins and financial uncertainty facing many farms, intergenerational transfer represents a period of extreme fragility in the survival of those operations.

Programs concerning farm transfer and retirement need to address the major concerns of families involving continuity of the farm and establishment of the next generation in the operation. Personal issues of each generation may need focus, because they may be neglected at times when they conflict with farm continuity. Such conflicts are major sources of stress for families, with major implications for both family and financial futures. Attorneys, farm management consultants, estate planners, and mental health and human service providers working with farm families involved in intergenerational operations should be aware of the relationship between critical psychosocial transitions and critical financial decisions.

—*Charles L. Griffin*

See also

Agricultural Law; Agriculture, Structure of; Family; Landownership.

References

Ballard-Reisch, Deborah S., and D. J. Weigel. "An Interaction-Based Model of Social Exchange in the Two-Generation Farm Family." *Family Relations* 40, no. 2 (April 1991): 225–231.

Hedlund, Dalva E., and Alan Berkowitz. "The Incidence of Sociopsychological Stress in Farm Families." *International Journal of Sociology of the Family* 9, no. 2 (July–December 1979): 233–243.

Kabacher, Judith Z., and V. Oliveira. *Structural and Financial Characteristics of U.S. Farms, 1992: 17th Annual Family Farm Report to Congress.* Agriculture Information Bulletin No. 72. Washington, DC: U.S. Department of Agriculture, Economic Research Service, Rural Economy Division, 1995.

Marotz-Baden, Ramona, Norah Keating, and Brenda Munro. "Generational Differences in the Meaning of Retirement from Farming." *Family and Consumer Science Research Journal* 24, no. 1 (September 1995): 29–47.

McEowen, Roger, and Neil E. Harl. *Principles of Agricultural Law.* Eugene, OR: Ag Law Press, 1996.

Munro, Brenda, Norah Keating, and Xiumei Zhang. "Stake in Farm and Family: A Two-Generation Perspective." *Canadian Journal on Aging* 14, no. 3 (Fall 1995): 564–579.

Russell, Candyce S., Charles L. Griffin, Catherine Scott Flinchbaugh, Michael J. Martin, and Raymond B. Atilano. "Coping Strategies Associated with Intergenerational Transfer of the Family Farm." *Rural Sociology* 50, no. 3 (Fall 1985): 361–376.

Salamon, Sonya. "Ethnic Communities and the Structure of Agriculture." *Rural Sociology* 50, no. 3 (Fall 1985): 323–324.

———. *Prairie Patrimony: Family, Farming. and Community in the Midwest.* Chapel Hill: University of North Carolina Press, 1992.

Irrigation

The application of water to crops, lawns, and gardens by artificial means, such as spreading, sprinkling, or dripping, to supplement natural precipitation. Irrigation supplements rainfall for plant growth. This entry describes the need for irrigation, development of irrigation technology, expansion of irrigation, irrigation costs, salinity control, and environmental impacts. References for the design and operation of irrigation systems are presented.

Need

Crop production consumes water by transpiration and evaporation from the soil. Irrigation supplements rainfall. In semiarid and subhumid areas, irrigation reduces the risk of low yields or crop failures and generally increases yields and quality. Most crops in arid areas cannot be produced without irrigation. Globally, irrigation plays a major role in providing food for the current world population of more than 5 billion. Irrigated agriculture will become more important as the world population is expected reach 9 billion by about 2030. Irrigated land in the United States produces about one-third of the value of crops on only one-seventh of the harvested cropland. Farmers practice irrigation where income from increased crop yield and quality exceeds capital and operating costs and a suitable renewable water supply is available.

Irrigation water requirements depend on the climate, or the evaporative demand, and rainfall received before and during the growing season. The need for irrigation water also depends on the capacity of soil to retain water between rain and irrigation events. Transpiration and evaporation deplete soil water. The combined process of transpiration by crops and evaporation from the soil is called evapotranspiration (ET). The daily ET rate depends on solar radiation intensity, humidity, wind speed, and the area of active transpiration on leaves, which is called the leaf-area index (LAI). The ET rate increases in the spring as solar radiation, air temperature, and LAI increase. It decreases after July in the Northern Hemisphere as solar radiation and air temperature decrease and crops mature. Irrigation assures germination and plant establishment. It is used for frost control and moistening of soils to permit the harvesting of root and tuber crops. Detailed information on the need for irrigation, its development and irrigation economics is available in a publication by irrigation specialists (Council for Agricultural Science and Technology [CAST] 1988).

Development of Technology

Farmers have practiced irrigation for thousands of years. In its beginnings, it enabled nomad tribes in semiarid and arid areas to settle in communities. Surface or gravity is the oldest irrigation method and still is used on most irrigated lands in the world. Surface systems distribute water by gravity. Infiltration occurs as water flows over the land guided by furrows or parallel dikes or is ponded in level basins surrounded by low dikes. Sprinkler systems distribute water through nozzles mounted on pressurized pipe, called laterals, made of aluminum. Initially, farmers moved laterals manually after applying water for 8 to 12 hours. Later, manufacturers attached wheels using the lateral pipe as the axle and installed automatic drain valves. After an irrigation set has occurred and water in the pipe has drained, farmers roll the entire lateral to the next set using a small engine to provide the power. This sprinkler system is used where tall crops such as corn are not grown. Manufacturers also mounted laterals much higher on sets of wheels, called towers. Each tower is powered either hydraulically or electrically. The lateral moves continuously while applying water. The most common moving lateral is the center pivot (CP) system, in which the lateral rotates about the pivot point that is also the water source. CP systems enable farmers to irrigate lands that they could not irrigate with surface methods. Farmers control most CP systems electronically, and therefore these systems have very low labor requirements.

The term *micro-irrigation* applies to several low-pressure systems such as drip or trickle, bubbler, and miniature spray. These systems apply water to each row or to individual vines or trees through emitters or small spray nozzles attached to pressurized plastic tubing. Micro-irrigation systems have dense plastic tubing networks to distribute water over fields. Most systems are controlled automatically using timers or soil water sensors to start and stop light, frequent irrigations. As a result, the range in soil water available to plants varies much less than with traditional surface irrigation and some sprinkler irrigation systems. Micro-irrigation has become the system of choice on new vineyards and many high-value vegetable crops that require good water control. Water quality is extremely important in all micro-irrigation systems. Filtration equipment is an essential component for removing sediment and debris to prevent plugging of the small emitters or spray nozzles.

Each irrigation system has advantages and disadvantages. When selecting a system, farmers consider capital and operating costs, crops to be grown, and expected increased crop yields and quality. Water consumption by most crops is about the same when irrigated with any well-designed and managed system. However, there can be large differences in the amounts of water applied, deep percolation below the root zone, and surface runoff. From a water balance viewpoint, most surface runoff and most deep percolation return to the groundwater or to rivers for reuse by downstream water users. The quality of the return flow, however, is degraded because it contains the same salt load that was in the irrigation water, but concentrated in a smaller volume.

Expansion

Irrigated land in the United States increased steadily from the mid-1940s until the 1980s. Most of this land is in 17 western states (see Figure 1). Increasing competition for water resources and declining groundwater levels decreased irrigated land in the southwestern states of Arizona, California, New Mexico, and Nevada. Depletion of groundwater caused the decline in irrigated land in the Great Plains mainly because of the decrease in the High Plains of Texas. Texas farmers returned some lands to dryland farming that were first irrigated in the 1950s and 1960s. CPs replaced many surface irrigation systems. Because they can handle smaller flow rates, less water is pumped; CP systems apply water uniformly, and they produce little or no surface runoff.

Florida's annual rainfall is about 50 inches, but farmers irrigate most high-value crops because of very sandy soils. More recently, Florida farmers converted many sprinkler systems to micro-irrigation systems. Most of the increase in irrigated lands in the eastern states has been in the north-central states of Michigan, Minnesota, and Wisconsin (see Figure 2). Sandy soil has been a major factor influencing expansion of irrigated

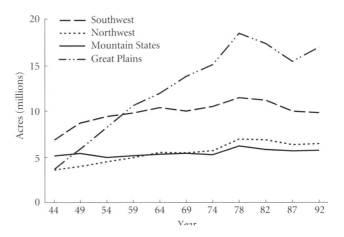

Figure 1. Irrigated Land in the Western States

Southwest states: Arizona, California, New Mexico, Nevada; Northwest states: Idaho, Oregon, Washington; Mountain states: Colorado, Utah, Wyoming; Great Plains states: Kansas, Montana, Nebraska, North Dakota, Oklahoma, South Dakota, Texas.

Source: U.S. Department of Commerce (various years).

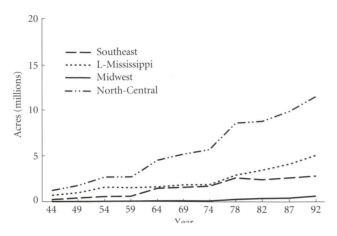

Figure 2. Irrigated Land in the Southeastern, Lower Mississippi, Midwestern, and North-Central States

Southeastern states: Alabama, Florida, Georgia, Kentucky, North Carolina, South Carolina, Tennessee, Virginia; lower Mississippi states: Arkansas, Louisiana, Mississippi, Missouri; Midwest states: Illinois, Indiana, Iowa, Ohio; North-Central states: Michigan, Minnesota, Wisconsin.

Source: U.S. Department of Commerce (various years).

lands. Groundwater has been the main source of water. Without a convenient and renewable source of water, farmers cannot irrigate, although potential increases in crop yields would offset capital and operating irrigation costs.

Costs

Irrigation increases production costs per acre but not necessarily the unit cost of production because of higher yields. Controlling crop quality with irrigation also can bring higher crop prices. Farmers amortize capital costs over the life of the investment. Operating costs, which include labor, maintenance, and fuel costs, vary with the system used. Labor costs are often highest for surface irrigation and sprinkler systems that require manual movement of laterals. Pumping costs may be high if water is pumped from deep groundwater or from surface sources at lower elevations. Additional pumping costs are involved where farmers pressurize water to distribute it through the sprinkler nozzles. Micro-irrigation systems typically operate at lower pressures than sprinkler systems, although many CPs now have low pressure spray nozzles.

Initial capital costs may be high for surface systems where extensive land leveling and smoothing are required, but maintenance costs after that are low. Water is supplied by gravity to most surface systems, so there are usually no pumping costs. Capital costs are highest for

micro-irrigation systems because of the dense tubing network to distribute water, the large number of small emitters and minisprinklers, filtration equipment, electronic controllers, and automated valves. Water for micro-irrigation systems essentially must be of drinking water quality to prevent plugging of small emitters and minisprinklers. Annual maintenance costs for most sprinkler systems range from 3 to 5 percent of the initial capital costs. For micro-irrigation systems, maintenance costs range from 2 to 4 percent, and for surface systems, they are about 1 percent.

Crops that are most profitable to irrigate are those that are sensitive to plant water stress and have high market value because irrigation enables quality control. In the arid Southwest, farmers irrigate most high-value crops, such as citrus, fruit orchards, grape vineyards, and vegetables. In the Great Plains, corn is a major irrigated crop. In the Southeast, farmers irrigate most vegetable crops because crop quality is a major factor affecting the market price. Overall, benefits of irrigation include higher and predictable yields, better and more uniform crop quality, and reduced farming risks.

Salinity Control

Soil salinity does not always increase with irrigation. All waters contain dissolved solids. Plants extract and transpire pure water, as does evaporation. ET therefore leaves dissolved salts in the soils that rain or excess irrigation must leach periodically. The salts originally in the irrigation water remain in the leachate, or drainage water, but become more concentrated in the return flow. Periodic leaching moves salt that has accumulated in the root zone downward. If natural drainage is sufficient, the effluent and salts drain naturally. Fine textured soils, or soils that have poor natural drainage, may need additional drainage capacity to ensure adequate salt control and to prevent waterlogging of the soil. Today, most subsurface drains consist of perforated, corrugated plastic tubing installed with machines. The addition of drainage increases irrigation costs, but this drainage may be essential for sustained agricultural production on some soils.

Environmental Impacts

Some societies practiced irrigation for centuries without degrading the environment. Transpiration is the main use of water in crop production and cannot be avoided. This process degrades the quality of remaining water because salts become more concentrated. Globally, major problems facing irrigated agriculture are waterlogging of soils and salinity, increasing competition for water, and water-related human diseases. Sustainable irrigated agriculture will require rehabilitation and modernization of existing projects and continual monitoring and evaluation of the performance of irrigated agriculture.

System Design and Operation

Guidelines for the design and operation of various irrigation systems are available from several sources (Jensen 1983; Elliott and Jensen 1997). Guidelines for managing irrigation systems, including the scheduling of irrigation using climate-soil-plant models, are available, as are guidelines to irrigate most farm crops (Hoffman, Howell, and Solomon 1990; Stewart and Nielsen 1990). The Council for Agricultural Science and Technology (1988) summarized guidelines for making effective use of water in irrigated agriculture. A comprehensive description of various irrigation systems, irrigation districts, and associated water rights issues can be found in recent articles by CAST (1988) and Replogle, Clemmens, and Jensen (1996).

—*Marvin E. Jensen*

See also

Conservation, Water; Dryland Farming; Groundwater; Horticulture; Hydrology; Rice Industry; Temperate Fruit Industry; Water Use.

References

Council for Agricultural Science and Technology. *Effective Use of Water in Irrigated Agriculture*. Ames, IA: Council for Agricultural Science and Technology, 1988.

Elliott, R. L., and Marvin E. Jensen, eds. *Design and Operation of Farm Irrigation Systems*. 2d edition. ASAE Monograph No. 3. St. Joseph, MI: American Society of Agricultural Engineering, 1997.

Hoffman, Glenn J., Terry A. Howell, and Kenneth H. Solomon, eds. *Management of Farm Irrigation Systems*. ASAE Monograph. St. Joseph, MI: American Society of Agricultural Engineering, 1990.

Jensen, Marvin E., ed. *Design and Operation of Farm Irrigation Systems*. ASAE Monograph No. 3. St. Joseph, MI: American Society of Agricultural Engineering, 1983.

Replogle, J. R., A. J. Clemmens, and Marvin E. Jensen. "Irrigation Systems: Part III, Water Supply." In *Water Resources Handbook*. Edited by Larry W. Mays. New York: McGraw-Hill, 1996.

Stewart, Bobby A., and Donald R. Nielsen, eds. *Irrigation of Agricultural Crops*. Agronomics Series No. 30. Madison, WI: American Society of Agronomy, 1990.

U.S. Department of Commerce. *Census of Agriculture, Part 51, United States Summary and State Data*. Washington, DC: U.S. Department of Commerce, Bureau of the Census (various years).

Labor Force

The number of workers potentially assignable for any purpose; the labor force consists of those persons who are employed or seeking employment, including men, women, and teenagers who are unskilled, uneducated, and consequently unemployed or underemployed. Current rural labor force trends are examined in this entry, with special emphasis on women, teenagers, and migrant farmworkers. Rural industrialization is suggested as one means of diversifying rural economies and providing additional labor opportunities. In 1990, there were 125,182,378 people 16 years and older in the U.S. civilian labor force. There were approximately 89,428,870 people employed for full-time wages in the United States. Of the 89 million, 68,085,993 were employed in urban areas and only 21,342,878 were employed in rural areas. The total unemployment rate in the United States in 1990 was 6.3 percent. In urban areas it was slightly higher, with a total of 6.4 percent, and rural areas had a total rate of 6.0 percent. Several demographic and economic influences have shaped the labor force since the 1960s, producing important historical trends that may have a significant impact on the future economy.

Trends

From 1950 to 1980, the labor force expanded by more than 44 million people, or by nearly 72 percent. In the late 1970s, the labor force was growing by 3 million people per year, primarily because of the baby boomers. After the very rapid growth of the 1970s, a slower rate of labor force growth began in the 1980s. The labor force expanded by about 17 percent during the 1980–1990 period, compared with a 29 percent increase in the previous decade. By 1992, there were 20 million more people in the labor force than in 1980 (Kutscher 1993).

Women began to enter the labor force in increasing numbers over the 1950–1980 span. In 1950, women represented less than 30 percent of all workers in America. By 1980, they had increased their share to more than 42 percent. Women's labor force participation rate—that is, women workers as a percentage of all women aged 16 and older—increased from 33.9 percent in 1950 to 51.5 percent by 1980. Growth was even faster for women aged 35 through 44. Labor force participation rates for women continued to increase in the 1980s. Yet by the mid- to late 1980s, the rate of growth had slowed among some age groups. Women in their 20s and 30s had greater stability in labor force participation rates in this period. The labor force participation rates for women in their 40s and 50s continued to increase appreciably over the 1980–1992 period. Labor force participation rates generally were lower for White women than for Black women, but rates for White women increased more rapidly. Labor force participation rates tended to be lower for Hispanic women than for either White or Black women (Kutscher 1993).

Men's labor force participation rate over the 1950–1980 span experienced a long-term but gradual decline from 86.4 percent in 1950 to 77.4 percent by 1980. This decline was more rapid among those aged 55 years and older. The labor force participation rates for Black men and White men tended to diverge over time, with rates for Black men declining more rapidly than those for White men. However, labor force participation declined among both minority and majority older men with lower educational attainment (Kutscher 1993).

Male and female teenagers aged 16 to 19 years old exhibited much year-to-year fluctuation in their labor force participation rates over the 1950–1992 period. Participation rates were lower for minority (Black, Hispanic,

Asian, and other) youths, particularly Black males, than for White youths. In 1980, minorities composed 18.1 percent of the labor force. By 1992, their share had increased to more than 22 percent, with non-Black minorities having the greatest and most rapid expansion in the labor force (Kutscher 1993). Since rural sectors are characterized by limited employment opportunities and higher rates of unemployment and account for a disproportionate amount of persistent poverty in the United States (Garrett, Ng'andu, and Ferron 1994), many local leaders see rural industrialization as an important way to improve the quality of life in rural areas.

Women

Traditionally, women have been placed in domestic roles, such as homemaker, caregiver, and expressive provider for the family. This is especially true among rural and farm families, where women's domestic roles have been the basic element of rural life. Yet the woman's role as a farmer in a sense has been invisible because women have been viewed as having no direct linkage to production (Keating and Little 1994). Despite the importance of the roles of rural women, they have been denied access to farm management roles and business decisions. Rural women presently are challenging the traditional family roles and are exploring the avenues of the capitalist system as a mechanism for survival and wage labor. They have been taking on more active roles in the business arena and are working to establish themselves in other facets of the rural labor force.

Ollenburger, Grana, and Moore (1989) suggested that farm women are presently more likely than nonfarm women to possess an active role in the wage labor force. They noted that factors such as educational background and marital status contribute to the amount of participation in the labor force in which farm women and nonfarm women engage. Lichter and McLaughlin (1995) asserted that, on average, the mass of rural (nonmetropolitan) workers fell behind their metropolitan counterparts in the labor force, especially those with limited educational skills. Consequently, women in the labor force in rural areas became increasingly marginalized in the labor structure and make up the mass of the unemployed and poor.

Poverty—the state of being poor or lacking the means for providing material needs or comforts—and unemployment among rural women is the center of much debate, bringing into question the structure of inequality within the labor force that has led to the feminization of poverty in nonmetropolitan areas. The "feminization of poverty" refers to the high percentage of females and

their children living without basic essentials and comforts and lacking the means of providing these needs. Rural women, particularly single mothers and the elderly, are identified today in America as those individuals who are affected most by pauperism (impoverishment and feminization of poverty) and unemployment. Elderly women in nonmetropolitan/rural areas have extremely high rates of poverty and lower incomes than their urban counterparts. In the 1980s, there was a decline in income by 0.6 percent in nonmetropolitan/rural areas and an increase by 6.4 percent in income in urban areas (McLaughlin and Holden 1993).

Nonmetropolitan women have fewer resources for economic survival than metropolitan women. Rural elderly women receive less social security and, on average, have a lower total income than urban elderly women (McLaughlin and Holden 1993). Thus, nonmetropolitan women, especially the elderly, are linked to poorer economic opportunities as a result of their residential location, presenting various economic limitations to those who are confined to nonmetropolitan/rural areas. The poverty rate in 1992 for nonmetropolitan (rural) single women was 37.3 percent, and for those women who had dependents, the poverty rate was 48.2 percent (U.S. Bureau of the Census 1992).

To combat these inequities, the U.S. government implemented policies targeting single, poor women and rural women with dependent children to enhance their participation in the labor force. Rural mothers were targeted because of the lack of health care benefits, medical benefits, and child care benefits that exist in nonmetropolitan areas. Low incomes carry the high risk of illness, limitations on mobility, and limited access to education, information, and training. Hence, poverty depends on individual factors and residential location (Lichter and McLaughlin 1995).

Women in all facets of rural America (elderly, single mothers, single women, and married women) encounter the challenges of pauperism (impoverishment) on a day-to-day basis. Lack of benefits and insufficient wage labor are only two of the issues having detrimental effects on the economic well-being of rural women. It is imperative that researchers direct their attention to female-headed households as they relate to the labor force and how they affect the labor market.

Teens

Because of the deteriorating labor market prospects of parents, the rise in single-parent families and the poverty associated with them, inadequate child support from noncustodial parents, and the erosion of government assistance, many nonmetropolitan teenagers currently are taking part in the paid labor force (Deseran and Keithly 1994). With the rise in service-related jobs, there are many positions that are considered undesirable for adults but are well suited for rural youths. Jobs requiring few skills, with nonstandard hours (evening and weekends) and low wages often are held by teenagers who are in school or have few job skills and little experience. Because they are most often confined to jobs near their homes when acquiring these positions, teenagers in rural areas actively participate in the local labor market.

The teenage laborer, characterized by a lack of work experience, is likely to be in school and lives with parents. Over 60 percent of high school seniors hold part-time jobs. Employment rates have been consistently lower for rural than for urban youths. Minority youths, particularly Black inner-city youths, still experience extreme levels of unemployment compared to other participants in the labor force (Deseran and Keithly 1994).

Family circumstances play a major role in most decisions concerning work, and for adolescents the family is by necessity central in the decision to enter the labor force. Teenage employment is driven to a large extent by desire for increased consumption of discretionary items (i.e., stereos, concert tickets) rather than necessities. Yet youths with unemployed parents and those from impoverished households (especially Black households in urban centers) are more likely to have jobs than their more affluent counterparts (Deseran and Keithly 1994).

Migrant Farmworkers

Just as teenagers are used to fill positions rural adults find undesirable, migrant workers, particularly illegal immigrants, provide the rural labor force with people willing to do jobs that no one else will do. Generally, living standards in rural areas are lower than those in the cities, yet U.S. agriculture has produced one set of conditions that is below even the lowest living standards. These conditions result from seasonal demands for labor to harvest perishable crops, particularly fruits, vegetables, cotton, and sugar beets (Horton, Leslie, and Larson 1994). Approximately 52 percent of migrant farmworkers work in vegetable, fruit, sugar cane, and grain field crops, and 3.5 percent work for tobacco growers. Fifty-seven percent of migrant farmworkers in the U.S. are citizens of Mexico, and only 26 percent of the total number of U.S. migrant labors are not Hispanic (Stuart 1992). Approximately

540,000 farmworkers, with up to 1 million additional members of their families, travel three major routes in search of work. Each migratory stream starts in the South and follows the harvests north (Horton et al. 1994).

The poverty and degradation under which migrant workers live remain hidden from the larger society because they are not permanent members of any community; thus their presence can be ignored for a short period each year. Since housing is typically provided for them by farm employers or by grower associations, they are removed from most direct contact with other members of the community. Because of their meager incomes, they live in shacks, hovels, hotels, roominghouses, cars, trailers, tents, or on the ground (Horton et al. 1994). In 1985, the average farmworker earned a total of $3,247 (Stuart 1992).

In a fairly common pattern, a recruiter promises these workers wages of $500 or more per week. The recruiter then takes the workers to the farmer or grower, who pays the recruiter between $300 and $500 per person. When they arrive, they are paid reasonable wages, but they are informed later that they can not leave until they have repaid the farmer the $300 to $500 fee. This amount is taken from their wages, and as the season progresses, workers also must pay the grower for room, board, clothing, cigarettes, and alcohol, all sold by the grower at extremely high prices. By the end of the season, the worker is averaging $5 a week for pocket money, with the rest of the "earnings" credited against what she or he owes the grower (Horton et al. 1994).

The children of migratory workers have fewer educational opportunities and lower educational achievement than any other group of Americans. Their school attendance is irregular because they must stay out of school to work (Horton et al. 1991). Findings show that 86 percent of migrant farm children do not finish high school, compared to 25 percent of other children in the country. Also, migrant farmworker children lag behind other children approximately 6 to 18 months in grade levels. Thus, about 15 percent of all migrant farm laborers are functionally illiterate, and the rate of school enrollment for farmworker children is lower than for any other group in the United States (Stuart 1992).

Injury is another major issue among migrant laborers. About 140,000 children under 14 years of age travel with their migrant parents. Another 119,000 migrant workers are between 14 and 17 years of age (Horton et al. 1991). Nearly 35 percent of children aged 5 to 14 have been injured in agricultural accidents. Sixteen states have no labor provisions specifically to protect farmworker children. Presently, at the age of 12 farmworker children lose federal child law protection (Stuart 1992).

Along with physical injury, there are several health risks to migrant laborers. The rate of parasitic disease among the children of migrant workers working in the United States is higher than it is for children in Guatemala, and the miscarriage rate for farmworkers is seven times the national average. Migrant workers are three times more likely than the general U.S. population to be exposed to toxic chemicals, and they have five times more cases of skin rash than other workers. More than 44 percent of the farmworker households in the United States have at least one disabled family member. Yet 19 states exempt agricultural workers from workers' compensation coverage. In 1985, there were 49 job-related deaths in agriculture per 100,000 and the average life expectancy of migrant agricultural workers was only 50 years (Stuart 1992). Technological displacement may change these numbers in that most harvesting now done by hand may soon be done by machines. Machines to pick vegetables, fruits, and berries are now in advanced stages of development (Horton et al. 1994).

Rural Industrialization

Community leaders view improved employment opportunities as a prime component in improving the quality of life in rural areas. Rural industrialization results in a diversified economy. A diversified economy enables the local labor market to withstand transient shifts in a specified industry because economic risks are distributed among several industries. Rural industrialization used to improve employment opportunities may affect the local occupational structure and thus the prestige, social class, mobility, and lifestyle of the population (Carter 1982). Rural industrialization may have positive impacts on the self-concepts of individuals moving into new jobs. But in order to recruit new industry, local leaders must provide much information on the advantages of the area for potential employers.

—*Jacqueline M. Davis-Gines and Anita D. Bledsoe*

See also
Dependence; Employment; Income; Inequality; Labor Unions; Migrant Farmworkers; Policy, Economic; Poverty; Rural Women; Underemployment; Work.
References
Carter, Keith A. "Inadequacies of the Traditional Labor Force Framework for Rural Areas: A Labor Utilization Framework Applied to Survey Data." *Rural Sociology* 47, no. 3 (Fall 1982): 459–474.

Deseran, Forrest A., and Diane Keithly. "Teenagers in the U.S. Labor Force: Local Labor Markets, Race, and Family." *Rural Sociology* 59, no 4 (Winter 1994): 668–692.
Garrett, Patricia, Nicholas Ng'andu, and J. Ferron. "Is Rural Residency a Risk Factor for Childhood Poverty?" *Rural Sociology* 59, no. 1 (Spring 1994): 66–83.
Horton, Paul B., Gerald R. Leslie, and Richard R. Larson. *The Sociology of Social Problems,* 11th ed. Englewood Cliffs, NJ: Prentice-Hall, 1994.
Keating, Norah C., and Heather M. Little. "Getting into It: Farm Roles and Careers of New Zealand Women." *Rural Sociology* 59, no. 4 (Winter 1994): 720–736.
Kutscher, Ronald E. "The American Work Force: 1992–2005. Historical Trends, 1950–92, and Current Uncertainties." *Monthly Labor Review* 116, no. 11 (November 1993): 3–10.
Lichter, Daniel T., and Diane K. McLaughlin. "Changing Economic Opportunities, Family Structure, and Poverty in Rural Areas." *Rural Sociology* 60, no. 4 (Winter 1995): 688–706.
McLaughlin, Diane K., and Karen C. Holden. "Nonmetropolitan Elderly Women: A Portrait of Economic Vulnerability." *Journal of Applied Gerontology* 12, no. 3 (Septermber 1993): 320–334.
McLaughlin, Diane K., and Carolyn Sachs. "Poverty in Female-Headed Households: Residential Differences." *Rural Sociology* 53, no. 3 (Fall 1988): 287–306.
Ollenburger, Jane C., Sheryl J. Grana, and Helen A. Moore. "Labor Force Participation of Rural Nonfarm and Urban Women: A Panel Update." *Rural Sociology* 54, no. 4 (Winter 1989): 533–550.
Stuart, Peggy. "Many Migrant Workers Face Bleak Prospects." *Personnel Journal* 71 (1992): 28.
U.S. Bureau of the Census. *1990 General Population Characteristics.* Washington DC: U.S. Government Printing Office, 1992.

Labor Unions

Organizations created to improve the economic position of workers. This entry examines the role and extent of organized labor activity in rural areas. It provides an overview of the economic functions of labor unions, issues involved in their formation, a brief history of unions, and their current status. The limited extent of union influence within the rural labor force is documented and discussed using both empirical evidence and arguments grounded in economic theory. The entry concludes with an evaluation of present trends in union influence and activity in light of major changes under way in workforce organization and labor-management relations.

Some Economic Issues

Labor unions enhance the bargaining power of individual workers through collective action. They extract economic surpluses from employers who are able to exert monopoly power in their output markets. A firm has monopoly power if it is the only or the major seller in an industry. Usually, this allows the firm to extract economic surpluses from its customers, and unions attempt to share in this surplus. Large firms are likely to have more market power than small firms and consequently are more likely to face collective action from their workers.

Subjects of union bargaining may include wages, benefits, or working conditions. Unions face a basic trade-off between raising wages (w) and guaranteeing employment (N). In simple models, unions are assumed to maximize the total wage bill ($w \times N$). Collective action also may be initiated by workers if the employer exercises undue power in labor-management negotiations. The employer's power may result from access to more information than that available to workers or from the fact that there is only one employer in a community or occupation. In general, the degree of competition in input and output markets and institutional factors such as federal regulation affect the economic viability of unions. Possible labor actions range from work slowdowns, sick-outs, work stoppages, and strikes to boycotts of goods.

Real costs are involved in organizing labor, and unions fail if costs of organizing exceed benefits. Economic benefits to the individual from becoming a union member include higher wages or better working conditions. In addition to paying dues, union members must accept collectively established policies and conditions, some of which they may not agree with. Thus, members experience a loss of individual freedom.

Union leaders bear the logistical costs of organizing workers. In addition, they face costs that arise in identifying and finding agreement for union goals among a majority of members and in subsequently bargaining with management to accomplish union objectives. Average costs per worker of organizing unions are lower (1) in firms with more employees, (2) in situations in which there are only a few key bargaining issues around which members can rally, and (3) where labor turnover is not excessive, as is usually the case in larger firms. Lower average costs are therefore another reason that workers in larger firms are more likely to be organized. Lower organizational costs also explain the greater tendency for specific occupational groups, such as coal miners, who are concerned not only about pay but also about focused issues such as safe underground working conditions, to be organized. Alternatively, as the number of issues involved in bargaining increases, benefits to any one member may be diluted.

A Brief History and Current Status

The first unions were formed in large cities such as Philadelphia and New York, where concentrations of workers in the same trade made collective action economically viable (Rees 1989). Unions subsequently spread to railroad workers and eventually to the first industrywide union, the United Mine Workers of America, in 1890. A peak in the unionized share of the non-agricultural workforce occurred in 1953, with 32.5 percent of the workforce unionized. Total membership peaked in 1975, with 22.2 million members (Rees 1989). Out of a total workforce of 105.1 million in 1993, 16.6 million (15.8 percent) were members of unions, whereas 18.6 million (17.7 percent) were represented by unions (U.S. Department of Labor 1994). There are presently 250 labor unions in the United States, with 176,000 employees and a payroll of $2.7 billion (U.S. Bureau of the Census 1993).

The five largest unions affiliated with the American Federation of Labor–Congress of Industrial Organizations are the Teamsters Union, with 1,379,000 members in 1991; followed by the American Federation of State, County, and Municipal Employees, with 1,191,000 members; the Union of Food and Commercial Workers, with 997,000 members; the Service Employees Union, with 881,000 members; and the United Auto Workers, with 840,000 members (U.S. Bureau of the Census 1993). In terms of worker characteristics, unionization rates are higher for male workers, African Americans, full-time workers, the 35–64 year age group, and workers with a high school diploma but no college degree (Curme, Hirsch, and MacPherson 1990).

In terms of industry, the highest unionization rate is found among government workers, followed by workers in communications and other public utilities and transportation (see table, p. 397). Nationally, government unionism is higher at the level of municipalities and townships than at the state and county levels (Hindman and Patton 1994, 110). The lowest union membership rate occurs in one of the industries most prevalent in rural areas, as measured by the percent of all jobs that are located in nonmetropolitan or rural areas: agricultural wage and salary workers. The last column in the table shows that 59.5 percent of these jobs are located in nonmetropolitan counties. In mining, the only other industry with a large share of jobs in nonmetropolitan counties, the unionization rate is 16 percent, which places that industry in a middle rank. The largest benefit to union membership, as measured by the ratio of union to nonunion wages and with no controlling for worker characteristics, is in construction (1.62), followed by retail trade (1.40), and transportation (1.32). No benefits are realized in mining (0.96) and in finance, insurance, and real estate services (0.98).

Considerable variation in unionization rates also exists across occupations. For example, approximately 25 percent of the blue-collar workforce consisting of precision production workers, machine operators, transportation workers, and handlers is unionized, compared with a rate of 40 percent for protective service occupations. The lowest rates occur among executive, administrative, managerial, and sales occupations and in farming, forestry, and fisheries. In this regard, it is important to note that the National Labor Relations Act, which encourages collective bargaining in addition to defining employee rights, explicitly excludes farmworkers (National Labor Relations Board 1992, 226). Farming, forestry, and fisheries workers are among the main beneficiaries of unionization when it does occur, as measured by weekly earnings. The largest earnings differential exists among handlers (where wages of unionized workers are 1.64 times those of nonunionized workers), the lowest among professional specialty occupations.

Influence in Rural Areas

Limited empirical information is available on union activity in rural areas because most research on labor unions and their effects has been carried out for urban areas. In part, this is because only 20 percent of employees work in a nonmetropolitan area and fewer than 2.5 percent work in rural areas (see table). When unions do exist in rural areas, they tend to be organized around extractive industries such as mining. Of the nearly 300 labor organizations listed in the *1988–1989 Directory of U.S. Labor Organizations,* only one is linked explicitly to farming: the United Farm Workers of America, with 30,000 members, which was headed by César E. Chávez and is active mainly in California (Gifford 1988). The only entry with the word *rural* in its title is the National Rural Mail Carriers Union, with 77,000 members.

Although unions have been active in agriculture historically, often organized around crops such as fruits and vegetables that require migrant laborers, their role is presently limited (see table; also Tweeten 1979, 282). It is difficult to organize diverse and individualistic farm families scattered across the United States, and many farmers probably would resist collective action to the extent that it implied loss of individual freedom.

Similarly, unions play a limited role among rural manufacturing workers. One important reason is that in recent years a large share of rural manufacturing activity in the United States relocated to the South, where antiunion sentiment traditionally has been strong and right-to-work (RTW) legislation further erodes the bargaining strength of unions. Under RTW laws, unions are unable to bar nonunionized workers from working in a plant (the so-called closed-shop phenomenon), so they have less control over the aggregate labor supply to the plant. Unions are strongest in the industrialized states of the western and northern United States, which tend not to have RTW laws. A further reason that labor unions are less important in rural areas is that firms tend to be smaller on average, largely because population densities are much lower, which in turn raises costs of organization. For example, rural counties on average have only 17.2 persons per square mile, compared with 70.9 in nonmetro, nonrural counties and 811.1 in metro counties.

The share of manufacturing workers belonging to unions is smaller in states in which a larger share of manufacturing labor is located in rural counties. More specifically, unionization rates of manufacturing workers are estimated to be 15 percent higher in urban than in rural areas (author's calculations using U.S. Bureau of the Census and Department of Commerce data). No more than 20 percent of the manufacturing labor force in right-to-work states is unionized. The fact that just over one-half of all manufacturing workers are unionized in the most heavily unionized state (Michigan) is evidence of the decline in union power relative to that in the past.

Trends Affecting Future Influence

A number of trends are under way in the American workforce to suggest that recent declines in the importance of unions for workers overall and rural workers in particular will continue or at least not be reversed. These include (1) high proportions of women—who are less likely to unionize—in the workforce; (2) more part-time employment; (3) increased overseas competition, particularly in durables goods manufacturing, which historically has been subject to more unionization; (4) deregulation, which reduced monopoly power in some industries; (5) antiunion sentiment among employers; and (6) increasing empowerment of workers, which reduces pressure to unionize. The last trend is perhaps the most important of all. In the future, the ability of workers and their managers to cooperate effectively and meaningfully in meeting domestic and international competition probably will be more important to the economic success of a business than whether or not the institutional framework guiding the worker-management relationship is based on the union model.

—*Stephan J. Goetz*

Basic Data on Union and Job Characteristics, by Industry and Occupation

	Total employment ('000s)	Percentage of Workers		Weekly Earnings ($)		Percentage of Total	
		Union Members[a]	Represented by Union[b]	Represented by Union	Not Unionized	Nonmetro and Nonrural	Rural
Industry							
Agricultural wage & salary workers[c]	1,472	1.6	2.1	n.a.	277	50.0	9.5
Mining	643	16.0	17.6	631	657	50.5	6.3
Construction	4,638	20.0	21.0	689	425	22.8	3.0
Manufacturing (durables)	10,790	20.7	21.9	523	480	22.7	2.2
Manufacturing (nondurables)	7,920	17.2	18.2	471	407	27.4	2.9
Transportation	3,650	28.7	30.2	624	472	17.8	2.0
Communication and public utilities	2,663	32.9	35.6	638	625	18.7	1.9
Wholesale trade	3,896	6.9	7.8	496	471	15.4	1.6
Retail trade	17,759	6.2	6.8	439	314	20.8	2.0
Finance insurance and real estate	6,783	1.9	2.6	481	490	12.4	1.2
Services	26,235	5.8	7.0	478	416	18.4	1.9
Government workers	18,618	37.7	43.8	596	498	19.6	2.3
Occupation							
Executive, administrative, and managerial	12,453	6.2	8.2	710	658	14.5	1.4
Professional specialty	14,715	22.3	26.3	683	681	16.5	1.6
Technical and related support	3,951	11.4	13.3	619	517	15.7	1.4
Sales	11,442	4.7	5.4	466	456	17.8	1.7
Administrative support	18,036	13.8	16.1	492	374	16.5	1.6
Protective service	2,178	40.1	43.0	628	404	18.7	1.9
Other service	13,193	9.5	10.7	369	253	22.9	2.5
Precision production	11,024	25.6	27.2	637	453	24.5	2.8
Machine operators	7,265	25.0	26.3	476	314	30.5	3.4
Transportation, etc.	4,552	26.8	28.4	581	398	28.1	3.6
Handlers, etc.	4,498	22.0	23.2	465	284	26.4	3.0
Farming, forestry, and fishing	1,759	5.1	5.7	413	264	50.7	9.8
Total employed	105,067	15.8	17.7	569	426	20.7	2.3
Total counties	3,111	—	—	—	—	75.2	23.5

Sources: Union membership and earnings data are from U.S. Department of Labor, *Employment and Earnings* (Washington, DC: U.S. Department of Labor, Bureau of Labor Statistics, January 1994) and are for the year 1993. Job breakdowns by nonmetro and nonrural and rural area are based on author's calculations using U.S. Department of Commerce, Bureau of Economic Analysis, Regional Economic Measurement Division (REIS) data for 1991. Employment estimates obtained from *Employment and Earnings* and REIS differ.
[a]Individuals who are members of unions or employee associations.
[b]Includes individuals in (*a*) but also those who are represented or covered by an association without being a member.
[c]Data in the last two columns include forestry and fisheries workers.

See also

Employment; Income; Labor Force; Migrant Farmworkers; Workers' Compensation.

References

Curme, Michael A., Barry T. Hirsch, and David A. MacPherson. "Union Membership and Contract Coverage in the United States, 1983–1988." *Industrial and Labor Relations Review* 44 (1990): 5–33.

Gifford, Courtney D. *Directory of U.S. Labor Organizations, 1988–89 Edition.* Washington, DC: Bureau of National Affairs, 1988.

Hindman, Hugh D., and David B. Patton. "Unionism in State and Local Governments: Ohio and Illinois, 1982–87." *Industrial Relations* 33, no. 1 (January 1994): 106–120.

National Labor Relations Board. "Rules and Regulations and Statements of Procedure." National Labor Relations Act and Labor Management Relations Act. Washington, DC: U.S. Government Printing Office, 1992.

Rees, Albert. *The Economics of Trade Unions.* 3d ed. Chicago: University of Chicago Press, 1989.

Tweeten, Luther G. *Foundations of Farm Policy.* 3d ed. Lincoln: University of Nebraska Press, 1979.

U.S. Bureau of the Census. *Statistical Abstract of the United States: 1993.* 113th ed. Washington, DC: U.S. Government Printing Office, 1993.

U.S. Department of Labor. *Employment and Earnings.* Washington, DC: U.S. Department of Labor, Bureau of Labor Statistics, January 1994.

Land Reform

The redistribution of land held by a few for the benefit of the many; the reshaping of property rights, land policy, and property taxation strategies to ensure social equity, community security, and environmental sustainability. This entry distinguishes several types of land reform and elaborates two types widely viewed as relevant abroad but less so in the United States, a view that is shown to be historically unfounded. Discussion of additional land policies needing reform now and in the future concludes the entry.

Distinct Traditions

Land reform has a broad spectrum of advocates. Conservatives support land reform for its contribution to capital formation, social tranquillity, and, where it applies, the expansion of private ownership. Radicals see land reform as a cure for unequal possession and power. Conservatives and radicals alike use land reform to purge vestiges of feudalism, real or imagined. Since by most accounts feudalism did not exist in America, one may ask why land reform occurred in our country's past and whether it is relevant to our future.

At least four distinct land reform traditions existed in American history. One consisted of mass resettlement and was typically a response to the land hunger generated by population growth. The second was truly redistributive and pitted the landless against landed oligopolies. The other two remaining land reforms redistributed control rather than ownership of land and will be noted here only in passing. One was land use planning reform, which employed the police powers of the state to regulate private lands. The other was public land management reform, which extended from acquisition and disposition practices to better public access and resource inventories, overhauled multiple use policies, and conservation of whole ecosystems.

Resettlement

The best remembered land reforms in American history involved massive human resettlement. Between 1790 and 1860, the U.S. population went from 4 to 31 million and 167 million acres of public domain were surveyed and sold. The blueprint was the Northwest Ordinance of 1787, which terminated feudal practices of entail, primogeniture, and escheatment in land inheritance; set aside land for veterans of the Revolutionary War; and prohibited slavery north of the Ohio River. It revised, extended, and reaffirmed Thomas Jefferson's vision of agrarian democracy based on a rectangular land survey with land set-asides for free public schooling. The soul of the republic, in this sweeping reform, was something unknown in Europe: an educated, smallholder electorate.

Homesteading and preemption (squatters' rights) acts had multiple origins. Abolitionists such as Garret Smith, laborites such as George Henry Evans, Free-Soilers from Sojourner Truth to Horace Greeley, and numerous followers of the Scotch-English land reformers lobbied the newly founded Republican Party to pass the Homestead Act of 1862. Such resettlement came at the expense of Indian cultures, irreversibly violated by settler encroachment and government efforts to force Jefferson's dream on Indians through the General Allotment Act of 1887.

Two other resettlement reforms are noteworthy. First, the Reclamation Law of 1902 was Washington's response to the Populist revolt of the 1890s. The Reclamation Act sought to adapt homesteading to arid western lands and quell criticisms that prior homesteading laws had done more to enrich railroads than assist homesteaders. The law was strikingly comprehensive. It offered financing for irrigation and drainage, reclamation districts that could possess and then sell land to settlers, and free long-term credit for land improvements. Its provisions included ability-to-pay arrangements for the poor, residency requirements to discourage absenteeism, and cooperatives to handle land transactions and land development. By 1920, close to 2 million acres of land had been reclaimed from desert for settlement. Yet the Reclamation Law ran awry. Ignoring strident public objections, large-scale western interests violated the residency and size restrictions of the law from the 1930s to the 1970s. Today, agribusiness is firmly entrenched in the arid West thanks to massive water subsidies wrung, legally and otherwise, from the Reclamation Law.

Second, the Resettlement Administration of the New Deal era was its response to the abject rural conditions of the Great Depression. Land reform was debated vigorously in 1930s within the Roosevelt administration and in Congress. The debate echoed in religious circles and among private-sector groups as diverse as the Southern Tenants Farmers League, which proposed legislation to nationalize all farmland, and the Nashville Agrarians, who eloquently defended the virtues of private smallholdings. The Great Depression occasioned the return of many Americans, previously drawn to cities, to the land. Under the 1935 Emergency Relief Appropriations Act, Washington established the Resettlement Administration, which, together with the Farm Security Administration, purchased nearly 2 million acres of land to redistribute to tenants and sharecroppers. These acres were clustered in some 200 settlements wherein settlers signed lease-purchase agreements with an option to buy, assisted by long-term, low-interest mortgages. Some 20,000 families benefited from the program.

Redistribution

Is there a place for land reform in contemporary rural America? Consider farmland ownership. Agriculture occupies nearly two-thirds of all private land in the United States (878 million acres) and remains the nation's largest single-land use category. This extraordinary resource is owned by just over 1 percent of the population, and within this 1 percent ownership is highly skewed: 4 percent of private owners own 47 percent of U.S. farmland, whereas the 30 percent with the least land claim 2 percent. Rental farmlands are almost as concentrated: 8 percent of landlords own over 50 percent of such lands. Trends in farm ownership concentration led the U.S. Office of Technology Assessment in 1986 to predict that by the year 2000 as few as 5,000 giant farms could dominate the landscape, leading to economic diseconomies and far-reaching rural community change.

In an era of strident property rights debate, many believe that land reform involving the forced breakup and restructuring of farmland ownership would be un-American. Yet there are many precedents for government condemnation of private property, urban and rural. The Continental Congress confiscated hundreds of square miles of Tory estates in Maine, New Hampshire, New York, Pennsylvania, Massachusetts, Georgia, South Carolina, and Virginia. Similarly, after the Civil War Union forces seized vast plantation holdings along the southeastern coast to redistribute among former slaves. More recently, eminent domain was upheld by the Supreme Court as a peacetime means to reduce public harm attributed to landed oligopolies. In land reforms in both Puerto Rico (1962) and Hawaii (1967), compulsory acquisition and redistribution of vast agricultural estates were defended by the courts. In both cases, former owners were compensated for their losses. The justices ruled that the reduction of gross land concentration yields public benefits such as lower land prices, a less skewed residential housing market, less urban sprawl, and enhanced public tranquillity and welfare.

The use of eminent domain for redistributive reform is not limited to offshore islands and agricultural monopolies. In 1977, heavy flooding in West Virginia prompted the state's Republican governor, John D. Rockefeller IV, to seek land and housing for flood victims by condemning coal company lands. In Mingo County, one of the hardest-hit areas, 64 percent of the real estate was owned by four out-of-state coal companies. In 1988, scarcity of affordable housing for the urban poor triggered use of eminent domain in Boston. The city's mayor and the Boston Redevelopment Authority granted a nonprofit housing organization eminent domain powers to reclaim vacant lots in the deteriorated Dudley Street Triangle. This transfer was upheld by the Massachusetts Superior Court. Once cleared and consolidated, the land transferred to a community land trust, which offered 99-year leases to home buyers and limited equity cooperatives.

Past and Future Policies

Despite legal and historical precedents, many view land reform as a remedy for poverty and foiled development abroad but not at home. The average American disassociates land-ownership from modern wealth and power. U.S. citizens resist regulation and recapture of windfalls from land speculation but plead for government relief when wipeouts beset them. Land reform is accepted in principle, though principally in someone else's backyard.

Two centuries of land reform suggest that the facts do not fit the common view. North America is not exempt from traditional land reforms or immune to new ones. Land concentration continues and will spawn new land reformers. So will unwise land policies. Glaring cases include federal land policy toward American Indians, nineteenth-century relic legislation such as the Mining Act of 1872, and the absence of social impact assessment for numerous federal land policies as required under the National Environmental Policy Act. Surprisingly, the United States lacks a nationwide land-ownership census, thereby obscuring important ownership inequalities. The Farmers Home Administration's loan and assistance programs for socially disadvantaged groups, including minorities and women, should be evaluated, publicized, and expanded.

At the level of states and localities, regulatory reform and innovation are in order. Creative laws and ordinances are needed for affordable housing (for example, density bonuses, inclusion of trailers/manufactured housing, and cluster zoning), as well as for environmental amenities (for example, well head and riparian area protection). Discrimination against property owners as the principal source of school taxes should be evaluated, as should the appraisal and assessment practices that yield property tax inequalities (as in the coal counties of Appalachia). A host of equity issues in land use controls, ranging from fair compensation to exclusionary practices, should be land reform priorities.

The nongovernmental sector has and will continue to sow land reform seeds. The Ford Foundation and several Boston-based foundations shared with Housing and

Urban Development the burden of the Dudley Street land purchases. Yale University offers ten-year subsidies to any of its 9,500 employees electing to reside in New Haven rather than its suburbs. Hundreds of community-sponsored agricultural organizations have sprung up across the continent. These provide quality produce from small local growers on a contract basis, linking land reform bioregionalism and agro-ecology. Churches of all faiths are seeking innovative ways to secure land and housing access for the least fortunate of their members.

Land reform in America is, in the end, a matter of value reform. Land speculation is an example. Jefferson sought a continent of yeoman farmers who would fortify the economy and protect the polity. In contrast, Alexander Hamilton, fearing national insolvency, urged the nation to substitute abundant land for scarce capital. The "monetizing of the land" cast speculation in the public interest, despite its excesses. With the exception of Henry George and the modern land trust movement, few American land reformers have challenged land speculation as threatening the common good. Thus, many today protest the uncompensated "taking" of private property for public purposes, while few favor the public recovery of windfall appreciation to property owners resulting from public policy or outright subsidies ("givings"). Failure to reform such value discrepancies will jeopardize advances in resettlement, reclamation, and redistribution of land in America.

—Charles C. Geisler and Chuck Matthei

See also
Agricultural Law; History, Rural; Land Stewardship; Theology of the Land.

References
Appalachian Land Ownership Task Force. *Who Owns Appalachia?* Lexington: University of Kentucky Press, 1983.
Callies, David C., and Laurence J. Aurbach. "Breaking up Land Oligopolies in the U.S.A." *Habitat International* 11, no. 1 (1987): 57–61.
Geisler, Charles C., and Frank J. Popper, eds. *Land Reform, American Style.* Totowa, NJ: Rowman and Allanheld, 1984.
George, Henry. *The Land Question, Property in Land, the Condition of Labor.* New York: Robert Schalkenbach Foundation, 1881.
Matthei, Chuck. "A 'Land Reform' Movement in the U.S.?" *Social Policy* (Spring 1992): 1–9.
Meyer, P. "Land Rush." *Harper's Magazine* 258 (January 1979): 45–60.
Mitchell, Harry L. *Mean Things Happening in This Land.* Totowa, NJ: Allanheld and Osmun, 1979.
Ostendorf, David. "Who Will Control Rural America?" *Christianity and Crisis* 48 (May 2, 1988): 156–159.
Sakolski, Aaron M. *Land Tenure and Land Taxation in America.* New York: Robert Schalkenback Foundation, 1957.
Zahler, Helene S. *Eastern Workingmen and National Land Policy.* New York: Columbia University Press, 1941.

Land Stewardship

Care of land under the assumption that regeneration of the resource base and maintenance of natural life processes are essential for the production of food and fiber for the support of generations yet to be born. Social justice, environmental stability, and resource renewal are the fundamental elements of land stewardship. An ethical frame of reference that gives meaning to the concept of land stewardship is based on certain value constructs. Without clarity about value assumptions, an ethical construct is without a foundation. Without an ethical orientation about what is considered by a society or a culture to be good, the concept of land stewardship is ambiguous. Values appropriate to the subject of agricultural ethics and the concept of land stewardship are inseparable. Stewardship of the land is the applied side of values and ethical designs. Land stewardship involves human understanding about what is of ultimate value and responsibility. This entry describes how land stewardship has been a challenge for nearly all of recorded history. Examples are offered of contemporary land stewardship issues that require moral judgments, and value foundations are laid for agricultural ethics and a normative construct. Contemporary land stewardship initiatives are listed.

The Challenge
From ancient times until now, humanity has been preoccupied with the question about how to care for the land. For example, at the beginning of the Hebrew scriptures is the mandate to care for the land for the sake of all generations (Genesis 1:28). In the book of Leviticus, the whole society is challenged to provide for the renewal of the land and all creatures that dwell upon it (Leviticus 25:24). Having dominion over the birds of the air and the creatures of the land and sea assumes responsibility to maintain the right order of all relationships within the sphere of one's influence. Thus, in this ancient literature the idea of stewardship involves caring for the land in ways that guarantee that all generations will inherit resources essential for their livelihood. Across the face of the North American continent, similar orientations were expressed within the cultures of indigenous people.

Recorded history reveals that every generation searches, sometimes desperately, for ways to feed and clothe itself without exhausting the resources necessary for the production of these essentials. The history of the rise and fall of civilizations is related directly to this challenge. Given the unprecedented growth in modern times of human populations, which now possess capital- and chemical-intensive agricultural technologies that were unimaginable even a half century ago, the challenge of land stewardship is more demanding than ever before. Since agriculture and the land are inextricably related, the most fundamental question associated with concepts about stewardship is, What is good agriculture? This question introduces the relatively new field of agricultural ethics. Without an adequately formulated agricultural ethic, including the field of environmental ethics, land stewardship is an ambiguous concept.

Ethics

Ethical thought is the body of moral principles and values that are recognized as important to the culture within which it emerges. Values and moral principles shape society's sense of acceptable behavior. Ethical standards provide society with a frame of reference to evaluate what it considers to be good. Agricultural ethics addresses the question of how society ought to understand good relationships between its agricultural methods and the land. The word *ought* suggests the existence of a moral imperative. *Good* points to normative thinking about what might be rather than what is. Agricultural ethics considers the philosophical, social, political, legal, economic, scientific, technological, and aesthetic aspects of agriculture and provides guidelines for the design and evolution of a responsible food system. Agricultural ethical thought is holistic. It works for coherence among means, values, and goals. The subject raises questions about the social and environmental consequences of the design of agriculture.

Examples of Contemporary Issues Requiring Moral Judgment

New agricultural issues of long-ranging impact emerge with every passing year; following are several examples. Soil loss continues to take its irrevocable toll, particularly in areas of high wind and rainfall in association with annual cropping systems. The loss is in spite of new efforts in minimum and no-till agriculture. The decline of plant and animal species resulting in weakened biological diversity continues to be experienced, particularly in areas dominated by large-scale monocropping systems that destroy habitat. Contemporary industrialized agriculture is highly dependent on fertilizers derived from a nonrenewable resource base of oil and gas. Since the introduction of petrochemicals into the agricultural system during World War II, toxic residues have accumulated to such an extent that pollution of water resources is now widespread and the normal function of soil microbiology

is altered. Concentrations in livestock production raise questions about animal welfare and the environmental impact of animal waste accumulations. The consolidation of agricultural commodity markets and food-processing industries has contributed in part to the decline in market opportunities for farmers. Biotechnology used to develop and patent animal strains and plant cultivars leaves some producers outside of the marketplace, while at the same time it increases the vulnerability of animals and plants to pathogens and parasitic infestations. Regulatory programs in cropland set-asides and production and price controls associated with every national farm bill are helpful to some and detrimental to others. Growing concentrations of landholdings raise fundamental questions about social justice.

These issues and many more illustrate the importance of reflection about agriculture and land stewardship. Avoiding judgment on these matters is becoming progressively more difficult. In the short run, social, environmental, and resource compromise is a reasonable option. However, when it comes to land stewardship on behalf of future generations, the need for ethical assessment becomes more obvious and urgent.

Value Foundations for Agricultural Ethics

An ethical frame of reference giving greater meaning to the concept of land stewardship is based on certain values. Values give meaning, purpose, coherence, and consistence to life. For example, many people embrace the ideal of a nurturing family as a primary value. The health of the family justifies one's investments in time, energy, and imagination. In contrast, throughout the modern industrialized world the driving value is economic growth. Individuals and nations value financial and physical growth as a primary value. This value has become the foundation block on which much current decision making is based. But economic growth is an inadequate value to sustain the life of the planet and to actualize a regenerative agriculture.

At least three values are essential to creating and maintaining regenerative relationships with the land. First, the health of the land is basic. Everything else depends on this premise. The term *land* means the life support systems of the biosphere itself (i.e., atmosphere, oceans, freshwater, flora, fauna, and soil). It is difficult to deny the primacy of the value of the health of the land. Although this value is obvious, Western culture has failed thus far to embrace it fully. When the fisheries of the seas are depleted, the consequences are obvious. But when it comes to soil loss over a period of one or two centuries as a consequence of wind and water erosion, salinization, alkalization, and water logging associated with irrigation in arid lands, or the loss of biological diversity associated with monoculture systems such as corn or soybeans, social understandings about the threat to the health of the land are, at best, ambiguous. Additionally, society is only beginning to comprehend the threat to the health of the land of global warming and the thinning of the ozone shield.

Second, the value concept of the welfare of future generations has come into play only recently in contemporary moral thought. The modern industrial world assumes that life becomes progressively better. Western culture accepts the idea that material progress at almost any cost is inherently good. Human populations double every 30 years, and increased appetites for resources are more devastating in their impact upon natural ecosystems. Thus, the need to overcome the popular definition of progress is urgent. Valuing the welfare of future generations is the basis for the ethical principle of sustainability. This is "development that meets the needs of the present without compromising the ability of future generations to meet their needs" (World Commission on Environment and Development 1987, 47). It is biological resource regeneration that allows for the maintenance of all ecological functions and thereby ensures the persistence of biological diversity.

Third, the value of the quality of relationships in human life can be considered a foundation block in ethical thinking. Quality relationships are based on the freedom to choose to be responsible for the care of people and land. Responsible human relationships with the land must be informed by sound ecological understandings of the workings of the fundamental processes of life within the biosphere. Sustainable agriculture requires regenerative management of the microbiotic communities that together compose the natural landscape. The goal is to enhance the resources essential for food and fiber production. Without enhancement of relationships within the human community, sustaining quality relationships with the land becomes difficult to envision. Quality relationships within human community and stewardship of the land itself are inseparable.

Toward a Normative Construct

If an agricultural ethic incorporates the values of the health of the land, the welfare of human community, and future generations, then "good agriculture" can be defined as an agriculture that provides food and fiber to sustain human life, enhance health, and maintain the integrity and stability of the natural system with which it interacts. Such an agriculture preserves species of plant and animal life, assures the health and fertility of the land for future generations, enhances personal and community relationships, and designs agricultural technologies for the regenerative production of food and fiber. The goals of such a normative agriculture are to (1) foster stability of the natural environment, (2) strengthen social and economic health and security of the rural community, and (3) enhance fertility of the land from generation to generation. Leopold (1970, 262) aptly explained: "A thing is right when it tends to preserve the integrity, stability, and beauty of the biotic community. It is wrong when it tends otherwise."

With such normative constructs in place, new frontiers in Western ethical thought come into view. Agricultural ethics points to the need to integrate moral thought and human values with the biological and physical principles and processes of biospheric life. Contrary to the general belief of Western people of recent centuries, humanity does not stand apart from nature. Progressively, moral thought is being defined, in part, by nature's wisdom.

An ethical framework involving normative thinking about values, purposes, goals, and long-range time horizons and being influenced by ecological understandings about how life within the biosphere is perpetuated provides content to the concept of land stewardship. Such stewardship involves human understandings about what is of ultimate value and responsibility. Land stewardship assumes regeneration of the resource base and maintenance of natural life processes that are essential to producing food and fiber for the support of the generations yet to be born. Social justice, environmental stability, and resource renewal are inseparable elements that are the foundation stones of the land stewardship concept.

Contemporary Initiatives

There are many organizations in the United States, from the local to the national level, that address the challenge of stewardship of the land. For example, organizations such as the Center for Rural Affairs (Walthill, Nebraska) or the Land Stewardship Project (White Bear Lake, Minnesota) advocate a greater degree of stewardship in American agriculture. They offer assistance to programs and projects in their regions to demonstrate new approaches in the quest for regenerative food systems. The Henry A.

Wallace Institute for Alternative Agriculture (Greenbelt, Maryland) promotes land stewardship in state and national farm policy. Other organizations aid the development of sustainable production and the marketing of organically grown food. Research in sustainable or regenerative agriculture is increasing at universities and land-grant colleges of agriculture. Of outstanding research significance is the work in herbaceous perennial polycultures of the Land Institute (Salina, Kansas). With regard to the issues associated with the value of human community, the Department of Philosophy of the University of Florida (Gainesville) has established a strong reputation in the field of agriculture and human values. Support for and practices in land stewardship continue to gain momentum in response to contemporary moral issues associated with agriculture.

—*C. Dean Freudenberger*

See also

Agriculture, Alternative; Animal Rights/Welfare; Conservation, Soil; Conservation, Water; Ethics; Land Reform; Policy, Agricultural; Policy, Environmental; Theology of the Land; Values of Residents.

References

Agriculture and Human Values (1984–present).

American Journal of Alternative Agriculture (1986–present).

Bailey, Liberty Hyde. *The Holy Earth*. New York: Christian Rural Fellowship, 1915, reprinted 1988. Columbus, OH: National United Methodist Rural Fellowship.

Berry, Wendell. *The Unsettling of America: Culture and Agriculture*. San Francisco: Sierra Club Books, 1977.

Bird, Elizabeth Ann R., Gordon L. Bultena, and John C. Gardner, eds. *Planting the Future: Developing an Agriculture That Sustains Land and Community*. Ames: Iowa State University Press, 1995.

Blatz, Charles V., ed. *Ethics and Agriculture: An Anthology on Current Issues in World Context*. Moscow: University of Idaho Press, 1991.

Freudenberger, C. Dean. *Food for Tomorrow?* Minneapolis: Augsburg, 1984.

Hartel, Peter G., Kathryn Paxton George, and James Vorst, eds. 1994. *Agricultural Ethics: Issues for the Twenty-First Century*. ASA Special Publication No. 57. Madison, WI: Soil Science Society of America, American Society of Agronomy, and Crop Science Society of America.

Hillel, Daniel. 1991. *Out of the Earth: Civilization and the Life of the Soil*. Berkeley and Los Angeles: University of California Press.

Leopold, Aldo. *A Sand County Almanac: With Essays on Conservation from Round River*. Reprint, New York: Ballantine Books, 1970.

Lowdermilk, W. C. *Conquest of the Land through 7000 Years*. Agriculture Information Bulletin No. 99. Washington, DC: U.S. Government Printing Office, 1975.

Lyle, John Tillman. *Regenerative Design for Sustainable Development*. New York: John Wiley and Sons, 1994.

Ponting, C. *A Green History of the World: The Environment and the Collapse of Great Civilizations*. New York: St. Martin's Press, 1991.

Soule, Judith D., and Jon K. Piper. *Farming in Nature's Image: An Ecological Approach to Agriculture*. Washington, DC: Island Press, 1992.

World Commission on Environment and Development. *Our Common Future*. New York: Oxford University Press, 1987.

Land Values

Estimates of the monetary units, usually per acre, at which land would change hands if placed on an open market. Land in farms is one of the most important categories of rural lands. Its value varies widely and is difficult to measure. Farm real estate values in the United States moved up sharply in the years prior to World War I, but declined until the Great Depression, when a long upward trend began. Land values dropped sharply in the early 1980s. The recovery that began in 1987 was still under way in the mid-1990s, but land values in many areas were still below record levels. Farmland values vary from a few hundred dollars per acre or less to thousands of dollars. The market value of land is difficult to determine and gave rise to the rural appraisal profession. This entry describes current trends in farm real estate values and cash rent values. Characteristics of the land market are examined, and the role of rural land appraisers is discussed.

Rural land may be classified by use for recreation, farming, and forestry. A fourth class is wasteland, which may have little economic use unless the potential exists for extraction of minerals or petroleum. The primary focus of this entry is on the value of farm real estate. This category of land consists of several subclasses: cropland, pasture or rangeland, and woodland. Farm buildings also are included in the estimates of the value of farm real estate published by the U.S. Bureau of the Census and the U.S. Department of Agriculture (USDA). Census estimates are made for counties, states, and the United States; those of the USDA are for states and the United States.

Trends

The census estimate of the value of U.S. farmland and buildings in 1850 was $11 per acre and by 1910 had increased 3.5 times to nearly $40, an annual compound rate of a little over 2 percent. Based on USDA estimates, U.S. farm real estate (land and buildings) values per acre nearly doubled from 1912 to 1920, then declined more than 50 percent by 1933 at the depths of the Great Depression. From this low point, U.S. farm real estate values began an upward trend that lasted nearly a half century. The per acre value in the peak year of 1981 was nearly 28 times the level in 1933, an annual compound rate of over 7 percent. Then came a reversal that ended in 1987, with farm real estate values 27 percent below 1981 levels. A gradual increase occurred from 1991 to 1995.

Mainline agricultural areas followed in a general way these historical movements in farm real estate values, but some states and areas went in opposite directions. For example, many northeastern states experienced continued gains in farm real estate values in the early to mid-1980s, whereas Iowa values declined by around 60 percent from 1981 to 1987. With 1977 = 100, the geographic diversity in movement of farm real estate values is seen in the following table.

The sharp drop in farm real estate values from 1981 to 1987 coincided with a period of great financial stress for many farmers in the Midwest. Interest rates on farm loans soared in the early 1980s and grain exports fell, as did farm incomes. Many farmers could not make the payments on loans they had taken out to buy land. In many cases, land values fell below the amount of debt against the land. Farmers and other owners lost the land, and lenders were unable to recover their loans. Not since the post–World War I period had so many midwestern farmers suffered such financial stress. Those hardest hit in both periods had borrowed to buy land during a period of double-digit inflation that ended in 1983; then, farm earnings declined and land values plummeted.

Per Acre Values

In absolute terms, the per acre value of U.S. farm real estate was $744 in 1994 (excluding Alaska and Hawaii). Of this amount, building values made up nearly 20 percent, leaving about $600 per acre as the value of the farmland. There is a tremendous variation in land values, even on a statewide basis. The average value of farm real estate in several Northeast states in the mid-1990s was $5,000 or more per acre, in contrast to an average of around $400 per acre in the Dakotas and under $200 per acre in Wyoming. Even within a given geographic area, variations exist. Average tillable land in central Indiana in 1995 was estimated to have a market value of around $1,700 per acre; in southeast Indiana that figure was only about $1,000. Even farms that are close together may have different values.

What accounts for differences in farmland values? First, any economic or marketable good must be both scarce and useful. Farmland is scarce because there is a limited quantity and because a relatively small amount is on the market at any given time. Farmland is useful when combined with labor, capital, and management to produce

Index of Average per Acre Value (in Dollars) of Farm Real Estate, by State and Region, 1987 and 1994 (1977 = 100)

	1987	1994
Northeast	168	217
Maine	214	261
New Hampshire	265	341
Vermont	209	237
Massachusetts	265	351
Rhode Island	186	293
Connecticut	200	263
New York	164	213
New Jersey	169	219
Pennsylvania	155	192
Delaware	134	211
Maryland	148	212
Lake	106	146
Michigan	119	156
Wisconsin	130	163
Minnesota	87	134
Corn Belt	82	117
Ohio	100	126
Indiana	89	124
Illinois	79	113
Iowa	62	105
Missouri	110	139
Northern Plains	102	153
North Dakota	111	149
South Dakota	123	200
Nebraska	95	151
Kansas	94	135
Appalachia	154	179
Virginia	165	191
West Virginia	147	166
North Carolina	166	178
Kentucky	142	185
Tennessee	151	171
Southeast	166	205
South Carolina	132	154
Georgia	153	169
Florida	186	256
Alabama	165	202
Delta	139	156
Mississippi	149	177
Arkansas	134	148
Louisiana	138	146
Southern Plains	167	158
Oklahoma	121	136
Texas	183	165
Mountain	148	187
Montana	127	192
Idaho	122	173
Wyoming	143	154
Colorado	144	168
New Mexico	154	238
Arizona	217	228
Utah	166	187
Nevada	214	204
Pacific	182	209
Washington	141	168
Oregon	158	216
California	205	227
48 states	126	157

Source: U.S. Department of Agriculture, Economic Research Service, *RTD Updates.* Washington, DC: U.S. Department of Agriculture, Economic Research Service, April 1994.

items such as crops, forage, fruit, and nuts. Second, land in some locations may be expected to become more useful in the future for home sites, shopping centers, and other nonagricultural uses. Third, farmland, like many other tangible goods, is generally thought to be a good inflation hedge and even may increase in value more than the inflation rate. Fourth, especially among farm people, there often is a personal satisfaction in owning land. The market value of farmland may be thought of as the sum of all the expected future returns discounted to the present. Of all these expected returns, land rent for agricultural use is the easiest to estimate.

Contract cash rent is the amount paid, usually annually, by the farm operator for the use of land. Property taxes and other landownership costs are subtracted to get net rent. Economic rent is the amount left after all production costs, including a payment for nonhired labor, have been subtracted from gross returns. Averaged over several years, these two measures of land rent should be similar; however, in any given year they may differ substantially because net cash rent is determined ahead of production, whereas economic rent is based on the value of production.

Gross cash rent per acre for cropland is reported annually by the USDA for most states and also is expressed as a percent of the land value per acre. Rents of around $25 per acre in 1994 were reported as averages in South Carolina, Oklahoma, and Montana, in contrast to around $110 in Illinois and Iowa. As a percent of land value, most state averages in the Corn Belt, plus Mississippi, Arkansas, Louisiana, Kentucky, Tennessee, Wyoming, and Washington, fell in the range of 5.5 to 7.0 percent. This rent-to-value percentage was under 4.0 percent in most states in the Northeast and Southeast. Some state averages were 8.0 percent or more. Allowance of 1.5 percentage points for taxes, insurance, and land maintenance costs would result in a net rental return of 4.0 to 5.5 percent in much of the heartland of the country and under 3.0 percent in much of the East. These relatively low rates of return indicate that landowners are paying for returns in addition to cash rent at current levels. This might be the expectation of higher future rents, but more likely it is the expectation of increasing land values, perhaps from inflation and increasing demand for nonagricultural uses of land.

The Market

Major characteristics of an efficient or well-functioning market include (1) many buyers and sellers, (2) grading standards that assure product uniformity, and (3) well-informed buyers and sellers. The land market falls far short of fully meeting these criteria. Buyers and sellers of land often are few. Buyer and seller may agree on the price, and other potential buyers or sellers may not even know about the sale until after the fact. In some areas, public land auctions are common and usually result in bringing together a number of potential buyers.

Land has so many characteristics affecting its value that establishing grades is extremely difficult. Farmland is sometimes classified by land productivity. Animal carrying capacity of rangeland and likely crop yields can be used to rate or classify land. In the Corn Belt, one often hears comments like, "This is 125 bushel land," meaning that likely long-term yields would average 125 bushels of corn per acre. Classification or grading based on productivity is useful especially when combined with sale price information in locations where nonfarm influences on value are somewhat uniform.

Both buyers and sellers tend to have limited information on the sale price of land. Such information is difficult to obtain. Land that changed owners can be identified from public records, and in some states the transaction price is on public record. Adjustments then must be made for differences between tracts of land in order to have a valid comparison of one tract with another. Information from the USDA, several state universities, and some other sources serve to give a general idea of land values and is useful in measuring changes over time in land values. In addition to land value and cash rent estimates, the USDA publishes information on acres per sale of farmland, characteristics of buyers and sellers, use before and after sale, and financing of land.

Rural Appraisal

Appraisers who specialize in rural land or farmland are available in most parts of the country. They collect information on market prices and characteristics of the property that are necessary for classification and analysis. This information provides the basis for estimates of the value of the subject farm, the farm being appraised. Adjustments are made in the prices to account for differences between comparable farms and the subject farm. Adjustments may be made for differences in date of sale, location, productive capacity, improvements, and farm size. The median value of several comparables then may be used as an estimate of the value of the subject property. This procedure is known as the sales comparison or market data approach to value.

Appraisers also use the income approach to value. An estimate is made of the return to farmland under typical management, divided by a capitalization rate, to arrive at an estimate of value. The capitalization rate represents the net return to investment in land and may be determined by analysis of farm operating records or land sales and rental information. For example, a 1994 study at Purdue University indicated that cash rent on average quality central Indiana cropland was 6.3 percent of the estimated land value (Atkinson and Cook 1994). If taxes and other annual landownership costs were 1.3 percent, the net return would be 5.0 percent. Capitalization of land rent of $110 per acre at 5.0 percent indicates a land value of $2,200 per acre ($110 ÷ .05).

Many rural appraisers are members of the American Society of Farm Managers and Rural Appraisers. Based on experience and completion of a rigorous plan of study, the designation Accredited Rural Appraiser is awarded. Other professional appraisal organizations tend to place more emphasis on commercial and residential appraisal.

—*Julian H. Atkinson*

See also
Agricultural and Resource Economics; Farm Management.
References
Atkinson, Julian H., and Kim Cook. "Land Values Jump by 10 Percent." *Purdue Agricultural Economics Report* (August 1994): 1–5.

Duffy, Michael D., and Chris Gingrich. *1994 Iowa Land Value Survey*. FM-1825. Ames: Iowa State University Extension, 1994.

Erickson, Duane E., and John T. Scott Jr., eds. *Farm Real Estate: Rights, Trends, Values, Methods of Sale, Finances, Appraisal, Investments*. NCR No. 51. Urbana-Champaign: University of Illinois, Cooperative Extension Service, 1990.

Hexem, Roger, ed. *Agricultural Resources: Agricultural Land Values and Markets: Situation and Outlook Report*. AR-31. Washington, DC: U.S. Department of Agriculture, Economic Research Service, June 1993.

Prevatt, J. Walter. *1994 Alabama Farmland Values and Cash Rents*. AECLV-94. Auburn, AL: Auburn University, July 1994.

Reynolds, John, and Stacey R. Linn. 1994 *Florida Agricultural Land Values Increase in the North and Decrease in the South*. Florida Food and Resource Economics Series, No. 119. Gainesville: University of Florida, Department of Food and Resource Economics Institute of Food and Agricultural Sciences, 1994.

Suter, Robert C. *The Appraisal of Farm Real Estate*. 3d ed. Lafayette, IN: Retus, 1992.

U.S. Department of Agriculture. Economic Research Service. "Agricultural Land Values." Pp. 1–8 in *RTD Updates*, no. 2. Washington, DC: U.S. Department of Agriculture, Economic Research Service, April 1994.

Land-Grant Institutions, 1862

Colleges and universities created by federal grants of land to each state in 1862 to provide education to a broad range of U.S. citizens primarily involved in agricultural and industrial work. This entry discusses the circumstances that gave rise to the establishment of land-grant institutions through the 1862 Morrill legislation and the subsequent development of research and extension programs through the Hatch Act of 1887 and the Smith-Lever Act of 1914. Past, present, and future challenges facing the land-grant institutions, as a result of the restructuring of agriculture and rural communities, are reviewed.

Creation of the Institutions

The Morrill-Wade Act of 1862 provided for the creation of land-grant colleges that would offer an education to a broad range of U.S. citizens primarily involved in agricultural and industrial work. It was not until 1890, however, with the passage of the second land-grant act, the Morrill-McComas Act, that provisions were made for this kind of education for African Americans through so-called separate but equal institutions. The designation *land grant* reflected the funding source that supported the establishment and development of land-grant colleges. The federal government provided that 30,000 acres of land (or the equivalent in land scrip) be allocated to each senator and representative in Congress. The land could be sold and the proceeds invested with the interest used to establish the colleges. Table 1 lists the institutions established under the Morrill Act of 1862, the year each institution was accepted by the state, the land acres received, and the scrip arrangements. Table 2 is a current list of the land-grant institutions and their locations.

The establishment of land-grant colleges reflected the convergence of a number of forces that brought about a true revolution in agriculture. One force was the push by educational reformers to ensure a relevant, affordable education for farmers' and laborers' children, who were virtually excluded from the more traditional, higher education institutions, which focused on providing instruction in the classics and arts to the urban elite. For the first time in history, states, through the 1862 Morrill legislation, were required to teach agriculture, mechanic arts, and military tactics. Another force was the desire, primarily by agricultural journalists and wealthy farmers, to apply science to agriculture. Their blossoming romance with science intersected with the national interest in having agriculture play a key role in spurring national growth and international trade.

Cotton was one of the crops focused on by the cooperative extension services developed at land-grant universities.

Early Struggles and Challenges

The ascending legitimacy of science and the pressing need for agriculture's contribution to national growth began to reverse the tide of public sentiment against the establishment of land-grant colleges. Traditional farmers, who were viewed as people with problems in need of the special attention of trained agricultural professionals, looked upon the colleges suspiciously and resisted their mission. Land-grant colleges struggled to define themselves for many years before consolidating their legitimacy. Many were considered no more than farm schools where students spent hours laboring with crops and animals for the sufficiency of the institution. Many of the concerns about the development of science within the land-grant colleges reflected broader national concerns about what the goal of science should be within a rapidly growing economy. Scientists returning from Germany and trained primarily in soil chemistry fought to keep the focus on basic research concerns, believing that this gave their research the air of legitimacy that more applied activities would not. Increasing pressures from client groups for research to fight crop pests and increase yields pressured many scientists into responding to concerns for immediate or at least shorter-term results. Research focused more on testing fertilizer and feed; analyzing seed, food, and drug products; and organizing farms that would model the best current cultivation methods. Questions about how to make agriculture scientific and how to train students to work as scientists preoccupied land-grant administrators and instructors for many years. Funded for the most part by the state through interest from the money generated by grants of land, many colleges struggled to finance buildings, equipment, and salaries.

The Creation of Agricultural Experiment Stations

The spiraling interest among commodity-specific market-oriented farmers, bankers, and people in business to put agriculture on a strong scientific footing culminated with the establishment of state agricultural experiment stations (SAESs) through the passage of the Hatch-George Act in 1887. The Hatch Act provided that applied research be conducted to improve agricultural production within each state. The legislation set precedent by providing support for applied agricultural research on a national scale. The Hatch Act distinguished itself from earlier legislation by providing formula funding; each state received annual allotments of money directly from the federal government, not through state treasuries dependent on interest from land-grant sales. The legislation specified that the SAESs be housed and administered within the land-grant college in each state. This gave the struggling institutions much-needed resources, a definitive mission, and the promise of full-fledged legitimacy.

By the turn of the century, agricultural science was coming into its own. Hatch money provided the foundational support that allowed land-grant programs outside of agricultural research to mature and science and liberal arts educations to be offered to an increasing number of students. Natural scientists in fields such as chemistry and biochemistry took positions within the experiment station and began the melding process that resulted in the creation of distinctive agriculture science disciplines such as agronomy, animal science, and plant pathology. The USDA, which also had been created in 1862, played a key role in administering Hatch programs and subsequent programs designed to spur agricultural research, extension, and instruction. Between 1889 and 1905, the number of workers in the SAESs more than doubled, with a larger complement of scientists better trained than pioneer scientists 20 years earlier.

The new scientists viewed themselves as professionals and as practitioners of science more than as attendants to farmers. The momentum generated by conflicts between those advocating original research through the SAESs and those wanting to generate practical information shaped compromises and accommodations that ultimately led to the professionalization of agricultural scientists. Central to this development was the role of the research entrepreneur, who in negotiating to minimize the explosion of demands that the experiment station scientist faced for information, speeches, and meetings, brokered the kinds of alliances with members of agricultural, political, and business communities that assured support for research. This helped to build a recognized base of knowledge and to satisfy farmers with immediate, useful findings.

With the passage of the Adams Act in 1906, a heightened commitment was made to original research in agriculture by the federal government. The act made it more difficult to use research funds for teachers' salaries, helping to free research scientists from teaching and exten-

sion obligations that often undermined the strength and value of their research. In spite of these developments, SAES scientists continued to be overwhelmed with demands for extension activities.

The Creation of the Cooperative Extension Program

Demonstration farms had been the ongoing response of experiment stations to public demands for practical information. However, the use of Hatch funds for this activity was expressly restricted in the Office of Experiment Station rulings in 1904 and 1909. Because farmer's institutes, another form of extension activity, brought about ever-increasing numbers of clients with increasing demands for sophisticated information from the SAES scientist, the federal government passed the Smith-Lever Act in 1914. The act provided support for a national extension system for rural adult vocational education through the deployment of specially trained agents who disseminated scientific knowledge to farmers and freed state researchers from their extension responsibilities.

The extension concept was originally conceived by Booker T. Washington and George Washington Carver, at the Tuskegee Institute, who developed the idea of a movable school to reach out to farmers and mobilized it in the form of the Jesup Agricultural Wagon for Better Farming. Seaman Knapp, professor of agriculture at Iowa State College, learned of the Tuskegee outreach effort and employed the concept to help cotton growers cope with the boll weevil invasion. He drew upon these experiences to provide leadership for the development of the cooperative extension network in 1914. In a notable departure from funding appropriations under the Hatch and Adams Acts, the Smith-Lever legislation required each state to match every dollar over an initial $10,000 for the annual federal grant. With the reorganization of the USDA in the mid-1990s, the Cooperative Extension Service was renamed the Cooperative State Research, Education, and Extension Service.

Strengthening Instruction

With research and extension missions clearly established within the White land-grant institutions, the more complete endowment and maintenance of the colleges provided for by the second Morrill Act of 1890 laid the foundation to bolster instructional programs. Until this time, only marginal support for teaching had been provided, especially within the southern states, where public education generally was weakly supported. The Morrill-McComas Act mandated that southern states designate

Land-Grant Institutions Established under the Morrill Act of 1862

Institution	Year Accepted by State	Land Acres Received	Acres Received in Scrip	Sale Price for Land or Scrip
Auburn University	1867	—	240,000	$216,000
University of Alaska	1929	336,000	—	—
University of Arizona	1910	150,000	—	—
University of Arkansas	1864	—	150,000	135,000
University of California	1866	150,000	—	732,233
Colorado State University	1879	91,600	—	185,956
University of Connecticut	1862	—	180,000	135,000
University of Delaware	1867	—	90,000	83,000
University of Florida	1870	—	90,000	80,000
University of Georgia	1866	—	270,000	242,202
University of Hawaii	1907*	—	—	—
University of Idaho	1890	90,000	—	129,615
University of Illinois	1867	—	480,000	648,442
Purdue University	1865	—	390,000	212,238
Iowa State University	1862	240,000	—	686,817
Kansas State University	1863	97,682	—	491,746
University of Kentucky	1863	—	330,000	164,746
Louisiana State University	1869	—	210,000	182,630
University of Maine	1863	—	210,000	116,359
University of Maryland	1864	—	210,000	112,504
University of Massachusetts	1863	—	360,000	236,287
Mass. Institute of Technology	1863	—	—	—
Michigan State University	1863	240,000	—	991,673
University of Minnesota	1863	120,000	—	579,430
Mississippi State University	1866	—	210,000	188,028
University of Missouri	1863	330,000	—	363,441
Montana State University	1889	140,000	—	533,148
University of Nebraska	1867	90,800	—	560,072
University of Nevada	1866	90,000	—	107,363
University of New Hampshire	1863	—	150,000	80,000
Rutgers, the State University	1863	—	210,000	115,945
New Mexico State University	1898	250,000	—	—
Cornell University	1863	—	990,000	5,460,000
North Carolina State University	1866	—	270,000	135,000
North Dakota State University	1889	130,000	—	455,924
Ohio State University	1864	—	630,000	340,906
Oklahoma State University	1890	350,000	—	835,637
Oregon State University	1868	90,000	—	202,133
Pennsylvania State University	1863	—	780,000	439,186
University of Puerto Rico	1908*	—	—	—
University of Rhode Island	1863	—	120,000	50,000
Clemson University	1868	—	180,000	130,500
South Dakota State University	1889	160,000	—	128,804
University of Tennessee	1868	—	300,000	271,875
Texas A&M University	1866	—	180,000	174,000
Utah State University	1888	200,000	—	194,136
University of Vermont	1862	—	150,000	122,626
Virginia Polytechnic Institute	1870	—	300,000	285,000
Washington State University	1889	90,000	—	247,608
West Virginia University	1863	—	150,000	90,000
University of Wisconsin	1863	240,000	—	303,594
University of Wyoming	1889	90,000	—	73,355
Total		3,766,082	7,830,000	18,250,408

*Land-grant institution not created under the Morrill Act of 1862 but entitled to participate in a fund created for agricultural colleges by the Second Morrill Act (1890) and the Nelson Amendment (1907).

Source: Brunner, Henry S. *Land-grant Colleges and Universities: 1862–1962.* Bulletin 1962, no. 13. Washington, DC: Government Printing Office, 1962.

Current 1862 Land-Grant Colleges and Universities

State	City	Institution
Alabama	Auburn	Auburn University
Alaska	Fairbanks	University of Alaska, Fairbanks
Arizona	Tucson	University of Arizona
Arkansas	Fayetteville	University of Arkansas, Fayetteville
California	Berkeley	University of California, Berkeley
California	Davis	University of California, Davis
California	Irvine	University of California, Irvine
California	Los Angeles	University of California, Los Angeles
California	Riverside	University of California, Riverside
California	San Diego	University of California, San Diego
California	Santa Barbara	University of California, Santa Barbara
Colorado	Fort Collins	Colorado State University
Connecticut	New Haven	Connecticut Agricultural Experiment Station
Connecticut	Storrs	University of Connecticut
Delaware	Newark	University of Delaware
District of Columbia	Washington	University of the District of Columbia
Florida	Gainesville	University of Florida
Georgia	Athens	University of Georgia
Guam	Agana	University of Guam
Hawaii	Honolulu	University of Hawaii, Manoa
Idaho	Moscow	University of Idaho
Illinois	Chicago	University of Illinois, Chicago
Illinois	Urbana	University of Illinois, Urbana-Champaign
Indiana	West Lafayette	Purdue University
Iowa	Ames	Iowa State University of Science Technology
Kansas	Manhattan	Kansas State University
Kentucky	Lexington	University of Kentucky
Louisiana	Baton Rouge	Louisiana State University
Maine	Orono	University of Maine
Maryland	College Park	University of Maryland, College Park
Massachusetts	Cambridge	Massachusetts Institute of Technology
Massachusetts	Amherst	University of Massachusetts, Amherst
Michigan	East Lansing	Michigan State University
Minnesota	Minneapolis	University of Minnesota
Mississippi	Mississippi State	Mississippi State University
Missouri	Columbia	University of Missouri, Columbia
Missouri	Rolla	University of Missouri, Rolla
Montana	Bozeman	Montana State University
Nebraska	Lincoln	University of Nebraska, Lincoln
Nevada	Reno	University of Nevada, Reno
New Hampshire	Durham	University of New Hampshire
New Jersey	New Brunswick	Rutgers, State University of New Jersey
New Mexico	State College	New Mexico State University
New York	Ithaca	Cornell University
North Carolina	Raleigh	North Carolina State University
North Dakota	Fargo	North Dakota State University
Ohio	Columbus	Ohio State University
Oklahoma	Stillwater	Oklahoma State University
Oregon	Corvallis	Oregon State University
Puerto Rico	San Juan	University of Puerto Rico, Rio Piedras
Rhode Island	Kingston	University of Rhode Island
South Carolina	Clemson	Clemson University
South Dakota	Brookings	South Dakota State University
Tennessee	Knoxville	University of Tennessee, Knoxville
Texas	College Station	Texas A&M University
Utah	Logan	Utah State University
Vermont	Burlington	University of Vermont
Virgin Islands	St. Thomas	University of the Virgin Islands
Virginia	Blacksburg	Virginia-Polytechnic Institute and State University
Washington	Pullman	Washington State University
West Virginia	Morgantown	West Virginia University
Wisconsin	Madison	University of Wisconsin, Madison
Wisconsin	Milwaukee	University of Wisconsin, Milwaukee
Wyoming	Laramie	University of Wyoming

Source: Brunner, Henry S. *Land-grant Colleges and Universities: 1862– 1962.* Bulletin 1962, no. 13. Washington, DC: Government Printing Office, 1962.

separate but equal institutions for African Americans to receive Morrill-McComas funds. It provided for the strengthening of instruction in the industrial and mechanic arts.

The Nelson Amendment of 1907 doubled the 1890 appropriations for teaching so that by 1912 each state received a permanent allotment totaling $50,000 annually. Because of the small number of teachers prepared to provide agricultural instruction within secondary schools, the Nelson Amendment directed that a portion of the funds be used to train teachers in the agricultural and mechanical arts. The Smith-Hughes Act of 1917 redoubled the commitment to teacher training programs at the land-grant colleges and to industrial and vocational education.

The Challenge of Responding to Changing Needs

From the turn of the century until the early 1920s, the land-grant colleges and the SAESs in particular enjoyed growing popular support, primarily because they responded to broader policy perceptions that remedying low agricultural production should be their main priority. However, beginning in 1920 problems with overproduction, price deflation, and the social consequences of changes in the structure of agriculture challenged the White land-grant institutions to reconsider their priorities. The federal government acknowledged and supported the key role of these institutions in helping to address these problems and passed the Purnell Act of 1925. It provided funds for SAES research in agricultural economics, rural sociology, and home economics. The social sciences received a cool reception within an institutional context where scientists were vying for legitimacy within the broader scientific community. The reordering of research priorities within rural sociology, for example, reflected institutional constraints. Major contributions by rural sociology during its early years within the experiment stations included community studies that documented the consequences of rural restructuring and how it disadvantaged particular groups and classes. In later years, these endeavors were scaled down as social scientists increasingly were called upon to conduct census counts and surveys, activities considered more scientific.

Since the passage of the first Morrill Act in 1862, the United States has been transformed into a country of urban dwellers. There has been a dramatic decline in the number of farmers, whereas farm size and corporate ownership have increased substantially. White land-grant institution programs, especially given the direction and momentum of experiment station research, have con-

tributed to the phenomenal changes that have taken place in rural America. Society as a whole has benefited from innovations in the use of chemicals, machines, and cultural practices that have increased production and controlled animal and crop pests, resulting in cheap, abundant food for domestic consumption and export. However, as a number of observers inside and outside of the White land-grant system assess, the costs of achieving great productivity have been high for marginal farmers, agricultural workers, many rural communities, and the environment. Observers note that the diminishing farmer client base and decreased support from federal sources have heightened the rate at which industry-university alliances have underwritten support for certain kinds of research often at odds with the needs and concerns of the public generally. Although the land-grant system appears to be buffeted by a variety of contradictory forces, hopeful observers believe that opportunities exist for land-grant institutions to optimize their complex, decentralized system; forge creative alliances with new agenda groups; and reframe agendas with older constituencies.

—*Rosalind P. Harris*

See also
Careers in Agriculture; Cooperative State Research, Education, and Extension Service; Education, Adult; History, Agricultural; Land-Grant Institutions, 1890; Rural Sociology.
References
Berry, Wendell. *The Unsettling of America: Culture and Agriculture.* San Francisco: Sierra Club Books, 1977.
Busch, Lawrence, and William B. Lacy. *Science, Agriculture, and the Politics of Research.* Boulder, CO: Westview Press, 1983.
———, eds. *The Agricultural Scientific Enterprise: A System in Transition.* Boulder, CO: Westview Press, 1986.
Convention of Friends of Agriculture Education (Chicago 1871). *An Early View of the Land-Grant Colleges.* Chicago: University of Illinois Press, 1967.
Danbom, David B. *The Resisted Revolution: Urban America and the Industrialization of Agriculture, 1900–1930.* Ames: Iowa State University Press, 1979.
Hadwiger, Don F. *The Politics of Agricultural Research.* Lincoln: University of Nebraska Press, 1982.
Kerr, Norwood A. *The Legacy: A Centennial History of the State Agricultural Experiment Stations, 1887–1987.* Columbia: University of Missouri, Missouri Agricultural Experiment Station, 1987.
Marcus, Alan I. *Agricultural Science and the Quest for Legitimacy: Farmers, Agricultural Colleges, and Experiment Stations, 1870–1890.* Ames: Iowa State University Press, 1985.
Pace, David W. *The Land Grant System: A Brief History of a Uniquely American Institution.* Lexington: University of Kentucky, Gaines Center for the Humanities, 1994, pp. 78–79.
Rosenberg, Charles E. *No Other Gods: On Science and American Social Thought.* Baltimore, MD: Johns Hopkins University Press, 1978.
Works, George, and Barton Morgan. *The Land-Grant Colleges.* Washington, DC: U.S. Government Printing Office, 1939.

Land-Grant Institutions, 1890

Colleges and universities created by federal grants of land to selected states in 1890 to provide education, primarily to African Americans involved in agricultural and industrial work. This entry provides a historical overview on the development of research, teaching, and extension programs at historically Black land-grant institutions. The entry discusses the historical forces that have shaped disadvantages for these institutions, as well as the distinctive current and future roles they have in rural America.

Funding Inequities

Congress passed the second Land-Grant College Act in 1890, which brought into existence segregated land-grant institutions for African Americans within the 16 southern and border states practicing both de jure and de facto racial discrimination. The table lists Black land-grant institutions and their dates of establishment. Although the 1890 institutions were established in principle to accomplish the tripartite mission of research, teaching, and extension that the 1862 historically White land-grant institutions had been established to accomplish, the system of racial discrimination that prevailed in the South after Reconstruction deprived them of the resources necessary to do so. This deprivation resulted in a very different trajectory of development for these institutions. For instance, federal formula funding under the Hatch Act of 1887 allowed White land-grant institutions to establish State Agricultural Experiment Stations (SAESs). This helped those institutions to develop the research capabilities necessary to be in the vanguard of the scientific revolution in American agriculture. Black land-grant institutions were denied access to Hatch funds for research, and federal funding was restricted to supporting teacher training and resident education within these institutions.

Emphasis on Teaching

The focus on teacher training and resident education within Black land-grant institutions was fueled by two different but interrelated forces. One was the poor educational environment in the South generally and for African Americans in particular. The majority of the land-grant institutions were located in areas where the public schools were either very poor or nonexistent. As a result, the majority of students attending Black land-grant institutions, up until the early years of the twentieth century, were at the primary and secondary levels. It was not until the late 1920s that the number of college students exceeded the high school and grade school enrollments.

Black Land-Grant Colleges and Universities and Tuskegee University

	Acres of Land Acquired	Founding Date
Alabama A&M University, Normal, AL	878	1875
Alcorn State University, Lorman, MS	1,700	1871
University of Arkansas, Pine Bluff, Pine Bluff, AK	275	1873
Delaware State College, Dover, DE	293	1891
Florida A&M University, Tallahassee, FL	404	1887
Fort Valley State College, Fort Valley, GA	645	1895
Kentucky State University, Frankfort, KY	320	1886
Langston University, Langston, OK	40	1897
Lincoln University, Jefferson City, MO	574	1866
University of Maryland, Eastern Shore, Princess Anne, MD	303	1886
North Carolina A&T State University, Greensboro, NC	800	1891
Prairie View A&M University, Prairie View, TX	1,400	1876
South Carolina State College, Orangeburg, SC	450	1872
Southern University and A&M College, Baton Rouge, LA.	875	1880
Tennessee State University, Nashville, TN	450	1909
Tuskegee University, Tuskegee, AL	5,189	1881
Virginia State College, Petersburg, VA	630	1882

Source: B. D. Mayberry, ed., *Development of Research at Historically Black Land-Grant Institutions* (Washington, DC: Bicentennial Committee of the Association of Research Coordinators and the U.S. Department of Agriculture, 1976).

The second force that conditioned the focus on teacher training and resident education within Black land-grant institutions was the belief that came to prevail in the South during the post-Reconstruction period—education for African Americans should be restricted to practical, vocational training involving extensive, manual-labor experiences. These kinds of programs were established at the Hampton Normal School (now Hampton University) by Samuel Chapman Armstrong in 1868 and later at Tuskegee Institute (now Tuskegee University) by Armstrong's student Booker T. Washington in 1881. Although neither of these schools was an official land-grant institutions, they were the models that the Black land-grant institutions subsequently attempted to emulate.

Teaching and teacher training became essential activities within Black institutions. Teachers such as Washington were key in disseminating ideas about the specific form that education should take for African Americans and could, in turn, reproduce these ideas through the design of their institutions and the activities of their students. Acceptance of this form of education helped to restrict African American social mobility within the South and served to mold an underclass that could be exploited to rebuild the cotton South after the war. Although there was great diversity among the Black land-grant institutions, from their beginnings they had in common the heritage of the practical-vocational orientation to education and consistently inadequate funding from state, federal, and private sources for research.

Forerunners in Extension

Extension activities were not supported for Black land-grant institutions by the Smith-Lever Act of 1914, which created the Cooperative Agricultural Extension Service, although the idea of a "movable school of agriculture" to reach out to farmers originated at Tuskegee Institute with Booker T. Washington and George Washington Carver. The "Jesup Agricultural Wagon for Better Farming," as the Washington-Carver concept came to be called, began operation in 1906, eight years before the Smith-Lever Act put the Extension Service in place. Carver and Washington conceived the idea for the Jesup wagon because both realized that it would be difficult to reach the many isolated farmers living in the Alabama countryside by trying to get them to attend the institute for instruction and support. Carver worked to create a horse-drawn wagon to carry plows, planters, seed varieties, sample fertilizers, and equipment to make butter and cheese. These items could be used by a faculty member from Tuskegee to give lectures and demonstrations.

Black land-grant institutions were not recognized or supported with Smith-Lever funds until the Food and Agriculture Act of 1977 was enacted. However, beginning in 1917 Seaman Knapp of the Federal Extension Service endorsed hiring "Negro farm agents" and "Negro home demonstration agents" to work in the counties with large Black populations. From this period on, a dual system of extension administration and implementation was enforced. Black agents were headquartered at the Black land-grant institutions and were supervised by a "Negro" state "leader," "director," or "district agent," who in turn was accountable to the White state director for the supervision of "Negro" agents in his charge.

The Impacts of Desegregation

With the desegregation mandate of 1954, Black land-grant extension programs were either eliminated or absorbed uncomfortably into White land-grant programs. Teaching programs in the Black land-grant institutions received increased federal support. With White institutions more accessible to African Americans, enrollments at Black institutions, especially in agriculture, began to decline. A greater number of African American agricultural students trained as researchers within White institutions instead of being restricted to roles as teachers.

Concerns about strengthening Black land-grant research capabilities to bring them to parity with agriculture programs at White land-grant institutions were at the center of proposals consistently made to the U.S. Department of Agriculture over the years by the 1890 President's Council. By 1967 the federal government had conceded that some support was in order. Between 1967 and 1971, Black land-grant institutions received an annual allocation of $283,000, or an average allocation per institution of $17,687.50, through the Cooperative State Research Service under Public Law 89-106. As discrete research grants, each grant was treated individually, and a system of yearly compliance was required for subsequent funding. Essentially, the allocations funded under Public Law 89-106 provided just enough money to whet the appetites of many Black land-grant research directors, but did not provide enough to develop substantial research programs.

By 1972 the yearly allocation to Black land-grant institutions had risen to $8,883,000. By 1977, the 1890 institutions had lobbied successfully for the provision of formula funds through the 1977 Farm Bill, Public Law 95-113, Section 1445 (also known as the Evans-Allen amendment or the Hatch Act for the Black land-grant institutions). It provided a formula fund for the annual authorization of research moneys to Black land-grant institutions. Evans-Allen funds are provided at an annual amount equal to 15 percent of federal funds provided to White land-grant institutions under the Hatch Act. As a result of the Evans-Allen formula, funding for Black land-grant institutions increased from $21,752,000 in 1977 to $49,300,000 in 1990.

The resulting lump sum and yearly appropriations from the federal government were continued under President Ronald Reagan's White House initiative to strengthen the educational and research programs of historically Black universities and colleges. These appropriations resulted in increased research activity at Black land-grant institutions, with a notable focus on issues of concern to limited-resource populations and small farmers specifically. For instance, Fort Valley State College in Georgia has projects to help small-scale, limited-resource farmers diversify and strengthen their operations. It designed programs to help poor rural residents overcome adverse economic conditions. Southern University in Louisiana has programs that focus on applied, action-oriented research and extension activities designed to help small farmholders and indigenous families. Alcorn University in Mississippi developed programs to increase income opportunities for low-income rural dwellers and address basic needs in rural development. Many Black land-grant institutions focused successfully on areas of traditional concern. In addition, many programs reflect an interest in nontraditional areas, such as the remote sensing research conducted at Alabama A&M University and research on aquaculture at Florida A&M University. Notable research accomplishments in the plant, animal, and rural social sciences have been made by scientists at Black land-grant institutions.

In 1977, measures were taken to strengthen extension programs at Black land-grant institutions through new authorizations provided in the Food and Agriculture Act of that year. The act provided for the direct allocation of formula funds to Black land-grant institutions at no less than 4 percent of funds included in Smith-Lever. It stipulated that Black land-grant and White land-grant institutions work together to develop statewide extension programs. To this end, Black land-grant and White land-grant institutions work under two memorandums of understanding (MOU), one between the U.S. Department of Agriculture and the respective institutions and the other among the institutions in respective states to better coordinate extension activities. Although both Black land-grant and White land-grant institutions are expected to meet the needs of limited resource populations, Black land-grant institutions have been especially directed in programmatic documents to respond to the needs of these groups.

International Involvements

Black land-grant institutions have been involved in overseas development activities. These activities were coordinated primarily through the Title XII Program administered by the U.S. Agency for International Development (USAID) since the late 1970s. Title XII amended the 1961 Foreign Assistance Act in 1975 to formalize relations between USAID and American universities. Title XII committed the federal government to using the resources and expertise of universities, particularly land-grant institutions, to relieve hunger and famine within postcolonial societies. Title XII was enacted in the wake of legislation passed in 1973 to redirect USAID's foreign assistance efforts toward the needs of the rural poor within these countries.

Title XII specified that university resources be employed to assist small-scale and limited-resource farmers in postcolonial societies with their food production concerns. The recognition that this had not been the priority for most land-grant institutions within the United States stimulated the development of legislative and programmatic mechanisms to help universities prepare to address the needs of limited-resource farmers through strengthening grants and project support grants. The latter were provided by memorandums of understanding and joint memorandums of understanding (JMOU) between universities and USAID. The JMOU arrangement was the primary mechanism for involving Black land-grant institutions in USAID projects. The JMOU program was developed to increase the presence of minority participants in overseas projects by increasing the involvement of Black land-grant institutions, the best source of minority agriculturalists. Title XII responded to governmentwide affirmative action mandates and provided mechanisms to compensate the perceived weaknesses of the Black land-grant institutions by linking Black land-grant and White land-grant institutions. This arrangement had satisfactory outcomes and drawbacks, such as making Black land-grant institutions subcontractors to White land-grant institutions that limited the Black institutions' access to resources and decision-making power.

Current Status and Future Directions

Several policies were enacted since the 1970s to compensate Black land-grant institutions for the historic lack of funding for research and extension programs and to shape new relational and task configurations between Black land-grant and White land-grant institutions. Despite these efforts, Black land-grant institutions continue as a subgroup of the land-grant system because of the economic and political forces that denied full citizenship to Africans freed from slavery after the Civil War.

With the continually changing rural landscape, however, there are unique opportunities for Black land-grant institutions to draw upon their legacies of self-determination, self-sufficiency, and community-centered agricultural development practices and to distinguish themselves in the newer priorities set by the U.S. Department of Agriculture. These priorities include sustainable agriculture, food safety, and rural development, all strengths of many Black land-grant institutions. By enhancing these programs and expanding their clientele base to include middle- and working-class Whites, Hispanics, and Native Americans, a good deal of which already has occurred, Black land-grant institutions will be in a unique position to support the agricultural and rural development needs of populations that are overlooked in most policy decisions. The often forgotten places of rural America—the "Black Belt" (14 census-designated states in the South where 33 percent or more of the population is African American), the Carolina Piedmont, the coastal plains, the Virginia tidewater, the Louisiana bayou, and the Mississippi and Tennessee River valleys—will be the focus of rural development policy deliberation. Black land-grant institutions will continue to be in the best position to keep the unique needs and interests of these regions present in the policy discourse.

—Rosalind P. Harris

See also

Careers in Agriculture; Cooperative State Research, Education, and Extension Service; Education, Adult; History, Agricultural; Land-Grant Institutions, 1862; Rural Sociology.

References

Anderson, James D . *The Education of Blacks in the South.* Chapel Hill: University of North Carolina Press, 1988.

Bond, Horace Mann. *The Education of the Negro in the American Social Order.* New York: Octagon, 1966.

Bullock, Henry A. *A History of Negro Education in the South: From 1619 to the Present.* Cambridge, MA: Harvard University Press, 1967.

Davis, John W. "The Negro Land-Grant College." *Journal of Negro Education* 2 (July 1933): 312–328.

Harris, Rosalind P. "Institutions under Influence: The Case of Knowledge Stratification within the U.S. Land-Grant System." *Southern Rural Sociology* 7 (1990): 70–85.

———. "Black Land-Grant Institutions and the Title XII Program: Is There Room to Maneuver?" *Agriculture and Human Values* 9, no. 1 (winter 1992): 67–71.

Mayberry, Bennie D. *A Century of Agriculture in the 1890 Land-Grant Institutions and Tuskegee University—1890–1990.* New York: Vantage Press, 1991.

———, ed. *Development of Research at Historically Black Land-Grant Institutions.* Washington, DC: Bicentennial Committee of the Association of Research Coordinators and the U.S. Department of Agriculture, 1976.

Schor, Joel. *Agriculture in the Black Land-Grant System to 1930.* Tallahassee: Florida A&M University, 1982.

Landownership

The possession of legal rights that may be exercised with regard to a specific geographic area. Rights in land, rather than mere possession, arise because of two unique features of land: its multiple uses and its perpetual life. This entry discusses some of these rights, as well as the obligations that go along with land-ownership. Various classes of landowners are identified, with special emphasis on farmland ownership. Farm operators farm land, under lease agreements, that they do not own. Our country was settled in such a way that we became a nation of family farmers. The family farm still predominates in the United States but has grown tremendously in terms of capital investment and volume of output.

Rights

Land may be defined as a specific area of the earth's non-water surface (although land may include streams, lakes, or ponds) that extends both upward and downward from the surface. The land's surface may change drastically, but it continues to exist, whereas other kinds of property wear out or become obsolete. Most goods or property do not have multiple simultaneous uses. An automobile may be used for transportation or scrap metal but not both at the same time. In contrast, this definition of land immediately suggests such multiple uses as growing crops, pumping oil from the subsurface, and transmitting electricity through the airspace. The right to use or not to use land for various purposes often is termed a *bundle of rights* similar to a bundle of sticks. Each stick represents a right in land that can be separated from the remainder of the bundle and used, sold, or leased. The sticks in this bundle include mineral rights, air rights, easements, rights of way, farming, and grazing.

Rights in land are said to be exclusive but not absolute: exclusive in the sense that property laws prevent anyone other than the owner from claiming or exercising the rights of the owner; not absolute in the sense that society, by way of the government, retains several of the sticks in the bundle of rights. Three of these include the rights to tax property, to enforce laws, and to take property, with compensation, for the public good (the right of eminent domain). A fourth right, escheat, allows government to take property upon the death of the owner who made no provision for its transfer and who has no heirs to claim the property under inheritance laws.

The right of government to tax property implies the obligation of the owner to pay taxes. The owner's general obligation is not to use property in such a manner as to harm others or violate their rights as citizens. In terms of rural land use, this was not viewed as much of a problem until the recent emphasis on the quality of the environment. Although there are risks of environmental damage from farming, especially water pollution resulting from erosion and the use of chemicals, the more widely publicized damages involving hazardous waste disposal, landfills, leaking underground fuel tanks, and chemical spills. And as livestock production became more concentrated, problems arose with regard to manure disposal and odors. Owners of agricultural land will face increasing obligations to protect the rights of others. Although the federal government regulates pesticide availability and use, many farmers seek to reduce the risk of water pollution from pesticides and fertilizer.

Who Owns Rural Land?

The federal government owns around 30 percent of the 2.3 billion–acre U.S. land area, making it the country's largest single landowner. Excluding Alaska, where the federal government owns 68 percent of the land, it owns more than 1 of every 5 acres. Forest and wildlife areas make up much of this acreage, followed mostly by low-value grazing land. The remainder consists of parks, national monuments, and military installations. Nearly 30 percent of the land classed as agricultural is owned by the federal government, but much of that is grazing and other land not considered to be in farms. Therefore, most of the land in farms, 90 percent or more, is privately owned.

Owners of Farmland

About 800 million acres of U.S. farmland are privately owned. Of this amount, somewhat less than one-half is cropland and most of the remainder is grazing land. Farmland ownership is concentrated. Owners of 1,000 acres and over in 1988 made up 4 percent of all owners, but they owned nearly 50 percent of the total acreage. Owners of under 50 acres account for 30 percent of all owners, but they own only 2 percent of the total acreage. One factor contributing to this concentration in ownership of farmland acreage is the use to which the land is suited. A family-operated ranch in the western United States may consist of 10,000 acres, whereas a family farm in the central Corn Belt may have 1,000 acres or less. Land values per acre tend to reflect this difference in productivity; therefore, ownership concentration in terms of value, rather than acreage, provides a better understanding of the nature of ownership concentration. Even so, considerable concentration exists. The 4 percent largest-acreage owners own 25 percent of the value in farms, down from nearly 50 percent in terms of acreage. The under-50-acre owners (30 percent of all owners) hold 11 percent of the value. These percentages have not changed much since 1945.

Farm operators own much, but not nearly all, of the land they farm. Nearly 40 percent of the privately owned land in farms is owned by nonoperators, 84 percent of whom are individuals who own two-thirds of the nonoperator-owned acreage. An additional 20 percent of this acreage is owned by partnerships and family corporations. Nonfamily corporations own only about 7 percent of the acreage, with 6 percent held by other legal entities such as estates and trusts. Of the individual nonoperator owners, 55 percent are 65 or more years old. Joint owners (mostly married couples) account for 29 percent of these owners; 40 percent are women, and 31 percent are men. Operator-owners are mostly individuals (89 percent) who, compared with nonoperator-owners, are younger and have larger average holdings of higher valued land.

Farming Nonowned Land

In addition to the 38 percent of all farmland owned by nonoperators, 4 percent is owned by operators and farmed by someone else. By farming region, land not owned by the operator ranges from 43 percent to 48 percent in the Pacific states and the Midwest and Plains states. The range is from 17 percent to 30 percent in other regions. In some Corn Belt areas, over 50 percent of the land farmed is not owned by the operator. What kinds of arrangements allow this separation of ownership and use? If we go back to the bundle of rights idea, one of the sticks is the right to farm the land and to produce crops or livestock. This right can be transferred for a specified time period to farm operators by means of a contract or a lease arrangement.

Kinds of Leases

Around 95 percent of all leases are of two types: share or cash. The share lease is one in which the landowner receives a specified percentage of the crops or gross income. In most cases, the landlord pays certain expenses in the same proportion as the crops are divided. These expenses are usually some or all of the variable crop expenses, except those related to machinery and labor. For example, in the Corn Belt the term *50–50 share lease* often is used to describe an arrangement in which the landlord pays land expenses, such as taxes and maintenance, plus 50 percent of costs of fertilizer, pesticides, seed, grain drying and hauling, and crop insurance. Crops or gross income is shared equally. On lower-quality land, the landlord may make a cash per acre payment, usually termed a *harvesting charge*. Adjustments for major differences in land quality may be made through a change in the percentage division of gross income and expenses. On low-quality land, the landlord's share may be 40 percent, and on high-quality land, 55 percent or 60 percent, although these higher percentages are not common.

Share leases result in a sharing of both risks and

rewards. In years of favorable yields or prices, incomes (rewards) may be favorable. But there is the risk that prices or yields will be so low that income will be much less than expected. Both tenants and landlords need the financial strength to get through the lean years in order to enjoy the years of favorable incomes.

As the name implies, cash leases provide payment of a specified amount per acre per year for the use of land. The tenant bears all the risk and reaps all the rewards. Risk may be shifted to the landlord by use of a flexible cash lease, an arrangement that provides for rent to move up and/or down from a specified base rent. This flexibility may be based on yield, product prices, or gross returns.

In the United States as a whole, about 65 percent of all leases are for cash, 30 percent are on a share basis, and the remainder includes those that are based on a fixed quantity of crops or in return for payment of taxes, upkeep, or other services. In the north-central United States (from the Dakotas to Ohio and Missouri on the south), about 55 percent of the leases are cash and 40 percent are on shares. The percentage of cash leases in other regions ranges from 64 to 85 percent. In many parts of the country, the trend has been toward more cash leases.

The Family Farm

A widely held philosophy among the founders and early leaders of our country was that those who tilled the soil should own it. Various measures were enacted by Congress to transfer the public domain to families who would live on the land suitable for farming, clear it, and make it productive. Public land was cheap, virtually free, and in spite of problems of land grabbers, speculators, and squatters, vast areas east of the Mississippi were settled before the Civil War. With continued settlement facilitated by the Homestead Act (1862), the nation became one of family farmers by the beginning of the twentieth century.

But with around 45 percent of the land now owned by nonoperators, has the family farm gone by the wayside? Some would say it has. Others would admit to changes (for example, fewer, larger farms; "industrialization" of some segments of livestock production; more rented land), but argue that our system of landownership allowed family farmers to adapt to change and still remain as producers of the vast majority of our food and fiber crops.

Farm numbers declined during much of this century, and farms became larger. Capital was substituted for labor as farms became mechanized. Expenditures increased for inputs such as fuel, improved seeds, and fertilizer. Larger machinery and reduced tillage systems further increased the acres that could be farmed per person. Much of U.S. farm production entered international markets with prices that reflected world production and demand. Production became more specialized; some farms grew only crops, whereas others produced livestock. Specialization occurred within crop and livestock production.

If some of these trends continue, and they probably will, does this mean the end of the family farm? Part of the answer is that farms a generation from now will be changed. Farms will be larger, more capital intensive, much more reliant on both electronic and biological technology; they probably will hire more labor and will have greater environmental concerns. These and other changes that we cannot foresee will bring changes in the family farm. One of the attributes of a system of family farms is the widespread ownership of land, much of it by farmers. Ownership of relatively small acreages of farmland by farmers and other individuals will provide the basis for the continued existence of family farms, even though they may decline in importance in specialized livestock production.

—*Julian H. Atkinson*

See also

Agricultural Law; Agriculture, Structure of; Intergenerational Land Transfer; Land Stewardship.

References

Barkley, Paul W., and Gene Wunderlich. *Rural Land Transfers in the United States*. AIB 574. Washington, DC: U.S. Department of Agriculture, Economic Research Service, 1989.

DeBraal, J. Peter. *Foreign Ownership of U.S. Agricultural Land*. Statistical Bulletin No. 879. Washington, DC: U.S. Department of Agriculture, Economic Research Service, 1994.

Erickson, Duane E., and John T. Scott, eds. *Farm Real Estate: Rights, Trends, Values, Methods of Sale, Finances, Appraisal, Investments*. NCR No. 51. Urbana: University of Illinois Cooperative Extension Service, 1990.

Ottoson, Howard W., ed.. *Land Use Policy and Problems in the United States*. Lincoln: University of Nebraska Press, 1963.

Rogers, Denise M. *Leasing Farmland in the United States: Agricultural Economics and Land Ownership Survey*. AGES-9159. Washington, DC: U.S. Department of Agriculture, Economic Research Service, 1991.

———. "Characteristics of Farmland Owners and Their Participation in the Farmland Market, 1970–1988." Pp. 43–47 in *Agricultural Resources: Agricultural Land Values and Markets: Situation Outlook and Report*. Edited by Roger Hexem. AR-26. Washington, DC: U.S. Department of Agriculture, Economic Research Service, June 1992.

Rogers, Denise, and Gene Wunderlich. *Acquiring Farmland in the United States*. AIB 682. Washington, DC: U.S. Department of Agriculture, Economic Research Service, 1993.

Suter, Robert C. *The Appraisal of Farm Real Estate*. 3d ed. Lafayette, IN: Retus, 1992.

Wunderlich, Gene. *Owning Farmland in the United States.* AIB 637. Washington, DC: U.S. Department of Agriculture, Economic Research Service, 1991.

Latinos

Modern term used in the United States to describe individuals born in, or descended from those born in, the Latin American countries, including South and Central America, Mexico, and the Spanish Caribbean. Most Latinos can be described as Hispanic, that is, coming from countries once part of the Spanish domains where Spanish is a common language. Latinos, primarily those from Mexico, have long been an important part of rural society in the U.S. Southwest. American rural communities received increasing numbers of immigrants from Central America and the Caribbean in the 1970s and 1980s, but their numbers still are small compared to those of Mexican origin. This entry reviews the history of Latino involvement in the U.S. countryside.

Historical Overview

From the European discovery of the New World until the early nineteenth century, the southwestern region of North America was part of the Spanish world. Latinos were displaced in the mid- to late 1800s by U.S. expansion into what is now the southwestern United States. Early in the twentieth century, the intense reintroduction and settlement of Latinos, mostly from Mexico, coincided with agricultural intensification in the region. The U.S. demand for Latino agricultural workers was institutionalized in the 1940s by the guest-worker program known as the Bracero Program. Following the termination of that formal labor agreement in the 1960s, Latinos began a process of permanent settlement in rural American communities, which continues unabated into the present. In the process, Latinos transformed many U.S. agricultural communities.

Not only have the number and distribution of Latin American–origin populations in rural America expanded in recent times, but also the circumstances of their presence and their influence on American rural society have been redefined. Most important, without the involvement of Latinos, many of the farm products that make up America's huge agricultural industry would not be grown. Their geographic proximity combined with conditions of poverty and unemployment in their home countries drives Latinos to seek work in the United States, but they are facilitated in this enterprise by the binational labor system formalized by the Bracero Program and by U.S. agriculture's insatiable demand for low-wage workers. The employment pattern so successful in the field-rich southwestern United States now is emulated all over the nation. Latinos harvest tobacco in Tennessee, peaches in Georgia and South Carolina, oranges and tomatoes in Florida, mushrooms in Pennsylvania, cucumbers in Michigan, apples in Washington and New York, and hops in Idaho. In the process, they are both forming and transforming rural American communities.

Spanish North America

Although nineteenth-century U.S. westward expansion typically is credited with settling what is now the U.S. Southwest, Mexican and Spanish pioneers first occupied the region in the 1700s as part of the northward expansion of New Spain. Through the presidios (military forts) and the mission system, New Spain's military and church "pacified" the indigenous occupants of the territory and enabled the establishment of pueblos (villages) and ranches (large farms) through the allocation of *mercedes de tierra* (land grants). New landowners staffed their farm enterprises with vaqueros (cowboys) from Mexico and local servants. California's coastal communities flourished by supplying the Galeón de Manila ships returning to the American continent from the Far East. Later, large cattle enterprises made a profitable business of trading hides and tallow for products of New England industries and whalers.

The Spanish/Mexican grasp in the regions now known as Texas, New Mexico, Arizona, Colorado, and California proved, however, to be tenuous. By the mid-nineteenth century, after Mexico's independence from Spain, vast northern territories were annexed by the United States. Following war with the United States over Texas, Mexico not only lost the Texas territory but also ceded the huge California and New Mexico territories in 1848. The agreement, the Treaty of Guadalupe Hidalgo (1848), reduced Mexico's area by one-half. While many Spanish-Mexican residents of the region moved back into Mexican territory, thousands of Mexican citizens were left to their fates in sparsely settled regions of a hostile country.

Dispossession

In stark contrast to their former status, the newly dispossessed Spanish-Mexicans became the working class in the service of the European American settlers who poured into the region. They were exploited further by corporations established as part of the globalized rapid

A Mexican farmer fertilizes the soil on this California farm.

capitalist expansion of the late 1800s and early 1900s. Latinos were marginalized from the richness of the growing economy and segregated into impoverished barrios within otherwise rapidly expanding and prosperous communities.

Unlike the legendary settlement of the Midwest by homesteading families that established small farms, American occupation of the Spanish-Mexican Southwest was driven by railroad interests and large, speculative investments. Much of the region, especially California, already was organized into latifundios (large landholdings) as a result of the Spanish grants. The power of corporate influence and capital turned the ranchos into huge corporate farms and ranches, hungry for labor.

Although the Treaty of Guadalupe Hidalgo guaranteed certain rights for the Mexican citizens remaining in the newly claimed U.S. territory (including landownership, citizenship, and retention of their Mexican culture and Spanish language), these provisions of the treaty were rarely honored. In the face of the dominant, expanding, and vigorous European American culture and population, the influence of Mexican culture and Mexican people greatly diminished. Throughout the late nineteenth century, the Mexican/Spanish population in the United States declined both in absolute numbers and in its share of the total population. Nevertheless, many remnants of Mexico are clearly visible in the architecture, communities, institutions, local customs, language, and people of the Southwest. The mission system in California was reconstructed as a set of museums, as were many presidios. But only in some isolated and distinct communities, such as the acequia (irrigation) towns along the Rio Grande in New Mexico, did the exotic ambiance of Spain and Mexico retain significant social importance.

The Beginning of Mexican Migration

New infusions of Latinos into the Southwest, especially Texas, California, and Arizona, did not begin until 50 years later, or about 1900. The extended Mexican Revolution, which began in 1910, greatly displaced the Mexican population. Driven to escape the war itself and its aftermath of economic and political instability, many Mexicans sought refuge in U.S. border towns, particularly in the Rio Grande valley of southeast Texas. U.S. prosperity and economic, especially agricultural, expansion provided an attractive alternative to the insecurity of living in revolutionary and postrevolutionary Mexico. Expanding agricultural interests in California, Texas, and the midwestern United States, driven by labor-intensive crops such as fruits, vegetables, cotton, and sugar beets, greatly increased demands for seasonal farm employment.

The Latino communities of southeast Texas became the headquarters for seasonal agricultural labor not only for cotton in Texas but also for fruit and vegetable crops in California and sugar beets in the Midwest. U.S. growers met their labor requirements by drawing first from the Mexican economic and political refugees in the border area and, later, from towns located deep in the Mexican countryside. Soon, Mexican migrants became the principal source of labor for much of American labor-intensive agriculture, curiously at a time when farm mechanization was displacing farmers in grain-growing areas. As a result of anti-Asian sentiment, the Chinese and Japanese immigrant labor that had been used heavily on the West Coast became completely unavailable. The Exclusion Acts of 1882 terminated Chinese immigration, and the Immigration Act of 1924 excluded the Japanese and many other groups, leaving Mexico as the only easily accessible source of immigrant workers. Mexican migrant laborers conveniently housed themselves in the Rio Grande valley or in rural Mexico during slow seasons and were easily mobilized to report to work when needed through a number of developing migrant recruitment and transportation streams.

This informal but effective labor supply system was briefly interrupted by the onset of the Great Depression in 1929, when more than 400,000 Mexicans, mainly farm laborers, were repatriated to Mexico. Once again their numbers in the United States declined; throughout the 1930s their labor was taken up by displaced U.S. farmers from the drought-plagued dust bowls of Texas, Oklahoma, Arkansas, and Missouri. But by 1941, the U.S. entry into World War II had created great demand for farm labor in America's agricultural fields as vast numbers of young men and women left for military service or factory work.

Establishment of a Binational Labor Force

Desperate for workers, the United States negotiated an executive agreement with Mexico in 1942. The agreement, formalized as Public Law 78 in 1951, allowed Mexican workers to enter the United States to fill the employment gap as part of the war effort. Under the Bracero (hired hand) Program, as the agreement came to be known, Mexican laborers were contracted and temporarily admitted for periods of work at guaranteed wages and conditions, especially in the agricultural, mining, and railroad industries. The agreement outlived the war. The number of contract braceros reached a high point of nearly 500,000 in 1956, and the program maintained large numbers until its demise in 1964.

Even after the Bracero Program was terminated, Mexican workers continued to influence U.S. agriculture and the demographics of rural America. The Mexican labor force, in continued demand by U.S. agricultural interests, unofficially sustained the program through undocumented migration from Mexico to American fields. Workers from rural Mexico still crossed the border (with U.S. acquiescence) in an uninterrupted flow, regularly circulating between their homes and U.S. fields in the cycles that had become traditional in many sending communities. Regular U.S. work became a standard economic strategy and significant source of family income, especially in the north-central and highland states of Michoacán, Jalisco, Guanajuato, and Zacatecas.

With widespread mechanization of cotton harvesting in Texas and relocation of much of the cotton-growing industry to California, workers based in depressed Texas border towns experienced substantial unemployment. Many moved their home base permanently to California or the industrial Midwest. But the migrant Mexican workers involved in American agriculture in the 1940s, 1950s, and 1960s did not have a significant impact on American rural communities. Most seasonal workers were transient, young, single men who moved from town to town with the harvests. They found temporary shelter in labor camps and farms and nearly always returned to their home communities in Mexico. Those who settled in U.S. rural environments formed small, marginalized *colonias* (neighborhoods) in rural towns, isolated from the majority Anglo population. Discouraged from building homes and lives by anti-immigrant attitudes, discrimination, and limited opportunities, these early rural Latino settlers soon moved on to urban residences and industrial employment in the booming cities of the 1960s and 1970s. However, in the absence of the structured labor contracts provided under the Bracero Program, these workers made significant strides in labor organization. Under the leadership of César Chávez, California Latino farmworkers spearheaded the establishment of the first effective union of agricultural workers, the United Farm Workers, earning a place in U.S. labor history and serving as an example to other organizing initiatives, such as the Farm Labor Organizing Committee in the Midwest.

Although Latino labor was central to the workings and expansion of U.S. agriculture and labor organization in the twentieth century, especially in California, it did not become a fixture and a social force of American rural society until the mid-1970s. Until that time, most seasonal farmworkers employed by U.S. farms trekked circularly from their home communities in rural Mexico or at the border, through various agricultural regions in rhythm with the growing cycles, and back to Mexico. Those who ventured to settle near employment sites soon were ushered out by the "revolving door" effect; unwelcomed, blacklisted settlers moved from rural environments and agricultural employment to seek better opportunities and socioeconomic mobility in urban areas and industrial or service jobs. They were further encouraged to leave by the pressure of the highly competitive labor supply continually emanating from Mexico, which, among other effects, kept agricultural wages down, labor organization weak, and working conditions poor. Hence, the early Mexican settlers only mildly affected the rural communities they briefly inhabited.

The Transformation of Rural America

A number of factors converged to change rapidly the number and influence of Mexican immigrant settlers in rural America, especially in California, in the 1970s. First, a radical change in popular diets created an unprecedented national and international demand for wholesome fresh fruits and vegetables. Much agricultural land was converted to grow these high-value specialty crops, which also are labor intensive and resistant to mechanization. Second, a strong inflationary trend greatly increased costs of farm production, including both energy costs and industrial and manufactured inputs, while conventional crops declined in value. As a result, a great incentive for high-value crops developed along with the impetus to replace high input costs with low labor costs. This phenomenon, well documented in California, reintensified farming and revitalized labor needs. An unprecedented number of former migrant workers and their families settled into the American agricultural landscape in response to increased employment opportunities, extended employment seasons, and deepening economic crises in their homelands.

The settlement of farmworkers is widespread throughout agricultural California, affecting the small cities and towns located in the state's central valley, coastal areas, and southern deserts. More than 500,000 immigrant farmworkers joined these communities, which now supply about one-half of the state's annual agricultural labor requirements. The newcomers radically transformed their settlements—demographically, politically, and culturally—as they became the majority populations in their communities. The demographic transformation of the town of Guadalupe in Santa Barbara County, located on the central California coast, is illustrative of events that overtook most agricultural settlements in California.

The internal dynamics of new Latino communities are unique in contrast with rural America at large, and

they are problematic. They have become Mexican communities where Mexican culture and Spanish language predominate. They are populated by young families with high fertility rates and strong aspirations to build new and better homes. But they also are places of concentrated and persistent poverty resulting from the low-wage, seasonal character of farm employment. Periodically these communities house a substantial portion of the remaining migrant, itinerant labor force that appears during the high-employment harvest season. Latino rural communities are places where the high aspirations of immigrants and the low opportunities of farm labor converge. Yet despite these limitations, many farmworkers have become homeowners, active members of their communities, and even independent farmers. Immigrant Mexican farmworkers have rooted themselves firmly in their new settlements and agricultural landscape as a result of changing agricultural employment opportunities.

The presence of growing Latino rural communities in California challenges many popular notions about the future of rural America, particularly the presumption of unavoidable rural to urban transition and the image of abandoned and aging towns. The existence of vigorous Latino settlements denies the stereotype of the nomadic, single male farmworker and his only transitional presence in agricultural employment and rural residences. Women make up about 30 percent of today's agricultural labor force. The communities in which farmworkers and their families live are filled with both hopeful opportunities for a rejuvenated rural society and depressing scenes of rural blight and poverty. But these stark contrasts are little known. Because Latino rural communities are well hidden, they suffer from political and public neglect.

In the course of the twentieth century, California experienced the Latinoization of its agricultural labor force to the extent that by 1996 nine out of ten farm workers were Latino. The state underwent the Latinoization of its rural communities as well during the 1980s and 1990s, so that most rural agricultural towns contain a large Latino component, which, in many cases, is now the majority. There is clear evidence that agricultural interests throughout the United States are successfully emulating California's agricultural development by, first, reorienting and reintensifying production to match new market demands and, second, by employing Latino laborers through both seasonal migrant and permanent immigration practices. This is true not only for states neighboring California and sharing the Southwest's natural environment, but also for midwestern states that have

**Guadalupe, California: Population
and Latino Representation, 1960–1990**

Year	Population	Latinos	Percentage Latino
1960	3,225	600	18
1980	3,632	2,713	74
1986	4,845	3,876	80
1990	5,479	4,547	83

Source: Juan-Vicente Palerm, *Farm Labor Needs and Farm Workers in California, 1970–1989* (Sacramento: California Agricultural Studies, Employment Development Department, 1991), p. 21.

previously experienced the presence of Latino farmworkers. Other states, especially along the eastern seaboard, are just beginning to develop their ties to a Latino labor force emanating from Mexico, Central America (especially Guatemala and El Salvador), and the Dominican Republic. Latino farmworkers and new Latino settlement communities are found in different stages of formation in such disparate locations as Yakima and Granger, Washington; Caldwell, Idaho; Hood River, Oregon; Twin Falls, Utah; Immokalee, Florida; the Delaware-Maryland-Virginia Peninsula; and Kennet Square in Chester County, Pennsylvania. The growth of Latino settlements suggests that the already significant presence of Latinos in modern U.S. agriculture and rural society will continue to increase and define, as in California, the rural mainstream. It will be necessary to monitor this process of rural transformation and to acknowledge and understand the importance, nature, and needs of the new rural Americans.

—*Juan-Vicente Palerm*

See also

Cultural Diversity; Culture; History, Rural; Labor Force; Migrant Farmworkers.

References

Camarillo, Albert. *Chicanos in a Changing Society: From Mexican Pueblos to American Barrios in Santa Barbara and Southern California, 1848–1930.* Cambridge, MA: Harvard University Press, 1979.

Commission on Agricultural Workers. *Report of the Commission on Agricultural Workers.* Washington, DC: U.S. Government Printing Office, 1993.

Galarza, Ernesto. *Merchants of Labor.* Santa Barbara, CA: McNally and Loftin, West, 1978.

Gamboa, Erasmo. *Mexican Labor and World War II: Braceros in the Pacific Northwest, 1942–1947.* Austin: University of Texas Press, 1990.

Gregory, James Noble. *American Exodus: The Dust Bowl Migration and Okie Culture in California.* New York: Oxford University Press, 1989.

Griffith, David, and Ed Kissam. *Working Poor: Farmworkers in the United States.* Philadelphia: Temple University Press, 1995.

Hoffman, Abraham. *Unwanted Mexican Americans in the Great Depression: Repatriation Pressures, 1929–1939.* Tucson: University of Arizona Press, 1974.

McWilliams, Carey. *Factories in the Field.* Boston: Little, Brown, 1939.

Palerm, Juan-Vicente. *Farm Labor Needs and Farm Workers in California, 1970–1989.* Sacramento: California Agricultural Studies, Employment Development Department, 1991.

Palerm, Juan-Vicente, and José Ignacio Urquiola. "A Binational System of Agricultural Production: The Case of the Mexican Bajío and California." Pp. 311–367 in *Mexico and the United States: Neighbors in Crisis. Proceedings from the Conference Neighbors in Crisis: A Case for Joint Solutions, February 1989.* Edited by Daniel G. Aldrich, Jr. and Lorenzo Meyer. San Bernardino, CA: Borgo Press, 1993.

Valdés, Dennis Nodín. *Al Norte: Agricultural Workers in the Great Lakes Region, 1917–1970.* Austin: University of Texas Press, 1991.

Leadership

The process of using influence to help groups achieve their goals. The availability of competent leadership is affected by the characteristics, behaviors, styles, and skills of local citizens and by the ways leadership functions are shared among the population. Leadership development programs with varying target audiences, content, and impacts strengthen individual and group leadership capabilities. The changing environment in American society in general and in rural communities in particular accentuates the need for strong leadership at the local level. Leadership and citizen involvement are key ingredients for addressing many problems that communities face today. No matter how competent a leader is, one person cannot take the responsibility or provide all the resources and expertise to solve a community's problems. Leadership development programs, whose target audiences vary widely, can help to ensure an adequate supply of effective leaders. This entry describes characteristics of leadership and leaders in rural America. It examines leadership development programs and their impacts on community life.

Characteristics of Rural America

Rural America faces major social and economic changes that provide challenges and opportunities for leaders, policymakers, and citizens at the community, state, and national levels. Leaders face the challenge of balancing environmental preservation, economic development, and increased opportunities for rural people. Professionals alone cannot accomplish this task. Local leaders must generate the ability to bring together people with diverse interests, develop a shared vision and goals, and achieve results ethically. Rural America faces many changes: a restructured global economy affecting rural industry competitiveness, increased diversity and heterogeneity, enhanced national emphasis on environmental sustainability, reduced power among rural residents who are becoming political minorities, and patterned in- and out-migration. These changes manifested themselves in communities in many different ways. Economic fluctuations affect farmers and local businesses by reducing their profitability, decreasing their tax base, and increasing their need for off-farm income. There are infrastructure deterioration, especially of roads and bridges; pressure on natural resources; needs for affordable, accessible health care; and pressures as people move in and out of the community.

Rural America needs leadership. It plays a key role in addressing community issues by locating the information and strategies needed. The critical need for agricultural and rural community leadership became increasingly apparent in the 1980s; there were fragmented, unproductive responses by individuals and communities to the "farm crisis." It was clear that people and communities needed improved capacities to frame problems and deal with hardships and conflicts. There was a lack of hope or positive vision for the future.

The lack of adequate individual and collective leadership and volunteerism compounds today's issues. People need help to build their capacity to address difficult issues. Rural communities differ widely in the strength of leadership from which they can draw. In some places, leaders emerge for almost every type of activity and projects and activities move forward effectively. But in other places, one project after another fails to develop beyond the discussion stage because no one assumes a leadership role. A sense of community and connectedness to a positive future creates a climate for success. Effective community leadership is based on a pattern of cooperative effort in which the leadership talents of every member of the group find an opportunity for use. One person cannot provide all the answers. For communities to flourish, each person must contribute leadership in some situations.

The rural community that suffers from a lack of leaders often can improve the situation by reducing at least three obstacles. The first obstacle is the belief that leaders are born, not made. Training and experience can develop the capacity to serve as leaders. The second obstacle is the idea that there is only one true leader. Most leadership talent is specialized; many people have expertise to contribute. The third obstacle is the continuation of current leaders as an "elite aristocracy." A conscious effort must be made to develop and encourage new, emerging leaders.

Characteristics of Rural Leaders

Rural leadership can be characterized in several ways. Traditionally, rural leaders have been men, although women are moving into leadership roles. The importance of involving all members of the rural community, including youths and adults, newcomers and established residents, and additional cultural or ethnic groups is beginning to be more widely recognized. Most communities have many voluntary organizations. Some organizations have little authoritarian structure; leaders are chosen by the members. Community officials frequently are volunteers whose role is facilitative rather than directive. Leaders and followers have a mutual influence on each other.

Certain behaviors or characteristics are closely associated with effective leadership, including perceptivity or interpersonal sensitivity, self-understanding, self-confidence, desire to lead, competence, and flexibility or adaptability. Effective leaders use behaviors or combinations of behaviors to suit the circumstances of particular situations. They facilitate friendly relationships; motivate followers to achieve goals; facilitate participation; promote goal achievement; provide recognition, benefits, and rewards; and establish external linkages.

A critical foundation view is that leadership is a shared function; no one individual has the abilities to carry out all these responsibilities. Citizen involvement and leadership are essential factors in solving the many social, economic, and infrastructure problems that face rural communities. Competencies or capacities that leaders need include at least five factors. First, a shared vision provides a context for action. Second, leaders must understand themselves as leaders, which involves self-knowledge, purpose and goals, and personal leadership attributes. Third, leaders must have tools and skills to manage change, such as communication, facilitation, mediation, negotiation, consensus building, process management, decision making, and problem solving. Fourth, leaders must have an ability to create environments that support decision making, risk taking, change, personal growth, and citizen participation. Fifth, they must have varied ways of thinking that are strategic, systematic, ethical, and proactive.

Another way to look at leadership in rural America is to consider some of the levels of leadership. First, community leadership involves influence, power, and input into public decision making over one or more spheres of activity. The leadership functions and skills are similar to those needed for organization leadership, but community leadership addresses concerns on a more complex level. Community leadership is more complex because of the many and varied groups, each with different viewpoints, agendas, and possibly competing interests. Second, team leadership is a process usually involving many people rather than one individual. It is a shared effort with many people contributing knowledge, skills, and other resources. Third, situational leadership stresses the interrelationships of behaviors and characteristics among leaders and group members and the situation in which they find themselves. The leader's behavior is associated with tasks, relationships, and the ability to be flexible. Leadership style needs flexibility to adjust to followers' ability and willingness to carry out specific activities.

Development Programs

There are many different definitions of leadership. Community leadership in rural America consists of three components: first, the process of using influence to help a group achieve its goals; second, the beliefs that individuals have about what makes effective leaders; and third, the qualities, behaviors, skills, and knowledge of persons regarded as effective leaders. Leadership is a subset of human action that is sensitive to shifting situational forces shaped by position and role. It is activated by the combining of motive with positional, personal, and other power resources. Leadership is both learned and earned.

Leadership development programs can help to ensure an adequate supply of effective leaders who can assist communities to provide a high quality of life for citizens. However, multiple providers and limited resources can result in no clearly defined and funded niche for leadership education. Programs are provided by land-grant universities and other colleges and universities, the Cooperative Extension Service, the Chambers of Commerce, and businesses, on a local or on a county- or statewide basis. Leadership development programs frequently are co-sponsored by several entities.

Target audiences vary widely. Agricultural and rural leadership programs usually target a small group of young, newly recognized leaders, with an emphasis on topics at the state, national, and international levels. Some specialized leadership programs address the needs of minority groups, where effective programs usually include an internship-type experience, an educational component, and placement or mentoring assistance. Other leadership programs are designed for women, youths, or adults and youths working as partners in community development.

The content of leadership development programs must be eclectic, drawing from many disciplines, theories, and practical experience or experiential learning. Several topics contribute to the education of potential leaders, including personal leadership skills, group process skills such as team building and conflict resolution, community development and planned change, specific community institutions and issues, standards of ethics and excellence, and the public policy process of understanding government structures and legislative process.

Several common educational goals guide the development of most rural and agricultural leadership programs. These are for participants to develop the ability to analyze public problems critically and objectively; gain knowledge of the economic, social, political, and cultural dimensions of public problems; enhance ability to solve public problems by improving leadership and group participation skills; and increase understanding of local, state, national, and international issues. Educational programs for beginning or emerging leaders frequently start with personal skill development, including self-esteem, self-confidence, and personal leadership styles; the programs then move on to interpersonal relationships and group process techniques.

Impacts of Development Programs

Evaluation of the impact of leadership development programs has been limited and fragmented. This is due, in part, to the intangible nature of leadership and the lack of a generally accepted definition of leadership in rural communities. Participants in leadership development projects are generally very positive. They indicate plans to use the information themselves and to listen to others, share their information, and encourage others to participate in leadership education. Individual change is recognized as a first step toward organizational and community change. In the Family Community Leadership program, for example, participants reported more trust, less negativity, more decisiveness, and a better understanding of group process. They reported initiating and organizing events and activities, serving more effectively on boards or committees, and in general being more willing to lead. Community leadership programs play an important part in helping citizens to improve their own self-image and skill levels and to enhance their participation in public-policy decisions and community actions.

Leadership in rural America occurs as part of a world that is so complex, interdependent, and interrelated that old patterns of leadership by one individual will no longer work. Citizens must become part of rural leadership and part of finding ways to improve community life. Leadership capabilities are developed through training, education, and experience.

—Katey Walker

See also
Development, Community and Economic; Education, Adult; Education, Youth.
References
Ayres, Janet S., R. Cole, C. Hein, S. Huntington, W. Kobberdahl, W. Leonard, and Dale Zetocha. *Take Charge: Economic Development in Small Communities*. Ames, IA: North Central Regional Center for Rural Development, 1990.
Brigham, Nancy. "Hitting Home: Results of the National Evaluation of the Family Community Leadership (FCL) Program." Pp. 125–135 in *Proceedings of the Association of Leadership*

Educators: Leadership and Service. Edited by C. Langone. Athens: University of Georgia, 1993.

Feeney, Marian, and Patricia Millar. *Community/Family Leadership Evaluation Project.* University Park: Pennsylvania State University, Northeast Regional Center for Rural Development, 1989.

Hoiberg, Otto G. *Leadership Development.* Lincoln: Nebraska Community Improvement Program, 1990.

Martin, Elizabeth, Deb Burwell, and Alexandra. Merrill. "The Lead Project in Rural Maine: Women Learning Personal Authority and Group Process through Experiential Training." Pp. 117–124 in *Proceedings of the Association of Leadership Educators: Leadership and Service.* Edited by C. Langone. Athens: University of Georgia, 1993.

Pulver, Glen C. "Elements of a Sustainable Rural Policy." Pp. 181–190 in *Increasing Understanding of Public Problems and Policies 1994.* Edited by Steve A. Halbrook and Teddee E. Grace. Oak Brook, IL: Farm Foundation, 1994.

Sheffert, Donna Rae, John L. Tait, and Gerald Miller. "Developing Interdisciplinary Leadership Education: The Minnesota-Iowa Experience." Pp. 160–178 in *Proceedings of the Leadership Development Seminar: People, Problems, and Solutions: The Leadership Connection.* Held in Milwaukee, WI, 18–19 August 1990. Edited by E. Bolton. Gainesville: University of Florida, Institute of Food and Agricultural Sciences, 1990.

Vandenberg, Lela, F. A. Fear, and M. Thullen. *Research-Practice Linkages in Extension Leadership Development Programs: Focus on Community Development Programs. A Report to the North Central Regional Center for Rural Development.* Ames: Iowa State University, 1988.

Walker, Katey, and Carol Young. "Volunteer Leadership Development: Changing Paradigms." Pp. 204–224 in *Leadership Development Seminar: Developing Human Capital through Extension Leadership Development Programs.* Edited by Elizabeth Bolton and Lynn White. Gainesville: University of Florida, 1989.

Libraries

See Public Libraries

Literacy

A complex set of skills that include the ability to read and interpret prose, documents, and quantitative data. This entry examines the nature of adult literacy in the United States, explores the problems of definition, reviews the history of literacy programs, and discusses issues relating to rural literacy education today. Adult illiteracy is increasingly recognized as a major problem in the United States. According to a recent national survey, 21 to 23 percent of U.S. adults (40 to 44 million out of 191 million) have low-level basic literacy skills. Many cannot write their names on a document, locate the time of an event on a schedule, or add the numbers on a bank deposit slip (Kirsch et al. 1993). This places low-level learners at great personal, social, and economic risk. Rural people are overrepresented in this group. Isolation, economic decline, and lack of educational opportunities amplify the difficulties of nonreading adults in rural communities. The diversity and complexity of contemporary rural life further aggravate the problem of illiteracy.

Nature of Rural Nonreading

Although exact statistics are unavailable, rural illiteracy rates in the United States (and elsewhere in the world) are believed to be higher than in urban areas. Although 28 percent of the U.S. population lives in rural areas, 42 percent of the functionally illiterate are rural, according to the Rural Clearinghouse (Spears 1993). Nonreading adults in North America, like elsewhere in the world, also are disproportionately poor and female and, in many cases come from culturally diverse groups.

Although the 1992 National Adult Literacy Survey (NALS) did not distinguish between rural and urban adult populations, it dramatically underscored the growing problem of adult illiteracy in the United States. NALS researchers identified three dimensions of literacy: the ability to read prose, interpret a document, and use numbers proficiently. Using scales to measure each dimension, researchers identified five levels of literacy skills required to perform increasingly complex tasks (Kirsch et al. 1993). The performance of 46 to 51 percent of U.S. adults placed them on the two lowest literacy proficiency levels. This means that approximately 50 percent of the adults living in the United States lack the skills needed to interpret the instructions on an appliance warranty or calculate the total purchase price on an order form (Kirsch et al. 1993). Critics have challenged some of the findings, but the study clearly showed that many adults in the United States have serious reading problems.

Problems of Definition

Discussions of rural literacy are complicated by issues of definition growing out of the complexity and multidimensional nature of what it means to be literate. Literacy, once defined merely as the ability to sign one's name, was replaced by definitions based on the capacity to read and write a simple passage. Adult literacy rates often are measured by the attainment of reading levels equal with a particular grade in school. In an analysis of literacy orientations, Fingeret (1992) labeled this approach "literacy as skills." Other definitions associate the accumulation of basic skills with the ability to function in society—functional literacy, or in Fingeret's terms, "literacy as tasks."

More recent definitions emphasize the ability of learners to participate in community—"literacy as social and cultural practices." Finally, Fingeret identified the emerging notion of basic education for social change with "literacy as critical reflection and action." People whose skills once would have been considered sufficient now would be considered illiterate by some definitions if they are unable to engage in critical reflection or participate fully in society.

The literature identifies at least two general approaches to literacy education: individual literacy and community-based literacy. From the perspective of the former, illiteracy prevents adults from obtaining adequate employment, and therefore income, which in turn denies them full access to a society's productive resources. Individual-based literacy education strategies emphasize the technical dimensions of reading and writing, which results in programs designed to help adults compensate for deficiencies in basic skills.

Inspired by Brazilian adult educator Freire (1970), others have linked the development of basic skills to the broader transformation of society. Variously called community-based literacy or critical literacy, participants learn basic skills through reflection upon the problems and issues facing their communities. As adult learners discuss these issues, they not only learn basic skills but also are motivated to participate in programs designed to change unjust social structures. Critical literacy's ultimate goal is to empower the poor and marginalized segments of society. Community-based literacy programs examine the social/cultural contexts of the learner that cause or contribute to illiteracy. Community-based solutions teach basic skills but also facilitate the process through which adult learners transform unjust structures and promote a reading society.

History of Adult Education

The history of literacy efforts in the United States reflects cycles of educational programs developed in response to social, economic, and political conditions—war, mass immigration, and social movements. Social reformers such as Jane Addams of Hull House designed urban adult education and social welfare programs for new immigrants from southern and eastern Europe at the end of the nineteenth century. "Americanization" programs operating through evening schools, factories, churches, and private organizations combined the teaching of skills with socialization into U.S. society. These immigrants developed reading and computational skills but also were consciously taught the customs and mores of their new country.

The need for trained soldiers and factory workers stimulated another round of literacy education programs during World War II. Adults with little formal education, many coming from rural areas, often lacked the technical skills required to read manuals, operate machines, or maintain equipment. The GI Bill and postwar boom fueled the rapid growth of higher education but underscored the inequalities among ethnic groups and social classes. Meanwhile, the growing awareness of illiteracy in the United States sparked a variety of programs designed to teach adults basic skills. Frank Laubach, for example, began literacy work overseas in the 1930s, which evolved into an international literacy program in the 1950s that now bears his name. Ruth Colvin established Literacy Volunteers of America in 1962 to combat adult illiteracy in her own Syracuse, New York, community. This grassroots initiative grew into a national volunteer tutor program. President Johnson's War on Poverty in the 1960s engaged the government in large-scale funding of basic skills training that included adult literacy. Southern states used stringent voter registration laws with literacy requirements to disfranchise African Americans. As a result, the civil rights movement promoted basic reading skills as part of its political strategy.

The influx of refugees from the war in Southeast Asia in the 1970s generated new literacy and English as a second language (ESL) programs funded through both public and private sources. Unlike the earliest refugees from Indochina, many who came to the United States later were not literate in any language. They needed basic literacy as well as English-language skills. Many church groups, such as the Lutheran Church Women, and other private organizations not only sponsored refugees for resettlement but also developed literacy and ESL programs designed to teach basic skills.

The growing recognition that U.S. workers' lack of basic skills is causing American companies to lose their competitive edge has led to a new round of educational programs beginning in the 1980s emphasizing workplace literacy. Intergenerational literacy programs reflect a relatively new trend in adult education, emphasizing a family-centered approach oriented toward community building. This approach aims to break the cycle of illiteracy by engaging parents and children as learning units.

Problems of Rural Nonreading

The complexity of literacy and societal issues makes it hard to generalize as to why millions of adults cannot read. Fitchen (1991) noted that the transformation of rural economies changed the employment picture and raised the stakes for those with inadequate formal education and basic skills. Formerly, when plants closed in rural communities, even relatively unskilled workers could find new employment. This is no longer the case. The downsizing of manufacturing and the restructuring of the labor force translate into tough times for rural communities. Companies considering moves into rural areas identify the lack of a trained workforce as a major limitation. Fitchen (1991, 80) described this mismatch between jobs and the potential workforce as "too large for training programs alone to resolve."

Rural adult learners participating in a Cornell University study (Capagrossi et al. 1994) blamed the schools. These adults felt that schools had lowered their standards and were graduating individuals with inadequate literacy skills. They argued that heavy workloads prevented teachers from spending adequate time on basic skills. Problem students sometimes monopolized teachers' time, while the needs of the learning disabled went unmet. The influx of immigrants needing basic skills often was high, placing increased pressure on the schools.

The Cornell study identified lack of economic opportunities as a significant barrier to rural literacy programs. Researchers found that most jobs commonly available in rural counties were low paying, often seasonal, and lacked health care and other benefits. Without the possibility of meaningful employment, nonreading adults had little motivation to invest their energy in adult literacy programs. At the same time, business and community leaders expressed their frustration at the lack of basic skills offered by potential employees, which made it difficult to attract new industries to the area. This dilemma increasingly has drawn adult educators to consider community-based literacy strategies.

Fingeret (1992) argued that the prevailing view of literacy education as a short-term crisis intervention undermines efforts to build a supportive infrastructure. The popular belief that literacy necessarily leads to employment is more myth than reality. It tempts policymakers to promote skills training without addressing the underlying question of what newly literate adults will be able to do with these new skills. Ferrell (1990) argued that literacy programs designed to improve the rural economy are vulnerable to funding cuts because of this public failure to understand the link between basic skills and viable communities.

Expanding rural populations with increasing special needs (for example, immigrants who need ESL programs, more people who are physically challenged, and more people who are elderly) place increasing pressure on already highly stressed social systems, as does the movement of people from large urban centers to rural communities in search of lower-cost housing and safer neighborhoods. Like many immigrants and refugees from abroad, these new residents often lack basic skills and therefore compete for the limited number of low-paying jobs that are locally available.

Rural literacy programs face several other unique challenges as well. Communities often lack public transportation, adequate communication systems (many rural poor do not have telephones), and local organizations designed to address community problems. These barriers prohibit many learners from attending classes or meeting with their tutors. Literacy tutors in one New York community identified low self-esteem, embarrassment, and fear as barriers to participation in adult literacy programs (Capagrossi et al. 1994). Nonreaders may conceal their lack of skills rather than participate in literacy programs. Although one may remain anonymous in the city, participation in a literacy program is difficult to hide in small rural communities. Lack of child care, aggravated by the increasing number of single-parent families, limits participation in rural literacy programs.

The Future

Illiteracy must be viewed as a product of economic, social, and cultural structures rather than solely as the result of individual deficiencies and failures. Spears (1993) argued that rural literacy programs must create networks of literacy practitioners who examine community problems. Community developers, planners, and educators in rural areas must shift from individual-based strategies to community-based literacy approaches that engage learners, educators, and their communities in solving local problems and promoting a reading society. Literacy skills refined through social action may transform rural communities.

—D. Merrill Ewert and Deborah Larson Padamsee

See also
Education, Adult; Employment; Poverty; Voluntarism.
References
Capagrossi, Douglas, D. Merrill Ewert, J. David Deshler, and Jennifer Greene. "Literacy and Community Development." *Community Development Report* 2, no. 3 (1994): 1–6.
Ferrell, Susan. "Adult Literacy Programs in Rural Areas." *ERIC Digest* (1990): 2–3.

Fingeret, Hanna A. *Adult Literacy Education, Current and Future Directions: An Update.* Information Series No. 355. Center on Education and Training for Employment. Columbus, OH: Center Publications, 1992.

Fitchen, Janet. *Endangered Spaces, Enduring Places: Change, Identity, and Survival in Rural America.* Boulder, CO: Westview Press, 1991.

Freire, Paulo. *Pedagogy of the Oppressed.* New York: Herder and Herder, 1970.

Kirsch, Irwin S., Ann Jungeblut, Lynn Jenkins, and Andrew Kolstad. *Adult Literacy in America: A First Look at the Results of the National Adult Literacy Survey.* Washington, DC: Office of Educational Research and Improvement, 1993.

Spears, Jacqueline. "Rural Clearinghouse: Rural Programs Survey." *Literacy Practitioner* 1, no. 2 (1993): 5–7.

Literature

Writings in prose or verse, either fiction or nonfiction. Rural literature comprises any of these forms that have as their subjects some aspect of country life. This entry traces the development of American rural literature from colonial days to the present.

Colonial Beginnings: 1588–1776

Rural writing in America began with the travel journals and promotional tracts written by New England's earliest adventurers, explorers, and colonists. These works, published in England, were generally written to promote immigration, secure funding for proposed colonies, or explain the failure of earlier attempts at colonization. Whatever the reasons for their publication, however, these were rural documents. Their subject matter, in most instances, was the land: its natural resources, its native population, and its prospects. Thomas Hariot's 46-page pamphlet *A Briefe and True Report of the New Found Land of Virginia* (London 1588), for example, described the Native Americans, the natural resources, and the types of crops already being produced in Virginia. John Smith's *A Description of New England* (1616) and *The Generall Historie of Virginia, New England, and the Summer Isles* (1624) provided descriptions of the climate, winds, soils, rivers, plants, animals, birds, fish, minerals, and Native Americans. The beginnings of American rural literature also may be found in colonists' diaries and autobiographies. William Byrd's secret journals, which were not published until 1841 (97 years after his death), provided descriptions, sometimes satirical, of rural life in colonial Virginia and North Carolina.

By the end of the colonial period, authors were beginning to write for an American audience. Jared Hariot's *Essays on Field-Husbandry in New England, As it is or may be ordered,* for example, was published in Boston in 1760. The first important handbook on agriculture, *Essays* advised farmers on stock breeding and the use of manure as a fertilizer and reminded them of the virtues of husbandry and its importance to the economy.

The New Republic: 1776–1829

The literature of the period immediately following the Revolutionary War reflected an almost narcissistic preoccupation with American life. Hugh Henry Brackenridge, for example, adapted the picaresque form of Miguel de Cervantes's *Don Quixote* to the American scene in *Modern Chivalry,* published in installments between 1792 and 1815. Poets Philip Freneau, William Cullen Bryant, and Samuel Woodworth used American rural scenes as topics for their poetry, whereas Washington Irving and James Fenimore Cooper made literary use of the new republic's recent past. Robert Thomas Bailey distilled the wit and rural wisdom of New England farmers in *The Farmer's Almanac.* The first issue of what is now called *The Old Farmer's Almanac* came off the press in 1793.

Western Expansion and the Antebellum Period: 1829–1860

From the earliest periods of North American colonization, explorers and colonizers were tempted to exaggerate when describing the New World. Sometimes the exaggerated descriptions were part of promotional schemes, but in many instances they were merely tall tales, created at the expense of the gullible for the enjoyment of the creator. An early example of the tall tale in rural literature is Samuel Peters's *General History of Connecticut* (1781). Peters anticipated Mark Twain and other Old Southwestern Humorists with tongue-in-cheek stories of frog migrations 40 yards wide and 4 miles long and rivers that ran fast enough to float crowbars. After 1840, as more land was opened to White settlement, the tall tale as an art form reached its fullest development. Representing themselves as faithful reporters of life in the frontier towns and camps in Tennessee, Alabama, Mississippi, Georgia, Arkansas, and Texas, a group of writers now known as Old Southwestern Humorists embellished their accounts with tales of legendary beasts and men that strain credulity.

In other areas, rural literature for the most part was represented by travel journals and accounts of frontier life. Caroline Kirkland's semifictional account of life in frontier Michigan, *A New Home—Who'll Follow?* appeared in 1839. Henry David Thoreau's *A Week on Concord and Merrimack Rivers,* published in 1849, was followed by his

Walden in 1854. *Hiawatha*, Henry Wadsworth Longfellow's romanticized interpretation of Native American life, came out in 1855.

In the years immediately preceding the Civil War, much of rural literature in America was preoccupied with a single issue: slavery. In the South, apologists for human slavery were constructing elaborate defenses of the southern patriarchal plantation system, while Northerners were busy with antislavery tracts. The proslavery southern literature, like slavery itself, did not survive the Civil War, while some of the antislavery literature did. George Fitzhugh's *Sociology for the South; or, the Failure of Free Society* has disappeared; Hariett Beecher Stowe's *Uncle Tom's Cabin* is still in print.

After the Civil War: 1865–1900

Rural writing, by its very nature, is regional writing because authors tend to write about that with which they are most familiar. This type of writing is called "local color" writing and is characterized by the authors' attempts to present in writing the features and characteristics of a particular locality and its inhabitants. In the period immediately following the Civil War, regional writing became increasingly popular, with the West represented by Bret Harte and Hamlin Garland; the South, by George Washington Cable, Joel Chandler Harris, and Mary Noailles Murfree; and New England, by Sarah Orne Jewett and Mary E. Wilkins Freeman. This trend continued, so that by the middle of the twentieth century each region of the United States had its own indigenous literature. In some instances, regions identified by their major crops (for example, the Cotton Belt) were represented by a body of prose and poetry.

The Early Twentieth Century: 1900–1929

At the turn of the century, many changes were taking place in America. The frontier had virtually disappeared, the great cattle ranches were being turned into small family farms, the sodbuster was taking the place of the cowboy, and across the nation cities were expanding into farmland as the nation became increasingly urbanized. Each of these factors in one way or another contributed to the development of two types of rural literature: westerns and farm novels/short stories.

As the frontier disappeared and the wide-open range and the old-time cowboy were replaced by the fenced homestead and the unhorsed farmer, fiction writers began to turn to the Old West as a source for their novels and short stories. The first genuine "western" story

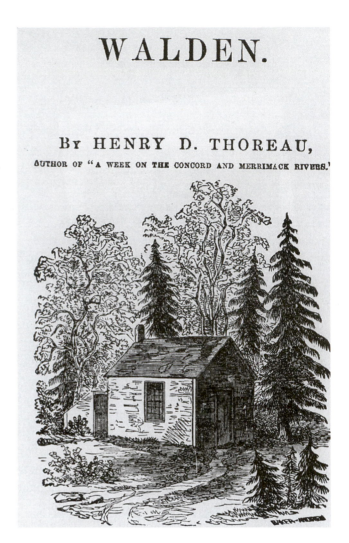

Travel journals and personal accounts such as Henry David Thoreau's Walden *characterized much rural literature in the nineteenth century.*

was Owen Wister's "Hank's Woman," published in *Harper's* magazine in 1892. Wister, a Philadelphia lawyer, was inspired to write "Hank's Woman" after a conversation with Theodore Roosevelt. Both men had spent time in the West, and both were concerned about the fact that no credible fiction about cowboys and ranchers had been written. In 1902, the cowboy hero of "Hank's Woman" became the title character for *The Virginian*. Subsequently, Wister's laconic cowhand became the model for the protagonists in Zane Grey's westerns. Wister's and Grey's novels still serve as templates for novels, short stories, movies, and television shows about an Old West as mythical as King Arthur's court. The persistence of the western, written by authors such as Louis L'Amour, suggests that for Americans the cowboy is the New World's knight on horseback, a swashbuckling, self-sufficient free spirit, the living embodiment of the American dream.

Although a few genuine studies of farm life were published between 1865 and 1900, farm fiction is a phenomenon of the twentieth century. Edward Eggleston's *Hoosier Schoolmaster* (1883), Joseph Kirkland's *Zury: The Meanest Man in Spring County* (1887), and Hamlin Garland's *Main-Travelled Roads* (1891) anticipated the later development of farm-related fiction, but the real beginning did not come until about the time of World War I. Willa Cather's *O Pioneers!* and Hamlin Garland's *A Son of the Middle Border* were published in 1913 and 1917, respectively, and each author followed with a series of novels set in Nebraska, Iowa, and the Dakotas. Farm fiction, in the form of short stories based on rural life, also developed rapidly during this period. This occurred, in part, because rural free delivery, begun in 1896, gave farm and ranch families access to national magazines, which, in turn, encouraged editors to publish stories about rural life.

Farm fiction came of age in the 1920s, with the publication of realistic farm novels such as Ellen Glasgow's *Barren Ground* (1925), Dorothy Scarbrough's *The Wind* (1925), and O. E. Rølvaag's *Giants in the Earth* (1927). Laura Ingalls Wilder's *Little House on the Prairie,* a still popular children's book, appeared in 1935. Between 1923 and 1935, five farm novels were awarded Pulitzer Prizes: Willa Cather's *One of Ours,* in 1923; Margaret Wilson's *The Able McLaughlins,* in 1924; Edna Ferber's *So Big,* in 1925; Louis Bromfield's *Early Autumn, in* 1927; and Josephine Johnson's *Now in November,* in 1935.

The Great Depression and World War II: 1929–1945

In *A Description Of New England,* written in 1616, John Smith articulated for perhaps the first time what has been called "the American Dream." Smith claimed that God had bestowed His blessings so freely "on them that will attempt to obtain them, as here [in America] every man may be master and owner of his own labor and land ... in small time. If he have nothing but his hands, he may ... by industry quickly grow rich." For many years, Smith's claim to a certain extent was sustained by an expanding frontier: exhausted land in one area could be abandoned for a new beginning further west. In the 1930s, however, it became obvious that the American Dream had somehow gone sour. On the Great Plains, drought and disastrous farming practices created what is now known as the Dust Bowl. The stock market crashed in 1929, signaling the beginning of the Great Depression, but the rural writers of this period were more concerned with the effects of industrialization and drought and the fate of tenant farm-

ers and small landholders than with the plight of Wall Street brokers. In the South, a group of writers cooperated on a manifesto opposing the industrialization of the South, *I'll Take My Stand: The South and the Agrarian Tradition, by Twelve Southerners,* which was published in 1930. John Steinbeck's *The Grapes of Wrath* (1939) and *Of Mice and Men* (1937) underscored the plight of tenant farmers and migrant farm laborers, while Lois Phillips Hudson's *The Bones of Plenty, A Novel* (published in 1962) recounted the fate of a North Dakota farm family forced from its land during the 1930s. Nonfiction accounts of the Depression years include Carey McWilliams's *Factories in the Fields: The Story of Migratory Farm Labor in California* (1939), and James Agee's and Walker Evans's *Let Us Now Praise Famous Men* (1941).

After World War II: 1945 to the Present

At the end of World War II, there was a renewed interest in rural life and country living. This was due in part to the nation's weariness with war followed by war; but in a larger sense it was simply the result of a rebirth of one of the nation's most persistent myths: the notion that men and women living a simple life in intimacy with the land can be in harmony with themselves and with one another. City dwellers, some with romantic—and unrealistic— ideas about farm life, and some with no other motive than a desire to exchange the urban "rat race" for what they perceived to be a simpler lifestyle, were relocating in rural areas, sometimes supporting their farming by writing witty accounts of their experiences. Betty McDonald's *The Egg and I,* published in 1945, and Helen and Scott Nearing's *Living the Good Life: How to Live Sanely and Simply in a Troubled World* (1954) are early examples of this back-to-the-farm literature. A more recent example is Marilyn and Tom Ross's *Country Bound! Trade Your Business Suit for Blue Jean Dreams,* published in 1992.

Another form of rural literature that gained in popularity during the postwar years is the country life essay. Country life essays range from simple celebrations of rural life, such as Annie Dillard's *Pilgrim at Tinker's Creek* (1974) and Noel Perrin's *First Person Rural: Essays Of A Sometime Farmer* (1978), to serious studies of rural life such as Kathleen Norris's 1993 collection of essays about rural life on the northern Plains, *Dakota: A Spiritual Geography,* or her *The Cloister Walk* (1996).

Rural literature since World War II has become increasingly regional, with local issues replacing local color as the characteristic of this type of writing. Two books published in 1995 may be used as cases in point:

Alston Chase's *In a Dark Wood: The Fight over Forests and the Rising Tyranny of Ecology* and Richard Manning's *Grassland: The History, Biology, Politics, and Promise of the American Prairies.*

Native American Works

The most significant development in rural literature in the postwar years has been the evolution of Native American literature. Until the late 1960s, when N. Scott Momaday's (Kiowa) *House Made of Dawn* was published, only a few works by Native Americans had been published. Most "Indian" stories prior to this time were written by Whites and, like James Fenimore Cooper's *Last of the Mohicans,* were more fantasy than fact. After *House Made of Dawn,* Native American fiction in particular became more realistic, as authors attempted to provide a picture of Native American life, past and present, or simply to depict the struggle of an essentially rural people trying to maintain a way of life in the face of constant pressure from an increasingly urban, industrialized society. Elizabeth Cook-Lynn's (Dakota) *From the River's Edge* (1991), for example, is the story of a Dakotah cattleman who struggles to maintain a traditional lifestyle as his land disappears under the water of a new lake created when a dam is built on the Missouri River. Other Native American writers who have contributed to the renaissance of Native American writing are James Welch (Blackfoot/ Gros Ventre), Louise Erdrich (Anishinaabe), Leslie Marmon Silko (Laguna Pueblo), Wendy Rose (Hopi/Miwok), Linda Hogan (Chickasaw), and Thomas King (Cherokee).

—Chandice M. Johnson Jr.

See also
American Indians; Arts; Cowboys; Culture; Films, Rural; Folklore; History, Rural; Music; Theatrical Entertainment; Values of Residents.

References
Blair, Walter, Theodore Hornberger, Jane E. Miller, and Randall Stewart. *American Literature: A Brief History.* Rev. ed. Glenview, IL: Scott, Foresman, 1974.

Fairbanks, Carol, and Sara Brooks Sundberg. *Farm Women on the Prairie Frontier: A Sourcebook for Canada and the United States.* Metuchen, NJ: Scarecrow Press, 1983.

Hayes, Robert G., ed. *Early Stories from the Land: Short-Story Fiction from Rural American Magazines, 1900–1925.* Ames: Iowa State University Press, 1995.

Hedges, Elaine, and William Hedges. *Land and Imagination: The Rural Dream in America.* Rochelle Park, NJ: Hayden Book, 1980.

Inge, M. Thomas, ed. *Agrarianism in American Literature.* New York: Odyssey Press, 1969.

Meyer, R. W. *The Middle Western Farm Novel in the Twentieth Century.* Lincoln: University of Nebraska Press, 1965.

Sherman, Caroline B. "The Development of American Rural Fiction." *Agricultural History* 12 (1938): 67–76.

Stone, Ted, ed. *One Hundred Years of Cowboy Stories.* Red Deer, Alberta: Red Deer College Press, 1994.

Livestock Industry

Economic activity that encompasses input suppliers (such as machinery, equipment, feed, and credit suppliers), livestock producers, processors of livestock and livestock products, and the distribution channels beyond the processors. This entry focuses primarily on the input supply (producer through the processor) components of the industry.

Impact on the Rural Community

The livestock industry can have a large impact on the economic base and activity of many communities through value-added production. Rural communities can have a direct-impact livestock industry development that meets the communities' goals and objectives for economic growth, while maintaining or improving their environment. Livestock production represents an important economic activity for many rural communities. For others, livestock production can be a dominant economic force but is not currently. Rural communities need to determine and evaluate their resource base and their strengths and identify areas for development. For some, these development areas will be in livestock production. In some cases, development represents maintaining an existing industry, whereas for others it represents movement into a new industry. Collaborative arrangements are needed among all community stakeholders to enhance the success of these efforts.

Many rural communities have the necessary ingredients to develop or maintain a strong livestock production industry, with their nearby access to grains and available quality labor and management. Another key ingredient, industry collaborative efforts, represents the missing link in many communities. For the livestock industry to be a dominant force, community stakeholders must consciously endorse the collaboration approach. Collaborative efforts necessitate that people direct and lead development. Support is needed; development will not happen without a focus.

Livestock and associated commodity production (such as milk, eggs, and wool) are widely dispersed throughout the United States. For example, the pork industry has annual U.S. marketings of about 88 million head per year. Cash receipts are about $10.1 billion per year, or 6.6 percent of all agricultural receipts. This generates about 746,080 jobs (Otto 1994). Total economic activity from pork production is about $48.7 billion annually.

Livestock production represents a value-adding industry, transforming base grain and forages into products of higher value. An example of the value-adding process is represented by pork production in a typical rural community trade area in the Midwest. In Iowa, 40,000 hogs typically are marketed per 100 square miles, a trade area common for many rural communities that are about 10 miles apart. Concentrated pork production areas would have a larger numbers of hogs. Most communities have additional livestock enterprises, such as beef and dairy; thus the overall livestock impact is larger. The increased value of pork over the homegrown feed that was fed to the hogs is $77.00 per head, or $3.08 million for the 40,000 hogs. With an average marketing weight of 250 pounds (2.5 hundredweight) and a live weight price of $44.00 per hundredweight, total revenue from pork production in the trade area would be $4.40 million. Given an output multiplier of 2.0 (Otto 1994), the $4.40 million generates another $4.40 million of revenue within the local economy. The pork producer buys groceries and clothes and pays the gas bill; the equipment dealer, the elevator personnel, and the consultant personnel spend their income in the community. In total, $8.80 million is generated. The selling of homegrown crops such as cash grain would have generated an income level of $1.32 million. The value of homegrown feed or $2.64 million of economic activity with a multiplier of 2.0. The production of pork dramatically increases this value and the income or economic base of the producing area or rural community. Livestock processing facilities will further expand the economic impact beyond that shown. Most rural communities also have other livestock enterprises; thus the impact of all livestock production is dramatically higher. Livestock production offers many opportunities for economic development and a value-adding process for rural communities.

Duffy (1992) has shown that a livestock production system can expand the economic base of a crop production operation. The latter can use effectively the manure from the livestock operation, while the livestock production operation adds value to the crops produced. For example, 400 acres of a corn-soybean rotation with 120 sows in a farrow-to-finish production system would generate a $39,320 return to management from the operation—compared to a $6,711 return to management for a 400-acre corn/soybean rotation without hogs.

Development

The livestock industry will continue to be influenced by many forces. There are many issues that affect its development and will require action on behalf of all rural community stakeholders. Rural communities and livestock producers will need continual evaluation and adjustments to maintain or improve their competitive position. Issues that can impact livestock producers and rural communities include livestock odors and environmental impacts; the movement toward larger and fewer livestock production operations; the need for cost-efficient livestock producers and businesses supporting the industry; industry access to financing, information, and technology at reasonable rates; the movement to collaborative industry arrangements; and the development of sustainable production systems.

Odors and Environmental Impacts. Livestock production is not the development panacea for all communities. A major issue on the horizon for livestock production is that of effectively handling the odors and waste that accompany livestock production. Key assets for some rural communities are a clean environment, freedom from odors, and low level of violence. These attract some urban residents to relocate into rural communities. This movement will put further pressure on livestock odor and environmental issues. Livestock production can be in competition with two of the key assets: the environment and odor. Discussion on community trade-offs will be needed. The need for effective livestock odor control will grow. Additionally, issues relating to effective animal waste storage use will increase in importance. Because of these conflicting problems, some communities will select livestock for a development base, whereas others will select other opportunities. Those selecting livestock will have to develop plans to effectively handle the odor and environmental issues. Socially and environmentally responsible production methods and standards will be needed. These standards will have to be well planned; standards that are too stringent will lead to industry decline, whereas standards that are not effective will lead to environmental decline, both of which will lead to the decline of the rural community.

The Movement to Larger and Fewer Operations. The movement to larger and fewer livestock production operations means firms that support businesses in rural communities will deal with fewer operators. All businesses, farm and support alike, must offer high-quality products at a low cost. Top management of the respective businesses and the rural community will be a necessity.

An industry with development or growth potential will require much coordination of the different functions or businesses. Among other items, this coordination would provide access to information, technology, and capital at competitive rates. The bottom line is that livestock production systems must be sustainable, both economically and environmentally. Many of the services needed for a sustainable industry can be provided by effective operation of businesses in the rural community. If they are not available, the farm operators will be forced to bypass the rural community to obtain the high-quality services needed at a reasonable cost.

Cost-Efficient Producers and Supporting Businesses. The livestock industry has many participants at the national and international levels. Thus, the industry's production costs must be competitive. The cost-competitiveness issue has received widespread attention, both within the United States (Hillburn et al. 1991) and between the United States and competing countries (Futrell 1991). U.S. producers can be very competitive in producing pork and other livestock. To maintain that competitive advantage, businesses supporting livestock production, the input suppliers (for example, feed, credit, and facilities), and the processors need to be operated cost effectively. They, too, have to be cost competitive in providing their services if a strong industry is developed. To capture the full economic impact from livestock production, rural communities have to assure that these services are available at competitive prices.

Access to Financing, Information, and Technology. The livestock industry is moving toward a greater level of specialization and coordination. This movement is occurring rapidly in the pork industry. Other livestock industries are experiencing this movement, but to a lesser degree. Rural communities represent an important link in establishing or maintaining a competitive livestock industry. Access to the best and most current information is an important ingredient in an industry remaining competitive. Businesses located in the community can be key participants in providing that information.

Another important participant in community development and the livestock production industry is the financial community. Adequate capital will be needed for the industry investment and remodeling necessary to maintain a cost leadership position. Financial institutions will have to evaluate their loan portfolios with respect to a community development impact. Moreover, community efforts may be needed to assure access to capital at competitive rates.

Collaborative Arrangements. Coordination activities range from those that are integrated through methods of ownership to various forms of formal or informal agreements to coordinate the livestock industry. Again, rural community stakeholders must be key participants in coordinating these efforts. A development within a coordinated industry uses contractual arrangements. These legal instruments are used to coordinate the livestock industry from the input supply, through the production, processing, and to the retailer or consumer. Coordinated activities are flexible and link many industry participants. For example, growth in contract hog production has been dramatic. Contract pork production grew from about 11 or 12 percent in 1989 to about 15 or 16 percent of U.S. domestic slaughter in 1992 (Rhodes and Grimes 1992), a 40 percent increase.

Development of Sustainable Production Systems. Production systems must be sustainable over time. For sustainability two primary issues have to be addressed: environmental sustainability and economic sustainability. Livestock systems are needed that maintain or improve the environment. Additionally, the systems will have to provide sufficient profit or economic return for the operation to remain in business over time. A lack of either the environmental or economic component will lead to a declining industry over time. A healthy industry cannot be sustained without fulfilling both parts.

The rural community that aggressively pursues the future has opportunities. Community stakeholders collectively have to determine areas for development potential and proceed in a well-organized fashion for development. Livestock production can be an effective development tool for many rural communities. They have the basic resources to convert products such as grain and forages into higher-value products and expanded economic activity. A coordinated approach involving all stakeholders will be required.

—*James B. Kliebenstein*

See also

Agricultural and Resource Economics; Animal Rights/Welfare; Development, Community and Economic; Environmental Protection; Environmental Regulations; Livestock Production; Marketing; Markets; Pasture; Poultry Industry; Ranching; Value-Added Agriculture.

References

Duffy, Michael. "The Role of Animal Production in Sustainability." *Leopold Letters* 4, no. 4 (Winter 1992): 9–11.

Futrell, Gene A. "The U.S. Pork Industry: How It Compares with Canada and Denmark." Washington, DC: U.S. Department of Agriculture, Economic Research Service, 1991.

Good, Keith, Chris Hurt, Kenneth Foster, John Kadlec, and Kelly Zering. "Comparative Costs of Hog Production in the Midwest and North Carolina." Paper presented at Pork Global Competitiveness Seminar, St. Louis, MO, January 9, 1995.

Hayes, Dermot, and Roxanne Clemens. "How the Danes Do It." *U.S. Meat Export Analysis and Trade News* (December 1994): 18–19.

Hillburn, Chris, James Kliebenstein, Emmett Stevermer, and Larry Trede. "A Comparison of Iowa Swine Production with Its Competition." Staff Paper No. 184. Ames: Iowa State University, Department of Economics, 1991.

Kliebenstein, James B., and Vernon D. Ryan. "Integrating Livestock Industry and Community Development Strategies." Pp. 113–130 in *The Livestock Industry and the Environment: Conference Proceedings*. Ames: Iowa State University, College of Agriculture, 1991.

Lasley, Paul. "Iowa Farm and Rural Life Poll, 1995 Summary Report." Pm-1628. Ames: Iowa State University, Extension Service, August 1995.

Otto, Daniel. "Economic Impact of Iowa's Livestock and Meat Processing Industries." Ames: Iowa State University, Department of Economics, 1994.

Rhodes, V. James, and Glenn Grimes. "Structure of U.S. Hog Production: A 1992 Survey." Agricultural Economics Report 1992–3. Columbia: University of Missouri, 1992.

Livestock Production

The raising of domesticated animals to produce specific commodities used by humans. Common livestock species include beef and dairy cattle, sheep, goats, swine, and poultry. Commodities produced by livestock in America include meat, milk, fiber, mechanical power (work), and pharmaceuticals. Livestock production in America is rapidly becoming industrialized.

History

Livestock production in rural America is changing dramatically. Various segments of animal agriculture have undergone or are undergoing the process of industrialization, or factory farming. Animal production is shifting from individual farmers to large corporations, with vertical integration of all phases of production and marketing under the control of a single company.

The traditional American family farm of the past typically had a variety of crop and livestock enterprises. Draft horses supplied power and traction. Forages and grains, such as oats, were grown to provide feed for work animals. Many farms had a small dairy herd to provide continual generation of cash (the monthly milk check). Cream often was separated on the farm, and pigs were raised on the skim milk. Beef cattle and sheep were raised to use forage growing in uncultivated areas, hillsides, woodlots, and crop residues. In the early twentieth century, mechanization with farm tractors occurred, a process that was completed by the end of the 1940s. This resulted in a dramatic decrease in draft horse numbers and consequently in a decline in the need to produce forage on the farm. This change coincided with the extensive employment of commercial fertilizers, further reducing the need for crop rotations involving leguminous forages. Mechanization reduced labor requirements and increased worker efficiency so that a farmer could farm more land than formerly was the case. Farm size increased, the numbers of farmers decreased, and specialization of production occurred. Farmers selected crops or livestock in which to specialize. In the case of livestock, automation (for example, milking machines) allowed expansion of dairy enterprises. Advances in disease control, nutrition, and animal waste management allowed the intensification of poultry and swine production with total confinement facilities. Developments in genetic engineering and biotechnology maintained and accelerated the trend of intensive livestock farming.

Industrialized Poultry Production

The industrialization of poultry production in the United States is virtually complete. Poultry meat (broiler chickens and turkeys) production is controlled entirely by a few vertically integrated companies. The factors responsible for this process are similar to those for other types of animal production. Poultry production is leading the way, although there is great controversy as to whether this is desirable.

The main types of poultry raised for meat are broilers (chickens) and turkeys. Small numbers of waterfowl (ducks and geese), pigeons (squab), guinea fowl, and game birds (quail, partridge, pheasants) are raised commercially. Broiler chickens have been genetically selected for heavily muscled (meaty) composition and rapid growth rate. Current strains of broiler chickens attain market weights at 5 or 6 weeks of age. Broilers are fed high-energy diets based on corn and soybean meal. They convert feed very efficiently to body weight gain, with a feed conversion efficiency of less than 2 kilograms of feed per 1 kilogram weight gain. About 75 percent of poultry meat production is from broilers, about 24 percent from turkeys, and 1 percent or less from water fowl, game birds, and other minor species. The industry is concentrated in areas close to feed resources and with low labor cost rates (for example, southeastern states such as Arkansas).

Vertical integration of poultry production implies that all components of production, processing, and mar-

Intensive production of broiler chickens in an industrial-scale poultry farm. The birds are grown under contract between the farmer and the vertically integrated poultry cooperation.

keting are controlled by one company, the integrator. Typically with broiler chickens, the integrator contracts with growers, who are provided chicks, feed, management instructions, and all other inputs. The grower provides the buildings and the labor. The integrator usually manufactures the feed in company-owned feed mills; dictates how and when birds will be raised; harvests the birds at the end of the feeding period, when they are five or six weeks of age; and decides how much the grower will be paid. The broilers are slaughtered and processed in a company-owned processing plant and marketed under the integrator's label. Usually the integrator owns feed mills, processing plants, breeder facilities, and marketing channels. Increasingly, integrators are moving to dominate an ever-widening array of inputs, including control of the production and processing of crops (such as corn and soybeans) used in the feeding program, housing and company stores for processing plant workers, and retail marketing of food products on a global basis. The production of poultry increasingly is being integrated into a total global food production system, with the entire process under the control of a few multinational corporations.

The industrialization of poultry production was facilitated by several attributes of chickens. Their reproductive process allows hatching of large numbers of birds at one time, so broilers can be raised on an all-in/all-out system. For example, 25,000 or more broiler chicks per building can be set up and the entire lot harvested five or six weeks later. Poultry produce a dry excreta, so high stocking densities can be used. Feed and water are provided automatically. The birds are raised under low light intensity, reducing their physical activity. In essence, they are meat machines.

Advantages of industrialized poultry production are the production of highly uniform, inexpensive broiler meat. There are favorable economies of scale in production of feed and other inputs. Disadvantages may be that poultry farming as a career has been eliminated. Contract growers are employees and have little management control or decision making. They assume a large burden of the risk in the enterprise, exemplified by the fact that the only segment of the entire industry not owned by the integrator is the facilities in which the birds are raised. Industrialized poultry production is designed to maximize profits and minimize risk for the integrators. The reverse often is true for the growers.

Thus, poultry meat production in rural America is no longer an activity engaged in by farmers. It is an industrial process controlled by vertically integrated multinational corporations. There is concern that, even though this system produces inexpensive meat in the supermarket, there may be hidden costs assumed by society at large, and short-term profits may be emphasized at the expense of sustainability. These hidden costs include extensive soil erosion and losses associated with intensive production of corn and soybeans to produce poultry feed, extensive air and water pollution from animal waste, and societal concerns regarding animal rights and animal welfare.

Eggs are produced by breeds of laying hens selected for high rates of egg production. Most layers are of the White Leghorn breed. In the United States, most laying hens are kept in small cages. As with broiler production, egg production systems are highly automated and vertically integrated. Caged layers often exhibit behavioral abnormalities (for example, feather picking, cannibalism, and hysteria). Intensive production of laying hens kept in small cages has led to considerable societal concern regarding the welfare of the birds. Some European countries have legislatively banned the use of layer cages and mandated that laying hens be kept under conditions that allow for more normal bird activity and behavior. These include free-range conditions and modified confinement with large pens and perches.

Industrialized Swine Production

In the 1990s, high-technology swine production became a very controversial issue in the United States. Large swine operations, referred to as swine megafarms, have been developed. These operations may have thousands of sows, with some of the largest farms having over 100,000 sows, producing 2 million or more pigs per year. Following the poultry model, these are largely corporate farms owned by corporations, in some cases the same companies that are industrial producers of poultry. In contrast to the situation with poultry, industrialized swine production generated tremendous public controversy, in part because of the odors associated with confinement production of pigs. Pollution of streams and rivers by failed

swine waste lagoons, pollution of groundwater, and severe air pollution problems led numerous states and counties to enact legislation blocking or restricting swine megafarms. There is concern that corporate farming will lead to the demise of family farmers and cause extensive changes in rural communities, as private farmers are replaced with megafarm employees. Industrialized swine production is highly automated, and much of the labor needs is provided by low-wage employees. There are concerns that industrialized swine production has societal costs of air and water pollution, disruption of the rural society and economy, and a lack of long-term sustainability resulting from the soil erosion and inefficient recycling of animal wastes associated with the separation of animal production from crop production.

Some societal concerns have been addressed concerning the location of swine megafarms in sparsely populated areas, mainly in the western United States. Industrial pig farms are locating increasingly in rural areas of states such as Utah, Wyoming, Colorado, Oklahoma, and Texas, far removed from populated areas. Although this relocation minimizes problems with swine odor, other concerns arise, including the excessive water demands in arid areas. Location of swine farms in areas far removed from centers of feed grain production eliminates recycling of animal wastes on cropland, resulting in a lack of integration of crop and livestock production. This has long-term implications for sustainability. There are also concerns with the high dependence on fossil fuel inputs with industrial agriculture.

Dairy Cattle Production

As with poultry and swine production, the dairy industry rapidly is undergoing the industrialization process. It is being concentrated in areas such as California, Arizona, New Mexico, and Idaho, where feed and environmental conditions are favorable for large confinement operations with herd sizes of several thousand to over 10,000 cows. Dairy production is technologically advanced, with widespread application of artificial insemination, computer-controlled milking machines, use of bovine somatotropin (bovine growth hormone) to stimulate milk production, and a high degree of sophistication of diet formulation to meet precisely nutrient requirements for high rates of milk production. The family dairy farm is being replaced by the corporate industrialized dairy.

The Holstein is the major dairy cow breed in the United States. Minor dairy breeds include the Jersey, Guernsey, Ayrshire, Brown Swiss, and Milking Shorthorn.

The Holstein became the dominant breed because of its high milk production capability and the low fat content of its milk. Sophisticated genetic programs for the selection of sires (bulls) used in artificial insemination of dairy cows resulted in a continual increase in average milk production per cow in the United States.

Milk from dairy cows is used for human consumption, either directly or indirectly in modified products such as cheese, yogurt, butter, and ice cream. With the increasing concern among Americans about the amount of fat in the human diet, the emphasis today is on low-fat dairy products. Low-fat (1 and 2 percent fat) and fat-free (skim) milk dominate the milk market. Reduced-fat cheese is available. With the reduced demand for milk fat, dairy marketing systems increasingly emphasize the solids-not-fat component of milk, with payment to dairy farmers based on milk protein production.

A new aspect of dairy production is the production of pharmaceuticals. By genetic engineering processes, human (or other) genes can be introduced into the genetic code of dairy cattle to cause them to produce human proteins in their milk. For example, various proteins in human blood can be produced in this way for medical uses. Use of transgenic dairy animals to produce pharmaceuticals for human medicine is in its infancy but shows great potential.

Beef, Sheep, and Goat Production

Beef cattle and sheep traditionally have been raised under extensive management systems, with cow herds and ewe flocks largely maintained on forage systems involving pasture, rangelands, and conserved forage or hay. The sheep industry has declined precipitously and now is relatively insignificant as an agricultural entity. Beef cattle production (cow-calf systems) has been a traditional activity on many farms. The industrialized production of swine and poultry, however, is having a major impact on the profitability of beef production. Poultry meat is achieving an increasing portion of the total market share for meat, largely at the expense of beef. Poultry meat has surpassed beef in per capita consumption, with poultry consumption continuing to increase and beef consumption decreasing. The increasing production of pork by swine megafarms will probably also have a negative impact on beef production. The beef industry is faced with choices of either industrializing, downsizing, or finding other ways to be economically competitive, such as developing niche and export markets. The livestock industry of rural America faces an identity crisis, as exemplified by challenges facing the beef industry. Animal production as a way of life, on the family farm or ranch, may cease to exist, except as a hobby.

The western U.S. cattle ranching industry is facing many other challenges. The grazing of cattle on rangelands, particularly public lands, has become very controversial. Environmental groups and organizations firmly oppose beef cattle production because of degradation of rangelands, destruction of wildlife habitat, predator control programs, and effects of riparian zone grazing on fish habitat. However, cattle ranching does discourage or buffer human degradation of rangelands (for example, urbanization, condominium sites, ski lodges, suburbs, and vacation homes), which threatens the integrity of much of the western United States and has particularly severe impacts on wildlife habitat. Thus, beef cattle ranching may warrant legislative or financial support (for example, subsidized public land grazing fees) to prevent urbanization of rural lands and maintain western cultural identity.

Sheep production in the United States has declined since 1940. Sheep are raised for meat, wool, and milk. Most U.S. production has been for meat (lamb) and wool. In arid rangeland areas, such as in Texas, wool production is emphasized. The Rambouillet, derived from French merino sheep, is the dominant wool breed. Range sheep generally are kept together as a flock (band or herd) under the control of a sheepherder. Sheepherders in the United States have generally been of European origin (Basques from Spain), with a recent trend for herders from South America and China. The range sheep industry has declined precipitously because of low economic returns and extensive losses to predators (coyotes and dogs). Increasing urbanization of western rangelands has intensified these problems.

Goats are raised for milk, meat, and fiber production. Dairy goats are kept to meet the limited demand for goat-derived dairy products such as milk and cheese. The majority of the goats raised commercially in the United States are Angora goats, produced primarily in Texas. Angora goats are the source of mohair, a luxury fiber. There is also some production of cashmere goats for cashmere, another expensive luxury fiber. There is current interest in the Boer breed, imported from South Africa. Boer goats have a more muscular composition than other breeds and are used for meat production. Hispanic peoples of the United States and Mexico consume significant quantities of goat meat. Recently there has been some production of dairy sheep in the United States. Sheep milk is used to produce certain specialty cheeses such as Roquefort.

New or Exotic Species

There is much interest in raising nontraditional animals, including bison, ratites (ostrich, emu, and rhea), rabbits, llamas, Boer goats, and numerous other minor species (yak, deer, water buffalo, and dairy sheep). This is particularly the case with part-time and hobby farmers who see minor species as opportunities to raise animals for profit. To a large degree, they are unable to raise traditional livestock profitably in competition with industrial producers. Thus, exotic species offer opportunities in niche market situations. With the possible exception of bison, these minor species are unlikely to have much impact on the total livestock production system. Bison ranching is becoming more important in western range areas because these animals are commonly perceived by many people more favorably than cattle, in part because bison are native to western North America. Bison production may become particularly important on lands owned by Native Americans to preserve cultural traditions and values.

Long-Range Outlook

Many challenges face animal agriculture. Probably the greatest is the increasing interest in vegetarianism. If a large proportion of the American public adopts vegetarianism, the demand for meat, milk, and eggs will be dramatically curtailed. There are numerous diet and health issues involving meat consumption, including animal fat, cholesterol, and coronary heart disease; obesity; and animal fat intakes related to various types of cancer. There is increasing evidence that a reduction in meat consumption by the American population would have favorable impacts on public health. Thus, it is likely that there will be reduced demand for animal products in the United States on a long-term basis.

The animal rights issue will have important implications for animal agriculture. The concept of animal rights is a direct result of the industrialization of agriculture. The development of intensive animal production techniques during the second half of the twentieth century led to widespread public concern for the welfare of the animals. Keeping hens in cages and veal calves in stalls, tethering sows in gestation stalls, and raising large numbers of animals in high stocking densities under confinement gave rise to organizations opposed to factory farming of animals. Increased awareness of these common animal production techniques led to skepticism and opposition to all types of animal production by many people. Concern for animal welfare under high-technol-

ogy animal agriculture is a significant driving force for the vegetarian movement.

There are numerous other controversial contemporary issues involving livestock production on a global basis, such as methane emissions from ruminants and global warming, tropical deforestation to produce pastures for cattle production, competition between humans and livestock for grain, use of hormones and chemical feed additives in animal production, genetic engineering of animals and production of transgenic animals, and monocultures and the loss of biodiversity. Intensive crop production to produce feed grains for animal feed caused high rates of soil erosion and inefficient use of fossil fuels. Modern, industrialized animal agriculture largely severed the traditional integration of crop and animal production, with possible adverse implications for long-term sustainability of agricultural resources.

Animal agriculture in rural America is in a period of dramatic change. Intensive, industrialized production of poultry and swine is changing the traditional face of American agriculture. The high economic efficiency of intensive production has contributed to the lack of economic viability of many family farms and mixed crop-livestock farms. Animal production is becoming concentrated on fewer but larger farms. Technological advances in genetic engineering, biotechnology in the feed industry, and advances in animal housing and management techniques have ushered in the era of high-technology, science-based animal agriculture. These efficiencies in animal production are counterbalanced by widespread societal concerns and fears of the ethical, social, and food safety implications of modern techniques of animal production. To a considerable extent, these concerns reflect the widespread uneasiness about our entire technology-based society. Societal concerns about modern animal agriculture were dramatically reinforced in 1996 by the apparent transfer of a fatal disease of cattle (bovine spongiform encephalopathy, or mad cow disease) to humans in Great Britain. This incident led to a dramatic decline in demand for British beef and worldwide concerns about meat safety.

Sustainable agriculture refers to the use of agricultural methods that preserve the integrity of the environment on a permanent basis. There is controversy as to whether modern intensive crop production in the United States is sustainable, as it is based on high inputs of nonrenewable fossil fuel and petroleum-derived chemicals and produces high rates of soil erosion, oxidative losses of humus, and loss of biodiversity. Livestock production contributes to these losses because much of the intensive agriculture in the United States is to produce corn and soybeans for animal feed. However, integration of livestock production into cropping systems involving production of forage crops and manure recycling could enhance the sustainability of American agriculture. Animal grazing lands offer greater possibilities for wildlife biodiversity than any other agricultural technique. In contrast, monocultures of grain and vegetable crops provide virtually no wild plant and animal habitat.

It is likely that there will be an increasing dichotomy in livestock production techniques in the United States, with one very large industrial sector and a traditional sector. Unless legislative action is taken to prevent industrialized agriculture, there is little likelihood that the current trend toward increasing intensification of animal production and toward technologically based production will change. Under current economic conditions, factory farming of livestock and poultry is clearly the most efficient and profitable system. The dichotomy arises because significant opportunities will exist in niche markets for organic meat, products from free-range production systems (e.g., free-range eggs), and products from other animal-friendly production systems. Although remnants of traditional farming and ranching lifestyles will remain, the bulk of America's plant- and animal-origin foods will be produced by intensive, industrialized, corporate agriculture.

—*Peter R. Cheeke*

See also

Agriculture, Alternative; Agriculture, Structure of; Agro/Food System; Animal Rights/Welfare; Biotechnology; Dairy Farming; Feedlots; History, Agricultural; Livestock Industry; Organic Farming; Pasture; Policy, Agricultural; Poultry Industry; Ranching; Wool and Sheep Industry.

References

Cheeke, Peter R. *Impacts of Livestock Production on Society, Diet/Health, and the Environment.* Danville, IL: Interstate, 1993.

Fraser, Andrew F., and Donald M. Broom. *Farm Animal Behavior and Welfare.* 3d ed. Philadelphia: Bailliere Tindall, 1990.

Hodges, J. "Sustainable Development of Animal Genetic Resources." *World Animal Review* 68, no. 3 (1991): 2–10.

National Research Council. *Managing Global Genetic Resources: Livestock.* Washington, DC: National Academy Press, 1993.

Pursel, Vernon G., Carl A. Pinkert, Kurt F. Miller, Douglas J. Bolt, Roger G. Campbell, Richard D. Palmiter, Ralph L. Brinster, and Robert E. Hammer. "Genetic Engineering of Livestock." *Science* 244 (1989): 1281–1288.

Rollin, B. E. "Animal Welfare, Animal Rights, and Agriculture." *Journal of Animal Science* 68 (1990): 3456–3461.

———. *Farm Animal Welfare: Social, Bioethical, and Research Issues.* Ames: Iowa State University Press, 1995.

———. "Bad Ethics, Good Ethics, and the Genetic Engineering of Animals in Agriculture." *Journal of Animal Science* 74, no. 3 (March 1996): 535–541.